Complete
BIOLOGY

W R Pickering

OXFORD

UNIVERSITY PRESS

OXFORD
UNIVERSITY PRESS

Great Clarendon Street Oxford OX2 6DP

Oxford University Press is a department of the University of Oxford.
It furthers the University's objective of excellence in research, scholarship,
and education by publishing worldwide in

Oxford   New York

Auckland   Cape Town   Dar es Salaam   Hong Kong   Karachi
Kuala Lumpur   Madrid   Melbourne   Mexico City   Nairobi
New Delhi   Shanghai   Taipei   Toronto

With offices in

Argentina   Austria   Brazil   Chile   Czech Republic   France   Greece
Guatemala   Hungary   Italy   Japan   Poland   Portugal   Singapore
South Korea   Switzerland   Thailand   Turkey   Ukraine   Vietnam

Oxford is a registered trade mark of Oxford University Press
in the UK and in certain other countries

© W. R. Pickering

British Library Cataloguing in Publication Data

Data available

ISBN-13: 978-0-19-914739-7
20 19 18 17 16 15 14

Printed and bound by Printplus, China

Acknowledgements

The publisher would like to thank the following for their kind permission to reproduce photographs:

Ardea: pp. **54** (top), **238**; Art Directors & Trip: pp. **57**, **90** (both), **150**, **243**, **262** (top right), **266** (top left), **289**, **307** (top), **313** (top right & lower right); Associated Press: pp. **130** (lower right), **143** (right); Biofotos/Heather Angel: pp. **54** (lower), **84**, **153** (left), **167** (top left, lower left & lower right), **230**, **231** (top & lower), **232**; John Birdsall: p. **143** (middle); Anthony Blake Photo Library: pp. **35** (top & lower), **303** (left), **307** (lower); Bridgeman Art Library: pp. **129** (top right), **211** (lower left); Martyn F. Chillmaid: p. **302** (top, middle, bottom); Sir Richard Doll: p. **82** (left); Geoscience: p. **47**; Courtesy Guinness World Records: p. **145** (right); Ronald Grant Archive: pp. **36** (top right), **62**, **106**; Holt Studios: pp. **159**, **173**, **174** (both), **176** (all), **179**, **180**, **216**, **248** (lower), **256**, **284**; Images of Africa: p. **145** (left); National Medical Slidebank: pp. **59**, **63**, **73** (left & right), **120**, **314**; Oxford Scientific Films: pp. **18** (left), **26** (top & lower), **33** (top), **59** (top), **129** (lower, lower middle & top), **162**, **229**, **237** (middle left), **252**, **264**, **273**, **278** (middle & lower), **281**, **283**; Rex Features: p. **330** (top & bottom); Science Photo Library: pp. **36** (lower left, right & top left), **61**, **66**, **67** (left & right), **72** (top & lower), **81**, **87** (right & left), **130** (left), **139** (top, middle top & lower), **147**, **159**, **160**, **189**, **200** (left & right), **211** (top, middle left & right, lower right), **215**, **219**, **237** (middle right), **261**, **278** (top), **280**, **285**, **294**, **295**, **296**, **313** (left), **314** (lower left), **315** (right & top right); Sporting Pictures: pp. **116**, **125**; Still Pictures: pp. **41** (top & lower), **82** (right), **266** (lower right), **321**, **329** (lower right); Tony Stone Images: pp. **8**, **71**, **94**, **98**, **101**, **129** (middle top & lower), **188**, **201** (left), **210**, **262** (lower left), **269**, **290**; Telegraph Colour Library: pp. **59** (lower), **79**, **137**, **139** (lower middle), **143** (left), **237** (lower right); Travel Ink: p. **286**; John Walmsley: p. **247**.

Cover photo: Telegraph Colour Library/K&K Ammann.

The illustrations are by:

Barking Dog Art, Julian Baker, Jeff Edwards, Fakenham Photosetting, Ian Foulis & Associates, Roger Gorringe, Nick Hawken, ODI, David Pattinson, and Halli Marie Verrinder.

Introduction

Biology is the study of life and living organisms. During the past few hundred years biology has changed from concentrating on the **structure** of living organisms (often by examining dead specimens!) to looking more at how they work or **function**. Over this time we have discovered much about health and disease, about the processes of plant nutrition which fuel the food chains, about the chemical basis of genetic information, and about controlling the activities of organisms to make products for humans. These advances in biological knowledge raise new issues, however. As people are healthier and live longer, the larger population places greater demands on the environment. The developing techniques of genetic engineering raise moral and ethical dilemmas about their use. Our increasing understanding of the complexities of ecology gives us more responsibility as 'stewards of the environment'.

In *Complete Biology* you will be studying the range of living organisms, the life processes that they carry out, and how these processes affect humans and have been exploited by us. This will help you to understand, and perhaps contribute to, the accelerating biological revolution which will increasingly affect all of our lives.

This book has been organised to help you find information quickly and easily. It is written in two-page units or 'spreads'. Each unit is a topic which forms part of a Dual Award Science or a Science: Biology syllabus. The Dual Award Science material is the 'core' of the syllabus, but different examination boards have chosen different topics to make up their 'extension' material. Your teacher will be able to tell you about the requirements of your syllabus.

Each person has their own way of working, but the following tips might help you to get the most from this book:

- Use the **contents** page - this will provide information on large topics, such as the brain or atmospheric pollution.
- Use the **index** - this will allow you to use a single word such as 'cerebellum' or 'ozone' to direct you towards pages where you can find most information about that word.
- Use the **questions** - this is the best way of checking whether you have learned and understood the material on each spread. There are short questions on each spread, and longer questions at the end of each chapter. Some of the shorter questions are harder than others – harder questions are identified by the icon ▢. The longer examination-style questions would all be the equivalent of the Higher grade standard at GCSE.

I hope that you enjoy using this book, and that it helps you to understand the world of biology. You, like every other living organism, are a part of this world - perhaps one day you will find yourself working to help others to understand more about it.

Ron Pickering   June 2000

Contents

Contents

1·1 Biology is the study of life and living organisms

The dawn of life

Scientists believe that the Earth was formed from an enormous cloud of gases about 5 billion years ago. Atmospheric conditions were harsh (there was no molecular oxygen, for example), the environment was very unstable, and conditions were unsuitable for life as we know it.

Many scientists believe that the first and simplest living organisms appeared on Earth about 2.8 billion years ago. These organisms probably fed on molecules in a sort of 'soup' (called the **primordial soup**) which made up some of the shallow seas on the Earth at that time. A question that has always intrigued scientists, philosophers and religious leaders is:

> What distinguishes these first living organisms from the molecules in the primordial soup?

In other words, what is life?

Characteristics of living organisms

You know that a horse is alive, but a steel girder is not. However, it is not always so obvious whether something is alive or not – is a dried-out seed or a virus particle living or non-living? To try to answer questions like this, biologists use a list of characteristics that living organisms show.

Living organisms:

- **Respire**
- show **Irritability** (sensitivity to their environment) and **movement**
- **Nourish** themselves
- **Grow** and **develop**
- **Excrete**
- **Reproduce.**

The opposite page gives more detail of the characteristics of life.

You may see other similar lists of these characteristics using slightly different words. You can remember this particular list using the word **RINGER**. It gives **Ringer's solution** it's name. This is a solution of ions and molecules that physiologists use to keep living tissues in – it keeps the cells alive.

As well as the characteristics in the 'ringer' list, living things have a **complex organisation** that is not found in the non-living world. A snowflake or a crystal of quartz is an organised collection of identical molecules, but even the simplest living cell contains many different complex substances arranged in very specific structures.

Living things also show **variation** – the offspring are often different from one another and from their parents. This is important in adaptation to the environment and in the process of **evolution**.

How the characteristics of life depend on each other

Each of the characteristics of life is linked to the others – for example, organisms can only grow if they are nourished. As they take nourishment from their environment, they may also produce waste materials which they must then excrete. To respond to the environment they must organise their cells and tissues to carry out actions. Because of the random nature of reproduction, they are likely to show variation from generation to generation.

Depending on energy

The organisation in living things and their ability to carry out their life processes depends on a supply of **energy**. Many biologists today define life as a set of processes that result from the organisation of matter and which depend on the expenditure of energy. In this book we shall see:

- how energy is liberated from food molecules and trapped in a usable form
- how molecules are organised into the structures of living organisms
- how living organisms use energy to drive their life processes.

Respiration is the process by which living cells release energy from organic molecules. The form of respiration that releases the most energy uses oxygen. Many organisms have **gaseous exchange** systems that supply their cells with oxygen from their environment.

Irritability (or **sensitivity**) is the ability to detect changes in the environment either inside or outside the organism, and to respond to them. These responses often involve movement.

Nutrition supplies an organism with the food it needs for respiration, growth, repair and reproduction. Plants make their foods using the process of photosynthesis, whilst animals obtain their foods 'ready-made' by eating them.

Growth and **development** are the processes by which an organism changes in size and in form. For example, as a young animal increases in size (as it grows), the relative sizes of its body parts change (it develops).

Excretion removes the waste products of processes such as respiration and nutrition from the organism's body.

Reproduction is the generation of offspring – new individuals. An organism may simply split into two, or reproduction may be a more complex process involving fertilisation. Reproduction makes new organisms of the same species as the parents. This depends on a set of chemical plans (the genetic information)

1 Approximately how many years passed between the formation of the Earth and the appearance of the first living organisms?

2 What sort of molecules do you think might have been present in the primordial soup?

3 **RINGER** is a word that helps people remember the characteristics of living organisms. Think of your own word to help you remember these characteristics.

4 Suggest *two* ways in which reproduction is essential to living organisms.

1·2 Water is an important biological molecule

Objectives

▸ To know that all living organisms are largely water, and that biological reactions always take place in an aqueous (watery) environment

▸ To understand that the biological properties of water result from the structure of the water molecule

▸ To list some of the biological functions of water

Water and life

Life first evolved in water for a number of reasons:

▸ The molecules that were used by living organisms, and that made up their structure, were dissolved in the first seas.

▸ In the muddy estuaries and shallow seas of the primitive Earth, the molecules could become concentrated enough to react together.

▸ Water acted as a protective shield for the first living organisms against the damaging ultraviolet rays from the Sun.

Recycling water

Life continues on this planet because water has special properties. In particular, all three states of water – solid ice, liquid water and gaseous water vapour – exist at the temperatures found on the Earth's surface. The temperature varies at different times and at different places on the planet, but the average temperature over the Earth's surface is about 16.5 °C. This means that ice, liquid water and water vapour are all present and are continually interchanging. Water is recycled between different parts of the environment, as shown in the water cycle below.

The special properties of water

The picture of the kangaroo shows the importance of the properties of water to living things.

The **high specific heat capacity** of water means that cells or bodies with a high water content tend to resist heating up or cooling down, even when the temperature of their environment changes.

Evaporation of water from a surface allows loss of heat. Water has a **high latent heat of vaporisation**.

Because water is **incompressible**, it provides excellent support. Water helps support a whole organism (e.g. a fish), or part of an organism (e.g. the eyeball, or the erect penis of a mammal).

Water is an excellent **lubricant**, for example in saliva or in the synovial fluid of movable joints.

Water is an excellent **transport medium** for many biological molecules, such as oxygen, glucose, amino acids, sodium ions and urea.

Water can be a **biological reagent**, for example in the processes of photosynthesis and digestion.

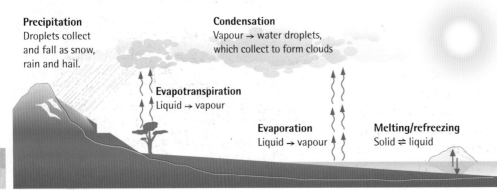

Precipitation
Droplets collect and fall as snow, rain and hail.

Condensation
Vapour → water droplets, which collect to form clouds

Evapotranspiration
Liquid → vapour

Evaporation
Liquid → vapour

Melting/refreezing
Solid ⇌ liquid

The water cycle is maintained by heat energy from the Sun.

Thermal properties

Water has a high specific heat capacity, which means that it takes a lot of energy to change its temperature. This property enables land-living animals and plants, which have a water content of 50–90%, to maintain a constant body temperature. Water also has a high latent heat of vaporisation – it takes a lot of energy to convert liquid water to water vapour at the same temperature. This property helps organisms to lose heat through sweating, the evaporation of water from the body's surface (see page 112).

Moving around

The small size of water molecules, and the fact that they are only bound to one another by fairly weak forces, means that water molecules are free to move quite easily. The movement of water molecules from one place to another is extremely important in living organisms. This will be discussed on page 24.

Sticking together

Water molecules tend to 'stick together' (to **cohere**). This means that continuous streams of water can be drawn up through the bodies of plants. Also, the surface of a body of water has a 'skin' which is relatively strong, and some organisms such as pond skaters can live on this surface.

A polar molecule that forms ions

Water is a **polar** molecule – the electrical charge within the molecule is not spread evenly. One part of the molecule is slightly more negative than the other part, as shown in the box above right.

Because its molecules are polar, water is a very good solvent for other polar molecules and ions. This means that water, for example in blood plasma, is an excellent medium for transporting materials around the bodies of living organisms.

Water molecules tend to separate into two charged particles or **ions**:

$$H_2O \rightleftharpoons H^+ + OH^-$$

The number of H^+ ions in a sample of water determines how acidic it is. Scientists use **pH** to describe how acidic a solution is. More H^+ ions make solutions more acidic and reduce the pH. The pH of a solution is very important for the processes of living organisms. The pHs of some important biological solutions are shown above right.

What makes water special?

The structure of the water molecule is the reason for water's special properties. Because the water molecule is polar, individual molecules have a weak attraction for one another. These weak attractions or **hydrogen bonds** are responsible for the thermal properties of water, for the fact that ice floats on liquid water, and for the cohesive properties of water.

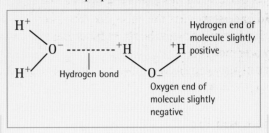

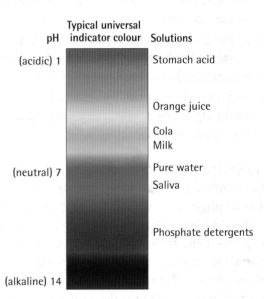

The pH of some solutions. The lower the pH, the more acidic is a solution (and the more H^+ ions it contains).

1 Give three biological functions of water.

2 Find out how water is involved in the processes of digestion and photosynthesis.

3 The kidney (see page 114) is involved in the control of blood pH. What might the kidney add to or remove from the blood to control its pH?

4 Suggest the biological implications if ice did not float on water.

5 Give one reason why phosphate detergents might be damaging to aquatic life.

1·3 All living things are made up of organic molecules

Objectives
- To understand that the structures of living things depend on the molecules that make them up
- To list the types of molecule found in living organisms

Organic molecules

Biological molecules are often called **organic molecules**, since many of them were discovered in living organisms. Chemists have found that these compounds all contain carbon atoms, along with other elements. Carbon atoms bond strongly to other carbon atoms, so organic molecules can be large and show a wide variety of chain and ring structures, with many carbon atoms bonded together. Organisms need organic molecules to:
- provide **energy** to drive life processes
- provide **raw materials** for the growth and repair of tissues.

Nutrition supplies living organisms with the molecules that they need. There are four main groups of organic chemicals used by living things:
- **carbohydrates**
- **lipids**
- **proteins**
- **nucleic acids.**

The diagram on the next page shows the structures of these different groups of organic molecules.

Basic biochemistry

Living organisms also contain inorganic molecules (such as water) and a number of ions. The study of the organic and inorganic molecules that make up living organisms is called **biochemistry**. The sum of all the chemical reactions in living organisms is sometimes called **metabolism**.

Large organic molecules are usually made up of lots of similar smaller molecules called **subunits**. The subunits can be split apart by a reaction called **hydrolysis**, which uses water. They can be joined together again, perhaps in new combinations, by a reaction called **condensation**, which produces water.

In this way living organisms can take molecules from their environment and rearrange them into shapes that suit their own particular requirements, as illustrated below.

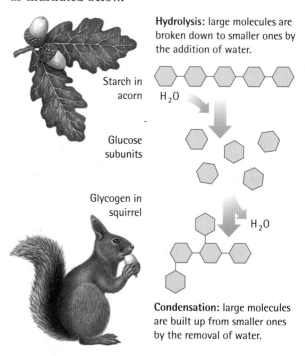

Starch in acorn

Glucose subunits

Glycogen in squirrel

Hydrolysis: large molecules are broken down to smaller ones by the addition of water.

H_2O

H_2O

Condensation: large molecules are built up from smaller ones by the removal of water.

The carbohydrate starch in the acorn is hydrolysed in the squirrel's cells into subunits called glucose. These are then built up into the carbohydrate glycogen by condensation reactions.

1 List the main groups of organic compounds found in living organisms. Suggest one important function for each group.

2 Using carbohydrates as an example, explain the meaning of the terms **hydrolysis** and **condensation**.

3 Some molecules such as glucose and amino acids are **soluble**, whereas others such as starch and fats are **insoluble**. Why is this physical property important in living organisms?

4 Some scientists would say that nucleic acids are the most important molecules in living cells; others might suggest that proteins are more important; and some might say that life could not continue without a supply of carbohydrates. Write a sentence in support of each of these points of view.

Carbohydrates

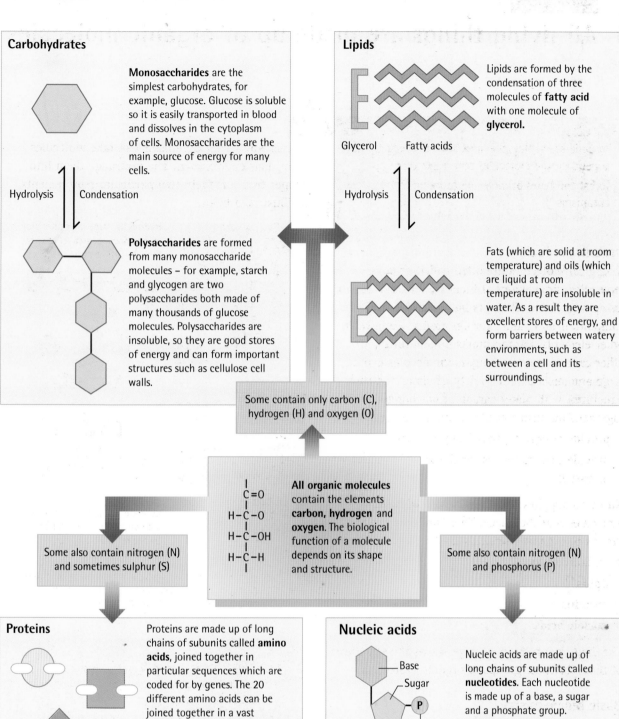

Monosaccharides are the simplest carbohydrates, for example, glucose. Glucose is soluble so it is easily transported in blood and dissolves in the cytoplasm of cells. Monosaccharides are the main source of energy for many cells.

Hydrolysis ⇅ Condensation

Polysaccharides are formed from many monosaccharide molecules – for example, starch and glycogen are two polysaccharides both made of many thousands of glucose molecules. Polysaccharides are insoluble, so they are good stores of energy and can form important structures such as cellulose cell walls.

Lipids

Lipids are formed by the condensation of three molecules of **fatty acid** with one molecule of **glycerol.**

Glycerol   Fatty acids

Hydrolysis ⇅ Condensation

Fats (which are solid at room temperature) and oils (which are liquid at room temperature) are insoluble in water. As a result they are excellent stores of energy, and form barriers between watery environments, such as between a cell and its surroundings.

Some contain only carbon (C), hydrogen (H) and oxygen (O)

$$\begin{array}{c} | \\ C=O \\ | \\ H-C-O \\ | \\ H-C-OH \\ | \\ H-C-H \\ | \end{array}$$

All organic molecules contain the elements **carbon, hydrogen** and **oxygen**. The biological function of a molecule depends on its shape and structure.

Some also contain nitrogen (N) and sometimes sulphur (S)

Some also contain nitrogen (N) and phosphorus (P)

Proteins

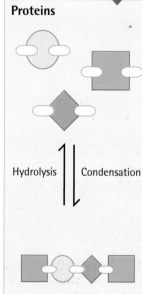

Proteins are made up of long chains of subunits called **amino acids**, joined together in particular sequences which are coded for by genes. The 20 different amino acids can be joined together in a vast number of different orders, and some proteins are thousands of amino acids long. The sequence of amino acids determines the shape of the protein molecule – some are long and thin (such as **keratin**, the protein in hair and nails), whilst others are more egg shaped or spherical (such as **haemoglobin**, the oxygen-carrying protein in red blood cells).

Amino acids are soluble so they are easily transported in living organisms, and can take part in reactions in the watery cytoplasm of the cell.

Hydrolysis ⇅ Condensation

Nucleic acids

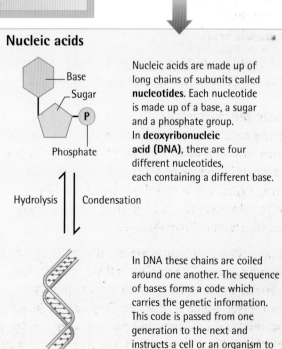

Base

Sugar

P

Phosphate

Nucleic acids are made up of long chains of subunits called **nucleotides**. Each nucleotide is made up of a base, a sugar and a phosphate group. In **deoxyribonucleic acid (DNA)**, there are four different nucleotides, each containing a different base.

Hydrolysis ⇅ Condensation

In DNA these chains are coiled around one another. The sequence of bases forms a code which carries the genetic information. This code is passed from one generation to the next and instructs a cell or an organism to carry out a particular task.

1·4 Testing for biochemicals

Objectives
▪ To describe simple chemical tests for the molecules of living organisms

Scientists often need to know whether or not a particular type of molecule is present in a solution. For example, a doctor might try to detect glucose in a urine sample (glucose in the urine suggests the patient has diabetes), or an environmental scientist might test for starch in the outflow from a food factory. There are a number of simple chemical tests that can be carried out on biological solutions. Some of these tests are described on the opposite page.

A special test for lipids
An important feature of fats and oils is that they are insoluble in water. This means that you cannot make an aqueous solution of a fat or oil on which to carry out a biochemical test. However, the fact that lipids are insoluble forms the basis of a **physical test.**

This is known as the **emulsion test:**

▪ 2 cm³ of ethanol are added to the unknown solution, and the mixture is gently shaken.
▪ The mixture is poured into a test tube containing an equal volume of distilled water.
▪ If a lipid is present, a milky-white emulsion is formed.

A milky emulsion shows that a lipid is present.

---

1   a What is the difference between a fat and an oil?
    b Both lipids and carbohydrates contain carbon, hydrogen and oxygen. How do they differ from one another?
    c Draw a diagram to show a molecule of fat. Suggest why it is possible to have many kinds of fat.

2   Here are the results of a series of tests on biological solutions.
    Suggest, giving your reasons, which of these solutions might be:
    a the washings from a laundry   d urine from somebody who has sugar diabetes
    b milk   e sweetened tea.
    c crushed potato solution

Solution	Colour after testing with reagent:			
	Iodine solution	Benedict's reagent	Biuret reagent	Benedict's reagent after acidification and neutralisation
A	Blue-black	Clear blue	Clear blue	Clear blue
B	Straw yellow	Orange	Purple	Orange
C	Straw yellow	Clear blue	Clear blue	Orange
D	Blue-black	Clear blue	Faint purple	Clear blue
E	Straw yellow	Orange	Clear blue	Orange

3   Describe the two types of control which are used in food tests and explain why they are needed.

Testing for vitamin C: using DCPIP
Vitamin C takes the colour out of a blue dye called DCPIP.

VITAMIN
C

The number of drops of vitamin C solution needed to make this happen depends on how concentrated the vitamin C solution is.

So
few drops: strong vitamin C solution

many drops: weak vitamin C solution

A **control** is needed to make sure that results are valid.

- To show that the test is working properly, a solution that is known to contain the substance is tested (for example, the Biuret reagent is used with a solution known to contain protein). This should give a positive result.

- To show that the test solutions are not contaminated, each test should be carried out on a sample of water. This should give a negative result.

To test for **protein,** a few drops of **Biuret reagent** are added to 2 cm³ of the unknown solution, and the mixture is gently shaken. A **mauve/purple** colour is a positive result (protein is present).

To test for **starch**, a few drops of **iodine solution** are added to 2 cm³ of the unknown solution, and the mixture is gently shaken. A **deep blue–black** colour is a positive result (starch is present).

To test for **glucose** (a **reducing sugar**), 2 cm³ of **Benedict's reagent** are added to 2 cm³ of the unknown solution, and the mixture is heated in a boiling water bath for 2–3 minutes. An **orange/brick–red** colour is a positive result (glucose is present).

When **making comparisons** between different solutions – for example, to compare the glucose content of different urine samples – it is important to carry out all tests under the same conditions. For example, a series of Benedict's tests should be performed:
- on equal volumes of unknown solutions
- using equal volumes of Benedict's solution
- with all mixtures heated to the same temperature
- for the same length of time.

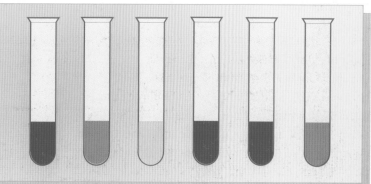

1·5 Enzymes control biochemical reactions in living organisms

Objectives

▶ To appreciate that biochemical reactions in living organisms must be controlled

▶ To understand how enzymes can act as biological catalysts

▶ To list and explain the factors that affect enzyme activity

▶ To list some examples of human exploitation of enzymes

Enzymes are biological catalysts

The sum of all the chemical reactions going on within a living organism is known as **metabolism**. **Anabolic** reactions build up large molecules from smaller ones, and usually require an input of energy. **Catabolic** reactions break down large molecules into smaller ones, and often release energy. The condensation of glucose molecules into the polysaccharide glycogen is an example of anabolism, and this happens in cells of the liver and skeletal muscle. The breakdown of glucose into carbon dioxide and water by respiration is an example of catabolism, and this also occurs in cells of the liver and skeletal muscle. What determines whether glucose molecules are built up into glycogen or broken down into carbon dioxide and water? The answer is **enzymes**. Enzymes are proteins, and they act as biological **catalysts** – they speed up reactions without themselves being affected by the reaction. The molecules that react in the enzyme-catalysed reaction are called **substrates**, and the molecules produced in the reaction are **products**. Different enzymes are involved in anabolic and catabolic reactions, and so the presence or absence of a particular enzyme controls what will happen to a particular molecule.

Enzymes and cells

Enzymes are synthesised in living cells. Most enzymes work inside the cell – examples of these **intracellular enzymes** are **catalase** (which breaks down harmful hydrogen peroxide in liver cells) and **phosphorylase** (which builds glucose into starch in plant storage cells). Other enzymes are made inside cells and then released from the cell to perform

their function – examples of these **extracellular enzymes** include the digestive enzymes such as **amylase** (which breaks down starch to maltose) and **lipase** (which breaks down fats to fatty acids and glycerol). Enzymes are **specific** – most enzymes work on one kind of substrate only. For example, proteases break down proteins but have no effect on carbohydrates or lipids, and lipases break down lipids but do not affect proteins or carbohydrates.

The mechanism of enzyme action (the lock and key hypothesis)

An **enzyme** is a protein, folded into a complex three-dimensional shape. The **active site** is the part of the enzyme that allows it to act as a catalyst, as shown below.

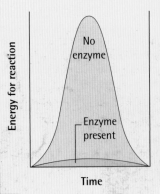

Molecules of substrate

Active site

Enzyme

The enzyme molecule is now free to bind with more molecules of substrate. Each enzyme molecule may be used many thousands of times.

Substrate molecules fit exactly into the active site of the enzyme. The active site brings the substrate molecules closer together.

Product

The substrates now react to form a molecule of product, which leaves the active site.

No enzyme

Enzyme present

Energy for reaction

Time

The enzyme lowers the energy needed for the reaction, and the reaction is then much more likely to take place.

Factors affecting enzyme activity

Temperature

Temperature affects the activity of enzymes since:

- a higher temperature speeds up the movement of substrate molecules, so that when they collide with the enzyme they have more energy and are more likely to bind to the active site. The enzyme activity increases with a rise in temperature, up to a point.

- the enzyme molecules themselves also gain in energy as the temperature rises so that they begin to vibrate. Eventually the enzyme molecules vibrate so much that they become **denatured** – they lose their three-dimensional shape and can no longer bind to their substrate. Because of this, high temperatures reduce enzyme activity. Each enzyme has an **optimum temperature**, which is a balance between these two effects, as shown in the graph below. Most human enzymes have an optimum temperature around 37 °C, whilst for most plants the optimum is rather lower at around 25 °C.

Denaturation is usually irreversible, and living cells make great efforts to keep the conditions suitable for their enzymes to work.

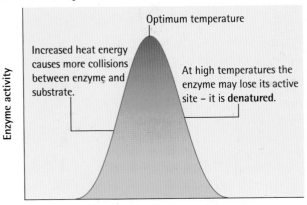

An enzyme-catalysed reaction gets faster, reaches a maximum rate and then slows down again as you increase the temperature.

pH

pH also affects enzyme activity since changing the acid or base conditions around an enzyme molecule affects its three-dimensional shape and can denature the enzyme. Each enzyme has its own **optimum pH**, as shown in the graph below, which depends on the environment in which the enzyme is working – **pepsin** is an enzyme that works in the stomach, and has an optimum pH around pH 2.0 (very acidic), whereas **amylase** works in the mouth and small intestine and has an optimum pH around 7.5 (slightly basic).

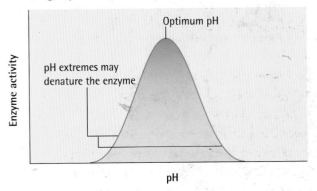

Activators and inhibitors

Some molecules change the likelihood of an enzyme being able to bind to its substrate. **Activators** make this binding more likely – for example, chloride ions are essential for the activity of salivary amylase. **Inhibitors** make it more difficult for the enzyme to bind to the substrate – for example, cyanide ions block the active sites of enzymes involved in respiration.

Humans exploit enzymes

Because enzymes are specific, and can be used over and over again, they are very useful in the fields of industry, food preparation and medicine (see page 312).

---

1 Copy and complete the following paragraph about enzymes.

Enzymes are _____ which speed up the biochemical _____ in living organisms. The enzymes themselves are not changed in these reactions, that is they are biological _____.

Enzymes are _____ – each one controls only one type of reaction. They are _____ by high temperatures and by extremes of pH.

2 Enzyme action is explained by the lock and key hypothesis (see box opposite). The example shows an enzyme that catalyses a condensation reaction – two small molecules are joined together to make a larger one. Redraw the diagram to show the action of an enzyme catalysing a hydrolysis reaction, and give an example of such an enzyme.

1·6 Enzyme experiments and the scientific method

What is the scientific method?

When scientists are faced with a problem, they tackle it using the **scientific method**. This starts off with an **observation**; for example, a farmer might notice that all his cows have stopped producing milk. The next step is to produce a **hypothesis**, a possible explanation for the observation (perhaps the cows' diet has been changed). Following this hypothesis, **predictions** are made, such as: *adding more protein pellets to the cows' feed will increase their yield of milk*. Then **experiments** are designed and carried out to test whether or not the predictions are true. The **data** (results of the experiment) are analysed and **conclusions** drawn. These conclusions will allow the experimenter to accept or reject the original hypothesis.

An illustration of the scientific method

In an experiment, apparatus is used to measure the effect of changing one factor (variable) on the value of a second factor (variable). For example, the experiment illustrated below is designed to test the hypothesis: *temperature affects the activity of catalase.*

Catalase is an enzyme that catalyses the breakdown of hydrogen peroxide:

> Hydrogen peroxide → oxygen + water

Catalase is present in potato tissue. Discs of potato are put into a solution of hydrogen peroxide. The catalase breaks down the hydrogen peroxide into water and oxygen, and the oxygen passes into the manometer. The changing level of the manometer fluid shows how much oxygen is being produced, and gives a measure of the activity of the enzyme. The rate of oxygen production is measured at different temperatures.

An identical **control** experiment is also set up, in which the manipulated variable (the temperature) is not changed. This confirms that the changes in temperature, and not an unknown variable, are causing the changes in enzyme activity. A control experiment ensures that the experiment is a **fair test**.

If the experimenter suspects that an error has been made, part of the experiment may be **repeated**. Taking a series of results and calculating the mean gives more accurate results than taking just one set, as any single inaccurate result then has less effect on the overall results.

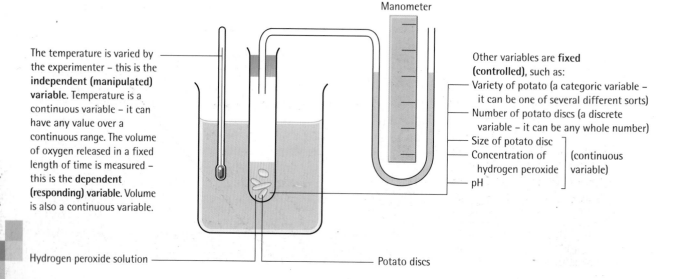

Manometer

The temperature is varied by the experimenter – this is the **independent (manipulated) variable**. Temperature is a continuous variable – it can have any value over a continuous range. The volume of oxygen released in a fixed length of time is measured – this is the **dependent (responding) variable**. Volume is also a continuous variable.

Other variables are **fixed (controlled)**, such as:
- Variety of potato (a categoric variable – it can be one of several different sorts)
- Number of potato discs (a discrete variable – it can be any whole number)
- Size of potato disc ⎤
- Concentration of   ⎥ (continuous
  hydrogen peroxide ⎥ variable)
- pH   ⎦

Hydrogen peroxide solution

Potato discs

Dealing with data: recording results

Raw data are gathered in a table during the experiment. They may then be manipulated (converted into another form), and are often displayed as a graph to allow the experimenter to draw conclusions from the results.

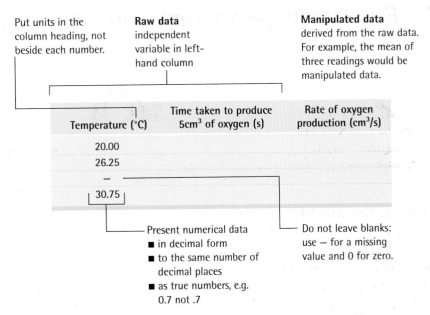

Put units in the column heading, not beside each number.

Raw data independent variable in left-hand column

Manipulated data derived from the raw data. For example, the mean of three readings would be manipulated data.

Temperature (°C)	Time taken to produce 5cm³ of oxygen (s)	Rate of oxygen production (cm³/s)
20.00		
26.25		
—		
30.75		

Present numerical data
■ in decimal form
■ to the same number of decimal places
■ as true numbers, e.g. 0.7 not .7

Do not leave blanks: use — for a missing value and 0 for zero.

Results are recorded in a table during the experiment. Give an informative title, such as: *The effect of temperature on the activity of catalase.*

Drawing a graph

A graph is a visual representation of data which often helps to make a relationship more obvious.

Evaluating an experiment

Scientists often look back at the results of their experiments and the methods used to gather them. This **evaluation** process is an important part of the scientific method because the scientist needs to be sure that the techniques and apparatus used have given the most reliable results before he or she draws conclusions from them.

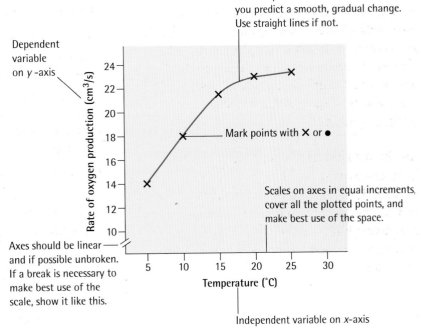

Join the points with a smooth curve if you predict a smooth, gradual change. Use straight lines if not.

Dependent variable on y-axis

Mark points with ✗ or ●

Scales on axes in equal increments, cover all the plotted points, and make best use of the space.

Axes should be linear and if possible unbroken. If a break is necessary to make best use of the scale, show it like this.

Independent variable on x-axis

Rule in the axes in black. Again, give an informative title.

---

1 Using the apparatus shown opposite, a student investigated the effect of temperature on the activity of the enzyme catalase. Here are his results:

a Copy and complete the table by calculating the rate of oxygen release.

b Present the data in the form of a graph.

c Explain the shape of the graph.

Temperature (°C)	Time taken to evolve 10 cm³ of oxygen (s)	Rate of oxygen release (cm³/s)
15	40	
25	20	
35	5	
45	20	
55	40	
65	120	
75	No gas evolved	

Organisms are made up of cells

Objectives

- To know that the basic unit of living organisms is the cell
- To know that all cells have certain features in common, but that there are differences between plant and animal cells
- To understand that the study of cells requires the use of a microscope

All living organisms are made up of units called **cells**. Although cells may take on very specialised functions, they have certain common features. These are shown on the opposite page. Both animal and plant cells have a **cell surface membrane**, **cytoplasm** and a **nucleus**. These three features can be seen on the photograph of a cheek cell below. In addition, plant cells have a **cellulose cell wall**, a **vacuole** and may have **chloroplasts**. These features can be seen on the photograph of the palisade cell below.

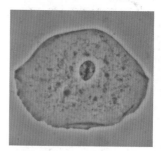

A cell from the inside of the cheek, viewed using a light microscope (magnified × 1500 times).

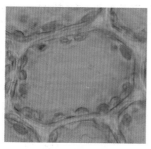

A palisade cell from a leaf, viewed using a light microscope (magnified × 500 times).

The light microscope

Cells are too small to see with the naked eye so a **microscope** is used to study them. Visible light passes through a suitable specimen, and a series of lenses magnify the image that is formed. A light microscope can give a useful magnification of about 400 times, which means the image seen is actually 400 times larger than the specimen. The contrast between different structures in the image can be improved by using dyes or stains. The nucleus of an animal cell, for example, shows up particularly well when stained with a dye called methylene blue.

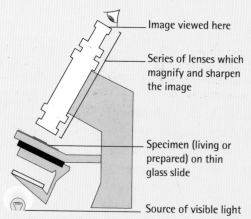

- Image viewed here
- Series of lenses which magnify and sharpen the image
- Specimen (living or prepared) on thin glass slide
- Source of visible light

A typical animal cell is about one-fortieth of a millimetre in diameter. This is rather a clumsy term, so scientists use smaller units: one metre (m) contains 1000 millimetres (mm), and one millimetre contains 1000 micrometres (µm). So a typical animal cell is about 25 µm in diameter.

---

1. Copy and complete this table by placing a tick if the structure is present and a cross if it is not.

2. A biology book said that 'the structure of a cell is closely related to its function'. Using both plant and animal examples, comment on the validity of this statement.

Structure	Liver cell	Palisade cell
Cell surface membrane		
Chloroplasts		
Cytoplasm		
Cellulose cell wall		
Nucleus		
Starch granule		
Glycogen granule		
Large, permanent vacuole		

Secretory vesicles containing cell products such as hormones or enzymes are much more common in animal cells.

Cytoplasm of animal cells is often denser, with many more organelles and dissolved substances.

Vacuoles are small and temporary. They can be involved with digestion (e.g. in phagocytes) or with excretion (contractile vacuoles may remove excess water).

Glycogen is the storage form of carbohydrates.

Animal cell features often relate to **heterotrophic nutrition** and high rates of **metabolic activity**.
e.g. liver cell

The absence of the cellulose wall means that animal cells may be **very irregular in shape**. The amount of cytoplasm that can be controlled by the nucleus is limited, so that animal cells may be **quite small** – about 25 μm in diameter.

Plant and animal cells have common features which relate to maintaining the characteristics of life.

Cell surface membrane which surrounds the cytoplasm. It controls the **entry and exit** of dissolved substances and separates the cell's contents from its surroundings.

Cytoplasm contains water, dissolved substances such as amino acids and sugars, and supports the various organelles (for example, mitochondria, ribosomes). The various metabolic reactions needed to sustain life (for example, respiration) take place within the cytoplasm and organelles.

Nucleus contains the genetic material (**DNA** which makes up **genes** on the **chromosomes**). This carries the coded instructions for controlling the activities and characteristics of the cell. The chromosomes only become visible during cell division.

Plant cell features oftenrelate to **autotrophic** nutrition.
e.g. palisade cell of leaf

The presence of the cellulose cell wall means that plant cells tend to be **regular in shape**. The presence of the vacuole means that plant cells may be **quite large** – often 60 μm (or 0.06 mm) in diameter.

Chloroplasts contain the pigment **chlorophyll** (for light absorption) and the **enzymes** necessary for the production of glucose by photosynthesis.

Large permanent vacuole contains water necessary to provide turgor pressure and may store ions and molecules.

Starch (in the cytoplasm or the chloroplasts) is the storage form of carbohydrates.

Cellulose cell wall provides structural support (pressure of cell contents leads to **turgidity**) and protects against damage caused by osmotic intake of water. The cell wall is **freely permeable to water and dissolved substances**.

The features of plant and animal cells allow these cells to carry out the basic processes of life. The differences between plant and animal cells are due to the differences in lifestyle between animals and plants, especially to their different methods of nutrition.

Basic principles

1

1·8 The organisation of living organisms

Objectives
- To understand that the body of a living organism is a highly organised structure
- To understand that cells, tissues, organs and systems represent increasing degrees of organisation in living organisms

Specialised cells

Large organisms are **multicellular** – they are made up of many cells. Different types of cell have particular structures designed to help them carry out different tasks and functions – they have become **specialised**. Some examples of specialised cells, and their functions, are shown in the table.

Cell type	Appearance	Functions and adaptations
Animal cells		
Red blood cell (page 61)		**Transports** oxygen from the lungs to the tissues where aerobic respiration occurs. The cytoplasm is filled with the pigment haemoglobin, which carries oxygen. The cells have no nucleus, leaving more space for haemoglobin, and they are very flexible (they can be forced through even the narrowest of blood vessels).
Muscle cell (page 124)		**Contracts** so that structures can be brought closer together. Muscle cells are long, and have many protein fibres in the cytoplasm. These fibres can shorten the cell when energy is available.
Sperm cell (page 132)		**Delivers** one set of chromosomes from the male to fertilise the female sex cell. The tail allows the sperm cell to swim towards the female sex cell, and the head carries the set of chromosomes from the male organism.
Motor nerve cell (page 89)		**Conducts nerve impulses.** The cell has a long fibre called an axon along which impulses travel, a fatty sheath which gives electrical insulation and a many-branched ending which can connect with many other cells.
Plant cells		
Root hair cell (page 160)		**Absorbs minerals and water** from the soil water. The cell has a long extension (a root hair) which increases the surface area for the absorption of materials.
Xylem vessel (page 162)		**Transports water and supports the plant.** The cell has no cytoplasm (so water can pass freely), no end wall (so that many cells can form a continuous tube) and walls strengthened with a waterproof substance called lignin.

Specialised cells combine to form tissues ...

Cells with similar structures and functions are massed together in **tissues**. Some plant and animal tissues are shown in the tables below.

Animal tissue	Main functions
Epithelium	Lines tubes such as the gut and covers surfaces such as the skin
Connective tissue	Binds and strengthens other tissues, such as tendons
Blood	Transports substances around the body, and defends against disease
Skeletal tissue	Supports and protects softer tissues, and allows movement
Nervous tissue	Sets up nerve impulses and transmits them around the body
Muscle tissue	Contracts to support and move the body

Plant tissue	Main functions
Epidermis	Protects against water loss, and may be involved in absorption of water and ions
Mesophyll	Photosynthesis
Parenchyma	Fills spaces between other plant tissues and may be involved in storage, as in the potato tuber
Vascular tissue	Transports materials through the plant body
Strengthening tissue	Supports the plant

... tissues combine to form organs ...

Several tissues may be combined to form an **organ**, a complex structure with a particular function, such as the small intestine shown right.

... organs combine to form organ systems

In complex organisms, several organs work together to perform a particular task. These organs form an **organ system**. Systems in animals and flowering plants are shown on the next two pages and below.

Each cell, tissue and organ in an organism has a specialised part to play (there is **division of labour**) but their activities must be coordinated.

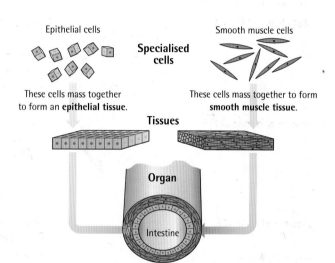

Epithelial cells   **Specialised cells**   Smooth muscle cells

These cells mass together to form an **epithelial tissue**.

These cells mass together to form **smooth muscle tissue**.

Tissues

Organ

Intestine

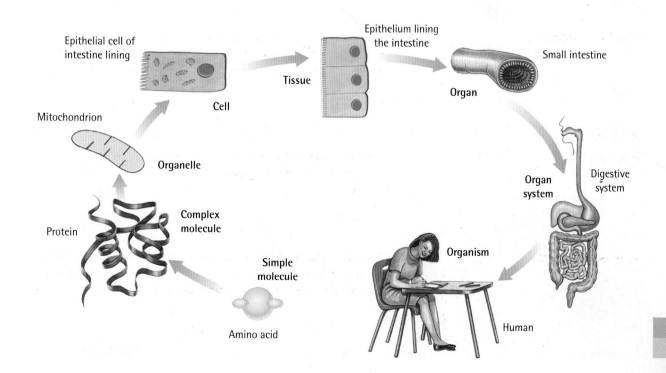

Epithelial cell of intestine lining

Mitochondrion

Organelle

Protein

Complex molecule

Simple molecule

Amino acid

Cell

Tissue

Epithelium lining the intestine

Organ

Small intestine

Organ system

Digestive system

Organism

Human

Animal organ systems are coordinated by the nervous and endocrine systems.

The nervous system is made up of the **brain, spinal cord, sense organs** and **peripheral nerves.** It conducts impulses to integrate the activities of other systems. It is the principal regulatory system.

The respiratory system consists of the **lungs** and **air passageways**. It maintains optimum concentrations of carbon dioxide and oxygen in the tissues.

The muscular system comprises **skeletal, cardiac** and **smooth muscle**. It is responsible for locomotion, movement of body parts, pumping of blood and internal movement of other materials. It maintains blood pressure and is responsible for the formation of tissue fluid.

The skeletal system consists of **bones** and **cartilage**. It supports the body, protects soft tissues and is the site of calcium storage and blood cell synthesis.

The reproductive systems comprise **testes** (male), **ovaries** (female) and associated structures. They produce and transfer gametes, and maintain secondary sex characteristics.

Skin, hair, nails and **sweat glands** protect the body against infection and dehydration, help control body temperature and receive stimuli about the external environment such as pressure and heat.

The circulatory system is composed of two subsystems. The **cardiovascular system** (heart, blood vessels and blood) is the transport system that carries many solutes, and the **lymphatic system** (lymph vessels and lymph) returns tissue fluid to the blood and helps defend against diseases.

The endocrine system consists of the **ductless glands**, many of which are under the influence of the pituitary gland. These regulate many body functions, and help to keep the composition of the blood constant.

The urinary system comprises the **kidneys, bladder** and associated **ducts**. These produce urine and remove it from the body. They remove toxins from the blood and maintain optimum solute concentrations.

The digestive system comprises the **mouth, oesophagus, stomach, intestines, liver** and **pancreas**. These organs ingest food, break it down mechanically and chemically, and absorb nutrients, so maintaining optimum concentrations of fuel molecules and raw materials for metabolism.

Plant organ systems allow great efficiency through division of labour.

The **reproductive system** consists of **flowers** which, when fertilised, produce **fruits**. These disperse the seeds containing the embryo, which will produce the next generation of plants.

The **epidermis** covers the plant and prevents the plant body drying out. This is vital for plants since they must be exposed to the drying effect of sunlight in order to photosynthesise.

Leaves form the main **photosynthetic system** that provides the organic compounds required for plant growth and development.

The **stem** contains the tube-like **vascular system**. This transports materials through the body of the plant. The stem is also strong enough to act as a support system, holding the leaves in the best position for photosynthesis and the flowers for pollination.

Roots are the **absorptive system** for the plant, taking up minerals and water from the soil and delivering them to the main vascular system. The roots are highly branched which helps anchor the plant in the soil.

---

1 Copy and complete the following paragraphs.

a Large numbers of _____ that have the same structure and function are grouped together to form _____, for example _____. Several separate tissues may be joined together to form an _____ which is a complex structure that can perform a particular task with great efficiency. In the most highly developed organisms, these complex structures may work together in _____. For example, the _____ in humans is responsible for the removal of the waste products of metabolism.

b The structure of cells may be highly adapted to perform one function, that is, the cells may become _____. One good example is the _____ which is adapted to carry oxygen in mammalian blood.

If the different cells, tissues and organs of a multicellular organism perform different functions they are said to show _____ of _____.

One consequence of this is the need for close coordination between different organs – this function is performed by the _____ and _____ systems in mammals.

c In plants, an example of a cell highly specialised for photosynthesis is the _____ which contains many _____. These cells are located in the organ called the _____. This organ also contains other tissues such as _____ which limits water loss and _____ which transports water and mineral ions to the leaf.

2 'The structure of an organ is related to its function'. Use one animal organ and one plant organ to illustrate this statement.

1·9 Movement in and out of cells

Objectives

- To understand that the contents of a living cell must be kept separate from its surroundings
- To know that the cell surface membrane can act as a barrier to some substances which might pass between a cell and its surroundings
- To understand the principles of diffusion, osmosis, active transport and phagocytosis

On page 18 we saw that the cell cytoplasm is surrounded by a **cell surface membrane**. This acts as a boundary between the cell contents and its surroundings – it has very little strength, but it plays a vital role in regulating the materials that pass in and out of the cell. Materials may pass in and out of cells by:

- **diffusion**
- **osmosis**
- **active transport**
- in special cases, **phagocytosis**.

Diffusion – 'mixing molecules'

Molecules and ions in a liquid or a gas move continuously. The movement is quite random, and the particles change direction as they bump into one another. The particles collide more often when they are close together (when they are **concentrated**) and so they tend to **diffuse**, or spread out, until they are spaced evenly throughout the gas or liquid. The movement of the particles is due to their own **kinetic energy**. When diffusion happens in living cells, the cells themselves do not have to expend any energy for it to take place.

If there is a region of high concentration and a region of low concentration, we can say that there is a **concentration gradient** between the regions. We can therefore define **diffusion** as:

- the movement of particles within a gas or liquid
- from a region of high concentration to a region of lower concentration (down a concentration gradient)
- until an equilibrium is reached.

Partially permeable membranes

Not all particles can diffuse through cell surface membranes. Sometimes the particles are too big, or they have the wrong electrical charge on them, or the chemical composition of the membrane prevents them passing across. The diagram below shows a **partially permeable membrane** – it is **permeable** to glucose and water but **impermeable** to protein.

Diffusion and life processes

Diffusion is the main process by which substances move over short distances in living organisms. Some of the life processes that involve diffusion are shown in the diagram above right.

Living organisms have certain adaptations to speed up diffusion:

- **Diffusion distances are short** – the membranes in the lungs, for example, are very thin so that oxygen and carbon dioxide can diffuse between the blood and the lung air spaces.
- **Concentration gradients are maintained** – glucose molecules that cross from the gut into the blood, for example, are quickly removed by the circulating blood so that their concentration does not build up and equilibrium is not reached.
- **Diffusion surfaces are large** – the surface of the placenta, for example, is highly folded to increase the surface area for the diffusion of molecules between a pregnant female and the developing fetus in her uterus.

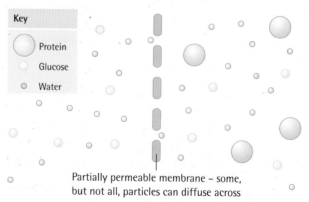

Key
- Protein
- Glucose
- Water

Partially permeable membrane – some, but not all, particles can diffuse across

The overall (net) movement of glucose and water molecules depends on their concentration gradient. Protein molecules cannot diffuse across this membrane, even though the concentration gradient suggests that they should move from right to left.

Life depends on the exchange of materials between different cells, and between cells and their surroundings. For example, a plant absorbs carbon dioxide from its surroundings by diffusion, and the carbon dioxide passes through the leaf to the photosynthesising cells by the same process.

From the lungs, oxygen enters the blood by diffusion. The continual movement of the blood keeps up a high concentration gradient between the air and the blood.

Glucose and amino acids pass from inside the gut into the blood, partly by the process of diffusion.

looks like a beanstalk to me!

Oxygen produced by photosynthesis diffuses out of the plant into the air. It enters the boy's lungs as he breathes in. The lungs are adapted to speed up the diffusion of oxygen into the blood, since they have thin surfaces with a very large surface area.

Mineral ions from the soil solution are absorbed by plant roots. This process depends upon diffusion as well as on active transport.

Many life processes depend on diffusion to move substances around. Diffusion has no 'energy cost' to a living organism.

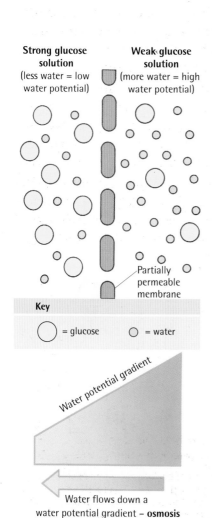

Strong glucose solution
(less water = low water potential)

Weak glucose solution
(more water = high water potential)

Partially permeable membrane

Key

◯ = glucose   ○ = water

Water potential gradient

Water flows down a water potential gradient – **osmosis**

Osmosis is a special case of diffusion

The biochemical processes in living cells always take place in a **solution**. A solution is made up of a **solvent** (the dissolving fluid) and a **solute** (the particles dissolved in the solvent). In living organisms, the solvent is water and the solution is called an aqueous solution.

Living cells are separated from their surroundings by the **partially permeable cell surface membrane**. The contents of the cell, the cytoplasm, is one aqueous solution and the surroundings of the cell, for example pond water, is another aqueous solution. If the two solutions do not have the same concentrations of various substances, molecules may move from one to the other by diffusion, if the membrane is permeable to these substances.

The diagram on the left shows two glucose solutions separated by a partially permeable membrane – this membrane will allow the diffusion of water molecules but not glucose (the solute) molecules. As a result water can move from the right, where there is a high concentration of water molecules, to the left, where there is a lower concentration of water molecules, by the process of diffusion. This diffusion of water is called **osmosis**, and will continue until a water equilibrium has been reached.

Because it is sometimes confusing to talk about water 'concentration', biologists use the term **water potential** instead. A solution with many water molecules has a **high water potential**, and a solution with few water molecules has a **low water potential**. In the diagram, a **water potential gradient** exists between the two solutions, and water molecules can flow down this gradient from right to left.

Osmosis can be defined as:

▪ **the diffusion of water molecules**

▪ **down a water potential gradient**

▪ **across a partially permeable membrane.**

Cells and osmosis

A cell is surrounded by a partially permeable membrane, and water may cross this membrane easily. If a cell is placed in a solution of lower water potential, water leaves the cell by osmosis. If the cell is placed in a solution of higher water potential, water enters by osmosis.

Plant cells and osmosis

If water enters a plant cell by osmosis the cytoplasm will swell, but only until it pushes against the cellulose cell wall, as shown below. A plant cell will not be permanently damaged by the entry of water. If water leaves a plant cell by osmosis the cytoplasm will shrink, but the cellulose cell wall will continue to give some support. Plant cells rarely suffer permanent damage by the loss of water. The effect of water gain or loss on whole plants is described on page 166.

Water potential of surroundings

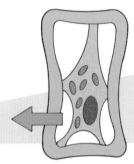 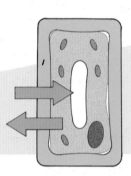 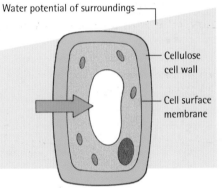

Cellulose cell wall

Cell surface membrane

Cell in solution of lower water potential than cell contents – water leaves by osmosis. The cytoplasm pulls away from the cell wall and the cell becomes **flaccid** ('floppy').

Cell in solution of equal water potential – no *net* movement of water; cytoplasm just presses against cell wall.

Cell in solution of higher water potential – water enters by osmosis. The cytoplasm pushes hard against the cell wall and the cell becomes **turgid** (firm).

Animal cells and osmosis

Animal cells have no cell wall, just a membrane. They are likely to suffer damage as a result of osmosis, as shown in the diagram below.

Osmosis is potentially damaging to animal cells, and animals have mechanisms to keep the blood plasma and the body fluids at the same water potential as the cytoplasm of cells. In mammals the kidney plays a vital part in this process of **osmoregulation** (see page 116).

Red blood cell

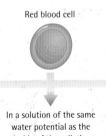

In a solution of lower water potential, the cell shrinks and becomes **crenated**

In a solution of the same water potential as the inside of the cell, the cell is in equilibrium

In a solution of higher water potential, the cell takes in water, swells and bursts (**haemolysis**)

The 'ghost' of a red blood cell; just the membrane is left behind

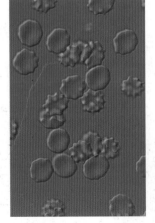

Crenated red blood cells

Red blood cells in equilibrium

Active transport requires energy to move materials

Molecules and ions can move from one place to another by diffusion, but only until an equilibrium has been reached. If no concentration gradient exists between the two places, no diffusion can occur – this means that if an equilibrium has been reached, useful particles cannot be absorbed by diffusion. **Active transport** is a method by which particles can cross membranes even against a concentration gradient. In active transport, protein molecules in the cell surface membrane pick up and carry particles across the membrane. These protein molecules are called **carriers**, and when they work they use energy supplied by the cell. Active transport is explained in the diagram below, and one important example of its use is the uptake of ions by plants (page 161). To summarise – active transport:

- can move molecules **against a concentration gradient** but
- **requires energy** and
- **involves protein carriers in membranes.**

Some cells use phagocytosis

Some particles are too large to cross a membrane by diffusion or by active transport. A few very specialised cells have developed a method for taking up these particles – the particles are literally engulfed by the cell surface membrane flowing around them. This process of **phagocytosis** is used by white blood cells, and is described on page 294.

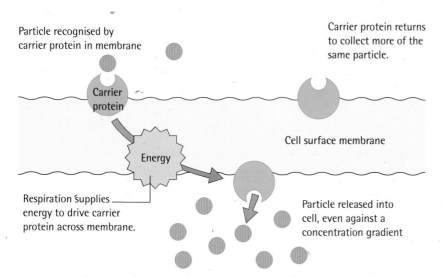

Particle recognised by carrier protein in membrane

Carrier protein

Energy

Respiration supplies energy to drive carrier protein across membrane.

Carrier protein returns to collect more of the same particle.

Cell surface membrane

Particle released into cell, even against a concentration gradient

Active transport uses energy to move substances against a concentration gradient. The protein carriers involved in active transport are rather like enzymes. They are able to recognise particular molecules and select them from a mixture. As a result active transport is specific, and the cell can 'choose' which molecules it will absorb from its surroundings.

1 Using an example, explain what is meant by a partially permeable membrane.

2 What is a concentration gradient?

3 Make a list of the processes in living organisms that are dependent on diffusion.

4 How are living organisms adapted to increase the possibility of diffusion?

5 Copy and complete the following paragraphs.
Animal cells contain _____, a semi-fluid solution of salts and other molecules, and are surrounded by a _____. When in distilled water, the animal cells _____ because the cell has a _____ water potential than the surrounding water. Plant cells do not have this problem because they are surrounded by a _____.

In the gut, soluble food substances such as _____ cross the gut lining into the capillaries by the process of _____, which is the movement of molecules down a _____. When an equilibrium is reached between the gut contents and the blood, glucose may continue to be moved using the process called _____, which consumes _____ and can move molecules _____ a concentration gradient.

The leaves of green plants obtain the gas _____, which they require for the process of photosynthesis, by the process of _____. They also lose the gas oxygen, produced during _____, by the same process.

6 Make a table that compares diffusion with active transport. Include one example of each process in your table. Under what circumstances would an organism use phagocytosis rather than diffusion or active transport?

1·10 Respiration provides the energy for life

Objectives

- To understand that energy is needed to carry out work
- To appreciate that different forms of energy can be interconverted
- To be able to list some of the energy-demanding processes in living organisms
- To describe how the process of respiration releases energy from chemical foods

Energy conversions in living things

Energy can be defined as 'the capacity for doing work'. The processes that keep organisms alive (for example, pumping ions from one side of a membrane to another) usually require work to be done. It is clear, therefore, that life requires energy.

Life also depends on energy **conversions**. The first and most important energy conversion in living things is **photosynthesis**. This process will be described in greater detail on page 148, but in energy terms it can be described simply as:

> Light energy from the Sun
> ⇓
> Converted in green plants
> ⇓
> Chemical energy in organic molecules

A second energy-conversion process releases the chemical energy stored in organic food molecules and converts it to energy forms that organisms use to stay alive. This process is called **respiration**. The diagram at the bottom of the page shows some of the energy conversions carried out by living organisms.

What is respiration?

Respiration involves the **oxidation** of food molecules, and energy is released during the process. These food molecules all contain carbon, hydrogen and oxygen and the complete oxidation process converts these to carbon dioxide and water. Complete oxidation occurs only if oxygen is present. For example:

> Glucose + oxygen → energy + carbon dioxide + water

So much energy is released in this process that if it was all released at once, the cell might be damaged. The energy is released in small 'packets' which can then drive the reactions that keep the cell alive. These energy packets act as a short-term store of energy. The one used most commonly by cells is a molecule called **adenosine triphosphate (ATP)**.

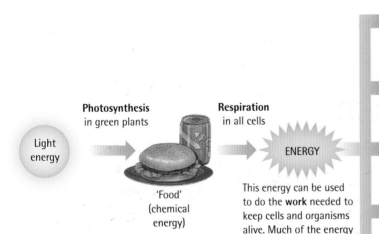

Photosynthesis in green plants

Respiration in all cells

Light energy

'Food' (chemical energy)

ENERGY

This energy can be used to do the **work** needed to keep cells and organisms alive. Much of the energy will eventually return to the environment as **heat**.

Growth: uses energy to synthesise large molecules from smaller ones (e.g. proteins from amino acids).

Maintenance of body temperature: all chemical reactions in the body release some heat, particularly reactions in the liver.

Active transport: moving molecules against a concentration gradient, e.g. ion uptake by roots.

Cell division: replication and separation of chromosomes is very energy demanding. A human replaces billions of cells every day.

Movement: contraction of muscle requires energy. The supply of energy will run out if food or oxygen is limited.

Living organisms obtain their food by nutrition (see page 34). They release energy from food in the process of respiration, and use it to carry out the work needed for life.

The reactions are summarised in the following equation.

glucose + oxygen
 |→ ATP → 'work' in cells
↓
carbon dioxide + water

This process, which releases energy in the presence of oxygen, is called **aerobic respiration** ('aerobic' means 'in air').

Anaerobic respiration – energy release in the absence of oxygen

Oxygen is not always available to a cell, for example, when the blood cannot deliver oxygen quickly enough during exercise. Energy can still be released from food molecules without oxygen by **anaerobic respiration**, but:

▪ the food molecule is only partly broken down

▪ much less energy is available to the cell from each food molecule (only about one-twentieth of the amount released by aerobic respiration).

The chemistry of respiration

Adenosine triphosphate or ATP is the 'energy currency' of the cell. Respiration produces ATP, which can then be used by the cell when and where it is needed. If ATP is used to perform work in the cell, it is broken down to **adenosine diphosphate (ADP)** and **phosphate (P)**. More energy from respiration will be needed to rebuild the ATP once more.

The release of energy by the oxidation of glucose takes place in many steps, as outlined in the flow diagram.

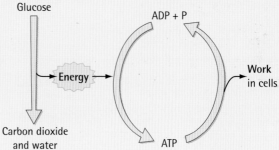

These first steps split the glucose molecule into two halves. Little energy is released (only enough to produce **two molecules of ATP**). The reactions take place in the **cytoplasm** of the cell, and do not need oxygen. No carbon dioxide is produced.

This step is different in animal cells (where lactic acid is produced) and in cells of fungi such as yeast (where ethanol and carbon dioxide are produced). No oxygen is needed – this is the end of **anaerobic respiration**, (see pages 124 and 302). These reactions take place in the cytoplasm.

Aerobic respiration – these steps are only possible if oxygen is present. A great deal of energy is released (another **36 molecules of ATP**), and many molecules of carbon dioxide are produced. These reactions all take place inside the **mitochondria**.

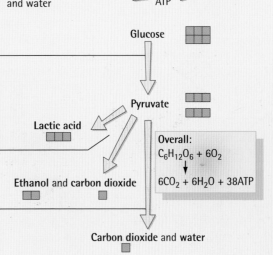

Overall:
$$C_6H_{12}O_6 + 6O_2 \rightarrow 6CO_2 + 6H_2O + 38ATP$$

1·11 The measurement of respiration

Objectives

- To explain how it is possible to detect the process of respiration

Since respiration is essential for life, an obvious 'sign of life' is that respiration is taking place. We can demonstrate that respiration is happening, and we can even measure how quickly it is going on.

The equation for aerobic respiration suggests methods that we might use to demonstrate this process.

Glucose + oxygen → energy + carbon dioxide + water

Oxygen consumption can be measured using a **respirometer**.

Energy release can be measured as the production of **heat**.

Involvement of enzymes can be demonstrated by the effects of temperature changes on respiration.

Carbon dioxide release causes:
- limewater to turn milky
- hydrogencarbonate indicator solution to turn from red → yellow-orange.

To demonstrate that respiration is going on, we need to use some living organisms. Germinating seeds are useful for this experiment since they are chemically very active (the fast growth during germination requires a great deal of energy). Animals such as blowfly larvae (maggots) or woodlice can also be used, although they are rather more difficult to handle.

Glucose consumption and water release

In theory, we could measure **glucose consumption** to demonstrate respiration, but this is difficult to do in a school laboratory. In a more advanced laboratory it is possible to provide an organism with radioactively labelled glucose and to measure how quickly the radioactive label ends up in carbon dioxide. Using up food leads to **loss of mass**, so this might provide a measure of respiration. However, mass is also lost by evaporation of water from an organism's body surfaces, so loss of mass is not a clear indicator of food use.

Respiration produces water, so this **release of water** itself might indicate that respiration is taking place. However, water can also evaporate from the surface of non-living things.

1 Measurement of oxygen consumption using a respirometer

The apparatus shown in the diagram on the next page is used.

a A measured mass of living organisms is put in the chamber.

b First the spring clip is open, so that an equilibrium of temperature and pressure is set up between the chamber and the surroundings.

c After five minutes or so, the spring clip is closed and the movement of the coloured liquid along the capillary tube is observed. The time taken for it to move a measured length along the tube is noted.

d The living organisms are removed and the experiment is repeated.

Using this apparatus, a group of students obtained the following data.

Experiment	Distance moved (mm)	Time taken (s)	Relative oxygen consumption (mm/s)
1 Seeds	39	100	
2 Seeds	42	100	
3 Seeds	24	60	
4 Maggots	46	90	
5 Maggots	55	100	
6 Maggots	30	60	

Principle: Carbon dioxide produced during respiration is absorbed by potassium hydroxide solution. If the system is closed to the atmosphere, a change in volume of the gas within the chamber must be due to the consumption of oxygen. The change in volume, i.e. the oxygen consumption, is measured as the movement of a drop of coloured liquid along a capillary tube.

Spring clip – when open, contents of chamber are in equilibrium with atmosphere.

Rubber stopper – can be made more airtight by smearing Vaseline along seal between chamber and stopper.

Filter paper wick ensures that maximum surface area of potassium hydroxide solution is available to contents of chamber.

Potassium hydroxide solution absorbs carbon dioxide evolved during respiration.

Graduated scale against which movement of coloured liquid can be measured

Coloured liquid – narrow-bore capillary tube means that any small change in volume of gas in chamber produces a large movement of liquid.

Gauze basket to hold respiring material must be porous to allow free exchange of gases.

Respiratory chamber has relatively low volume, so that changes in volume due to respiration are significant enough to be measured.

Weighed amount of respiring material – the mass, m, of the respiring material should be known so that results can be compared with other experiments.

Glass rod to keep respiring material out of direct contact with potassium hydroxide solution

---

2 Measurement of carbon dioxide release

To detect carbon dioxide released by respiring organisms, we can use an **indicator solution.** For example **hydrogencarbonate indicator** is purple at high pH (alkaline), red around neutral pH and orange-yellow at low pH (acidic). The diagram shows the apparatus.

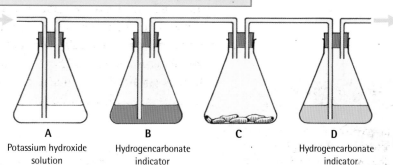

A	B	C	D
Potassium hydroxide solution	Hydrogencarbonate indicator		Hydrogencarbonate indicator

---

[1] a In experiment **1** why did the students take more than one set of readings for each group of organisms?

b Calculate the mean relative oxygen consumption for the seeds and for the maggots. Suggest a reason for the difference.

[2] The students repeated the experiment with no living organisms in the chamber. The coloured liquid did not move at all. Why was this important?

[3] In an extension of this investigation, the students measured the effect of temperature on the rate of

oxygen consumption by the maggots. They obtained the following results:

Temperature (°C)	Relative oxygen consumption (mm/s)
15	0.3
25	0.6
35	1.1
45	0.8
55	0.2
65	0.0

a Plot these results on a graph, and explain the shape of the curve.

b In this investigation, identify the **manipulated variable** and the **responding variable.**

c suggest any **fixed variables.** (Refer to page 16 if you are unsure about these terms.)

In experiment 2:

[4] What is the purpose of the potassium hydroxide solution?

[5] What does the indicator solution in flask B show?

[6] How can you explain the change in flask D?

[7] Suggest a control for this investigation, and explain why it is a suitable control.

[8] Suggest any visible change that might happen in flask **C.** Explain your answer.

1·12 Questions on basic principles

1 **a** The bar chart opposite shows the percentage of each of the main elements in the human body.
Convert this data into:
i a table   **ii** a pie chart.
Which do you think is the better way of showing the data? Explain why.

b These elements are mostly present in the body as part of compounds. The proportions of the main groups of compounds in a human body are shown in the table.

  i Which is the most abundant compound?

  ii Which compound contains most of the nitrogen in the body?

  iii Which compound contains most of the oxygen?

  iv Which compound contains most of the carbon?

  v The total of these compounds does not add up to 100%. Suggest another organic compound that forms a proportion of the remainder.

  vi Try to find out which structure(s) in the body contain most of the calcium.

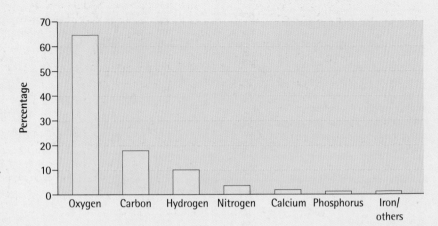

The main elements in the human body.

Compound	Approximate percentage in the body
Fats	14%
Proteins	12%
Carbohydrates	1%
Water	70%

2 **a** The properties of enzymes were investigated using the simple experiment shown opposite.
Which of the following conclusions are valid from these results?

  i The enzyme reaction occurs more quickly at 30 °C than at 20 °C.

  ii The enzyme in saliva is inactivated by boiling.

  iii Saliva contains an enzyme which digests starch.

  iv Boiled saliva contains an enzyme which digests starch.

b What is the purpose of tube **D**?

c How could you increase the validity of these results?

d What is the product of starch digestion present in tubes **A** and **B** after 20 minutes? Describe a simple biochemical test for this substance.

Time of test for starch

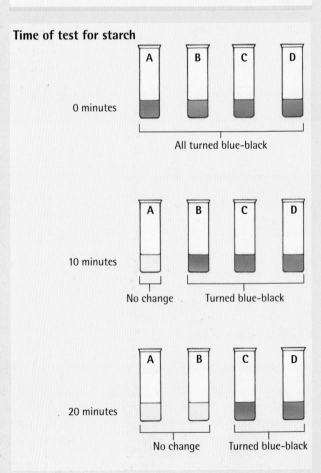

Four test tubes were set up:

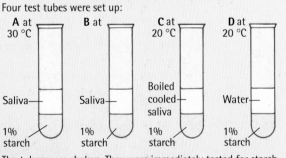

The tubes were shaken. They were immediately tested for starch by adding one drop of iodine solution to one drop of the mixture in a specimen tube. The test was repeated at intervals.

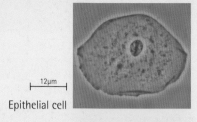

Epithelial cell

├─ 12μm ─┤

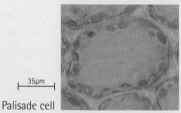

├─ 35μm ─┤

Palisade cell

3 Look at these photomicrographs (photographs taken through a microscope).

a List three differences between the epithelial and palisade cells, and three common features which they share. Why are there differences between these cells?

b Use the scales to calculate the following in μm:

i the height of the palisade cell
ii the width of the palisade cell
iii the width of the epithelial cell at its widest point
iv the length of a single chloroplast
v the length of an animal cell nucleus.

c Show your working in each case:

i Assume that the epithelial cell is a sphere. Calculate its volume (volume of sphere $= 4/3\pi r^3$).
ii Assume that the palisade cell is a cylinder. Calculate its volume (volume of cylinder $= \pi r^2 h$).
iii How much greater is the volume of the plant cell than that of the animal cell? Express your answer as a ratio.

4 In an investigation to measure the speed of diffusion, cubes of gelatin which had been stained purple with an indicator solution were placed in dilute acid as shown in the diagram. The time taken for each cube to turn completely orange is shown in the table.

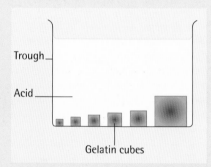

Trough

Acid

Gelatin cubes

Length of side of cube (mm)	Time taken to turn orange (s)	Surface area of cube (total of 6 sides) (mm²)	Volume of cube (mm³)	Surface area to volume ratio (surface area ÷ volume)
1	20			
2	41			
3	76			
4	104			
5	188			
10	600			

a Copy and complete the table. Plot a graph of surface area to volume ratio against time taken to turn orange. Plot time taken on the vertical axis.

b What do the results suggest about the efficiency of diffusion in supplying materials to the centre of an organism's body?

c Suggest methods which organisms might use to improve the supply of materials by diffusion. Try to provide examples of these methods.

5 A student carried out an investigation based on the one in the diagram using a range of sugar solutions. He obtained the results below right.

a Copy and complete the table, and present the results in a suitable graph.

b Use the graph to calculate the sugar concentration inside the potato cells. Explain your answer.

c Why is it useful to present the results in terms of 'percentage change' in length?

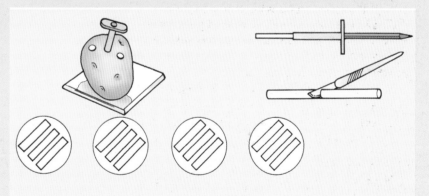

Concentration of sugar solution (mol/dm³)	Length of cylinder at start (mm)	Mean length (mm)	Length of cylinder after 24 hours (mm)	Mean length (mm)	Percentage change
0.0	50, 50, 50		54, 52, 55		
0.1	50, 49, 50		53, 52, 53		
0.2	50, 50, 50		51, 52, 51		
0.3	50, 51, 49		49, 49, 49		
0.4	50, 50, 50		47, 47, 48		
0.5	50, 51, 51		45, 47, 46		

Basic principles

2·1 Food and the ideal diet: carbohydrates, lipids and proteins

Objectives
- To understand why organisms require food
- To list the constituents of an ideal diet
- To know the functions of each component of an ideal diet

Food

All living organisms are made up of molecules, organised so that they can carry out the characteristics of life. Food supplies them with:

- molecules that are the **raw materials** for repair, growth and development of the body tissues
- molecules that can be oxidised in respiration, and act as a **source of energy**
- elements and compounds that enable the raw materials and energy to be used efficiently.

All living organisms need food, but some, green plants in particular, can manufacture their own organic molecules. These organisms are said to be **autotrophic** (or 'self feeding'). Green plants use a form of autotrophic nutrition called **photosynthesis** to supply them with all the organic molecules they need (see page 148). Other organisms cannot make their own food, and must take in food molecules from their surroundings. These molecules have been made by another organism, so living things that feed in this way are said to be **heterotrophic** (or 'other feeding'). Humans, like all animals, are totally dependent on other organisms for their food.

A balanced diet

The total of the molecules or **nutrients** that we need is called the **diet**. A **balanced diet** provides all the nutrients, in the correct amounts, needed to carry out the life processes. If the diet does not provide all the nutrients in the correct proportions, a person may suffer from **malnutrition** (see page 40, for example).

Food can be analysed to find out what chemicals it contains, using quite simple chemical techniques (see page 13). A balanced diet should contain the correct proportions of **carbohydrates**, **lipids**, **proteins**, **vitamins** and **minerals**, **water** and **dietary fibre**. We shall look at each in turn.

Carbohydrates

Carbohydrates, for example glucose or starch, are the main **energy source** for living cells. Some cells, such as those of the nervous system, cannot use any other molecules as an energy source, and would die without carbohydrate. Carbohydrate should make up about $5/7$ of the solid part of the diet, and ideally no more than $2/7$ of the carbohydrate should be refined sugars such as glucose. Refined sugars are absorbed very rapidly, giving a sudden boost of 'energy source'. Starch is digested and absorbed more slowly, giving a steady supply of energy source. Starches are called **slow-release carbohydrates**. Plants have a relatively high carbohydrate content – potatoes, rice, bread and pasta are very rich sources of starch. Refined sugars are common in sweets, desserts and many soft drinks.

These foods are high in carbohydrate.

Lipids

Lipids include **fats** and **oils**, such as those found in butter and cheese, and **cholesterol**, found in egg yolk for example. Animal foods such as meat are a rich source of lipids, along with some nuts and seeds. Fats and oils are another **energy source**, and are particularly valuable as an **energy store** because they are insoluble in water. They also provide **insulation** – electrical insulation around the nerves and thermal insulation beneath the skin – and form part of **cell membranes**. Some lipids (see page 11) contain **saturated fatty acids** (more common in animal foods) and others contain **unsaturated fatty acids** (with at least one carbon – carbon double bond – more common in plant foods). The wrong balance of saturated and unsaturated fatty acids in our diet can contribute to diseases of the circulation. Fats should not make up more than $\frac{1}{7}$ of our solid diet, and saturated fats should be less than half this.

These foods provide lipids.

Proteins

Proteins have many roles in humans, for example:

- as **catalysts** (enzymes)
- as **transport molecules** (for example, haemoglobin in the blood)
- as **structural materials** (such as in muscles)
- as **hormones** (for example, insulin)
- in **defence against disease** (antibodies).

Proteins are long chains of **amino acids** (see page 11), and 20 different amino acids are needed to make up all the different proteins in the human body. Some of these amino acids must be supplied in the diet – these are the **essential amino acids**. Others can be manufactured by biochemical reactions in the cells. Proteins from animal sources usually contain all 20 amino acids, but plant proteins often lack one or more of the essential amino acids. Protein from a wide variety of sources should make up about $\frac{1}{7}$ of our solid diet. Meat, fish, eggs and cheese are good sources of animal protein; peas and beans are good sources of plant protein.

These foods have a high proportion of proteins.

One of the best plant sources of protein is the soya bean. This contains very little fat (unlike most animal sources, such as red meat) and so is suitable for people with health problems caused by fat. Soya

beans can be flavoured and textured to make them taste and feel like meat – this **textured vegetable protein** is used as 'artificial' meat in some vegetarian dishes. Microorganisms can also provide a source of protein for humans and other animals (see page 304).

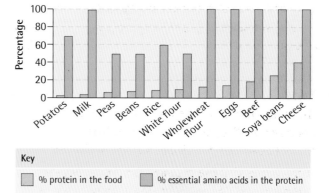

Key

▢ % protein in the food   ▢ % essential amino acids in the protein

The protein values of some common foods.

Essential amino acids – cry baby

One factor that determines how comfortable babies feel is the supply of a 'pleasure chemical', called **serotonin** in the brain (see neurotransmitters, page 89). An essential amino acid called **lysine** is needed to make serotonin. Lysine is in short supply in some artificial milks. Babies fed on these milk substitutes can't manufacture enough serotonin, they feel uncomfortable and they CCCCRRRRRRRRRRYYYYYYYYYY! Natural mother's milk contains an adequate supply of lysine.

Vegetarians must ensure that their diet contains a wide range of protein sources since very few plants contain all the essential amino acids. An ideal vegetarian meal containing all the essential amino acids is baked beans on toast (which also contains a high proportion of dietary fibre).

1. Give three reasons why living organisms need food.
2. Write one sentence to explain the difference between autotrophic and heterotrophic nutrition.
3. What is a balanced diet?
4. Which are the main energy foods for humans?
5. State four functions of proteins, using particular examples to illustrate your answer.

Food and the ideal diet: vitamins, minerals, water and fibre

Vitamins and minerals

Vitamins and minerals are essential for the body to be able to use the other nutrients efficiently. They are needed in only very small amounts. There are many different vitamins and minerals, and they are usually provided in the foods of a balanced diet.

Vitamin C is a water-soluble vitamin found in green leafy vegetables such as spinach, and in citrus fruits such as oranges, lemons and limes. Vitamin C is essential for the formation of the connective tissues of the body. If someone does not have enough of a particular vitamin or mineral in the diet, they can suffer from a **deficiency disease**. For example, **scurvy** is caused by too little vitamin C, and people with scurvy have loose teeth and their wounds do not heal well. Vitamin C also protects cells from ageing.

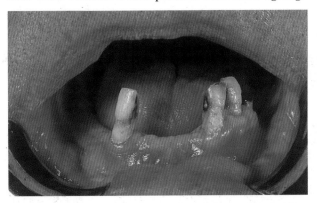

This person has scurvy, caused by insufficient vitamin C in the diet.

Vitamin D is a fat-soluble vitamin found in fish liver oils and in milk. It can also be made by the body, just beneath the top layer of the skin, as long as the person is exposed to sunlight. People who live in sunny parts of the world can usually make enough vitamin D to last through the winter. Vitamin D is needed for the efficient uptake and use of calcium ions – if there is a shortage of vitamin D, calcium cannot be incorporated into teeth and bones. People affected by the vitamin D deficiency disease called **rickets** have weak legs which may bend under the weight of their body. Vitamin D is fat soluble, so people who take in too little fat in their diet can suffer from vitamin D deficiency.

Iron is a mineral required for the synthesis of **haemoglobin**, the pigment in red blood cells that transports oxygen around the body. Iron also has other functions, such as helping mitochondria to release energy during respiration. Iron is plentiful in red meat, especially in liver, and is 'added' to food

Iron is needed to make haemoglobin, the pigment that makes red blood cells red.

People who have insufficient iron in the diet may become anaemic. Anaemic people look pale, and feel very tired.

when metal utensils are used in cooking – the amount of iron in a piece of beef is doubled when the meat is minced in an iron mincer ready for making burgers! Since iron is essential for the proper functioning of red blood cells, a deficiency causes a reduced ability to transport oxygen. This deficiency disease is called **anaemia**. A person affected by anaemia feels tired and weak.

Calcium forms part of the structure of bones and teeth, it is needed for muscles to contract and it plays a part in the clotting of the blood. Good sources of this mineral are milk, cheese and fish, and a shortage in the diet leads to **rickets**, the same deficiency disease caused by insufficient vitamin D.

Water

Water forms about 70% of the human body. Two-thirds of this water is in the cytoplasm of cells, and the other third is in tissue fluid and blood plasma. Humans lose about 1.5 litres of water each day, in urine, faeces, exhaled air and sweat – this must be replaced by water in the diet. It is obtained in three main ways:

- as a drink
- in food, especially salad foods such as tomatoes and lettuce
- from metabolic processes (think back to the equation for aerobic respiration – water is one of the products).

A loss of only 5% of the body's water can lead to unconsciousness, and a loss of 10% would be fatal. We shall look further at how the body conserves water on page 116.

Fibre

Dietary fibre is the indigestible part of food, largely cellulose from plant cell walls, which provides bulk for the faeces. Plenty of fibre in the diet stretches the muscles of the gut wall and helps push the food along by peristalsis (see page 46). A shortage of fibre can cause constipation, and may be a factor in the development of bowel cancer.

Summary of a balanced diet

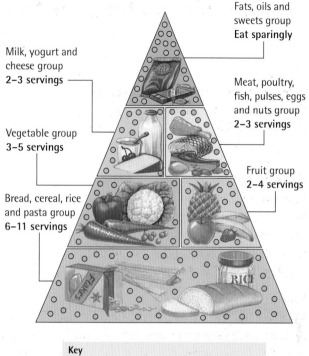

Key

- ○ Fat (naturally occurring and added to food)
- ○ Sugars (added to food)

Food guide pyramid: choosing to eat these amounts of different kinds of foods each day provides a balanced diet.

---

1. Table 1 shows the daily energy needs of different people. Table 2 shows the energy content of four foods.
   a What is the daily energy need for an active 8-year-old boy?
   b How many grams of Food 3 would meet the energy needs of an office worker?
   c How much more energy does a labourer need than a male office worker each day? Show your working.
   d i From the foods given in Table 2, which ONE would be the best for the labourer to eat? Give a reason for your choice.
   ii If the labourer ate only the food you have suggested in your answer to i, what is the least amount he should eat to meet his daily energy need? Show your working.
   e The heat energy in foods can be measured experimentally by burning food under a known mass of water. The temperature rise of the water is recorded. The number of joules received by the water from 1 gram of food can be calculated using the following formula:

   Heat gained by water from Y grams of food
   $$= \frac{\text{mass of water} \times \text{temperature rise} \times 4.2}{Y} \text{ J per g}$$

   Use the following data and the formula to work out the number of joules released from 1 gram of food which caused the rise in temperature of the water
   Mass of water = 20 g
   Temperature rise = 18 °C
   Mass of food = 2 g   *[MEG June 1994 (part)]*

Person	Occupation	Daily energy need (kJ)
Active girl aged 8 years	School girl	8 000
Active boy aged 8 years	School boy	8 400
Woman	Office worker	9 500
Man	Office worker	10 500
Active girl aged 15 years	School girl	11 800
Active boy aged 15 years	School boy	14 700
Man	Labourer	18 900

Table 1

Food	1	2	3	4
Energy content (kJ per 100 g)	3 800	130	1 050	400

Table 2

2·3 Food is the fuel that drives the processes of life

Objectives

▶ To know that food has an energy value
▶ To know how to calculate the energy value of different foods
▶ To understand that different people have different demands for energy

Measuring the energy in food

Energy is released from food by respiration, which is an oxidation process, similar in some ways to combustion – if food is combusted (burned), it releases energy, mainly as heat. We can work out the energy value of any particular type of food by assuming that respiration releases the same amount of energy in total as combustion does. The energy value is found using a **food calorimeter** or **bomb calorimeter**, shown in the diagram opposite.

A weighed sample of food is completely burned in an atmosphere of oxygen. The heat released by this combustion is transferred to a known volume of water, which rises in temperature as a result. The energy value of the food can be calculated as follows:

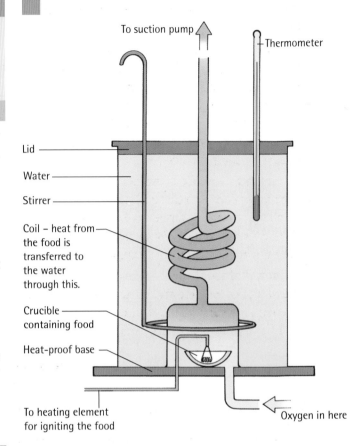

To suction pump
Thermometer
Lid
Water
Stirrer
Coil – heat from the food is transferred to the water through this.
Crucible containing food
Heat-proof base
To heating element for igniting the food
Oxygen in here

$$\text{Energy value of food in calories per gram} = \frac{\text{temperature rise (°C)} \times \text{volume of water (cm}^3)}{\text{mass of food sample (g)}}$$

$$\text{Energy value in kilojoules per gram} = \frac{\text{energy value in calories per gram}}{1000} \times 4.2$$

Energy values of different foods

The three main energy-providing organic molecules found in food are fats, carbohydrates and proteins. Each has a different energy value:

Fats	39 kJ/g
Proteins	20 kJ/g
Carbohydrates	17 kJ/g

Carbohydrates provide most of our energy, not because there is most energy available per gram in carbohydrates, but because we eat more grams of carbohydrates than of proteins or fats.

Units of energy

The SI unit of energy is the joule (J). The amount of energy contained in food is measured in either joules (J) or calories (cal).

1000 J = 1 kJ (kilojoule)   1000 cal = 1 kcal (kilocalorie)

A calorie is an older unit of energy that is still often used. A calorie is the amount of energy needed to raise the temperature of 1 cm^3 of water by 1 °C.

1 calorie = 4.2 joules

Joules and calories are small amounts of energy so kilojoules and kilocalories are more frequently used to describe the energy values of foods. In popular nutrition guides, the calories referred to are actually kilocalories and are often spelt Cal, with a capital C.

The energy content information given on the packaging of many foods has been calculated by burning a sample of the food in a food calorimeter.

Our energy requirements

The total of all the chemical reactions in the body is called **metabolism**. It is driven by the energy from respiration, so the amount of energy needed depends on how many metabolic reactions a person is carrying out. The amount of metabolism depends on three factors:

- the processes required simply to stay alive. These processes include breathing, excretion, thinking and keeping a constant body temperature. The energy consumed in one day by these processes is called the **basal metabolic rate (BMR)**. The BMR is different for males and females, and gets less as a person gets older.
- the amount of **activity** or **exercise** – this requires muscular work and extra temperature regulation. This energy demand can be very little (in a sedentary office worker, for example) or very great (in a road worker, for example).
- the amount of food eaten – eating food means extra work for the digestive system and the liver. The energy demand simply caused by eating is called the **dynamic action of food**.

$$\text{Energy requirement per day} = \text{BMR} + \text{activity} + \text{dynamic action of food}$$

The bar chart below illustrates the energy demands for different people. Three factors affect the body's energy requirements – **age**, **sex** and **occupation**.

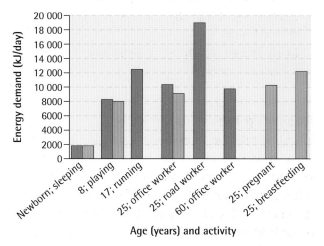

Energy requirements for different people.

Key
Male   Female

Energy in food

A class of students used the apparatus shown here to investigate the energy content of a peanut.
They first recorded the temperature of the water (T_1) and weighed the nut.
The nut was held in a Bunsen burner flame until it caught fire, and then placed under the boiling tube.
The students recorded the maximum temperature the water reached (T_2), and then repeated the experiment twice more. A typical set of results from one pair of students is shown in the table at the bottom of the page.

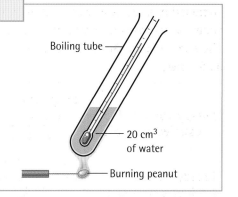

Boiling tube

20 cm³ of water

Burning peanut

---

1. a Copy and complete the table of results.
   b Add a further column and include the energy value of the peanut in kJ/g.
   c Calculate the mean energy value of the peanut as found by these students. Why is the mean value more valid than any single value that they obtained?

   d Can you suggest any improvements to the apparatus so that the students' value might be closer to the 'professional' one (24.5 kJ/g)? Redraw the apparatus showing your suggestions.
   e What features of the method helped to improve the validity of the results? How could the students have treated the results differently to improve their validity further?

T_1 (°C)	T_2 (°C)	$T_2 - T_1$ (°C)	Volume of water (cm³)	Energy transferred to water (kcal)	Mass of nut (g)	Energy value (kcal/g)
22	78				0.45	
22	74				0.52	
21	75				0.47	

2·4 Balancing energy intake and energy demand

Objectives

- To understand that different people have different demands for energy
- To understand that energy intake must be balanced by energy use

Malnutrition means literally 'bad feeding'. This 'bad feeding' could include:

- eating foods in the wrong proportions, for example, gaining too many kilojoules from fats and too few from carbohydrates
- eating too much of all foods, so having a balanced diet but consuming more than is needed
- having too little food.

If the diet contains more energy than the body needs, the excess will be stored as **glycogen** or **fat**; if it contains less energy than the body needs, then the body's own tissues will be broken down to be respired. The diagram below shows the importance of an **energy balance**.

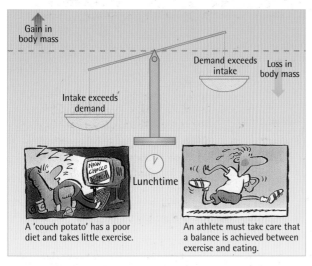

A 'couch potato' has a poor diet and takes little exercise.

An athlete must take care that a balance is achieved between exercise and eating.

Storing excess food: overnutrition

The body can store a limited amount of glycogen, which allows the body to continue working even if the last meal was some time ago. However, the body can store an almost unlimited amount of fat to help the body survive periods without food. Our food intake should not be so great that we store an unhealthy amount of fat. A person whose fat storage is beyond a healthy limit is said to be **obese**.

The 'ideal' body mass differs from person to person, and depends on height and age. A person who is obese is at risk from a number of life-shortening diseases, including **diabetes, breathing difficulties, atherosclerosis** (narrowing of the arteries) and **arthritis**. Obesity is one of the most widespread results of malnutrition in the western world.

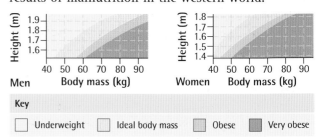

The ideal body mass should fall within the range shown in these charts (designed for adults who have reached their full height).

Losing body mass

The energy balance diagram shows that to lose body mass, it is necessary to reduce energy intake below energy use. This can be done in two ways:

- by eating less 'high-energy' food, which will **reduce the energy intake**
- by taking more exercise, which will **increase the energy use**.

The best approach is to combine both methods, controlling the diet and also taking more exercise. Many people who rely on diet alone have great difficulty in controlling their body mass.

Malnutrition can also mean undernutrition

In the developing countries of the world, many people have diets which are neither adequate nor balanced. In other words, they do not receive enough energy to drive metabolism, nor do they take in the nutrients they need for growth and development. These people, often children, suffer from many deficiency diseases – shortage of iron means they are often anaemic, and a limited supply of vitamin C means that many of them have scurvy, for example. The most obvious signs of their malnourished state, however, are often caused by **protein deficiency**. There are two extremes of protein deficiency – **kwashiorkor** and **marasmus**.

Kwashiorkor

In kwashiokor, the child may not have received enough of its mother's milk (often because another child has been born) and may be forced onto a diet that is too high in carbohydrate (often maize). As a result the child may eat enough 'energy' food, but because the diet is poor in protein when its body should be developing quickly, the mental and physical development of the child may be impaired.

Marasmus

In marasmus, the child has symptoms of general starvation – there is not enough 'energy' food or enough protein. All the body tissues waste away, and the child becomes very thin with a wrinkled skin.

Causes and treatments

Kwashiorkor and marasmus are both serious conditions. They are common in countries where drought conditions have led to poor harvests, or where people have left their homes because of civil war. Aid offered to these people must include both energy foods and the nutrients needed for growth. Powdered milk is often provided, because it is light and easy to transport. However it must be rehydrated with clean water otherwise water-borne diseases such as cholera (see page 286) may result.

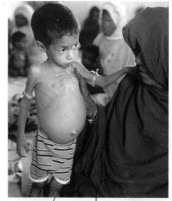

This child has kwashiorkor. The absence of protein means that muscle development is very slow, and the limbs have a stick-like appearance. The swollen abdomen is caused largely by water from the blood plasma remaining behind in the body tissues. The liver is also swollen because it is working hard to make the proteins needed by the body from an inadequate dietary supply.

Marasmus is caused by insufficient levels of all nutrients in the diet.

---

1 The table below shows the energy value of a number of products from the Mars company.

a Copy and complete the table to show the energy value of each product in kJ/100 g (take care – some energy values are shown for 25 g; others are for whole bars or packets).

b Draw a bar chart showing the products in descending order of energy value (the one with the highest energy value on the left).

c For a 50 g portion which product would be:
  i the least fattening
  ii the most fattening?

d A Mars bar weighs 65 g. What is its energy value in kilojoules?

e While sitting watching television, a boy of 15 uses about 6 kJ per minute.
  i How long would it take him to use all the energy obtained from the Mars bar?
  ii What is he using this energy for?

f While playing football the same boy uses, on average, 30 kJ per minute. How long would it take him to use up the energy obtained from the Mars bar?

g A football match lasts for 90 minutes. If the boy ran for half of the game, would he have used more energy or less than the Mars bar provided? How could his body cope with any difference between energy demanded and energy supplied?

Name of product	Energy value (kJ/25 g, unless otherwise stated)	Energy value (kJ/100 g)
Bounty, 60 g	490	
Maltesers	504	
Mars	454	
Milky Way	490	
Minstrels, 49 g	870	
Snickers	504	
Treets, 42 g	1040	
Twix	504	

2·5 Nutrition converts food molecules to a usable form

Objectives
- To know that the process of nutrition involves several stages
- To know the basic layout of the human alimentary canal

Nutrition involves a sequence of processes

Living things obtain food molecules from the environment. These molecules are not usually exactly the same as the biological molecules the organism needs to carry out its life processes. The processes of nutrition convert the food molecules into a form that can be used by the organism. In humans and many other animals, these processes take place in the **alimentary canal** (sometimes called the **gut**). The alimentary canal is a specialised tube running from the front of the animal (starting at its **mouth**) to the rear (ending at its **anus**). While the food is inside the tube it is not available to the body tissues. The food molecules must be changed into a form that can cross the gut wall and then be transported to the places where they will be used or stored. The processes of nutrition are described in the diagram below.

The alimentary canal is highly specialised in humans. The food molecules are converted to a usable form in a clear sequence, with each part of the gut being adapted to carry out particular functions. The layout of the alimentary canal is shown in the diagram opposite, and we shall see how its organs work in the next few pages.

1. List, in their correct sequence, the processes that make up nutrition.
2. What is the difference between the following?
   a chemical and mechanical digestion
   b absorption and assimilation
   c egestion and excretion
3. Why are the epiglottis and the soft palate important in efficient feeding?
4. Name three glands that add juices to the alimentary canal.

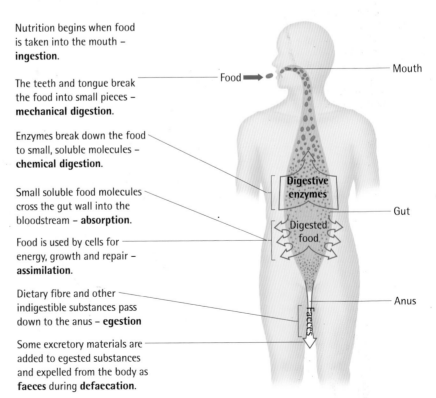

Nutrition begins when food is taken into the mouth – **ingestion**.

The teeth and tongue break the food into small pieces – **mechanical digestion**.

Enzymes break down the food to small, soluble molecules – **chemical digestion**.

Small soluble food molecules cross the gut wall into the bloodstream – **absorption**.

Food is used by cells for energy, growth and repair – **assimilation**.

Dietary fibre and other indigestible substances pass down to the anus – **egestion**

Some excretory materials are added to egested substances and expelled from the body as **faeces** during **defaecation**.

Food — Mouth

Digestive enzymes

Digested food — Gut

faeces — Anus

Nutrition is a sequence of processes involving ingestion, digestion, absorption and egestion.

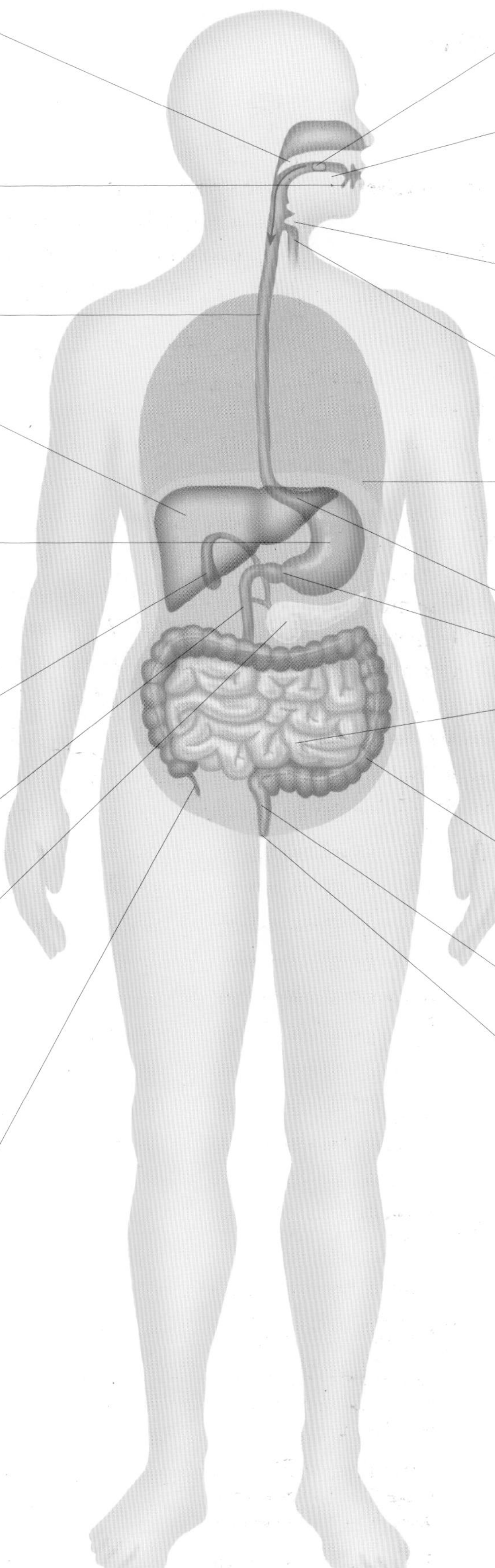

Soft palate – closes off the nasal cavity during swallowing to prevent food entering this cavity.

Salivary glands – three pairs, produce saliva and pour it into the mouth through **salivary ducts**.

Oesophagus – muscular tube which helps food move to stomach by peristalsis.

Liver – produces **bile**, which helps to neutralise acidic chyme and also emulsifies fats. Important in assimilation.

Stomach – muscular bag which stores food for a short time, and mixes food with acidic digestive juices to form the creamy liquid called **chyme**.

Gall bladder – stores bile before pouring it into duodenum through the **bile duct**.

Duodenum – first part of the small intestine, where semi-liquid food is mixed with pancreatic juice and bile.

Pancreas – produces pancreatic juice (contains enzymes, mucus and hydrogencarbonate which neutralises acidic chyme) which is poured into the small intestine through the **pancreatic duct**.

Caecum
Appendix] no known function in humans

Bolus of food – produced by teeth, tongue and saliva during **mastication**.

Tongue – involved in mastication and then in pushing bolus to back of mouth ready for swallowing. Also has taste buds which help in choosing food.

Epiglottis – flap of muscle which closes the entry to the trachea during swallowing.

Trachea (windpipe) – allows air to pass to lungs from mouth and nose.

Diaphragm – a feature of mammals. It is a sheet of muscle which separates the chest cavity from the abdomen.

Cardiac sphincter ⎤ retain food
Pyloric sphincter ⎦ in stomach

Ileum – longest part of the small intestine, where digested food is absorbed into the blood and lymphatic system.

Large intestine – (wider than the small intestine)

The **colon** is part of the large intestine. It reabsorbs water from gut contents; also absorbs some vitamins and minerals.

Rectum – stores faeces before expelling them at a convenient time.

Anus – exit for faeces; defaecation is controlled by two anal sphincters.

INGESTION

DIGESTION

ABSORPTION

EGESTION

Objectives

- To understand the part played by teeth and the tongue in preparing food for the alimentary canal

Mastication produces a bolus

The first stage in processing food for use by the organism is taking the food into the gut. Once the food has been caught or collected, and perhaps cooked or processed in some other way, it is placed in the mouth. Here it is cut up by the teeth, and the pieces are mixed with saliva by the tongue. This cutting and mixing is called **mastication**, and produces a ball of food called a **bolus**. The bolus is swallowed and passed on to the next parts of the gut. The teeth play an important role in mastication, and it should be no surprise that:

- the structure of a tooth is closely related to its function

- there are different types of teeth adapted to deal with all types of food.

Human teeth and their function

The structure and function of a human tooth are shown in the diagram below. This type of tooth is called a molar, found towards the back of the jaw. The diagram above right shows the four different types of human teeth, and the part each of them plays in mastication.

The teeth in the skull

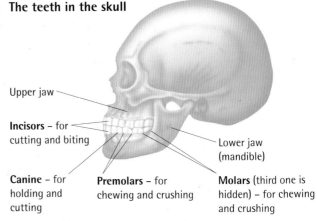

Upper jaw

Incisors – for cutting and biting

Canine – for holding and cutting

Premolars – for chewing and crushing

Lower jaw (mandible)

Molars (third one is hidden) – for chewing and crushing

Side view of the four types of tooth

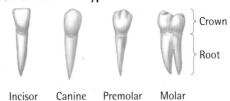

} Crown

} Root

Incisor Canine Premolar Molar

Surface view of the lower jaw

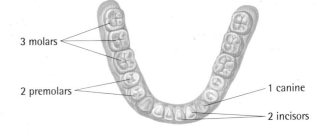

3 molars

2 premolars

1 canine

2 incisors

Enamel – the hardest tissue in the body. Produced by **tooth-forming cells** and made of calcium salts. Once formed, enamel cannot be renewed or extended.

Cement – similar in composition to dentine, but without any canals. It helps anchor the tooth to the jaw.

Pulp cavity contains:
- **tooth-producing cells**
- **blood vessels**
- **nerve endings** which can detect pain.

Crown

Neck

Root embedded in jawbone

Dentine – forms the major part of the tooth. Harder than bone and made of calcium salts deposited on a framework of **collagen fibres**. The dentine contains a series of fine canals which extend to the pulp cavity.

Gum – usually covers the junction between enamel and cement. The gums recede with age.

Periodontal membrane – bundles of collagen fibres, anchoring the cement covering of the tooth to the jawbone. The tooth is held firmly but not rigidly. The periodontal membrane has many nerve endings which detect pressures during chewing and biting.

Vitamin C deficiency impairs production of collagen fibres, including those in the periodontal membrane, so that the teeth become loose and may fall out – a classic symptom of scurvy.

Nutrition and health

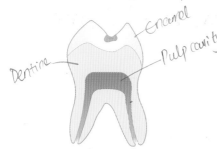

Decay begins in enamel – **no pain.**

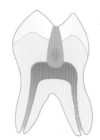

Decay penetrates dentine and reaches pulp – **severe toothache.**

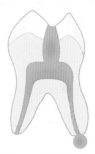

Bacteria now infect pulp and may form abscess at base of tooth – **excruciating pain.**

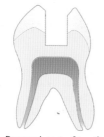

Decayed part of tooth is drilled out by a dentist.

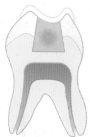

Hole is filled with amalgam or plastic, and may be coated with plastic.

Two sets of teeth

Humans, like other mammals, have two sets of teeth during their life. The first set is the milk dentition, which begins to grow through the gums one or two teeth at a time at around five months old. By about 18 months most children have a set of 20 teeth – there are fewer molars ('cheek teeth') than in an adult since the jaw is too small to hold any more. Between the ages of seven and twelve years these milk teeth fall out and are replaced by larger adult teeth. Eight new cheek teeth are added, with a further four (the wisdom teeth) appearing at the back of the jaw by about the age of 17 years. The individual now has the complete adult or permanent dentition of 32 teeth.

Western-style malnutrition may cause dental decay

A diet that provides too much energy can cause obesity (see page 40). Much of this energy-rich food will be in the form of refined sugars such as sucrose (cane sugar) which is used to sweeten many foods. These sugars may also be used by bacteria in the mouth to carry out their own life processes.

The bacteria produce a sticky matrix which traps food particles and forms a coating of **plaque** on the teeth. The bacteria in the plaque convert sugars in the food to acids. These acids remove calcium and phosphate from the enamel, allowing bacteria to reach the softer dentine beneath. This is the start of **dental decay** or **dental caries**. The dentine decays rapidly and the pulp cavity may become infected. The tooth will need dental treatment, as shown in the diagrams on the left.

Dental decay, and the gum disease that often goes along with it, can be prevented by:

- eating food with a low sugar content
- regular and effective brushing of teeth at least twice a day to prevent the build-up of plaque – plaque begins to reform after about 24 hours
- if brushing is not convenient, finishing a meal with a crisp vegetable or fruit, followed by rinsing with water.

The mineral fluoride can be added to drinking water. Tests have shown that this mineral reduces the risk of dental decay, although some people say that they should not be forced to consume it.

1 How do we know that a tooth is a living structure?

2 Imagine yourself on a British warship several hundred years ago. Explain, simply, why the sailors were losing their teeth.

3 a What is dental caries?
  b How does it begin?
  c Suggest **two** ways in which caries can be prevented or reduced.

2·7 Digestion prepares useful food molecules for absorption

Objectives

- To know that digestion converts large insoluble molecules into smaller, soluble molecules
- To understand that enzymes catalyse the breakdown of food
- To list examples of enzymes involved in digestion of carbohydrates, proteins and fats, and to know where they perform their tasks
- To understand that undigested food must be expelled from the gut

The diet contains three types of food molecule in large amounts – carbohydrates, proteins and fats. When ingested, these molecules may be too large to cross the gut wall and too insoluble to be transported in the watery blood plasma. **Digestion** is the process that converts these ingested foods into a form that can be absorbed and transported.

Digestive enzymes

In digestion, food molecules are broken down by **hydrolysis** reactions (breakdown with water), catalysed by a series of enzymes. There are different enzymes for the hydrolysis of each food type; each enzyme works in different regions of the gut. The basic process of hydrolysis is the same for all the food molecules:

Carbohydrate digestion begins in the mouth

The saliva contains an enzyme called **salivary amylase** (a carbohydrase). This enzyme catalyses the conversion of the insoluble polysaccharide starch to the soluble simpler sugar called maltose:

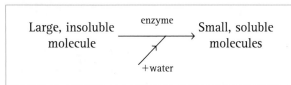

The saliva also contains mucus, which lubricates the food, and hydrogencarbonate, which provides the ideal conditions of pH (alkaline) for amylase to work. The starch is not usually all converted to maltose in the mouth since the food does not remain there for very long.

Passing to the stomach

Mastication produces a bolus of food, as we saw on page 44. The tongue pushes the bolus to the back of the mouth, and it is then swallowed (see opposite page) and enters the **oesophagus**. The oesophagus or gullet is a muscular tube leading from the mouth to the stomach. The bolus is forced down the oesophagus more quickly than can be explained by gravity alone. (It is even possible to swallow food when standing on your head!) Waves of muscular contraction push the bolus down towards the stomach, as shown in the diagram below. These waves of contraction are known as **peristalsis**, and they occur throughout the length of the gut. The reason why fibre is important in the human diet is that without it the gut contents are very liquid, and the muscles of the gut cannot squeeze the food along by peristalsis.

Cross-section of gut showing muscle layers

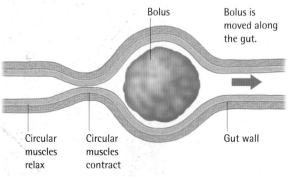

Longitudinal section of gut showing peristalsis

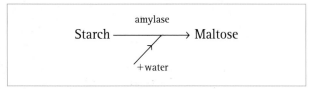

Peristalsis is a wave of muscular contraction that moves food along the gut. Mucus lubricates the bolus, helping it to move along.

Protein digestion begins in the stomach

The stomach is a muscular bag with a lining that contains digestive glands. These glands produce three important secretions:

- **mucus**, which protects the walls of the stomach from attack by gastric (stomach) juices
- pepsin, a **protease** or protein-digesting enzyme
- **hydrochloric acid**, which provides the acidic conditions needed for the action of pepsin.

Inside the stomach the food is churned up with the gastric juices. The long protein molecules are broken down by hydrolysis to smaller molecules called peptides, as shown in the diagram below.

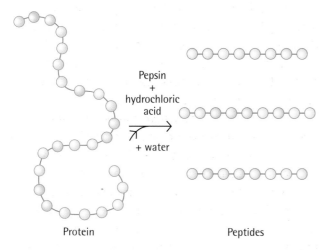

Pepsin
+
hydrochloric
acid

+ water

Protein

Peptides

The pH in the stomach is too low (too acidic) for the action of amylase, so the digestion of carbohydrate comes to a halt whilst the food is in the stomach. The churning action of the stomach muscles mixes the food into a creamy liquid called **chyme**. Once the food is sufficiently liquid, it squeezes past a second ring of muscle at the foot of the stomach, the **pyloric sphincter**, and enters the **duodenum**, the first part of the small intestine.

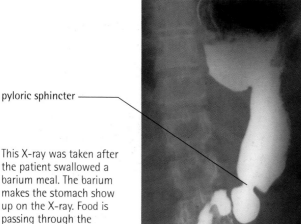

pyloric sphincter

This X-ray was taken after the patient swallowed a barium meal. The barium makes the stomach show up on the X-ray. Food is passing through the pyloric sphincter.

The swallowing reflex

It is important that the bolus of food travels down the oesophagus and not down the trachea (windpipe), or it might block the trachea and prevent breathing. A flap of muscle, the **epiglottis**, is forced across the top of the trachea whenever food is swallowed, ensuring food does not enter the trachea. We don't have to think about this swallowing reflex, but it can be overruled if we try to eat and talk at the same time!

At the bottom of the oesophagus, just where it joins the stomach, is a ring of muscle called the cardiac sphincter. When the bolus reaches this sphincter, the ring of muscle relaxes to allow the bolus through into the stomach. If the stomach contents pass upwards through this sphincter and make contact with the wall of the oesophagus, they cause a burning sensation known as 'heartburn'.

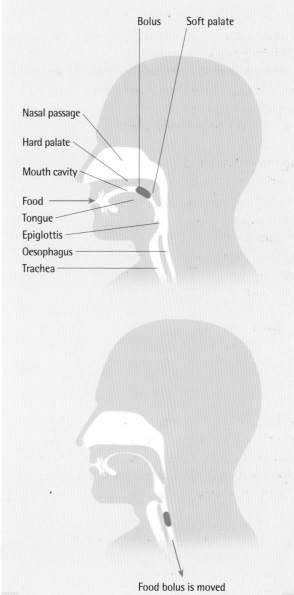

Bolus   Soft palate

Nasal passage

Hard palate

Mouth cavity

Food

Tongue

Epiglottis

Oesophagus

Trachea

Food bolus is moved down the oesophagus.

Digestion of food molecules is completed in the small intestine

The liquid chyme contains partly digested food molecules. The digestion of these food molecules is completed in the small intestine, using digestive juices which contain:

- enzymes from the pancreas
- enzymes from the intestine wall
- bile from the liver.

The enzymes from the pancreas carry out three tasks – **amylase** completes the conversion of starch to maltose, **protease** completes the breakdown of peptides to amino acids, and **lipase** converts fats to fatty acids and glycerol. These enzymes work best at around pH 8 (slightly alkaline conditions), and the juice from the pancreas also contains hydrogencarbonate which neutralises the acid coming through from the stomach.

Lipase is helped in its action by **bile**, which is made in the liver and stored in the gall bladder from where it is released when needed. Bile **emulsifies** the fats – it converts them from large globules into much smaller droplets, giving a greater surface area for the lipase to work on, as shown in the diagram.

Bile also contains hydrogencarbonate to help neutralise the acid from the stomach. Enzymes on the wall of the small intestine include **maltase**, which completes the breakdown of maltose to glucose. All the starch has now been converted to glucose. The table opposite lists the digestive juices and their actions.

Water and digestion

The digestive juices are largely made up of **water** – this is one of the major demands for water within the body. This water is the solvent for the biochemical reactions of digestion and is also used in the hydrolysis reactions that split up the large, insoluble food molecules. The juices also contain **mucus** which protects the wall of the gut from being digested by its own enzymes.

Egestion removes undigested food

Food may contain some molecules that cannot be digested by the enzymes of the human gut. Examples include substances in plant cells, such as the cellulose in cell walls and the lignin in xylem vessels (see page 162). Water is first absorbed from the gut contents that remain after digestion, and this indigestible food is then expelled. This process is called **egestion**. Some excreted materials, such as salts in the bile, may be added to the indigestible foods to form the **faeces**. The faeces are stored temporarily in the rectum. When full, the rectum sets off a reflex action which causes its muscles to contract and squeeze the faeces out through the anus. Humans have a sphincter at the anus which can prevent this **defaecation** happening at an inconvenient time! The control of this sphincter has to be learned, and babies simply fill their nappies when the rectum is full.

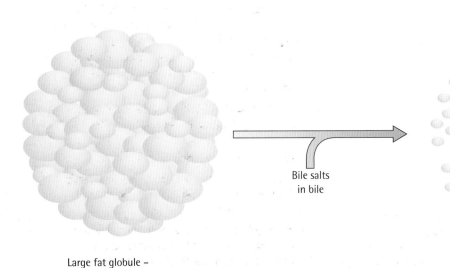

Bile salts
in bile

Large fat globule –
relatively small surface area

Many small fat droplets –
relatively large total surface area

Emulsification of fats provides a larger surface for lipase to act on.

Region of gut	Digestive juice	Enzymes	Substrate	Product(s)	Other substances in juice	Function of other substances
Mouth	Saliva from salivary glands	Salivary amylase	Starch	Maltose	Hydrogencarbonate	Alkaline (pH 7.5) environment for amylase
Stomach	Gastric juice from glands in wall of stomach	Pepsin	Proteins	Peptides	Hydrochloric acid	Acidic (pH 2) environment for pepsin; kills bacteria
Small intestine (duodenum)	Pancreatic juice from pancreas	Pancreatic amylase Trypsin (a protease) Lipase	Starch Peptides Emulsified fats	Maltose Amino acids Fatty acids and glycerol	Hydrogencarbonate	Neutralises chyme: alkaline environment for enzymes
	Bile from liver (stored in gall bladder)	None			Bile salts	Emulsifies fats – converts globules to smaller droplets
					Hydrogencarbonate	Neutralises chyme
Small intestine (ileum)	Intestinal juice from cells on villi	Maltase Lactase Sucrase	Maltose Lactose Sucrose	Glucose Glucose and galactose Glucose and fructose		

The human digestive juices and their actions.

1 In 1822 Alexis St Martin, a Canadian fur trapper, was wounded in his left side by a shotgun blast. Luckily the accident occurred close to an army fort where one of the surgeons, William Beaumont, was able to treat St Martin. The wound healed very slowly, and left a small hole in the side of the young man. Beaumont realised that this gave him a unique opportunity to study what was happening in his patient's stomach.

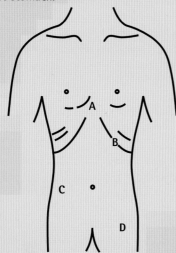

a Which letter on the outline above represents the most likely position of the hole?

b Beaumont described one of his investigations as follows: 'Juice was extracted from the stomach and placed in a small vial. A solid piece of boiled, recently salted beef weighing three drachms was added. The vial was corked and kept under controlled conditions. A similar piece of beef was suspended on a string into the man's stomach.'

  i Suggest one condition around the vial that Beaumont would have kept constant.
  ii What control experiment should Beaumont have performed?
  iii Why did Beaumont use 'boiled, salted beef'?

c After two hours, Beaumont recorded the following results: 'Beef in vial – the cellular texture seemed to be entirely destroyed, leaving the muscular fibres loose and unconnected, floating about in fine, small shreds, very tender and soft. Beef in stomach – I drew out the string, but the meat was all completely digested and gone.'

Use your knowledge of digestion to explain the difference between the changes in the vial and those in the stomach.

2 The liver produces a liquid which is added directly to the partly digested food in the small intestine.
a Name the liquid.
b Describe how it helps digestion.

3 Describe, in the correct sequence, how the protein and starch in a ham sandwich are broken down ready for absorption.

4 Digestive juices contain enzymes, water and some other substances. Name two of these other substances. State which digestive juice contains them, and state what function they perform.

Objectives

- To understand that digested food in the gut is still 'outside' the body
- To know how the small intestine is adapted to the function of absorption of digested food
- To understand the part played by the liver in the assimilation and distribution of absorbed foods

Absorption of the products of digestion

Enzymes in the gut convert large, insoluble molecules to small, soluble molecules. These soluble molecules are transported across the lining of the gut into the bloodstream, a process called **absorption**. They can then be distributed to the parts of the body where they will be used.

Most absorption happens from the **ileum**, the lower part of the small intestine. The ileum is very well adapted to perform this task:

- It is **very long**, about 6 m in an adult human, so food takes a long time to pass through it, and there is enough time for absorption to occur.
- The surface of the ileum is **highly folded**, which gives a much larger surface area for absorption than a simple tube would.

The lining of the ileum is folded into hundreds of thousands of tiny finger-like structures, the **villi**, which project out into the liquid digested food. The structure of a villus, and its adaptations to increase absorption, are shown in the diagram below.

Following absorption in the small intestine, the contents of the gut are little more than water and indigestible matter. Most of the water is reabsorbed into the bloodstream from the colon, part of the large intestine. Some minerals and vitamins are also absorbed here.

The liver and assimilation

Digested food is absorbed into the bloodstream. Each type of absorbed food has a particular function in the body, so it is important that food molecules of the right type are available at the right time in the right place. The **liver** 'sorts out' digested food molecules, and all foods absorbed into the capillaries of the villi are sent first to the liver. The veins leaving the villi join together into one blood vessel called the **hepatic portal vein** ('hepatic' means 'to do with the liver' and 'portal' means 'carrying'). This arrangement, shown in the

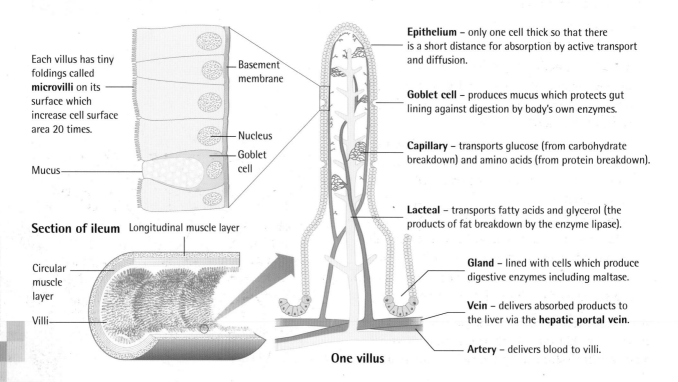

Each villus has tiny foldings called **microvilli** on its surface which increase cell surface area 20 times.

Mucus

Basement membrane

Nucleus

Goblet cell

Section of ileum Longitudinal muscle layer

Circular muscle layer

Villi

One villus

Epithelium – only one cell thick so that there is a short distance for absorption by active transport and diffusion.

Goblet cell – produces mucus which protects gut lining against digestion by body's own enzymes.

Capillary – transports glucose (from carbohydrate breakdown) and amino acids (from protein breakdown).

Lacteal – transports fatty acids and glycerol (the products of fat breakdown by the enzyme lipase).

Gland – lined with cells which produce digestive enzymes including maltase.

Vein – delivers absorbed products to the liver via the **hepatic portal vein**.

Artery – delivers blood to villi.

diagram below, means that the liver can sort out absorbed food molecules and make sure that the other tissues of the body receive exactly what they need.

Blood returned to general circulation through **hepatic vein**. This blood contains a **constant** and **ideal** concentration of food molecules such as glucose and amino acids.

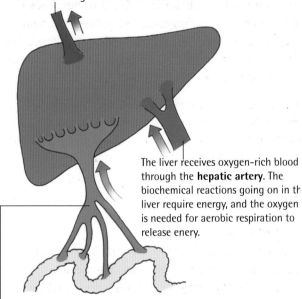

The liver receives oxygen-rich blood through the **hepatic artery**. The biochemical reactions going on in th liver require energy, and the oxygen is needed for aerobic respiration to release enery.

Blood from the intestine is delivered to the liver in the **hepatic portal vein**. This blood contains **variable** and **possibly dangerously high** concentrations of food molecules, depending on what has been absorbed from the gut.

The liver has many functions – at least 500 different biochemical reactions go on inside its cells. These functions include:

- manufacture of bile, which is important for the digestion of fats
- storage of glucose as glycogen
- interconversion of glucose and glycogen, which keeps the glucose concentration constant for the working tissues of the body
- interconversion of amino acids – the liver can convert some amino acids into others that the body might require in a process called **transamination**
- excretion of excess amino acids – the amino part of the amino acid is removed in a process called **deamination** and excreted in the urine as urea
- removal of old red blood cells from the circulation and storage of the iron they contained.

A combination of transamination and deamination makes sure that there is always a 'pool' of amino acids available for use by the cells of the body.

As a result of these and other activities, the liver provides ideal concentrations of food molecules for the working of the body tissues. Each type of tissue uses food molecules for different purposes – for example, muscle cells manufacture muscle protein, bone cells take up calcium and phosphate to make bone, and all cells use glucose to release energy by respiration. The processes of using up food molecules in these various ways are together called **assimilation**.

Alcohol and the liver

The liver receives all the molecules that the gut absorbs from food. As well as useful molecules such as glucose and amino acids, this may include harmful molecules such as drugs or poisons. **Alcohol** is a drug (a molecule that affects the normal working of the body – see page 98) which passes quickly to the liver after being absorbed from the stomach and ileum. The cells of the liver convert this alcohol to another substance which does not pass through to the rest of the body's circulation. Unfortunately, in working to protect the other tissues, the liver is likely to harm itself. The substance produced from alcohol can be dangerous to liver cells in high concentrations and can cause a serious disease called cirrhosis of the liver. If the liver is damaged by excessive alcohol consumption, then the whole body is affected. For example, the blood glucose concentration cannot be controlled efficiently if the liver has been damaged.

Alcohol has other effects on the body – these are described on page 98.

1. In what way is the blood supply to the liver unusual?

2. Name two substances stored in the liver, and two that are converted to different substances.

3. How is the structure of the villus adapted to its function?

4. What are goblet cells? Where else do you think they might be found apart from in the gut?

5. Some microorganisms infect the gut lining so that water cannot be absorbed. What effect(s) might this have on the infected person?

2·9 Carnivores and herbivores are well adapted to their diet

Objectives

- To appreciate that mammals have specialised guts to deal with particular diets
- To understand that carnivores must deal with protein-rich meals at long intervals
- To understand that herbivores must deal with nutrient-poor diets eaten continuously

Mammals have adapted to make the most of many different food sources. Humans have a 'general purpose' gut that can deal with a wide variety of foodstuffs in their diet. Organisms that have a diet like humans are called **omnivores** ('all eaters'). Some mammals have become specialised to eat just the flesh of other animals. These are the **carnivores** ('meat eaters') and their gut is adapted to deal with foods that are very rich in protein, sometimes with long gaps between meals. Other mammals have become specialised to eat only plants. These are the

herbivores ('herb eaters') and their gut is adapted to deal with almost continuous feeding on vegetation, which is rather low in nutrient value. These different mammals show several types of adaptation to their diet:

- The **teeth** may be adapted, both in number and in shape.
- The **movement of the jaw** may be adapted for killing, biting or long-term chewing.
- The **structure of the intestine** may be adapted to allow storage or more efficient digestion of food.
- There may be partnerships with **symbiotic bacteria** (see page 57).
- Food may be **redigested** to obtain maximum value from it.

Adaptations of carnivores and herbivores to their specific diets are shown in the diagrams.

Adaptations of a carnivore

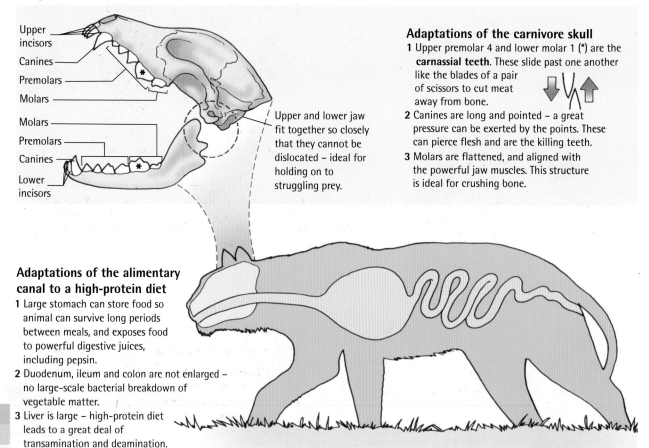

Upper incisors
Canines
Premolars
Molars
Molars
Premolars
Canines
Lower incisors

Upper and lower jaw fit together so closely that they cannot be dislocated – ideal for holding on to struggling prey.

Adaptations of the carnivore skull

1 Upper premolar 4 and lower molar 1 (*) are the **carnassial teeth**. These slide past one another like the blades of a pair of scissors to cut meat away from bone.
2 Canines are long and pointed – a great pressure can be exerted by the points. These can pierce flesh and are the killing teeth.
3 Molars are flattened, and aligned with the powerful jaw muscles. This structure is ideal for crushing bone.

Adaptations of the alimentary canal to a high-protein diet

1 Large stomach can store food so animal can survive long periods between meals, and exposes food to powerful digestive juices, including pepsin.
2 Duodenum, ileum and colon are not enlarged – no large-scale bacterial breakdown of vegetable matter.
3 Liver is large – high-protein diet leads to a great deal of transamination and deamination.

Adaptations of herbivores

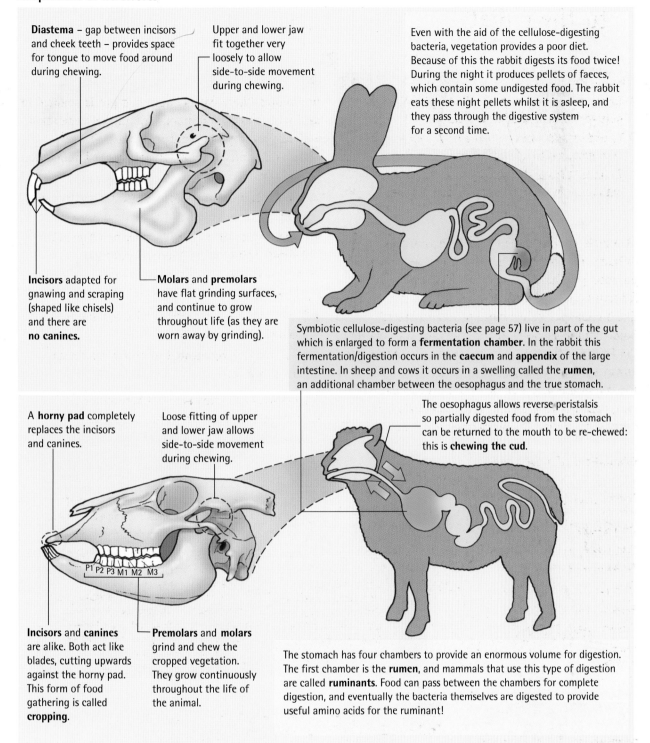

Diastema – gap between incisors and cheek teeth – provides space for tongue to move food around during chewing.

Upper and lower jaw fit together very loosely to allow side-to-side movement during chewing.

Even with the aid of the cellulose-digesting bacteria, vegetation provides a poor diet. Because of this the rabbit digests its food twice! During the night it produces pellets of faeces, which contain some undigested food. The rabbit eats these night pellets whilst it is asleep, and they pass through the digestive system for a second time.

Incisors adapted for gnawing and scraping (shaped like chisels) and there are **no canines.**

Molars and **premolars** have flat grinding surfaces, and continue to grow throughout life (as they are worn away by grinding).

Symbiotic cellulose-digesting bacteria (see page 57) live in part of the gut which is enlarged to form a **fermentation chamber**. In the rabbit this fermentation/digestion occurs in the **caecum** and **appendix** of the large intestine. In sheep and cows it occurs in a swelling called the **rumen**, an additional chamber between the oesophagus and the true stomach.

A **horny pad** completely replaces the incisors and canines.

Loose fitting of upper and lower jaw allows side-to-side movement during chewing.

The oesophagus allows reverse peristalsis so partially digested food from the stomach can be returned to the mouth to be re-chewed: this is **chewing the cud**.

P1 P2 P3 M1 M2 M3

Incisors and **canines** are alike. Both act like blades, cutting upwards against the horny pad. This form of food gathering is called **cropping**.

Premolars and **molars** grind and chew the cropped vegetation. They grow continuously throughout the life of the animal.

The stomach has four chambers to provide an enormous volume for digestion. The first chamber is the **rumen**, and mammals that use this type of digestion are called **ruminants**. Food can pass between the chambers for complete digestion, and eventually the bacteria themselves are digested to provide useful amino acids for the ruminant!

---

1. Name one carnivore, and describe how its teeth and jaws are adapted to its method of feeding.

2. Why do rabbits eat their own faeces?

3. Carnivores often have a large stomach and an active liver. Why?

4. **a** What is a ruminant?
   b Why is reverse peristalsis important to ruminants?

5. Make a table comparing the teeth, jaw movement and gut features of an omnivore, a carnivore, a gnawing herbivore such as a rabbit, and a cropping herbivore such as a sheep.

2·10 Engulfing, filter feeding and fluid feeding

Objectives

- To understand that not all organisms obtain food in the same way as humans do
- To know that some small organisms engulf their food by flowing their body around it
- To give examples of filter feeders – organisms that obtain small particles of food from their environment
- To give examples of fluid feeders – organisms that obtain their food in liquid form

In the animal kingdom there is a huge variety of feeding mechanisms, reflecting the wide variety of food available – organisms have adapted to make use of almost every food there is. Humans take in most of their food in the form of large particles. Many other organisms feed differently, using food sources that humans cannot (or will not!) exploit.

Filter feeders collect small particles

Many organisms live in aquatic environments, particularly the sea. There are enormous numbers of food particles, together known as **plankton**, floating in the water. Many organisms have evolved methods of capturing this plankton, using **filter feeding**. A large volume of water is passed through a net or sieve, and the plankton is filtered out from the water. The food particles are then passed on to a digestive system and the water is returned to the environment. Some examples of filter feeders are shown in the photographs below. The largest animal ever to have lived, the blue whale, feeds in this way, illustrating the richness of the sea as a food source.

Baleen plates

The blue whale swims through the sea with its mouth open, collecting an enormous volume of water. The mouth is then partly closed and the tongue moves upwards to push the water out through the baleen ('whalebone') plates. The plankton is trapped behind the plates, licked off by the tongue and then swallowed.
The largest living fish, the basking shark, also feeds in this way.

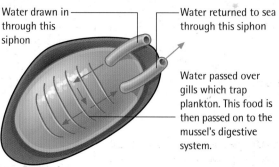

Water drawn in through this siphon

Water returned to sea through this siphon

Water passed over gills which trap plankton. This food is then passed on to the mussel's digestive system.

A mussel (shown in the drawing with one shell removed) has a system for collecting plankton by filtration.

Filter feeders come in many shapes and sizes, but they all use some form of sieve to collect plankton from water.

Amoeba engulfs its prey

Small single-celled organisms such as *Amoeba* can engulf small particles of food, for example bacteria, by 'flowing' their body around them. This is similar to the way in which these animals move (see page 129).

White blood cells called phagocytes engulf invading organisms to remove them from the body (see page 294).

Many insects feed on fluids

Insects are the most successful organisms on this planet. They are present in enormous numbers and, despite our best efforts, humans have not been able to eliminate any one insect species. One of the reasons why insects are so successful is that they have evolved to make the most of a wide variety of food stuffs. The mouthparts of different types of insect show how well they have adapted to different foods. The most basic type of mouthpart (probably the type which the first insects on Earth had) is good for chewing. Many other types of mouthparts have developed from this basic type, and several of them are very efficient at dealing with liquid foods. Insects with this type of mouthpart are examples of **fluid feeders**. The diagram below shows some insect mouthparts specialised for fluid feeding.

1. What is plankton? Describe how one named organism can feed on plankton.

2. Suggest which digestive enzymes will be secreted into the feeding vacuole of an *Amoeba*.

3. Describe **two** ways in which insect mouthparts can be adapted for feeding on fluids.

4. Why do fluid feeders need relatively few digestive enzymes, but sometimes need anticoagulants in their saliva?

The mouthparts of fluid-feeding insects are adaptions of the basic chewing mouthparts.

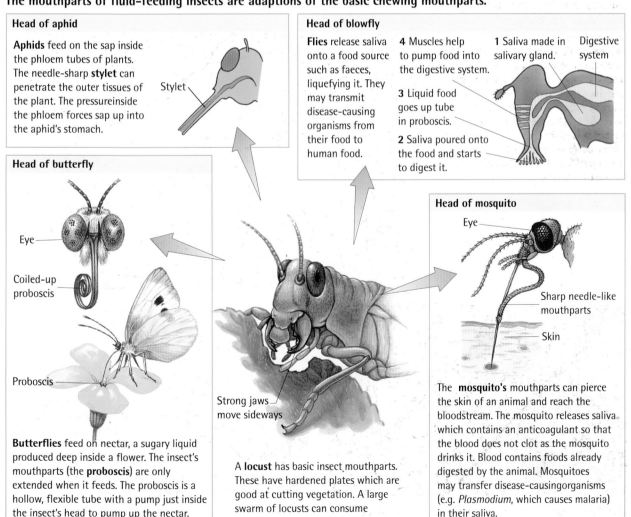

Head of aphid

Aphids feed on the sap inside the phloem tubes of plants. The needle-sharp **stylet** can penetrate the outer tissues of the plant. The pressure inside the phloem forces sap up into the aphid's stomach.

Stylet

Head of blowfly

Flies release saliva onto a food source such as faeces, liquefying it. They may transmit disease-causing organisms from their food to human food.

4 Muscles help to pump food into the digestive system.

3 Liquid food goes up tube in proboscis.

2 Saliva poured onto the food and starts to digest it.

1 Saliva made in salivary gland.

Digestive system

Head of butterfly

Eye

Coiled-up proboscis

Proboscis

Butterflies feed on nectar, a sugary liquid produced deep inside a flower. The insect's mouthparts (the **proboscis**) are only extended when it feeds. The proboscis is a hollow, flexible tube with a pump just inside the insect's head to pump up the nectar.

A **locust** has basic insect mouthparts. These have hardened plates which are good at cutting vegetation. A large swarm of locusts can consume 20 000 tonnes of vegetation in a day.

Strong jaws move sideways

Head of mosquito

Eye

Sharp needle-like mouthparts

Skin

The **mosquito's** mouthparts can pierce the skin of an animal and reach the bloodstream. The mosquito releases saliva which contains an anticoagulant so that the blood does not clot as the mosquito drinks it. Blood contains foods already digested by the animal. Mosquitoes may transfer disease-causing organisms (e.g. *Plasmodium*, which causes malaria) in their saliva.

Decomposers, parasites and symbiosis

- To understand that some organisms obtain their food by the decomposition of animal and plant remains
- To know that parasites obtain their food from another living organism
- To appreciate that some organisms live together in a feeding relationship which benefits them both

All heterotrophic organisms take in ready-made organic food molecules. They need a diet containing large amounts of fats, proteins and carbohydrates, as well as some other substances in smaller quantities. However, not all heterotrophic organisms feed as we do, by consuming food and breaking it down by digestion.

Saprotrophic organisms feed on dead and decaying material

No organism lives for ever. Each is born, may reproduce itself and eventually dies. Why is the world not covered with a deep layer of dead leaves, insects, snails, humans and other organisms? The answer is that a group of heterotrophic organisms called **saprotrophs** feed on this dead and decaying material. Most saprotrophs are **decomposers**, and many are bacteria or fungi. Decomposers release enzymes onto their food outside their body and then absorb the soluble food molecules, as shown on page 229 (fungi).

Decomposers are extremely important, because:

- They prevent the build-up of dead organisms or organic wastes – for example, they are used in the treatment of human sewage (see page 266).
- They recycle molecules which would otherwise be 'locked up' in the bodies of dead organisms, playing a vital role in the nitrogen and carbon cycles (see pages 254 and 256).
- They are used by humans in, for example, the production of some foodstuffs such as cheese (see page 306).

Parasites feed on the living body of another organism

A typical predator, such as a fox or a lion, will kill its prey and then eat it (usually in one go). Parasites, on the other hand, do not kill their prey and may continue to feed from it on many occasions. The parasite may live inside the prey or **host** organism, such as a tapeworm in a human's gut, or on the surface of the host, such as a flea on a dog. Parasites that live in the gut of their host have a regular supply of ready-digested food, so need no digestive system of their own. However, they have to cope with the harsh environment inside the host's gut. Some adaptations to the parasitic way of life are shown in the diagram below.

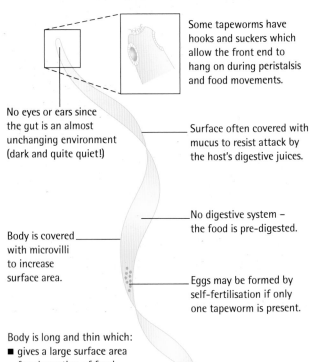

Some tapeworms have hooks and suckers which allow the front end to hang on during peristalsis and food movements.

No eyes or ears since the gut is an almost unchanging environment (dark and quite quiet!)

Surface often covered with mucus to resist attack by the host's digestive juices.

No digestive system – the food is pre-digested.

Body is covered with microvilli to increase surface area.

Eggs may be formed by self-fertilisation if only one tapeworm is present.

Body is long and thin which:
- gives a large surface area for absorption of food
- allows food to 'flow' past, so that the tapeworm is not washed away.

Body is pale, since there is no advantage in being brightly coloured in a dark environment.

Body wall has active transport systems for uptake of food molecules even against a concentration gradient.

A tapeworm is a parasite that is well adapted to life in its host's gut.

Organisms of different species may live together for their mutual feeding benefit

Some heterotrophic organisms obtain their food from another living organism but, unlike a parasite, offer something in return. This 'give and take' relationship is called **symbiosis** ('living together') or **mutualism**. For example, bacteria of the genus *Rhizobium* live in swellings called nodules on the roots of pea plants. The bacteria receive sugars from the pea plant, and donate nitrates to the pea plant (see page 256). Another example is the symbiosis between gut bacteria and cattle, shown below.

Summary of feeding relationships

The table below summarises parasitic, saprotrophic and symbiotic feeding relationships.

Parasite, e.g. tapeworm in mammal's gut	Saprotroph, e.g. fungi decomposing a log	Symbiotic relationship, e.g. bacteria in gut of cow
Involves two organisms, the parasite and its host	Involves one organism – the food is dead	Involves two organisms
Only the parasite gains – the host may be harmed by the relationship	Only the saprotroph gains from the relationship	Both organisms gain from the relationship

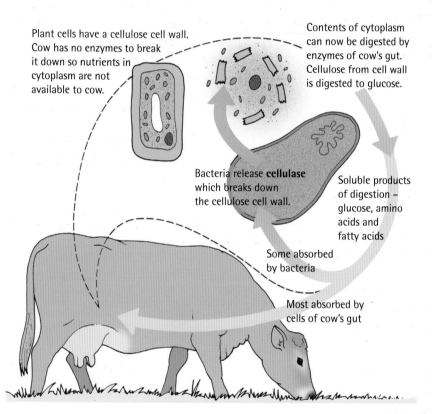

Plant cells have a cellulose cell wall. Cow has no enzymes to break it down so nutrients in cytoplasm are not available to cow.

Contents of cytoplasm can now be digested by enzymes of cow's gut. Cellulose from cell wall is digested to glucose.

Bacteria release **cellulase** which breaks down the cellulose cell wall.

Soluble products of digestion – glucose, amino acids and fatty acids

Some absorbed by bacteria

Most absorbed by cells of cow's gut

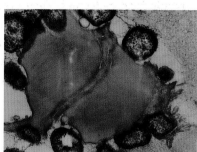

Symbiosis: both cow and bacteria gain from the relationship in which bacteria break down cellulose. Here, the bacteria are surrounding the plant material to digest it.

Lichens are able to live on bare rock. A lichen is made up of two organisms living in a symbiotic relationship. One is a fungus, which can anchor itself to rock and can decompose the rock to release important minerals. The other is an alga, which can make organic foods by photosynthesis. The fungus supplies support and minerals to the alga, and the alga supplies sugars and amino acids to the fungus.

1. Name one compound that a gut bacterium might gain from the contents of a cow's stomach.
2. Suggest two ways in which decomposers affect the human environment.
3. Name the enzymes released from the cells of a decomposer. Name the substrate and the product(s) of each of them.
4. Describe three ways in which a tapeworm is adapted to its parasitic way of life.

Nutrition and health

57

Questions on nutrition and health

Food	Energy (kJ)	Animal protein (g)	Plant protein (g)	Calcium (mg)	Iron (mg)	Vitamin C (mg)
Biscuits	2000	2	5	100	1.5	0
Bread	900	0	9	100	1.7	0
Butter	3000	0.5	0	15	0.2	0
Cheese	1600	26	0	800	0.4	0
Cucumber	40	0	0	25	0.3	8

Table 1

1 John and Paul were eating their school lunch.
Later, they decided to look up the nutritional value of some of the foods in a book. The book had a table showing what 100 g of each food contains.

a Use Table 1 above and your biological knowledge to answer the following questions.

　i Which food shown in the table would be the best for preventing scurvy?

　ii John ate a sandwich containing 100 g of bread, 50 g of cheese and 10 g of butter.
　　How much energy did he take in?
　　Show how you work out your answer.

b Paul had been complaining of pain after eating and so went to the doctor.

The doctor wanted to find out if Paul was allergic to any foods.

She asked Paul to eat two different foods at each meal and record whether he suffered any pain afterwards.

This is what he noted down.

Food eaten	Pain
Bread and butter	yes
Bread and cheese	yes
Cheese and biscuits	yes
Cheese and cucumber	no
Bread and cucumber	yes

　i The doctor asked Paul to complete a chart.
　　Using Paul's notes, copy and complete the chart according to the key given. The result for bread and butter has been done for you.

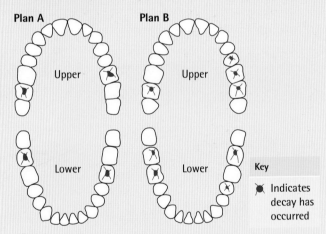

Key
× no pain
✓ pain
— not tested

　ii From the chart the doctor could identify the foods to which Paul was allergic. Which are they?

　iii Use Table 1 to identify which substance in the foods was the cause of the allergy.

　iv The doctor said that the substance which caused Paul's allergy was destroying the villi in his small intestine. She said that this might slow down Paul's growth.
　　Explain why the destruction of the villi may slow down Paul's growth.

[MEG (June 1996)]

2 The diagrams below show plans of the teeth in the upper and lower jaw. Plan A is from a 27-year-old woman called Hannah; plan B is from a 27-year-old woman called Caitlin.

Plan A　　Plan B

Upper　　　Upper

Lower　　　Lower

Key

✹ Indicates decay has occurred

The two women live in different towns. In one town the natural drinking water contains fluoride salts, but there are no fluoride salts in the drinking water of the other.

a Which woman lives in the town with fluoride in the drinking water? Support your answer with numerical data.

b Suggest other reasons for the difference in the number of decayed teeth between the two women.

c Why is it important that both plans are from women, and each is aged 27?

d Explain why decay is more likely in the cheek teeth.

e How would these plans have been different if they had been taken when the women were 10 years old?

3 The table below shows the effect of pH on the time taken for the complete breakdown of a starch solution in the presence of an enzyme.

pH	5.0	5.5	6.0	6.5	7.0	7.5	8.0	9.0
Time taken (min)	20.00	15.00	8.00	4.00	1.25	1.25	3.00	8.00
Rate of reaction								

a Copy and complete the table. Assume that the rate of reaction is the same as $1/_{\text{time taken}}$.

b Plot the results in the form of an appropriate graph.

c What is the optimum pH for this enzyme?

d Name one region of the gut where this pH would be found. How is this pH kept constant?

e Suggest two chemical tests that could be carried out on samples of the solution to show that starch is being broken down.

f In this experiment pH is the manipulated or independent variable, and rate of reaction is the responding or dependent variable. Suggest three fixed variables which must be kept constant if these results are to be valid.

4 Study the following table. It shows the number of deaths in Paris from 1934 to 1966. Wine was rationed during the Second World War, and wine production was not back to normal until the early 1950s.

a Plot these results on a suitable graph.

b Do the results suggest any link between alcohol consumption and cirrhosis? Support your answer with figures from the table.

Year	Deaths (number per 100 000 population)	
	All causes	Cirrhosis of liver
1934	1000	45
1938	1010	44
1942	1435	6
1946	1100	7
1950	1000	23
1952	998	35
1958	1012	43
1962	1000	42
1966	1188	45

5 During the 16th and 17th centuries, sailors were as likely to die from the disease **scurvy** as from enemy action. A chance observation that sailors who were transporting citrus fruits did not develop scurvy led Admiral Nelson to insist that all British ships should carry plenty of limes on long voyages. (This is why British sailors were called 'Limeys'.)

Clearly limes and other citrus fruits contained a substance that prevented scurvy, but it was not until the middle of the 20th century that this substance was shown to be **ascorbic acid** (also called **vitamin C**). At that time an American surgeon called John Crandon carried out an experiment on himself:

1 He cut himself with a sterile scalpel – the cut healed in 3 or 4 days.

2 He had no vitamin C in his diet for 3 months – a similar cut took 3 months to heal.

3 He had no vitamin C for 6 months – a cut would not heal at all.

Do you think that Crandon's results were valid? How could this experiment have been improved?

We now know that long-term deficiency in vitamin C makes it difficult for the body to manufacture the connective tissues that hold body structures together – thus skin damage is difficult to repair. The recommended daily amount (RDA) of vitamin C is the amount required to prevent scurvy, but many scientists believe that vitamin C has other functions in the body and that this RDA is probably too low. Higher doses of vitamin C help the immune system to fight off viruses, prevent cells ageing, and prevent anaemia by increasing the absorption of iron from food.

6 An American doctor called Joseph Goldberger was working in a prison when he noticed that some of the convicts had a strange disease. Some were mentally ill and almost all had skin rashes, especially around the neck. At that time many diseases were believed to be caused by germs, but Goldberger was convinced that these rashes were caused by poor diet. He tested this hypothesis on himself by eating powdered skin rash from one patient and faeces from another. Goldberger reasoned that if the disease was due to a germ he would catch it, but if it was due to poor diet he wouldn't. Goldberger remained healthy, suggesting that the disease was caused by poor diet. Incidentally, Goldberger then performed the experiment on his wife, with the same results!

Later experiments suggested that the convicts were suffering from a shortage of vitamin B_3, or niacin. Liver and fish are rich in vitamin B_3, but neither was present in the convicts' diet.

Design an experiment to investigate Goldberger's observation that poor diet caused skin rashes. Suggest a suitable hypothesis, give the variables in your experiment and describe a control which would improve the validity of your results.

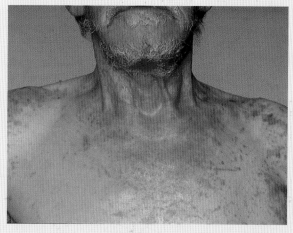

The rash around the neck is typical of pellagra, a deficiency disease caused by too little vitamin B_3 in the diet

Transport systems in animals use blood as the transport medium

All living organisms require energy, which is released from food and oxygen in the process of respiration. All living cells in the body (for example in the brain, liver, kidney and muscle) need energy, and so glucose and oxygen must be transported throughout the body. In some small animals (especially those with a flat body such as the flatworm in the photograph), substances are transported in and out of the body, and from one tissue to another, by the process of **diffusion**.

The flatworm is very thin and has a high surface area to volume ratio. Its volume is made up of working cells that need various substances including oxygen, which can diffuse in across the large surface. The distance from the surface to all the cells is small.

Large complex organisms, such as humans, have a small surface area in relation to their relatively large volume. As a result, cells near the centre of the body are some distance away from contact with the atmosphere, and may also be some distance from the gut where food is digested. Cells inside such large organisms cannot gain enough oxygen and glucose by diffusion alone.

A mass flow system

To supply oxygen and glucose, as well as other substances, large organisms have a specialised **transport system**. This system, called the **blood vascular system** in all vertebrate animals, is an example of a **mass flow system**. A mass flow system carries large volumes of fluid to all parts of the organism. A system like this has four parts:

▪ a **medium** – the fluid that flows in the system and carries materials around the body. This is the **blood**.

▪ a **system of tubes** that carries the fluid from place to place. These are the **arteries** and **veins**.

▪ a **pump** that supplies pressure to keep the fluid moving through the tubes. This is the **heart**.

▪ **sites of exchange** that allow materials delivered by the blood to enter the tissues that need them. These are the **capillaries**.

A whale has a large surface area, but its volume is too large for materials to be moved to and from its body cells by diffusion. It has a circulatory system made up of 4000 dm³ of blood, pumped through 50 000 km of blood vessels by a heart the size of a small car, which beats 40 000 times a day. The main artery can be 20 m long and wide enough for a child to crawl through!

Blood is the circulatory medium

The average adult human has about 5 dm³ of blood, which contains a number of blood cells suspended in a watery liquid (**plasma**). If a sample of blood taken from the body is allowed to stand, and a chemical added to prevent it clotting, it will separate into layers as shown opposite.

If a drop of blood is placed on a microscope slide and stained with a special dye, these different types of cell can be seen, as the photograph below shows.

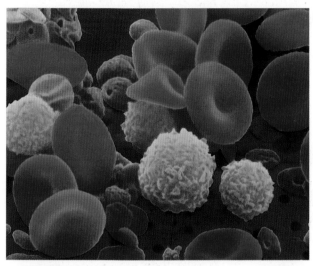

Blood cells dyed so that the different types can be distinguished: red blood cells: red; white blood cells: yellow; platelets: pink.

Blood cells are first formed in the bone marrow of long bones such as the femur (thigh bone), although they may go on to other parts of the body before they become fully developed. The structure and function of different types of blood cell are shown in the table below.

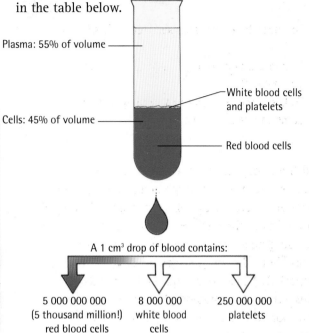

Plasma: 55% of volume

White blood cells and platelets

Cells: 45% of volume

Red blood cells

A 1 cm³ drop of blood contains:

| 5 000 000 000 (5 thousand million!) red blood cells | 8 000 000 white blood cells | 250 000 000 platelets |

The red blood cells sink to the bottom, and the white blood cells and platelets settle on top of the red blood cells, rather like a layer of dust. The plasma forms a clear, straw-coloured layer at the top.

Cell type	Appearance	Function	How the structure is suited to the function
Red blood cells (erythrocytes)		■ Transport oxygen from lungs to all respiring tissues. Prepare carbon dioxide for transport from all respiring tissues to lungs.	■ Contain **haemoglobin**, an iron-containing pigment which picks up oxygen at the lungs and lets go of it at the tissues. ■ Have no nucleus, leaving more space for haemoglobin. ■ Cells are small and flexible, so can squeeze through narrow capillaries.
White blood cells: phagocytes		■ Remove any microorganisms that invade the body and might cause infection. The phagocyte engulfs the microorganism (see page 294).	■ Irregular shaped nucleus allows cell to squeeze through gaps in walls of capillaries. ■ Enzymes in cytoplasm digest microorganisms once engulfed. ■ Sensitive cell surface membrane can detect microorganisms.
White blood cells: lymphocytes		■ Produce antibodies – proteins that help in the defence against disease (see page 296).	■ Large nucleus contains many copies of genes for the control of antibody protein production.
Platelets		■ Cell fragments involved in blood clotting.	■ Can release blood-clotting enzymes (see page 295).

Functions of the blood

The table on page 61 shows that one function of red blood cells is the transport of the respiratory gases, oxygen and carbon dioxide, between the lungs and the respiring tissues. The plasma also has transport functions. This watery liquid carries dissolved food molecules such as glucose and amino acids, waste materials such as urea, and some control molecules such as hormones. Because the plasma is largely water, it has a very high specific heat capacity (see page 9). This means that the plasma is able to distribute heat around the various parts of the body.

Defence against disease is another important function of the blood. The different roles of the blood are summarised below.

Functions of the blood

Regulatory functions – homeostasis
Blood solutes affect the water potential of the blood, and thus the water potential gradient between the blood and the tissue fluid. The size of this water potential gradient is largely due to sodium ions and plasma proteins. The blood solute level **regulates the movement of water** between blood and tissues.

Water plays a part in the **distribution of heat** between heat-producing areas such as the liver and areas of heat loss such as the skin.

Blood also helps to maintain an **optimum pH** in the tissues.

> Too much alcohol in the blood can cause water to leave brain cells, causing the pain and sensation of thirst called a **hangover!**

Protective functions
Platelets, plasma proteins (e.g. fibrinogen) and many other plasma factors (e.g. Ca^{2+} ions) protect against **blood loss** and the **entry of pathogens** by the clotting mechanism.

White blood cells protect against **disease-causing organisms**:
- **phagocytes** engulf them
- **lymphocytes** produce and secrete specific antibodies against them.

Transport functions
Soluble products of digestion/absorption (such as glucose, amino acids, fatty acids, vitamins and minerals) are transported from the gut to the liver and then to the general circulation.

Waste products of metabolism (such as urea, creatinine and lactate) are transported from sites of production to sites of removal, such as the liver and kidney.

Respiratory gases (oxygen and carbon dioxide) are transported from their sites of uptake or production to their site of use or removal.

Hormones (such as insulin) are transported from their sites of production in the glands to the target organs where they have their effects.

Support function
Erection of the penis is achieved by filling large spongy spaces with blood. The penis becomes flaccid when blood flows out quicker than it flows in.

Dracula is based on a 15th-century prince of Romania. He may have consumed blood because he suffered from **porphyria**, an inability to synthesise some compounds including the haem group of haemoglobin. People with porphyria also have a marked sensitivity to daylight and abnormal development of the teeth.

The blood detectives

A scientist who specialises in the study of blood is called a **haematologist**. A haematologist can tell a great deal from a tiny sample of blood. For example:

- **Anaemia**, an inability to transport enough oxygen, can be detected by noting a lower than normal number of red blood cells.

- **Sickle cell anaemia** shows some red blood cells shaped like sickles, as the photograph below illustrates.

- **Leukaemia**, a cancer of white blood cells, can be detected by high numbers of oddly shaped white blood cells.

- **AIDS** may be detected in its early stages by the presence of antibodies to the human immunodeficiency virus (HIV) in the plasma – the affected person is HIV positive. In the later stages of the disease, the number of white blood cells is very much reduced.

- **DNA fingerprinting**, which can be important in criminal investigations, can be carried out on nuclei extracted from white blood cells.

- **Diabetes** may be detected by a high glucose concentration in the plasma.

- **Eating disorders** may be detected by higher than normal concentrations of urea in the plasma.

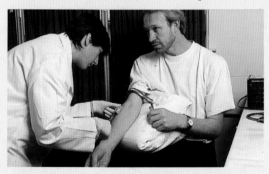

Using modern techniques of biochemistry, a single drop of blood can yield information about all the conditions described above.

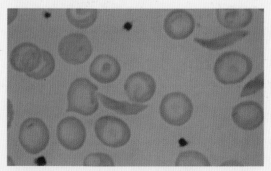

Sickle-shaped red blood cells show the person has sickle cell anaemia. A sickle is a long hooked tool used for cutting crops.

1. Why do large organisms require a transport system?

2. A sample of human blood is collected and placed in a tube and centrifuged. The blood separates into two distinct layers.

   a What are the two layers?

   b Suggest one dissolved food substance found in the upper layer. Choose a substance for which there is a simple chemical test. Describe the test for this substance, and state what a positive result would be.

   c There is a third, rather thin, layer between the two main components. What is this layer made of?

3. 'The structure of a cell is closely related to its function.' Is this statement correct for blood cells? Explain your answer.

4. The table shows the cell composition of three samples of blood.

Cell count (number per mm³)	Sample from		
	Jill	Jenny	Jackie
Red blood cells	7 500 000	5 000 000	2 000 000
White blood cells	500	6000	5000
Platelets	250 000	255 000	50

   a Which person is most likely to have lived at high altitude recently? Explain your answer.

   b Which person would be the most likely to become ill if exposed to a virus? Explain your answer.

   c Which person's blood is least likely to clot efficiently? Explain your answer.

   d Which person is likely to have an iron deficiency in her diet? Explain your answer.

   e These three samples were all taken from 23-year-old women. Explain why this makes comparisons between them valid.

3.2 The circulatory system

Objectives

- To understand that the blood is directed around the body in a set of vessels
- To know the structure and function of arteries and veins
- To understand why humans have a double circulatory system
- To know the names of the main arteries and veins in the human body

Blood vessels – arteries and veins

Blood flows around the body in a system of tube-like **blood vessels**, arranged in such a way that they all eventually lead back to the heart. The blood flows *away* from the heart in vessels called **arteries**, and it flows back *towards* the heart in vessels called **veins**. Joining the arteries and veins are the **capillaries**, and we shall look at these on page 66.

In humans (and in many other animals), the main artery is called the **aorta** and the main vein is called the **vena cava**. The structure and functions of arteries and veins are shown in the table below.

The human double circulation

The human circulation is outlined at the top of the page opposite. The arrangement is called a **double circulation** because the blood passes through the heart twice for each complete circuit of the body. The blood flows to the lungs under high pressure (so a large volume of blood flows past the lung surfaces in a short time). Then, having picked up oxygen at the lungs, the blood receives another 'boost' of pressure from the heart to drive it out to the tissues, where the oxygen is needed.

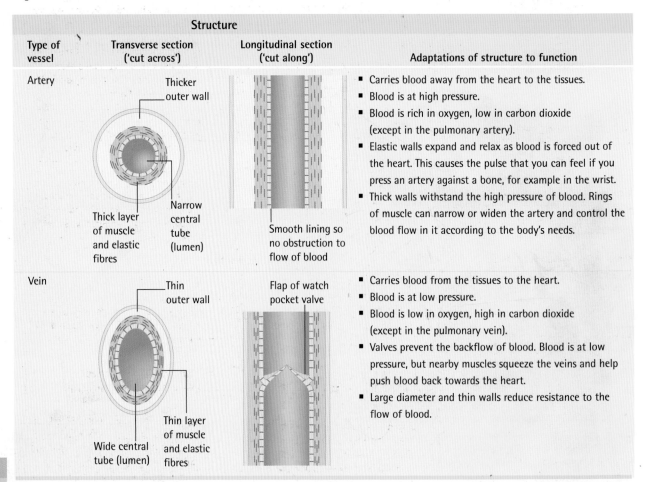

Type of vessel	Structure — Transverse section ('cut across')	Structure — Longitudinal section ('cut along')	Adaptations of structure to function
Artery	Thicker outer wall; Thick layer of muscle and elastic fibres; Narrow central tube (lumen)	Smooth lining so no obstruction to flow of blood	• Carries blood away from the heart to the tissues. • Blood is at high pressure. • Blood is rich in oxygen, low in carbon dioxide (except in the pulmonary artery). • Elastic walls expand and relax as blood is forced out of the heart. This causes the pulse that you can feel if you press an artery against a bone, for example in the wrist. • Thick walls withstand the high pressure of blood. Rings of muscle can narrow or widen the artery and control the blood flow in it according to the body's needs.
Vein	Thin outer wall; Wide central tube (lumen); Thin layer of muscle and elastic fibres	Flap of watch pocket valve	• Carries blood from the tissues to the heart. • Blood is at low pressure. • Blood is low in oxygen, high in carbon dioxide (except in the pulmonary vein). • Valves prevent the backflow of blood. Blood is at low pressure, but nearby muscles squeeze the veins and help push blood back towards the heart. • Large diameter and thin walls reduce resistance to the flow of blood.

The structure and functions of arteries and veins.

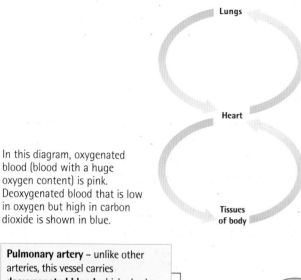

Lungs

Heart

Tissues of body

In this diagram, oxygenated blood (blood with a huge oxygen content) is pink. Deoxygenated blood that is low in oxygen but high in carbon dioxide is shown in blue.

1 State two differences between arteries and veins, and say how these differences are related to the functions of these blood vessels.

2 Look at the diagram below. Follow the path of the red blood cell in the renal artery around the circulation and back to the renal artery. How many times does it pass through the heart? List the blood vessels and chambers of the heart that the cell passes through.

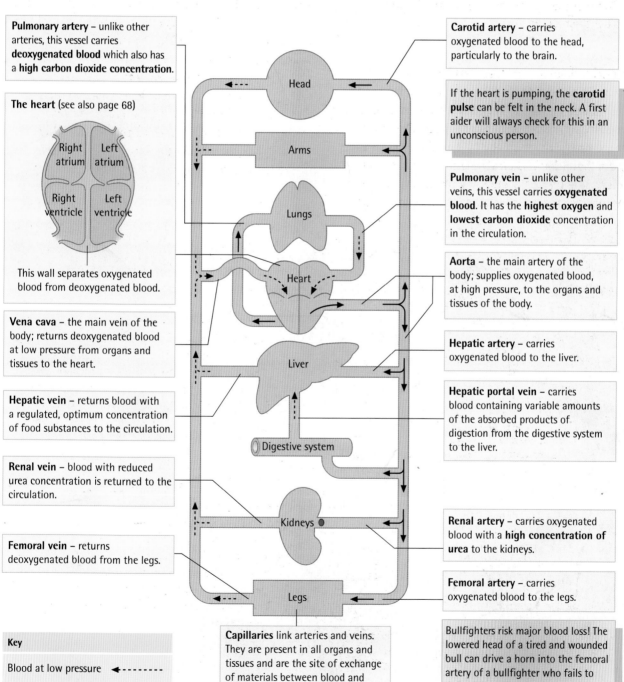

Pulmonary artery – unlike other arteries, this vessel carries **deoxygenated blood** which also has a **high carbon dioxide concentration**.

The heart (see also page 68)

| Right atrium | Left atrium |
| Right ventricle | Left ventricle |

This wall separates oxygenated blood from deoxygenated blood.

Vena cava – the main vein of the body; returns deoxygenated blood at low pressure from organs and tissues to the heart.

Hepatic vein – returns blood with a regulated, optimum concentration of food substances to the circulation.

Renal vein – blood with reduced urea concentration is returned to the circulation.

Femoral vein – returns deoxygenated blood from the legs.

Head

Arms

Lungs

Heart

Liver

Digestive system

Kidneys

Legs

Carotid artery – carries oxygenated blood to the head, particularly to the brain.

If the heart is pumping, the **carotid pulse** can be felt in the neck. A first aider will always check for this in an unconscious person.

Pulmonary vein – unlike other veins, this vessel carries **oxygenated blood**. It has the **highest oxygen** and **lowest carbon dioxide** concentration in the circulation.

Aorta – the main artery of the body; supplies oxygenated blood, at high pressure, to the organs and tissues of the body.

Hepatic artery – carries oxygenated blood to the liver.

Hepatic portal vein – carries blood containing variable amounts of the absorbed products of digestion from the digestive system to the liver.

Renal artery – carries oxygenated blood with a **high concentration of urea** to the kidneys.

Femoral artery – carries oxygenated blood to the legs.

Bullfighters risk major blood loss! The lowered head of a tired and wounded bull can drive a horn into the femoral artery of a bullfighter who fails to deflect the bull with his cape.

Key

Blood at low pressure ◄------

Blood at high pressure ◄——

Capillaries link arteries and veins. They are present in all organs and tissues and are the site of exchange of materials between blood and tissue fluid (see next page).

Circulation

65

3·3 Materials are exchanged between blood and tissues at the capillaries

Objectives

▪ To understand that substances carried in the blood must leave the circulation to reach the tissues

▪ To know that materials are exchanged between tissues and blood in the capillary beds

▪ To know how the structure of the capillaries is suited to the transfer of materials between blood and tissues

Tissue fluid leaves the capillaries

To reach the cells that need them, dissolved substances carried in the blood must leave the blood vessels and enter the tissues. At the same time, waste materials produced by the tissues need to enter the blood to be carried away. Dissolved substances move between the blood and tissues by **diffusion** across the walls of very fine blood vessels called **capillaries**. Networks or **beds** of capillaries extend through all the tissues, so every body cell is near to a capillary. The capillary beds are adapted to their function of exchange of substances in a number of ways:

▪ the walls of the capillaries are only one cell thick – substances do not have very far to diffuse through them

▪ the capillaries are highly branched so they cover an enormous surface area, giving more 'space' for diffusion to occur

▪ the capillary beds are constantly supplied with fresh blood, keeping up the concentration gradients of dissolved substances between blood and tissues. Without these concentration gradients diffusion could not occur.

The diagram shows how materials are exchanged between the blood and the tissues, and how **tissue fluid** is formed.

Artery – delivers oxygenated blood, rich in nutrients and at high pressure. Can be narrowed or widened to control blood flow (for example, during exercise). Continuous supply of blood keeps up the concentration gradients of substances between the blood plasma and the tissue fluid.

Cells of tissue
Need: oxygen and nutrients such as glucose and amino acids.
Produce: wastes such as carbon dioxide and some useful products such as hormones.

Vein – carries away deoxygenated blood, low in nutrients and at low pressure. Has high concentration of waste products.

Tissue fluid
▪ formed from plasma
▪ contains no blood cells or plasma proteins.

Capillary has:
▪ wall only one cell thick
▪ very large surface area

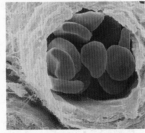

Capillary walls are about 1 μm thick. The central tube (lumen) may only be the same diameter as the red blood cells, so they have to squeeze through the capillary in single file as they unload their oxygen.

→ Formation of lymph

Useful substances move out from plasma – formation of tissue fluid

Substances collected from cells

Remember how substances cross membranes

Diffusion is:
▪ the movement of molecules
▪ down a concentration gradient
▪ until equilibrium is reached.

Osmosis is:
▪ the movement of water
▪ down a water potential gradient
▪ across a partially permeable membrane.

Problems with the return of tissue fluid

The diagram below shows in detail how tissue fluid is formed and returned to the blood. If anything goes wrong with this return of tissue fluid, the tissues swell up.

In **elephantiasis**, a parasitic worm lodges in the lymph vessels in the groin and causes fluid to build up in the legs.

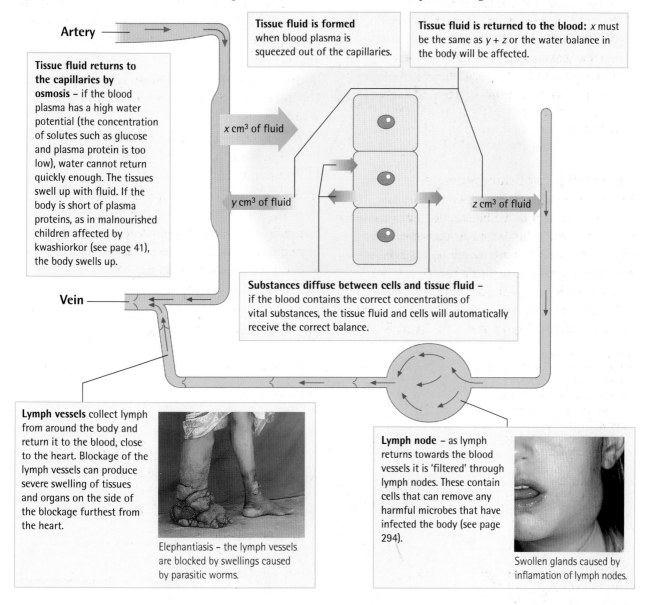

Artery

Tissue fluid is formed when blood plasma is squeezed out of the capillaries.

Tissue fluid is returned to the blood: x must be the same as $y + z$ or the water balance in the body will be affected.

Tissue fluid returns to the capillaries by osmosis – if the blood plasma has a high water potential (the concentration of solutes such as glucose and plasma protein is too low), water cannot return quickly enough. The tissues swell up with fluid. If the body is short of plasma proteins, as in malnourished children affected by kwashiorkor (see page 41), the body swells up.

x cm³ of fluid

y cm³ of fluid

z cm³ of fluid

Vein

Substances diffuse between cells and tissue fluid – if the blood contains the correct concentrations of vital substances, the tissue fluid and cells will automatically receive the correct balance.

Lymph vessels collect lymph from around the body and return it to the blood, close to the heart. Blockage of the lymph vessels can produce severe swelling of tissues and organs on the side of the blockage furthest from the heart.

Elephantiasis – the lymph vessels are blocked by swellings caused by parasitic worms.

Lymph node – as lymph returns towards the blood vessels it is 'filtered' through lymph nodes. These contain cells that can remove any harmful microbes that have infected the body (see page 294).

Swollen glands caused by inflamation of lymph nodes.

---

1 This diagram represents a group of body cells and some parts of the circulatory system. The arrows show movement of fluids.

a Name the fluids contained in spaces **A**, **B** and **C**.

b Name two substances that the cells remove from the fluid in **B**. Suggest two substances that the cells might add to the fluid in **B**.

c Describe how the fluid in **C** is returned to the circulation.

d Give a reason why the process shown at **D** might be inefficient. What would be the result of this for the body? How could it be corrected?

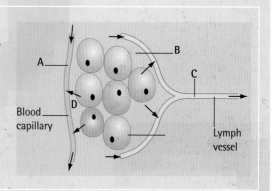

A

B

C

D

Blood capillary

Lymph vessel

The heart is the pump for the circulatory system

Objectives

- To know that the blood is pumped around the circulatory system by the action of the heart
- To know that the heart is a muscular organ with four chambers
- To understand how the flow of blood through the circulation is maintained

The heart of a mammal pumps blood through the circulatory system. It provides the pressure that forces the blood through arteries, capillaries and veins. The pressure is generated by the squeezing of the walls of the heart against the incompressible fluid blood. The heart walls can squeeze the blood because they are made of **muscle**, and the muscle contracts rhythmically.

A double pump

The heart is divided into two sides, each of which acts as a pump. The right side of the heart pumps deoxygenated blood coming from the tissues out to the lungs. The left side pumps oxygenated blood coming from the lungs out to the tissues. A much greater pressure (about five times as much) is needed to force blood out to the extremities of the body than is needed to drive blood to the lungs. Because of this, the left side of the heart is much more muscular than the right side.

Even though the two sides of the heart generate different pressures, they work in the same way and have the same parts, as shown in the diagram below.

Pulmonary arteries – carry deoxygenated blood to the lungs.

Semilunar valves – prevent blood running back into the ventricles when pressure falls during relaxation.

Vena cava – the main vein of the body; returns deoxygenated blood from the head and lower body to the right atrium.

Right atrium – receives deoxygenated blood from the vena cava. The **pacemaker** is found in the wall of the right atrium.

Three flaps of tricuspid valve – prevent blood flowing back from ventricle to atrium during contraction.

Tendons which are tightened to make sure that the valve does not turn inside out when the ventricle walls contract.

Chamber of **right ventricle**

Aorta – the main artery of the body; carries oxygenated blood out to the tissues. Blood pressure is at its highest in the aorta, and the strongest pulse is felt here.

Wall of right ventricle – less muscular than left ventricle since it need only force blood along the pulmonary arteries to the lungs.

Pulmonary vein – returns oxygenated blood from the lungs. A vein from each lung join together before entering the left atrium.

Left atrium – receives oxygenated blood returning from the lungs. Atria have thin walls since they need only pump blood to the ventricles.

Two flaps of **bicuspid valve** – when this valve is closed and the ventricle contracts, the blood **must** leave through the aorta.

Chamber of **left ventricle**

Wall of left ventricle – thick and muscular since it must force blood through the arteries to all the tissues of the body.

Think about it! The left ventricle can push out about 70 cm³ of blood with each beat, and in a normal healthy person at rest the heart beats 70 times per minute. How much blood is pumped out of the heart per hour? How much per day?

Key

Deoxygenated blood	◄- - - Blood at low pressure
Oxygenated blood	◄—— Blood at high pressure

Note that:

- The **atrium** receives blood at low pressure from the veins (comming from the lungs or tissues).
- The **ventricle** pumps blood at high pressure out to the arteries (to the lungs or tissues).
- **Valves** make sure that the blood flows in the right direction.

The beating of the heart is controlled by a pacemaker

In a healthy person the heart beats about 70 times a minute during normal levels of activity. This rate is enough to supply blood containing oxygen and nutrients to tissues.

The muscular walls of the heart differ from other muscles in that they never become tired or **fatigued**, because each contraction of the heart is immediately followed by a relaxation. Even when the heart is beating at its fastest during severe exercise (see page 71), the period of relaxation allows the muscle to recover so it does not fatigue.

The pattern of contraction and relaxation is kept going by electrical signals sent from a region of the heart called the **pacemaker**. This is a specialised piece of tissue in the wall of the right atrium. It is sensitive to the swelling of the heart wall as blood enters the heart from the main veins. The signals from the pacemaker make sure that:

- the atria contract just before the ventricles, so that blood flows from atria to ventricles
- the heartbeat is fast enough to meet the demands of the tissues for oxygen and nutrients, and for the removal of wastes.

If the pacemaker does not work as well as it should, an artificial electronic pacemaker can be fitted inside the chest (see box opposite).

Artificial pacemakers – help for the heart

The beating of the heart is controlled by the natural pacemaker in the wall of the right atrium. If this pacemaker is damaged, pumping goes on automatically at about 30 beats per minute. This is less than half the normal rate, and is only enough to keep a very inactive person alive.

An artificial pacemaker can help people whose natural pacemaker does not work well. This artificial pacemaker is made up of a box containing batteries and an electronic timing device. It is placed in a cavity under the muscle of the upper chest as shown below, and a wire is fed down a vein into the right ventricle. The timing device sends a small electrical charge which triggers the beating of the heart. This is set to give a basic rate of 72 beats per minute. The latest pacemakers can sense changes in breathing, movement and body temperature, and make exactly the right adjustments to heart rate. The battery in the pacemaker is usually replaced every year or so, under local anaesthetic.

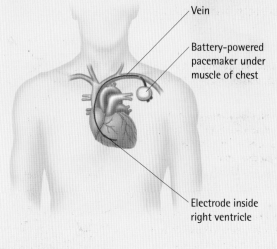

Vein

Battery-powered pacemaker under muscle of chest

Electrode inside right ventricle

An artificial pacemaker.

---

1 a Name the chamber of the heart that receives blood from the lungs.

b Explain what happens to the blood in the ventricles when the muscle in the ventricle walls contracts.

c The muscle around the atria is thinner than the muscle around the ventricles. Suggest a reason for this.

2 A doctor listening to the heartbeat through a stethoscope hears two sounds as the blood flows through the heart: 'lup-dup lup-dup lup-dup'.

a From your knowledge of the working of the heart, suggest how these two sounds are produced.

b The doctor records 72 beats per minute. How long a period would there be between two consecutive 'lup' sounds? Explain your answer.

3·5 Control of blood pressure and the benefit of exercise

Objectives

☞ To understand how the flow of blood through the circulation is maintained

☞ To understand how the regular beating of the heart can be adjusted according to the body's needs

Blood pressure

As the ventricles of the heart contract they force blood at high pressure into the arteries. This pressure needs to carry blood to the working tissues, but it must not be so high that it damages the blood vessels. Blood pressure can be varied, such as to force more blood to muscles during exercise. The blood pressure is raised by:

☞ making the ventricles contract more powerfully

☞ narrowing the diameter of the arteries.

Stress or excitement also raise the blood pressure. A diet with too much saturated fat can cause high blood pressure by clogging up the arteries.

Measuring blood pressure

The blood pressure naturally goes up and down during the heart's cycles of contraction and relaxation. The blood pressure is highest when the ventricles contract (**systolic pressure**) and lowest when the heart walls are relaxed as blood returns into the atria (**diastolic pressure**). A person's blood pressure is expressed as a fraction, systolic pressure divided by diastolic pressure. A typical healthy young person would have a blood pressure around 120/80 – this means that systolic pressure is 120 mm of mercury and diastolic pressure is 80 mm of mercury.

The high pressure generated when the ventricles contract forces blood out into the arteries. The elastic walls of the arteries expand and then relax. This causes a **pulse** in the arteries – this can be felt wherever an artery can be pressed against a solid surface, such as a bone. The pulse should always be felt with the index or ring fingers, since the thumb has a pulse of its own. There is no pulse in the veins since the blood no longer has spurts of pressure (it is now a long way from the heart) and the walls of veins are not elastic.

Blood flow through the veins

The pressure generated by the beating of the heart, together with the elastic recoil of the walls of the arteries, drives the blood out to the tissues. At the capillaries, some of the plasma leaks across the capillary walls to form the tissue fluid (see page 67). As a result of this the volume of blood in the vessels falls, and so too does its pressure. The pressure is no longer great enough to return the blood to the heart through the veins. How does blood return to the heart? There are a number of factors that help it to flow in the veins, as shown in the diagram below.

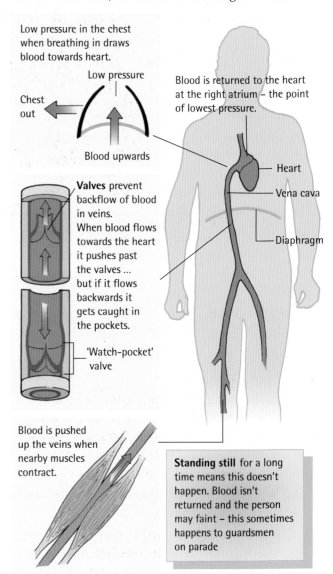

Low pressure in the chest when breathing in draws blood towards heart.

Low pressure

Chest out

Blood upwards

Valves prevent backflow of blood in veins. When blood flows towards the heart it pushes past the valves ... but if it flows backwards it gets caught in the pockets.

'Watch-pocket' valve

Blood is pushed up the veins when nearby muscles contract.

Blood is returned to the heart at the right atrium – the point of lowest pressure.

Heart

Vena cava

Diaphragm

Standing still for a long time means this doesn't happen. Blood isn't returned and the person may faint – this sometimes happens to guardsmen on parade

Blood from the veins is returned to right atrium of the heart via the vena cava. At this point blood pressure is at its lowest.

DANGER!
Exercise, especially if sudden and unplanned, can overstress the heart. This can lead to chest pain (**angina**) or even death. Those who are especially at risk include:
■ the elderly
■ people with coronary heart disease (CHD).
■ people who do not exercise regularly.

Anticipation of exercise such as a warm-up can prepare the body for action. The hormone **adrenaline**:
■ increases blood flow to muscles, and reduces blood flow to 'non-vital' organs such as the gut
■ allows the heart to expand more to give 'deeper' beats – greater volume of blood is forced out with each beat.

During exercise the concentration of carbon dioxide in the blood rises. This is detected automatically (no 'thought' is necessary) by the brain, and nerve messages are sent out to...

Long-term benefits
Regular, carefully planned training can:
■ increase the size of the heart
■ increase the power of heart muscle
■ keep artery walls flexible
■ increase the size of capillary beds, including the ones that supply the heart muscle itself.

The heart, which beats more quickly and more deeply, pumping more blood out into the circulation each minute.

The capillary beds, which can be opened up in vital working organs such as muscle, and closed down in non-vital organs such as the gut.

Sphincter muscles control blood flow to capillaries.

Result?
More **oxygen** and **more glucose** can be delivered for **respiration** in working muscles.

Well trained athletes often have a lower pulse rate than people who are less fit because their heart and circulation are more efficient.

The heart and exercise

During strenuous exercise such as running, the muscles work hard. They need more oxygen and glucose to release energy by respiration, so they need an increased circulation of blood to supply the oxygen and glucose. This is achieved in two ways:

▪ **the heart pumps more blood each minute** – it beats more quickly and more deeply

▪ **sphincters control the distribution of blood** – rings of muscle open to increase the blood flow to the muscles, and close to decrease the blood flow to less important areas such as the gut.

1 During exercise the heart pumps out a greater volume of blood per minute than at rest. Suggest two ways in which the heart can increase the volume of blood pumped out.

2 'Exercise has both short- and long-term effects on the heart.' Explain what is meant by this statement.

3 When a doctor takes a patient's blood pressure the result is expressed as two figures, for example, 120/80 mm of mercury. Explain why there are two figures.

Circulation

71

3·6 Coronary heart disease

Objectives

- To know that the heart muscle requires a supply of oxygen, glucose and other nutrients
- To know that the heart muscle has its own blood supply through the coronary arteries
- To understand that factors such as lifestyle, diet and family history may affect the efficiency of the coronary arteries
- To know that coronary heart disease is one of the major causes of death in the developed world

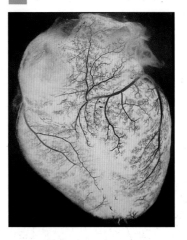

Cast of the heart showing the coronary circulation

The supply of blood to the heart muscle

Heart muscle contracts to push blood through the vessels of the circulation. This contraction is work, and it requires energy. The energy is made available by aerobic respiration, so the working cells of the heart need glucose and oxygen for respiration.

The blood passing through the chambers on the left side of the heart carries oxygen and glucose, but the heart cells cannot use these because the muscular walls are very thick and the blood is too far away. The heart muscle has its own blood supply, delivered to capillary beds in the walls of the heart through the **coronary arteries**. The coronary arteries branch off from the aorta, just where the aorta leaves the left ventricle. The heart therefore has a high-pressure supply of blood loaded with oxygen and glucose. Once these useful substances have been

removed by the heart muscle cells and replaced with wastes such as carbon dioxide, the blood returns to the circulation through **coronary veins** which pour blood into the vena cava. The coronary circulation is shown below left. The photograph above shows a cast of the heart with all the coronary circulation picked out after the heart muscle has been removed.

Coronary heart disease

If any of the coronary arteries become blocked, the supply of blood to the heart muscle may be interrupted. The heart muscle cells are deprived of glucose and oxygen, and poisonous wastes such as lactic acid build up (see page 29). Part of the heart muscle stops contracting, causing a **heart attack**. This can be damaging or even fatal, since other tissues in the body no longer receive their supplies of oxygen and nutrients if the heart stops beating.

What causes the coronary arteries to become blocked? The photographs at the top of the next page compare a section of a healthy coronary artery with one that has been narrowed by atheroma so that blood flow through it is restricted. This person has **coronary heart disease (CHD)**.

The risk of developing CHD is increased by:

- **poor diet** – high levels of cholesterol or saturated fatty acids in the blood
- **poor lifestyle** – smoking, lack of exercise, stress
- **genetic factors** – being male; having a family history of heart disease.

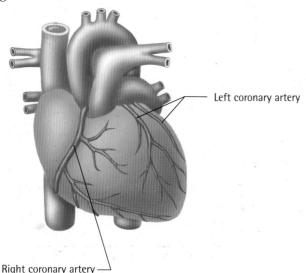

Left coronary artery

Right coronary artery

The coronary arteries branch off the aorta, supplying the surface of the heart with oxygenated blood at high pressure.

Anyone with a genetic risk of developing heart disease should obviously take care that he or she does not have a poor diet or lifestyle. Many middle-aged men, the highest risk group, help to prevent heart disease by taking half an aspirin a day (this seems to help stop small clots forming which could block the arteries) and/or by drinking a small quantity of alcohol (red wine may be the most beneficial).

If a doctor suspects that a patient has CHD, an **angiogram** is carried out. This gives a picture of the state of these arteries (see below). If the coronary arteries are blocked, a **coronary artery bypass** operation may be carried out, as shown right.

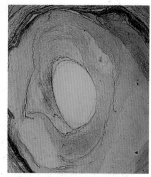
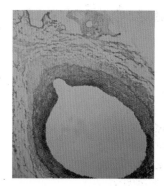

The coronary artery on the left is healthy, but the one on the right is blocked by atheroma.

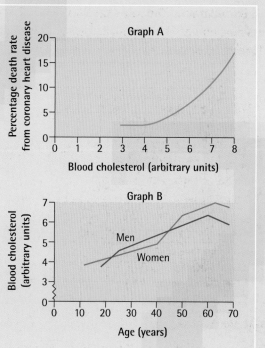

Aortic arch

Grafted 'bypass'

Blocked part of coronary artery

Coronary artery

In a coronary artery bypass operation a blood vessel is removed from another part of the body and stitched into place between the aorta and the unblocked part of the coronary artery. Sometimes an artificial vessel is used. The bypass increases blood flow and reduces the likelihood of angina (chest pain).

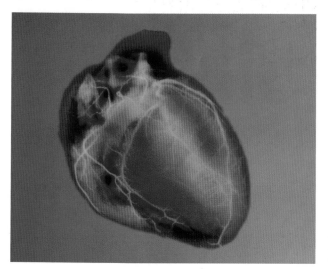

1 a The heart muscle has its own supply of blood from vessels that run all over its surface. What is the name of these vessels?

b In some people these vessels can become blocked with a fatty substance containing cholesterol. Explain the effects that blocking these blood vessels would have.

2 Look at the graphs. Graph A shows the relationship between the death rate for CHD and the blood cholesterol level. Graph B shows the relationship between cholesterol levels and age, for men and women.

a At which ages do men and women show the same blood cholesterol level?

b Use the information in the graphs to explain why the death rate from CHD is higher for men than for women between the ages of 25 and 45 years.

c Use the graphs to determine the level of blood cholesterol that would keep the death rate from CHD at a minimum.

d What does your answer to c suggest about cholesterol as the only cause of CHD?

e What sort of person is most at risk from CHD?

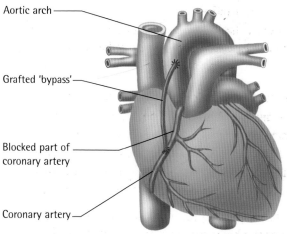

[1] Read the following article carefully, then answer the questions based on it.

Blood plasma carries red blood cells, white blood cells and platelets to all parts of the body. It also carries many solutes (dissolved substances) – these include oxygen, carbon dioxide, urea, hormones, glucose and amino acids.

In a normal healthy person the number of white blood cells may vary, but is usually no more than 8000 per mm^3 of blood. If a person has an infection, the number of white blood cells may rise to 40 000 per mm^3 of blood.

In a healthy person living at sea level there are about 5 000 000 red blood cells per mm^3 of blood. The cells are regularly replaced from the bone marrow. Old, worn out red blood cells are removed from the blood by the liver, after about 120 days of carrying out their function. Each cell carries oxygen from the lungs to the tissues, combined with a protein called haemoglobin. Haemoglobin will also combine with carbon monoxide, a gas in car exhaust fumes and cigarette smoke. Carbon monoxide combines with haemoglobin about 250 times more readily than oxygen does, and the combination does not break down.

a Name two soluble substances transported in the blood plasma. For each substance you name, suggest where it might be coming from and where it might be going to.

b What is the maximum number of white blood cells normally found in 1 mm^3 of blood? What can cause this number to increase?

c In a healthy person, what is the ratio of red blood cells to white blood cells?

d Name two sources of carbon monoxide.

e What happens to the amount of oxygen transported if a person breathes in carbon monoxide? Explain your answer.

f How long would it take the blood of the person in part e to regain its full ability to carry oxygen? Explain your answer.

g Liver is a good dietary source of iron. Why?

[2] Name the blood vessel in a human that has:

a the highest pressure

b the highest oxygen concentration

c the highest carbon dioxide concentration

d the highest temperature when the body is at rest

e the function of removing deoxygenated blood from the leg

f the highest concentration of glucose following a meal

g blood at high pressure but with a low oxygen concentration.

[3] These diagrams are concerned with the exchange of materials between the blood and tissues.

Part of the circulatory system

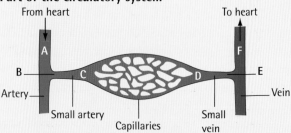

Sections through blood vessels *(not to scale)*

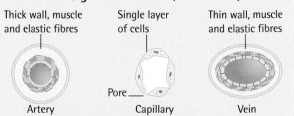

Average blood pressure at different positions in the circulatory system

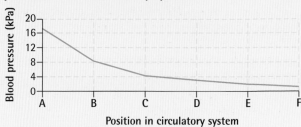

a What happens to the blood pressure as the blood travels from A to F?

b The highest pressure is found in the artery. Why is this important for the delivery of materials to the cells?

c Veins have structures along them, not shown in the diagram, to help return blood to the heart. What are these structures called?

d How can the small arteries help control the distribution of blood to tissues which have a high demand for oxygen and nutrients?

e Use information shown in the diagrams to explain how the structure of capillaries allows substances to pass from them to surrounding cells.

[4] List the blood vessels and chambers of the heart through which:

a a molecule of glucose absorbed through the gut passes on its way to an active muscle in the leg

b a red blood cell passes as it delivers oxygen from the lungs to the brain and returns to be oxygenated again.

5 On a visit to a sports physiology laboratory, a student underwent a series of tests. He was made to exercise on a rolling road, and the following information was collected.

Heart rate (beats per minute)	Total heart output (dm³ per minute)	Output per beat (cm³)
55	4.0	
70	4.8	
80	5.2	
90	5.6	
120	6.0	
140	6.0	
150	5.8	
170	4.6	

a Copy the table and complete it by calculating the output per beat for each heart rate value.

b Plot a graph of total output (vertical axis) against heart rate (horizontal axis). On the same graph plot output per beat (vertical axis) against heart rate.

c Describe the relationship between:
  i heart rate and total output
  ii heart rate and output per beat.

d **i** Even during severe exercise, the heart rate seldom rises above 140 beats per minute. Use the data in the table to explain why this is so.
  ii Well trained athletes can keep up a heart rate of 170 beats per minute. Suggest how their output per beat may be different from that of an untrained person such as the student.

e Distance runners often have low resting heart rates. How might this be of advantage to them?

f Increased total output means that more blood can be delivered to active tissues. As heart rate increases, so does breathing rate. Suggest why.

6 The bar chart below shows how the risk of CHD varies in different parts of the world.

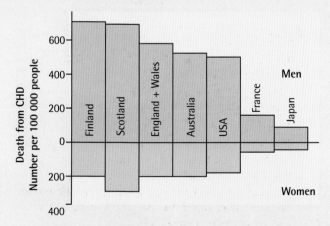

A USA citizen is almost three times as likely to develop CHD as a French citizen. Medical scientists suggested that this difference could be due to either diet or inheritance. They set up a study of 1000 French nationals who had emigrated to the USA, and who had taken up the American lifestyle, including diet.

a How many of these people would you expect to develop CHD if:
  i diet is responsible
  ii inheritance is responsible?

b All the people in this study were male, and non-smokers. Why was this important to the validity of the results?

7 The following tables show the effects of smoking and blood cholesterol levels on the risk of developing CHD.

Cigarettes smoked per day	Relative risk of CHD
0	1
5	1.2
10	1.5
15	2.0
20	2.5
25	2.9
30	3.2

Effect of smoking.

Cholesterol level	Relative risk of CHD
Male, normal	1
Female, normal	0.3
Male, 30% above normal	1.4
Male, 45% above normal	2.0
Male, 75% above normal	3.1

Effect of blood cholesterol level.

a Plot the two sets of results in an appropriate way.

b **i** Which appears to carry greater risk, smoking 10 cigarettes per day or having a blood cholesterol level 45% above normal?
  ii How much more likely is a man who smokes 30 cigarettes per day and has a 75% higher than normal blood cholesterol level to develop CHD than a non-smoking woman with normal blood cholesterol level?

8 Suggest how:
a lifestyle
b diet
c inheritance
may cause problems with the circulatory system.

Objectives

- To understand why living organisms must obtain oxygen from their environment, and why they must release carbon dioxide to their environment
- To know the properties of an ideal gas exchange surface
- To be able to identify the parts of the human gas exchange system

Property of surface	Reason
Thin (ideally one cell thick)	Gases have a short distance over which to diffuse.
Large surface area	Many molecules of gas can diffuse across at the same time.
Moist	Cells die if not kept moist.
Well ventilated	Concentration gradients for oxygen and carbon dioxide are kept up by regular fresh supplies of air.
Close to a blood supply	Gases can be carried to and from the cells that need or produce them.

Exchanging oxygen and carbon dioxide

Respiration uses oxygen to 'burn' (oxidise) food and so release the energy that cells need to stay alive. Respiration produces carbon dioxide and water vapour as waste products:

$$\text{Glucose} + \text{oxygen} \rightarrow \text{energy} + \text{carbon dioxide} + \text{water}$$

Living organisms must be able to take oxygen from the air and get rid of carbon dioxide to the air. Swapping oxygen for carbon dioxide in this way is called **gas exchange** (or **gaseous exchange**).

Gas exchange takes place through a **gas exchange surface**, also known as a **respiratory surface**. The diagram below shows how the process happens. The properties of an ideal respiratory surface are given in the table on the right.

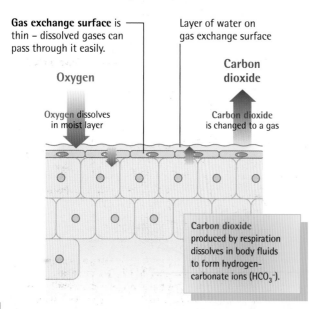

Gas exchange surface is thin – dissolved gases can pass through it easily.

Layer of water on gas exchange surface

Oxygen

Oxygen dissolves in moist layer

Carbon dioxide

Carbon dioxide is changed to a gas

Carbon dioxide produced by respiration dissolves in body fluids to form hydrogen-carbonate ions (HCO_3^-).

A gas exchange surface allows cells to obtain the oxygen they need for respiration, and get rid of the carbon dioxide they produce.

Gas exchange in humans

Like other mammals, humans are active and maintain a constant body temperature. This means they use up a great deal of energy. Mammals must have a very efficient gas exchange system.

The gas exchange system in humans is shown opposite and is made up of:

- a **respiratory surface** – membranes lining the alveoli (air sacs) in the lungs
- a **set of tubes** to allow air from the outside to reach the respiratory surface. This set of tubes has many branches, and is sometimes called the 'bronchial tree'.
- a **blood supply** (carried by the pulmonary artery and pulmonary vein) to carry dissolved gases to and from the respiratory surface
- a **ventilation system** (the intercostal muscles and the diaphragm) to keep a good flow of air over the respiratory surface.

1. What are the properties of an ideal gas exchange surface?

2. List the structures through which a molecule of oxygen passes to get from the atmosphere to the cytoplasm of a named working cell.

3. Most larger animals transport oxygen in red blood cells. What are the advantages of transporting oxygen in this way? How is a red blood cell adapted to its function of oxygen transport?

4. What is the difference between respiration and gas exchange?

Gas exchange

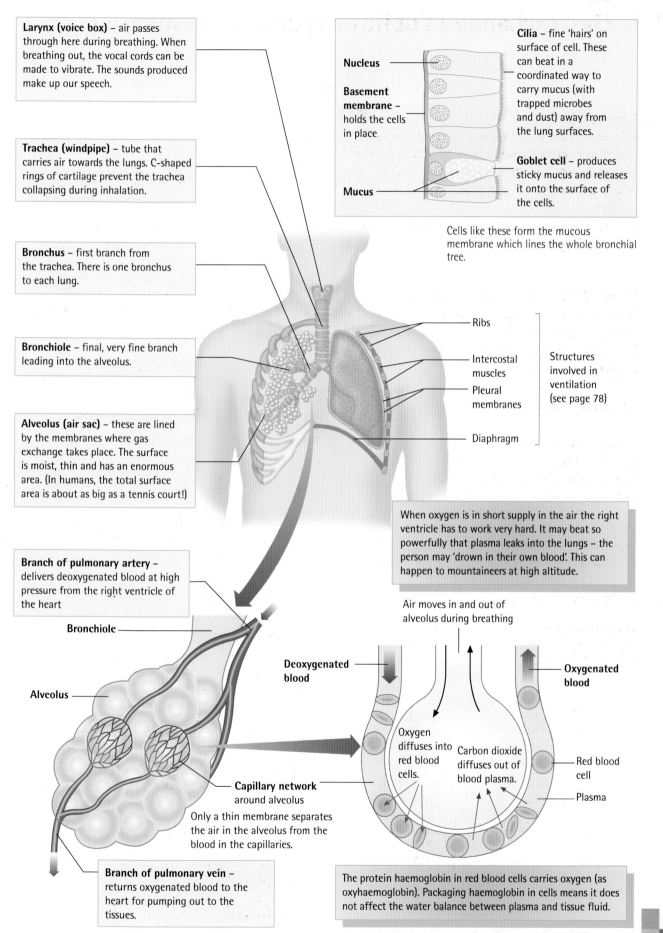

Larynx (voice box) – air passes through here during breathing. When breathing out, the vocal cords can be made to vibrate. The sounds produced make up our speech.

Trachea (windpipe) – tube that carries air towards the lungs. C-shaped rings of cartilage prevent the trachea collapsing during inhalation.

Bronchus – first branch from the trachea. There is one bronchus to each lung.

Bronchiole – final, very fine branch leading into the alveolus.

Alveolus (air sac) – these are lined by the membranes where gas exchange takes place. The surface is moist, thin and has an enormous area. (In humans, the total surface area is about as big as a tennis court!)

Nucleus

Basement membrane – holds the cells in place

Mucus

Cilia – fine 'hairs' on surface of cell. These can beat in a coordinated way to carry mucus (with trapped microbes and dust) away from the lung surfaces.

Goblet cell – produces sticky mucus and releases it onto the surface of the cells.

Cells like these form the mucous membrane which lines the whole bronchial tree.

Ribs

Intercostal muscles

Pleural membranes

Diaphragm

Structures involved in ventilation (see page 78)

When oxygen is in short supply in the air the right ventricle has to work very hard. It may beat so powerfully that plasma leaks into the lungs – the person may 'drown in their own blood'. This can happen to mountaineers at high altitude.

Branch of pulmonary artery – delivers deoxygenated blood at high pressure from the right ventricle of the heart

Bronchiole

Alveolus

Air moves in and out of alveolus during breathing

Deoxygenated blood

Oxygenated blood

Oxygen diffuses into red blood cells.

Carbon dioxide diffuses out of blood plasma.

Red blood cell

Plasma

Capillary network around alveolus

Only a thin membrane separates the air in the alveolus from the blood in the capillaries.

Branch of pulmonary vein – returns oxygenated blood to the heart for pumping out to the tissues.

The protein haemoglobin in red blood cells carries oxygen (as oxyhaemoglobin). Packaging haemoglobin in cells means it does not affect the water balance between plasma and tissue fluid.

Gas exchange

77

4·2 Breathing ventilates the lungs

Objectives

- To understand the muscular movements involved in the ventilation of the lungs
- To know how the efficiency of breathing can be measured
- To understand how breathing is affected by exercise
- To appreciate that the function of the lungs may sometimes need to be supported

Breathing is the set of muscular movements that gives the respiratory surface a constant supply of fresh air. This means there is always a concentration gradient between the blood and the air in the alveoli for both oxygen and carbon dioxide.
As shown below, breathing is brought about by:

- the action of two groups of muscles – the **intercostal muscles** and the **diaphragm**
- the properties of the **pleural membranes** that surround the lungs.

The pleural membranes 'stick' the outside of the lungs to the inside of the chest cavity. The lungs themselves do not have any muscles, but the 'stickiness' of the pleural membranes means that the lungs will automatically follow the movements of the chest wall. If the volume of the chest cavity increases, the volume of the lungs will increase at the same time. The pressure inside the lungs will decrease as the volume gets bigger.

Air always moves down a pressure gradient, from a region of higher air pressure to a region of lower air pressure. If the air pressure in the lungs is less than the pressure of the atmosphere, air will move into the lungs along a pressure gradient. In the same way, if the air pressure in the lungs is greater than the pressure of the atmosphere, air will move out of the lungs along a pressure gradient.

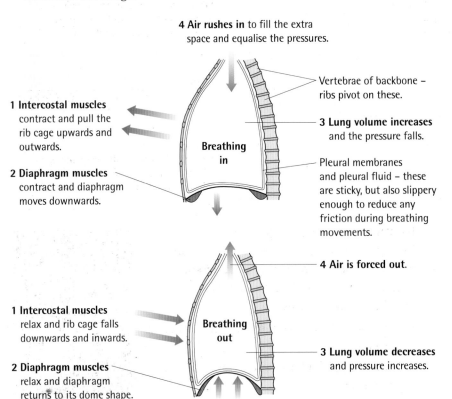

4 Air rushes in to fill the extra space and equalise the pressures.

Vertebrae of backbone – ribs pivot on these.

1 Intercostal muscles contract and pull the rib cage upwards and outwards.

Breathing in

3 Lung volume increases and the pressure falls.

2 Diaphragm muscles contract and diaphragm moves downwards.

Pleural membranes and pleural fluid – these are sticky, but also slippery enough to reduce any friction during breathing movements.

4 Air is forced out.

1 Intercostal muscles relax and rib cage falls downwards and inwards.

Breathing out

2 Diaphragm muscles relax and diaphragm returns to its dome shape.

3 Lung volume decreases and pressure increases.

Summary:
Extra lung volume created by
- rib cage moving up and out
- diaphragm moving down

↓

Pressure falls

↓

Air rushes into lungs

There are **two** sets of intercostal muscles. The **external** intercostal muscles contract during breathing in. The **internal** intercostal muscles are used during coughing and sneezing, for example.

The intercostal muscles ('intercostal' means 'between the ribs') and the diaphragm work together to alter the volume of the chest cavity. Changing the volume of the chest cavity will automatically change the pressure of air inside it. (It is a law of physics that pressure × volume is a constant – in other words, if pressure increases then volume must decrease, and vice versa.)

Gas exchange

Air is breathed in, gas exchange happens in the alveoli, and the air is breathed out again. The composition of the inspired (breathed-in) air is therefore different from the composition of the expired (breathed-out) air, as shown in the table.

Component of air	Inspired (inhaled) air (%)	Expired (exhaled) air (%)	Reason
Oxygen	21	18	Oxygen has diffused from the air in the alveoli into the blood.
Carbon dioxide	0.04	3	Carbon dioxide has diffused from the blood into the air in the alveoli.
Nitrogen	78	78	Nitrogen gas is not used by the body.
Water vapour	Very variable	Saturated	Water evaporates from surfaces in the alveoli.
Temperature	Very variable	37 °C	Heat is lost to the air from the lung surfaces.

Composition of inhaled and exhaled air.

Measuring the efficiency of the lungs

The amount of air that enters and leaves the lungs is measured using a **spirometer**. A person breathes in and out of a mouthpiece connected to a chamber. Inside the chamber a piston moves up and down, and its movements are measured electronically. The changes in volume during breathing are plotted on a graph called a **spirogram**, shown below.

A spirogram gives a great deal of information about someone's breathing and the efficiency of their lungs. The lung volumes are expressed in the SI unit dm^3. 1 dm^3 is the same as 1 litre.

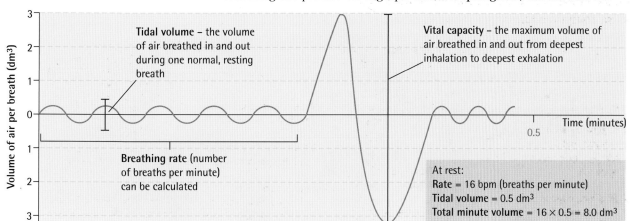

Tidal volume – the volume of air breathed in and out during one normal, resting breath

Vital capacity – the maximum volume of air breathed in and out from deepest inhalation to deepest exhalation

Volume of air per breath (dm^3)

Time (minutes)

Breathing rate (number of breaths per minute) can be calculated

At rest:
Rate = 16 bpm (breaths per minute)
Tidal volume = 0.5 dm^3
Total minute volume = 16 × 0.5 = 8.0 dm^3

Exercise and breathing

During exercise the muscles work hard, and need to release more energy by respiration. Greater volumes of air must therefore be breathed in and out, by:

■ increasing the **breathing rate** – more breaths per minute

■ increasing the **tidal volume** – more air per breath.

These two changes can increase the volume of air passing in and out of the lungs from the typical 8 dm^3 per minute at rest to 50–60 dm^3 per minute during strenuous exercise.

1 Explain the part played by the intercostal muscles and diaphragm in breathing.

2 What can be learned from a spirogram?

3 Why are there differences in the oxygen and carbon dioxide compositions of inhaled air and exhaled air?

The effect of exercise on breathing can be measured by this apparatus.

4·3 Smoking and disease

Objectives
▪ To understand that smoking tobacco is harmful to health
▪ To list some of the harmful components of tobacco smoke and the damage they cause
▪ To understand why it is so difficult to give up smoking

The risks of smoking

Many national advertising campaigns stress that smoking is harmful. At the same time, the manufacturers of cigarettes emphasise the 'glamorous' side of smoking. However, manufacturers have to include, by law, a statement on their advertisements and cigarette packets that 'smoking can seriously damage your health'.

Life insurance companies routinely ask 'Do you smoke?' because they are aware that smokers are more likely to die younger. Whether or not to take up smoking is the most important health decision that many of us will ever make. For this reason everyone should know about the possible effects of smoking. Nobody who starts smoking now can say 'But I didn't know the risks' when they suffer the effects of their smoking habit later in life.

How is smoking harmful?

Smoking is inhaling the smoke from burning tobacco (and paper). This smoke can harm the lungs and respiratory passages for a number of reasons:

▪ it is hot
▪ it has a drying effect
▪ it contains many harmful chemicals.

The heat and dryness irritate the lungs, but the main dangers of smoking come from the chemicals in the burning tobacco. There are over 1000 known chemicals in tobacco smoke. These include tars, carbon monoxide, sulphur dioxide, nicotine and even small quantities of arsenic and plutonium! When doctors treat lung diseases with medicine, the molecules of the medicine are delivered in a spray; the droplets of water in the spray carry the medicine down through the respiratory tubes and deep into the lungs. Burning tobacco produces tiny

droplets of water too, and these carry the harmful chemicals deep into the lungs in just the same way as a medicine spray. It would be hard to find a more efficient way of delivering harmful chemicals to the lungs than smoking! Some of these dangerous chemicals, and the effects they have on the body, are shown on the opposite page.

Why is it so difficult to give up smoking?

In many ways nicotine is the most dangerous of the chemicals in tobacco smoke. As well as affecting the heart and blood pressure directly, nicotine makes a person become **addicted** to smoking. Addiction comes in two forms:

▪ in **physical addiction**, the body cannot function properly in the absence of the chemical because it has partly replaced a natural body chemical

▪ in **psychological addiction**, the addicted person links smoking with comfort or lack of stress – when they feel stressed they may automatically reach for a cigarette.

1 How is smoke harmful to the lungs?

2 What is the difference between physical and psychological addiction? How can smokers be helped to overcome their addiction?

3 Suggest three harmful effects of smoking other than damage to the lungs and breathing passages.

4 Why are smokers more likely to develop infections of the lungs than non-smokers?

5 Draw a single cube with a side of 10 cm, and then the same cube divided into smaller cubes each with a side of 1 cm.
  a How many small cubes fit into the large cube?
  b What is the surface area of each small cube?
  c What is the total surface area of all of the small cubes?
  d What is the surface area of the large cube?
  e Use your answers to explain why emphysema sufferers are often very breathless.

Gas exchange

Free radicals are extremely dangerous chemicals that damage proteins and DNA. They cause ageing of cells (smokers are often 'wrinkled', inside and out!) but smokers can reduce their effects with high doses of vitamin C.

Nicotine is the chemical that causes **addiction**. It is also a **stimulant** which makes the heart beat faster and at the same time makes blood vessels narrow. Together these two effects **raise blood pressure** (causing long-term damage to the circulation). The increased heart rate increases the demand for oxygen, but carbon monoxide (see below) reduces oxygen availability – so heart muscle is more likely to be damaged.

Cancer of the mouth and larynx is 5 times more likely in smokers than non-smokers. Cancer of the tongue and oesophagus is particularly common in smokers who drink alcohol. **Laryngitis** (infection of the larynx) is more common in smokers than non-smokers. Laryngitis causes a husky voice, and makes speaking difficult and painful.

Cilia are destroyed which means that mucus accumulates in the respiratory tubes. Dust and microbes, trapped in the mucus, slide down towards the lungs making the person cough. This coughing inflames the lining of the bronchi, causing **bronchitis**. A smoker is 20 times more likely to develop bronchitis than a non-smoker is.

Mucus, microbes and cell fragments build up

Carbon monoxide reduces the oxygen supply

Oxygen combines with haemoglobin to form **oxyhaemoglobin** in red blood cells. Carbon monoxide (CO) reduces oxyhaemoglobin formation because it binds very tightly to haemoglobin, and the effect is permanent since **carboxyhaemoglobin is very stable**. This:

■ reduces aerobic respiration (bad for sport)
■ reduces oxygen transport across the placenta (babies born to smokers have low birth-weight).

Carbon monoxide poisoning is especially likely when car engines are allowed to run in enclosed spaces (such as garages) and when the atmosphere is of poor quality (e.g. in smog).

Lung cancer is 10 times more likely in a smoker than a non-smoker. The tumour (see page 196) invades other tissues. This causes pain and loss of function of other tissues, often resulting in death.

The lung of a smoker destroyed by cancer (left), and a normal lung (right)

Tar causes cancer, which is uncontrolled division of cells. These cells, usually those lining the lower part of the bronchus, grow through the basement membrane and invade other tissues.

Tar is also an **irritant** which makes coughing more likely. This causes physical damage to the lungs, and makes the effects of emphysema even worse. Other irritants in tobacco smoke include **smoke particles**, **ammonia** and **sulphur dioxide**.

Smoking causes other diseases including:
■ cancer of stomach, pancreas and bladder
■ loss of limbs – amputated because of poor circulation
■ coronary heart disease
■ lower sperm counts in men.

Emphysema results when the walls of the air sacs are destroyed. This happens because smoke affects white blood cells which then destroy lung tissue. When the walls break down there is less surface for gas exchange, and breathing becomes very difficult. Somebody with emphysema may only be able to walk 2 or 3 metres before becoming breathless. Emphysema is almost unknown in non-smokers.

Healthy alveoli

Alveoli in person with emphysema

Gas exchange

4·4 How do we know that smoking causes disease?

Sir Richard Doll's research into smoking

We know today that smoking causes disease, but how have we found this out? The diseases could result from living in a polluted environment, or exposure to chemicals at work, or diet, or any number of other factors.

Sir Richard Doll was an **epidemiologist** – he studied patterns in the distribution of diseases. He was particularly interested in comparing the habits and environment of people who developed lung disease with people who did not. His results were very valuable because he collected data in a scientific way, removing many variables from his studies. For example:

- he carried out many of his studies on doctors, so he could rule out profession as a cause of lung disease
- he separated data for people living in cities from those living in the countryside, so environment was not causing large differences between people in one study group.

Some examples of epidemiological studies that related lung disease and early death to smoking tobacco are shown on the opposite page. The box shows some data about smoking in Britain and other countries.

Sir Richard Doll carried out epidemiological research on lung diseases.

Some disturbing data

Fewer boys are taking up smoking in the UK than 20 years ago (good news) but more girls are now smoking (bad news). Can you suggest reasons for these changes?

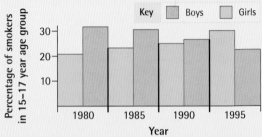

Cigarette sales in the UK have fallen because people are becoming more aware of the health risks of smoking. Advertising campaigns emphasise the dangers, and smoking is banned in many public places to reduce 'passive smoking' (breathing in someone else's cigarette smoke). Tobacco companies are focusing on selling to developing countries where people are less aware of the health risks. The rise in lung disease in Britain in the 1980s and 1990s will be repeated in 20 years' time in these countries.

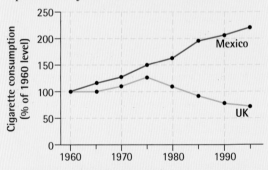

The number of cigarettes sold in the UK and in Mexico, 1960–1995.

The cigarette companies are now targeting countries such as Africa to increase their profits.

Evidence linking smoking with lung cancer

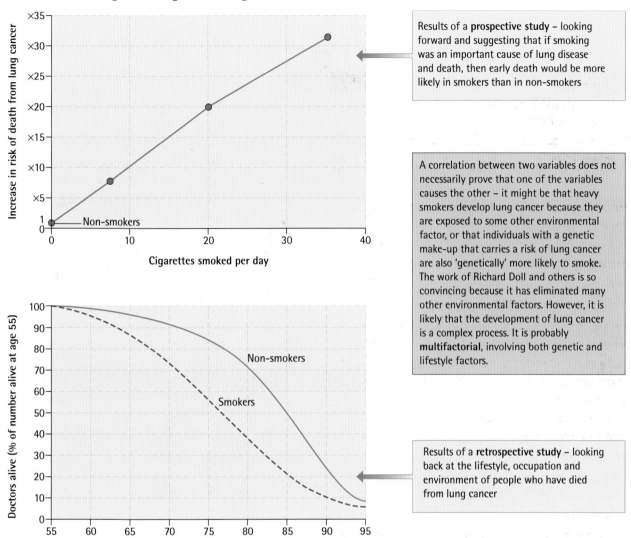

Results of a **prospective study** – looking forward and suggesting that if smoking was an important cause of lung disease and death, then early death would be more likely in smokers than in non-smokers

A correlation between two variables does not necessarily prove that one of the variables causes the other – it might be that heavy smokers develop lung cancer because they are exposed to some other environmental factor, or that individuals with a genetic make-up that carries a risk of lung cancer are also 'genetically' more likely to smoke. The work of Richard Doll and others is so convincing because it has eliminated many other environmental factors. However, it is likely that the development of lung cancer is a complex process. It is probably **multifactorial**, involving both genetic and lifestyle factors.

Results of a **retrospective study** – looking back at the lifestyle, occupation and environment of people who have died from lung cancer

In 1962 the Royal College of Physicians published a report on smoking and health, which suggested a clear link between cancer and smoking. For example, among a sample of doctors living in similar-sized cities, those who smoked regularly were more likely to develop cancer of the lung.

---

1 What is meant by the term epidemiology?

2 Suggest two factors other than cigarette smoking that might increase the risk of developing lung cancer.

3 How much more likely to die of lung cancer is a person who smokes 25 cigarettes a day than someone who does not smoke at all?

4 One epidemiological study has suggested that living close to power lines can cause leukaemia. How would you try to prove this link?
   ▪ Which populations would you study?
   ▪ How old would they be?
   ▪ Which sex?
   ▪ Which occupation?
   ▪ How about their diet?
   In what way do you think the results of your study might be useful?

5 In a typical laboratory experiment, data are collected by manipulating one variable and measuring the responding change in another, with all other identifiable variables kept constant (see page 16). Why can this approach not be used to investigate the effect of smoking on the development of lung disease in humans?

Gas exchange

83

4·5 Gas exchange in other animals

Objectives
- To realise that other organisms may not need such an efficient surface as a mammal does
- To recall the gas exchange systems in earthworms, insects and fish

This photograph shows the earthworm's shiny mucus-covered skin.

Cross-section of earthworm

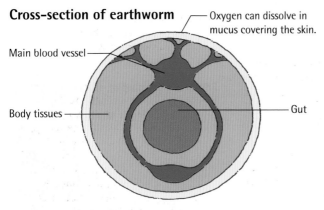

- Oxygen can dissolve in mucus covering the skin.
- Main blood vessel
- Body tissues
- Gut

Earthworms use their skin as a gas exchange surface. Earthworms are not very active and can gain enough oxygen in this way to drive the limited amount of respiration they carry out.

Cross-section of one segment, showing part of tracheal system

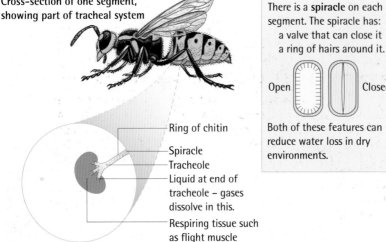

- Ring of chitin
- Spiracle
- Tracheole
- Liquid at end of tracheole – gases dissolve in this.
- Respiring tissue such as flight muscle

There is a **spiracle** on each segment. The spiracle has:
- a valve that can close it
- a ring of hairs around it.

Open   Closed

Both of these features can reduce water loss in dry environments.

Gas exchange in insects relies on tubes that go directly to the tissues.

Gas exchange is necessary to supply oxygen for the release of energy by respiration, and to remove the carbon dioxide formed. The more energy an organism uses, the more efficient its system of gas exchange needs to be. Mammals have a sophisticated gas exchange system. Simpler animals also respire and therefore need some form of gas exchange system.

Gas exchange in earthworms

The shape of an earthworm, like a long thin cylinder, means that it has quite a high surface area to volume ratio. Gas exchange can happen fast enough over the relatively large surface to supply respiration within the volume of the worm's body. The gas exchange system in earthworms simply uses the **skin**, which is kept moist with a layer of mucus. The earthworm is the simplest animal to have a transport system with closed blood vessels. It uses this system to transport gases between the skin and the respiring tissues, as outlined in the diagram opposite.

Gas exchange in insects

Insects are active animals, and so need a lot of oxygen. The system for gas exchange is different from that of any other group of animals. Insects have a system of tubes that lead directly from the outside atmosphere to the working tissues (see left). The tubes, called **tracheoles**, lead from holes called **spiracles** along the side of the insect's body and are kept open by stiff rings of a material called **chitin**.

Gases are not transported by blood – oxygen and carbon dioxide gases diffuse along the tubes. Diffusion is slow, so the tracheoles must be short. This is why insects are quite small. Larger insects can move the abdomen up and down to pump air in and out, but the 'monsters' shown in some science fiction films could not supply themselves with oxygen! The insect gas exchange system is shown on the left.

Gas exchange in fish

Fish obtain their oxygen from water, which has a lower concentration of oxygen than the air. Fish have an efficient gas exchange system with the following features:

- The gas exchange surface is the **gills** – there are four gills on each side of the head.
- The gills are held in chambers on each side of the head. They are very delicate structures and are covered by a muscular flap called the **operculum**.
- Water is forced back over the gills, and then out behind the operculum. This one-way flow of water is extremely effective for gas exchange.
- A set of blood vessels, with capillaries into the gills, transports oxygen and carbon dioxide.

The gas exchange system in a fish is outlined in the diagram below.

The table below compares the gas exchange systems in earthworms, insects, fish and mammals.

Organism	Name of gas exchange surface	Is there any ventilation?	Is blood involved?
Earthworm	Skin	No	Yes
Insect	Tracheoles	Very little	No
Fish	Gills	Yes	Yes
Mammal	Lungs	Yes	Yes

The gills of a fish are efficient at extracting oxygen from water.

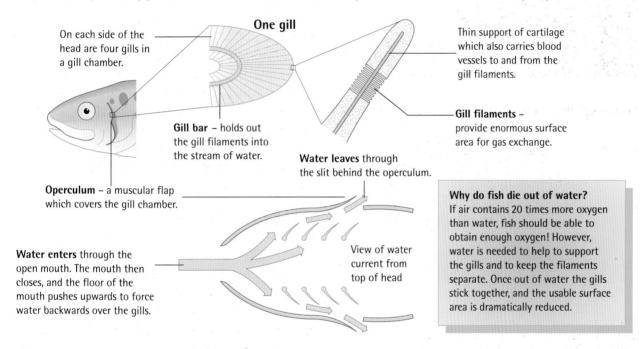

One gill

On each side of the head are four gills in a gill chamber.

Thin support of cartilage which also carries blood vessels to and from the gill filaments.

Gill bar – holds out the gill filaments into the stream of water.

Gill filaments – provide enormous surface area for gas exchange.

Water leaves through the slit behind the operculum.

Operculum – a muscular flap which covers the gill chamber.

Water enters through the open mouth. The mouth then closes, and the floor of the mouth pushes upwards to force water backwards over the gills.

View of water current from top of head

Why do fish die out of water?
If air contains 20 times more oxygen than water, fish should be able to obtain enough oxygen! However, water is needed to help to support the gills and to keep the filaments separate. Once out of water the gills stick together, and the usable surface area is dramatically reduced.

---

1 Copy and complete the following paragraph.
All living organisms require _____ which is released from the process of _____. The most efficient form of this process requires the gas _____ and produces the waste gas _____. To keep this energy-releasing process going the organism must have a gas exchange surface – this surface has certain properties. These are a large _____, a _____ membrane so that diffusion distances are short and a _____ layer (since cells die if they dry out). In addition the most advanced systems have a means of _____ to move the gases over the surface, and are close to a _____ supply to transport gases between the surface and the living tissues.

2 Explain the following features of the insect gas exchange system:
a there are hairs and valves at the spiracles
b insects have no red blood cells in their blood.

3 Water contains only about one-twentieth of the oxygen concentration found in air. How do fish remove enough oxygen from the water in which they live?

4·6 Questions on gas exchange

1 Two boys were asked to take part in an investigation into the effect of exercise on breathing. The number of breaths they took in each half minute was measured and recorded, first of all while sitting still, then when recovering from two minutes of hard exercise. The results are shown in the table below.

Time (minutes)	Activity	Number of breaths in each half minute	
		Tom	Alan
0.0		7	8
0.5		7	8
1.0	Sitting still	7	8
1.5		7	8
2.0			
2.5			
3.0	Exercise (step-ups)		
3.5			
4.0		24	24
4.5		23	17
5.0		18	13
5.5		15	10
6.0	Recovery (sitting)	12	10
6.5		12	9
7.0		10	8
7.5		8	8
8.0		8	8
8.5		7	8

a Draw a graph to show the changes in breathing rate over the time period of this investigation. Plot both lines on the same axes.

b Which boy appears to be fitter? Explain your answer.

The teacher of the class was interested in the changes in breathing during the exercise period. She used a sensor, computer interface, monitor and printer to obtain the following information on another member of the class.

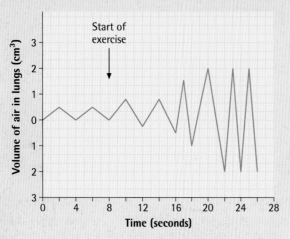

c What is the ratio of the volume of a breath during exercise to the volume of a breath at rest?

d Calculate the rate of breathing, in breaths per minute, during strenuous exercise.

e Using the data gathered, describe two effects of exercise on breathing.

f The computer could also measure the effects of exercise on heart rate. Suggest what these effects might be.

g What is the benefit to the body of the effects described in **e** and **f**?

2 These diagrams show apparatus that can be used to explain the mechanism of breathing.

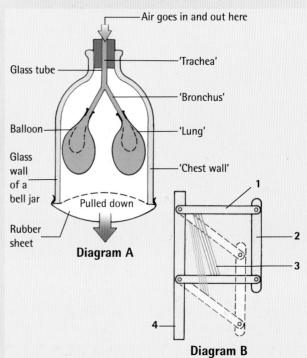

Diagram A

Diagram B

Look at diagram **A**.

a What does the rubber sheet represent?

b What will happen to the balloons when the rubber sheet is pulled downwards?

c What phase of the breathing cycle is represented when the rubber sheet is allowed to return to its resting position?

d In what way is this model an incomplete demonstration of the mechanism of breathing?

Look at diagram **B**.

e What parts of the human ventilation system do the labels **1–4** represent?

f Use the information in your answers to **a–e** to comment on the statement: 'Breathing in is an active process, but breathing out is completely passive.'

3 Copy the following paragraph and complete it by filling in the missing words.

Deoxygenated blood arrives at the lungs in the _____ artery. Oxygen has been removed from the blood by cells that are _____ to release _____ needed to carry out their functions. This blood also contains a relatively high concentration of the gas _____, which is carried dissolved in the plasma as _____ ions. Each artery branches many times to form _____, which are well adapted to allow the exchange of gases because they are _____-walled and have a very large _____. These small vessels lie very close to the _____ of the lungs, and it is here that gas exchange takes place. The gas _____ moves out of the blood and the gas _____ moves into the blood. Both gases move by the process of _____. Oxygenated blood then leaves the lungs in the _____ vein that returns blood to the heart at the chamber called the _____.

4 This table shows the causes of death of cigarette smokers in Great Britain.

Cause of death	Percentage of deaths
Lung cancer	8
Bronchitis and emphysema	17
Circulatory diseases	20
Other causes (not related to smoking)	55

a What percentage of smokers dies from smoking-related diseases?

b Present the data in the form of a bar chart *or* a pie chart. Which will display the information in the best way? Explain your choice.

c Emphysema is a disease caused by smoking. The photographs below show normal lung tissue and lung tissue from a person with emphysema.

   i Describe two differences between the normal lung tissue and the lung tissue from a person with emphysema.

   ii How will these differences affect the supply of oxygen to the blood in the person with emphysema?

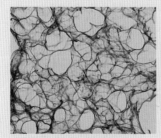
Lung tissue from a person with emphysema (×40).

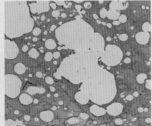
Normal lung tissue (×40).

5 Two students wished to investigate how insects breathe. They counted the breathing movements of locusts in different situations, using the apparatus shown below.

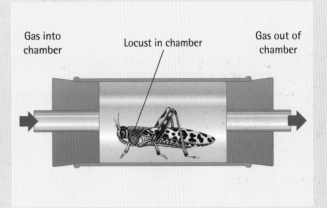

Gas into chamber   Locust in chamber   Gas out of chamber

They obtained the results shown in the table.

Condition around locust	Number of breathing movements per minute/ mean of five observations
Normal air	16
Dry air	3
Air exhaled by student	37

a Plot a bar chart of these results.

b Why did the students repeat their observations to get five results?

c The teacher wanted to know if they had kept other variables fixed. Which factors should they have kept as fixed variables?

d Explain the results they obtained.

5·1 Coordination: the nervous system

Working together

There are millions of cells and scores of different tissues and organs in the body of an animal such as a mammal. The cells and organs do not all work independently – their activities are **coordinated**, which means that they work together, carrying out their various functions at certain times and at certain rates, according to the needs of the body.

Coordination in mammals is achieved through two systems, each with its own particular role. The **nervous system** deals with rapid but short-lasting responses, whereas the **endocrine system** brings about slower, longer lasting responses. The two systems are compared in the table below.

The nervous system

In mammals and other vertebrates, the nervous system is arranged as shown in the diagram on the left. It consists of a **brain** and **spinal cord**, which together form the **central nervous system (CNS)**, connected to the various parts of the body by the **peripheral nervous system**. This is made up of **nerves**, collections of many long thin nerve cells called **neurones**.

Information flows along the nervous system as follows. A **receptor** detects a change in conditions (a **stimulus**). A message is carried from the receptor to the CNS by a **sensory neurone**. After processing, a message is sent from the CNS to an organ (an **effector**) that carries out a **response**. A **motor neurone** carries this message.

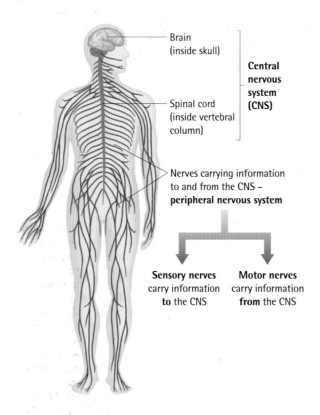

Brain
(inside skull)

Central nervous system (CNS)

Spinal cord
(inside vertebral column)

Nerves carrying information to and from the CNS – **peripheral nervous system**

Sensory nerves carry information **to** the CNS

Motor nerves carry information **from** the CNS

The arrangement of the human nervous system.

The endocrine and nervous systems compared.

Comparison	Nervous system	Endocrine system
Speed of action	Very rapid	Can be slow
Nature of message	Electrical impulses, travelling along nerves	Chemical messengers, travelling in the bloodstream
Duration of response	Usually completed within seconds	May take years before completed
Area of response	Often confined to one area of the body – the response is **localised**	Usually noticed in many organs – the response is **widespread**
Examples of processes controlled	Reflexes such as blinking; movement of limbs	Growth; development of reproductive system

Nerves and neurones

All the information carried by the nervous system travels along specialised cells called neurones (sometimes just called nerve cells). The structure of a single neurone, and the ways in which it is adapted to its function of carrying information, are shown on the right.

Nerve impulses

Messages pass along neurones in the form of **electrical impulses**, which travel very quickly from one end of a nerve cell to the other. In a living mammal the impulses always travel along a neurone in a certain direction. They are then passed on to another neurone, to a muscle cell or to a gland cell. The end of the neurone is separated from the next cell by a tiny gap, visible under a microscope, and the impulses can only cross this gap in one direction. This gap, called a **synapse**, acts like a valve as explained in the diagram below.

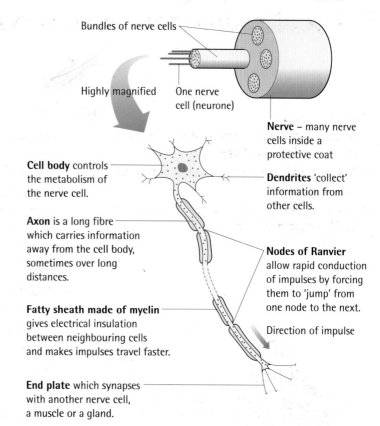

Bundles of nerve cells

Highly magnified   One nerve cell (neurone)

Nerve – many nerve cells inside a protective coat

Cell body controls the metabolism of the nerve cell.

Dendrites 'collect' information from other cells.

Axon is a long fibre which carries information away from the cell body, sometimes over long distances.

Nodes of Ranvier allow rapid conduction of impulses by forcing them to 'jump' from one node to the next.

Fatty sheath made of myelin gives electrical insulation between neighbouring cells and makes impulses travel faster.

Direction of impulse

End plate which synapses with another nerve cell, a muscle or a gland.

A nerve is made of many neurones. This **motor neurone** carries information from the CNS to an effector.

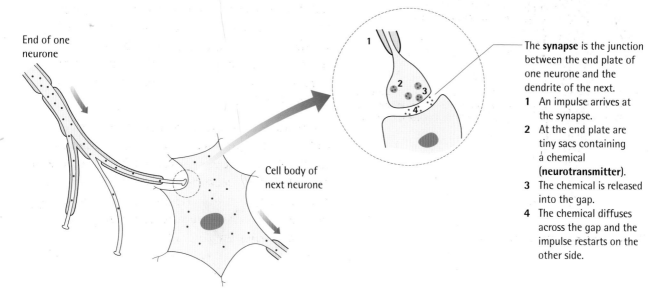

End of one neurone

Cell body of next neurone

The **synapse** is the junction between the end plate of one neurone and the dendrite of the next.

1 An impulse arrives at the synapse.
2 At the end plate are tiny sacs containing a chemical (**neurotransmitter**).
3 The chemical is released into the gap.
4 The chemical diffuses across the gap and the impulse restarts on the other side.

Impulses travel along a neurone in the direction that allows the mammal to respond to changes in its environment. They can only pass across the synapse in this direction.

1 Suggest two similarities and two differences between the endocrine system and the nervous system. What is the importance of these differences?

2 Explain how the structure of a neurone is related to its function.

3 Explain the difference between:
   a motor and sensory neurones
   b central and peripheral nervous systems.

4 How does a nerve impulse:
   a pass along a neurone   b cross a synapse?

5·2 Neurones can work together in reflex arcs

Objectives
- To understand that neurones work together in a reflex arc
- To understand that all reflex arcs are important for survival

Neurones act together in many complex ways to bring about the correct response to a stimulus. The simplest type of response is called a **reflex action**. A reflex action is a rapid automatic response to a stimulus, for example jerking your hand away from a sharp or hot object. The nerve pathway involved in the reflex action is called a **reflex arc**, shown in the diagram on the opposite page.

Reflexes and survival

All reflex actions have evolved to help us survive. The table below lists four reflexes, and shows how each helps us survive.

The size of the pupil can change quickly and automatically in response to changes in the intensity of light. This reflex action, described in more detail on page 103, prevents damage to the retina.

Name of reflex	Stimulus	Response	Survival value
Coughing	Particles making contact with the lining of the respiratory tree	Violent contraction of the diaphragm and internal intercostal muscles	Prevents lungs being damaged or infected, so that gas exchange remains efficient
Pupil reflex	Bright light falling on the retina	Contraction of the circular muscles of the iris	Prevents bleaching of the retina so that vision remains clear
Knee jerk	Stretching of the tendon just under the knee, holding the kneecap in place (a doctor may tap this tendon to test the reflex)	Contraction of the muscles of the upper thigh so that the leg straightens	The leg can support the body's weight during walking
Swallowing	Food particles making contact with the back of the throat	Contraction of the muscle of the epiglottis, which closes off the entrance to the trachea	Prevents food entering the respiratory pathway, so that the lungs are not damaged

1 The diagram opposite shows the route taken by nerve impulses to bring about the knee-jerk reflex.
a Name the structure tapped by the hammer. How does this set off the reflex action?
b Name the structure that carries impulses towards the spinal cord.
c Which structure A–E is responsible for the response in this reflex action?
d The distance between structure B and the spinal cord is about 30 cm. Assuming that the impulses travel at 100 m/s, how long should it take for an impulse to travel through this reflex arc?
e Careful measurement suggests that the actual time taken for the impulse to travel through this arc is 2 or 3 times this value. Can you explain why?

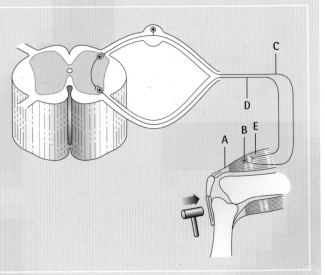

The **reflex arc** is the basic working unit of the nervous system. It links **receptors** to **effectors** via the **integrators** of the central nervous system. Note that the sequence is always the same:

Receptor → sensory neurone → central nervous system → motor neurone → effector

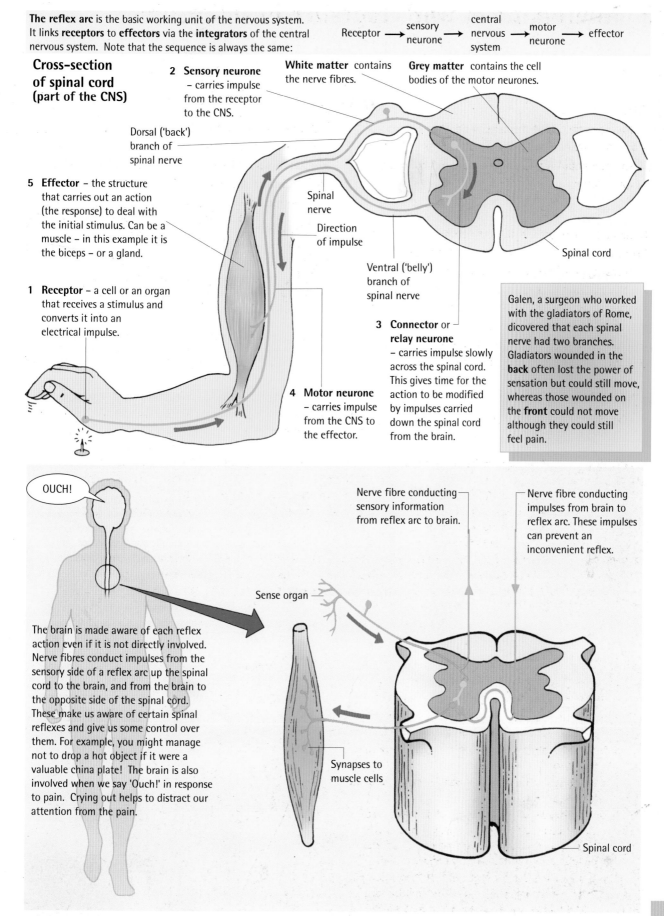

Cross-section of spinal cord (part of the CNS)

White matter contains the nerve fibres.

Grey matter contains the cell bodies of the motor neurones.

2 Sensory neurone – carries impulse from the receptor to the CNS.

Dorsal ('back') branch of spinal nerve

Spinal nerve

Direction of impulse

Ventral ('belly') branch of spinal nerve

Spinal cord

5 Effector – the structure that carries out an action (the response) to deal with the initial stimulus. Can be a muscle – in this example it is the biceps – or a gland.

1 Receptor – a cell or an organ that receives a stimulus and converts it into an electrical impulse.

3 Connector or **relay neurone** – carries impulse slowly across the spinal cord. This gives time for the action to be modified by impulses carried down the spinal cord from the brain.

4 Motor neurone – carries impulse from the CNS to the effector.

Galen, a surgeon who worked with the gladiators of Rome, dicovered that each spinal nerve had two branches. Gladiators wounded in the **back** often lost the power of sensation but could still move, whereas those wounded on the **front** could not move although they could still feel pain.

OUCH!

The brain is made aware of each reflex action even if it is not directly involved. Nerve fibres conduct impulses from the sensory side of a reflex arc up the spinal cord to the brain, and from the brain to the opposite side of the spinal cord. These make us aware of certain spinal reflexes and give us some control over them. For example, you might manage not to drop a hot object if it were a valuable china plate! The brain is also involved when we say 'Ouch!' in response to pain. Crying out helps to distract our attention from the pain.

Nerve fibre conducting sensory information from reflex arc to brain.

Nerve fibre conducting impulses from brain to reflex arc. These impulses can prevent an inconvenient reflex.

Sense organ

Synapses to muscle cells

Spinal cord

Even a simple reflex such as withdrawing the hand from a sharp object involves many neurones, and this diagram is very much over-simplified.

5·3 Integration by the central nervous system

Objectives
- To understand that the central nervous system integrates and coordinates the responses of the body

The central nervous system (CNS) processes information from receptors and passes instructions to effectors to tell the organism how to respond. This complex series of operations, referred to as **integration**, is outlined below.

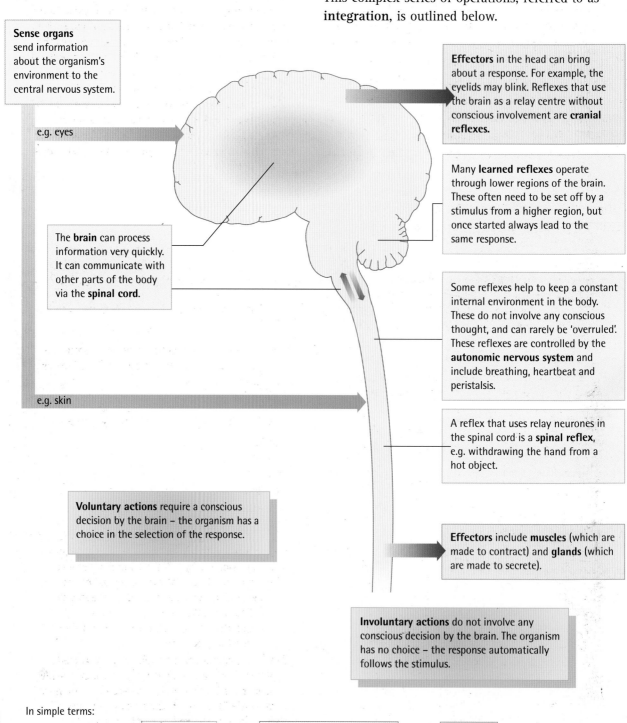

Sense organs send information about the organism's environment to the central nervous system.

e.g. eyes

The **brain** can process information very quickly. It can communicate with other parts of the body via the **spinal cord**.

e.g. skin

Effectors in the head can bring about a response. For example, the eyelids may blink. Reflexes that use the brain as a relay centre without conscious involvement are **cranial reflexes.**

Many **learned reflexes** operate through lower regions of the brain. These often need to be set off by a stimulus from a higher region, but once started always lead to the same response.

Some reflexes help to keep a constant internal environment in the body. These do not involve any conscious thought, and can rarely be 'overruled'. These reflexes are controlled by the **autonomic nervous system** and include breathing, heartbeat and peristalsis.

A reflex that uses relay neurones in the spinal cord is a **spinal reflex**, e.g. withdrawing the hand from a hot object.

Voluntary actions require a conscious decision by the brain – the organism has a choice in the selection of the response.

Effectors include **muscles** (which are made to contract) and **glands** (which are made to secrete).

Involuntary actions do not involve any conscious decision by the brain. The organism has no choice – the response automatically follows the stimulus.

In simple terms:

Stimulus ⟶ **Sense organ** ⟶ **Central nervous system** ⟶ **Effector** ⟶ **Response**

Coordination and response

Involuntary actions

Reflexes concerned with the 'housekeeping' tasks of the body, such as breathing, do not reach the conscious level of the brain. They are dealt with by the **autonomic** branch of the nervous system.

Responses may be more complex than a simple reflex arc. For example, the CNS may store information as **memory** and then compare an incoming stimulus with a previous one. It chooses the correct response for this particular situation, and sends information out to the effectors to bring about the appropriate action. Each time a particular stimulus leads to a certain response, the impulse passes along the same route, so that reflex actions become **learned reflexes**. Talking and cycling are examples of learned reflexes. Whether or not a reflex has been learned, it is an **involuntary action** – a particular stimulus always leads to the same response.

Voluntary actions

During evolution, the front of the spinal cord became highly developed to form the brain. The advanced development of the brain, particularly those parts that deal with learning, sets mammals (and especially humans) apart from 'lower' animals. The brain is involved in **voluntary actions**, in which a conscious choice is made about the response to a particular stimulus.

Conditioned reflexes

Conditioned reflexes are learned reflexes in which the final response has no natural relationship to the stimulus. In an experiment, a Russian scientist, Ivan Pavlov, rang a bell when he fed dogs. The dogs then salivated in response to the bell, even when no food was given. The natural stimulus the food had been replaced by an unnatural one, (the sound of the bell). Conditioned reflexes can be 'unlearned' if the unnatural stimulus is not repeated with the natural one – if the food was produced without the bell over a period of time, the dogs would no longer salivate at the sound of the bell.

---

1 Reaction times for a class were measured using a computer to calculate the time taken for each student to press the space bar after seeing a light. The table opposite shows the results for student 1.

a Calculate the mean reaction time of this student. Why is the mean value useful?

The mean class results are shown in the table below. (You have just calculated the result for student 1.)

Attempt	1	2	3	4	5	6	7	8	9	10
Reaction time (ms)	330	340	290	320	320	280	270	290	400	260

b Place the students' reaction times into groups by copying and completing the table below. Draw a bar chart of the results.

Reaction time (ms)	Number of students in group
110–150	
160–200	
210–250	
260–300	
310–350	

Student number	Reaction time (ms)	Student number	Reaction time (ms)
1		16	150
2	220	17	300
3	130	18	140
4	220	19	230
5	210	20	150
6	250	21	190
7	190	22	180
8	200	23	240
9	220	24	120
10	240	25	170
11	140	26	160
12	280	27	190
13	210	28	210
14	330	29	270
15	270	30	200

c The teacher suggested that this reaction time could affect driving ability – a motorcycle travelling at 55 km/h would cover about 15 m in a second. How far would the motorcycle travel before:
  i the student with the shortest reaction time pulled the brake lever
  ii the student with the longest reaction time pulled the brake lever?

d In a further experiment a loud noise was made at the same time as the light was shown. Eventually the student began to respond when just the noise was made. How does this result explain the meaning of the term 'conditioned reflex'?

The brain is the processor for the central nervous system

The central nervous system (brain and spinal cord) integrates the working of receptors and effectors to bring about appropriate responses. The brain controls all our voluntary actions and many of our involuntary actions. It is also the seat of awareness, knowledge, emotion and learning.

The structure of the brain

The **brain** develops as a swelling at the anterior (front) end of the spinal cord. In humans it weighs about 1.4 kg and is the most complex organ known. The brain is largely composed of neurones, typically containing about 25 000 000 000 cells, each connected to as many as 1000 others, forming a total of up to 10^{14} synapses. As well as these neurones, the brain contains many other cells with supporting roles – some form a barrier to prevent infection, others secrete cushioning fluids – and a well developed blood supply delivers the vital supplies of oxygen and glucose.

Grey matter

The brain gives instructions for responses by the body, some simple involuntary actions, others resulting from intelligent decisions. The brain delays the flow of information around the nervous system slightly. This is because the neurones of which it is made are not fast-conducting neurones covered by a myelin sheath. The absence of the fatty myelin sheath around the nerve fibres in the brain gives brain tissue a grey appearance, hence the name 'grey matter'.

Organisation of the brain

The brain is a highly organised structure, and contains three types of 'centre':

- **sensory centres** receive incoming messages from the sense organs
- **motor centres** carry instructions from the brain to the effectors, such as muscles and glands
- **association centres** interpret the information delivered to the sensory centres and make sure that appropriate instructions are given via the motor centres.

Magnetic resonance imaging

Magnetic resonance imaging (MRI) is a technique used by doctors for scanning the body, including the brain. This technique can be used to locate areas of brain damage, disease or unusual brain activity. The results can be used in research, for example to relate a loss of body function to an area of brain damage, and in medicine, for example to examine the effects on the brain of a particular treatment.

MRI is much less damaging to patients than the techniques that were available previously. Brain surgery is extremely complex, and may cause more damage than benefit as there are areas of the brain with unknown function. X-rays cannot be used to study the brain as the soft tissues in the brain do not show up without injection of dense materials. MRI works by measuring changes in positions of molecules in the body after being exposed to a strong magnetic field.

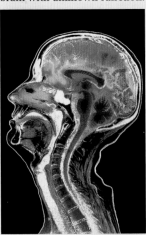

This MRI scan shows **atrophy** (shrinkage and wastage away) of the brain in the dark red area at the top.

Some association centres are little more than a collection of relay neurones involved in **cranial reflexes** such as blinking (see page 92) – the brain is acting like an extension of the spinal cord. Other association centres are more complex, involving the **learning centres** which can compare incoming information with previous experience.

Mapping the brain – assigning a function to an area of the brain

The different functions of the brain have been studied extensively, making it possible to produce maps such as the one below showing the positions of sensory, association and motor regions. These maps are updated as advances in medical technology make it possible to study the brain without damaging it, using **non-invasive techniques**.

1 Name the parts of the brain responsible for:
   a control of breathing and heartbeat
   b aggressive behaviour
   c learning a foreign language.
2 How is the brain protected?
3 How does information reach the brain, and how is it carried away to other parts of the body?
4 a Magnetic resonance imaging (MRI) is a non-invasive technique. What does this mean?
   b What information can now be obtained using techniques such as MRI which could not be obtained before this technology was available?

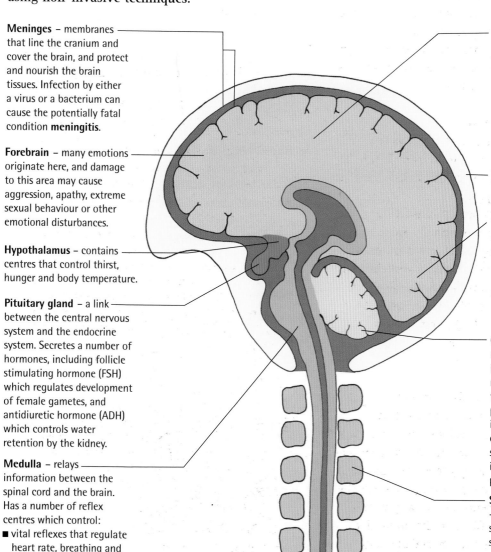

Meninges – membranes that line the cranium and cover the brain, and protect and nourish the brain tissues. Infection by either a virus or a bacterium can cause the potentially fatal condition **meningitis**.

Forebrain – many emotions originate here, and damage to this area may cause aggression, apathy, extreme sexual behaviour or other emotional disturbances.

Hypothalamus – contains centres that control thirst, hunger and body temperature.

Pituitary gland – a link between the central nervous system and the endocrine system. Secretes a number of hormones, including follicle stimulating hormone (FSH) which regulates development of female gametes, and antidiuretic hormone (ADH) which controls water retention by the kidney.

Medulla – relays information between the spinal cord and the brain. Has a number of reflex centres which control:
■ vital reflexes that regulate heart rate, breathing and blood vessel diameter
■ non-vital reflexes that coordinate swallowing, salivation, coughing and sneezing.

Cerebral cortex has motor areas to control voluntary movement, sensory areas which interpret sensations and association areas to link the activity of motor and sensory regions. The cortex is the centre of intelligence, memory, language and consciousness.

The **cranium** is the part of the skull that encloses and protects the brain.

Visual centre – this area of the cerebral cortex:
■ interprets impulses from the optic nerve (is responsible for vision)
■ has the connector neurones for both accommodation and the pupil reflex (see page 103).

Cerebellum – coordinates movement using sensory information from position receptors in various parts of the body. Helps to maintain posture using sensory information from the inner ear. Can control learned sequences of activity involved in dancing, sport and in playing musical instruments.

Spine (vertebral column) – composed of 33 separate small bones (**vertebrae**) which surround and protect the spinal cord. At each joint between the vertebrae, two **spinal nerves** carry sensory information into the spinal cord and motor information out of it.

5·5 Drugs and disorders of the nervous system

Objectives
- To know what is meant by a drug
- To be able to list the main types of drug
- To understand the effects of some drugs on the nervous system
- To appreciate that the nervous system may not always work perfectly

Types of drug

A **drug** is a chemical substance that can alter the way in which a part of the body works. A **medicine** is a chemical treatment for an illness or disorder. All medicines contain drugs, for example, aspirin tablets contain the drug acetylsalicylic acid, but not all drugs are medicines. Nicotine and alcohol are drugs, for instance, but are not usually thought of as medicines.

There are many drugs, affecting different parts of the body. Some drugs act directly on the nervous system. These are often grouped according to the effect they have, for example:

- **Stimulants** promote (speed up) the action of the nervous system. Stimulants usually make the drug user feel more confident and alert, and include **amphetamines**, **caffeine** and **nicotine**.

- **Depressants** inhibit (slow down) the action of some part of the nervous system. The user feels sleepy and less anxious, but may become dependent on the drug. Examples of depressants are **barbiturates**, **alcohol** and **cannabis**.

- **Narcotics** act like depressants but particularly target the brain. They work as pain-killers and may bring about a feeling of drowsy well-being or **euphoria**. Narcotics such as **heroin** are very likely to bring about drug dependence in the user.

- **Analgesics** are mild pain-killers. **Aspirin** and **paracetamol** are widely used analgesics.

- **Hallucinogens** alter the passage of impulses through the brain, causing unusual sensations. These drugs include **LSD** and some **solvents**.

Some of these drugs and the effects that they have are described on the opposite page.

Social drugs may be abused

A drug that is taken for non-medical reasons can be described as a **social** or **recreational drug**. Examples include legal drugs, such as nicotine in cigarette smoke, and alcohol, and illegal drugs, such as amphetamines and LSD. These drugs are taken for the pleasurable sensations that they give the user. Users may become **dependent** on the drugs because they are unwilling to give up these pleasurable sensations. This **psychological** or **emotional addiction** may then be followed by a **physical addiction**. A person becomes physically addicted to a drug when the drug is necessary for the normal working of the body. If the person cannot get the drug, then he or she will get **withdrawal symptoms**. Someone suffering withdrawal from heroin, for example, may vomit, tremble, sweat profusely and have severe abdominal pain after as little as four hours without the drug.

The dangers of abusing social drugs

Many casual users of social drugs soon become dependent upon them (physically and/or psychologically), so that the drug becomes a dominant feature of everyday life. The user will do almost anything to satisfy the desire for the effects of the drug, and this may lead to problems such as:

- malnourishment as the drug depresses the appetite
- financial problems – drugs can be expensive and users often resort to stealing
- infections from shared needles used to inject drugs, including HIV and hepatitis
- dangers from other substances mixed with the drugs.

The drug may also lead to dangerous behaviour such as poorly coordinated driving after drinking alcohol or erratic behaviour when using a hallucinogen.

Drugs may affect the central and peripheral nervous system

Alcohol affects emotional centres in the forebrain. It acts as a **depressant** and overrules normal social restraints. At low concentrations alcohol therefore 'lifts' social inhibitions.

Solvents may work by dissolving away part of the membrane surrounding sensory cells. As the cells 'burst' they send off pleasurable sensations to the brain, *but these sensory cells cannot be replaced.* **Aerosol**-based solvents can kill by the cooling effect they have on the respiratory system. This cooling constricts the breathing tubes and no air reaches the lungs.

At high concentrations, **alcohol** depresses the life-support centres in the medulla. Breathing may stop, causing brain damage or even death.

Nicotine is a **stimulant** which mimics the natural neurotransmitters in the part of the nervous system concerned with control of heartbeat and blood pressure.

Aspirin does not affect the nervous system directly but inhibits an enzyme involved in the response that leads to inflammation.

The brain is affected by several groups of drugs:
- **Narcotics** such as heroin mimic the action of the body's natural pain-killers. This gives a pleasurable sense of well-being (a 'high').
- **Hallucinogens** upset the normal memory pathways in the association areas so that a normal stimulus may 'connect to' an unusual response and the user may experience **hallucinations** (vivid waking dreams).
- **Alcohol** can upset normal sleep patterns by reducing the levels of a 'calming agent' in the brain.

Alcohol slows down impulses in peripheral nerves, causing slower reactions. It also affects nerves that control blood flow to the skin, causing flushing of the skin.

Many drugs have their effects at synapses
Synapses transfer nerve impulses as chemicals called **neurotransmitters** (see page 89). Stimulants such as **caffeine** increase the concentration of these chemicals, while depressants such as **Valium** make it more difficult for these chemicals to cross the synaptic gap. Note: **Valium** may be prescribed as an antidepressant, but this refers to its effects on the individual rather than its chemical action

Ecstasy

- Ecstasy is known by many other names, including 'Disco burgers', 'Doves', 'Dennis the Menace' and 'Fantasy'.
- It provides a 'feeling of energy' which can enable people to dance for long periods. This causes **dehydration** – users need to drink a pint of non-alcoholic liquid each hour.
- Death or disability can result from high body temperatures, **but** rapid rehydration has also caused some deaths.
- Ecstasy is one of the most commonly 'cut' drugs. This means it is mixed with other substances, and its quality is extremely variable.
- Long-term use has been shown to reduce the number of nerve cell connections in the brain. This causes memory loss and inability to perform simple tasks.
- Is a powerful stimulant and so is especially dangerous for anyone with high blood pressure, heart problems or epilepsy.
- Affects coordination so users should never drive or use machinery.

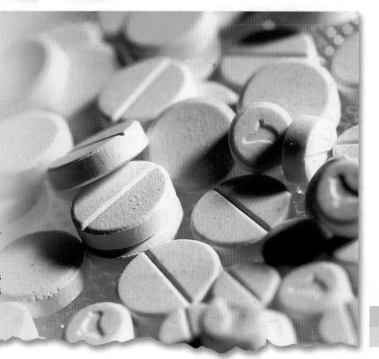

Alcohol is the most widely used drug

Alcohol is an unusual drug in that it is widely available legally in many countries. Even young people that cannot buy alcohol legally may still be able to obtain it quite easily. Apart from some cultures which ban alcohol, very few people have never tried the drug, and most young people would not consider it a 'drug of abuse'. However, alcohol can be an addictive drug, and causes great harm when used in excess. Most people greatly underestimate how much alcohol they drink. The effects of alcohol on the body extend beyond the nervous system – these are described in the diagram below.

Alcohol has widespread effects throughout the body.

Cardiovascular effects include **anaemia** (alcohol poisons bone marrow) and increased **deposits of fat** in the coronary arteries.

Skin blood vessels dilate so warm blood flows to the skin. The body feels warm and comfortable, but **hypothermia** may result at low environmental temperatures.

One unit of alcohol is the amount that can be processed by the liver in one hour in the average person (see page 51). This is equivalent to one glass of wine, half a pint of beer, or one measure of spirits.

Sex organs are stimulated but do not work well. Sperm count may be reduced.

Intestines are irritated, causing indigestion, nausea, diarrhoea and ulcers.

In pregnant women, alcohol may cross the placenta to the unborn child. The child may develop slowly, especially its nervous system (this is called **fetal alcohol syndrome**).

Liver cells work harder to detoxify the alcohol. Cells lining blood vessels are damaged causing **cirrhosis** – liver function begins to fail.

Many effects on the nervous system – see page 97.

Kidneys cannot reabsorb water very well. Too much water is excreted and the body becomes dehydrated (this is responsible for the headache following a drinking bout).

Cancer of the tongue and oesophagus are much more likely in heavy drinkers (especially if they also smoke).

Because alcohol is a depressant, **withdrawal** leads to tremors, high pulse rate, sweating and visual hallucination. This is called **delirium tremens** (the DTs) and is treated with sedatives and multivitamins.

Disorders of the nervous system

We have seen that many drugs have their effects by altering the activity of the nervous system. The nervous system may also be damaged by medical conditions. Some of these are more likely in old age (such as Alzheimer's disease), some may strike at any time (such as multiple sclerosis), some are caused by infection (such as meningitis) while others may result from an injury (such as a broken back). Such problems may cause great hardship to the affected person, and to those who care for them.

1. a Several drug types affect the brain. These include stimulants, depressants, narcotics and hallucinogens. Give one example of each, and describe how it affects the brain.

   b What is the difference between psychological and physical addiction to a drug?

   c What is meant by drug tolerance?

   Some drug users suggest that ordinary people are drug dependent. They claim that people who drink six or more cups of coffee per day may experience withdrawal symptoms if they stop. These symptoms are said to include headaches and poor concentration.

   d Design an experiment that would allow you to investigate the validity of this claim. State clearly the manipulated and responding variables, and say how you would manipulate or record them. Suggest some fixed variables that might improve the validity of your data.

2. Alcohol is a powerful and widely used drug. It affects the central nervous system, slows down reflex actions and causes small blood vessels in the skin to dilate. Most alcohol is absorbed in the small intestine, although its rapid effects are partly explained by the observation that up to 30% of it may be absorbed from the stomach. Alcohol is broken down in the liver, and most of it appears as carbon dioxide and water.

   A medical student was given six units of alcohol to drink, then blood samples were taken over the next five hours. The table shows the blood alcohol level (BAL) over the time of the experiment.

Time since drinking (hours)	BAL (mg of alcohol per 100 cm³ of blood)
0.0	0.0
0.5	70
1.0	135
1.5	140
2.0	115
3.0	75
4.0	50
5.0	40

   a Use these data to plot a graph.

   b i What would be the likely BAL after 2.5 hours?

   ii The legal limit for driving is a BAL of 80 mg per 100 cm³ of blood. For how long would this student be above this limit?

   iii How would driving be affected by a BAL of 100 mg per 100 cm³ of blood?

   c Suggest one visible effect of the dilation of blood vessels in the skin.

   d The liver detoxifies (breaks down) alcohol, and much of it is lost as carbon dioxide and water. How would these substances be lost from the body? Suggest one long-term effect of alcohol consumption on the liver.

   e People who drink large amounts of alcohol over long periods often become malnourished. In particular they may be deficient in calcium and vitamin C. What symptoms might be seen in such people?

   f What is delirium tremens? Does this condition suggest that alcohol is a stimulant or a depressant? Explain your answer.

3. Illegal or controlled drugs are classified in the UK into three groups – A, B and C. Group A contains the most harmful drugs, including the opiates such as heroin. Drugs seized by police and customs are put into these categories for the purposes of keeping records. The table shows the number of drug seizures by the police in the UK in 1980, 1985 and 1990.

   a i Suggest one reason for classifying a drug as a group A drug.

   ii Calculate the percentage increase in the total quantity of cocaine seized by the police between 1980 and 1990. Show your working.

   iii Identify three main trends in the information shown in this table.

   b Drug dependence is characterised by personal neglect – poor nutrition, lack of care in personal hygiene and being willing to share needles during injections. Infections such as hepatitis are common, as are vitamin deficiencies. Heroin users are 50 times more likely to commit suicide than non-users. A female user who becomes pregnant may pass on the dependence to her child. Users who are denied access to the drug show violent withdrawal symptoms that include convulsions, diarrhoea and vomiting.

   i What factors contribute to the early death of heroin users?

   ii Following withdrawal, users are treated with methadone (a drug similar to heroin but less likely to case dependence) and multivitamin supplements. Why?

Seizures of group A drugs in the UK.

Drug	Number of seizures			Quantity seized (kg)		
	1980	1985	1990	1980	1985	1990
Cocaine (Group A)	365	510	1410	4.2	6.7	49.6
LSD (Group A)	244	448	1772	0.003	0.006	0.020
Heroin (Group A)	612	3003	2321	1.8	32.2	26.9
Cannabis resin	6218	13734	43474	312.2	469.8	57164
Amphetamines	706	3401	4490	5.0	50.2	222.7

Receptors and senses: the eye as a sense organ

- To understand that receptors are the first stage in reflex arcs
- To know the different types of stimulus to which a mammal is sensitive
- To know that a sense organ combines receptors with other cells
- To know the structure and function of the eye

Receptors detect changes in the environment

A **stimulus** is a change in the environment that affects an organism. All living organisms are **sensitive** – they can respond to stimuli. Animals, including mammals, have a nervous system which receives information from the environment, decides how to respond and then tells the body. A **receptor** is a part of the nervous system that is adapted to receive stimuli. Receptors can be classified according to the type of stimulus they respond to, as shown in the table.

Receptor type	Responds to stimulus	Example in humans
Photoreceptor	Light	Rod cells in retina of eye
Chemoreceptor	Chemicals	Taste buds
Thermoreceptor	Changes in temperature	Thermoreceptors in skin
Mechanoreceptor	Mechanical changes such as changes in length	Hair cells in ear

Classification of receptors.

Receptors are transducers

All receptors are **transducers**, which means they convert one form of energy into another. They convert the energy of the stimulus (such as light energy) into the kind of energy that the nervous system can deal with (electrical impulses). The general principle of receptor action is outlined in the diagram opposite.

The senses

Our **senses** are our ability to be aware of different aspects of the environment. For example, the sense of sight allows us to be aware of light stimuli, detected by photoreceptors. The photograph opposite shows the different human senses, and the stimuli to which they are sensitive.

The receptor cells that provide our senses do not work on their own. They need a supply of blood to deliver nutrients and oxygen and remove wastes. Receptors may need help in receiving the stimulus, and receptor cells are often grouped together with other tissues to form a **sense organ**. The other tissues allow the receptor cells to work efficiently.

The working of the eye illustrates the involvement of other tissues in the operation of a sense organ, as described opposite.

Note that the senses are detected by receptors in structures on the outside of the body, and mainly around the head. This is because the stimuli come from outside the body, and the head is often the first part of the body that goes into a new environment. There are also many **internal** receptors inside the body. These detect blood temperature and pH, for example, and are vital in the process of homeostasis (see page 110).

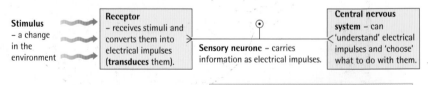

Think about it! We are not aware of any stimulus until the impulse reaches the correct area of the brain. The receptor can be working perfectly but unless the sensory nerve and brain are working, the 'sense' will be incomplete – we 'see' with our brain as much as our eyes.

All receptors work in the same way – they convert one form of energy (the stimulus) into another form that the nervous system can understand.

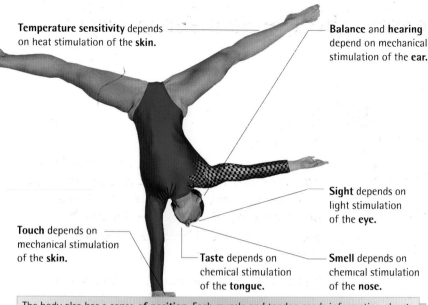

Temperature sensitivity depends on heat stimulation of the **skin**.

Balance and **hearing** depend on mechanical stimulation of the **ear**.

Sight depends on light stimulation of the **eye**.

Touch depends on mechanical stimulation of the **skin**.

Taste depends on chemical stimulation of the **tongue**.

Smell depends on chemical stimulation of the **nose**.

The body also has a **sense of position**. Each muscle and tendon sends information about how stretched it is to the central nervous system (CNS). The CNS interprets this so that we 'know' where each part of the body is in relation to the other parts (see how easy it is to clasp your hands behind your back, or to touch your nose with your eyes shut).

The eye as a sense organ

The eye is an example of a sense organ. It contains:

- **receptors** – the rod and cone cells on the retina
- **systems for making the most of the light stimulus**, including the lens and the iris
- its own **blood supply** and **physical protection** via the choroid and the sclera.

The diagram below shows the arrangement of the structures in the eye.

Together control light intensity on the retina (see page 103)

Pupil – the circular opening which lets light into the eye. It appears black because the choroid is visible through it.

Iris – the coloured part of the eye which can expand and contract to control the amount of light that enters the eye.

Together control light focusing on the retina (see overleaf)

Ciliary muscle **Suspensory ligament** **Lens**

Sclera – the tough outer coat which protects the eye against damage. The muscles that move the eye in its socket attach to the sclera.

Choroid – a darkly coloured layer which reduces reflections inside the eye and contains blood vessels which help to nourish the cells of the retina.

Retina – contains the light-sensitive cells, the rods and cones.

Cornea – a transparent layer responsible for most of the refraction (bending) of light rays that enter the eye.

Yellow spot (fovea) – this area has the highest density of cones and thus offers **maximum sharpness** but only works at full efficiency in **bright light**.

Optic nerve – composed of sensory neurones which carry nerve impulses to the **visual centre** at the rear of the brain.

Aqueous humour – watery fluid which supports the cornea and the front chamber of the eye.

Vitreous humour – a jelly-like substance which helps to keep the shape of the eyeball, supports the lens and keeps the retina in place at the back of the eye.

Blind spot – at the exit point of the optic nerve. There are no light-sensitive cells here so light falling on this region cannot be detected.

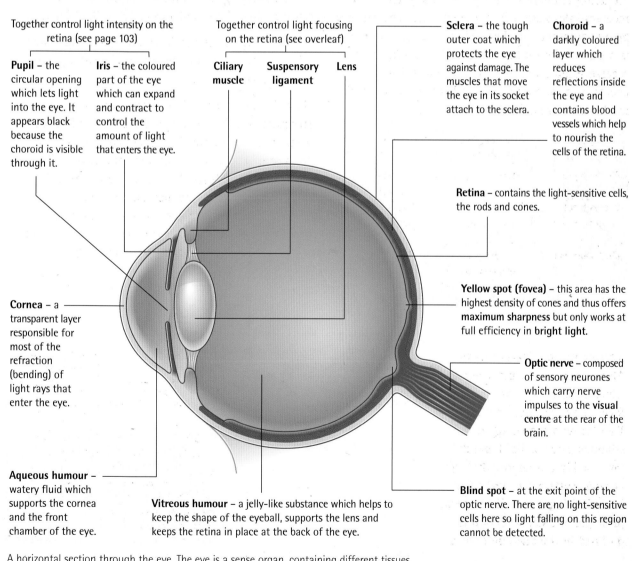

A horizontal section through the eye. The eye is a sense organ, containing different tissues working together to perform one function.

Rods and cones are photoreceptors

The retina contains two types of light-sensitive cell, **rods** and **cones**, as shown in the diagram.

Rod cells are packed most tightly around the edge of the retina. Objects are seen most clearly at night **by not looking directly at them.**

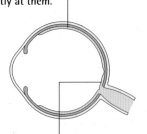

Cone cells are packed most tightly at the centre of the retina. Objects are seen most clearly during daylight **by looking directly at them.**

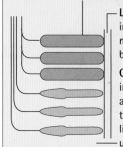

Rods provide black-and-white images. Several rods may be 'wired' to a single sensory neurone in the optic nerve, giving great sensitivity at low light intensity (night vision), but images lack detail.

Layer of pigment prevents internal reflection which might lead to multiple or blurred images.

Cones provide detailed images, in colour (there are three types, sensitive to red, green and blue light). Cones only work under high light intensity.

How a sharp image is formed on the retina

An **image** is formed when rays of light from an object are brought together (**focused**) onto the retina, as shown here.

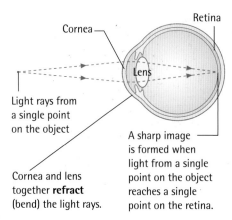

Cornea

Retina

Lens

Light rays from a single point on the object

Cornea and lens together **refract** (bend) the light rays.

A sharp image is formed when light from a single point on the object reaches a single point on the retina.

The image formed on the retina is **inverted** (upside down) and **diminished** (smaller than the object). The brain 'corrects' this inversion and reduction in size. This process is called **integration.**

Accommodation – adjusting for near and distant objects

The amount of **refraction** (bending) of the light is adjusted depending on the distance between the object and the eye. The light rays coming from very distant objects are parallel. They only need to be refracted a little to form a single, sharp, focused image on the retina. However, the lens does not need to be very powerful for this. The light rays coming from close objects are diverging. They need to be refracted more to form a sharp image on the retina, and the lens needs to be more powerful. The ability of the lens system to produce a sharp image of objects at different distances is called **accommodation**. As people get older the lens becomes less elastic and loses its ability to change

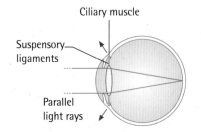

Ciliary muscle

Suspensory ligaments

Parallel light rays

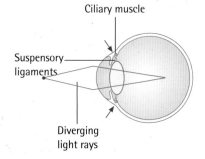

Ciliary muscle

Suspensory ligaments

Diverging light rays

Distant object
- Light needs to be **refracted** (bent) **less.**
- Ciliary muscles **relax**, eyeball becomes spherical.
- Ligaments are **tight.**
- Lens is pulled **long and thin.**

Close object
- Light must be **greatly refracted** (bent).
- Ciliary muscles **contract**, pull eyeball inwards (eyeball 'bulges' forward).
- Ligaments **relax.**
- Lens becomes **short and fat.**

Relaxed or waking eyes are set for viewing distant objects so that images of close objects (such as alarm clocks!) are blurred.

Eyestrain is caused by long periods of close work. The ciliary muscles are contracting against the pressure of fluid in the eyeball.

shape. This makes it harder to refocus quickly on objects at different distances. Smokers may experience this problem earlier than non-smokers because smoke 'ages' molecules in the lens.

The iris controls the light intensity at the retina

Light falls on the retina and stimulates the rods and cones to produce nerve impulses. These travel to the brain along the optic nerve. It is important that the rod and cone receptor cells are not over-stimulated. If too much light fell on them they would not recover in time to allow continued clear vision. The iris contains muscles that alter the size of the pupil, thereby controlling the amount of light that falls on the retina. This control is automatic, and is a good example of a reflex action (see page 90). This **pupil reflex** is explained in the diagram opposite.

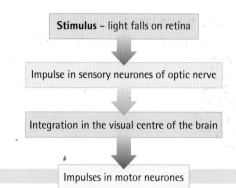

Stimulus – light falls on retina

Impulse in sensory neurones of optic nerve

Integration in the visual centre of the brain

Impulses in motor neurones

Low light intensity – radial muscles of iris contract and the pupil is opened wider, so more light can enter and reach the retina.

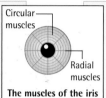
Circular muscles

Radial muscles

The muscles of the iris

High light intensity – circular muscles of iris contract and the pupil is reduced in size, so less light can enter and the retina is protected from bleaching.

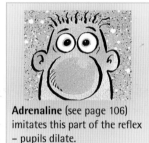
Adrenaline (see page 106) imitates this part of the reflex – pupils dilate.

Heroin (see page 96) imitates this part of the reflex – pupils constrict.

The pupil reflex prevents bleaching of the retina by regulating the amount of light that enters the eye.

---

1. What is a transducer? Explain how:
   a taste buds   b rod cells
   can be called transducers.

2. Copy and complete this paragraph.
   Light rays from an object are refracted by the _____ and the _____ which focus the light rays onto the _____. The amount of light that reaches this light-sensitive layer is controlled by the _____ which is able to adjust the size of the _____ (the black 'hole' in the front of the eye). There are two types of light-sensitive cells, the _____, which are responsible for _____ vision in low light intensity, and the _____, which are responsible for _____ vision in _____ light intensity. The image formed on the _____ is _____ and _____ than the object, but the nerve impulses that pass along the _____ nerve to the brain are interpreted so that they make sense. The ability of the brain to compare incoming information with previous experience, and to set off the correct response, is called _____.

3. Bimla was sitting in a well-lit room. She covered one eye with an eye patch. A pencil was held in front of her eye for 10 seconds. Bimla focused on it and at the same time the thickness of her eye lens was measured using an optical instrument. The pencil was then moved a different distance from the eye. This was repeated over a short period. The results are shown in the table.

Distance from eye (cm)	Thickness of lens (mm)
10	4.0
20	3.6
30	3.2
50	2.9
100	2.7
150	2.6
200	2.6

a Name the structures in the eye that bring about the change in the thickness of the lens.

b In this investigation, which is the manipulated variable and which is the responding variable?

c Suggest two important fixed variables. Explain why they must be fixed.

d How could the experiment be improved to make the data more valid?

5·7 The endocrine system

A second control system

The responses controlled by the nervous system happen quickly, but there are some responses that go on over a long period of time. Growth and development, for example, continue for years. Animals have a second coordination system, the **endocrine system**, which carries out this sort of control.

Ductless glands

The endocrine system is a series of organs called **glands**, which secrete chemicals called **hormones**. The endocrine glands are ductless glands – they secrete their hormones directly into the bloodstream. (Other glands, such as those in the digestive system, secrete substances through a duct or tube.) The hormones, once released, travel in the blood to any part of the body that is supplied with blood. The hormones affect only their **target organs,** as outlined in the diagram below.

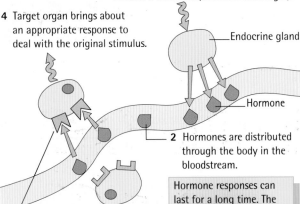

1 Stimulus affects endocrine gland so that it releases a hormone (chemical messenger).

4 Target organ brings about an appropriate response to deal with the original stimulus.

Endocrine gland

Hormone

2 Hormones are distributed through the body in the bloodstream.

Hormone responses can last for a long time. The hormones are eventually removed from the blood. Some (such as adrenaline) pass into the urine; others (such as sex hormones) are first altered chemically by the liver.

3 Receptors on the cell membranes of the target organ recognise the circulating hormone molecules. Cells with different receptors are not affected by the hormone, so only the specific target organ can respond to the hormone.

The mechanism of hormone action.

Hormones control puberty in humans

Hormones control long-term processes, and often have widespread effects on the body. At **puberty** a person becomes physically able to reproduce. The development of sexual maturity is a good example of a hormone-controlled process.

As a young person develops physically, certain signals are processed by the brain, which then instructs the pituitary gland to stimulate the **primary sex organs** – the testes in males and the ovaries in females. Sex hormones - **oestrogen** (in females) and **testosterone** (in males) - are released into the bloodstream and circulate throughout the body. They only affect the target organs which have receptors that recognise them. These target organs then carry out responses, such as the growth of body hair, which may continue for many years. The effects of these hormones at puberty are explained further in the diagram opposite.

Hormone production is under feedback control

The production and secretion of hormones is accurately controlled by **feedback** – the hormones regulate their own production. As the level of hormone in the blood rises, it switches off (**inhibits**) its own production so that the level never gets too high. As the level of hormone in the blood falls, it switches on (**stimulates**) its own production so that the level never gets too low. **Feedback control** is very important in biology, particularly in homeostasis (see page 110). It is outlined in the diagram opposite.

Human growth hormone

Sometimes the endocrine system does not function properly. An example is **pituitary dwarfism** – a person fails to grow and develop properly because of a lack of a hormone called **human growth hormone**. Treatment has been considerably improved in recent years by the production of human growth hormone by bacteria. This process is described on page 218.

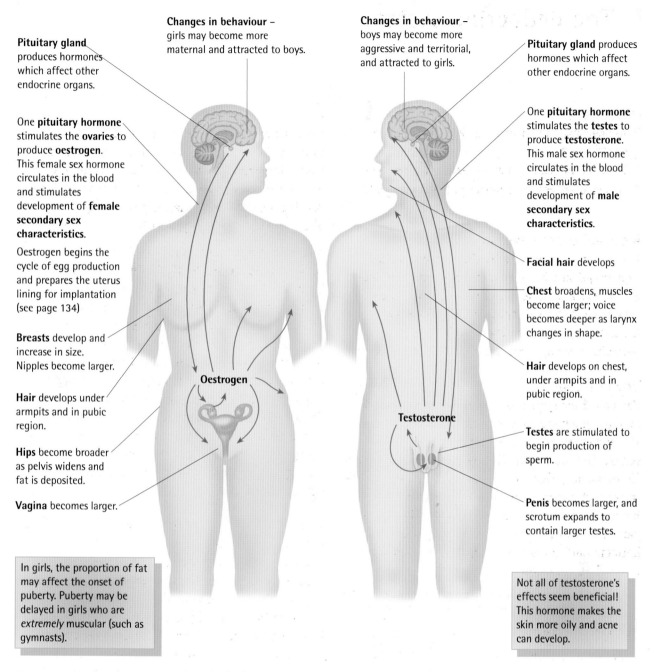

Pituitary gland produces hormones which affect other endocrine organs.

One **pituitary hormone** stimulates the **ovaries** to produce **oestrogen**. This female sex hormone circulates in the blood and stimulates development of **female secondary sex characteristics**.

Oestrogen begins the cycle of egg production and prepares the uterus lining for implantation (see page 134)

Breasts develop and increase in size. Nipples become larger.

Hair develops under armpits and in pubic region.

Hips become broader as pelvis widens and fat is deposited.

Vagina becomes larger.

Changes in behaviour – girls may become more maternal and attracted to boys.

Oestrogen

Changes in behaviour – boys may become more aggressive and territorial, and attracted to girls.

Pituitary gland produces hormones which affect other endocrine organs.

One **pituitary hormone** stimulates the **testes** to produce **testosterone**. This male sex hormone circulates in the blood and stimulates development of **male secondary sex characteristics**.

Facial hair develops

Chest broadens, muscles become larger; voice becomes deeper as larynx changes in shape.

Hair develops on chest, under armpits and in pubic region.

Testosterone

Testes are stimulated to begin production of sperm.

Penis becomes larger, and scrotum expands to contain larger testes.

In girls, the proportion of fat may affect the onset of puberty. Puberty may be delayed in girls who are *extremely* muscular (such as gymnasts).

Not all of testosterone's effects seem beneficial! This hormone makes the skin more oily and acne can develop.

Oestrogen and testosterone are hormones – they are chemical messengers secreted directly into the bloodstream and bring about widespread and long-lasting effects.

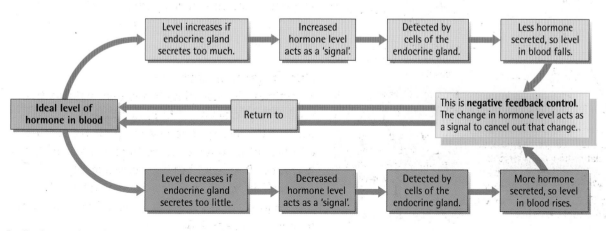

Feedback control regulates hormone levels in the blood.

Adrenaline

One hormone that has been widely studied is **adrenaline**. This substance seems to bridge the gap between nervous and endocrine control. It is definitely a chemical messenger, and is released directly into the bloodstream, yet its actions are often very rapid indeed and may only last for a very short time. The widespread and instant effects of adrenaline are described below.

| **Skin becomes pale** as blood is diverted away. |

| **Deeper, more rapid breathing** and airways become wider. |

| **Heart beats more rapidly.** |

| **Blood** is diverted away from digestive system to muscles by using sphincters (see page 71). |

| **Adrenal glands** (on top of the kidneys) release the hormone adrenaline. |

| **Glycogen in muscles** is converted to **glucose**, and released into the blood. |

Adrenaline is known as the 'flight or fight' hormone, released when the body is given a shock.

The overall effect is to provide more glucose and more oxygen for working muscles – preparation for action!

Control of blood glucose level

One of the functions of adrenaline is to increase the concentration of glucose in the blood for respiration. However, constant high concentrations of glucose in the blood are harmful.

The ideal concentration of glucose in the blood is normally maintained by two further hormones, **insulin** and **glucagon**. These are secreted by cells in the pancreas in response to changes in blood glucose concentration. They affect liver, fat tissue and muscle.

- **Insulin** is released when blood sugar is too high. It stimulates the removal of glucose from the blood.
- **Glucagon** is released when blood sugar is too low. It stimulates the release of glucose into the blood.

Insulin controls the conversion of **glucose** to **glycogen**; glucagon controls the conversion of **glycogen** to **glucose**. Glucose is a simple sugar and is soluble in blood plasma and cell cytoplasm. Glycogen is a polysaccharide (see page 11) and is insoluble. Glucose is therefore the usable form of carbohydrate and glycogen is the storage form of carbohydrate. The way in which the blood glucose level is kept within safe limits is shown in the diagram on the opposite page.

HORMONES AND SPORT

Athletes can improve their performance with the use of hormones. Although this is strictly illegal and may be harmful, some atheletes are willing to take the risk in the pursuit of sporting success. Some 'abused' hormones are listed below.

Hormone	Sporting benefit	Possible harm to user
Adrenaline	Improved immediate performance, especially in 'power' events such as sprinting.	Rise in blood pressure may be harmful to the circulation.
Anabolic steroids	Increased growth of muscle. Allows rapid recovery between training sessions – more training can be completed.	Act as feedback inhibitors of 'natural' steroid production. May cause loss of sexuality, hair loss and possibly increase risk of cancer.
EPO (erythropoeitin)	Increase rate of production of red blood cells, so allowing more oxygen to be carried by the blood.	Blood 'thickens' and the rise in blood pressure can lead to strokes.

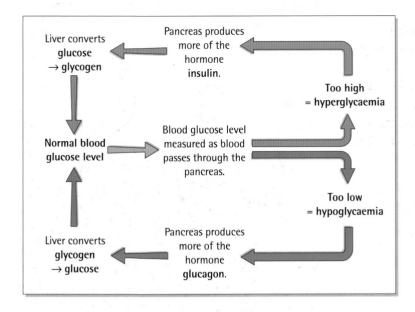

Liver converts glucose → glycogen

Pancreas produces more of the hormone **insulin**.

Too high = hyperglycaemia

Normal blood glucose level

Blood glucose level measured as blood passes through the pancreas.

Too low = hypoglycaemia

Liver converts glycogen → glucose

Pancreas produces more of the hormone **glucagon**.

Blood glucose level

Glucose is the cells' main source of energy, and it must always be available to them for respiration ...

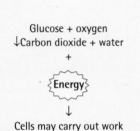

Glucose + oxygen
↓Carbon dioxide + water
+
Energy
↓
Cells may carry out work

... so the body keeps a constant amount of glucose in the blood. This **blood glucose level** is usually maintained at about 1 mg of glucose per cm³ of blood.

What is diabetes?

Diabetes is a condition in which the blood glucose concentration is higher than normal.

- It is usually the result of the pancreas failing to secrete enough insulin.

- Symptoms include
  - excessive thirst, hunger or urine production
  - sweet smelling breath
  - high 'overflow' of glucose into urine (test with **Clinistix**).

- Long-term effects if untreated include
  - premature ageing
  - cataract formation
  - hardening of arteries
  - heart disease.

- Treatment is by regular injection of pure insulin – much of this is now manufactured by genetic engineering (see page 218).

- A diet that contains too much fat and too much sugar can also cause a form of diabetes. This type of diabetes can be controlled by adjusting the diet to limit fat and sugar, and does not need injection of insulin. This 'non-insulin-dependent' diabetes is a common problem for obese people.

Clinistix are thin strips of plastic with a small pad at the bottom. The pad contains an enzyme and a dye. If glucose is present the enzyme uses it to change the colour of the dye. A Clinistix dipped into a urine sample from a diabetic person will give a positive result within seconds. Clinistix are an excellent example of the medical uses of enzymes (see page 15).

Blood glucose level is under feedback control by the hormones insulin and glucagon.

1. Copy and complete the following paragraph.

   A human exposed to a severe shock responds by producing the hormone _____. This hormone causes the storage polysaccharide _____ to be converted to _____, a soluble sugar used to release energy via respiration. Aerobic respiration requires _____ as well as this sugar, and more of this gas is made available because the hormone causes _____ and _____ breathing. The body makes the most of its resources by adjusting blood flow to different organs – less blood flows to the _____, for example, and more

   flows to the _____. The face of a shocked person shows three effects of this hormone – the skin _____, the pupils _____ and the hair _____. Because of these effects this hormone is often called the _____ or _____ hormone.

2. A dangerously aggressive animal is unlikely to fit into society. Aggression may be an important part of puberty in male animals, and may help to win females. Explain how negative feedback (feedback control) would keep aggression within acceptable limits in a young male animal.

5·8 Questions on coordination and response

1 Study the diagram below, then answer the questions that follow.

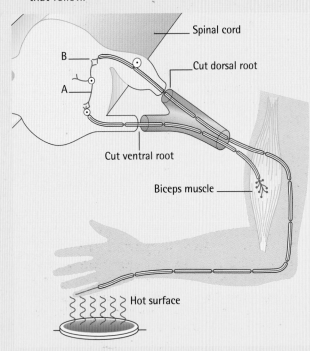

- Spinal cord
- B
- A
- Cut dorsal root
- Cut ventral root
- Biceps muscle
- Hot surface

a Name the type of neurone labelled **A**. What important function does it have?

b Name the gap labelled **B**.

c In what form is a message transmitted:
  i along a nerve fibre
  ii across the gap **B**?

d Give two examples of spinal reflexes, two of cranial reflexes and one conditioned reflex.

e How would sensation in the limb be affected if:
  i the dorsal root (branch) was cut
  ii the ventral root was cut?

f Would a reflex action occur in the limb when the dorsal root was being cut? Explain your answer.

g Name the parts **C–G** on the diagram of a sensory neurone below. State two ways in which this neurone differs from a motor neurone.

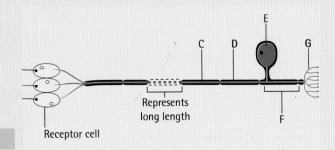

- C
- D
- E
- G
- Represents long length
- F
- Receptor cell

2 A group of students suggested that coffee is enjoyable because it speeds up the heart rate. They gave several groups of people different amounts of coffee one morning and collected the following information.

Number of cups of coffee drunk	Heart rate (beats per minute) Total	Mean
0	74, 76, 72, 72, 78, 68	
1	78, 78, 82, 72, 72, 70	
2	78, 78, 79, 87, 80, 72	
3	80, 82, 78, 81, 78, 76	
4	76, 78, 88, 90, 88, 86, 78	
5	80, 90, 88, 88, 94, 92	

a **i** Copy and complete the table by calculating the mean heart rate for each of the test groups.
  ii Present your data in a suitable graphical form.
  iii Does this data support the hypothesis that coffee affects the heart rate?
  iv Suggest three precautions that the students should have taken to ensure that their data were valid.

b How could you use epidemiology to investigate the hypothesis that heroin dependence in women leads to lower birth mass of children? Why is an epidemiological approach necessary to use in this sort of investigation?

3 An experiment similar to that in question 3 on page 103 was carried out. Data from a number of subjects were used to draw the graph below.

a At what age does the lens more or less lose the ability to change shape?

b What effect will this have on the person's eyesight?

c From the information in the graph, suggest why senior citizens (people over the age of 60) do not have to keep getting new glasses for reading.

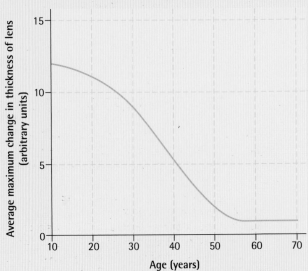

Average maximum change in thickness of lens (arbitrary units) vs Age (years)

d In the condition called **cataract** the lens becomes very cloudy and must be removed. Which structure will now be the only way to converge light onto the retina? How will this operation affect a person's eyesight?

e Scientists know that cigarette smoking hardens the arteries. Some scientists believe that smoking also hardens the lens, making a change of shape more difficult. How could you investigate this hypothesis? What controls would you need?

4 a Copy the diagram of the eye. Use arrows and the letters listed below to label the diagram.

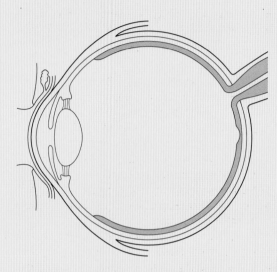

A Layer containing rods and cones
B Muscles controlling the amount of light entering the eye
C The source of tears
D A black layer containing blood vessels
E A very thin layer which protects the surface of the eye from bacteria
F A tough white protective layer

b In bright light the iris changes shape to reduce the size of the pupil.
  i What is the advantage of this?
  ii For this purpose, name the stimulus, receptor, coordinator and effector. Copy and complete the diagram below.

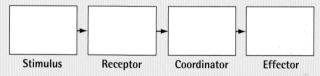

| Stimulus | Receptor | Coordinator | Effector |

c Rosie went from bright light into a dark room. The graph opposite shows the dimmest light in which she could see during the first half hour after entering the room.
  i How long was it before Rosie's eyes were completely 'used to the dark'?
  ii Rosie's friend, Matilda, suggests that Rosie's eyes become 'used to the dark' because her iris changes shape. From the evidence in the graph, do you think that this is likely? Explain your answer.

5 Normal blood glucose level is 1 mg per cm³. Ten people with normal blood glucose levels were tested for blood glucose and plasma insulin levels over a period of six hours. The mean values for these measurements were calculated and recorded. The test period included two meals and a session of exercise. The results are shown in the table below.

Time (hours)	Activity	Blood glucose level (mg per cm³)	Plasma insulin level (µg per cm³)
0	Meal eaten	1.0	10
0.5		1.5	20
1.0		1.0	40
1.5		0.8	25
2.0	Exercise started	0.8	15
2.5	Exercise finished	1.2	10
3.0		1.0	20
3.5		1.0	10
4.0	Meal eaten	1.0	10
4.5		1.4	20
5.0		1.0	35
5.5		0.8	40
6.0		0.8	10

a Present all the data in the form of a graph.

b What effect does the period of exercise have on the blood glucose and plasma insulin levels? Explain your answer.

c Suggest two other hormones that would change in concentration in the blood during exercise. Why are these hormones important?

d Why is it good experimental technique to:
  i take mean values for blood glucose and plasma insulin levels
  ii use only subjects with normal glucose levels?

e How long after a meal does it take for the blood glucose level to return to normal?

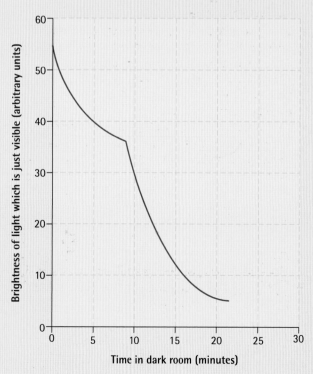

Brightness of light which is just visible (arbitrary units)

Time in dark room (minutes)

Homeostasis: maintaining a steady state

The cells in any living organism will only function properly in the correct conditions. The conditions *outside* the body (the **external environment**) are continuously changing – for example, temperature on a cool day might vary from 0 °C out of doors to 20 °C indoors. The body has mechanisms for adjusting conditions *within* the body (the **internal environment**) so that conditions around the cells remain constant.

Keeping the internal environment constant

The blood cells lie in the blood plasma, and other cells are surrounded by tissue fluid (see page 66). Conditions in the blood (and therefore in the tissue fluid) are maintained at an **optimum** – the best values for the cells to function. Keeping constant conditions in the tissue fluid around the cells is called **homeostasis**.

Homeostasis involves several organs, but the basic principle is always the same, as shown below. The diagram on the right shows some of the organs involved in homeostasis, and the particular conditions in the tissue fluid which they regulate.

Cells change the composition of the tissue fluid as they remove food and oxygen and add carbon dioxide and other wastes.

Heart supplies the constant pressure needed to deliver blood to the tissues, and to form the tissue fluid.

Skin – the main organ for control of heat exchange (see page 112).

Kidneys regulate levels of water and salt (**osmoregulation**) and remove urea and other wastes (**excretion**) (see pages 114–16).

Lungs regulate exchange of carbon dioxide and oxygen.

Intestines supply soluble foods and water.

Liver regulates the levels of many solutes in the blood, and removes poisons.

Many organs play a part in homeostasis. (A more accurate diagram of the human circulation is given on page 65.)

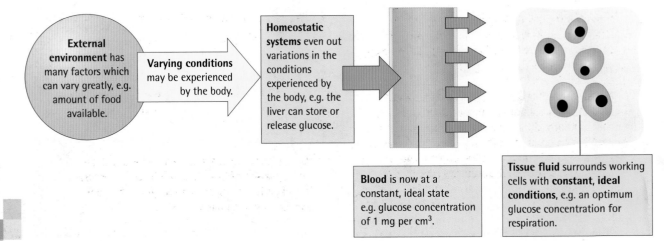

External environment has many factors which can vary greatly, e.g. amount of food available.

Varying conditions may be experienced by the body.

Homeostatic systems even out variations in the conditions experienced by the body, e.g. the liver can store or release glucose.

Blood is now at a constant, ideal state e.g. glucose concentration of 1 mg per cm^3.

Tissue fluid surrounds working cells with **constant, ideal conditions**, e.g. an optimum glucose concentration for respiration.

Homeostasis

How is homeostasis brought about?

The work of these organs must be coordinated to achieve homeostasis. Information about the conditions in the body is continuously fed to the brain from **sensory receptors** around the body.

For example, if the body temperature rises, temperature receptors in the skin send information to the brain. In response, the brain starts off mechanisms that will lower the body temperature again. The same temperature receptors 'inform' the brain when the temperature is back to normal. Homeostasis depends on this continual **feedback** of information, as explained in the diagram below.

To summarise:

- Homeostasis is the maintenance of a constant internal environment.
- Homeostasis involves control by negative feedback.
- In negative feedback, a change sets off a response that cancels out the change.

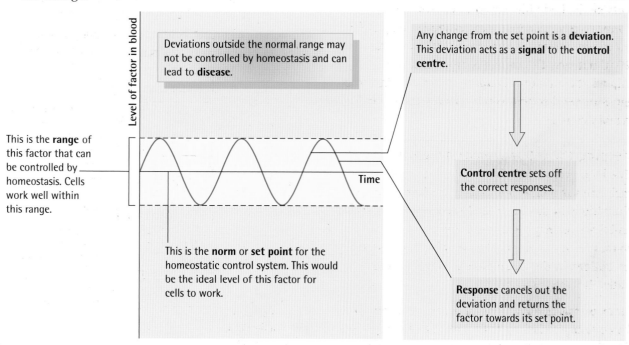

In homeostasis, deviation from a set point acts as the signal that sets off the correction mechanism. This negative feedback keeps variable factors within the narrow range suitable for life.

1 Copy and complete the following paragraph.

Cells work best when conditions around them remain constant. Cells are bathed in _____ fluid, and many systems work to keep the composition of this fluid constant. Each system has _____, which detect any changes from the _____ (the ideal conditions for the cells). The changes are then communicated to the _____, usually along _____ neurones. The central control area then sets off the correct responses. These responses cancel out the original change and so this sort of control is often called _____.

2 Copy and complete the following table.

Homeostatic organ	Factor controlled
Liver	
Lungs	
	Water content of blood
	Heat loss or gain
Intestines	

3 Use the principle of feedback control to compare the regulation of blood glucose level in humans (see page 107) with the maintenance of a stable temperature in an aircraft cabin.

6·2 Control of body temperature

Objectives

- To understand why body temperature must be controlled
- To know the difference between endotherms and ectotherms
- To understand the part played by the skin in control of temperature
- To appreciate that control of body temperature is an example of negative feedback

The importance of a constant temperature

Many biological and physical processes are affected by temperature. For example:

- enzymes work best at their optimum temperature, and are denatured by wide deviations from this

- cell membranes become more fragile as temperature rises

- diffusion rates are increased by higher temperatures, and decreased by lower ones

- liquids such as blood become more viscous (thicker) as the temperature falls.

Most animals *control* their body temperature. Some are ectotherms ('outside heat') – they can only control their body temperature by their behaviour. A lizard, for example, basks in the sun to gain heat, or seeks shade when it is too hot.

Birds and mammals are **endotherms** ('inside heat') – they can maintain a constant body temperature by generating heat internally. Humans have several mechanisms which work non-stop to balance heat production against heat loss, as shown in the diagram below. This balance is achieved by a **temperature control centre** in the **hypothalamus**, a region of the brain. The diagram opposite shows the negative feedback systems that control body temperature in an endotherm.

The role of the skin

As the barrier between the body and its environment, the skin is also the main organ concerned with heat loss and heat conservation.

An endothermic animal maintains an ideal body temperature by balancing heat losses and heat gains.

Metabolism – many biochemical reactions, especially **respiration**, in the liver **generate heat**.

Movement **generates heat** by **respiration** and **friction** within the muscles.

Excretion: urine and faeces are at body temperature. Heat is **lost** when they are expelled from the body.

Heat is lost when water **evaporates** from the lungs and sweat evaporates from the skin.

Convection – transfer of heat to and from the body on air currents. Can be increased by 'fanning' air past the body.

Radiation – transfer of heat in the form of rays, usually infra-red rays.

Conduction – transfer of heat by direct contact with another object such as a cold rock or a hot oven door.

Heat can be **gained or lost** by these processes.

Fat! Fat is an important compound in temperature control:
- each fat molecule provides about twice as much energy in respiration as a molecule of either protein or carbohydrate
- fat stores under the skin insulate against heat loss.

Heat gains	Heat losses
Respiration	Evaporation
Conduction	Excretion
Convection	Conduction
Radiation	Convection
	Radiation

37°C

If heat gains exceed heat losses the body temperature will rise – may cause **hyperthermia**.

If heat losses exceed heat gains the body temperature will fall – may cause **hypothermia**.

Homeostasis

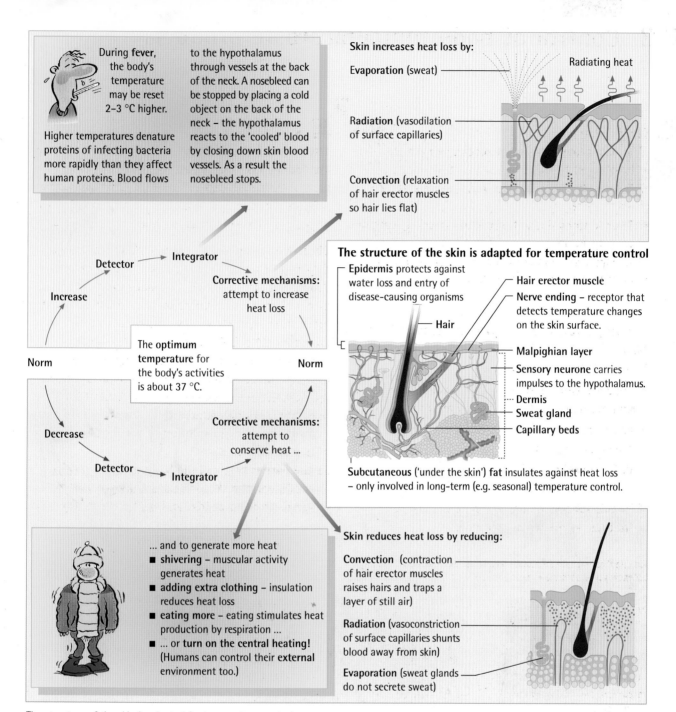

During **fever**, the body's temperature may be reset 2–3 °C higher.

Higher temperatures denature proteins of infecting bacteria more rapidly than they affect human proteins. Blood flows

to the hypothalamus through vessels at the back of the neck. A nosebleed can be stopped by placing a cold object on the back of the neck – the hypothalamus reacts to the 'cooled' blood by closing down skin blood vessels. As a result the nosebleed stops.

Skin increases heat loss by:

Evaporation (sweat)

Radiating heat

Radiation (vasodilation of surface capillaries)

Convection (relaxation of hair erector muscles so hair lies flat)

Detector → Integrator

Corrective mechanisms: attempt to increase heat loss

Increase

The **optimum temperature** for the body's activities is about 37 °C.

Norm

Norm

Decrease

Corrective mechanisms: attempt to conserve heat …

Detector → Integrator

The structure of the skin is adapted for temperature control

Epidermis protects against water loss and entry of disease-causing organisms

Hair

Hair erector muscle

Nerve ending – receptor that detects temperature changes on the skin surface.

Malpighian layer

Sensory neurone carries impulses to the hypothalamus.

Dermis

Sweat gland

Capillary beds

Subcutaneous ('under the skin') **fat** insulates against heat loss – only involved in long-term (e.g. seasonal) temperature control.

… and to generate more heat
- **shivering** – muscular activity generates heat
- **adding extra clothing** – insulation reduces heat loss
- **eating more** – eating stimulates heat production by respiration …
- … or **turn on the central heating!** (Humans can control their **external** environment too.)

Skin reduces heat loss by reducing:

Convection (contraction of hair erector muscles raises hairs and traps a layer of still air)

Radiation (vasoconstriction of surface capillaries shunts blood away from skin)

Evaporation (sweat glands do not secrete sweat)

The structure of the skin is adapted for temperature control

Hypothermia

In extreme heat loss, the body will protect the vital **core** organs in the centre of the body, even if this means that the extremities of the body suffer. If the core temperature falls below 35 °C then **hypothermia** results. This can damage the brain permanently. Hypothermia is a particular risk for mountaineers (exposed to low temperatures and wind), swimmers (water conducts heat away from the body) and the elderly (who tend to be less active and so generate less heat from respiration).

1. What is the difference between an endotherm and an ectotherm?
2. Which structures in the skin are effectors in the control of body temperature?
3. How can the body gain heat?
4. Explain how evaporation aids heat loss from the body.
5. How can subcutaneous fat help in temperature control?

6·3 Excretion: removal of the waste products of metabolism

Objectives
- To understand that living cells produce wastes
- To name some human waste products
- To name the organs involved in excretion
- To understand the functions of the kidney

Homeostasis means keeping a constant environment around the cells of the body. This involves providing cells with essential raw materials, but also means removing waste products. These waste products can be very toxic (poisonous), for example:

- **Carbon dioxide**, produced during respiration, dissolves in plasma and tissue fluid to form a weak acid (carbonic acid, H_2CO_3) which can denature enzymes and other proteins at high concentrations.

- **Urea**, produced in the liver during deamination of excess amino acids, can denature enzymes.

The body expends a great deal of energy getting rid of these wastes, and has several specialised organs for this function of **excretion**.

The role of the kidney
The kidneys are specialised organs that:

- remove the toxic waste product **urea** from the circulating blood – they carry out **excretion**
- regulate the **water content** of the blood – they carry out **osmoregulation**.

The structure of the kidneys is well adapted to enable them to carry out these processes.

- Each kidney receives a good supply of blood at high pressure through the **renal artery**.
- Each kidney contains hundreds of thousands of tubes, the **nephrons**, that can filter substances from the blood.
- Each kidney has an exit tube, **the ureter**, to carry away the **urine** (a solution of wastes dissolved in water).
- The kidney is under close control by a **feedback system** so that water saving is always exactly balanced to the body's needs.

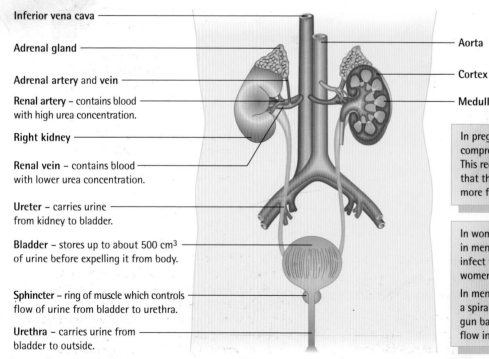

Inferior vena cava

Adrenal gland

Adrenal artery and vein

Renal artery – contains blood with high urea concentration.

Right kidney

Renal vein – contains blood with lower urea concentration.

Ureter – carries urine from kidney to bladder.

Bladder – stores up to about 500 cm³ of urine before expelling it from body.

Sphincter – ring of muscle which controls flow of urine from bladder to urethra.

Urethra – carries urine from bladder to outside.

Aorta

Cortex

Medulla

In pregnant women the bladder is compressed by the expanding uterus. This reduces its storage capacity so that these women have to urinate more frequently than normal.

In women the urethra is shorter than in men. This means that bacteria can infect the bladder more easily in women than in men.

In men the inside of the urethra has a spiral groove (like the rifling in a gun barrel), which makes the urine flow in a narrow stream.

The kidneys receive blood from the renal artery, remove urea and a variable amount of water from it and return the 'modified' blood to the circulation through the renal vein. The wastes removed from the blood are eventually expelled from the body through the urethra after being stored in the bladder.

Homeostasis

The structure of the kidney

The kidneys and their blood vessels are located in the abdomen, as shown in the diagram opposite. The kidneys produce urine constantly, which passes to the **bladder**.

The functional unit – the nephron

Each kidney contains hundreds of thousands of long tubes called **nephrons**, each with its own branch of the renal artery and vein. Each nephron works in exactly the same way, so the function of the kidney can be explained by considering the working of just one nephron, as shown below.

The kidney is made up of many nephrons (kidney tubules). Substances are filtered out of the blood into the nephron. Useful molecules and most of the water are reabsorbed into the blood.

About 180 dm³ of water filters through to the nephrons every day. Only about 1.5 dm³ is lost as urine because the rest of it is returned to the blood.

Branch of renal artery – blood containing **water** plus **useful molecules** plus **water** is delivered from the circulation.

Branch of renal vein – blood containing useful molecules and water but cleared of wastes is now returned to the circulation.

Bowman's capsule – blood is filtered under high pressure (ultrafiltration). Wastes plus some useful molecules plus some water are filtered into the nephron (kidney tubule).

First coiled tubule – useful molecules plus most of water are **selectively reabsorbed** into the blood.

Collecting duct – kidney can reabsorb water from here and return it to the blood according to the body's demands, under the influence of **anti-diuretic hormone (ADH).**

Urine containing **wastes** dissolved in a small volume of **water.**

Loop of Henlé alters salt concentrations in the medulla to aid reabsorption of water from the collecting ducts.

Position of nephron in kidney

Medulla (contains loops of Henlé and collecting ducts).

Cortex (contains Bowman's capsules and coiled tubules).

Key
- water
- waste
- useful molecules

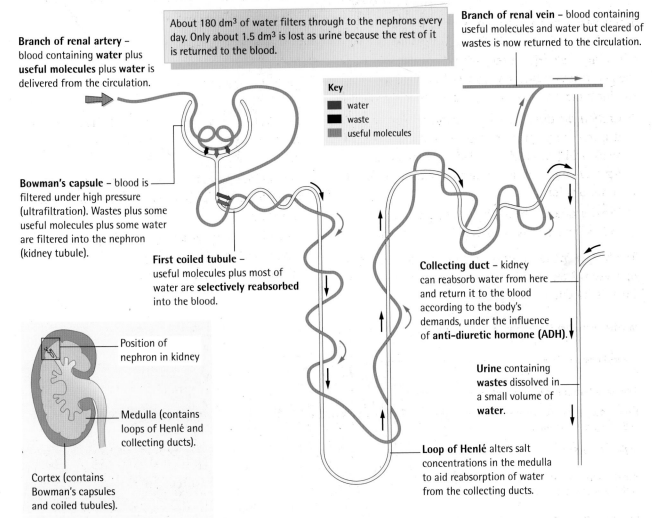

---

1. Define the terms excretion and osmoregulation.

2. Name two waste products of metabolism. State their source and how they are removed from the blood.

3. Copy and complete the following paragraph.
   The main excretory organ in the mammal is the _____. There are two of these, each supplied with blood through the _____ and each composed of many thousands of tubules called _____. Each of these tubules receives materials from the blood after filtration in the _____ capsule. The tubules then remove useful substances such as _____ from this filtrate by the process of _____. The remaining waste or excess materials pass down the tubule and leave the excretory organ via the _____. They are collected for temporary storage in the _____. Eventually a dilute solution of these wastes, the urine, leaves the body through the _____.

6·4 Osmoregulation and the treatment of kidney failure

Objectives
- To explain how body water is regulated
- To explain how kidney disease can be treated

Osmoregulation

The final part of each nephron, the **collecting duct**, removes water from the filtered solution passing down inside the tubule and returns it to the blood. The body can control the amount of water that is returned to the blood in this way, and balance it with the amount of water taken in in the diet and the amount of water lost from the body by other means. This vital control of water balance is called **osmoregulation**. Water is the most common substance in the body, and has many functions (see pages 8–9). The average daily intake and loss of water by different methods is outlined in the diagram below. The amount of water reabsorbed into the blood from the collecting ducts, and therefore the amount of water lost in the urine, is controlled by **antidiuretic hormone**. This is another example of control by negative feedback, as described in the diagram at the top of the page opposite.

Kidney failure

Damage to the kidneys, perhaps through infection or following an accident, can stop the nephrons working efficiently. The body can no longer control the composition or amount of urine formed, so the content of the blood plasma and tissue fluid is not kept at its optimum. Death may follow quite quickly if the kidney failure is not corrected. Two types of treatment are available:

- **dialysis** using a kidney machine (an artificial kidney)
- **kidney transplant**.

Dialysis and the artificial kidney

A kidney machine takes a patient's blood, 'cleans' it and returns the blood to the circulation. This process is called **dialysis**. Wastes diffuse out of the blood, across a partially permeable membrane, into a fluid that is constantly renewed. In this way urea is removed from the blood without altering any of its other features. The diagram on the opposite page shows the workings of a kidney dialysis machine.

The water excreted in the urine is adjusted so that total water intake and total water loss are balanced.

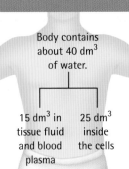

Intake varies greatly depending on the type of food available. Some desert animals gain 90% of their water from respiration. Camels don't store water in their hump, but fat. Water is released when the fat is respired.

Water intake

Drinks	1500 cm^3
Water in foods	800 cm^3
From respiration	200 cm^3

Body contains about 40 dm^3 of water.

15 dm^3 in tissue fluid and blood plasma

25 dm^3 inside the cells

Water loss

Urine	1500 cm^3
Sweat	500 cm^3
Exhaled air	400 cm^3
Faeces	100 cm^3

Isotonic sports drinks provide rapid rehydration. They contain:
- **glucose and salts**, which are quickly absorbed so that
- **water** follows by osmosis.

Volume of urine is greatly reduced if more water is lost through sweating.

Diarrhoea can greatly increase water loss. Severe cases can cause death by dehydration.

Homeostasis

Water content rises too high – blood plasma becomes **less** concentrated.

Optimum water level in blood plasma

Return to normal

Kidney reabsorbs **more** water into blood, excretes less water in urine.

Thirst centre in hypothalamus is **less** stimulated.

Jockeys long to be light!
Jockeys or boxers who want to get down to ideal weight for their sport can take drugs that interfere with ADH. Less water is reabsorbed, more is lost in the urine and the body loses weight.

Hangover! Alcohol reduces the effect of ADH on the kidney. Water is not reabsorbed and the body becomes dehydrated. Dehydrated brain cells cause a headache.

Pituitary gland releases **more** ADH.

Pituitary gland releases **less** ADH.

Kidney reabsorbs **less** water into blood, excretes **more** water in urine.

Return to normal

Water content falls too **more** – blood plasma becomes **more** concentrated.

Thirst centre in hypothalamus is **more** stimulated.

Antidiuretic hormone (ADH) helps to regulate the amount of water in the body by feedback control.

Kidney transplants

A **kidney transplant** involves surgically transferring a healthy kidney from one person (the **donor**) to a person with kidney failure (the **recipient**). It is relatively simple to connect up the donor kidney in the recipient's body, but a problem arises with **tissue rejection**. The recipient's immune system will attack the donor kidney and slowly destroy it (see page 299) unless the recipient takes drugs to stop this happening. Blood groups and tissue types of donors and recipients are carefully matched to reduce the likelihood of rejection. Successful kidney transplants have advantages over dialysis treatment:

- In the long term, a transplant is much cheaper.
- The patient's life is less disrupted once they have recovered from the operation.

1. The body must maintain a water balance.
   a Why does the body need water?
   b How is water gained by the body?
   c How is water lost by the body?
2. The water balance of the body is maintained by negative feedback. Explain what this term means.
3. What is meant by the term water potential? Use a flow diagram to explain how measurement of the blood water potential allows control of the body's water balance.
4. Why is a kidney transplant considered better than dialysis? What problems are associated with kidney transplantation?

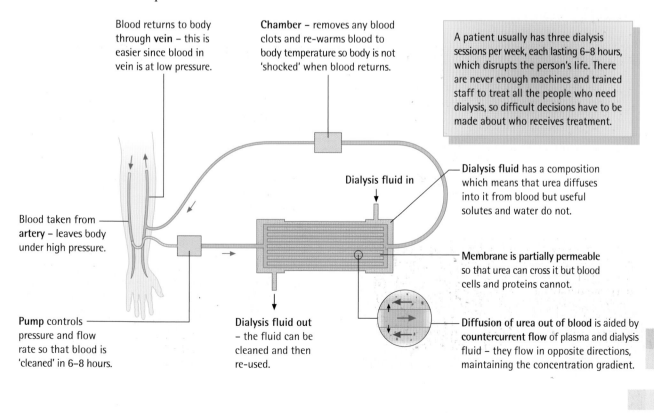

Blood returns to body through **vein** – this is easier since blood in vein is at low pressure.

Chamber – removes any blood clots and re-warms blood to body temperature so body is not 'shocked' when blood returns.

A patient usually has three dialysis sessions per week, each lasting 6–8 hours, which disrupts the person's life. There are never enough machines and trained staff to treat all the people who need dialysis, so difficult decisions have to be made about who receives treatment.

Dialysis fluid in

Dialysis fluid has a composition which means that urea diffuses into it from blood but useful solutes and water do not.

Blood taken from **artery** – leaves body under high pressure.

Membrane is partially permeable so that urea can cross it but blood cells and proteins cannot.

Pump controls pressure and flow rate so that blood is 'cleaned' in 6–8 hours.

Dialysis fluid out – the fluid can be cleaned and then re-used.

Diffusion of urea out of blood is aided by **countercurrent flow** of plasma and dialysis fluid – they flow in opposite directions, maintaining the concentration gradient.

Homeostasis

117

6·5 Questions on homeostasis

1 **a** What is hypothermia?

b Why are old people particularly at risk from hypothermia?

c Why do you think children lose heat very quickly?

2 This diagram shows how body temperature is controlled.

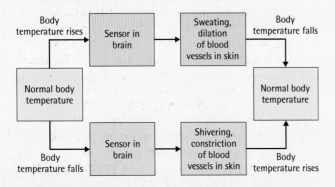

a Use this information to explain how humans control body temperature.

b Explain how shivering affects body temperature

c How does the liver contribute to body heat?

d Use the diagram to explain the meaning of 'negative feedback'.

3 If a person's kidneys are diseased he or she may have a kidney transplant. The transplanted kidney is connected to blood vessels which go into and out of the leg.

a Copy and complete the diagram below to show clearly how the artery, vein and tube carrying urine should be connected in a transplant operation.

b Sometimes a transplanted kidney is rejected. Explain why rejection may occur.

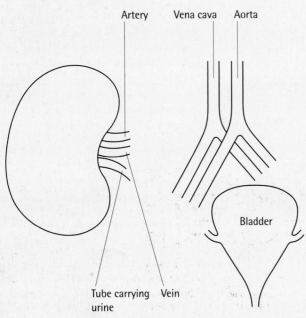

c Below is a record of how much urine a healthy man produced each day during one week. The man's diet included the same amount of water each day.

Day	Volume of urine produced (cm³)
Monday	1540
Tuesday	1470
Wednesday	1510
Thursday	1240
Friday	1450
Saturday	1770
Sunday	1520

i Calculate the average (mean) volume of urine produced each day.

ii Suggest, with reasons, why the amount of urine produced was quite different on two of the days.

d Explain how the kidneys prevent sugar and useful ions being lost from the blood.

(NEAB June 1992)

4 A person who suffers kidney failure may be treated every few days by dialysis. This uses an artificial kidney machine. The diagram shows the working of a kidney machine. In this machine a special solution flows around the outside of an inner tube which carries the patient's blood.

a How is the waste substance urea removed from the blood by dialysis?

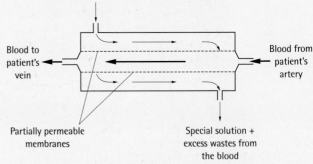

b **i** It is better for the body if a kidney transplant operation is performed instead of having to undergo dialysis every few days. Apart from the improved convenience, why is a kidney transplant better than dialysis treatment?

ii It is important to match carefully the tissue type of the kidney donor and of the patient before doing a kidney transplant. What would happen after the transplant if this matching were not done?

(SEG June 1992)

5 The table below summarises information about the excretion of urea by three mammals which live in different habitats.

Mammal	Habitat	Urine concentration (units urea per litre) urine	Length of kidney tubules
Beaver	Aquatic	500	Short
Human	Land	1150	Medium
Desert rat	Land (desert)	6000	Long

a What was the concentration of human urine?

b Which mammal had the most dilute urine?

c How many times more concentrated is the urine of the desert rat than that of the beaver? Show your working.

d What is the relationship between the length of kidney tubules and the amount of water available to each of the mammals in its habitat?

e What is the relationship between urine concentration and the amount of water available to each of the mammals in its habitat?

f One of the functions of a mammalian kidney tubule is to reabsorb water. The reabsorbed water may be important for survival. Suggest how the length of the kidney tubule may play a part in making beavers and desert rats successful in their particular habitats.

(MEG)

6 a During an investigation into heat loss, four tubes were set up as shown in the diagram below.

The same volume of very hot water was placed in each tube.

The temperature of each tube was recorded every two minutes for 10 minutes.

The results are shown in the table below.

	Temperature (°C)			
Time (mins)	Tube A	Tube B	Tube C	Tube D
0	83	84	82	83
2	81	83	81	80
4	80	82	80	75
6	78	82	79	71
8	75	81	78	66
10	72	80	76	61

i During the investigation, the thermometers were kept in the middle of the tubes and did not touch the glass.
Suggest a reason for this.

ii Explain the difference in the rate of temperature fall in tubes **A** and **B**.

b i A new born baby is sometimes wrapped in aluminium foil. Use the results of the investigation in part **a** and your own knowledge to explain why this is done.

ii Explain why it could be harmful to go out in wet clothing on a windy day.

c Sweating is an important method of controlling the temperature of the body. Use the results of the investigation in part **a** and your own knowledge to explain how sweating helps to keep the body cool.

d i On a hot day, we sweat more but produce less urine than on a cold day, even if we drink the same amount of liquid. The change in the volume of urine produced is controlled by antidiuretic hormone (ADH).
Explain how ADH helps to maintain the correct amount of water in our bodies.

ii The control of the water level in the body by ADH is an example of negative feedback.
What is meant by **negative feedback**?

(Edexcel June 1997)

7 a What is homeostasis?

b Copy and complete this table to explain how the kidneys, lungs, liver and skin are involved in this process.

c For any one of the organs that you have described in your table, suggest how negative feedback is involved in its operation.

Name of organ	One body 'factor' controlled by this organ

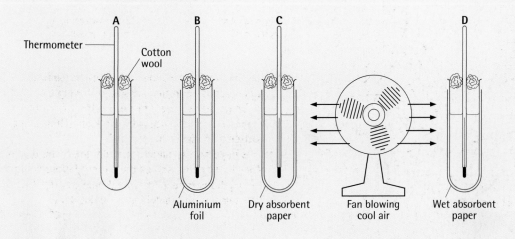

7.1 The skeleton

Bone and cartilage

The **skeleton** is made up of hard tissue that is formed by living cells. The diagram below shows the relationship between the living bone cells and the hard materials that give stiffness to the bone.

As well as bone there are other tissues in the skeleton, each with a particular function. **Cartilage** is relatively hard but more flexible than bone. Hard bone is made from cartilage by adding more and more calcium salts. Throughout the life of a mammal, the skeleton contains an increasing amount of calcified tissue (hard bone). In a newborn mammal, parts of the skeleton are made of cartilage and are therefore rather soft. This allows some movement of the bones of the baby's skull during birth so that it can pass through the narrow gap in the mother's pelvic girdle.

Some vertebrates have hardly any bone at all – for example, sharks and rays have a skeleton that is largely cartilage, although some of this cartilage is strengthened by the addition of calcium salts.

Types of skeleton

Vertebrates (animals with a backbone) such as mammals have an **endoskeleton** – the hard skeletal material is on the inside of the body and the softer, less dense muscle and connective tissue are on the outside. Other organisms have different kinds of skeleton. Insects and crustaceans, for example, have the hard, protective material on the outside of the body with the softer tissues on the inside. This **exoskeleton** has the major disadvantage that it limits growth. Some organisms have no real protective skeleton at all, but they still need some firm material to push or pull against when they move. These soft-bodied animals, such as slugs and earthworms, use their body fluid as a **hydroskeleton**. The features of an exoskeleton and a hydroskeleton are shown opposite, along with a simplified diagram of a human endoskeleton.

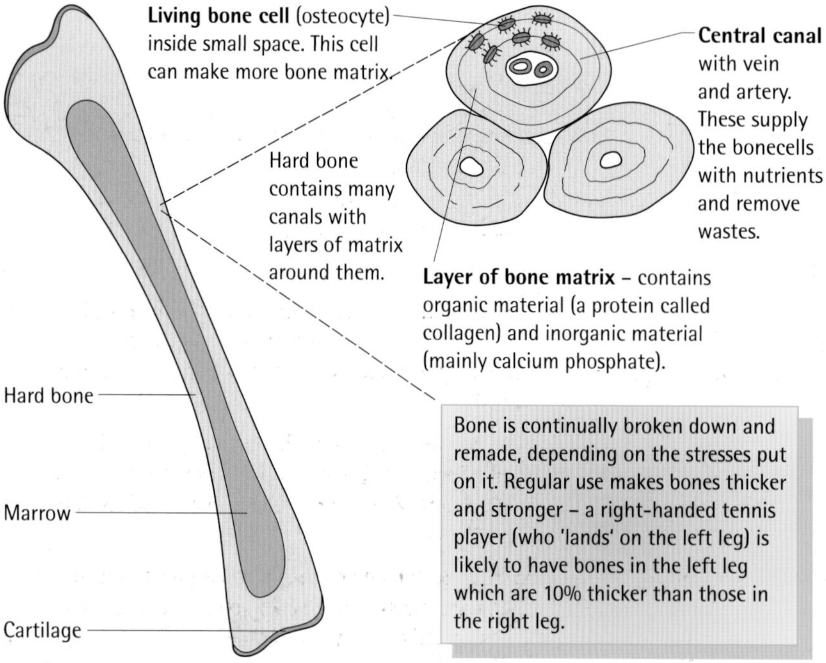

Living bone cell (osteocyte) inside small space. This cell can make more bone matrix.

Central canal with vein and artery. These supply the bonecells with nutrients and remove wastes.

Hard bone contains many canals with layers of matrix around them.

Layer of bone matrix – contains organic material (a protein called collagen) and inorganic material (mainly calcium phosphate).

Hard bone

Marrow

Cartilage

Bone is continually broken down and remade, depending on the stresses put on it. Regular use makes bones thicker and stronger – a right-handed tennis player (who 'lands' on the left leg) is likely to have bones in the left leg which are 10% thicker than those in the right leg.

Bones can be fragile
Manufacture of bone by the body requires:
- calcium
- phosphate
- amino acids
- hormones
- vitamin D.

As a person gets older the bones become more fragile. In **osteoporosis**, cavities appear in the bone.

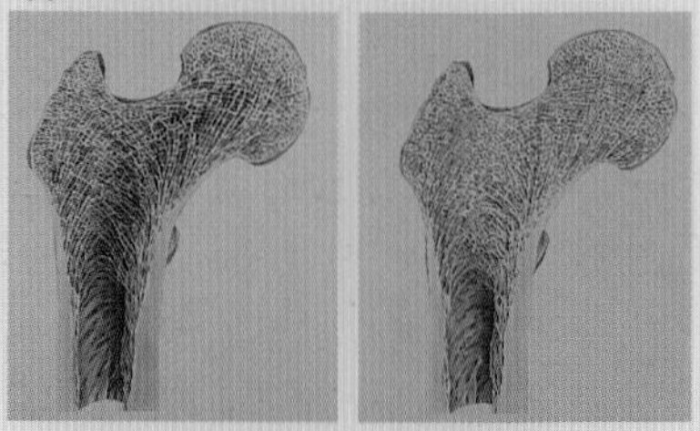

Top of osteoporitic femur Normal femur. showing enlarged spaces in bone.

Women are protected against osteoporosis by oestrogen. After the menopause this can be supplied by **hormone replacement therapy (HRT)**.

Because bone is a hard tissue, it may seem non-living. However, bone is a living tissue.

Movement

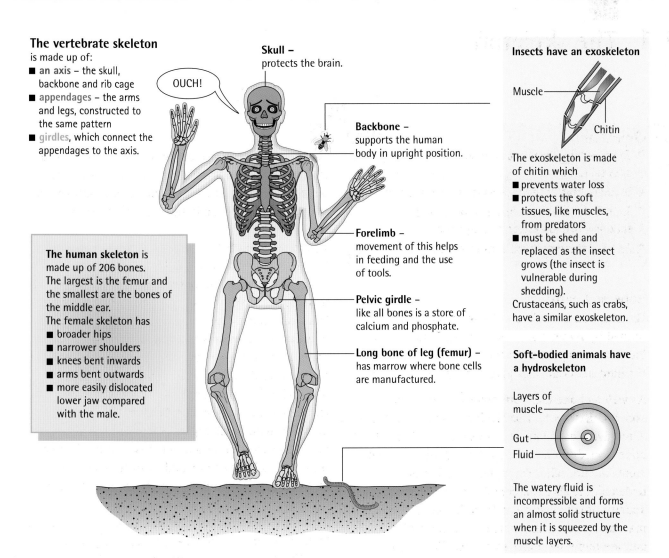

The vertebrate skeleton
is made up of:
- **an axis** – the skull, backbone and rib cage
- **appendages** – the arms and legs, constructed to the same pattern
- **girdles**, which connect the appendages to the axis.

OUCH!

Skull –
protects the brain.

Backbone –
supports the human body in upright position.

Forelimb –
movement of this helps in feeding and the use of tools.

Pelvic girdle –
like all bones is a store of calcium and phosphate.

Long bone of leg (femur) –
has marrow where bone cells are manufactured.

The human skeleton is made up of 206 bones. The largest is the femur and the smallest are the bones of the middle ear.
The female skeleton has
- broader hips
- narrower shoulders
- knees bent inwards
- arms bent outwards
- more easily dislocated lower jaw compared with the male.

Insects have an exoskeleton

Muscle

Chitin

The exoskeleton is made of chitin which
- prevents water loss
- protects the soft tissues, like muscles, from predators
- must be shed and replaced as the insect grows (the insect is vulnerable during shedding).
Crustaceans, such as crabs, have a similar exoskeleton.

Soft-bodied animals have a hydroskeleton

Layers of muscle

Gut

Fluid

The watery fluid is incompressible and forms an almost solid structure when it is squeezed by the muscle layers.

Like all vertebrates, humans have an endoskeleton, whereas insects have an exoskeleton and worms have a hydroskeleton.

The functions of the skeleton

The skeleton of any vertebrate has the following functions:

- **Support** – for animals that live on land, the air does not support softer tissues like muscle and so the hard, incompressible bone holds the rest of the body in position.

- **Protection** – vital tissues and organs can be protected from physical damage by a covering of bone. For example, the brain is protected from shock inside the skull and the heart and lungs are protected inside the rib cage.

- **Movement (locomotion)** – bones meet at **joints** (see page 122) which form levers. Muscles pull on these levers to move the body.

- **Storage** – both calcium and phosphate are stored in the bone.

- **Manufacture of blood cells** – the marrow inside some of the bones makes blood cells.

1. Explain the difference between the following pairs of terms:
   a bone and cartilage
   b endoskeleton and exoskeleton
   c axis and appendage.

2. Describe how the human skeleton is involved in support, protection and movement. What property of bone makes each of these functions possible?

3. Which components of the diet play a part in bone formation? Which other component of the diet might play a part in bone function? Explain your answer.

4. What are the advantages and disadvantages of the hard exoskeleton of an arthropod? How are these disadvantages overcome?

Movement

7·2 Joints in the skeleton allow movement

Objectives

▪ To understand the functions of the skeleton
▪ To understand the part played by the skeleton in movement
▪ To understand that muscles work by contraction
▪ To understand that efficient movement at a joint is achieved by antagonistic pairs of muscles

The rigidity of the skeleton is ideal for support and protection, but for movement the skeleton must be flexible. This is possible because of joints.

The pentadactyl limb

The human arm and leg have a similar arrangement of bones and joints. They are examples of **pentadactyl limbs** – they have five digits ('penta' = five, 'dactyl' = finger). The diagram below shows the basic structure of a pentadactyl limb, and how the forelimbs of a human and other vertebrates have become adapted from it.

The pentadactyl limb is an example of an **homologous structure** – it is adapted from a common original type.

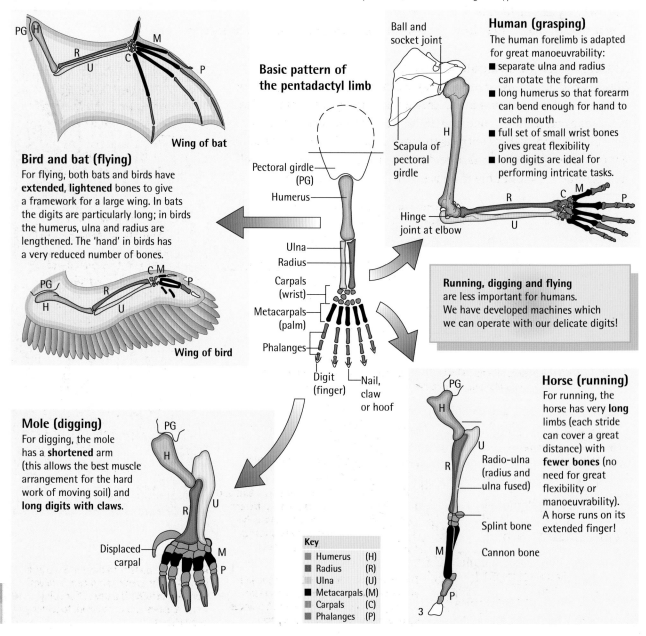

Bird and bat (flying)
For flying, both bats and birds have **extended, lightened** bones to give a framework for a large wing. In bats the digits are particularly long; in birds the humerus, ulna and radius are lengthened. The 'hand' in birds has a very reduced number of bones.

Wing of bat

Wing of bird

Basic pattern of the pentadactyl limb

Pectoral girdle (PG)
Humerus
Ulna
Radius
Carpals (wrist)
Metacarpals (palm)
Phalanges
Digit (finger)
Nail, claw or hoof

Human (grasping)
Ball and socket joint
The human forelimb is adapted for great manoeuvrability:
■ separate ulna and radius can rotate the forearm
■ long humerus so that forearm can bend enough for hand to reach mouth
■ full set of small wrist bones gives great flexibility
■ long digits are ideal for performing intricate tasks.

Scapula of pectoral girdle

Hinge joint at elbow

Running, digging and flying are less important for humans. We have developed machines which we can operate with our delicate digits!

Mole (digging)
For digging, the mole has a **shortened** arm (this allows the best muscle arrangement for the hard work of moving soil) and **long digits with claws**.

Displaced carpal

Horse (running)
For running, the horse has very **long** limbs (each stride can cover a great distance) with **fewer bones** (no need for great flexibility or manoeuvrability). A horse runs on its extended finger!

Radio-ulna (radius and ulna fused)

Splint bone

Cannon bone

Key
■ Humerus	(H)
■ Radius	(R)
■ Ulna	(U)
■ Metacarpals	(M)
■ Carpals	(C)
■ Phalanges	(P)

3

Movement is made possible by joints

A **joint** is a part of the skeleton where two bones meet. There are several types of joint in the body, but the type that allows the greatest amount of movement is called the **synovial joint**, shown in the diagram opposite.

The direction and amount of movement possible at a synovial joint depend on:

- the shape of the bones at the point where they **articulate** (come together)
- how much movement is allowed by the ligaments that bind the two bones together.

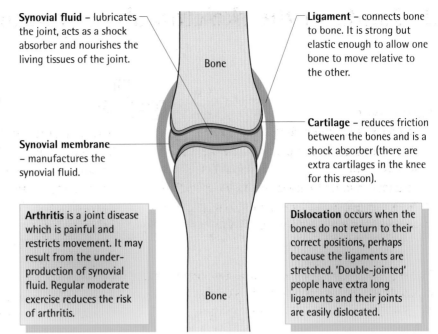

Synovial fluid – lubricates the joint, acts as a shock absorber and nourishes the living tissues of the joint.

Synovial membrane – manufactures the synovial fluid.

Bone

Bone

Ligament – connects bone to bone. It is strong but elastic enough to allow one bone to move relative to the other.

Cartilage – reduces friction between the bones and is a shock absorber (there are extra cartilages in the knee for this reason).

Arthritis is a joint disease which is painful and restricts movement. It may result from the under-production of synovial fluid. Regular moderate exercise reduces the risk of arthritis.

Dislocation occurs when the bones do not return to their correct positions, perhaps because the ligaments are stretched. 'Double-jointed' people have extra long ligaments and their joints are easily dislocated.

A synovial joint allows free movement between bones.

Muscles work in antagonistic pairs

Muscles can only cause movement by **contracting** (shortening) – they can only pull, they cannot push. Muscles are arranged in pairs which have opposing actions – one muscle contracts to move a bone in one direction, and the other contracts to move it back. These pairs of muscles are called **antagonistic pairs**. The diagram below shows the action of antagonistic muscles in the movement of the human forearm.

A flexor muscle contracts to bend the limb.

Biceps (flexor) contracts

Triceps (extensor) relaxes

An extensor muscle contracts to straighten the limb.

Biceps (flexor) relaxes

Triceps (extensor) contracts

Tendons connect muscle to bone. They are inelastic so that they transmit the contraction of the muscles to the bone, which moves.

TAKE NOTE! For muscle and bone to work as a machine the ends of the muscle must be attached to different bones. The tendon must go across the joint.

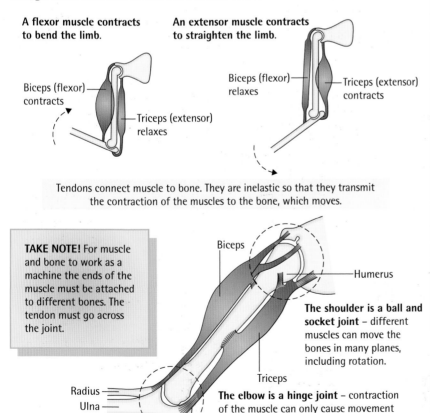

Biceps

Humerus

Triceps

Radius

Ulna

The shoulder is a ball and socket joint – different muscles can move the bones in many planes, including rotation.

The elbow is a hinge joint – contraction of the muscle can only cause movement in a single plane (the forearm can be moved up or down in the plane of this page).

1. The diagram below shows a section through a ball and socket joint in the human hip.
   a Name the tissue S.
   b The ligament is involved in holding the bones together. As well as being strong, suggest another important property of the ligament.
   c What is the function of the synovial fluid?

Synovial fluid

Head of femur

S

Ligament

Movement, whether of the whole body, a single limb or even of an organ, involves **work**. A **machine** is a device for doing work; muscles and bones work together as machines.

7·3 Contraction of muscles requires energy

Objectives

- To know that respiration is the source of energy for muscular work
- To understand that anaerobic respiration is less efficient than aerobic respiration and produces a toxic product
- To understand that exercise is limited by the build-up of lactic acid

How muscles contract

Muscles contract and pull on bones to move the skeleton. Muscles are collections of very long **muscle fibres**. A powerful microscope shows that each muscle fibre is made up of interlocking filaments of two different proteins called **actin** and **myosin**. When a nerve impulse arrives at a muscle fibre from a motor neurone, the actin and myosin filaments slide over each other and shorten the muscle fibre, as shown in the diagram below. When lots of fibres shorten at the same time, the muscle contracts.

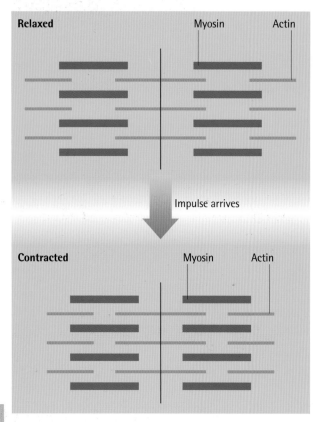

The actin and myosin filaments slide over each other and shorten the muscle when a nerve impulse is received.

Muscular work requires energy

Aerobic respiration

Work must be done to contract muscle. **The energy** for this comes from **aerobic respiration**. The equation shows how this energy is released:

$$\text{Glucose} + \text{oxygen} \rightarrow \text{energy} + \text{carbon dioxide} + \text{water}$$

The oxygen comes from the air. It is taken in at the lungs and carried around the body in the blood, pumped by the heart. Glucose comes from food digested in the gut, and is also carried in the blood. Muscles have extensive capillary beds to supply glucose and oxygen for respiration, and to carry away carbon dioxide. The blood also carries away heat that is produced during respiration.

Anaerobic respiration

When we work very hard our muscles use up a lot of energy. The heart and lungs, even working flat out, cannot supply enough oxygen to provide this energy by aerobic respiration. Muscles can release energy from food without using oxygen, by a process called **anaerobic respiration**:

$$\text{Glucose} \rightarrow \text{energy} + \text{lactic acid}$$

Anaerobic respiration has two drawbacks:

- It gives only about one-twentieth of the energy per glucose molecule that aerobic respiration yields.
- Lactic acid is poisonous – if it builds up in the cells it inhibits muscular contraction, which leads to fatigue and, eventually, death.

This harmful lactic acid is carried out of the muscles in the blood. It is transported around the body to the heart, liver and kidneys where it is oxidised to **pyruvate**, which can be used to release energy by aerobic respiration. The heart, the liver and the kidneys will need extra oxygen to get rid of this lactic acid, provided by the deep fast breathing that follows hard exercise. This extra oxygen is the **oxygen debt**.

Movement

The diagram below shows the part played by aerobic and anaerobic respiration during rest, exercise and recovery.

Rest – all respiration is aerobic. Normal breathing and heart rates can supply the tissues with all the oxygen they need.
Glucose + oxygen → energy + carbon dioxide + water

Heart rate
70 beats per minute

Breathing
15 breaths per minute

Hard exercise – respiration is mainly anaerobic. Very high breathing and heart rates still cannot provide the muscles with enough oxygen for aerobic respiration.
Glucose → energy + lactic acid

Heart rate
140 beats per minute

Breathing
50 breaths per minute

The muscles are getting energy without 'paying' for it with oxygen. They are running up an **oxygen debt**.

Recovery – paying off the oxygen debt. The breathing and heart rates remain high, even though the muscles are at rest. The extra oxygen is used to convert the lactic acid into carbon dioxide and water, paying off the oxygen debt.

Heart rate
140 beats per minute falling to normal after some minutes

Breathing
50 breaths per minute falling to normal after some minutes

Panting and rapid heartbeat continue until the lactic acid has been removed. Physically fit people recover faster.

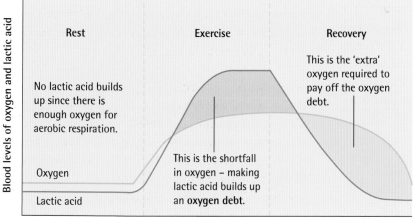

Blood levels of oxygen and lactic acid

Rest — No lactic acid builds up since there is enough oxygen for aerobic respiration.

Exercise

This is the shortfall in oxygen – making lactic acid builds up an **oxygen debt**.

Recovery

This is the 'extra' oxygen required to pay off the oxygen debt.

Oxygen

Lactic acid

Time (min)

Trained athletes can exercise for longer than confirmed couch potatoes before they build up an oxygen debt.

The last 50–60 m of a 400 m race are fuelled completely by anaerobic respiration, building up an oxygen debt.

1 The concentration of lactic acid (lactate) in the blood of a runner was measured at intervals before, during and after she ran for 10 minutes. The results are shown in the table below.

Time (minutes)	Concentration of lactic acid (arbitrary units)
0	18
10	18
15	56
25	88
35	42
50	21
65	18

a Plot this information in the form of a graph.

b What was the lactic acid concentration at the end of the run?

c For how long did the concentration of lactic acid increase after the end of the run?

d Why did the blood still contain lactic acid after the run?

e In which tissues was the lactic acid produced?

f How long after the run was it before the oxygen debt was paid off?

7·4 Moving through the air

Objectives
- To know how birds are adapted for flight
- To understand the importance of feathers as an aid to flight
- To understand the mechanism of flight

The air is not very dense, so it offers little support to an organism moving through it. Birds are well adapted to move through the air. They have:

- large **wings** with **feathers** which provide a large surface of the correct shape to provide **lift**
- a **light skeleton** and a **streamlined shape**
- powerful **flight muscles** and efficient **muscle–bone machines** to move their wings.

Feathers and wings

Flying demands a great deal of energy. Feathers provide thermal insulation, so the bird can keep its body temperature high (muscles work more efficiently when they are warm) without losing too much heat to the environment. Birds are **endothermic** (see page 112), and keep their body temperature steady at around 41 °C. The features of feathers, particularly their arrangement in the wings, are described in the diagram opposite.

Bones and muscles

The large surface area of the wing is due to the long flight feathers, and to the extended bones of the forelimb. Adaptations of the bird's skeleton to flight are shown in the diagram below.

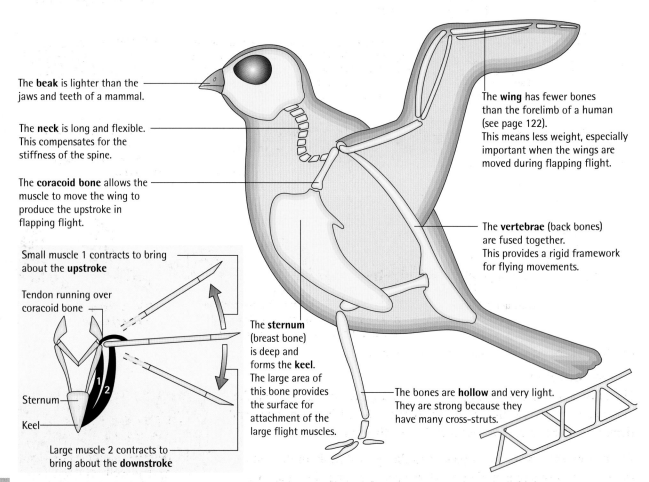

The **beak** is lighter than the jaws and teeth of a mammal.

The **neck** is long and flexible. This compensates for the stiffness of the spine.

The **coracoid bone** allows the muscle to move the wing to produce the upstroke in flapping flight.

The **wing** has fewer bones than the forelimb of a human (see page 122). This means less weight, especially important when the wings are moved during flapping flight.

The **vertebrae** (back bones) are fused together. This provides a rigid framework for flying movements.

Small muscle 1 contracts to bring about the **upstroke**

Tendon running over coracoid bone

Sternum

Keel

Large muscle 2 contracts to bring about the **downstroke**

The **sternum** (breast bone) is deep and forms the **keel**. The large area of this bone provides the surface for attachment of the large flight muscles.

The bones are **hollow** and very light. They are strong because they have many cross-struts.

The skeleton of a bird shows many adaptations to flight. The flight muscles can make up to 20% of a bird's weight – they form the 'breast' meat of a chicken or turkey. A large muscle provides the powerful downstroke, and a smaller muscle gives the upstroke.

Movement

Feathers and wings are adapted for flight. The wing provides an enormous surface area to lift the bird against the force of gravity pulling it down towards the ground.

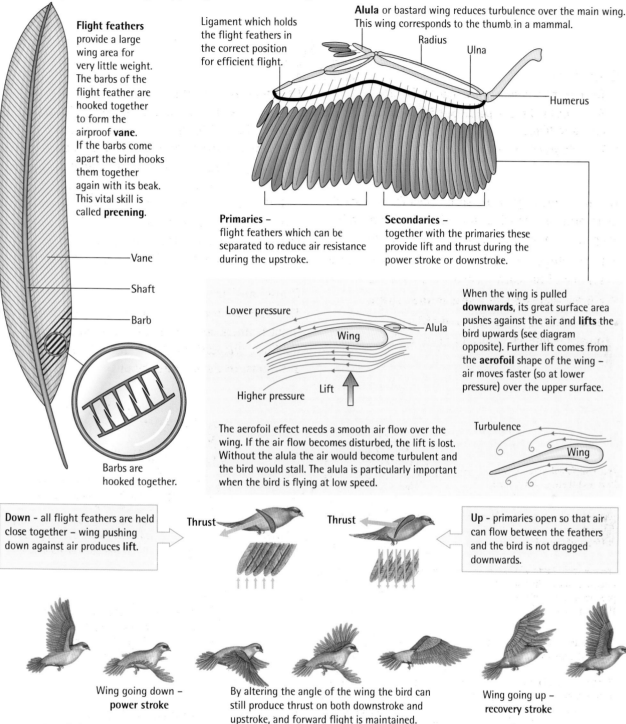

Flight feathers provide a large wing area for very little weight. The barbs of the flight feather are hooked together to form the airproof **vane**. If the barbs come apart the bird hooks them together again with its beak. This vital skill is called **preening**.

Vane

Shaft

Barb

Barbs are hooked together.

Alula or bastard wing reduces turbulence over the main wing. This wing corresponds to the thumb in a mammal.

Ligament which holds the flight feathers in the correct position for efficient flight.

Radius

Ulna

Humerus

Primaries – flight feathers which can be separated to reduce air resistance during the upstroke.

Secondaries – together with the primaries these provide lift and thrust during the power stroke or downstroke.

Lower pressure

Wing

Alula

Lift

Higher pressure

When the wing is pulled **downwards**, its great surface area pushes against the air and **lifts** the bird upwards (see diagram opposite). Further lift comes from the **aerofoil** shape of the wing – air moves faster (so at lower pressure) over the upper surface.

The aerofoil effect needs a smooth air flow over the wing. If the air flow becomes disturbed, the lift is lost. Without the alula the air would become turbulent and the bird would stall. The alula is particularly important when the bird is flying at low speed.

Turbulence

Wing

Down - all flight feathers are held close together – wing pushing down against air produces **lift**.

Thrust

Thrust

Up - primaries open so that air can flow between the feathers and the bird is not dragged downwards.

Wing going down – **power stroke**

By altering the angle of the wing the bird can still produce thrust on both downstroke and upstroke, and forward flight is maintained.

Wing going up – **recovery stroke**

Bird flight has alternating power strokes and recovery strokes.

Flying techniques

The most obvious type of flight is called **flapping flight**, in which the bird moves the wings up and down to generate **lift** (upward force) and **thrust** (forwards force), as outlined in the diagram above.

The **downstroke** is the main **power stroke**, providing both lift and thrust. The **upstroke** is more of a **recovery**, returning the wing to a position ready for another downstroke. Some birds can also use the upstroke to provide thrust, by changing the angle of the wing.

1 List three adaptations of birds to flight.

2 Describe how wings can generate both lift and thrust during flight.

Movement

7·5 Moving through water

Objectives
- To understand why movement in water causes some difficulties
- To understand how fish are adapted for movement in water
- To know how some unicells move through water

Water is very much more dense than air, so it is more difficult for an organism to push its way through water than it is through air. On the other hand, the water offers more support than air for the organism's body, and something firm to push against. Water is a suitable environment for many organisms (see page 8). They have developed a number of ways of moving through the water.

Fish

Fish are highly adapted to movement through water – indeed they cannot live in any other environment. They have:

- a streamlined shape to reduce water resistance
- a broad tail and tailfin to push the fish through the water
- additional fins to prevent unwanted movement
- a swim bladder to control vertical movement
- an arrangement of muscles and a flexible backbone that allow the fish to push its tail against the water.

The adaptations of fish to swimming are explained in the diagram below.

Fish show many adaptations to moving through water.

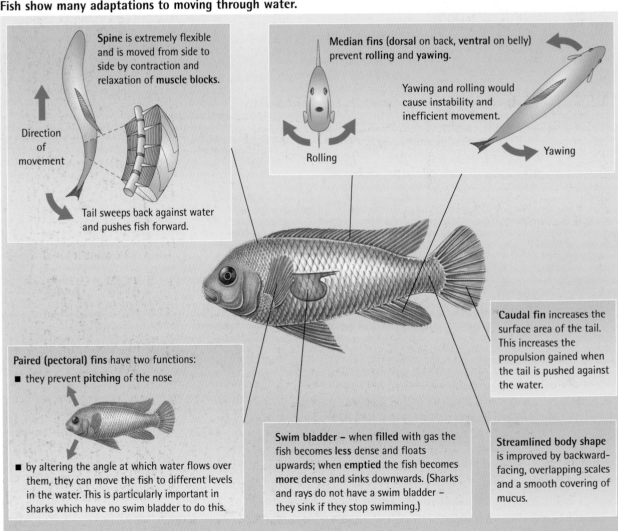

Spine is extremely flexible and is moved from side to side by contraction and relaxation of **muscle blocks**.

Direction of movement

Tail sweeps back against water and pushes fish forward.

Median fins (**dorsal** on back, **ventral** on belly) prevent **rolling** and **yawing**.

Yawing and rolling would cause instability and inefficient movement.

Rolling

Yawing

Caudal fin increases the surface area of the tail. This increases the propulsion gained when the tail is pushed against the water.

Paired (pectoral) fins have two functions:
- they prevent **pitching** of the nose
- by altering the angle at which water flows over them, they can move the fish to different levels in the water. This is particularly important in sharks which have no swim bladder to do this.

Swim bladder – when filled with gas the fish becomes **less** dense and floats upwards; when **emptied** the fish becomes **more** dense and sinks downwards. (Sharks and rays do not have a swim bladder – they sink if they stop swimming.)

Streamlined body shape is improved by backward-facing, overlapping scales and a smooth covering of mucus.

Unicellular organisms

An enormous number of unicells (single-celled organisms) live in water. A few examples, and the methods that they use for movement, are described in the diagrams.

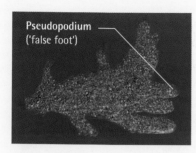

Pseudopodium ('false foot') – the cytoplasm inside the *Amoeba* can flow into the bulge at the front of the animal. It is rather like toothpaste being squeezed along its tube. In this way the animal 'oozes' very slowly from place to place.

Amoeba (×1000)

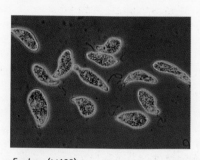

Flagellum – can beat with a whip-like motion against the water and move the *Euglena* rather erratically from place to place

Euglena (×100)

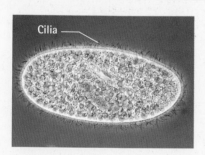

Cilia on the surface of the *Paramecium* beat with a rhythm which drives the animal through the water. The cilia are held stiffly, rather like oars, on the power stroke and then allowed to relax on the recovery stroke.

Paramecium (×225)

1 **a** Why is it difficult to move through water?
   b What feature of water aids movement through it?

2 How does the movement of *Euglena* differ from that of *Amoeba*?

3 Copy and complete the following paragraph.
Fish show many adaptations to movement through water. The body has a _____ shape, and _____ which face backwards to reduce resistance. The body is muscular and the flexibility of the _____ allows side-to-side movement. This side-to-side movement causes the _____ to propel the fish through the water. The fish remains stable because of the presence of _____, for example the _____ prevent pitching and the _____ prevent yawing and rolling. Finally the _____ can be filled with air to provide buoyancy.

Something fishy – evolving in water

During the evolution of animal life, many animal types have lived in water. The problem for them has always been the same – water is a very dense medium to swim through. It should be no surprise that the same solution to this problem has appeared many times in the history of living things. The ichthyosaur (a marine dinosaur), dolphin, shark and seal all have very similar streamlined shapes with flattened structures to drive them through the water in the most stable way.

This situation, with a number of organisms from different classification groups showing similar shapes and structures, is called **convergent evolution**.

7·6 Questions on movement

1 Heating a bone to about 250 °C in an oven removes protein from the bone. The protein is burned to oxides of carbon, sulphur and nitrogen. Immersing a bone in hydrochloric acid (HCl) for 24 hours removes inorganic substances from the bone. The minerals form soluble salts in the acid.

a Which minerals are required for bone formation?

b Which organic molecule forms about 50% of bone structure?

c How can you tell that a bone is a living structure?

d Several students were investigating the composition of bone, using both heating and immersion in HCl. They obtained the following results.

Type of bone	Treatment	Mass before (g)	Mass after (g)	Percentage change in mass
Chicken	Heating	18.2	9.8	
Chicken	Immersion in HCl	16.4	8.7	
Turkey	Heating	22.4	11.9	
Turkey	Immersion in HCl	20.0	9.6	
Lamb	Heating	23.0	13.0	
Lamb	Immersion in HCl	22.8	10.0	
Rabbit	Heating	21.4	12.0	
Rabbit	Immersion in HCl	21.4	9.4	

i Copy and complete the table by adding the data for percentage change in mass.

ii Calculate the average proportion of mineral material in the samples of bones tested.

2 The photo shows an X-ray picture of a human elbow.

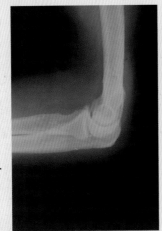

a Why do the bones show up more clearly than the surrounding tissues?

b Sketch the photograph and draw on it a flexor muscle, and a tendon attached to the muscle.

c Explain how antagonistic muscles work to bend the arm at the elbow.

d Name one other human joint in which the movement is similar to that of the elbow.

3 a Name two substances whose concentration would increase in a muscle as it contracts repeatedly.

b Name two substances, essential to a muscle for its repeated contraction, which are delivered to it by the bloodstream.

New body parts

A recent operation on a damaged thumb has given hope for the replacement of many damaged or diseased body parts. A factory worker in the USA had crushed the tip of his thumb. The severed thumb was temporarily attached to the patient's chest to keep the skin alive. Surgeons then built a framework for the damaged part, using sea coral carved into the correct shape. The coral is honeycombed with tiny channels, and was filled with a mixture of calcium alginate and some bone cells taken from the patient's arm. The calcium alginate, a chemical from seaweed, is a growth medium for the bone cells and the coral was chosen because it slowly breaks down naturally.

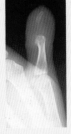

The bone cells start to grow in the coral.

The recreated thumb.

The research workers who carried out this operation have already grown and transplanted more than 20 body parts in laboratory animals, including blood vessels, heart valves, tendons and ligaments. Their work first hit the headlines when they grew and transplanted the cartilage of an ear onto a mouse. The benefits of using laboratory animals for growing tissues such as these are that:

- the new tissue can be grown in very carefully controlled conditions
- the immune system of a mouse can be suppressed to prevent rejection
- if the tissue can be grown on the mouse, it should also grow on another mammal.

One of the team now believes that they have the experience and knowledge to try more human experiments.

A human ear transplanted onto a mouse.

4 Read the text box on the left.

a Transplanting the body's own cells gives one great advantage. What is it?

b Tendons and ligaments seem particularly straightforward to grow and transplant. How could this be an advantage to sports men and women?

c Why is it important that the growth medium contains calcium?

d The growth medium also contains a source of energy. Why is this important?

5 Copy and complete the following paragraph.

Air is not very dense, and so does not give much _____ to organisms moving through it. Birds are very well adapted to moving through the air – they have a _____ skeleton to reduce the effects of gravity, _____ which provide insulation and _____ with a large surface area, and powerful flight muscles. These muscles are attached at one end to an extension of the breast bone called the _____. The bigger of the two muscles contracts to pull the wing _____ and the smaller of the two muscles operates over a pulley system to pull the wing _____. The wings flap through a cycle of power stroke, which provides both _____ and _____, and recovery stroke. During the recovery stroke the _____ flight feathers are separated to limit the tendency of the bird to be pushed downwards.

6 Look at the pictures below. Flapping flight demands a great deal of energy, but there are alternative energy-saving methods of flight. Gliding and soaring is a very economical method of flying. Once the bird is in the air, the aerofoil shape of its wings means that it can glide in the air for some time without flapping its wings. This is particularly important for large, heavy birds that find flapping flight very difficult. Some large birds cannot even get off the ground with flapping flight, and just launch themselves into the air from cliffs or very tall trees. Large birds of prey such as _____ glide and soar, making use of upcurrents of air caused by heat _____. Sea birds such as the _____ take advantage of upcurrents as the air rises at a cliff.

These are energy-saving forms of flight available for large birds

Large birds of prey use **thermals**. These are spiral columns of warm air caused by the uneven heating of the land beneath them, e.g. **buzzard**.

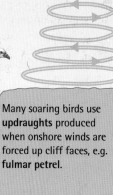

Fastest windspeed about 15 m above sea surface

Bird now rides in fastest windstream, e.g. **albatross**.

Many soaring birds use **updraughts** produced when onshore winds are forced up cliff faces, e.g. **fulmar petrel**.

Momentum is used to regain height.

Bird glides downwards, gaining momentum.

Slowest windspeed because of friction between air and surface of sea.

Reproduction

Objectives
- To define the term 'sexual reproduction'
- To know the steps involved in sexual reproduction
- To describe the human reproductive systems

Reproduction may be sexual or asexual. In **sexual reproduction**, genetic information from two parents combines to produce a new individual. Humans, like all other mammals, only use sexual reproduction. Sexual reproduction produces individuals that are different from each other. The process involves a number of stages, as shown in the diagram below.

The male reproductive system
The male reproductive system has two functions:
- to manufacture the male gametes
- to deliver them to the site of fertilisation.

The male gametes, called **spermatozoa**, or **sperm** for short, are manufactured in the **testes**. These are enclosed in a sac of skin, the **scrotum**, which hangs outside the body between the legs. This position helps protect the testes from physical damage, and more importantly keeps them at a temperature

2–3 °C lower than body temperature, ideal for development of the sperm. The sperm are delivered inside the female body through a series of tubes that eventually release the sperm from the tip of the **penis**. The male reproductive system lies very close to the part of the excretory system that removes urine from the body; indeed the urethra is a tube used to expel urine and seminal fluid from the body. A valve prevents this happening at the same time! The two systems together are called the **urinogenital system**. The male reproductive system, is shown in the diagram opposite.

The female reproductive system
In addition to producing female gametes, the female reproductive system receives male gametes. It provides a site for fertilisation and for the development of the zygote. The female gametes, called **ova**, are produced one at a time by the two **ovaries**. The ovum travels along the **oviduct** or **Fallopian tube** towards the **uterus**. It may be fertilised while in the oviduct. The zygote grows and develops into a baby in the uterus. The female reproductive system is shown in the diagram opposite.

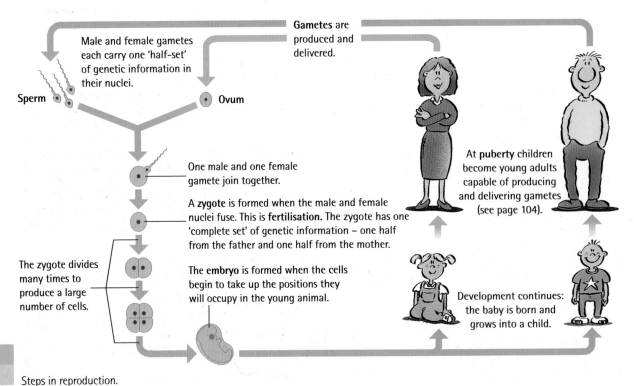

Male and female gametes each carry one 'half-set' of genetic information in their nuclei.

Gametes are produced and delivered.

Sperm

Ovum

One male and one female gamete join together.

A **zygote** is formed when the male and female nuclei fuse. This is **fertilisation**. The zygote has one 'complete set' of genetic information – one half from the father and one half from the mother.

The zygote divides many times to produce a large number of cells.

The **embryo** is formed when the cells begin to take up the positions they will occupy in the young animal.

At **puberty** children become young adults capable of producing and delivering gametes (see page 104).

Development continues: the baby is born and grows into a child.

Steps in reproduction.

The male urinogenital system.

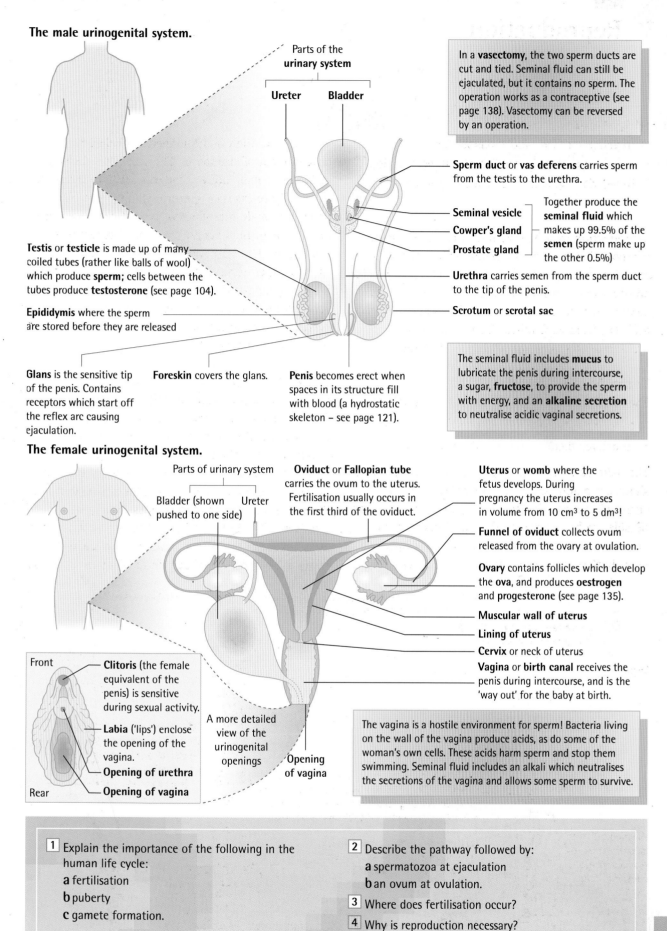

Parts of the urinary system

Ureter   **Bladder**

In a **vasectomy**, the two sperm ducts are cut and tied. Seminal fluid can still be ejaculated, but it contains no sperm. The operation works as a contraceptive (see page 138). Vasectomy can be reversed by an operation.

Sperm duct or **vas deferens** carries sperm from the testis to the urethra.

Seminal vesicle
Cowper's gland
Prostate gland

Together produce the **seminal fluid** which makes up 99.5% of the **semen** (sperm make up the other 0.5%)

Urethra carries semen from the sperm duct to the tip of the penis.

Scrotum or **scrotal sac**

Testis or **testicle** is made up of many coiled tubes (rather like balls of wool) which produce **sperm**; cells between the tubes produce **testosterone** (see page 104).

Epididymis where the sperm are stored before they are released

Glans is the sensitive tip of the penis. Contains receptors which start off the reflex arc causing ejaculation.

Foreskin covers the glans.

Penis becomes erect when spaces in its structure fill with blood (a hydrostatic skeleton – see page 121).

The seminal fluid includes **mucus** to lubricate the penis during intercourse, a sugar, **fructose**, to provide the sperm with energy, and an **alkaline secretion** to neutralise acidic vaginal secretions.

The female urinogenital system.

Parts of urinary system

Bladder (shown pushed to one side)   Ureter

Oviduct or **Fallopian tube** carries the ovum to the uterus. Fertilisation usually occurs in the first third of the oviduct.

Uterus or **womb** where the fetus develops. During pregnancy the uterus increases in volume from 10 cm³ to 5 dm³!

Funnel of oviduct collects ovum released from the ovary at ovulation.

Ovary contains follicles which develop the **ova**, and produces **oestrogen** and **progesterone** (see page 135).

Muscular wall of uterus
Lining of uterus
Cervix or neck of uterus
Vagina or **birth canal** receives the penis during intercourse, and is the 'way out' for the baby at birth.

Front

Clitoris (the female equivalent of the penis) is sensitive during sexual activity.

Labia ('lips') enclose the opening of the vagina.

Opening of urethra

Opening of vagina

Rear

A more detailed view of the urinogenital openings

Opening of vagina

The vagina is a hostile environment for sperm! Bacteria living on the wall of the vagina produce acids, as do some of the woman's own cells. These acids harm sperm and stop them swimming. Seminal fluid includes an alkali which neutralises the secretions of the vagina and allows some sperm to survive.

1 Explain the importance of the following in the human life cycle:
   a fertilisation
   b puberty
   c gamete formation.

2 Describe the pathway followed by:
   a spermatozoa at ejaculation
   b an ovum at ovulation.

3 Where does fertilisation occur?

4 Why is reproduction necessary?

Reproduction

8·2 The menstrual cycle

The testes produce sperm continually at a rate of about 100 000 000 per day from puberty to old age. Women produce only one ovum per month during their reproductive life, from puberty to middle age. The two ovaries take it in turns to produce an ovum, and one ovary releases a mature female gamete every 28 days. The cycle of producing and releasing mature ova is called the **menstrual cycle** (from the Latin word *menstrua* meaning month).

The menstrual cycle is a long-term process controlled by a number of hormones, which:

- prepare the uterus to receive any fertilised ova
- control the development of mature ova.

Hormones affect the wall of the uterus
During the menstrual cycle the wall of the uterus goes through four phases, under the influence of two hormones, **oestrogen** and **progesterone**. During the first phase, which lasts about five days, the lining of the uterus is shed, accompanied by a loss of blood. This time is a woman's **period**, or more correctly the **menstrual phase** or **menstruation**. The other phases of the cycle prepare the uterus to receive and protect a zygote, and are shown in the diagram below.

4 Premenstrual phase
The uterus lining degenerates as the **progesterone** concentration starts to *fall* **unless embryo implantation** has occurred, in which case **progesterone** (from the corpus luteum) keeps the lining intact to begin pregnancy.

In humans the cycles of the two ovaries are out of phase. **Each ovary** ovulates every 56 days but **each woman** ovulates every 28 days.

1 Menstruation
The uterus lining is shed, and blood and fragments of tissue leave the body through the vagina. Menstruation is triggered by a *decrease* in the concentration of **progesterone**.

Blood is lost during menstruation and needs to be replaced during the repair phase. Menstruating women therefore have a high requirement for **iron** in their diet. If this requirement is not met they can become **anaemic**.

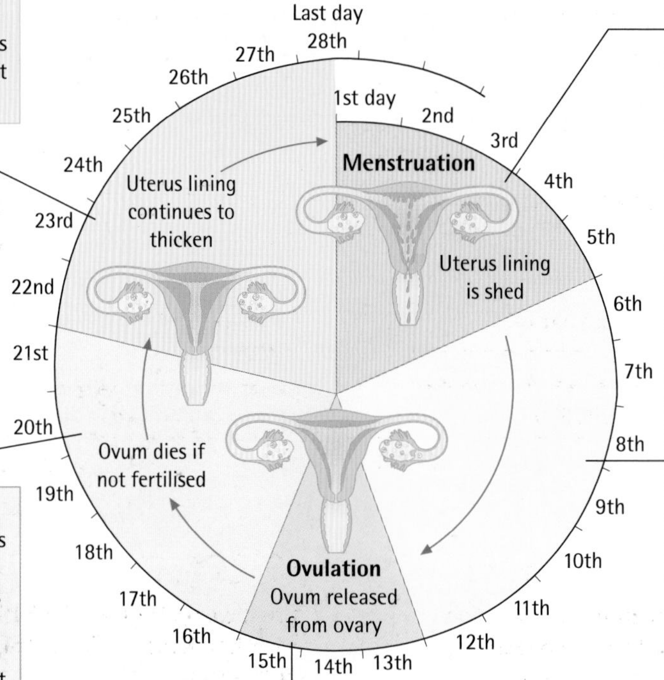

Last day
28th
27th
26th
25th
24th
23rd
22nd
21st
20th
19th
18th
17th
16th
15th 14th 13th
12th
11th
10th
9th
8th
7th
6th
5th
4th
3rd
2nd
1st day

Uterus lining continues to thicken

Menstruation

Uterus lining is shed

Ovum dies if not fertilised

Ovulation
Ovum released from ovary

2 Repair phase
More blood vessels grow in the lining of the uterus, and the lining thickens and becomes more stable. These changes are triggered by an *increase* in the concentration of **oestrogen**.

3 Receptive phase
The lining of the uterus and its blood vessels are now well developed. If fertilisation has occurred the embryo can become buried or **implanted** in this lining. This optimum set of conditions for implantation remains for 6–7 days after ovulation, and is maintained by an *increasing* concentration of **progesterone**.

Following the development of a Graafian follicle (see top of next page), an ovum (egg) is released into the oviduct. **Ovulation** occurs at the *peak* of **oestrogen** concentration and is triggered by a hormone from the pituitary gland.

The release of the ovum is accompanied by a slight increase in body temperature – some women are actually aware of the moment of ovulation.

Reproduction

Hormones control the development of ova

The ova develop from cells lining the ovary. This is triggered by follicle stimulating hormone (FSH) released from the pituitary gland. FSH causes a special cell in the ovary to produce a sac around itself. The fluid-filled sac and the developing ovum inside it are together called a **Graafian follicle**. Once the follicle is mature, and there is a high concentration of oestrogen, it moves to the surface of the ovary and bursts, releasing the ovum into the funnel of the oviduct. This process is called **ovulation**. The remaining cells of the Graafian follicle become a structure known as the **corpus luteum**, which produces the hormone progesterone. This hormone keeps the wall of the uterus in good condition for the development of a zygote if implantation has occurred. It also prevents FSH secretion which prevents the release of any more mature ova by feedback inhibition. This ensures that only one fertilised ovum develops in the uterus at any one time. The processes taking place in the uterus and the ovary and their control by hormones are summarised in the diagram below.

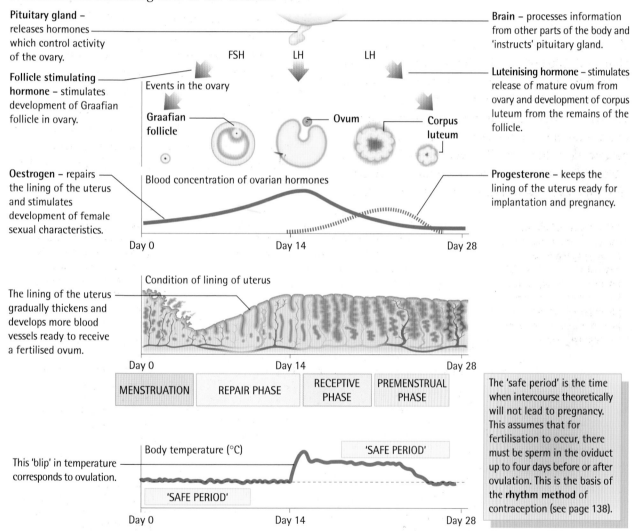

Pituitary gland – releases hormones which control activity of the ovary.

Follicle stimulating hormone – stimulates development of Graafian follicle in ovary.

Oestrogen – repairs the lining of the uterus and stimulates development of female sexual characteristics.

Brain – processes information from other parts of the body and 'instructs' pituitary gland.

Luteinising hormone – stimulates release of mature ovum from ovary and development of corpus luteum from the remains of the follicle.

Progesterone – keeps the lining of the uterus ready for implantation and pregnancy.

FSH   LH   LH

Events in the ovary

Graafian follicle   Ovum   Corpus luteum

Blood concentration of ovarian hormones

Day 0   Day 14   Day 28

The lining of the uterus gradually thickens and develops more blood vessels ready to receive a fertilised ovum.

Condition of lining of uterus

Day 0   Day 14   Day 28

| MENSTRUATION | REPAIR PHASE | RECEPTIVE PHASE | PREMENSTRUAL PHASE |

This 'blip' in temperature corresponds to ovulation.

Body temperature (°C)   'SAFE PERIOD'

'SAFE PERIOD'

Day 0   Day 14   Day 28

The 'safe period' is the time when intercourse theoretically will not lead to pregnancy. This assumes that for fertilisation to occur, there must be sperm in the oviduct up to four days before or after ovulation. This is the basis of the **rhythm method** of contraception (see page 138).

---

1 Define the terms **menstruation** and **ovulation**. What is the link between these processes?

2 Describe the role of the hormones FSH, LH, oestrogen and progesterone in the control of the menstrual cycle.

3 Use the term **feedback inhibition** to explain why contraceptive pills contain the hormone progesterone.

4 a List the phases of the menstrual cycle.
  b How long does the cycle last?
  c At what time in the cycle does ovulation occur?

8·3 Copulation and conception

Objectives
- To understand the difference between copulation and conception
- To describe the events of fertilisation
- To describe the processes of *in vitro* fertilisation and artificial insemination by donor
- To understand some of the moral and ethical questions posed by human intervention in reproductive processes

Ovulation provides a female gamete

During ovulation each month, an ovum is released from one of the ovaries. The ovum moves slowly along the oviduct towards the uterus. This movement is brought about by:

- **peristalsis** – rhythmic contractions of muscles in the wall of the oviduct
- **cilia** – fine hair-like structures on the lining of the oviduct which sweep the ovum along.

Sexual intercourse or copulation delivers male gametes to the female reproductive system.

It takes 4–7 days for the ovum to reach the uterus, and during this time fertilisation may take place in the oviduct (see below).

Copulation delivers male gametes

Before intercourse, sexual stimulation causes blood to flow into the man's penis. The penis becomes erect and hard enough to enter the woman's vagina (helped by lubricating fluids released by the walls of the vagina). This is called **copulation** or **sexual intercourse**. The rubbing of the tip of the penis (the **glans**) against the wall of the vagina sets off a reflex action that releases stored sperm from the testes, and squeezes them by peristalsis along the sperm ducts and the urethra. As the sperm pass along these tubes, seminal fluid is added to them and the complete **semen** is ejaculated in spurts from the tip of the penis. About 3 or 4 cm³ of semen is ejaculated, and this contains about 300 000 000 sperm. The diagram below illustrates how the male and female gametes arrive at the same place.

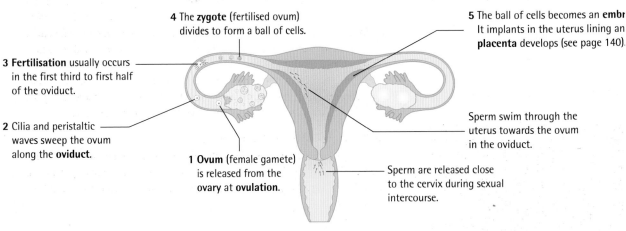

3 Fertilisation usually occurs in the first third to first half of the oviduct.

4 The **zygote** (fertilised ovum) divides to form a ball of cells.

5 The ball of cells becomes an **embr**[yo]. It implants in the uterus lining an[d] **placenta** develops (see page 140).

2 Cilia and peristaltic waves sweep the ovum along the **oviduct**.

1 Ovum (female gamete) is released from the **ovary** at **ovulation**.

Sperm swim through the uterus towards the ovum in the oviduct.

Sperm are released close to the cervix during sexual intercourse.

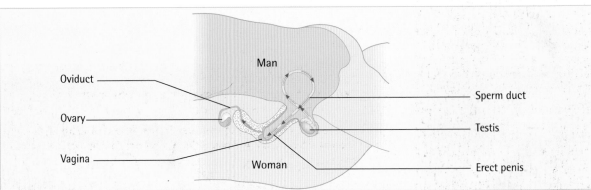

Oviduct

Ovary

Vagina

Man

Woman

Sperm duct

Testis

Erect penis

1 Sperm swim towards ovum.

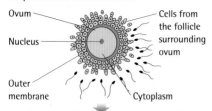

Ovum · Cells from the follicle surrounding ovum · Nucleus · Outer membrane · Cytoplasm

2 Remaining follicle cells are scattered by sperm.

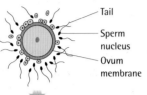

Tail · Sperm nucleus · Ovum membrane

3 One sperm passes through the outer membrane. A barrier forms to prevent entry of more than one sperm.

4 Head of sperm crosses ovum cell membrane.

5 Sperm nucleus and ovum nucleus fuse at fertilisation. A zygote has been formed.

Fertilisation is the fusion of ovum and sperm.

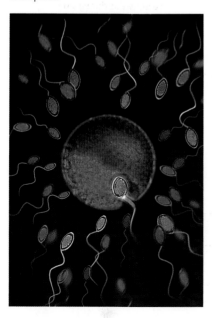

Fertilisation is the fusion of ovum and sperm

Fertilisation is the joining together (fusion) of an ovum and a sperm. The new cell contains a set of genetic material from the mother and a set from the father. Fertilisation takes place in the oviduct, and although several hundred sperm may reach the ovum, only one of them will penetrate the membrane that surrounds it. Once this has happened a series of changes takes place:

- The ovum membrane alters to form a barrier to the entry of other sperm.
- The head of the sperm (the male nucleus) moves towards the nucleus of the ovum and the two fuse (join together).
- The fertilised ovum or **zygote** now starts to divide, first into two cells, then into four, and so on. It continues to move towards the uterus.

The events of fertilisation are summarised in the diagram opposite.

Conception is the implantation of the ball of cells

About six days after fertilisation the ball of cells, now called an **embryo**, becomes embedded in the thickened lining of the uterus. **Conception**, the beginning of the development of a new individual, takes place when this embedding or **implantation** is complete. Once the embryo is attached to the lining of the uterus, some of its outer cells combine with some of the mother's cells and a **placenta** begins to develop.

Infertility treatment

In vitro fertilisation (IVF)

The term *in vitro* means 'in glass', and is used to describe a procedure that takes place outside the body in some form of laboratory glassware. In *in vitro* fertilisation, an ovum is fertilised outside a woman's body in a special kind of dish (not a test tube, although the technique is sometimes called 'test-tube fertilisation'). The fertilised ovum is placed in the woman's uterus to develop. This procedure is used to treat couples who are unable to conceive. For example, a woman's oviducts may be blocked, preventing sperm reaching the ovum, or making it difficult for a fertilised ovum to get to the uterus.

Artificial insemination by donor (AID)

If a couple is unable to conceive naturally due to a problem with the man's sperm, they may try AID. Sperm from a donor is obtained from a sperm bank (where it is stored) and is inserted into the woman's uterus close to her time of ovulation.

1 Define the terms conception, copulation and fertilisation. In what order do these events occur?

2 It is possible for humans to intervene in the process of reproduction. Suggest how IVF and AID raise ethical problems for the medical profession.

8·4 Contraception

Objectives
- To define contraception
- To know about different methods of contraception
- To evaluate the effectiveness of different methods of contraception

Preventing pregnancy

Contraception (which literally means 'against conceiving') is defined as 'deliberately preventing pregnancy'. It is quite natural for two people who love each other to want to have intercourse (to 'make love' or 'have sex'). However, they may not want to have a baby. Using contraception allows a couple to choose when to have children and is an essential part of **family planning**.

Contraception may depend on:

- an understanding of the body's natural cycles (e.g. the **rhythm method**)
- a physical barrier between ovum and sperm (e.g. the **condom**)
- a chemical (e.g. a **pill**, or a **spermicide**)
- a surgical procedure (e.g. **vasectomy**).

The rhythm method: natural contraception

Couples who use the rhythm method avoid having intercourse during the **fertile period**. Instead they wait for the **safe period**, when fertilisation is unlikely to result. The diagram on page 135 shows the safe period. There are several methods of working out the time of ovulation:

- **Calendar method** – the time of ovulation is calculated after keeping a record of when the last six or more periods started.
- **Temperature method** – the woman measures her body temperature and looks for changes at ovulation.
- **Mucus method** – the woman notes changes that take place in the mucus lining of the vagina and cervix at ovulation.

The table opposite shows that the rhythm method is not very reliable. However, it is acceptable for religious groups opposed to artificial methods of contraceptiom.

Male contraceptive methods

There are three methods of contraception for men:

- **Withdrawal (coitus interruptus)** – the penis is withdrawn from the vagina before ejaculation. This method is unreliable as small amounts of semen can leak out before the ejaculation.
- **Vasectomy** – the sperm ducts are cut or tied in a surgical operation (see page 133).
- **Condom or sheath** – this is a thin rubber covering that is fitted over the erect penis before intercourse. It prevents sperm being released into the vagina, and also protects against sexually transmitted diseases (see page 293).

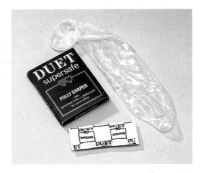

The condom or sheath is unrolled over the erect penis, and semen is collected in the end.

Female contraceptive methods

The main methods of contraception used by women are shown in the diagram opposite.

Which method is best?

Choosing a method of contraception depends on a number of factors, including age, religious belief and whether a long- or short-term method is required. The table compares the failure rates of the different methods in the form of HWY, the number of pregnancies likely if a hundred women used the same method for one year.

Method of contraception	Failure rate (HWY)
No method used	54
Rhythm method	15
Condom	8–10
Diaphragm with spermicide	2–3
IUD	1
Contraceptive pill	1
Female sterilisation	0
Vasectomy	0

Female sterilisation is difficult to reverse and should only be considered by couples who are sure that they do not want any more children.

Female sterilisation
The oviducts are tied and cut during an operation. Released ova cannot reach the part of the oviduct where sperm are present.
- A permanent method which is 100% reliable.

IUD (intrauterine device) or coil
This is a plastic-coated copper coil which may be left in the uterus for months or even for years. Strings attached to the lower end allow the coil to be removed via the vagina.
- Quite reliable, particularly for women who have already had children.
- Irritates the lining of the uterus so that implantation of the zygote does not occur.

A capsule inserted just beneath the skin can release progestogen over a 3 or 4 month period. This is useful for women who might forget to take the contraceptive pill.

The contraceptive pill
There are two kinds of contraceptive pill. The **mini-pill** contains **progestogen** (synthetic progesterone) which causes changes in the uterus lining so that implantation of a zygote is difficult. The **combined pill** contains **oestrogen** and **progestogen**, and prevents ovulation.
- Almost 100% reliable if used according to instructions.
- Diarrhoea or vomiting can remove the pill from the gut before it has been absorbed fully, reducing its effectiveness.

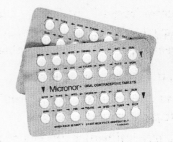

Spermicide
A chemical, applied as a cream, gel or foam, which kills sperm.
- Very unreliable on its own but makes barrier methods of contraception more effective.

Diaphragm or cap
A thin rubber barrier with a springy outer ring to ensure a close fit. Prevents sperm from entering the uterus.

- Very reliable if properly fitted and used with a spermicide.
- Correct size must be used – requires a trial fitting at a family planning clinic.
- Must be fitted before intercourse and remain in place for 6 hours afterwards.

Female condom or 'Femidom'
A thin sheath which lines the vagina, and prevents entry of sperm. The 'closed' end has a ring to make fitting easier, and the ring at the open end lies flat against the labia.

Morning-after contraception
These are pills used after intercourse has taken place. They are not for regular use, but a doctor might prescribe them if there is a risk of unwanted pregnancy which might lead to an abortion at a later date. The morning-after pill contains hormones which cause the uterus lining to be shed. It is taken 48–72 hours after intercourse. A **coil** fitted within 72–96 hours of intercourse usually prevents pregnancy as well.

Methods of contraception for women include physical, chemical and surgical methods.

1. List the methods of contraception mentioned on these two pages. Mark each one P, C or S for physical, chemical or surgical.

2. Which contraceptive method(s) might be suitable for a short-term relationship?

3. Why is sterilisation unsuitable for a short-term relationship?

4. Why do you think the rhythm method has such a high rate of failure?

8·5 Pregnancy: the role of the placenta

Objectives
- To know the sequence of events in the development of a baby
- to understand the role of the placenta

Growth and development

From the time of conception it takes about nine months, or 40 weeks, for a fertilised ovum to become a fully formed baby. This progress involves two closely linked processes:

- **growth** – the repeated division of the zygote to provide the many cells that make up the baby
- **development** – the organisation of the cells into tissues and organs.

During growth, the zygote divides into many identical cells – one zygote at conception becomes 30 million million cells at birth! This type of cell division is called **mitosis** (see page 194). Each cell also takes up its correct position in the embryo. The cells become organised into tissues (see page 21) and start to take on special functions such as nerve cells and skin cells.

A controlled environment

The time taken for the development of a baby from an implanted zygote is called the **gestation period**. The developing fetus needs a stable environment which is provided by the **placenta**, a structure that is only found in mammals. The placenta forms early in pregnancy, partly from the lining of the uterus, and partly from the outside cells of the developing embryo. The fetus is attached to the placenta by the **umbilical cord** as shown below. It is surrounded by the **amniotic sac** which is filled with **amniotic fluid**; this protects the fetus from knocks and bumps.

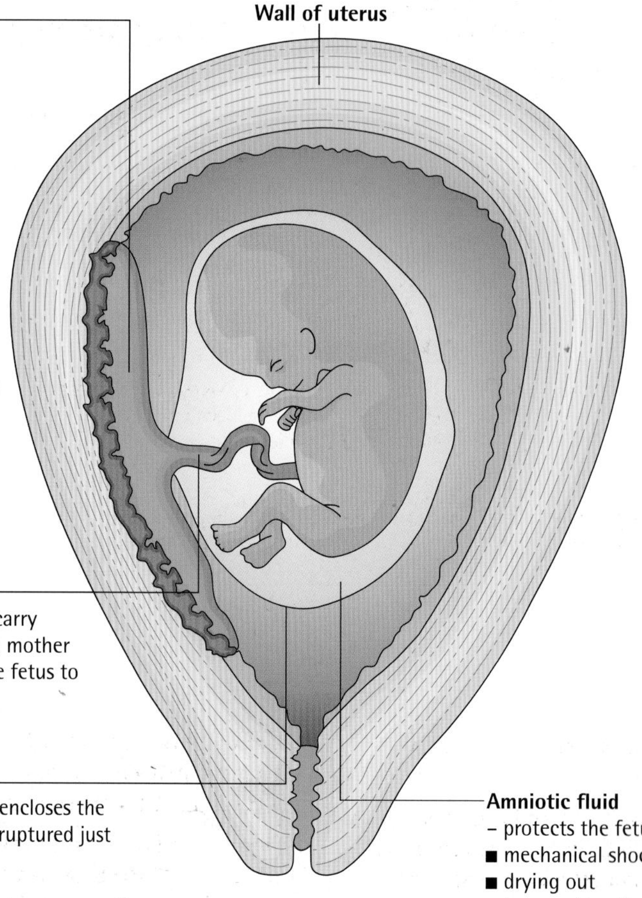

Placenta – this disc-shaped organ has a number of functions:
- exchange of soluble materials such as foods, wastes and oxygen between mother and fetus
- physical attachment of the fetus to the wall of the uterus
- protection
  (1) of fetus from mother's immune system
  (2) against dangerous fluctuations in mother's blood pressure
- secretion of hormones which maintain the lining of the uterus as the corpus luteum breaks down by the third month.

Umbilical cord – contains blood vessels which carry materials for exchange between mother and fetus. The cord connects the fetus to the placenta.

Amnion – the membrane that encloses the amniotic fluid. This is ruptured just before birth.

Wall of uterus

Amniotic fluid – protects the fetus against
- mechanical shock
- drying out
- temperature fluctuations.

Amniocentesis is a test to check for abnormalities of the fetus. A sample of amniotic fluid is collected in a syringe through the abdominal wall of the mother. The fluid contains cells from the fetus, which are cultured and then analysed. There is a risk of miscarriage following the test.
- The procedure is usually offered to older women because fetal abnormalities are more common in older mothers.
- The test gives information about chromosome mutation (e.g. Down's syndrome) and gene mutation (e.g. cystic fibrosis).
  Usually carried out at 16–18 weeks.

The placenta protects and nourishes the developing fetus.

Reproduction

The placenta begins to develop at implantation and after about 12 weeks it is a thick, disc-like structure with finger-like projections called **villi** that extend deep into the wall of the uterus. The placenta continues to grow to keep pace with the developing fetus and is about 15 cm across, weighing about 500 g, at the time of birth. After the baby has been born the placenta, amniotic sac and umbilical cord are expelled from the uterus as the **afterbirth**. The structure of the placenta, and some of its functions, are illustrated in the diagram below.

Exchange of materials across the placenta

At the placenta, materials are exchanged quickly and selectively between the mother's blood and that of the fetus to keep a constant internal environment inside the fetus. The placenta has adaptations that make this process efficient, as outlined in the diagram below. Towards the end of pregnancy, protective antibodies also cross the placenta so that the baby has some immunity to certain diseases.

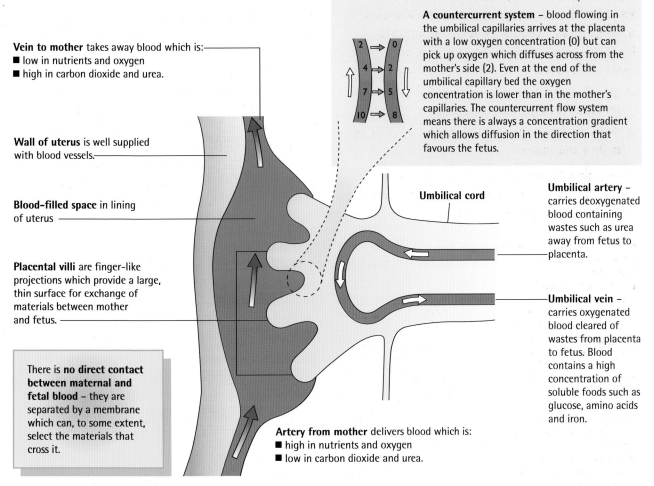

A countercurrent system – blood flowing in the umbilical capillaries arrives at the placenta with a low oxygen concentration (0) but can pick up oxygen which diffuses across from the mother's side (2). Even at the end of the umbilical capillary bed the oxygen concentration is lower than in the mother's capillaries. The countercurrent flow system means there is always a concentration gradient which allows diffusion in the direction that favours the fetus.

Vein to mother takes away blood which is:
■ low in nutrients and oxygen
■ high in carbon dioxide and urea.

Wall of uterus is well supplied with blood vessels.

Blood-filled space in lining of uterus

Placental villi are finger-like projections which provide a large, thin surface for exchange of materials between mother and fetus.

There is **no direct contact between maternal and fetal blood** – they are separated by a membrane which can, to some extent, select the materials that cross it.

Umbilical cord

Umbilical artery – carries deoxygenated blood containing wastes such as urea away from fetus to placenta.

Umbilical vein – carries oxygenated blood cleared of wastes from placenta to fetus. Blood contains a high concentration of soluble foods such as glucose, amino acids and iron.

Artery from mother delivers blood which is:
■ high in nutrients and oxygen
■ low in carbon dioxide and urea.

The placenta is the site of exchange – useful substances such as glucose and oxygen pass from mother to fetus and wastes such as urea and carbon dioxide move in the opposite direction.

---

1. What name is given to the complete period from fertilisation to birth?

2. The growth of the fetus is due to an increase in the number of cells of which it is made. A newborn baby has about 30 million million cells. Remember that each cell divides into two, and each of those two into two more (a total of four), and so on. Calculate approximately how many divisions were necessary to produce the baby from the zygote.

3. Cell division is only part of the overall process of production of the baby. Which other process runs alongside cell division? Define this process.

8·6 Birth and the newborn baby

Objectives
- To describe the events leading to birth
- To describe the early care of a young baby
- To appreciate the benefits of breast feeding

Hormones are responsible for birth

The sequence of events that leads to the birth of a baby is called **labour**. Labour begins with the **contractions** of the uterus muscle. These contractions are:

- prevented by **progesterone** – the level of this hormone *falls* as birth approaches
- stimulated by **oxytocin**, a hormone released from the pituitary gland of the mother
- helped by **oestrogen** (which makes the uterus more sensitive to oxytocin) – the level of this hormone *rises* as birth approaches.

Labour

By the end of pregnancy the baby normally lies with its head against the cervix. At first the contractions come every 20 minutes or so, but as birth approaches they become more frequent and more powerful. The contractions cause the amniotic membrane to break and release the amniotic fluid – this is known as breaking the waters – and the cervix to dilate (get wider). The first stage of labour is complete when the cervix is wide enough for the baby's head to pass through. Labour continues as the baby's head is pushed past the cervix into the vagina, which is now acting as a birth canal. From now on the process is quite rapid and needs only gentle contractions by the mother, helped by the midwife or the obstetrician (doctor who specialises in birth). The birth process is quite traumatic for the baby, and it may become short of oxygen as the umbilical cord is compressed by the walls of the birth canal. The baby's heartbeat is monitored during birth, and the blood soon reoxygenates once the baby begins to breathe. When the baby is breathing properly the umbilical cord is clamped (to prevent bleeding) and cut. The placenta comes away from the wall of the uterus and leaves the vagina as the **afterbirth**.

Feeding the newborn baby

When a newborn baby is placed close to its mother's breast it sucks at the nipple. This is known as the **suckling reflex**. Suckling stimulates the mother's brain to release more oxytocin. The hormone causes tiny muscles in the **mammary glands** to squeeze out milk. This process is **lactation.**

The mother's milk is an ideal food for the baby – it contains all the nutrients the baby needs in the correct proportions. It also contains some antibodies from the mother which help to protect the baby during its early months. Milk made in the first few days is called **colostrum.** It contains mainly antibodies and very little food. The mother continues to produce milk as long as the baby suckles. A newborn baby cannot eat solid food because it has no teeth and its digestive system is not developed enough to deal with solids. At around four to six months when the first teeth are starting to appear, the baby can begin to eat some solid food. The gradual changeover from milk to a solid food diet is called **weaning**.

Twins

Humans usually give birth to a single baby. Occasionally two embryos develop together, each with its own placenta and umbilical cord, resulting in **twins**. There are two kinds of twins, and they arise in different ways, as shown in the diagram opposite.

Very occasionally three or more ova are released and fertilised at the same time, resulting in a multiple birth. This is quite common in women who have been treated with a **fertility drug.** The uterus cannot expand enough to contain several fetuses growing and developing at the same time, and the mother often gives birth early, usually around the seventh month of the pregnancy. Increasingly, medical care (including the use of incubators) means that the babies may survive.

The development of twins.

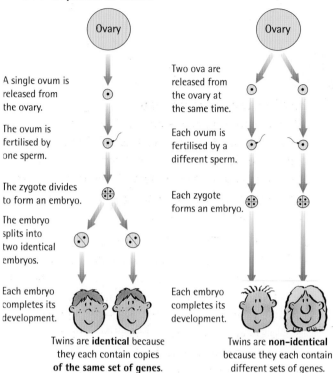

A single ovum is released from the ovary.

The ovum is fertilised by one sperm.

The zygote divides to form an embryo.

The embryo splits into two identical embryos.

Each embryo completes its development.

Twins are identical because they each contain copies of the same set of genes.

Two ova are released from the ovary at the same time.

Each ovum is fertilised by a different sperm.

Each zygote forms an embryo.

Each embryo completes its development.

Twins are non-identical because they each contain different sets of genes.

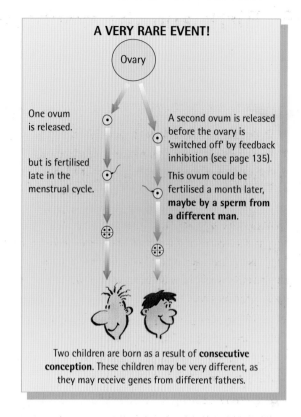

A VERY RARE EVENT!

One ovum is released.

but is fertilised late in the menstrual cycle.

A second ovum is released before the ovary is 'switched off' by feedback inhibition (see page 135).

This ovum could be fertilised a month later, **maybe by a sperm from a different man.**

Two children are born as a result of **consecutive conception.** These children may be very different, as they may receive genes from different fathers.

Identical twins have the same genes.

Non-identical twins are no more alike than any other brothers and sisters.

Multiple births can happen naturally, or following treatment with fertility drugs.

1. Describe the role of hormones in the birth and early growth of a human baby.

2. Copy and complete the following paragraph about the birth of a human baby.

   An expectant mother knows when she is about to give birth because her _____ begins to experience waves of contraction. These contractions are caused by an increased release of the hormone _____ from the pituitary gland, and become more and more powerful as the concentration of the hormone _____ falls. Eventually the contractions are so powerful that the _____ dilates, the _____ bursts and the 'waters' are released. Further powerful contractions push the baby through the _____ or birth canal (usually head first, but occasionally feet or bottom first in what is called a breach birth). Once the baby has been delivered it is important that it takes deep breaths because it may have been deprived of _____ as the _____ cord is compressed during delivery. This cord is clamped and cut, and relatively mild contractions of the uterus cause the _____ to come away from the wall of the uterus and pass out of the vagina as the _____.

3. Consider this list of statements about identical twins, and say whether each is true or false.

   a They each have the same genes.

   b They are formed from two separate ova.

   c They each have their own placenta and umbilical cord.

   d They may be of the same sex or different sexes.

   e They are also known as fraternal twins.

   f They are formed from a single fertilised egg that splits in two.

8·7 Growth

Objectives

- To understand how growth can be measured
- To understand that there is considerable variation in the rate of human growth
- To understand how a growth curve is constructed
- To appreciate some of the factors that affect growth in humans

- Calculate the **mean** to minimise the influence of any one individual result.

- Select the correct **parameter** (feature) to measure. **Standing height** is the most commonly used linear measurement, but does not take account of growth in other directions (such as girth – waist measurement) or of growth in different parts of the body. **Body mass** is better in many ways than a linear measurement since it takes volume into account, and therefore includes growth of all body parts. However, body mass measurements do not distinguish between true tissue growth (such as the addition of protein to muscle) and temporary changes (such as fat deposition or variable water intake).

How do you know whether you are 'growing up' properly? Schools and medical practices make 'growth measurements' to check that a child or young person is growing. These measurements are compared with the expected growth for a person of the same age and sex. Clearly it is very important to know what the expected measurement should be, and to be certain that all the measurements are taken under the same conditions.

Measurement of growth

Growth curves such as the one shown below are useful for comparing measurements from different people. They are made by measuring some feature of many individuals and plotting the results against time. There are some important points to consider:

- Take **samples** from populations, for example, collect data from every tenth student on a school's alphabetical register.

What is normal growth?

Everybody wants to be normal. Many young people are anxious about their size (Why aren't I as tall as him?) or their development (Shouldn't I be shaving? When will my periods start?). Children and young people grow and develop at different rates, and reach different sizes. Many factors determine size, as illustrated opposite, so it should be no surprise that 'normal' covers a very wide range.

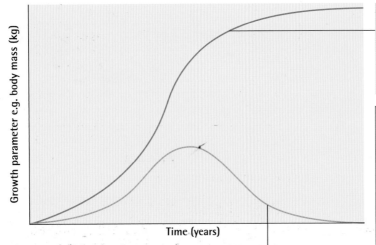

Actual growth curve – this is the **increase** in the measured parameter over a period of time. The general pattern is typically an S-shaped curve – growth starts slowly, speeds up during puberty, then slows and stops altogether when adulthood is reached, typically in the early twenties.

Time (years)	Mass (kg)	Growth increment (kg)
9	32.0	
10	33.0	1.0
11	34.5	1.5
12	36.5	2.0
13	40.0	3.5
14	45.0	5.0
15	48.5	3.5
16	50.5	2.0
17	52.0	1.5
18	53.0	1.0

Rate of growth curve – this is another way of showing the basic growth curve. It describes the **change** in the measured parameter that takes place during successive time intervals – it plots growth increments against time. It is useful for comparing the growth of different parts of the body.

A growth curve is a graph with time on the x (horizontal) axis and the measured parameter such as height or body mass on the y (vertical) axis.

Genes – many genes on several different chromosomes affect body size.
For example sex-linked genes mean that:
- men are **usually** taller than women
- girls are **rarely** taller than their father.

Hormones – both the **type** of hormone and **when it is secreted** may affect final body size. **Sleep** is vital because growth hormone is secreted faster when the body is at rest.

Growth Hormone

Human growth hormone can be given to children at the lower end of the height range. This hormone is made by genetic engineering.

Racial origins can make great differences to body size – probably both **genes** and **nutrition** are involved.

Nutrition – both **type** and **quantity** of nutrients, and the period of time for which they are available, affect final body size.

FULL FAT MILK

Great variation in body size

Many factors affect growth, so there is a wide variation in 'normal' size. Many doctors also believe that psychological well-being can influence growth. A stress-free and caring environment may be very significant in the normal growth and development of a young person.

Growth patterns in humans

Several stages can be recognised during the growth and development of a human from birth to adulthood. These can be simply described on a general growth curve as infancy, childhood, puberty, adolescence and adulthood, as shown opposite. However, a general growth curve for a human does not show:

- changes in **growth of individual organs**
- changes in **proportions**
- effects of **growth spurts**.

These additional factors make it very difficult to say what is 'normal' growth for a human.

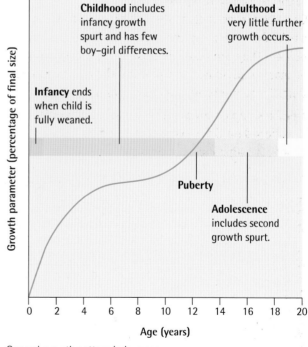

General growth pattern in humans.

---

1. What are the factors that may affect the growth of an individual?

2. What factors should be considered when producing a growth curve?

3. List the stages, in order, that occur in the growth and development of a human from birth to adulthood.

1 The graph below shows the levels of the hormones oestrogen and progesterone in a woman's blood during a month when she becomes pregnant.

Use the information in the graph and your own knowledge to answer the questions below.

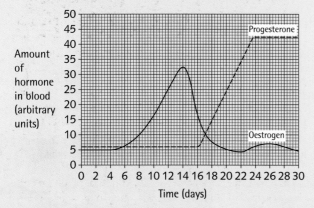

Amount of hormone in blood (arbitrary units)

Time (days)

a When are the levels of oestrogen and progesterone equal?

b Which process occurred between day 0 and day 5?

c Give ONE function of each of these hormones.
 i Oestrogen
 ii Progesterone

d What evidence from the graph shows that an ovum was fertilised?

e Copy the graph. Draw a line between day 16 and day 30 to show a probable level of progesterone which would be found in the woman's blood if she had NOT become pregnant.

f How does the lining of the uterus help in the development of a fertilised ovum?

(Edexcel June 1996)

2 The diagram below shows the reproductive organs of the human male after an operation called a 'vasectomy' has been performed. Following a vasectomy, the man can still ejaculate fluid produced by the prostate and Cowper's glands.

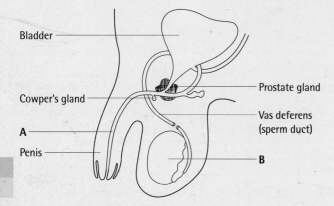

Bladder

Cowper's gland

A

Penis

Prostate gland

Vas deferens (sperm duct)

B

a Name parts **A** and **B**.

b Put an 'X' on the diagram to show where sperms are made.

c **i** In what way are the reproductive organs of the male with the vasectomy different from those of a normal, untreated male?
 ii Explain how this will act as a method of contraception.

d A man infected with the human immuno-deficiency virus (HIV) may transmit AIDS (acquired immuno-deficiency syndrome) to another person. The virus is transmitted in body fluids. Following a vasectomy, is it still possible for an infected man to pass AIDS to another person? Explain your answer.

(SEG June 1991)

3 The following table provides information about the body temperature of a young woman on each day throughout a single menstrual cycle.

a Plot all of this information in the form of a graph.

b **i** What is the range of the body temperature during the cycle?

Day of menstrual cycle		Body temperature (°C)
1		36.5
2		36.2
3	Menstruation	36.2
4		36.2
5		36.2
6		36.2
7		36.3
8		36.2
9		36.4
10		36.3
11		36.2
12		36.1
13		36.2
14	Ovulation	36.2
15		36.5
16		36.7
17		36.8
18		36.7
19		36.7
20		36.8
21		36.7
22		36.6
23		36.6
24		36.7
25		36.6
26		36.6
27		36.7
28		36.6

ii These measurements were made at the same time each day, in the same room and while the woman was wearing the same dressing gown. Why is this important?

c i The times of menstruation and ovulation are shown in the table. What changes in temperature coincide with these events?

ii How could this information be used:
(a) as a method of contraception
(b) to help increase the chance of conception?

d Which other methods of contraception are available to a woman? Why are these methods more successful than the one outlined in part **c**?

4 Below is a diagram of part of a human placenta.

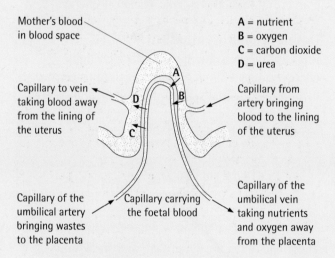

Mother's blood in blood space

A = nutrient
B = oxygen
C = carbon dioxide
D = urea

Capillary to vein taking blood away from the lining of the uterus

Capillary from artery bringing blood to the lining of the uterus

Capillary of the umbilical artery bringing wastes to the placenta

Capillary carrying the foetal blood

Capillary of the umbilical vein taking nutrients and oxygen away from the placenta

Use the information in the diagram to describe the flow of blood and exchange of dissolved nutrients, gases and excretory products which take place in the placenta. Your description should start with blood flowing from the foetus to the placenta.

(MEG June 1994)

5 The temperature of the human fetus whilst in the uterus is about 0.5 °C above that of its mother. At birth it emerges into a relatively cool, dry atmosphere and immediately encounters a problem of temperature control.

a Suggest why the temperature of the fetus is above that of its mother.

b Explain how the following help the newborn baby to control its temperature:
i from about the fifth month of pregnancy onwards a layer of subcutaneous fat is developed by the fetus
ii at birth the blood vessels to the baby's skin constrict very quickly.

c A baby born prematurely is less able to control its body temperature and must be kept in an incubator (see photograph).
i A constant temperature is maintained within the incubator, using a thermostat and an electric heater. Use this example to explain the meaning of the term negative feedback.
ii Suggest two functions of the hood that covers the incubator.

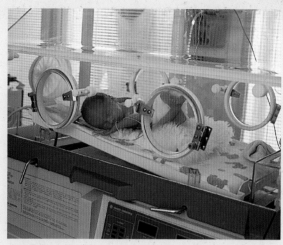

An incubator provides a constant warm environment for a premature baby.

d The premature baby must be fed through a plastic tube going through its nostril into its stomach.
i The food supplied to the baby contains substantial quantities of carbohydrate and protein. Suggest one function of each of these substances in the body of the newborn baby.
ii Name one substance normally supplied across the placenta in the late stages of pregnancy which the artificial diet is unlikely to supply. What problem might this cause for the newborn baby?

6 The table below shows the average height of boys and girls up to the age of 18 years.
a Plot this information as a pair of standard growth curves. Use the same axes for boys and girls.
b On the graph indicate the periods which correspond to weaning, childhood, puberty and adolescence.
c When does the most rapid growth take place?
d At what age are girls generally taller than boys?

Age (years)	Average height (cm)	
	Boys	Girls
0 (at birth)	52	51
1	76	75
2	88	88
3	97	97
4	103	103
5	110	110
6	118	117
7	125	122
8	131	128
9	135	133
10	141	140
11	145	146
12	150	153
13	156	158
14	164	161
15	169	162
16	172	162
17	174	162
18	175	162

Reproduction

147

9·1 Photosynthesis and plant nutrition

Objectives
- To understand that plants, like all living organisms, must receive nourishment
- To know the basic definition for photosynthesis
- To know word and symbol equations for photosynthesis
- To remember that a plant body has organs that are well suited to carry out particular functions

Plants need food

All living organisms need food. Animals take in 'ready-made' food which they digest. They use the digested products for energy and to build new cells and tissues. Plants also require raw materials for building tissues and a source of energy. They manufacture everything they need out of simple ions and compounds available in the environment. The building up of complex molecules from simpler substances (**synthesis**) requires energy and enzymes. The enzymes are in the plant's cells, and the energy comes from sunlight. The process is therefore called **photosynthesis**. An outline of plant nutrition is shown in the diagram below.

Chloroplasts are energy transducers

Plants can absorb and use light energy because they have a green pigment, **chlorophyll**, contained in **chloroplasts** in some of their cells. Chlorophyll allows the energy in sunlight to drive chemical reactions. Chloroplasts act as **energy transducers**, converting light energy into chemical energy.

Defining photosynthesis

Photosynthesis is the process in which light energy, trapped by chlorophyll, is used to convert carbon dioxide and water into glucose and oxygen.

$$\text{Carbon dioxide} + \text{water} \xrightarrow[\text{chlorophyll}]{\text{light energy}} \text{glucose} + \text{oxygen}$$

$$6CO_2 + 6H_2O \xrightarrow[\text{chlorophyll}]{\text{light energy}} C_6H_{12}O_6 + 6O_2$$

These equations summarise photosynthesis:

These equations are simplified, and show only glucose as a food product of photosynthesis. In fact plants can make all of their food compounds by photosynthesis and other chemical processes.

Plants are **autotrophic** (self-feeding) – they take simple substances from their environment and use light energy to build them up into complex food compounds.

SUN

Light energy

Carbon dioxide
from the atmosphere

Water from the soil

Minerals such as nitrate, phosphate and magnesium from the soil

Oxygen – a waste product released to the atmosphere

The plant makes **Complex food compounds** which may be used for energy, growth, repair and reproduction. They include:
- **glucose**
- **starch** } contain carbon, hydrogen and oxygen (C, H, and O).
- **amino acids and proteins** } contain nitrogen as well as C, H and O
- **nucleic acids** – contain phosphorus as well as C, H, O and N
- **lipids** – contain C, H and O

Animals depend on plants
Autotrophic nutrition provides:
- a supply of **complex food compounds** which can be eaten by heterotrophic organisms, including animals
- a supply of **oxygen** which is essential for aerobic respiration in all organisms, including animals.

Photosynthesis and transport in plants

Some of the glucose produced is stored in the plant cells as **starch**. The experiment below shows how a starch test can be used to demonstrate the conditions needed for photosynthesis.

To demonstrate that some factor is necessary for the production of starch, the plant must have no starch to begin with. The plant is placed in a dark cupboard or box for 48 hours. It uses any starch that is already in its leaves and is now **destarched**.

Test for starch in leaves

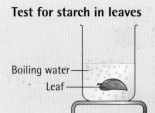

(a) Leaf is boiled in water for about 2 minutes. Purpose: to break down cell walls and to stop the action of enzymes within the leaf. Also allows easier penetration by ethanol.

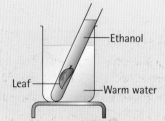

(b) Leaf is warmed in ethanol until leaf is colourless. Purpose: to extract the chlorophyll, which would mask observations later. (Chlorophyll dissolves in ethanol but not in water.)

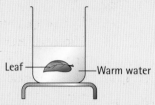

(c) Leaf is dipped into warm water (briefly). Purpose: to soften the now brittle leaf, and allow penetration by iodine solution.

(d) Leaf is placed on white tile and iodine solution added. Purpose: iodine shows the presence (blue–black) or absence (orange–brown) of starch; colours are shown against the white tile.

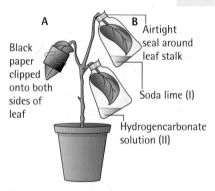

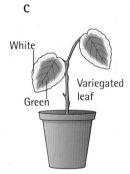

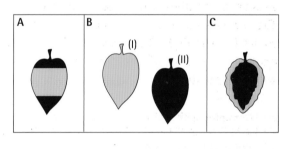

Testing leaves for starch.

These questions are about the diagram above.

1. Before testing for starch, the leaf is warmed in ethanol. The ethanol turns green. Why is this?

2. A group of students wanted to investigate the conditions needed for photosynthesis. They set up the three experiments shown as A, B and C. Each of the plants was given the same light conditions.
   a What does the result of experiment A suggest?
   b Soda lime removes carbon dioxide from the atmosphere, and hydrogencarbonate slowly releases it. What do the results of experiment B suggest about carbon dioxide and starch formation?
   c What is the purpose of experiment C?
   d From experiments A, B and C, list the factors necessary for starch formation by photosynthesis.

3. The students' teacher asked for some further tests to be completed before accepting their results as valid.
   a How could the students show that there was no starch in the leaves at the start of the experiment?
   b The teacher suggested that the black paper attached to the leaf in experiment A prevented the leaf from absorbing gases, and that was why no starch had been produced in the covered area. How could the students disprove this theory?

4. What additional experiment could be set up to show that the formation of starch by photosynthesis depends on the activity of enzymes? (There is a clue given in one part of the diagram above.)

9·2 The rate of photosynthesis

Measuring photosynthesis

The most straightforward way of showing whether or not photosynthesis has occurred is to test for the presence of starch. Starch is a product of photosynthesis and the blue–black colour of the iodine test is a simple method for detecting it. Unfortunately this is an 'all-or-nothing' test, that is, the colour is just as dark with a small amount of starch as it is with a large amount. The iodine test is said to be **qualitative** – it only shows whether or not starch is present. To find out *how quickly* photosynthesis is going on, we need to use a **quantitative** test.

The basic equation for photosynthesis is:

$$\text{Carbon dioxide} + \text{water} \xrightarrow[\text{chlorophyll}]{\text{light energy}} \text{glucose (starch)} + \text{oxygen}$$

This shows that as well as starch, there is another product of photosynthesis – oxygen. It is quite easy to measure amounts of oxygen, and so the production of oxygen can be used as a quantitative test for photosynthesis.

Analysing the design of an experiment

The simplest apparatus for measuring oxygen release is shown in the diagram below left. This method depends on counting the number of oxygen bubbles given off in a fixed length of time.
Apparatus that can be used to measure the *volume* of oxygen released in a fixed length of time is shown on the opposite page. When looking at this, remind yourself of the principles of experimental technique (see page 16).

Tracing photosynthesis

The rate of photosynthesis can be estimated by measuring how much carbon dioxide a plant absorbs. This is done using a radioactively labelled form of carbon dioxide, $^{14}CO_2$. Labelled carbon dioxide is absorbed by the leaf cells and converted into labelled carbohydrates in exactly the same way as 'normal' carbon dioxide. A Geiger counter is used to detect how much radioactive material has been incorporated by the plant in a fixed length of time – the rate of photosynthesis. This method is useful for studying the rate of photosynthesis in a 'real-life' situation – in the middle of a crop field, for example – where it is not possible to collect and measure volumes of oxygen.

Using radioactive tracers can also provide information about other compounds that plants make following photosynthesis (see page 157), and about how plants transport food substances from one place to another in the plant (see page 162).

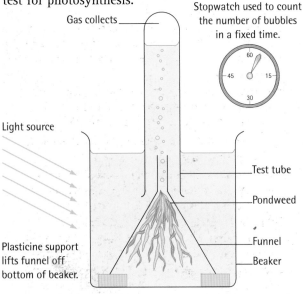

Stopwatch used to count the number of bubbles in a fixed time.

Gas collects

Light source

Plasticine support lifts funnel off bottom of beaker.

Test tube

Pondweed

Funnel

Beaker

Experiment for a simple quantitative estimation of photosynthesis.

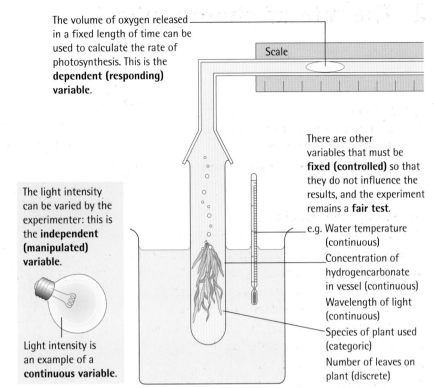

The volume of oxygen released in a fixed length of time can be used to calculate the rate of photosynthesis. This is the **dependent (responding) variable**.

Scale

The light intensity can be varied by the experimenter: this is the **independent (manipulated) variable**.

Light intensity is an example of a **continuous variable**.

There are other variables that must be **fixed (controlled)** so that they do not influence the results, and the experiment remains a **fair test**.

e.g. Water temperature (continuous)

Concentration of hydrogencarbonate in vessel (continuous)

Wavelength of light (continuous)

Species of plant used (categoric)

Number of leaves on plant (discrete)

A more accurate method for measuring the rate of photosynthesis. This apparatus can be used to investigate the effect of light intensity on the rate of photosynthesis.

1 What important assumption about the bubbles is being made when using the method shown on the page opposite to measure the rate of photosynthesis?

2 Using the apparatus above, Samantha and Jane obtained the results shown in the table.

a Plot this information in the form of a graph.

Light intensity (arbitrary units)	Volume of oxygen released (mm³/minute)
1	7
2	14
3	21
4	28
5	34
6	39
7	42
8	44
9	45
10	45

b At what light intensity did the plant produce 25 mm³ of oxygen per minute?

c What levels of light intensity had the greatest effect on the rate of photosynthesis? How could this information be useful to a grower of greenhouse tomatoes?

Samantha and Jane wanted to investigate whether the wavelength of the light would affect

photosynthesis, and decided that they could use the same apparatus.

d What would be the manipulated variable in this investigation? How could the two students manipulate this variable?

e What would be the fixed variables in this investigation?

f The students decided to repeat their experiment, and then to pool their results with the results of other students in the same class. Why was this pooling of results important?

g The teacher said that if the students were going to pool their results then they must remove the plants from the apparatus and weigh them. Why should they do this?

h State the manipulated, responding and fixed variables in an investigation into the effect of temperature on the rate of photosynthesis.

3 This question is about the box 'Tracing photosynthesis' on the opposite page.

a What important assumption is being made when using the rate of uptake of $^{14}CO_2$ as a measure of the rate of photosynthesis?

b Why is it important that radioactively labelled carbon dioxide, $^{14}CO_2$, is treated by leaf cells in exactly the same way as 'normal' carbon dioxide?

c Which process might release $^{14}CO_2$ from the plant?

9·3 The leaf and photosynthesis

Features of the leaf

In order to photosynthesise efficiently a leaf needs:

- a method for **exchange of gases** between the leaf and its surroundings
- a way of **delivering water** to the leaf
- a system for the **removal of glucose** so that it can be transported to other parts of the plant
- an efficient means of **absorbing light energy**.

The diagram below shows how the structure of the leaf meets these requirements.

Features of the plant

Each leaf is adapted for photosynthesis, and the leaves of whole plant are arranged to maximise the amount of photosynthesis that can take place.

- The leaves grow so that they shade one another as little as possible, but also leave hardly any gap through which light can pass. Such a **leaf mosaic** is shown in the photograph on the opposite page.
- The plant can detect the direction of light, and grow so that its leaves are always in the best position to absorb light – this is described on page 170.

Chloroplast structure and photosynthesis

Chloroplasts are only found inside the cells of green plants. They make the plant green, because they contain the green pigment chlorophyll. The diagram opposite shows the structure of a chloroplast.

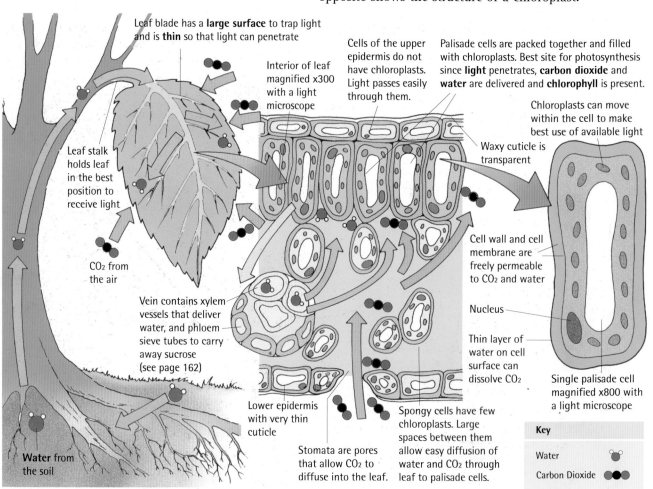

Leaf blade has a **large surface** to trap light and is **thin** so that light can penetrate

Interior of leaf magnified x300 with a light microscope

Cells of the upper epidermis do not have chloroplasts. Light passes easily through them.

Palisade cells are packed together and filled with chloroplasts. Best site for photosynthesis since **light** penetrates, **carbon dioxide** and **water** are delivered and **chlorophyll** is present.

Chloroplasts can move within the cell to make best use of available light

Waxy cuticle is transparent

Leaf stalk holds leaf in the best position to receive light

Cell wall and cell membrane are freely permeable to CO_2 and water

Nucleus

CO_2 from the air

Vein contains xylem vessels that deliver water, and phloem sieve tubes to carry away sucrose (see page 162)

Thin layer of water on cell surface can dissolve CO_2

Single palisade cell magnified x800 with a light microscope

Lower epidermis with very thin cuticle

Stomata are pores that allow CO_2 to diffuse into the leaf.

Spongy cells have few chloroplasts. Large spaces between them allow easy diffusion of water and CO_2 through leaf to palisade cells.

Water from the soil

Key

Water

Carbon Dioxide

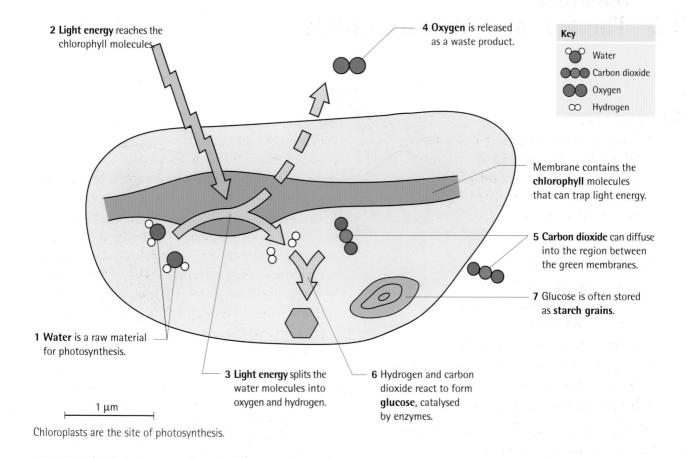

2 Light energy reaches the chlorophyll molecules.

4 Oxygen is released as a waste product.

Key

○◉○	Water
●●●	Carbon dioxide
●●	Oxygen
○○	Hydrogen

Membrane contains the **chlorophyll** molecules that can trap light energy.

5 Carbon dioxide can diffuse into the region between the green membranes.

7 Glucose is often stored as **starch grains**.

1 Water is a raw material for photosynthesis.

3 Light energy splits the water molecules into oxygen and hydrogen.

6 Hydrogen and carbon dioxide react to form **glucose**, catalysed by enzymes.

1 μm

Chloroplasts are the site of photosynthesis.

---

1. Chlorophyll appears green because it absorbs other colours from visible light. Which colours must chlorophyll absorb in order to appear green?

2. Use the scale on the diagram above to calculate:
   a the actual length of a chloroplast
   b the magnification of this diagram.

3. How could you prove that chloroplasts contain starch grains?

4. Photosynthesis tends to slow down above about 30 °C. How does the diagram above help to explain this observation?

5. Look at the photograph below.

The leaves on a plant are arranged in a leaf mosaic.

   a How does it explain the term **leaf mosaic**?
   b The veins transport materials in and out of the leaf. They also contain woody material. How does this adapt the leaf for efficient photosynthesis?

6. The photograph below shows a vertical section through a leaf. It has been stained and photographed through a light microscope.

Vertical section through a leaf.

   a Identify the structures 1–7. Explain how structures 3, 4 and 7 adapt the leaf to efficient photosynthesis.
   b The photograph has been magnified 100 times. What is the true thickness of the leaf? How is this thickness important in efficient photosynthesis?

153

9·4 The control of photosynthesis

Objectives
- To understand that photosynthesis is affected by a number of different factors
- To appreciate that photosynthesis is affected most by the factor that is in shortest supply – the limiting factor
- To know that an understanding of limiting factors can be used in the efficient growth of greenhouse crops

Requirements for photosynthesis

The process of photosynthesis depends upon:
- the availability of light
- the presence of a pigment to absorb the light
- a supply of carbon dioxide and water
- a temperature suitable for enzyme activity.

The need for each of these requirements or **factors** is outlined in the diagram below.

If any of these factors is in short supply, the rate of photosynthesis will be less than its maximum possible rate. One factor can cause a 'bottleneck' in the overall process as shown at the top of the page opposite. The factor that is furthest from its optimum level is controlling the rate of the overall process. This factor is called the **limiting factor**. The limiting factor varies at different times and under different conditions.

- In Britain, during the summer, light and temperature may be ideal for photosynthesis but the carbon dioxide concentration may be the limiting factor.

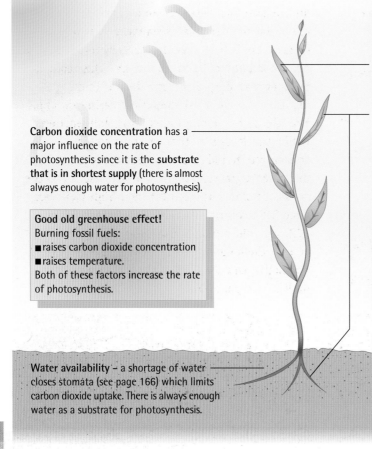

Availability of light – light provides the energy that drives photosynthesis (by splitting water molecules).
The light energy absorbed by a plant depends on:
- the **intensity** of the light source
- the **wavelength** of the light
- the **length of time** (duration) that the light is available.

Chlorophyll is essential for the absorption of light energy. The synthesis of chlorophyll requires **magnesium ions**, which must be supplied from the soil.

Temperature affects the rate of enzyme activity. A 10°C rise in temperature can cause a doubling in the rate of enzyme activity (although higher temperatures cause denaturation). This is important both in **leaves** (enzymes involved directly in photosynthesis) and in **roots** (enzyme systems involved in active transport of mineral ions – see page 161).

Carbon dioxide concentration has a major influence on the rate of photosynthesis since it is the **substrate that is in shortest supply** (there is almost always enough water for photosynthesis).

Good old greenhouse effect!
Burning fossil fuels:
- raises carbon dioxide concentration
- raises temperature.
Both of these factors increase the rate of photosynthesis.

Poisons and photosynthesis
Photosynthesis may be inhibited by poisons, e.g.
- paraquat (a weed killer) prevents light energy being used to convert carbon dioxide to sugars
- sulphur dioxide (in acid rain) damages the palisade cells of the leaf.

Water availability – a shortage of water closes stomata (see page 166) which limits carbon dioxide uptake. There is always enough water as a substrate for photosynthesis.

Well balanced plants! Plants are autotrophic ('self-feeding') and can carefully regulate their food production. Plants need nitrate to be able to convert glucose from photosynthesis into amino acids. If there is a shortage of nitrate, the plant will reduce its rate of photosynthesis since it will need fewer sugars to make amino acids.

Factors affecting photosynthesis.

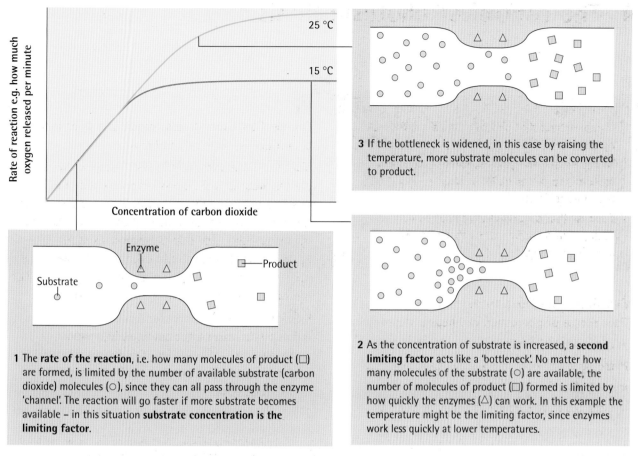

1 The **rate of the reaction**, i.e. how many molecules of product (□) are formed, is limited by the number of available substrate (carbon dioxide) molecules (○), since they can all pass through the enzyme 'channel'. The reaction will go faster if more substrate becomes available – in this situation **substrate concentration is the limiting factor**.

2 As the concentration of substrate is increased, a **second limiting factor** acts like a 'bottleneck'. No matter how many molecules of the substrate (○) are available, the number of molecules of product (□) formed is limited by how quickly the enzymes (△) can work. In this example the temperature might be the limiting factor, since enzymes work less quickly at lower temperatures.

3 If the bottleneck is widened, in this case by raising the temperature, more substrate molecules can be converted to product.

Limiting factors control the rate of reactions in living organisms.

- During any 24-hour period, light will be the limiting factor from dusk to dawn.
- During a British winter, plants may not photosynthesise on a bright, sunny day because temperature is the limiting factor.

The availability of water is rarely a limiting factor for photosynthesis, since there are so many other physiological processes in plants that depend on water that these processes will usually halt in a water shortage before photosynthesis does.

Controlling the limiting factors

In an open field, there is very little that farmers can do to speed up photosynthesis – they cannot change the degree of cloud cover or warm up the air, for example. However, in an enclosed environment such as a greenhouse, it is possible to control the factors affecting photosynthesis and so get the maximum yield from crops. This requires an understanding of the principle of limiting factors – it is no good simply increasing the light availability by having lights on in dull weather without making sure that carbon dioxide concentration and temperature are adequate, for example. A greenhouse grower will also try to use strains of plants selected for their high yield (see page 216), control any potential pests (see page 272) and will probably use automatic systems to control the factors that might limit the crop yield. The management of a greenhouse ecosystem is outlined on page 274.

1. List the three most important factors that control the rate of photosynthesis.
2. The burning of fossil fuels can both help and hinder photosynthesis. Explain this statement.
3. Which ion deficiency is most likely to affect photosynthesis? Why?
4. What is a limiting factor? Which limiting factor is most likely to affect photosynthesis:
   a on a cloudy, spring day
   b on a bright, sunny day in winter
   c in the middle of a crop field on a sunny, warm July day?

9·5 Photosynthesis and the environment

Objectives

- To understand that plants both photosynthesise and respire
- To understand that these processes affect the composition of the atmosphere
- To appreciate that photosynthesis plays an important part in the carbon cycle

Photosynthesis and respiration

From the equation for photosynthesis (see page 148) we know that this process removes carbon dioxide from the atmosphere and at the same time releases oxygen. This is the opposite of the exchange of gases in respiration:

Glucose + oxygen → carbon dioxide + water

Green plants both photosynthesise and respire:

- if photosynthesis exceeds respiration (in the light) plants will, overall, remove carbon dioxide and add oxygen
- if photosynthesis is less than respiration (in the dark) plants will, overall, remove oxygen and add carbon dioxide.

Demonstrating gas exchange

The overall change in carbon dioxide levels in the atmosphere can be demonstrated using **hydrogencarbonate indicator**, as shown in the diagram below. Carbon dioxide produces a weak acid, **carbonic acid**, in water and this indicator is sensitive to the changes in pH caused by the acid.

In the dark, the rate of respiration greatly exceeds the rate of photosynthesis – the plant cells are living on the sugars they manufactured during previous periods of photosynthesis. As the light intensity increases after dawn, there comes a point where the rates of respiration and photosynthesis exactly balance one another and there is no net uptake or loss of carbon dioxide or oxygen. This is called the **compensation point**, and at this point the glucose consumed by respiration is exactly balanced by the glucose produced during photosynthesis. Beyond the compensation point the plant begins to gain glucose, as photosynthesis exceeds respiration.

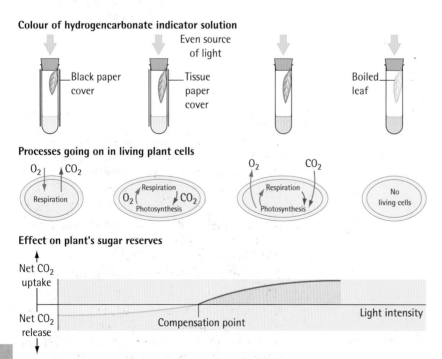

Experiment to demonstrate the effect of light intensity on the balance between photosynthesis and respiration.

As **carbon dioxide concentration decreases**, the indicator solution turns purple.

pH rises (less acidic)

pH falls (more acidic)

As **carbon dioxide concentration increases**, the indicator solution turns orange–yellow.

Hydrogencarbonate indicator reacts to changes in carbon dioxide in the air.

Photosynthesis and transport in plants

The products of photosynthesis

Plants manufacture all of their food requirements, starting from the glucose molecule. The diagram shows some of the products that the plant makes.

These products are available to the plant, and to any organism that eats the plant. An animal that eats plant material will use most of it to obtain energy by respiration. The carbon dioxide released as a waste product is then available for plants as a substrate for photosynthesis. An atom of carbon in carbon dioxide could be taken in by a plant, built up to a complex food molecule, and then eaten by an animal which breaks it down to carbon dioxide again. Thus atoms are **recycled** between simple and complex molecules, through the bodies of plants, animals and other living organisms. The **carbon cycle** is described simply in the diagram at the bottom of the page, and more fully on page 254.

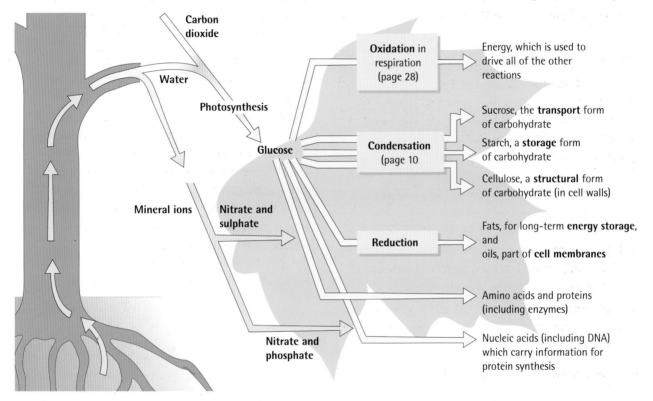

Plants produce all their food molecules from the products of photosynthesis by metabolic reactions.

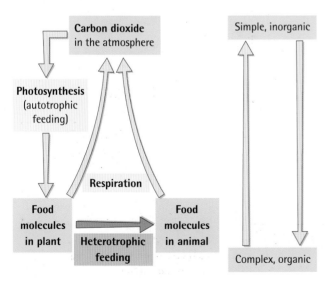

Photosynthesis and the carbon cycle – carbon is recycled between simple inorganic and complex organic compounds.

1. Name an indicator that can be used to measure carbon dioxide concentrations in solution. What colour change would you predict for this indicator in the presence of an actively photosynthesising plant? Explain your answer.

2. What is meant by the term compensation point? Why is it important that a grower of greenhouse crops should understand this term?

3. 'Photosynthesis provides plants with sugars' – is this true, and is it the whole story?

4. Plants take up carbon dioxide, which they convert to carbohydrate. Explain how it is possible for the plant to take in the same molecule of carbon dioxide more than once.

Plants need a number of minerals. The plant uses minerals to make food molecules such as amino acids, proteins and nucleic acids out of the carbohydrates made by photosynthesis (see page 157). Plants absorb minerals from the soil in the form of **ions**. The mechanism of ion uptake is described on page 160. Here we shall consider *why* the ions are required, and how scientists might work out the function of each different mineral nutrient.

Minerals in soil

The minerals present in soil depend on the type of rock beneath the soil and on the decomposition of animal and plant remains lying on the soil.

Minerals are taken out of the soil by plants, and are also washed out by rain. In natural, uncultivated soils there is a balance between the formation and the loss of mineral ions, as shown below.

In *cultivated* soils the ground is prepared and then the crop is harvested. There are few plant remains left to decompose and replace the minerals taken up into the plant body. Levels of minerals such as nitrate and phosphate fall, so farmers add these back in the form of **fertilisers**. These may be **natural fertilisers**, such as sewage sludge, animal manure or compost, or they may be **artificial fertilisers**. The most common artificial fertiliser is NPK fertiliser which contains three main nutrients – nitrogen (**N**), phosphorus (**P**) and potassium (**K**). The role of each of these minerals, and the effect on the plant of mineral deficiencies, is shown in the diagram on the opposite page.

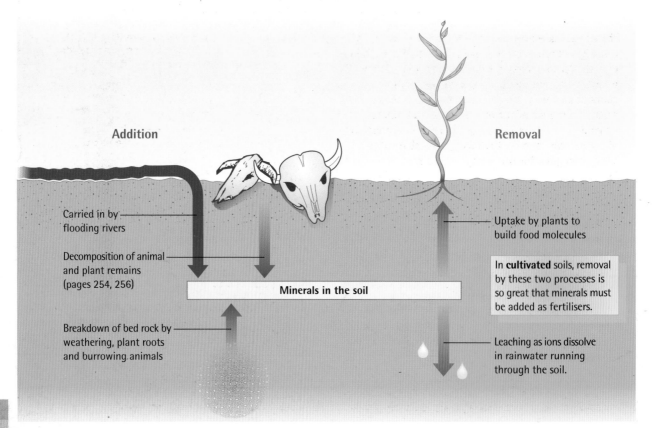

Addition

Removal

Carried in by flooding rivers

Decomposition of animal and plant remains (pages 254, 256)

Breakdown of bed rock by weathering, plant roots and burrowing animals

Minerals in the soil

Uptake by plants to build food molecules

In **cultivated** soils, removal by these two processes is so great that minerals must be added as fertilisers.

Leaching as ions dissolve in rainwater running through the soil.

Minerals are added to the soil and also removed by natural processes.

Magnesium is absorbed from the soil as **magnesium ions (Mg^{2+})**. Magnesium forms part of the chlorophyll molecule. Deficiency causes **chlorosis** – the leaves turn yellow, usually from the bottom of the plant first.

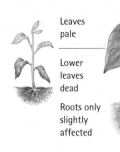

Leaves turn pale green or yellow.

Roots normal

Potassium is absorbed from the soil as **potassium ions (K$^+$)**. Deficiency of potassium causes poor growth of flowers and fruit. Extra potassium is added to crop plants before they start to fruit.

No fruit

Dead edges and spots on leaves

Normal roots

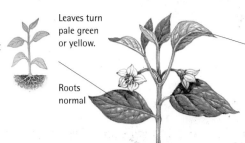

Nitrogen is absorbed from the soil as **nitrate ions (NO$_3^-$)** or **ammonium ions (NH$_4^+$)**. Because nitrogen is required for so many food molecules, especially proteins (including enzymes), deficiency causes severe symptoms. The whole plant is stunted, with a weak stem and yellowing, dying leaves.

Leaves pale

Lower leaves dead

Roots only slightly affected

Phosphorus is absorbed from the soil as **phosphate ions (PO$_4^{3-}$)**. Deficiency causes a lack of DNA, membrane lipids and ATP. Lack of ATP affects active uptake of other minerals by the roots.

Purple leaves

Roots poorly developed

Nitrogen probably has the greatest effect on plant growth. Farmers use expensive NPK fertilisers to replace nitrogen removed from the soil when crops are harvested.

Dried sea-bird droppings (**guano**) are an excellent source of phosphate! Entire islands in the Pacific Ocean have been stripped of guano built up over tens of thousands of years – the guano is used as agricultural fertiliser.

Plant growth and mineral deficiencies.

Plants and minerals – investigation

The apparatus shown on the right can be used to investigate the effects of mineral deficiencies on plant growth. Cereal plants of equal age and size are grown in a series of culture solutions. One of the solutions contains all known mineral nutrients in the correct proportions; each of the others is missing a single mineral. All the vessels are placed in identical conditions of temperature and light intensity, and the plants are allowed to grow for equal lengths of time.

1. Why is the vessel surrounded by black paper?

2. The bubbled air supply provides oxygen to the roots. Why might this be important in mineral uptake?

3. What is the manipulated variable in this investigation, and what is the responding variable?

4. Suggest some fixed variables, and state how you would attempt to control them.

5. Cereal plants such as grasses are useful in this sort of investigation, since many identical plants can be obtained from a single clump. Why is this important in providing valid data?

6. The plant nutrients used in this investigation are supplied as salts. How could you make up a culture solution that is only lacking a single element?

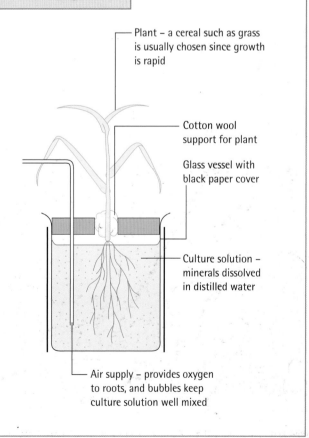

Plant – a cereal such as grass is usually chosen since growth is rapid

Cotton wool support for plant

Glass vessel with black paper cover

Culture solution – minerals dissolved in distilled water

Air supply – provides oxygen to roots, and bubbles keep culture solution well mixed

9·7 Uptake of water and minerals by roots

Objectives
- To understand that water may enter and leave cells by osmosis
- To understand that dissolved substances may enter and leave cells by diffusion and active transport

Plants need water and minerals

Plants need to obtain certain raw materials from their environment. The roots of the plant are adapted to absorb both minerals and water from the soil. **Water** is essential to support the plant, as a reagent in many biochemical reactions and also as a transport medium (see page 8). The diagram below shows how water enters the plant through **root hair cells**.

Minerals have a number of individual functions and together have a great effect on the water potential of the plant tissues. Minerals from the soil are absorbed in the form of **ions**, for example, magnesium enters the root as Mg^{2+} ions and nitrogen enters as nitrate NO_3^- ions. If the soil solution contains higher concentrations of these ions than the root hair cell cytoplasm, the ions can enter by diffusion (see page 24). However, plants can continue to take up ions even if the concentration gradient is in the wrong direction, that is, if the concentration of the ions is higher inside the cell than in the soil solution.

Leaves have a large surface area for photosynthesis. When the stomata are open, water is lost by evaporation from spongy mesophyll cells (see page 166).

Roots have an enormous surface area and penetrate between the particles of soil.

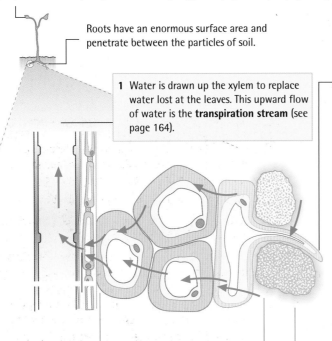

1 Water is drawn up the xylem to replace water lost at the leaves. This upward flow of water is the **transpiration stream** (see page 164).

Root hair cells have an enormous surface area. This helps them absorb water and minerals from the soil. The photograph shows root hair cells magnified ×300.
The root hairs are very delicate and easily damaged.
When plants are transplanted they recover much more quickly if the roots are kept in a ball of soil or compost so that the root hairs are not disturbed.

Note: Water movement through the plant occurs in the sequence 1–2–3–4: it **begins** with loss from the leaves, and is **completed** with water absorption from the soil solution.

2 Water (with any substances dissolved in it) is forced to cross the membrane and cytoplasm of cells of the **endodermis**. The cell walls in the endodermis contain a waxy material which makes them impermeable to water. This allows the membranes of the endodermis cells to **select** which substances can enter the xylem and be distributed through the body of the plant.

3 Water crosses the living cells of the **cortex** by (a) osmosis through the cells and (b) 'suction' through the freely permeable cellulose cell walls. Almost all of the water moves across the cortex by route (b).

4 Water enters root hair cells by **osmosis**, from the thin film of water surrounding the particles of soil. The soil water has a **higher water potential** than the cytoplasm of the root hair cell, so that water moves down a water potential gradient (see page 25).

Uptake of water by root hair cells.

Osmosis: a reminder

A cell's membrane, controls the entry and exit of materials to and from the cell (see page 26). A typical plant cell such as that found in the mesophyll layer of the leaf has a high concentration of solutes. As a result water will enter a plant cell by osmosis from an environment with a high water potential, until the water inside the cell forces the cell membrane up against the cellulose cell wall.

When a plant cell contains plenty of water, the internal pressure of the cell contents against the cell wall supports the cell. The cell is said to be **turgid**, and turgidity helps support the plant. If the plant does not have a good supply of water, the cells lose their turgidity and slowly collapse. The cells are said to be **flaccid** and the plant is wilted.

Experiments on the uptake of ions also show that:

▪ the cells can select which ions enter from the soil solution

▪ any factor that affects respiration, for example lack of oxygen or low temperature, can reduce the uptake of ions. The diagram opposite shows some results that support these observations.

The explanation of these observations is that the root hair cells use **active transport** to carry out the selective uptake of ions against a concentration gradient, using energy from respiration (see page 26).

Active transport: application

To increase crop yields, farmers may drain fields that are liable to flooding. If the soil is not waterlogged, more oxygen in soil air spaces is available to the plants, so the rate of aerobic respiration in root cells is faster. This provides more energy for active transport, so that the growing plants will more quickly absorb mineral ions present in the soil. Farmers may also cover their fields with black polythene. This absorbs heat and helps to raise the soil temperature, so that seed germination and ion uptake by young roots will be faster.

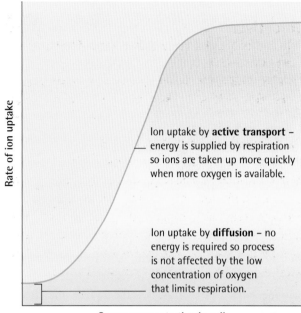

'Plateau' suggests that active transport of ions is limited by some other factor that limits respiration, such as temperature.

Ion uptake by **active transport** – energy is supplied by respiration so ions are taken up more quickly when more oxygen is available.

Ion uptake by **diffusion** – no energy is required so process is not affected by the low concentration of oxygen that limits respiration.

Rate of ion uptake (y-axis)

Oxygen concentration in soil (x-axis)

Ion uptake depends on respiration.

1 Does a solution containing many molecules of dissolved sugar and amino acids have a high or a low water potential? Explain your answer.

2 Define osmosis in terms of water potential.

3 How does the strength of the cellulose cell wall help plants to support themselves?

4 A scientist investigated the uptake of magnesium ions by the roots of young cereal plants. He made the following observations:

a The rate of uptake was increased by raising the temperature, so long as it did not exceed 40 °C.

b Uptake stopped if the roots were treated with cyanide, an ion that prevents respiration.

c Ions were taken up even if they were present at a lower concentration in the solution around the roots than in the root cells themselves.

d If ion uptake continued for some time, the concentration of sugars in the root cells decreased.

What conclusions can be drawn from each of these observations?

Objectives

☞ To appreciate that water and dissolved substances are transported around the plant in specialised transport tissues

Xylem and phloem

Substances need to be transported for long distances throughout a plant's body – sugars, for example, are produced in the photosynthesising cells of the leaves and may need to be transported to storage cells in the roots. The water and ions absorbed by the roots may be required by cells at the growing tip (the **meristem**) of the shoot. These long-distance transport functions are carried out by two specialised plant tissues – the **xylem** and the **phloem**. These are tubes running through the plant,

collected together in groups in the **vascular (transport) bundles,** as shown in the diagram opposite.

Moving vital substances from sources to sinks

The transport tissues are arranged in the stem and root as shown opposite, to offer:

☞ the most efficient transport of materials from **sources** (where they are taken in or made) to **sinks** (where they are used or stored)

☞ the most effective support in air (the stem) and soil (the root).

The transport functions of xylem and phloem have been investigated in a number of ways, as shown in the diagram below.

A section of the stem shows that the stylet has entered the phloem, and no other tissue

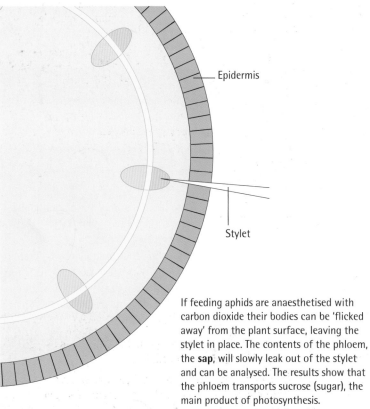

Epidermis

Stylet

If feeding aphids are anaesthetised with carbon dioxide their bodies can be 'flicked away' from the plant surface, leaving the stylet in place. The contents of the phloem, the **sap,** will slowly leak out of the stylet and can be analysed. The results show that the phloem transports sucrose (sugar), the main product of photosynthesis.

Demonstrating that xylem is the tissue of water transport and phloem is the tissue of sugar transport. In another experiment, plants supplied with radioactively labelled carbon dioxide ($^{14}CO_2$) produce radioactively labelled sugars. Testing with a Geiger counter shows that this radioactivity is confined to the phloem.

Application: aphids eat themselves to death!
Many insecticides kill useful insect species as well as pests. **Systemic** insecticides are sprayed onto the plant and absorbed into the phloem tissues, so they only kill aphids.

TOXOBUG (SYSTEMIC)

Transport of the products of photosynthesis
Aphids (greenfly) are serious pests of many crops. They can take food meant for the growing regions of plants by inserting their mouthparts (the **stylet**) into the plant tissues.

162

Xylem tissue contains long **xylem vessels** adapted for the rapid transport of **water** and **dissolved mineral ions.** Movement is always **up** the stem.

Longitudinal section of xylem vessels

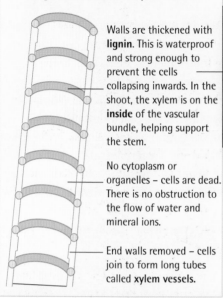

Walls are thickened with **lignin.** This is waterproof and strong enough to prevent the cells collapsing inwards. In the shoot, the xylem is on the **inside** of the vascular bundle, helping support the stem.

No cytoplasm or organelles – cells are dead. There is no obstruction to the flow of water and mineral ions.

End walls removed – cells join to form long tubes called **xylem vessels.**

Cambium tissue (see page 194) contains cells which divide by mitosis to produce more phloem and xylem.

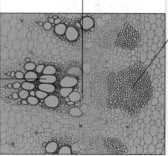

Vascular bundle (× 100).

Phloem tissue contains **sieve tubes** and **companion cells.** It is adapted for transport of the **organic products of photosynthesis** i.e. sugars (transported as **sucrose**) and amino acids.

Longitudinal section of phloem sieve tubes

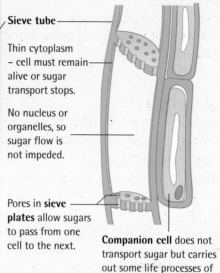

Sieve tube

Thin cytoplasm – cell must remain alive or sugar transport stops.

No nucleus or organelles, so sugar flow is not impeded.

Pores in **sieve plates** allow sugars to pass from one cell to the next.

Companion cell does not transport sugar but carries out some life processes of the sieve tubes.

Stem – vascular bundles are arranged in a ring with soft cortex in the centre, helping to support the stem.

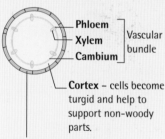

Phloem
Xylem   } Vascular bundle
Cambium

Cortex – cells become turgid and help to support non-woody parts.

Epidermis – protects against infection by viruses and bacteria, and dehydration.

Direction of transport varies with the seasons!
Sucrose is transported **from** stores in the root **to** leaves in spring, but **to** stores in the root **from** photosynthesising leaves in the summer and early autumn.

NOTICE
Sugar can move up and down phloem at the same time.

Root – root hairs are extended cells of the epidermis.

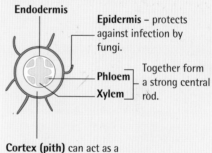

Endodermis

Epidermis – protects against infection by fungi.

Phloem
Xylem   } Together form a strong central rod.

Cortex (pith) can act as a winter store for starch.

The transport tissues xylem and phloem are arranged in vascular bundles. They transport water and dissolved substances around the plant.

---

1. Name the two vascular tissues in flowering plants. Which tissue divides to form the vascular tissues?

2. What is a **source**? Suggest two examples in a flowering plant.

3. Why does the direction of sugar transport vary from season to season?

4. Why must sugar be transported to **sinks** such as growing points and roots?

5. Many dyes are water soluble. Xylem vessels reach up from roots to flower petals. How could these two observations be useful to a florist?

Water movement through the plant: transpiration

Objectives

- To recall that water movement through a plant begins with water loss from the leaves
- To understand that water is lost from leaves via the stomata, through which the exchange of gases between the leaf and the atmosphere also occurs
- To describe how the leaf surface most involved in water loss can be identified
- To understand how environmental conditions can affect water movement through plants

Evaporation from leaves

Water evaporates from the parts of a plant that are exposed to the atmosphere – for example, the whole shoot system of a terrestrial plant and the upper leaf surfaces of a floating aquatic plant. The greatest loss of water takes place through the **stomata** (singular **stoma**), minute pores on the leaf surface (see page 166). There are usually more stomata on the lower surface of leaves than on the upper surface. The lower surface is less exposed to

Water movement through a plant begins with evaporation from the leaf surface. 98% of the water taken up by a plant is lost to the atmosphere by transpiration.

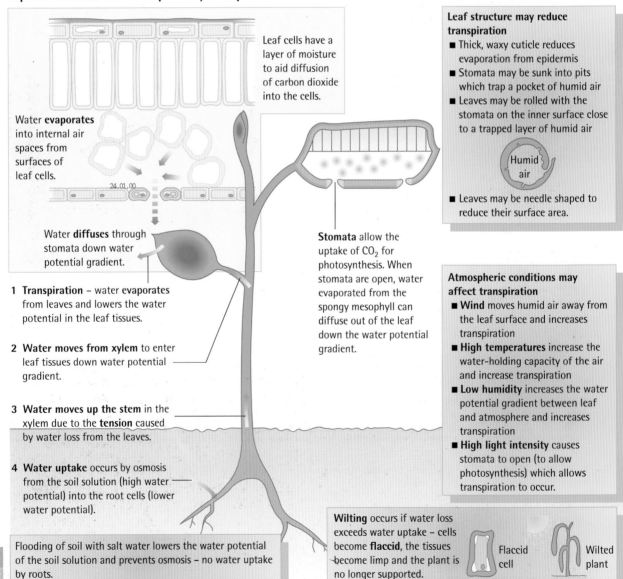

Leaf cells have a layer of moisture to aid diffusion of carbon dioxide into the cells.

Water **evaporates** into internal air spaces from surfaces of leaf cells.

Water **diffuses** through stomata down water potential gradient.

24.01.00

1 **Transpiration** – water evaporates from leaves and lowers the water potential in the leaf tissues.

2 **Water moves from xylem** to enter leaf tissues down water potential gradient.

3 **Water moves up the stem** in the xylem due to the **tension** caused by water loss from the leaves.

4 **Water uptake** occurs by osmosis from the soil solution (high water potential) into the root cells (lower water potential).

Flooding of soil with salt water lowers the water potential of the soil solution and prevents osmosis – no water uptake by roots.

Leaf structure may reduce transpiration
- Thick, waxy cuticle reduces evaporation from epidermis
- Stomata may be sunk into pits which trap a pocket of humid air
- Leaves may be rolled with the stomata on the inner surface close to a trapped layer of humid air

Humid air

- Leaves may be needle shaped to reduce their surface area.

Stomata allow the uptake of CO_2 for photosynthesis. When stomata are open, water evaporated from the spongy mesophyll can diffuse out of the leaf down the water potential gradient.

Atmospheric conditions may affect transpiration
- **Wind** moves humid air away from the leaf surface and increases transpiration
- **High temperatures** increase the water-holding capacity of the air and increase transpiration
- **Low humidity** increases the water potential gradient between leaf and atmosphere and increases transpiration
- **High light intensity** causes stomata to open (to allow photosynthesis) which allows transpiration to occur.

Wilting occurs if water loss exceeds water uptake – cells become **flaccid**, the tissues become limp and the plant is no longer supported.

Flaccid cell

Wilted plant

the warming effects of the Sun's radiation, which would speed up the evaporation rate. Loss of water from the leaf is shown in the diagram on the opposite page.

Water cannot diffuse *into* the leaf through the stomata, because the air spaces inside the leaf are completely saturated. Instead, water must be absorbed from the soil solution and drawn up through the plant (see page 160). This flow of water through the plant to replace the losses by evaporation from the leaf is called the **transpiration stream**, shown in the diagram on the opposite page.

Investigation of water loss from leaf surfaces

Cobalt chloride paper is blue when dry, and pink when wet. It is handled with forceps to avoid dampness from the fingers affecting its colour. The paper is attached to the upper and lower leaf surfaces using microscope slides. The paper attached to the lower surface of the leaf turns pink, showing that water is lost mainly from the lower surface. This technique gives a *qualitative (non-quantitative)* comparison.

Measuring the mass changes of leaves can be used to give a quantitative comparison of water loss from different leaf surfaces. A number of leaves are smeared with Vaseline as shown in the diagram below. They are weighed and then left in a drying atmosphere for 48 hours, and reweighed at intervals. Some typical results from this investigation are shown in the table.

Leaf number	Initial mass (g)	Final mass (g)	Percentage change in mass
1	4.2	4.1	
2	4.6	4.4	
3	3.9	2.5	
4	4.1	2.5	

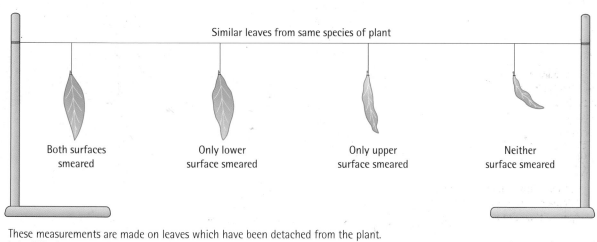

Similar leaves from same species of plant

Both surfaces smeared   Only lower surface smeared   Only upper surface smeared   Neither surface smeared

These measurements are made on leaves which have been detached from the plant. It is difficult to measure water loss from the leaves of an intact plant, but relatively simple to measure water uptake using a **potometer** (see page 168).

Questions 1 to 4 refer to the investigation above.

1. Copy the table above. Calculate the percentage change in mass for each leaf.

2. Why did leaf 3 lose a greater proportion of its mass than leaf 2?

3. Why was it important that leaves of the same species were used?

4. How could the results be made more reliable or valid?

5. Copy and complete the following paragraph.
   The movement of water through the plant begins at the leaf surface, and a stream of water called the _____ is drawn up through the plant to replace these losses. The gas _____ is required for photosynthesis, and enters the leaves through pores called _____. These pores allow the loss of _____ to the atmosphere, and leaves show many adaptations to reduce this loss. These adaptations include _____, _____ and _____.

6. List four functions of water in the plant that make water loss a disadvantage.

9·10 The leaf and water loss

Objectives

- To understand that stomata are opened to allow carbon dioxide to enter the leaf, and that this allows water vapour to diffuse out of the leaf
- To describe adaptations of leaves to reduce water losses

Stomata and water loss

Water is lost by evaporation and diffusion from the leaf surface. This water loss happens because the stomata need to open so the leaf can take in carbon dioxide as a raw material for photosynthesis. Plants can open and close the stomata, which helps to minimise water loss whilst allowing photosynthesis to continue. The position and operation of the stomata is explained in the diagram below, which also reviews the adaptations of the leaf to photosynthesis.

Adaptations of plants

The diagrams opposite show how plants may be adapted to the availability of water.

Waxy cuticle reduces water loss. It is thicker on the upper surface since this surface is usually more exposed to the warming rays of sunlight.

Upper epidermis – a complete covering which is usually one cell thick. It is transparent to allow the free passage of light, and has the major function of preventing the entry of disease-causing organisms such as bacteria and fungi.

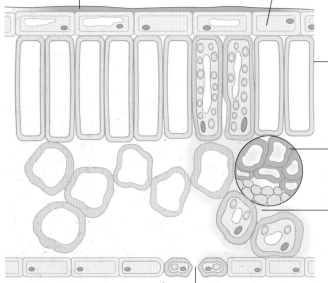

Palisade mesophyll – tall thin cells arranged in columns and separated by very narrow air spaces. Cells contain many chloroplasts, and the dense packing of these cells allows the absorption of the maximum amount of light energy.

Vein – the transport system in and out of the leaf. The **xylem** vessels deliver water and mineral salts, and the **phloem** sieve tubes carry away the organic products of photosynthesis.

Spongy mesophyll – these cells are rather loosely packed, and are covered with a thin layer of water. The air spaces between them aid the diffusion of gases through the leaf. The air spaces are saturated with water vapour so water diffuses out of the leaf.

Stomata – these minute pores are mainly present in the **lower epidermis.** This surface is less exposed to the Sun's radiation so that evaporation of water is kept to a minimum. The stomata can be closed when no carbon dioxide intake is needed (in the dark, for example).

When a plant is short of water, the guard cells become flaccid, closing the stoma.

When a plant has plenty of water, the guard cells become turgid. The cell wall on the inner surface is very thick, so it cannot stretch as much as the outer surface. So as the guard cells swell up, they curve away from each other, opening the stoma.

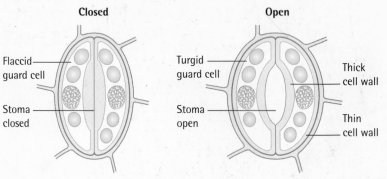

Closed	Open
Flaccid guard cell	Turgid guard cell
	Thick cell wall
Stoma closed	Stoma open
	Thin cell wall

Leaf structure is a compromise between maximising photosynthesis and minimising water loss.

Adaptations of plants to reduce water loss in different environments.

Cacti are well adapted to hot, dry environments.

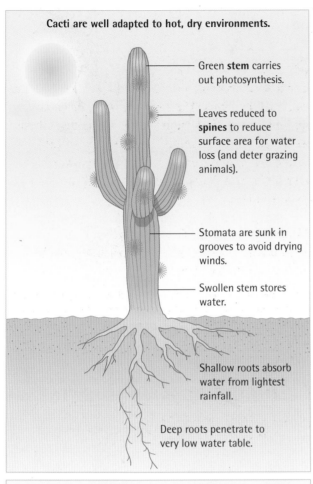

Green **stem** carries out photosynthesis.

Leaves reduced to **spines** to reduce surface area for water loss (and deter grazing animals).

Stomata are sunk in grooves to avoid drying winds.

Swollen stem stores water.

Shallow roots absorb water from lightest rainfall.

Deep roots penetrate to very low water table.

Aquatic plants have leaves with:

■ little lignin in the xylem, since the leaf is supported by the water
■ a very thin cuticle, since water conservation is not a problem
■ stomata on the **upper** surface to allow CO_2 uptake from the atmosphere.

Wilting and leaf fall

When water is in short supply, plants may reduce water loss by:

■ wilting – leaves collapse and stomata close to reduce heat absorption and evaporation/ diffusion of water
■ leaf fall – in very severe conditions, e.g. when water is frozen during winter, plants allow the leaves to fall off so that no water loss can occur. No photosynthesis can take place, but the plants can remove chlorophyll from the leaves for storage before allowing leaves to fall.

Modern Christmas trees are bred so that the needles don't fall – a disadvantage in a natural habitat, but good news when clearing up after Christmas!

---

1 The diagram shows a leaf of marram grass, a plant that grows in dry, windy environments on sand dunes. The photograph shows a transverse section of marram grass leaf as seen under a microscope.

a Copy the diagram of the leaf, and draw a line to show the direction in which a transverse section is cut.

b The positions of several stomata are labelled on the photograph. If sufficient light is available, oxygen is released from the leaf through the stomata.
 i Name the process that produces oxygen.
 ii Which gas is consumed during this process?
 iii Name and define the process by which the oxygen moves from leaf to atmosphere.

c When the stomata are open, water vapour will also be lost from the leaf's internal surfaces. Use the diagram and the photograph to suggest three ways in which the structure of the marram grass leaf helps to reduce water loss.

d Give three reasons why plants require water.

e Why is it particularly important that a plant growing in sand dunes should reduce water loss?

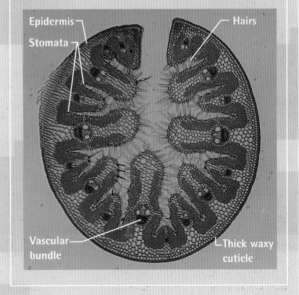

Epidermis

Hairs

Stomata

Vascular bundle

Thick waxy cuticle

Questions on photosynthesis and transport in plants

1 The diagram shows apparatus which can be used to investigate the effect of different light intensities on the rate of photosynthesis.

Bubbles of gas containing oxygen were produced by the pond plant during photosynthesis. These bubbles rose to the top of the test-tube. This forced water into the capillary tube, causing the air bubble to move along the tube.

The lamp was placed at different distances from the plant. The intensity of light reaching the test-tube, and the distance moved by the air bubble in 4 minutes, were measured and recorded each time the lamp was moved.

The syringe was used to bring the bubble back to 0 on the scale, at the start of each 4 minute period.

The results are shown in the table.

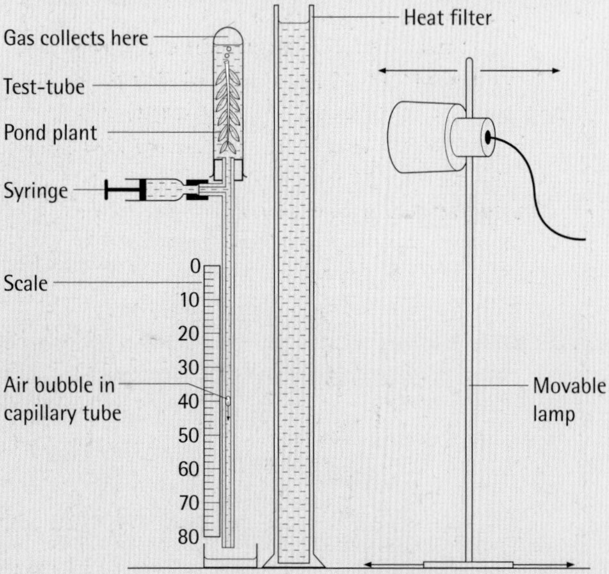

a Plot the results as a graph.

b Why was a heat filter needed?

c Each time the lamp was moved to a new position, an interval of 5 minutes was allowed before starting to time a 4 minute period for movement of the air bubble. Suggest a reason for this 5 minute interval.

d Suggest why the rate of movement of the air bubble was the same at 6.0 units as at 7.0 units of light intensity.

e Suggest why the air bubble did not move when the light intensity was 0.5 units.

f Suggest a suitable control for this investigation.

Diagram labels:
- Gas collects here
- Test-tube
- Pond plant
- Syringe
- Scale
- Air bubble in capillary tube
- Heat filter
- Movable lamp

Scale markings: 0, 10, 20, 30, 40, 50, 60, 70, 80

light intensity/ arbitrary units	distance moved by bubble in the 4 min period/ mm
0.5	0
1.0	6
2.0	18
3.0	30
4.0	42
5.0	54

(IGCSE June 1997)

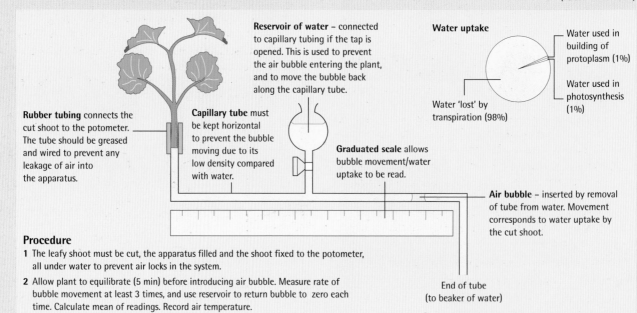

Reservoir of water – connected to capillary tubing if the tap is opened. This is used to prevent the air bubble entering the plant, and to move the bubble back along the capillary tube.

Water uptake
- Water used in building of protoplasm (1%)
- Water used in photosynthesis (1%)
- Water 'lost' by transpiration (98%)

Rubber tubing connects the cut shoot to the potometer. The tube should be greased and wired to prevent any leakage of air into the apparatus.

Capillary tube must be kept horizontal to prevent the bubble moving due to its low density compared with water.

Graduated scale allows bubble movement/water uptake to be read.

Air bubble – inserted by removal of tube from water. Movement corresponds to water uptake by the cut shoot.

End of tube (to beaker of water)

Procedure

1 The leafy shoot must be cut, the apparatus filled and the shoot fixed to the potometer, all under water to prevent air locks in the system.

2 Allow plant to equilibrate (5 min) before introducing air bubble. Measure rate of bubble movement at least 3 times, and use reservoir to return bubble to zero each time. Calculate mean of readings. Record air temperature.

3 Rate of water uptake per unit area of leaves can be calculated by measuring leaf area.

The bubble potometer measures water uptake (water loss by transpiration plus water consumption for cell expansion and photosynthesis).

2 This question is about water uptake by plants.

Using the potometer shown at the bottom of the opposite page, a student investigated the factors that influence water uptake by a plant. He obtained the following results:

Environmental condition	Time taken for bubble to move 10 cm (minutes)	Rate of bubble movement (cm per minute)
A High light intensity	6	
B High humidity (plant enclosed in clear plastic bag)	18	
C Wind (electric fan blowing over plant surface)	2	
D Dark and windy	19	
E Dark and low humidity	20	

a Copy the table. Calculate the rate at which the bubble moves and complete the third column. Plot these results in the form of a bar chart.

b Plants require light for photosynthesis. They 'anticipate' the need for carbon dioxide uptake during photosynthesis by opening their stomata under appropriate conditions. Does this help to explain the results of experiment A? Explain your answer.

c Water is lost from leaves by evaporation and diffusion if the stomata are open, and a suitable water potential gradient exists. Use this information to explain the results of experiments B and E.

d Explain the results of experiments C and D.

3 Copy and complete the following paragraphs.

a The cells of green plants absorb water by _____. Plant cells rely on water for _____, as a medium for biochemical reactions, as a _____ and as a raw material for _____.

b Water is obtained by plants from the soil solution. The water enters the plant through its _____. These structures are well adapted to the absorption of water. There are _____ growing on their epidermis which greatly increase the _____ over which water absorption can take place. In addition to water, these structures also absorb _____ such as _____ which is required for the synthesis of chlorophyll and _____ which is required for the manufacture of amino acids and proteins. These substances are absorbed by a process called _____ since it requires a supply of energy.

c Water is used as a transport medium for both ions and sugars. Mineral ions are transported within the main water flow through the plant in the _____ tissue. Sugars are transported in the living cells of the _____. These specialised tissues are grouped together into _____ bundles.

4 This question is about support in plant cells.

The plant cells are in the root of a carrot.

The following diagram shows three carrot root cells placed in a concentrated sugar solution.

a i Name the parts of the cell labelled A, B and C.
 ii What is filling the space labelled D on the diagram?

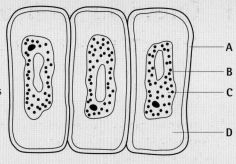

Concentrated sugar solution outside the cells

— A
— B
— C
— D

b Below are descriptions of plant cells which have turgor pressure and plant cells which do not.

List the **three** descriptions of cells with turgor pressure.
- the cell membrane is pressed against the cell wall
- the cell membrane is not in contact with the cell wall
- the cell wall is stretched
- the cell wall is not stretched
- the vacuole is pushing against the cytoplasm
- the vacuole is not pushing against the cytoplasm

c People do not like buying carrots which are split.

Scientists can use a wedge test to find out how easily a carrot splits.

The diagram shows a wedge test.

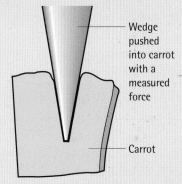

Wedge pushed into carrot with a measured force

Carrot

The graph shows the results of many wedge tests.

 i What does the graph tell you about the relationship between turgor pressure and the amount of force needed to split carrot roots?

 ii Suggest why carrots grown in low-rainfall areas are less likely to split.

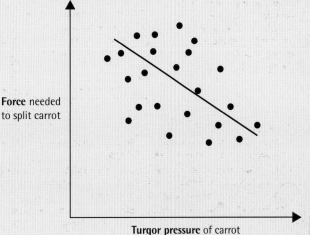

Force needed to split carrot

Turgor pressure of carrot

(MEG June 1998)

10·1 Sensitivity and movement in plants

Objectives

- To recall that plants, like all living things, are sensitive to their environment
- To know that plants respond to stimuli by changes in their growth patterns
- To know that plant growth responses are controlled by hormones
- To appreciate the importance of plant growth responses
- To understand how plant hormones may be used commercially

Plants respond to their environment

Plants respond to their environment – they show **sensitivity (irritability)**. Plant responses are rather slow compared with those of animals – plants respond to **stimuli** (to changes in their environment) by changing their growth patterns. These growth responses enable a plant to make the most of the resources available in its environment.

Plants respond to many stimuli, but two are of particular importance: **light** (the photo-stimulus) and **gravity** (the geo-stimulus). A growth response carried out by a plant in response to the direction of a stimulus is called a **tropism**.

A **positive** response is a growth movement towards the stimulus, and a **negative** response is a growth movement away from the stimulus. For example:

- a stem growing towards light is a **positive phototropism**
- a stem growing upwards (away from gravity) is a **negative geotropism**
- a root growing downwards (away from light but towards gravity) is a positive geotropism but a negative phototropism.

Roots are **positively geotropic**:

- They grow into the soil, which provides a source of water and mineral ions.
- They provide an extensive system of support and anchorage for the plant.

Shoots are **positively phototropic**:

- Leaves are in the optimum position to absorb light energy for photosynthesis.
- Flowers are lifted into the position where they are most likely to receive pollen. They will be held out into the wind, or may be more visible to pollinating insects.

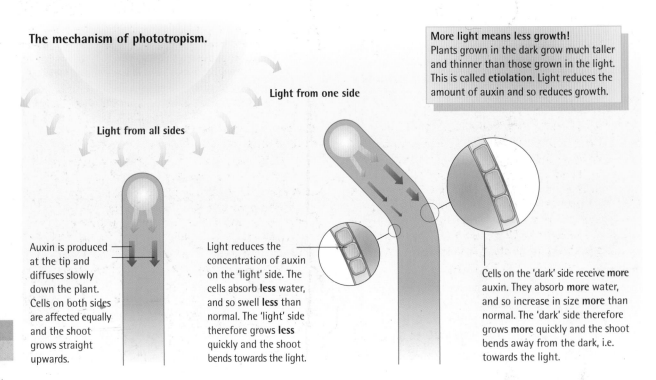

The mechanism of phototropism.

Light from all sides

Light from one side

> **More light means less growth!**
> Plants grown in the dark grow much taller and thinner than those grown in the light. This is called **etiolation**. Light reduces the amount of auxin and so reduces growth.

Auxin is produced at the tip and diffuses slowly down the plant. Cells on both sides are affected equally and the shoot grows straight upwards.

Light reduces the concentration of auxin on the 'light' side. The cells absorb **less** water, and so swell **less** than normal. The 'light' side therefore grows **less** quickly and the shoot bends towards the light.

Cells on the 'dark' side receive **more** auxin. They absorb **more** water, and so increase in size **more** than normal. The 'dark' side therefore grows **more** quickly and the shoot bends away from the dark, i.e. towards the light.

Plant movement and reproduction

Phototropism is controlled by auxin

Growth is a relatively slow response to a stimulus in animals (see page 104) and plants. Growth in plants is controlled by **plant hormones** or **plant growth substances**. These are sometimes grouped together as **'auxin'**, which means 'growth substance'. The following observations have been made about auxin:

- If the tip of a young shoot is cut off, the shoot can no longer respond to stimuli. This suggests that the tip produces the auxin.

- A shoot responding to a stimulus always bends *just behind* the tip. The auxin appears to travel from the tip (where it is made) to a region behind the tip (where it has its action).

- When shoot tips are exposed to light from one side, auxin accumulates on the 'dark' side of the shoot. The auxin is somehow affecting the growth of the 'dark' side of the shoot.

The role of auxin in phototropism is shown in the diagram at the bottom of the page opposite.

Plant hormones have commercial uses

Humans put their knowledge of how hormones work in plants to good use. Being able to control the growth of plants is valuable, since plants are at the base of all human food chains. Some examples of the commercial use of plant hormones are illustrated in the diagram below.

Synchronised fruiting – spraying hormone onto fruits can make them develop at the same rate. This allows efficient picking of the crop by machine.

This happens naturally! One ripe fruit in a bowl releases a hormone gas which makes the other fruit ripen.

Weeds can be killed – spraying with high concentrations of hormone upsets normal growth patterns. Different plant species are sensitive to different extents, so this weed killing can be selective, e.g. grasses may be killed when shrubs survive.

Agent Orange worked like this! During the Vietnam war, hormone sprays were used to clear areas of vegetation and make bombing of bridges and roads easier. These sprays can also be used to clear vegetation from overhead power lines, where removal by hand could be expensive and dangerous.

Seedless fruits can be produced – a hormone spray can make fruits such as apples and grapes develop **without fertilisation**. Since no fertilisation has taken place, no seeds are formed. This also reduces the grower's dependence on pollinating insects.

Cuttings can be stimulated to grow roots. In this way a valuable plant can be cloned (see page 184) to provide many identical copies.

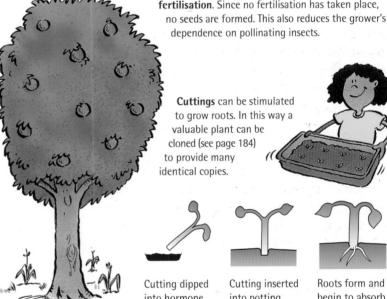

Cutting dipped into hormone rooting powder

Cutting inserted into potting compost

Roots form and begin to absorb mineral ions and water

Copy and complete the following paragraphs.

1. The _____ of a growing shoot produces a plant hormone or _____. This substance causes cells behind the tip to _____ by the absorption of _____. When the shoot is lit from one side, more _____ accumulates on the dark side. As a result the cells _____ more and the shoot bends towards the light. This response is called _____ and offers several advantages to the plant, including greater access to light energy to drive the process of _____.

2. Plant hormones have many commercial uses. These include:
   - the stimulation of _____ on cuttings, which allows growers to produce many _____ of valuable plants
   - the control of _____, which allows growers to harvest economically with machinery
   - the destruction of _____, which could otherwise compete with crops for _____, _____ and _____. Careful selection of hormone concentrations allows this destruction to be _____: only pest plants are killed.
   - the production of _____ fruits, since the hormone can make the plant develop a fruit without _____ taking place.

10·2 Reproduction in flowering plants: flowers

Objectives
- To understand the part played by flowers in the life of a flowering plant
- To be able to identify the parts of a typical flower
- To be able to state the functions of the parts of a flower

An individual plant, like any other living organism, eventually dies. For a *species* of plant to survive, the *individual* plants must be able to replace themselves. This is the process of **reproduction**, an essential part of the life cycle of the plant.

Sexual reproduction in plants

Flowering plants, as their name suggests, are able to reproduce using highly adapted structures called **flowers**. The life cycle of a flowering plant is outlined below.

Flowering plants reproduce sexually. The following list shows the stages that can be recognised in the reproduction of flowering plants.

- The young plant develops reproductive organs.
- Sex cells (gametes) develop inside the reproductive organs.
- The male sex cells are transferred to the female sex cells.
- Fusion of male and female sex cells (fertilisation) occurs, and a zygote is produced.
- The zygote develops into an embryo.
- The embryo grows into a new young plant, and the cycle starts all over again.

Whereas animals move around freely (they are **motile**), plants live in a fixed position. In plants:

- Male gametes may have to be carried some distance to meet female gametes.
- Young plant embryos may have to be carried some distance to get away from their parents!

Most plants are **hermaphrodite**, that is, they have male and female sexual parts on the same individual. This means that the male gametes only have to travel a short distance to the female gametes.

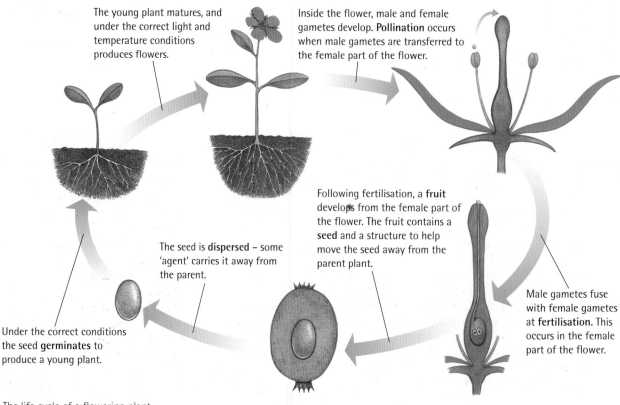

The young plant matures, and under the correct light and temperature conditions produces flowers.

Inside the flower, male and female gametes develop. **Pollination** occurs when male gametes are transferred to the female part of the flower.

Following fertilisation, a **fruit** develops from the female part of the flower. The fruit contains a **seed** and a structure to help move the seed away from the parent plant.

Male gametes fuse with female gametes at **fertilisation**. This occurs in the female part of the flower.

The seed is **dispersed** – some 'agent' carries it away from the parent.

Under the correct conditions the seed **germinates** to produce a young plant.

The life cycle of a flowering plant.

The formation of flowers

A flower is formed from a bud, which is a collection of cells at the end of a flower stalk. The cells receive hormone messages from the main plant body, and gradually develop into four rings of specialised leaves – the flower. These have the sole function of forming sex cells and making sure that fertilisation occurs.

The structure of a typical insect-pollinated flower is shown in the diagram below.

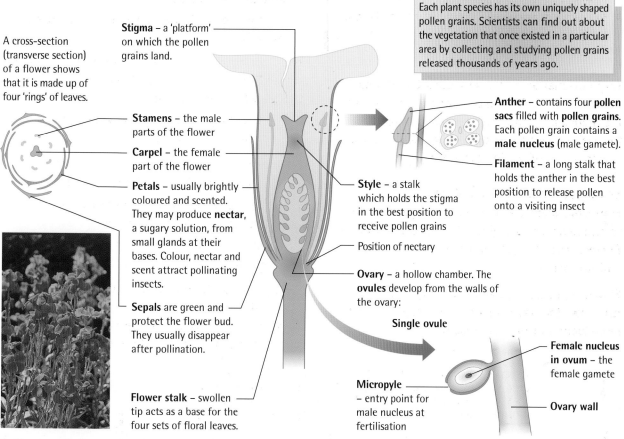

A cross-section (transverse section) of a flower shows that it is made up of four 'rings' of leaves.

Stigma – a 'platform' on which the pollen grains land.

Each plant species has its own uniquely shaped pollen grains. Scientists can find out about the vegetation that once existed in a particular area by collecting and studying pollen grains released thousands of years ago.

Stamens – the male parts of the flower

Carpel – the female part of the flower

Petals – usually brightly coloured and scented. They may produce **nectar**, a sugary solution, from small glands at their bases. Colour, nectar and scent attract pollinating insects.

Sepals are green and protect the flower bud. They usually disappear after pollination.

Flower stalk – swollen tip acts as a base for the four sets of floral leaves.

Anther – contains four **pollen sacs** filled with **pollen grains**. Each pollen grain contains a **male nucleus** (male gamete).

Filament – a long stalk that holds the anther in the best position to release pollen onto a visiting insect

Style – a stalk which holds the stigma in the best position to receive pollen grains

Position of nectary

Ovary – a hollow chamber. The **ovules** develop from the walls of the ovary:

Single ovule

Micropyle – entry point for male nucleus at fertilisation

Female nucleus in ovum – the female gamete

Ovary wall

The structure of a flower: the wallflower. A flower grows from a flower bud and is specialised to produce and release the male and female gametes.

1. Look at the table on the right. Match each part of a flower to its function. Write the letter and number to show your answer, for example, (a)-5.

2. Copy and complete the following paragraph.
The life cycle of a flowering plant has a number of stages. A young plant develops when a seed _____. The plant matures until it produces a _____ which is a collection of leaves specialised for _____. Male gametes are transferred to the female part of the flower by _____ and fuse with female gametes at _____. Following this process the ovary develops into a _____ which contains a _____ and a structure to help move it away from the parent plant. This process, which is called _____, requires some agent or vector to remove the seed from the parent plant.

Flower parts	Functions
(a) pollen	1 to support the anther
(b) flower stalk	2 to secrete a sugary solution
(c) style	3 to contain the female gametes
(d) filament	4 to protect the flower in bud
(e) anther	5 to deliver the male gamete
(f) sepal	6 to form a base for the flower
(g) petal	7 to hold up the stigma
(h) nectary	8 to attract insects
(i) ovary	9 to produce pollen
(j) sepal	10 to receive pollen

Plant movement and reproduction

10·3 Pollination: the transfer of male sex cells to female flower parts

Objectives

- To define the term pollination
- To understand the difference between self-pollination and cross-pollination
- To describe how flowers may be adapted to pollination by insects or wind
- To describe how honey bees are adapted as insect pollinators

Self-pollination and cross-pollination

For sexual reproduction to occur, the male gametes must be transferred to the female part of the flower – this transfer is the process of **pollination**. The transfer may come about within the same flower (self-pollination) or from one flower to another of the same species (cross-pollination), as shown in the diagram on the right.

Cross-pollination offers many advantages, and some species make sure that it happens.

- Some have special proteins on the surface of the stigma that prevent pollen tubes forming if the pollen comes from the anthers of the same plant. These are **self-sterile** plants.

- In some plants, the anther and the stigma are so far away from one another in the flower that it is not very easy for pollen to travel from the anther to the stigma of the same flower.

- A few plants, such as ash, willow and holly, have separate male and female plants.

Pollination by wind and insects

Whether self- or cross-pollination occurs, some agent or vector is needed to carry the pollen grains from the anthers to the stigma. This agent is most often an insect or the wind. Flowers show many adaptations to successful **insect pollination** or **wind pollination**. Some of the insects that act as pollinators have also become adapted to make the most of their relationship with flowers. The table on the opposite page shows how some plants are adapted for pollination by insects or plants. The honey bee feeds on nectar and pollen. The diagram on the next page shows how it is adapted as a pollinating insect.

In **self-pollination** pollen is transferred from anther to stigma **of the same plant**. This is very efficient (the pollen doesn't have to travel very far) but does not offer much chance of genetic variation (see page 000).

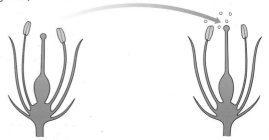

In **cross-pollination** pollen is transferred from anther to stigma **of another plant of the same species**. This is risky (pollen may never reach the other plant) but offers a greater chance of genetic variation than self-pollination.

Cross-pollination is the only possibility for flowers that are not hermaphrodite. Sometimes a plant has only male or only female flowers. This is **very** risky, since plants of the opposite sex may not be nearby, but offers a very great chance of genetic variation.

Pollination.

Wind-pollinated flowers such as this grass have small, inconspicuous petals. The anthers and stigmas hang outside the flower.

Plant movement and reproduction

Part of flower	Insect-pollinated (e.g. wallflower)	Wind-pollinated (e.g. grass)	Reason
Petals	Usually large, brightly coloured, scented, often with nectaries. Guide lines may be present.	Small, green or dull in colour, no scent or nectaries	Insects are attracted to colour and scent. Guide lines direct insects to nectaries, past anthers.
Anthers	Stiff, firmly attached and positioned where insects must brush against them	Hang loosely on long thin filaments	Wind is more likely to dislodge pollen from exposed, dangling anthers than from enclosed ones
Pollen	Small amounts of large, sticky grains	Enormous quantities of light, smooth pollen grains	Sticky grains attach to hairs on insect's body. Larger amounts from wind-pollinated flowers mean pollination is more likely.
Stigma	Usually flat or lobe-shaped, and positioned where insect must brush against them	Long and feathery, and hanging outside flower	Feathery stigmas form a large network to catch pollen being blown past the flower

The honey bee is adapted as an insect pollinator.

Wings allow the bee to move between food source and hive.

Hairs on body hold the sticky pollen grains.

Head

Eyes detect colour on flowers.

Antennae detect scent from flowers.

Sucking tube collects nectar.

Hind legs

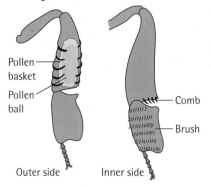

Pollen basket

Pollen ball

Comb

Brush

Outer side

Inner side

The hind legs collect pollen. The comb and brush remove pollen from the body and pass it to the pollen basket on the opposite leg. The bee then carries the **pollen ball** back to the hive. Pollen is an excellent protein source.

Intestine

Salivary glands

The honey bee ferments a mixture of nectar and saliva to produce honey.

Honey is an excellent energy source, and can be stored at the beehive.

The flower is pollinated by bees:
- the coloured petals signal a source of food
- nectar is deep in the flower
- bee mouthparts are too short to reach the nectar
- bee pushes its body deep into the flower, and pollen rubs off from anther
- bee flies to another flower. Pollen is rubbed off its body onto the stigma of the second flower: cross-pollination has taken place.

Experimental design: using models

Scientists use **models** of living organisms to study one or two features of the organism. Living organisms may have features that other organisms can detect, but that humans cannot. These might affect the results of an experiment, so a model is easier to study.

Two students were interested in why honey bees visit wallflowers. One of them believed that the *colour* of the flower, attracted the bees but the other was convinced that it was the *scent*.

1 Design an experiment to determine whether colour or scent is the more important stimulus to the honey bees. In your design:
- devise suitable models for the wallflowers
- clearly state the manipulated and the responding variables
- suggest any variables that should be fixed, and say how you would fix them
- consider whether there are any controls that you might use
- draw a table that would be suitable for the presentation of your data.

Plant movement and reproduction

Objectives

- To define the process of fertilisation
- To understand the role of the pollen tube
- To recall which parts of a flower form the fruit
- To understand that a seed contains a food store as well as an embryo

Fertilisation follows pollination

Pollination is complete once the pollen released from an anther has landed on the stigma of the same or another flower. The next step in the plant's reproductive process is **fertilisation**, the fusion of the male and female gametes. The diagram opposite shows how the nucleus from the pollen grain travels down a **pollen tube** to combine with the nucleus of the ovum.

The formation of fruit and seed

After the male nucleus has fused with the ovum, the resulting **zygote** divides many times to produce an **embryo**. The development of a seed and the structure of the embryo are described in the diagram on the opposite page.

Once fertilisation is complete, the developing seed sends hormone messages to the flower, and a number of changes take place:

- The sepals and petals wither away, and may fall off.
- The stamens, stigma and style wither away.

These structures have now completed their function, and would use up valuable food compounds if they remained.

- The wall of the ovary changes. It may become hardened and dry, or fleshy and succulent, and in the wallflower it forms a leathery pouch.

The ovary is now called a **fruit**. A fruit is a fertilised ovary, and has the function of dispersing the seeds away from the parent plant, as we shall see on page 178.

Pollen grain – chemical signals released by the stigma ensure that a pollen tube is only produced when pollen lands on a stigma of the same species.

Pollen tube grows down through the style and acts as a channel to deliver the male gamete from the pollen grain to the female gamete in the ovule.

Ovary wall – ovules are attached to the inside of the ovary wall by a short stalk.

Ovule contains the female gamete, and some other cells which may develop into food reserves.

Stigma

Style

Fertilisation occurs when the haploid male and female gametes fuse to form a diploid zygote.

Fertilisation also triggers some other cells in the ovule to divide rapidly and form a food store inside the seed.

Micropyle – a gap in the covering of the ovule. The tip of the pollen tube locates this gap and the male gamete enters the ovule through it.

Note that only one fertilisation is shown here. Each ovule needs its own pollen grain and pollen tube to be fertilised. A plum has only one ovule in each ovary, a wallflower has a few tens and a poppy may have thousands of ovules in one ovary!

Stages in the development of a fruit

Tomato flowers – the petals are still obvious.

After fertilisation, the petals have fallen off, the stigma and style have withered and the carpel is beginning to swell.

In the ripe fruit, the ovary wall is swollen and succulent. What do you think is the purpose of the bright red colour?

Plant movement and reproduction

The formation of seed and fruit following fertilisation.

 After successful fertilisation the sepals, petals and anthers wither away. The stigma and style also wither so that only the ovary remains on the flower stalk.

Seed coat (testa) prevents drying out of the embryo.

Cotyledons (seed leaves) may form the food store for the embryo. There is **one** seed leaf in monocotyledons such as grasses, or **two** in dicotyledons such as peas and beans.

Endosperm – tissue which forms the food store in cereal crops.

Ovary wall may become dry and hard (in a Brazil nut, for example), very soft and fleshy (in a plum, for example) or form a leathery pouch (as in the wallflower).

Plumule (young shoot)
Radicle (young root)
together with the cotyledons these make up the **embryo**. The embryo develops into a new young plant after germination.

Fertilised ovule develops into a seed, with the zygote forming the embryo.

Micropyle – a small hole in the testa which allows the entry of water and oxygen as the seed germinates.

Remember!
- The **carpel** becomes the **fruit**.
- The **ovule** becomes the **seed**.

Fruit or vegetable?
If it's been formed following **F**ertilisation it's a **F**ruit; if there's no sex in**V**olved it's a **V**egetable. Potatoes and carrots are vegetables but tomatoes are fruits.

Not all seeds are edible
Seeds contain stores of carbohydrate, fat, protein, minerals and other food compounds. These are used up by the embryo as it develops into a young plant, but also form an excellent food source for animals (including humans). But note ...
- Uncooked castor oil seeds contain a deadly poison, **ricin**, which was used to kill the Romanian dissident Georgi Markov.
- Almonds contain **cyanide**. Don't eat too much marzipan since this is made from almond paste!

---

1. In one sentence, explain the difference between pollination and fertilisation.

2. Draw a simple diagram of a typical hermaphrodite flower. On your diagram label:
   a the parts that fall off after fertilisation
   b the parts that develop into a fruit.

3. Define the word 'seed'.

4. Classify each of the following as:
   a fruit b seed or c neither fruit nor seed.
   Tomato, cucumber, Brussels sprout, baked bean, runner bean, celery, pea, grape

5. Two students suggested that the wallflower cannot produce fruits unless pollination has taken place. Their teacher showed them how to prevent bees reaching the flowers by covering the flowers in a fine mesh bag, and how to transfer pollen with a fine paintbrush.
   a Describe how the students could carry out an experiment to test their hypothesis.
   b Suggest how they could modify their experiment to test whether self- or cross-pollination produced more seeds in the wallflower.

   In your answer be sure to describe any controls which they could include, and any steps they could take to ensure that their results were valid.

10·5 Dispersal of seeds and fruits

Objectives
▪ To define the term dispersal
▪ To describe how fruits and seeds may be adapted for dispersal
▪ To understand why dispersal is necessary

Dispersal of seeds and fruits.

Remember! Both **pollination** and **dispersal** use animals and/or wind as 'agents'. Make certain that you can distinguish these processes.

An adult plant with well developed root and shoot systems is well adapted to exploit the resources of the environment.

Competition for limited resources is reduced by a range of methods of **seed dispersal**.

By wind

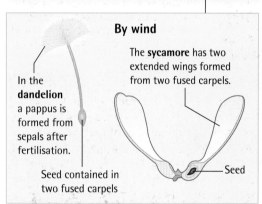

In the **dandelion** a pappus is formed from sepals after fertilisation.

The **sycamore** has two extended wings formed from two fused carpels.

Seed contained in two fused carpels

Seed

By an explosive mechanism
e.g. lupin

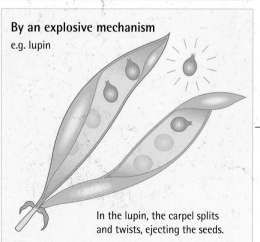

In the lupin, the carpel splits and twists, ejecting the seeds.

By animals

Avens actually produces a **false** fruit because the style (not just the ovary) is involved in dispersal.

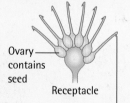

Ovary contains seed

Receptacle

Hooked style is lignified (woody) and attaches to hair or fur of animals.

In the **plum**, succulent flesh offers a food reward to animals.

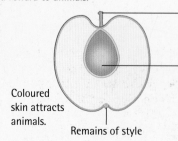

Coloured skin attracts animals.

Remains of style

Pedicel – the stalk which attached the fruit to the adult plant

Seed is resistant to the digestive juices of the animal, and passes out in the faeces.

By water

In the **coconut**, the fibrous ovary wall allows the fruit to float in water.

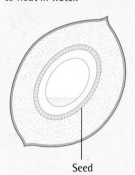

Seed

Seeds need to be dispersed away from the parent plant

After fertilisation, the seeds are attached to the parent plant. Before it can germinate and develop into a new young plant, the seed (enclosed in the fruit) must be separated from its parent plant. If the young plant remains close to its parent, it would need to **compete** with the parent for resources such as light energy, water and carbon dioxide. The parent plant has some means of **dispersing** the seeds and fruits, that is, separating them from the parent so they are far enough away to avoid competition. Fruits may be adapted in different ways to aid dispersal of the seeds, as shown in the diagrams on the opposite page. Agents that disperse fruits include wind, water and animals.

Lots of fruits increase the chances of success

Any method of seed dispersal is very risky. The seeds may fall beneath the parent plant, and be out-competed for vital resources, or they may land in a place that is entirely unsuitable for germination and growth. Plants produce enormous numbers of fruits, which makes it more likely that at least a few will land in a suitable place for germination and development. A single mature oak tree, for example, might produce a million acorns (oak fruits) in a single year!

Lines of weakness which allow the ovary to split open as the wall dries out

Seeds are exposed to the wind

The wallflower disperses its seeds using the wind. The fruit dries out, and then splits along lines of weakness. The seeds are now exposed to the wind, and blow away from the parent plant.

---

1 During a class investigation, a group of students measured the time taken for a dropped dandelion fruit to reach the ground, and also the distance travelled by the fruit in that time.

Time taken (s)	Distance travelled (cm)
6	100
9	140
3	65
14	200
7	105
7	95
9	135
11	170
2	45
8	165

a Plot this information as a scatter graph.

b Is there any relationship between the time spent floating and the efficiency of dispersal of the dandelion fruit?

c Look at the photograph of dandelion fruits. Is there any feature of the fruit that would be likely to increase the length of time it spent floating?

d The teacher insisted that the students dropped all of the fruits from the same height, and in the same corner of the laboratory. Why?

Dandelion fruits are dispersed by wind.

10·6 Germination of seeds

Dispersal allows plants to spread their seeds so they can develop without competition from their parents. A seed is made up of an embryo and a food store, all enclosed within a seed coat. If environmental conditions are suitable, the embryo will begin to use the food store in the seed and grow into a new young plant. This development of a seed to a new young plant is called **germination**.

Conditions for germination

A seed needs the following to germinate:

- a **supply of water**
- **oxygen** for **aerobic respiration** (see page 28)
- a **temperature suitable** for the enzymes involved in germination (see page 15).

These requirements are explained more fully in the diagram below.

Some seeds have other requirements as well as the ones shown in the diagram. A few need particular conditions of light (for example, lettuce).

Start here!

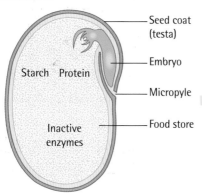

Start of germination

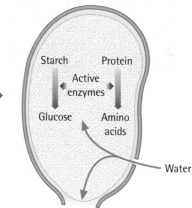

Germination proceeds

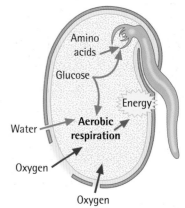

Dormant seed – embryo and food stores are surrounded by an impermeable seed coat. The micropyle is the only gap in the seed coat.

Environmental factors that affect germination are very similar to those that affect enzyme activity. This indicates that **germination is a process controlled by enzymes.**

Water enters through the micropyle and:
- activates enzymes to convert insoluble stores to soluble foods
- makes tissues swell so that the testa is split open.
Enzymes work at their **optimum temperature**.

Water and oxygen enter through gaps in the testa. Oxygen and glucose enable aerobic respiration, which releases energy. The embryo is able to grow as it receives raw materials and energy.

Dormancy will continue if the embryo in the seed does not experience the right conditions:
- if kept in anaerobic conditions
- if kept dry
- if kept cool.
Oxygen and water cannot reach the embryo if the testa remains impermeable. Some seeds must pass through an animal's gut (where digestive juices are present) before the testa is weakened enough for the seeds to germinate.

Seeds kept dry in a vacuum, as in seed packets, can be stored for long periods

Conditions for germination.

Dormancy

If a seed does not experience ideal conditions for germination immediately, it will not die. Most seeds can survive long periods of poor conditions, only germinating when conditions improve. Seeds survive in a resting state called **dormancy** during which they use hardly any food. The very low water content of seeds allows them to remain dormant, and the availability of water is one of the conditions that allows a seed to escape dormancy and germinate.

Structural changes during germination

Many biochemical processes go on inside the seed during germination. There are also external changes that can easily be seen as a seed begins to develop into a young plant. Different types of seed germinate in different ways. We shall take the broad bean as an example.

The broad bean shows **hypogeal germination**. 'Hypogeal' means 'below the ground' ('hypo' sounds like 'low' and 'geo' refers to 'earth'). The seed remains below the ground throughout the whole process. The stages involved in hypogeal germination are described in the diagram below.

The seedling must start to photosynthesise before all the food stores are used up. For this reason each seed type has an optimum depth for planting. If a seed is planted too deep, the shoot can't get above the ground before all the reserves are used up. Very tiny seeds (lettuce for example) often require a light signal to trigger germination. They will not germinate unless they are close to the surface of the soil, where they are in less danger of using up their food stores too quickly.

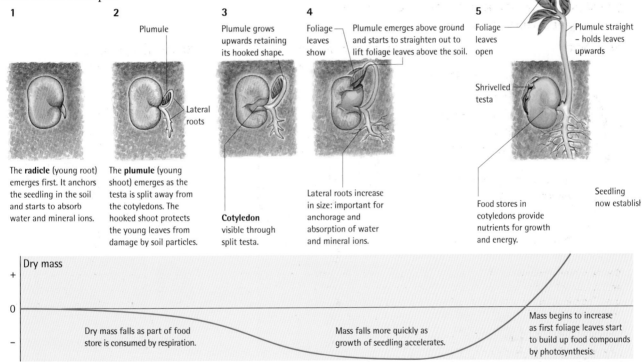

1

The **radicle** (young root) emerges first. It anchors the seedling in the soil and starts to absorb water and mineral ions.

2

Plumule

Lateral roots

The **plumule** (young shoot) emerges as the testa is split away from the cotyledons. The hooked shoot protects the young leaves from damage by soil particles.

3

Plumule grows upwards retaining its hooked shape.

Cotyledon visible through split testa.

4

Foliage leaves show

Plumule emerges above ground and starts to straighten out to lift foliage leaves above the soil.

Lateral roots increase in size: important for anchorage and absorption of water and mineral ions.

5

Foliage leaves open

Plumule straight – holds leaves upwards

Shrivelled testa

Food stores in cotyledons provide nutrients for growth and energy.

Seedling now established

Dry mass

+

0

–

Dry mass falls as part of food store is consumed by respiration.

Mass falls more quickly as growth of seedling accelerates.

Mass begins to increase as first foliage leaves start to build up food compounds by photosynthesis.

Germination of the broad bean. Dry mass is used as a measure of the food stores because wet mass would include water absorbed from the soil, and the amount of water absorbed and lost can vary greatly.

1 Copy and complete the following paragraph.

Before germination, a seed must absorb _____ from the soil. The seed coat is impermeable to this substance, and it enters through a hole called the _____. This absorption causes the seed to _____ and split the _____. The gas _____ can now enter, which is necessary for _____. The energy from this process, together with soluble food compounds, allows the _____ to grow. The young root or _____ appears first and grows downwards by _____, providing _____ and absorbing water and minerals for the seedling. The young shoot or _____ appears next. This grows upwards and eventually bursts through the soil. The first _____ leaves develop and the seedling is able to produce its own food by _____.

2 How would you attempt to prove that germination is controlled by enzymes?

Objectives

▪ To understand that plants can reproduce asexually

▪ To understand some of the benefits of vegetative propagation

▪ To describe examples of vegetative propagation

Sexual reproduction provides variation

The plant life cycle shown on page 172 shows sexual reproduction, which depends on the fusion of male and female **gametes**. Sexual reproduction consumes energy that otherwise could be used by the parent plant. However, it also leads to **variation** (see page 210). Sexual reproduction occurs in all advanced organisms.

Asexual reproduction can be advantageous

Plants arrive in new locations by the dispersal of seeds. There are occasions, however, when a plant would benefit from simply producing many copies of itself. For example:

▪ When a single plant arrives in a new habitat it can occupy this habitat if many copies can be produced quickly.

▪ When a plant is well suited to its habitat, any variation might be a disadvantage.

Many plants are able to reproduce **asexually** – without gametes, pollination, fertilisation and dispersal. This form of asexual reproduction, also known as **vegetative propagation**, is outlined in the diagram below.

Vegetative propagation has certain features.

▪ The new miniature plant is formed by copying cells from the parent plant (by **mitosis**, page 194), and has characteristics identical to its parent.

▪ The miniature plant can be nourished by the parent plant until it is established enough to live independently.

▪ The plant does not need to produce any flowers.

Many different methods of vegetative propagation happen naturally. Two common examples are described in the diagrams opposite – the formation of **runners** and **stem tubers**. As well as being organs of vegetative propagation, tubers also store food when photosynthesis is easy. The food can then be used for growth at the beginning of the following year when photosynthesis might be slower. This allows the plant to **perennate**, or live on from year to year. For this reason, tubers are also known as **organs of perennation**.

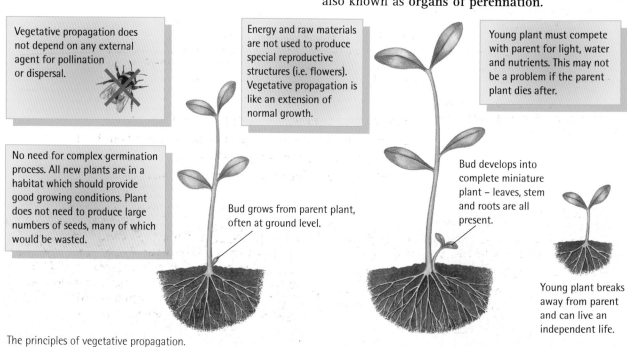

Vegetative propagation does not depend on any external agent for pollination or dispersal.

Energy and raw materials are not used to produce special reproductive structures (i.e. flowers). Vegetative propagation is like an extension of normal growth.

Young plant must compete with parent for light, water and nutrients. This may not be a problem if the parent plant dies after.

No need for complex germination process. All new plants are in a habitat which should provide good growing conditions. Plant does not need to produce large numbers of seeds, many of which would be wasted.

Bud grows from parent plant, often at ground level.

Bud develops into complete miniature plant – leaves, stem and roots are all present.

Young plant breaks away from parent and can live an independent life.

The principles of vegetative propagation.

Tuber in winter

Scar where potato was attached to shoot

New shoot beginning to develop – these make the 'eyes' on the potato.

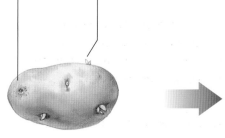

These 'seed' potatoes are allowed to produce short shoots, then planted to produce a new potato crop. They are not true 'seeds' as they were not formed by fertilisation.

Plant in summer

The shoots have developed enough to photosynthesise. They send food compounds along underground shoots, the tips of which swell to form 'new' potatoes.

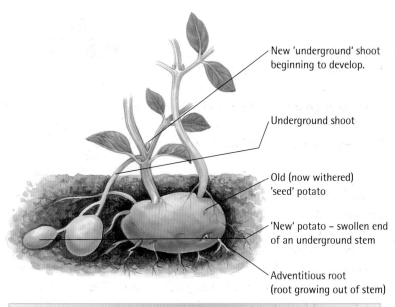

New 'underground' shoot beginning to develop.

Underground shoot

Old (now withered) 'seed' potato

'New' potato – swollen end of an underground stem

Adventitious root (root growing out of stem)

The 'new' potatoes are identical to the parent and to one another so they are all susceptible to the same diseases. The Irish famines of the nineteenth century resulted from blight fungus infecting almost all of the potato crop.

Bud on strawberry runner – can develop into another plant if it touches the ground and forms roots.

Plants are smaller the further they are from the parent plant since:
■ they are younger
■ they are 'last in line' for food compounds transported along the runner.

Terminal (end) bud on runner

Each parent plant produces runners so a dense patch of plants forms, crowding out other competitor species. Once the plants are established some vertical shoots produce flowers and, eventually, fruits.

Lateral (sideways) shoot is called a runner. Eventually the runner rots away, and the new plant exists independently.

Where the runner touches the ground it forms **adventitious roots**. Soon normal leafy shoots develop from the rooted runner.

Vegetative propagation. Potatoes reproduce using tubers; strawberries use lateral shoots called runners.

Sexual and asexual reproduction compared

Sexual reproduction and vegetative propagation both have advantages and disadvantages. Many plants make the best of both worlds, and reproduce both sexually and asexually.

1 Name two food compounds that could be detected in the transport system of a strawberry runner.

2 Suggest two storage compounds that would be present in a potato tuber. Describe simple chemical tests that would allow you to confirm their presence.

3 The two examples of vegetative propagation shown above both rely on shoots growing away from the parent plant. Given a razor blade, a red water-soluble dye and a microscope, describe how you would show that these underground or sideways-growing structures are in fact shoots and not roots.

10.8 Artificial propagation

Objectives
▪ To understand some of the benefits of vegetative propagation
▪ To appreciate how humans have exploited vegetative propagation

People use their knowledge of vegetative propagation to increase stocks of plants. Sometimes they use natural methods, for example by dividing up clumps of bulbs, or sometimes they carry out a process that would not happen in nature, such as taking cuttings from a particularly desirable plant. **Artificial propagation** is a form of plant propagation that would not occur naturally (in plants living in the wild). Stem cuttings and tissue culture are both examples of artificial propagation. These techniques are outlined in the diagrams below and opposite.

Clones and cloning

The most obvious feature of vegetative propagation is that there is no mixing of genetic material from different parents. The offspring are therefore identical to one another. A population of genetically identical individuals produced from a single parent is called a **clone**. Members of the clone have the same characteristics as the parent, which is very useful if the parent plant is well suited to particular environments, or is desirable to consumers. In natural conditions a clone may be at a disadvantage since any environmental change – a disease for example – could eliminate *all* members of the clone if the parent had no resistance to this change. Despite these disadvantages, artificial propagation and the production of clones is a very widely used practice in modern agriculture and horticulture.

A **cutting** is produced by cutting off a short piece of stem just below a point where a leaf joins the stem. The cutting is trimmed so that only two or three leaves remain.

Many ornamental house plants are produced using stem or leaf cuttings. The compost is usually replaced with a jelly containing minerals, hormones to stimulate rooting and growth, and sometimes glucose to provide an energy source for the developing roots.

The cuttings are put into a rooting compost, and then covered with a clear polythene cover. This:
- prevents excessive loss of water (which cannot be replaced without roots)
- prevents entry of fungal spores which might infect the cuttings.

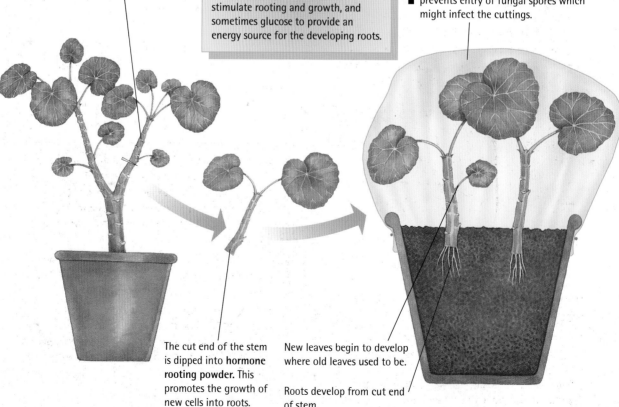

The cut end of the stem is dipped into **hormone rooting powder**. This promotes the growth of new cells into roots.

New leaves begin to develop where old leaves used to be.

Roots develop from cut end of stem.

Geraniums can be artificially propagated by stem cuttings.

Remove **meristem** (growing point) from plant with desirable characteristics.

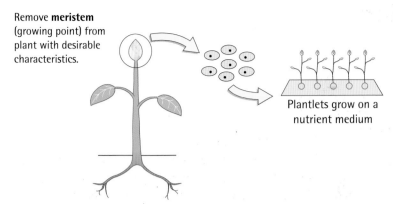

Plantlets grow on a nutrient medium

The tissue is sterilised (with sodium hypochlorite solution) and broken up into cells. The cell walls are removed (using the enzyme cellulase) to produce **protoplasts** (plant cells without cell walls). These can be treated with plant hormones to make them divide.

This method is ideal for plants that are to be transported. For example, rubber 'trees' can be started in Britain then transferred to Malaysia for planting.

Tissue culture allows many individuals to be grown in a small space.

Auxin concentration (parts per million)	Initial length of stem piece (mm)	Final length of stem piece (mm)	Change of length (mm)	Percentage change in length
0	20	21		
1	20	22		
2	20	23		
5	20	25		
0	20	26		

A group of students used some geranium stems for an experiment on auxins. If a section of stem is placed in auxin solution, the effect of this plant hormone can be detected by measuring the change in length of the stem.

1 a Why is it important to measure the pieces of stem before they are placed in the auxin solution?

b It is not important that the pieces of stem were removed from the solution after *exactly* 24 hours, but it is important that they each spent *exactly* the same amount of time in the solution. Why?

The results obtained are given in the table above.

c   i Copy the table and complete the final two columns.

ii Plot a graph to illustrate the effect of auxin concentration on stem length.

iii The diagrams show a piece of stem before and after floating in another auxin solution.

Use the diagram and your graph to calculate the concentration of this auxin solution.

2 Auxins can be used in rooting powders. The diagrams on the right show the stages of an investigation using rooting powder.

a Suggest why the piece of plant stem was split before it was placed in rooting powder (stage 2).

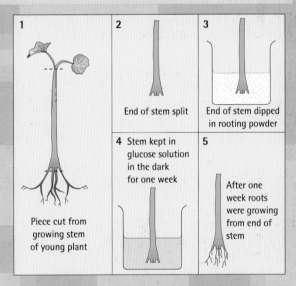

b Suggest why the piece of plant stem needed to be kept in glucose solution in stage 4.

c Redraw stage 1 to suggest how the students could have modified their technique if they wished to demonstrate the process of artificial propagation.

d Suggest one advantage and one disadvantage of an artificial propagation technique such as this one.

e When stem sections like these are placed in growing solution, they are usually surrounded by a clear plastic container. Why are they enclosed in this way? Why is it important that the container is clear?

Plant movement and reproduction

1 A student carried out an experiment on the direction of growth of the root of a germinating seed and the shoot of a seedling. Fig. 1a shows the experiment when first set up. The electric motors slowly turn the cork base and the plant pot. Fig. 1b shows the experiment after two days. The root and shoot received the same amount of light from all directions.

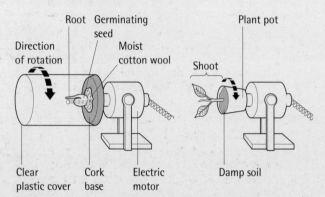

Fig. 1a

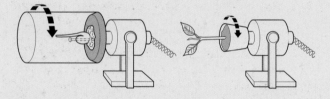

After 2 days

Fig. 1b

a Suggest why a clear plastic cover was provided for the root but not for the shoot.

b i Copy the diagram below and complete it to show how the root and shoot would appear 24 hours **after the motors were switched off.**

ii Name the responses shown by the root and the shoot that you have drawn and explain how the responses have come about.

iii Suggest why these responses were **not** shown in Fig. 1b.

(IGCSE June 1997)

2 A second student wished to extend the investigation in question 1. This student had read that roots were affected both by light and by gravity, and wanted to find out which of the two stimuli was the more powerful. Suggest how this student might use the apparatus shown in question 1 to decide whether gravity or light had the greater influence on young roots.

3 The drawing shows a section through a broad bean seed which had been soaked in water for 48 hours and then cut lengthways.

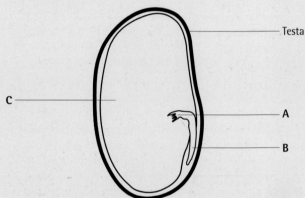

a i Name the structures labelled A, B and C.

ii Predict the likely results of dropping iodine solution onto chopped up pieces of each of A, B and C.

b Ten broad bean seeds (**Batch A**) were dried in an oven to constant mass. The total mass of the seeds was measured and recorded.

A second batch of ten broad bean seeds (**Batch B**) was allowed to germinate and grow for **8 days**. This batch was then dried in an oven to constant mass and the total mass measured and recorded.

The results are shown in Table 1.

Batch	
A (10 seeds) mass/g	B (10 seeds) mass/g
47.25	27.08

Table 1

i Explain why the total mass of **Batch B** seeds is considerably less than that of the **Batch A** seeds.

ii Predict the result of a similar experiment in which a batch of ten seeds was germinated and allowed to grow for **20 days** before being dried in an oven to constant mass.

Explain the reasoning on which your prediction was based.

c During an investigation on seed germination and growth, twenty pea seeds were placed in damp sawdust in each of four plant pots. The top of each plant pot was covered with a thin film of plastic. The thin film of plastic was a different colour for each plant pot. The four plant pots were placed in the same laboratory for four weeks.

Table 2 summarises the results of this investigation.

Description of plastic film covering each plant pot				
	Red	Green	Clear (not coloured)	Black
Original number of seeds	20	20	20	20
Number of seeds germinating	18	17	18	20
Number of plants surviving one week	18	16	17	20
Number of plants surviving four weeks	18	4	17	0

Table 2

i 'Photosynthesis occurs equally well in white light and red light'.
Comment on the truth of this statement, giving your reasons.

ii State **TWO** other conclusions which can be reached by comparing results in Table 2.

(MEG June 1992)

4 Strawberry plants are able to reproduce asexually by means of runners. A runner produced in early summer gives rise to a new plant, which in turn produces a runner to give rise to a second new plant and so on. This process is summarised in the diagram.

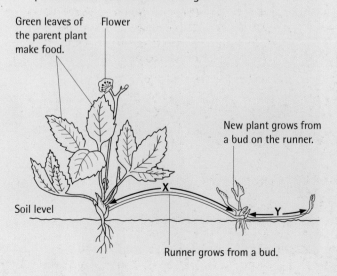

Green leaves of the parent plant make food.

Flower

New plant grows from a bud on the runner.

Soil level

X

Y

Runner grows from a bud.

a Ten different strawberry plants were taken and the lengths of the runners **X** and **Y** (shown in the diagram) were measured. The results are shown in the table.

Plant number	Length of runner Y/mm	Length of runner X/mm
1	400	200
2	350	280
3	420	260
4	610	260
5	640	340
6	600	250
7	340	240
8	460	270
9	600	250
10	520	290

i Using the data in the table, calculate the average (mean) lengths for runner **X** and for runner **Y**. **Show your workings.**

ii Calculate the difference in mean length between runner **X** and runner **Y**. **Show your workings.**

iii The lengths of the runners **X** in the table vary considerably. Suggest **TWO** possible causes of this variation.

iv Predict how the results would be different from those shown in the table if measurements were taken of the runners between the second and third new plants. Explain why there would be this difference.

b What else has to happen to the plant shown in the diagram for the process of asexual reproduction to be completed?

c A fruit grower found that one particular strawberry plant survived two weeks of heavy winter frosts. Suggest why the grower would be more likely to obtain frost resistant strawberry plants by the asexual method shown in the diagram rather than by using seeds produced by the flower.

d i Describe briefly how the strawberry plant produces food to send to its developing strawberries.

ii Name the plant tissue through which soluble food products are transported along the runner to the new plants.

(MEG Nov. 1991)

5 'Seed' potatoes are normally kept in a dry, dark, cool location to prevent them sprouting too soon. Design an experiment that would allow you to determine the minimum temperature required for sprouting. Identify:

a the manipulated variable

b the responding variable and

c the fixed variables.

How would you manipulate **a**, measure **b** and fix **c**?

Inherited and acquired characteristics

Living organisms vary in many ways. For example, humans all have the same general shape and the same set of body organs, but some features differ from one person to the next, such as height, weight, eye and hair colour, shape of nose, language, knowledge and skills. These are examples of **individual variation**.

Some of these features that vary from person to person may be inherited from the parents. Examples of these **inherited** (or **hereditary**) **characteristics** include the tendency to develop some diseases, such as cystic fibrosis, and the permanent colour of the skin. Some, such as a temporary suntan or a scar, cannot be inherited – these are called **acquired characteristics**. Many acquired characteristics can be changed (for example, body mass can be changed by an adjustment to the diet). Inherited characteristics cannot usually be altered (except temporarily).

Genetics

The study of inherited characteristics, and the way they are passed on from one generation to another, is called **genetics**. Our knowledge of the subject of genetics is expanding extremely rapidly, and this knowledge depends upon our understanding of the molecule DNA (see page 190).

When we study inheritance we are looking for answers to several important questions:

- What is a characteristic? Why does a cell or organism develop a certain characteristic?
- How can characteristics be passed on accurately from one cell to another?
- How are the characteristics of two different organisms combined at fertilisation?
- How do characteristics vary from one organism to another and from one generation to another?

Answers to questions such as these help us in many ways, for example to increase our understanding about genetic diseases, and to develop techniques to 'add' desirable characteristics to our domestic animals and plants.

Sexual reproduction and inheritance

The production of offspring by sexual reproduction always involves the **production of gametes** and **fertilisation** (see page 132). In sexual reproduction:

- The only part of the male gamete (sperm in mammals) that goes to form the zygote is the **nucleus**.
- The gametes are formed by **cell division**.
- The young organism develops from a single fertilised egg by **cell division**.

So, if we are to understand how characteristics are passed on during reproduction, we should look carefully at the structure of the nucleus, and how the nucleus behaves during cell division.

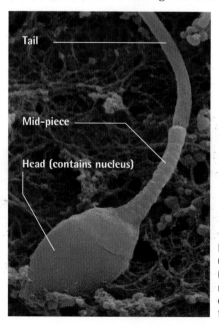

Tail

Mid-piece

Head (contains nucleus)

Human sperm ×1000. Only the 'head' (containing the nucleus) enters the egg at the time of fertilisation.

The contents of the nucleus

Special stains can be used to show up the contents of the nucleus. If the cell is not actually dividing, these contents are rather indistinct, but as the cell begins to divide the contents show up as a series of thread-like structures. As the threads shorten they take up the stain. For this reason they were called **chromosomes** (literally 'coloured bodies'). The structure of a chromosome is outlined below.

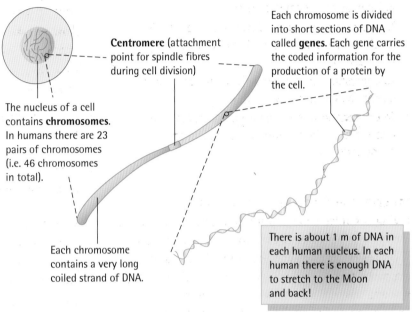

Centromere (attachment point for spindle fibres during cell division)

Each chromosome is divided into short sections of DNA called **genes**. Each gene carries the coded information for the production of a protein by the cell.

The nucleus of a cell contains **chromosomes**. In humans there are 23 pairs of chromosomes (i.e. 46 chromosomes in total).

Each chromosome contains a very long coiled strand of DNA.

There is about 1 m of DNA in each human nucleus. In each human there is enough DNA to stretch to the Moon and back!

The structure of a chromosome.

A great deal of evidence suggests that the chromosomes carry **genetic information** – the information that gives the particular characteristics to a cell:

- If sections of chromosome are transferred from one cell to another, the characteristics of the recipient cell change.
- If chromosomes are deliberately damaged, the characteristics of the cell change.
- In some cells, the chromosomes are seen to swell when proteins are being manufactured in the cell.
- The only difference between the nuclei of male and female cells is the presence of one particular chromosome (see page 208). (Males and females certainly have different characteristics!)

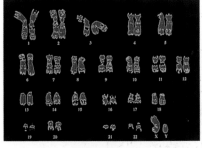

A **karyotype** – a photograph of human chromosomes arranged in pairs. The 23rd pair is an X and a Y chromosome – this cell comes from a male.

1 Look around your class. This group of humans shows many variations between individuals. Suggest one variation that is inherited and one that is acquired.

2 Find three newspaper articles that include the words 'gene', 'genetic' or 'inheritance' in their headings. Summarise one of the articles in three or four sentences.

3 a What is a chromosome? What evidence is there that chromosomes carry genetic information?

b When can chromosomes be observed? Explain why this is possible.

11·2 DNA, proteins and the characteristics of organisms

Objectives
- To know that cell characteristics depend on proteins
- To understand the principle of the genetic code
- To be able to describe the replication of DNA

Characteristics depend on proteins

It has been discovered that the characteristics that a cell or organism possesses depend on the **proteins** that the cell can manufacture. For examples of this, look at the picture at the top of the opposite page.

For cells to specialise in the many different ways that they do, they must make different proteins. The instructions as to which proteins should be manufactured at any one time in a cell are carried as **genes** on the **chromosomes**. Chemical tests have shown that chromosomes are largely composed of the enormous molecule called **deoxyribonucleic acid** or DNA for short. In other words:

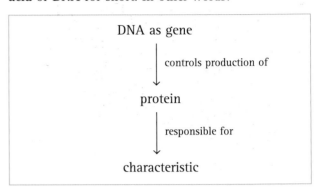

DNA as gene
↓ controls production of
protein
↓ responsible for
characteristic

DNA carries its instructions as coded messages using just four different chemical compounds called **nucleotide bases** or organic bases (see page 11). The names of the bases are shown in the diagram below, but you only need to remember their initial letters (A, T, G and C) to understand how the code works.

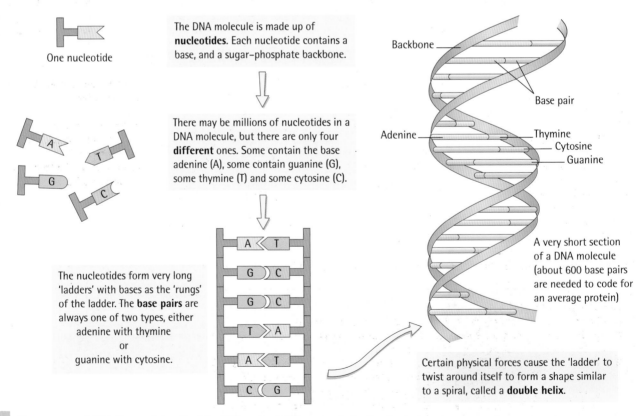

One nucleotide

The DNA molecule is made up of **nucleotides**. Each nucleotide contains a base, and a sugar–phosphate backbone.

There may be millions of nucleotides in a DNA molecule, but there are only four **different** ones. Some contain the base adenine (A), some contain guanine (G), some thymine (T) and some cytosine (C).

The nucleotides form very long 'ladders' with bases as the 'rungs' of the ladder. The **base pairs** are always one of two types, either adenine with thymine
or
guanine with cytosine.

Backbone

Base pair

Adenine

Thymine
Cytosine
Guanine

A very short section of a DNA molecule (about 600 base pairs are needed to code for an average protein)

Certain physical forces cause the 'ladder' to twist around itself to form a shape similar to a spiral, called a **double helix**.

The structure of DNA. The exact length of the DNA molecule is known only for the simplest of organisms, such as bacteria. It is very important to remember that: **adenine** always pairs with **thymine**, and **guanine** always pairs with **cytosine**.

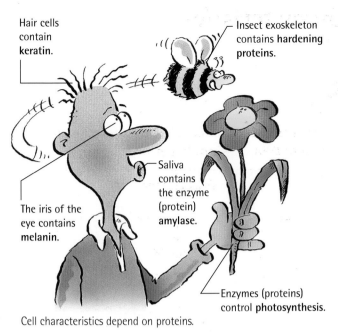

Hair cells contain **keratin**.

Insect exoskeleton contains **hardening proteins**.

The iris of the eye contains **melanin**.

Saliva contains the enzyme (protein) **amylase**.

Enzymes (proteins) control **photosynthesis**.

Cell characteristics depend on proteins.

Base pairing can explain how DNA is replicated

For one organism to pass on characteristics to its offspring, it must be able to copy the coded instructions for these characteristics and hand them on. In other words, DNA in the chromosomes must be copied or **replicated**. This replication must be carried out with great accuracy, since a change in characteristics might be harmful to the organism. The base pairing rule means that the coded sequence on one chain of the double helix automatically determines the coded sequence on the other chain, ensuring accurate replication. The principles of DNA replication are outlined below.

The replication of DNA is a vital part of cell division. It is particularly obvious in copying division (mitosis), as we shall see on page 194.

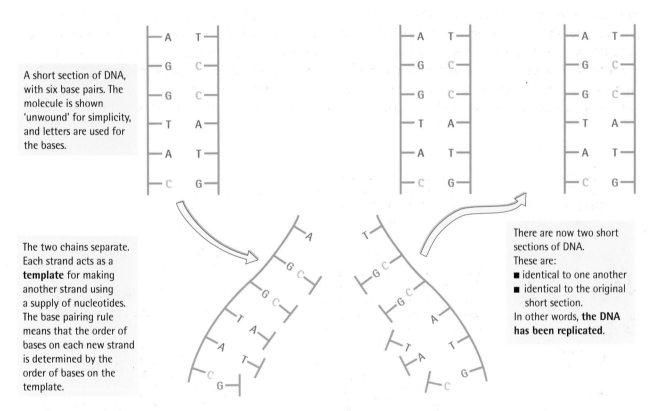

A short section of DNA, with six base pairs. The molecule is shown 'unwound' for simplicity, and letters are used for the bases.

The two chains separate. Each strand acts as a **template** for making another strand using a supply of nucleotides. The base pairing rule means that the order of bases on each new strand is determined by the order of bases on the template.

There are now two short sections of DNA. These are:
■ identical to one another
■ identical to the original short section.
In other words, **the DNA has been replicated**.

DNA replication is essential for characteristics to be passed from one generation of cells to the next.

The discovery of DNA
The discovery of DNA structure depended on the work of many scientists. These included
■ **Rosalind Franklin:** she made many measurements on DNA, using patterns obtained by directing a beam of X-rays onto crystals of this molecule.
■ **James Watson and Francis Crick:** used the measurements made by Franklin, and results of the chemical analysis of DNA which showed that the number of (adenine + guanine) bases was always equal to the number of (thymine + cytosine) bases, to produce a working model of the DNA molecule. This model was the double helix which we are familiar with. Watson and Crick were awarded the Nobel prize (the highest scientific award) for their work on DNA. Sadly, Rosalind Franklin died before her part in the discovery of DNA structure was properly recognised.

Inheritance and evolution

11·3 How the code is carried

Objectives
- To understand that the genetic code is carried as a sequence of bases on the DNA molecule
- To understand the need for a messenger molecule in protein synthesis
- To define the terms transcription and translation

DNA 'code words' for amino acids

How does the DNA in the genes instruct the cell to make particular proteins? The following points are important in understanding this link:

- Each gene carries a series of coded instructions ('code words') for the synthesis of proteins.
- Each 'code word' on the DNA is made up of three bases (three 'letters') in a certain sequence.
- Each 'code word' – called a **triplet** – corresponds to a **single amino acid in a protein**.

The sequence of bases in DNA is therefore a series of coded instructions for the building up of amino acids into proteins. The proteins then give the cell or organism a particular characteristic. This relationship between DNA bases and amino acids is called the **genetic code**, and is outlined below.

A DNA strand carries instructions in the form of three-letter 'code words' called triplets.

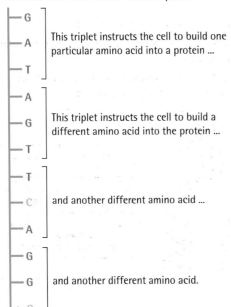

This triplet instructs the cell to build one particular amino acid into a protein ...

This triplet instructs the cell to build a different amino acid into the protein ...

and another different amino acid ...

and another different amino acid.

The four different bases in DNA can be arranged in enough different triplets to code for all 20 amino acids normally found in a cell.

Passing the messages to the ribosomes

This coded information in the genes is located on the chromosomes, which are in the nucleus. You may remember that the protein-manufacturing stations, called **ribosomes**, are found outside the nucleus, in the cytoplasm. How does the code pass from the nucleus to the ribosomes in the cytoplasm? It is carried by another type of nucleic acid, called **messenger RNA (mRNA)**.

Transcription and translation

The mRNA is made by a process called **transcription**, which literally means 'cross writing'. The base sequence in the DNA is **transcribed** into another base sequence in the mRNA, using very similar base pairing rules to those used in the replication of DNA. There is one important difference – RNA never contains the base thymine (T). Thymine is replaced by a fifth base called **uracil (U)** so instead of the base pair A–T used in DNA replication, in transcription we have the base pair A–U.

Once it has been made, the mRNA leaves the nucleus and travels to the ribosomes. The sequence of bases in the mRNA is used to build up a sequence of amino acids into a protein in the ribosome. This process is called **translation** – it involves rewriting the language of bases into a language of amino acids. The processes of transcription and translation are outlined in the diagram on the next page.

Summary of replication, transcription and translation

It is quite easy to confuse the various processes involving nucleic acids. Remember:

- Replication makes a DNA copy, using DNA.
- Transcription makes mRNA, using DNA.
- Translation makes protein, using mRNA.

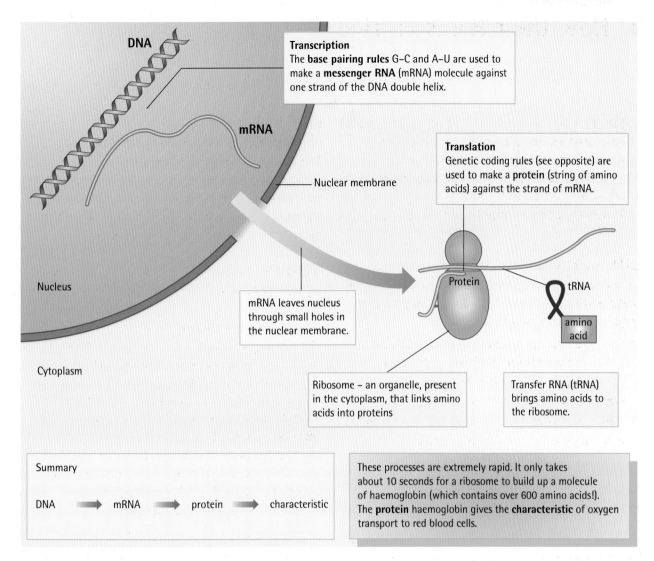

DNA

Transcription
The **base pairing rules** G–C and A–U are used to make a **messenger RNA** (mRNA) molecule against one strand of the DNA double helix.

mRNA

Translation
Genetic coding rules (see opposite) are used to make a **protein** (string of amino acids) against the strand of mRNA.

Nuclear membrane

Protein

tRNA

amino acid

Nucleus

mRNA leaves nucleus through small holes in the nuclear membrane.

Cytoplasm

Ribosome – an organelle, present in the cytoplasm, that links amino acids into proteins

Transfer RNA (tRNA) brings amino acids to the ribosome.

Summary

DNA ➡ mRNA ➡ protein ➡ characteristic

These processes are extremely rapid. It only takes about 10 seconds for a ribosome to build up a molecule of haemoglobin (which contains over 600 amino acids!). The **protein** haemoglobin gives the **characteristic** of oxygen transport to red blood cells.

How information in DNA codes for characteristics in cells.

---

1. What are the subunits of a nucleic acid called?

2. Name the four bases in DNA.

3. DNA exists as a double helix. Name the base pairs that hold the double helix together. Why is base pairing important?

4. Define the term DNA replication.

5. Name four proteins that give particular characteristics to named cells.

6. Name one process of which DNA replication is a vital part.

7. The diagram on the right represents the behaviour of DNA strands during the early part of cell division.

   Use the information in the diagram to help you answer the following questions.

a Identify the organic bases X and Y.

b Name and describe, in detail, the process shown in the diagram.

c What is the importance of the SEQUENCE of organic bases along a DNA strand?

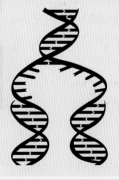

Key:

Organic base	Symbol
Adenine (A)	▶
X	◀
Y	▶
Guanine (G)	◀

(Edexcel June 1995)

11·4 Cell division

Objectives

- To understand why it is necessary to copy genetic material accurately
- To know that copying division is called mitosis, and results in cells with an identical number and type of chromosomes as their parent cells
- To know how chromosomes behave during mitosis
- To know where mitosis takes place in the bodies of mammals and flowering plants
- To understand the need for a special cell division in the formation of haploid gametes

on when cells divide. Each chromosome has a partner, forming **homologous pairs**. Both chromosomes in an homologous pair have the same genes in the same positions. The diagram below shows cell division in which the new cells are copies of the parent cell – **mitosis**.

Mitosis is for growth

Both plants and animals grow by mitosis.

- In animals each tissue provides its own new cells when they are needed.
- In plants cell division in the **cambium** increases the plant girth (the plant gets thicker), and cell division in the **meristems** at the tips of the roots and shoots leads to an increase in length.

Mitosis is copying division

Characteristics are transmitted from one generation of cells to the next. For this to happen, the chromosomes must be accurately copied and passed

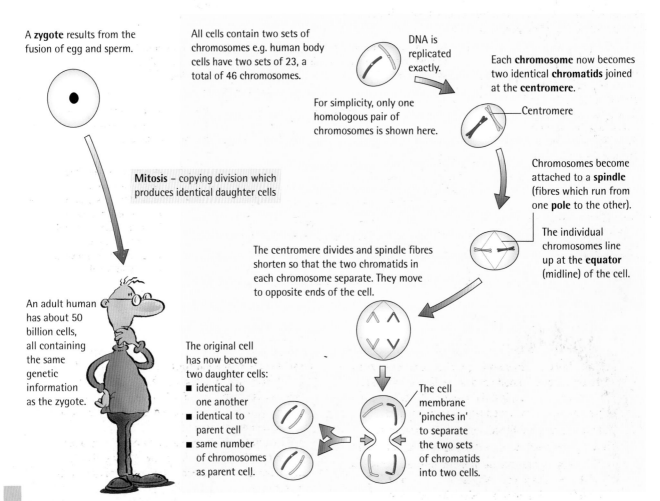

A **zygote** results from the fusion of egg and sperm.

All cells contain two sets of chromosomes e.g. human body cells have two sets of 23, a total of 46 chromosomes.

For simplicity, only one homologous pair of chromosomes is shown here.

DNA is replicated exactly.

Each **chromosome** now becomes two identical **chromatids** joined at the **centromere**.

Centromere

Chromosomes become attached to a **spindle** (fibres which run from one **pole** to the other).

The individual chromosomes line up at the **equator** (midline) of the cell.

Mitosis – copying division which produces identical daughter cells

The centromere divides and spindle fibres shorten so that the two chromatids in each chromosome separate. They move to opposite ends of the cell.

An adult human has about 50 billion cells, all containing the same genetic information as the zygote.

The original cell has now become two daughter cells:
- identical to one another
- identical to parent cell
- same number of chromosomes as parent cell.

The cell membrane 'pinches in' to separate the two sets of chromatids into two cells.

Mitosis – copying division. Note that cell division is a continuous process. Although the diagram shows mitosis in a series of stages, in reality each stage merges into the next one.

Inheritance and evolution

Meiosis is reduction division

During sexual reproduction (see page 132) two gametes fuse to form the zygote. The gametes must contain only one set of chromosomes, otherwise the zygote would have twice as many chromosomes as it needed! This principle is outlined in the diagram on the left.

Each cell of an organism has a fixed number of chromosomes within the nucleus. The number of chromosomes in a normal body cell is the **diploid number** (or $2n$); the number of chromosomes in a gamete is the **haploid number** (or n). **Fertilisation is the fusion of haploid gametes to restore the diploid number in the zygote**. Gametes are formed by a type of cell division called **meiosis** or **reduction division**, shown in the diagram below.

Meiosis only happens in the gamete-producing organs: the testes and the ovaries in animals, and the pollen sacs of the stamens and the ovules in the ovary in plants.

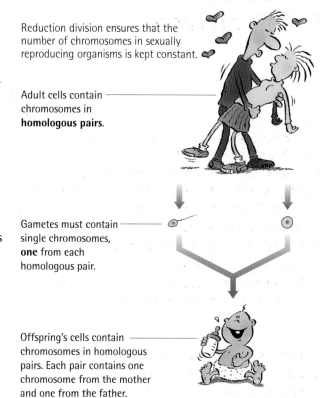

Reduction division ensures that the number of chromosomes in sexually reproducing organisms is kept constant.

Adult cells contain chromosomes in **homologous pairs**.

Gametes must contain single chromosomes, **one** from each homologous pair.

Offspring's cells contain chromosomes in homologous pairs. Each pair contains one chromosome from the mother and one from the father.

Meiosis is called reduction division because it halves the number of chromosomes in cells.

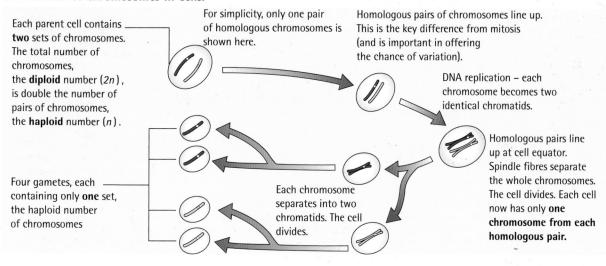

Each parent cell contains **two** sets of chromosomes. The total number of chromosomes, the **diploid** number ($2n$), is double the number of pairs of chromosomes, the **haploid** number (n).

For simplicity, only one pair of homologous chromosomes is shown here.

Homologous pairs of chromosomes line up. This is the key difference from mitosis (and is important in offering the chance of variation).

DNA replication – each chromosome becomes two identical chromatids.

Homologous pairs line up at cell equator. Spindle fibres separate the whole chromosomes. The cell divides. Each cell now has only **one chromosome from each homologous pair**.

Four gametes, each containing only **one** set, the haploid number of chromosomes

Each chromosome separates into two chromatids. The cell divides.

---

1. Cells in bone marrow undergo mitosis. Some of these cells become red blood cells, to replace those lost as they wear out. A typical red blood cell lasts for 120 days before it is removed from the circulation.
   a Suggest why red blood cells last for a short time.
   b Which organ removes red blood cells from blood?
   c This organ stores the main metal ion that forms part of the red blood cell. Which ion is this, and what molecule is it a part of inside the red blood cell?

   d The human circulation contains about 5 dm^3 of blood. Each dm^3 of blood contains 5 000 000 red blood cells. (1 dm^3 = 1 000 000 mm^3.)
     i Calculate how many red blood cells there are in the human circulation.
     ii The total number of red blood cells is replaced every 120 days. Calculate how many cells are replaced each day. How many are replaced each second?

11·5 Cancer is uncontrolled cell division

Objectives

- To know that cancer results from a failure to control cell division
- To understand how a tumour develops and causes damage to the body
- To understand how cancer may be treated

For most of the time cells are not dividing – they are carrying out whatever is their normal function. Cells only start to divide when the body needs them to. Scientists are very interested in how the cell 'knows' when it must divide. The diagram below outlines the life cycle of a liver cell.

Dividing out of control causes problems

If a group of cells divides too often, the 'extra' cells may compete for nutrients with nearby cells from another tissue. The tissue will not perform its proper function and the organism may die. Cells dividing out of control may form a lump of cells called a **tumour**, as shown in the diagram on the opposite page.

What causes cancer?

The rate of cell division by mitosis is normally very strictly controlled. Cells touch one another as they fill up the available space, and the cells then 'switch off' their process of division. This is called **contact inhibition** and involves proteins on the cell surface membrane. Cell division may get out of control for a number of reasons:

- The cell may not have the gene to produce the correct cell surface protein. This is a **genetic tendency**, and explains why some types of cancer such as breast cancer tend to run in families.
- The protein may be inactivated in some way. This usually occurs because of an **environmental factor**, and explains why certain lifestyles or occupations carry a higher risk of cancer. Smoking tobacco, for example, increases the risk of cancer of the lung, and drinking lots of alcohol increases the risk of cancer of the oesophagus.

Scientists believe that most types of cancer only develop when several factors are present. For example, a person might be carrying a gene that makes their lung cells more likely to divide, but the presence of chemicals in tobacco smoke makes the gene run out of control. Any substance that causes cancer to develop is called a **carcinogen** (literally a 'cancer maker'). The involvement of external factors in the development of lung cancer is explained on page 80.

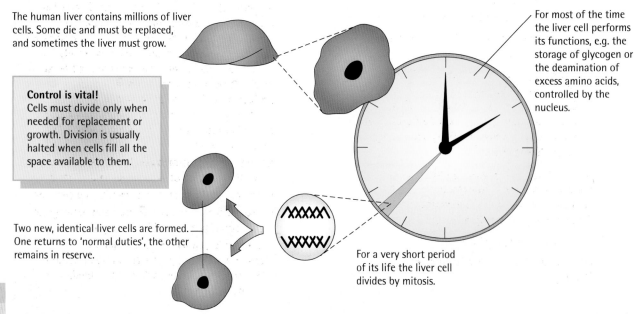

The human liver contains millions of liver cells. Some die and must be replaced, and sometimes the liver must grow.

Control is vital!
Cells must divide only when needed for replacement or growth. Division is usually halted when cells fill all the space available to them.

Two new, identical liver cells are formed. One returns to 'normal duties', the other remains in reserve.

For most of the time the liver cell performs its functions, e.g. the storage of glycogen or the deamination of excess amino acids, controlled by the nucleus.

For a very short period of its life the liver cell divides by mitosis.

The life cycle of a liver cell

Inheritance and evolution

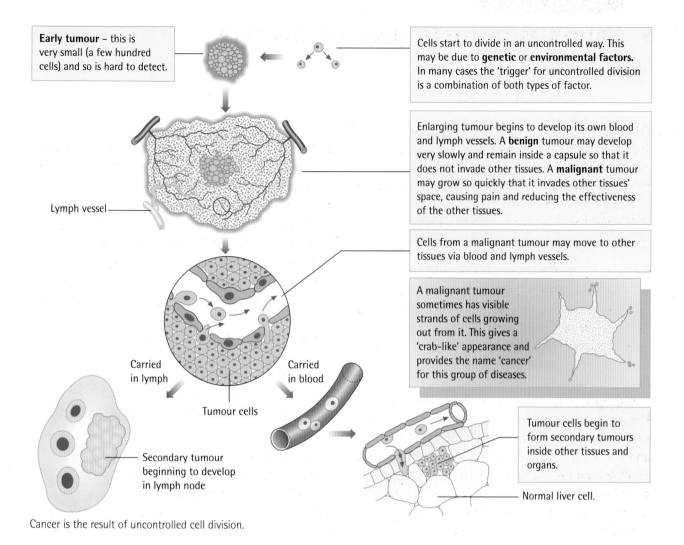

Early tumour – this is very small (a few hundred cells) and so is hard to detect.

Cells start to divide in an uncontrolled way. This may be due to **genetic** or **environmental factors.** In many cases the 'trigger' for uncontrolled division is a combination of both types of factor.

Enlarging tumour begins to develop its own blood and lymph vessels. A **benign** tumour may develop very slowly and remain inside a capsule so that it does not invade other tissues. A **malignant** tumour may grow so quickly that it invades other tissues' space, causing pain and reducing the effectiveness of the other tissues.

Lymph vessel

Cells from a malignant tumour may move to other tissues via blood and lymph vessels.

A malignant tumour sometimes has visible strands of cells growing out from it. This gives a 'crab-like' appearance and provides the name 'cancer' for this group of diseases.

Carried in lymph

Carried in blood

Tumour cells

Tumour cells begin to form secondary tumours inside other tissues and organs.

Secondary tumour beginning to develop in lymph node

Normal liver cell.

Cancer is the result of uncontrolled cell division.

The treatment of cancer

If a cancer is detected early enough it can often be treated. Treatment tries to gain control of the cancer cells in the following ways:

- hormone treatment for breast cancer
- surgery to remove a tumour if a single organ or tissue is affected
- chemotherapy – using medicines to stop cell division. Most of these chemicals also damage healthy cells, so they may have side-effects. Monoclonal antibodies (see page 298) may target chemotherapy to cancer cells very specifically, reducing side-effects.
- radiotherapy – using ionising radiation to kill rapidly dividing cells. The radiation must be aimed very carefully at the tumour to avoid damage to rapidly dividing healthy cells.
- gene therapy (see page 221)
- boosting the patient's own immune system (see page 296)

1 Read this passage and then answer the questions. Skin cancer is the second most common cancer in the UK. Most skin cancers are curable, although the most serious form (**malignant melanoma**) can be fatal if not treated early. Skin cancer is caused when ultraviolet radiation affects the division of cells just below the surface of the skin – getting sunburned is extremely dangerous. People with fair skin and red hair are most at risk, whilst dark-skinned people are protected by the pigment **melanin** in their skin. Ozone high in the atmosphere filters out much of the harmful ultraviolet radiation before it reaches the Earth.

a Suggest why Australia and New Zealand have the highest rates of skin cancer in the world.

b Why do you think many skin cancers are curable?

c Suggest why we should worry about damage to the ozone layer caused by some pollutants.

d How could you use the technique of epidemiology (see page 82) to find out whether skin cancer was more affected by heredity or by environment?

11·6 Variation

Objectives
- To recall that living organisms differ from one another
- To distinguish between continuous and discontinuous variation

Living organisms differ from one another. Even members of the same species have slightly different sets of characteristics. Some of these differences are inherited from their parents, and others are the result of the environment. Scientists who study variation are interested in questions such as:

- Are all of the variations of the same type?
- How do the variations come about?
- How are the variations in characteristics passed on from parents to offspring?
- What is the importance of these variations?

There are two types of variation – **discontinuous variation** and **continuous variation**.

Discontinuous variation
Characteristics that show discontinuous variation have several features:

- An organism either has the characteristic or it doesn't have it. There is no range of these characteristics between extremes. An organism can easily be placed into definite categories, and there is no disagreement about the categories.
- These characteristics are usually **qualitative** – they cannot be measured.
- They are the result of genes only – they are not affected by the environment.

An example of discontinuous variation is shown in the diagram above right.

Continuous variation
Characteristics that show continuous variation have different features:

- Every organism within one species shows the characteristic, but to a different extent. The characteristic can have any value within a range. Different scientists might well disagree about which category any single organism falls into.

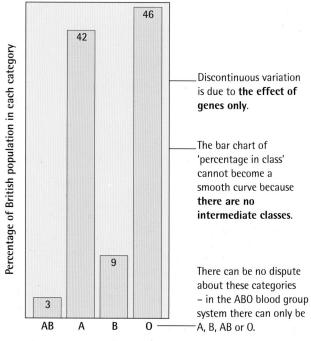

Discontinuous variation is due to **the effect of genes only**.

The bar chart of 'percentage in class' cannot become a smooth curve because **there are no intermediate classes**.

There can be no dispute about these categories – in the ABO blood group system there can only be A, B, AB or O.

Human blood groups are an example of discontinuous variation. Another example is gender – you are either male or female.

- These characteristics are usually **quantitative** – they can be measured.
- They result from several genes acting together, or from both genes and the environment.

An example of continuous variation is shown in the diagram at the top of the opposite page.

Characteristics can be both discontinuous and continuous
Some characteristics are difficult to classify as either discontinuous or continuous variation. Human hair colour, for example, appears in a range from black to blond with many intermediate colours (it shows continuous variation as a result of the involvement of many genes). However, the gene for red hair is masked by every other hair colour gene (which gives a discontinuous situation – hair is either red or not red). Eye colour can be identified as brown or not brown, which would classify it as a discontinuous variation, or it can be put into a range of many intermediate classes, which would make it a continuous variation. A simple guideline is: 'if it can be measured and given a numerical value, it is a continuous variation'.

Inheritance and evolution

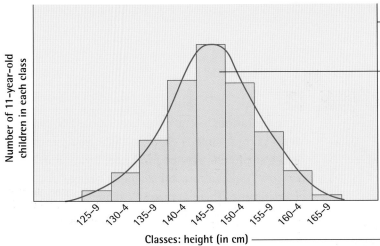

Number of 11-year-old children in each class

Classes: height (in cm)

Classes: 125–9, 130–4, 135–9, 140–4, 145–9, 150–4, 155–9, 160–4, 165–9

Continuous variation is due to the combined effects of **genes** and the **environment**.

The bar chart of 'number in class' can be redrawn as a smooth curve because there are **many possible intermediate classes between the two extremes** (the curve becomes smoother if the classes become smaller, e.g. 1 cm rather than 5 cm).

There could be a dispute about the boundary of these classes. One observer might use, for example, 127–31, 132–6, etc. rather than the boundaries shown.

Human height is an example of continuous variation. Other examples include quantitative characteristics such as chest circumference, body mass and hand span.

Francis Galton was a cousin of Charles Darwin. He investigated intelligence as an example of phenotype, and believed that 'nature' (genotype) was much more important than 'nurture' (environment). He suggested that:
a children from families where the parents were uneducated would always have low intelligence
b females were less intelligent than males – he suggested the 'ideal' child would be born to 'a man of genius and a woman of wealth'.
His ideas have rightly been updated, but he does deserve some credit – his studies showed that identical twins were genetically the same.

Phenotype and genotype

Variations in characteristics allow us to recognise different organisms, and to place them in different categories (see page 224). The overall appearance of an organism is a result of the characteristics that it has inherited from its parents and the characteristics that result from the effects of the environment. The following equation summarises this:

> **Phenotype** = genotype + effects of the environment
> the observable characteristics of an organism
> the full set of genes it possesses

Some characteristics result from both genes and environment. For example, a bean seedling has the genes to develop chlorophyll (and turn green) but it won't do so unless it receives enough light. A young mammal has the genes to develop a rigid bony skeleton, but it won't do so unless it receives calcium in its diet.

1 Copy and complete the following paragraph.
Variation occurs in two forms, _____, which shows clear-cut separation between groups showing this variation, and _____, in which there are many intermediate forms between the extremes of the characteristic. The first of these is the result of _____ alone, whilst the second is also affected by _____ factors. The sum of the genes that an organism contains is called its _____ and the total of all its observable characteristics is called the _____.
The two are related in a simple equation: _____ equals _____ plus _____.

2 Which of the following is an example of discontinuous variation?
Body mass, chest circumference, blood group, hairstyle, height
Explain:
a why you chose one of these characteristics
b why you rejected the others.

3 Two students in the first year of secondary school were carrying out a mathematical investigation. They decided to measure the heights of all of the other students in their class. The results are shown in the table below.
a Plot these results as a bar chart.
b Does this illustrate continuous or discontinuous variation? Explain your answer.
c Suggest one characteristic that the students could have recorded to illustrate the other kind of variation.

Height category (cm)	Number in category
121–125	2
126–130	4
131–135	9
136–140	6
141–145	4
146–150	1

Inheritance and evolution

199

Causes of variation

- To identify mutation and sexual reproduction as sources of variation
- To understand that mutations may involve whole chromosomes or genes within them
- To recognise that environmental factors may increase the likelihood of mutation

Permanent changes to the phenotype

Permanent characteristics that can be inherited are due to the genetic make-up of an organism. This may be altered, thereby increasing variation, as a result of **mutation** or of **sexual reproduction**.

Mutation

A **mutation** is a change in the type or amount of DNA and can arise because of:

- mistakes in the copying of DNA as cells get ready to divide – pairing with the 'incorrect' base
- damage to the DNA – some environmental factor might alter the bases present in the DNA
- uneven distribution of chromosomes during the division of cells.

Gene mutations occur when part of the DNA on a single chromosome is changed. As a result a defective protein may be produced, or no protein at all. This can lead to a considerable change in a characteristic. There are many examples, including **sickle cell anaemia**, shown opposite. **Chromosome mutations** occur when cell division fails to work with complete accuracy (see diagram below).

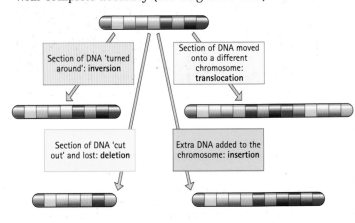

Section of DNA 'turned around': **inversion**

Section of DNA moved onto a different chromosome: **translocation**

Section of DNA 'cut out' and lost: **deletion**

Extra DNA added to the chromosome: **insertion**

Don't worry! 'Repair enzymes' in cells continually check the DNA and try to correct these mutations

Types of chromosome mutation

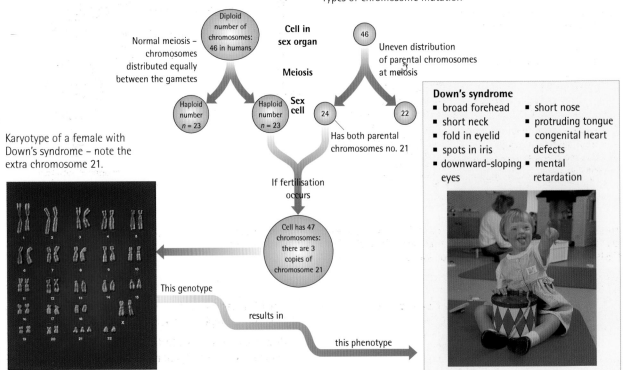

Normal meiosis – chromosomes distributed equally between the gametes

Diploid number of chromosomes: 46 in humans

Cell in sex organ

Meiosis

Haploid number *n* = 23

Haploid number *n* = 23

Sex cell

46

Uneven distribution of parental chromosomes at meiosis

24

22

Has both parental chromosomes no. 21

If fertilisation occurs

Cell has 47 chromosomes: there are 3 copies of chromosome 21

Down's syndrome
- broad forehead
- short neck
- fold in eyelid
- spots in iris
- downward-sloping eyes
- short nose
- protruding tongue
- congenital heart defects
- mental retardation

Karyotype of a female with Down's syndrome – note the extra chromosome 21.

This genotype

results in

this phenotype

Chromosome mutation and Down's syndrome

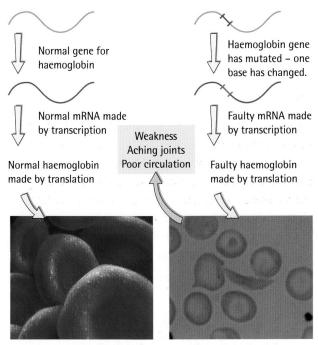

Normal gene for haemoglobin

↓

Normal mRNA made by transcription

↓

Normal haemoglobin made by translation

Haemoglobin gene has mutated – one base has changed.

↓

Faulty mRNA made by transcription

↓

Faulty haemoglobin made by translation

Weakness
Aching joints
Poor circulation

Sickle cell anaemia (A sickle has a curved blade for cutting grass.)

Beneficial mutations

Not all mutations are harmful. Many of them give benefits to the organisms that have them, and aid adaptation to the environment (see page 212). Some may cause harm in one environment but be a benefit in another!

Radiation can increase mutation rates

Mutations occur spontaneously (for no apparent reason), though they are very rare events. However, a number of factors (called **mutagens**) can increase the rate of mutation. Important mutagens are:

- **radiation** – gamma, ultraviolet and X-radiation can all damage DNA and so cause mutations
- **chemicals** – tars in tobacco smoke, high concentrations of some preservatives and some plant control hormones can cause mutation.

Mutations may be linked with cancer (see page 196). A mutagen that causes uncontrolled cell division is called a **carcinogen** ('cancer maker').

Sexual reproduction leads to variation

Sexual reproduction mixes up genetic material in three ways, as shown below, producing new genotypes and so variations in phenotype.

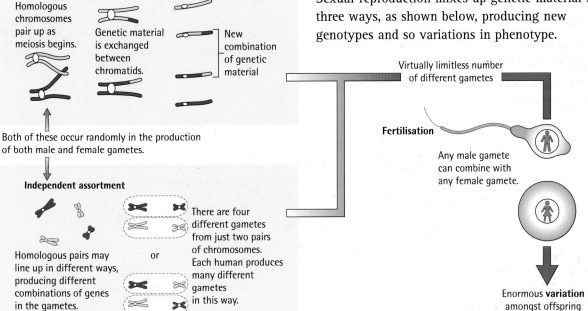

Crossing over

Homologous chromosomes pair up as meiosis begins.

Genetic material is exchanged between chromatids.

New combination of genetic material

Both of these occur randomly in the production of both male and female gametes.

Independent assortment

Homologous pairs may line up in different ways, producing different combinations of genes in the gametes.

or

There are four different gametes from just two pairs of chromosomes. Each human produces many different gametes in this way.

Virtually limitless number of different gametes

Fertilisation

Any male gamete can combine with any female gamete.

Enormous **variation** amongst offspring

Crossing over, **independent assortment** and **fertilisation** all lead to variation. There is very little chance that any two gametes from one individual will be identical. The combined effects of mutation and sexual reproduction lead to enormous variation between individuals..

1. What is a gene mutation? Give an example of:
   a a harmful
   b a beneficial
   gene mutation.

2. What is a carcinogen?
   Give two examples of carcinogens.

3. How does sexual reproduction lead to variation amongst members of a population?

Inheritance and evolution

11.8 Inheritance

Objectives
- To recall the features of sexual and asexual reproduction
- To be able to define the terms gene and allele, homozygous and heterozygous, dominant and recessive

Reproduction: a reminder

Living organisms can pass on their characteristics to the next generation (**reproduce**) in two ways.

Asexual reproduction:
- involves only one parent organism
- all the characteristics of this one parent are passed on to all of the offspring
- many organisms reproduce asexually when conditions are favourable (e.g. when there is plenty of food), and build up their numbers quickly.

Sexual reproduction:
- requires two organisms of the same species, one male and one female
- each individual produces sex cells (**gametes**)
- sexual reproduction always involves **fertilisation** – the fusion of the gametes
- offspring receive some genes from each parent, so shows a mixture of parental characteristics.

In sexual reproduction, a mixture of genes is passed from parents to offspring. This handing down of genes is not random, and there are certain rules that govern how genes will be passed on and which ones will show up in the offspring.

The inheritance of characteristics

Chromosomes carry genetic information as a series of **genes**, such as the gene for eye colour, the gene for earlobe shape and the gene for hair texture. Each chromosome in the nucleus of a diploid organism has a partner that carries the same genes. Such a pair of chromosomes is called an **homologous pair**.

Each chromosome in a pair may carry alternative forms of the same gene. These alternative forms are called **alleles**. For example, the gene for eye colour has alleles that code for blue or brown. If both alternative alleles are present in a particular cell nucleus, then the cell is **heterozygous** for that characteristic. On the other hand, if the nucleus carries the same allele on both members of the homologous pair, then the cell is **homozygous**. The meaning of these genetic terms is outlined in the diagram at the top of the next page.

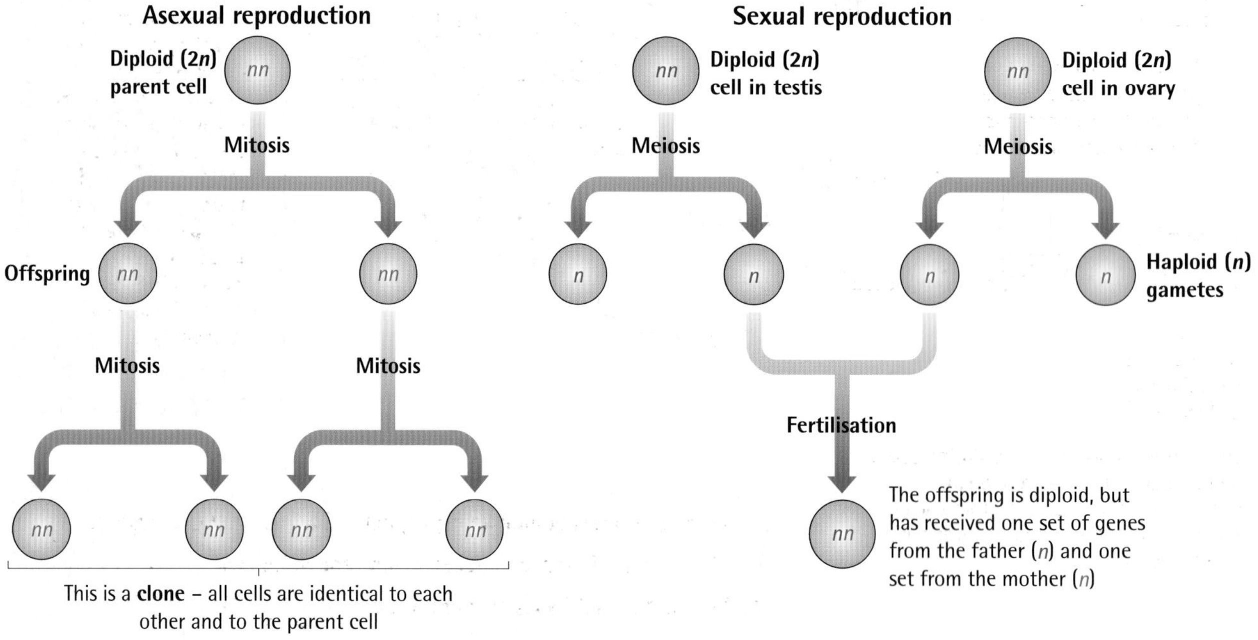

Asexual reproduction

Diploid (2*n*) parent cell *nn*

Mitosis

Offspring *nn*   *nn*

Mitosis   Mitosis

nn   *nn*   *nn*   *nn*

This is a **clone** – all cells are identical to each other and to the parent cell

Sexual reproduction

nn Diploid (2*n*) cell in testis   *nn* Diploid (2*n*) cell in ovary

Meiosis   Meiosis

n   *n*   *n*   *n* Haploid (*n*) gametes

Fertilisation

nn The offspring is diploid, but has received one set of genes from the father (*n*) and one set from the mother (*n*)

Organisms can reproduce asexually or sexually.

Inheritance and evolution

202

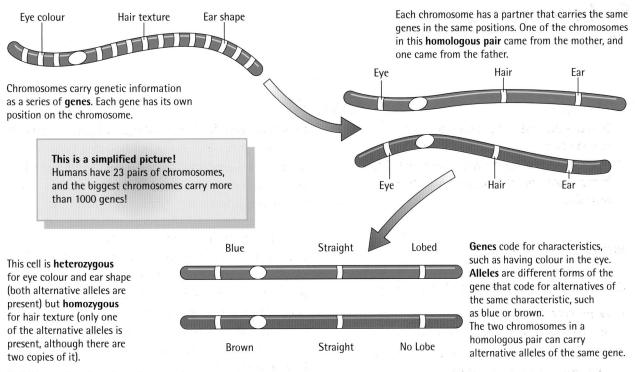

Eye colour   Hair texture   Ear shape

Chromosomes carry genetic information as a series of **genes**. Each gene has its own position on the chromosome.

This is a simplified picture!
Humans have 23 pairs of chromosomes, and the biggest chromosomes carry more than 1000 genes!

Each chromosome has a partner that carries the same genes in the same positions. One of the chromosomes in this **homologous pair** came from the mother, and one came from the father.

Eye   Hair   Ear

Eye   Hair   Ear

Blue   Straight   Lobed

Brown   Straight   No Lobe

This cell is **heterozygous** for eye colour and ear shape (both alternative alleles are present) but **homozygous** for hair texture (only one of the alternative alleles is present, although there are two copies of it).

Diploid organisms have homologous pairs of chromosomes in the nucleus.

Genes code for characteristics, such as having colour in the eye. **Alleles** are different forms of the gene that code for alternatives of the same characteristic, such as blue or brown.
The two chromosomes in a homologous pair can carry alternative alleles of the same gene.

In a heterozygous cell, when the members of the homologous pair separate during meiosis the gametes will contain different alleles. This means that when gametes fuse at fertilisation, the resulting zygote may have a number of different possible allele combinations. The production of gametes and the formation of different zygotes in this way are explained in the diagram below.

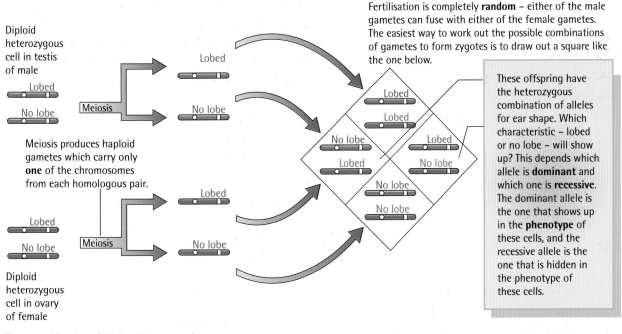

Diploid heterozygous cell in testis of male

Lobed
No lobe

Meiosis

Lobed
No lobe

Meiosis produces haploid gametes which carry only **one** of the chromosomes from each homologous pair.

Lobed
No lobe

Meiosis

Lobed
No lobe

Diploid heterozygous cell in ovary of female

Lobed
No lobe
Lobed
No lobe

Lobed
Lobed
No lobe   Lobed
Lobed   No lobe
No lobe
No lobe

Fertilisation is completely **random** – either of the male gametes can fuse with either of the female gametes. The easiest way to work out the possible combinations of gametes to form zygotes is to draw out a square like the one below.

These offspring have the heterozygous combination of alleles for ear shape. Which characteristic – lobed or no lobe – will show up? This depends which allele is **dominant** and which one is **recessive**. The dominant allele is the one that shows up in the **phenotype** of these cells, and the recessive allele is the one that is hidden in the phenotype of these cells.

The recombination of alleles during sexual reproduction gives rise to a great variation among offspring. This leads to the evolution of new strains, races and, eventually, new species.

1 Define the terms homologous pair, heterozygous and homozygous.

2 What is the difference between a gene and an allele?

3 What is a meant by a dominant allele?

11·9 Studying patterns of inheritance

Objectives
- To understand the method for describing genetic crosses
- To know the result of crosses involving two heterozygous parents
- To understand the principle of the test cross

Scientists called **geneticists** study the inheritance of characteristics by carrying out breeding experiments. There is a conventional pattern for describing the results of such experiments – a sort of genetic shorthand, shown in the example below.

At fertilisation, any male gamete can fuse with any female gamete

Drawing out chromosomes carrying alleles of genes is very time-consuming. Geneticists write out the stages of crosses using symbols to replace the chromosomes and genes. These symbols should always be identified at the start of a cross.

Let **B** = brown and **b** = blue.

The **capital** letter is used for the **dominant** allele.

Brown (**B**) and blue (**b**) are **alleles** of the **gene** for eye colour.

Consider a cross between a homozygous brown-eyed man (**BB**) and a homozygous blue-eyed woman (**bb**):

Parents	BB	×	bb

Gametes   (B) and (B)   (b) and (b)

At fertilisation   (B)   (b)

Remember, gametes are **haploid** so receive only one allele from the two present in the parent cell.

↓
Bb

A male gamete fuses with a female gamete

↓
Bb

This **genotype** would give a brown-eyed **phenotype**, since brown is **dominant** to blue.

First generation (called the **F_1 generation**)

Now consider a cross between two heterozygous parents (**Bb**), i.e. with the same genotype as the F_1 above:

Parents	Bb	×	Bb

Gametes   (B) and (b)   (B) and (b)

At fertilisation, any male gamete can fuse with any female gamete

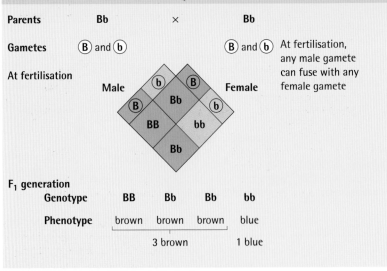

F_1 generation

Genotype	BB	Bb	Bb	bb
Phenotype	brown	brown	brown	blue

3 brown   1 blue

The inheritance of eye colour. There are two important points about this cross.

(1) These results are **probabilities**. The offspring *should* be in the 3:1 ratio shown, but each fertilisation is random so they may not be. This ratio is more likely to be seen in very large numbers of offspring. For human families a 3:1 ratio is unlikely since very few mothers give birth to four children at one time.

(2) Every cross between the same two parents is a different event. If two heterozygous parents produce a child with blue eyes (a 1/4 probability) there is still a 1/4 probability that their next child will have blue eyes.

In theory a cross between two heterozygous parents should produce offspring in the ratio of 3 showing dominant to 1 showing recessive. This can be restated as: 'The probability of any offspring showing dominant is 3/4 or 75%; the probability of it showing recessive is 1/4 or 25%'.

Test cross

In the eye colour example, both of the genotypes BB and Bb give the same phenotype – brown eyes. It might be important to know whether a particular organism is homozygous or heterozygous, particularly in the breeding of domestic animals. To do this, geneticists use a **test cross** (often called a **back cross to the recessive**). The principle is outlined on the right.

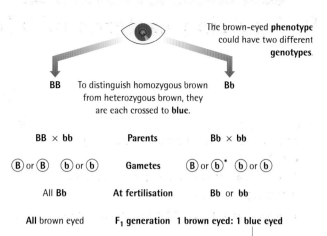

The brown-eyed **phenotype** could have two different **genotypes**.

| BB | To distinguish homozygous brown from heterozygous brown, they are each crossed to **blue**. | Bb |

BB × bb	**Parents**	Bb × bb
Ⓑ or Ⓑ Ⓑ or Ⓑ	**Gametes**	Ⓑ or Ⓑ* Ⓑ or Ⓑ
All Bb	**At fertilisation**	Bb or bb
All brown eyed	**F₁ generation**	**1 brown eyed : 1 blue eyed**

*The heterozygous brown can supply the **b** allele for a gamete even though it is 'hidden' in the phenotype of the diploid parent.

If **any** offspring showing the recessive characteristic result from a test cross, the parent **must** have been heterozygous.

A test cross can distinguish different genotypes with the same phenotype.

Monohybrid cross and the work of Gregor Mendel

A genetic cross like the one described on the left, in which a single pair of alleles is transmitted to the next generation, is called a **monohybrid cross**. The first quantitative information about inheritance came from monohybrid crosses carried out by an Austrian monk called **Gregor Mendel** (1822–84) more than 100 years ago. His work is outlined below. Mendel's work was not discovered by other scientists until after his death. Modern genetics is based on his results.

Mendel: Why was he successful?

He chose a suitable organism for study	**He only studied discontinuous variations**	**He studied one characteristic at a time**

The garden pea:
     was available in **pure-breeding strains** – these show a certain characteristic unchanged for many generations (we now call them **homozygotes**)
     usually self-pollinates but can be artificially cross-pollinated – so Mendel could control the parents in his crosses
 ■ breed quickly – Mendel soon had many results to analyse
 ■ show many clear-cut characteristics – Mendel was easily able to distinguish different phenotypes.
	This meant that there were no confusing 'intermediate' forms and made it easier for Mendel to record the results of a cross. For example:
	 ■ pea stems are either **tall** or **short**
	 ■ pea pods are either **yellow** or **green**
	 ■ pea seeds are either **round** or **wrinkled**.

		Mendel began his work by looking at one characteristic and ignoring the rest. This made it easier for him to see the rules or laws which governed inheritance.
		
		 When studying colour of pod, he ignored stem length and seed shape, for example.

Mendel's first experiments
He crossed pure-breeding tall with pure-breeding short plants, then crossed the offspring with each other:

Parents   Tall × Short
        ↓
F₁   All tall
(Tall is dominant to short)

Then

F₂ generation   F₁ tall × F₁ tall
        ↓
3 tall : 1 short

1. Draw a diagram to explain how two brown-eyed parents can have a blue-eyed child.

2. Gregor Mendel suggested that a cross between two heterozygous individuals produces offspring in a ratio of 3 showing the dominant characteristic to 1 showing the recessive characteristic. Explain why such crosses rarely give an exact 3:1 ratio.

3. Use a suitable example to explain the value of a test cross.

- To know some examples of inherited diseases
- To understand inheritance when neither allele is dominant

Cystic fibrosis is caused by a recessive allele.

Let **N** = normal allele and **n** = mutant (cystic fibrosis, CF) allele.

If both parents are carriers (heterozygous):

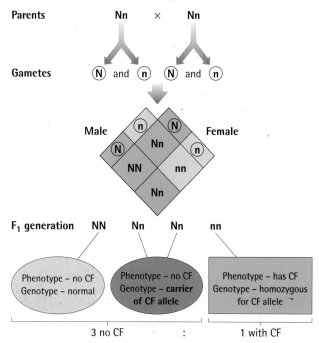

F₁ generation NN   Nn   Nn   nn

Phenotype – no CF
Genotype – normal

Phenotype – no CF
Genotype – **carrier of CF allele**

Phenotype – has CF
Genotype – homozygous for CF allele

3 no CF   :   1 with CF

Inherited diseases

There are several important medical examples of monohybrid inheritance, including cystic fibrosis, Huntington's chorea and sickle cell anaemia.

- **Cystic fibrosis** is caused by a **recessive** allele. Heterozygous individuals are not affected by the condition, but they are **carriers** of the allele. People with cystic fibrosis have an imbalance of chloride ions across the membranes of cells lining some of the major passageways of the body. This imbalance causes mucus to build up, congesting the lungs and airways and blocking the pancreatic duct so that digestion is limited.

- **Huntington's disease** is caused by a **dominant** allele so that heterozygous individuals are affected by the condition. The disease affects the central nervous system. There are no symptoms until middle age, but then there is a rapid loss of coordination, leading to death.

- **Sickle cell anaemia** is a condition in which a homozygote has the disease, but a heterozygous individual may gain some benefit in certain environments (see also page 201).

The inheritance of these three conditions is described on these two pages.

Huntington's disease is caused by a dominant allele.

This condition is caused by a **dominant** allele, so a heterozygote will develop the disease.

Let **H** = allele for disease (Huntington's disease) and **h** = normal allele.

If one parent is heterozygous, and the other is homozygous normal:

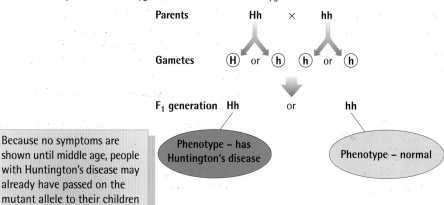

F₁ generation Hh   or   hh

Phenotype – has Huntington's disease

Phenotype – normal

Because no symptoms are shown until middle age, people with Huntington's disease may already have passed on the mutant allele to their children before knowing they have the disease.

Polydactyly (a condition in which a person has more than five fingers and toes on each hand or foot) is another example of an inherited disease caused by dominant allele. This condition is inherited in the same way as Huntington's disease, but does not have the same lethal results.

Homozygous dominant individuals are very rare. These people **do** show early symptoms, and die very young (or may be spontaneously aborted).

Sickle cell anaemia – carriers are anaemic but are resistant to malaria.

Sickle cell anaemia is caused by a recessive allele.
Let **S** = normal allele and **s** = sickle cell allele.
Consider a cross between two heterozygous parents:

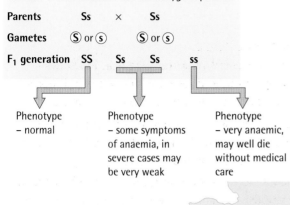

Parents	**Ss**	×	**Ss**
Gametes	Ⓢ or Ⓢ		Ⓢ or Ⓢ
F₁ generation	SS	Ss Ss	ss

Phenotype
– normal

Phenotype
– some symptoms
of anaemia, in
severe cases may
be very weak

Phenotype
– very anaemic,
may well die
without medical
care

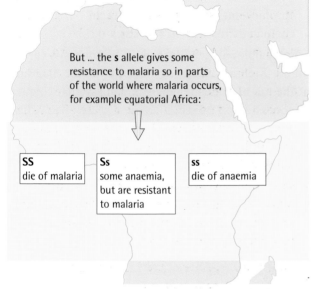

But ... the **s** allele gives some resistance to malaria so in parts of the world where malaria occurs, for example equatorial Africa:

SS die of malaria	**Ss** some anaemia, but are resistant to malaria	**ss** die of anaemia

Codominance

Some genes have more than two alleles. For example, the gene controlling the human ABO blood groups has three alleles, given the symbols I^A, I^B and I^O. Neither of the I^A and I^B alleles is dominant to the other, although they are both dominant to I^O. This is called **codominance**. It results in an extra phenotype when both alleles are present together. The genotypes and phenotypes are shown in the table.

Genotype	Phenotype
$I^A I^A$ or $I^A I^O$	Blood group A
$I^B I^B$ or $I^B I^O$	Blood group B
$I^A I^B$	Blood group AB
$I^O I^O$	Blood group O

The human blood groups are easily detected by a simple test on a blood sample.

---

1 Cystic fibrosis is a common inherited disease caused by a recessive allele. A blood test can detect this allele. A man and his wife were both found to be carriers of the cystic fibrosis allele.

a What is meant by a carrier of the allele?

b Draw a genetic diagram to show the inheritance of cystic fibrosis in any children of this couple. What is the chance that a child will have cystic fibrosis?

2 Huntington's chorea (HC) is caused by a dominant allele (**H**) – the other allele (**h**) results in normal working of the central nervous system. This diagram shows how one family is affected by HC.

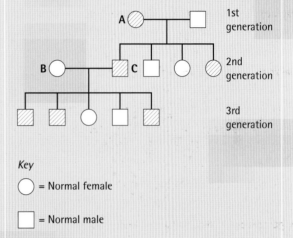

Key

◯ = Normal female

☐ = Normal male

◢ = Affected female

a What was the genotype of the grandmother, **A**? Explain your reasoning.

b Draw a genetic diagram to show how parents **B** and **C** passed on HC to their children.

c If parents **B** and **C** have a sixth child, what are the chances that it will have HC?

d Most serious genetic diseases are caused by recessive alleles. Explain why a dominant allele that causes a serious disease may quickly disappear from a population.

3 a Draw a genetic diagram to explain the inheritance of blood group in the Wilson family. Mr Wilson has the genotype $I^A I^B$ and Mrs Wilson has the genotype $I^O I^O$.

b What is the probability of the Wilsons' first child being female?

c What is the probability of this child being female and having blood group A?

d A person with alleles I^A and I^B shows the effect of both alleles in the phenotype. What term is used to describe this?

Sex is determined by X and Y chromosomes

- To understand how sex is determined and inherited in humans
- To know that some genes are sex linked
- To understand the pattern of inheritance of sex-linked genes

The photograph on page 189 shows a complete set of human chromosomes (a karyotype). When all of the chromosomes are arranged in pairs, there may be two left over which differ in size and do not form an homologous pair. These are the **sex chromosomes**. The importance of these sex chromosomes is outlined below.

Note that:

- The man's sperm determines the sex of his children since the woman can only produce gametes with an X chromosome.
- The sex chromosomes carry genes concerned with sexual development, such as development of the sex organs and position of fat stores.
- The sex chromosomes also carry a few genes that code for characteristics that are not concerned with sex. Since these genes are carried on the sex chromosomes, they may show their characteristics only in one sex.

For example the gene for **colour blindness** is carried on the X chromosome, as illustrated in the diagram at the top of the page opposite. We say that colour blindness is **sex linked**.

The inheritance of sex

Each human body cell has 46 chromosomes. There are 22 **pairs** of chromosomes plus another two chromosomes which may not look alike. These are the **sex chromosomes**. Female cells have two sex chromosomes that are alike (called XX) and male cells have two sex chromosomes that are not alike (XY).

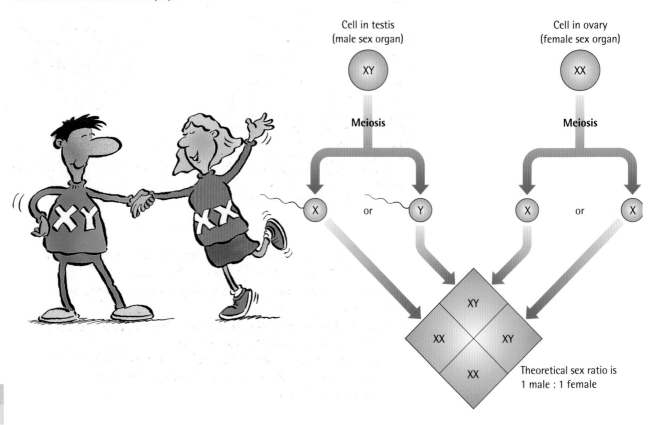

Cell in testis (male sex organ) — XY — Meiosis — X or Y

Cell in ovary (female sex organ) — XX — Meiosis — X or X

	XY
XX	XY
	XX

Theoretical sex ratio is 1 male : 1 female

The inheritance of sex-linked characteristics

One well known sex-linked characteristic is **haemophilia** This is a disease in which the blood fails to clot properly. It is an X-linked condition. The inheritance of this disease is shown opposite. Red–green colour blindness is inherited in a similar way – there are many more males than females who cannot distinguish red from green.

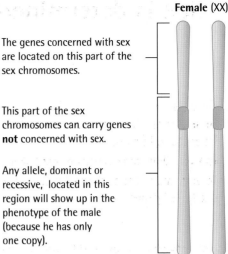

Male (XY)   Female (XX)

The genes concerned with sex are located on this part of the sex chromosomes.

Gene for colour vision – the recessive allele causes colour blindness.

This part of the sex chromosomes can carry genes **not** concerned with sex.

Any allele, dominant or recessive, located in this region will show up in the phenotype of the male (because he has only one copy).

Any gene carried on the sex chromosomes is sex linked.

The inheritance of haemophilia

Let **H** = normal allele and
   h = mutant allele.

Because these alleles are carried on the X chromosome, it is necessary to show the sex chromosomes in the pattern of inheritance. For example,

Female

$X^H X^h$

Female, so two X chromosomes   Heterozygous for haemophilia gene

Male

$X^H Y$ — Remember – no 'haemophilia' gene on the Y chromosome.

Male, so only **one** X chromosome

Two unaffected parents can produce a son with haemophilia.

Note that a daughter with haemophilia ($X^h X^h$) could only be produced if **both** parents contributed X^h gametes – if the father had haemophilia. In this case his condition would be known and the daughter's condition might be expected.

Consider a cross between a carrier woman and a normal man:

Parents $X^H X^h$ × $X^H Y$

Female – normal phenotype but a carrier of the mutant allele   Male – normal phenotype

Gametes X^H X^h X^H Y

F₁ generation

$X^h X^H$

$X^H X^H$ $X^h Y$

$X^H Y$

Key

Carrier female   Normal male/female

Male with haemophilia

1 Use a simple genetic diagram to explain why there are approximately equal numbers of male and female babies.

2 Why are males more likely to have red–green colour blindness than females?

3 Haemophilia is a sex-linked characteristic. The diagram above shows how the allele for haemophilia is inherited.

  a Explain why the mother is described as a carrier of this condition.

  b If she has one child, what is the probability of her having a haemophiliac son?

Variation and natural selection: the evolution of species

Objectives
- To understand the meaning of adaptation, and to provide examples of this
- To realise that Darwin's theory benefited from the ideas of other scientists

Adaptation

As we have seen, living organisms differ from one another. Some of these variations make an organism well suited to its environment, some make no difference, and others make the organism *less* well suited to its environment. An organism that is well suited to make the most of the limited resources within its environment is said to show **adaptation** to its environment, as shown opposite. The cactus, polar bear and camel are all well adapted to their environments – see pages 167 and 239.

A lion has adaptations that enable it to capture prey efficiently. These are:

- structural (e.g. teeth and claws)
- biochemical (e.g. extra protein-digesting enzymes)
- behavioural (e.g. hunting in groups).

The work of Charles Darwin

Charles Darwin (1809–82) was a British naturalist who took part in a world voyage on a ship called HMS *Beagle*. The voyage, which began in 1831 and lasted for five years, allowed Darwin to see many examples of adaptations. His most famous observations were made on the Galapagos Islands off the west coast of South America. Some species seemed to have adaptations to life on particular islands, but had similarities, and Darwin suspected that they all originated from a single species. An example is shown above right.

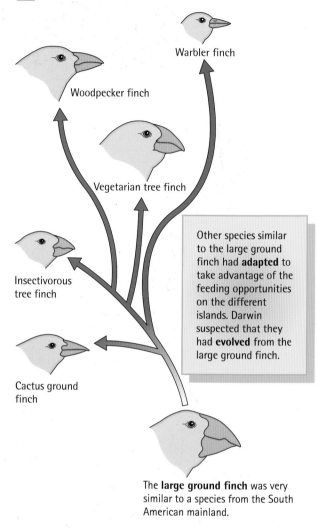

Woodpecker finch

Warbler finch

Vegetarian tree finch

Insectivorous tree finch

Cactus ground finch

Other species similar to the large ground finch had **adapted** to take advantage of the feeding opportunities on the different islands. Darwin suspected that they had **evolved** from the large ground finch.

The **large ground finch** was very similar to a species from the South American mainland.

Finches of the Galapagos islands show adaptations to the food resources on the different islands.

Evolution by natural selection

At the time that Darwin lived, most people believed that each species was fixed, and had been put on Earth in its current form by a creator – God. Darwin thought that species were not fixed, and that they changed through time to produce new species. He called this changing through time **evolution**. At first he was unable to convince other scientists because he could not suggest a **mechanism for evolution**. However, he eventually published his ideas in a famous book, *The Origin of Species by Means of Natural Selection*. An outline of the events leading to this publication is shown on the opposite page.

As a result of many observations made during his voyage on HMS *Beagle*, Charles Darwin began to think that living organisms could change in structure. Darwin suggested that species became adapted to meet the challenges of their environment.

The Rev. Thomas Malthus was a mathematician who showed that populations of living organisms would increase indefinitely unless they were kept in check by limited resources.

Charles Lyell was a geologist who showed that the Earth's rocks were very old. He pointed out that rocks of different ages contained the fossilised remains of different animals and plants.

Darwin proposed a mechanism of evolution by natural selection

Darwin was stung into action, and published his ideas in *The Origin of Species*.

Alfred Russell Wallace was a professional animal collector working in Malaysia. He wrote to Darwin, and Darwin realised that Wallace had reached the same conclusions about natural selection.

Darwin and *The Origin of Species*

1 What is meant by the term adaptation?

2 Name one animal and one plant with which you are familiar, and describe how each is adapted to its environment.

Objectives
- To understand how adaptation leads to natural selection

Darwin's ideas about natural selection can be summarised under a number of headings, as shown in the diagram below.

Natural selection may lead to new species

Some organisms are better suited to their environment than others. These organisms will be more likely to survive and breed than some of their competitors. Because of this, the characteristics they possess will become more common in the species over successive generations. If we consider one such characteristic, for example neck length in antelopes, we should be able to draw a graph showing how this characteristic is distributed in the population (see page 198). If the environment applies a **selection pressure** such as a limited availability of leaves for food, one part of the population may be favoured. In a few generations' time the graph may look rather different, as shown on the opposite page. If two populations of this antelope were separated from one another, natural selection might favour different adaptations in the two environments. Eventually the two different populations of antelope could have so many different adaptations that they can no longer interbreed – they are said to be different **species**.

Alternative theories of evolution

Early scientists and religious leaders believed that a creator had placed all living organisms on the Earth in their present-day forms. Even once the evidence for evolution had been accepted, not everyone agreed with Darwin's idea of natural selection. Jean Baptiste Lamarck was a Frenchman who lived about 70 years before Darwin. He believed that organisms adapted to their environment by 'use and disuse', that is, a giraffe might gain a long neck by stretching up for food in a tall tree. However, Lamarck was never able to show how these acquired characteristics could be passed on from one generation to another. The major difference between the theories of Darwin and Lamarck was that:
- **Lamarck** suggested that the environment *caused* the variations
- **Darwin** suggested that the environment *selected* the variations, which had arisen purely by chance.

Over-production – all organisms produce more offspring than can possibly survive, and yet populations remain relatively stable.
e.g. a female peppered moth may lay 500 eggs, but the moth population does not increase by the same proportion!

Struggle for existence – organisms experience environmental resistance i.e. they compete for the limited resources within the environment.
e.g. several moths may try to feed on the same nectar-producing flower.

Variation – within the population there may be some characteristics that make the organisms that have them more suited for this severe competition.
e.g. some moths might be stronger fliers, have better feeding mouthparts, be better camouflaged while resting or be less affected by rain.

Survival of the fittest – individuals that are most successful in the struggle for existence (i.e. that are the best suited/adapted to their environment) are more likely to survive than those without these advantages.
e.g. peppered moths: dark-coloured moths resting on soot-covered tree trunks will be less likely to be captured by predators than light-coloured moths.

Advantageous characteristics are passed on to offspring – the well-adapted individuals are more likely to breed than those that are less well-adapted – they pass on their genes to the next generation. This process is called **natural selection**.
e.g. dark-coloured moth parents will produce dark-coloured offspring.

Evolution by means of natural selection

Height is a characteristic that shows **continuous variation** in antelopes.

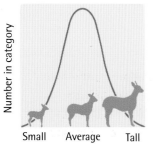

When food is only available from high branches, **natural selection** picks out the taller antelopes.

Many generations later

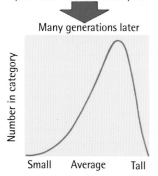

The formation of new species

Forming new species
Two populations of the same species could be separated, e.g. by a mountain range. Different **selection pressures** might exist on opposite sides.

Natural selection by **predators**, who can see tall antelopes more easily, favours the small antelopes.

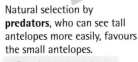

Many generations later

Natural selection by **food availability** on high trees only, favours the tall antelopes.

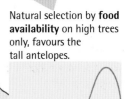

Many generations later

The two populations now have so many different adaptations that they cannot interbreed. They have now become two species, e.g. the dik-dik and giraffe in east Africa.

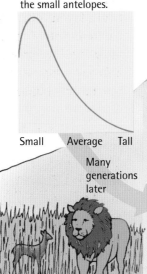

1 Using only the following information, answer questions **a** to **d**.

Cepaea is a type of snail which shows considerable variation in its shell colour. The basic colour can be yellow, brown, fawn, pink, orange or red. Over the top of this basic colour up to five bands of a darker colour may occur, around the shell. Colour of shell provides camouflage for the snail because some colours are more difficult to see than others against the background.

Cepaea is an important part of the diet of thrushes. These birds collect snails and break open their shells by banging them on a stone. Thrushes tend to use the same stone, called an 'anvil', whenever feeding in a particular area.

It is possible to collect the remains of the shells and count the number of each shell type. It is also possible to collect the live snails in the same area and count the numbers of each shell type.

Collections of both live snails and broken shells were made in an area where the ground layer plants gave a fairly evenly coloured background. The results are shown in the table.

a How many more live, unbanded *Cepaea* were collected than banded?

b Suggest an explanation for thrushes taking more banded snails even where there appear to be more unbanded snails in the live populations.

	Number of snails			
	Banded	Unbanded	Total	% Banded
Live snails	264	296	560	47.0
Shell remains from 'anvils' in the area	486	377	863	56.0

c Which type of shell, banded or unbanded, would you expect to occur most frequently in a live snail population
  i amongst dead leaves in a wood?
  ii amongst grasses growing on a sand dune?

d The main points of the theory of evolution by natural selection are listed below.
  A The number of offspring is far greater than the number surviving to adult stage.
  B Variation exists among the offspring.
  C Some variations are useful and help the organisms to survive.
  D Competition occurs between the offspring.
  E Only those surviving can breed.
  Natural selection can change the proportions of the different colours in a snail population. Use the five points A to E above to describe how this change might come about.

(MEG June 1992)

Natural selection in action

Objectives
- To provide examples of natural selection in action today
- To outline evidence that evolution has occurred

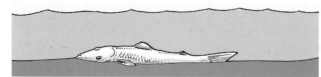

1 Organisms die – bodies sink to the bottom of the sea, and become covered with sediment.

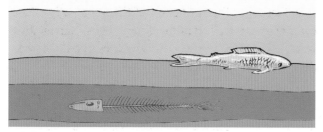

2 Sediment hardens and the remains turn to stone. New layers, containing newer remains, form over the old.

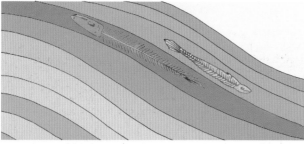

3 Rock layers (**strata**) fold and are raised up out of the sea. They are now exposed to wind and rain.

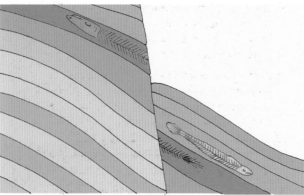

4 Erosion, and faults in rocks, expose the different strata and the fossils they contain.

How fossils form. Fossils of different ages show different structures, but similarities between them suggest that one form evolved into another.

Evolution occurs over very long periods of time. Evidence from fossils suggests that it took many millions of years for the modern-day form of the horse to evolve, for example. The horse takes several years to produce the next generation, but organisms that breed more rapidly, such as microorganisms and insects, should show adaptations much more quickly. Bacteria have evolved to be resistant to antibiotics (see page 310), and insect pests on crops have developed resistance to the chemicals used to control them. Some populations of rats have evolved resistance to **warfarin**, a chemical used to control rodents.

Evidence for evolution: fossils tell the story

When organisms die, their remains usually decompose and their bodies disappear. Sometimes, however, parts of them are turned into rock, forming **fossils**. The best fossils are found in **sedimentary rocks**, which were formed from sediments such as sand or mud at the bottom of ancient seas. The oldest sedimentary rocks, and therefore the oldest fossils, are found in the deepest layers of rock. The study of fossils, called **palaeontology**, provided much of the early evidence that organisms had evolved from earlier forms.

Evolution of the horse

The fossil record has given us clues about the evolution of the horse, as shown on the page opposite.

Evolution may be reversed

The evolution of the dark, or **melanic**, form of the peppered moth was described on page 212. After years of smoky pollution the dark form was more common in industrial areas than the light form. However, after the Clean Air Act the emission of smoky pollution became strictly controlled and trees gradually lost their smoky covering. Light-coloured lichens were able to grow on trees as pollution levels fell, and soon the dark form of the moth became more obvious to predators! In most areas of the UK the light form of the moth is now more common than the dark form (see opposite).

Inheritance and evolution

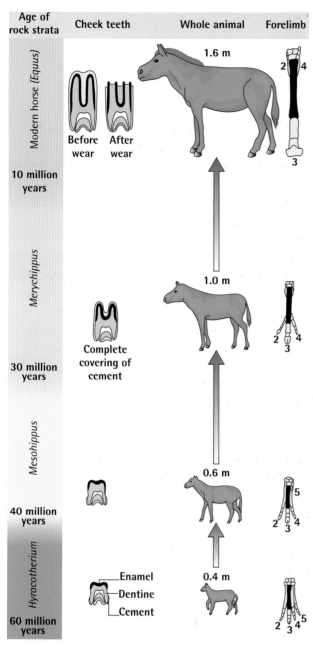

Age of rock strata	Cheek teeth	Whole animal	Forelimb

Modern horse (Equus)

Before wear — After wear

1.6 m

2 3 4

10 million years

Merychippus

Complete covering of cement

1.0 m

2 3 4

30 million years

Mesohippus

0.6 m

2 3 4 5

40 million years

Hyracotherium

Enamel
Dentine
Cement

0.4 m

2 3 4 5

60 million years

The evolution of the horse: clues from the fossil record

Light and dark (melanic) forms of the peppered moth

Extinction

Evolution continues to adapt organisms to their environment. If there are rapid changes to the environment, organisms may not evolve quickly enough to adapt. They will no longer be successful in exploiting the resources of their environment, and the species may become **extinct**. Many living organisms have become extinct during the history of the Earth.

For example, during the Mesozoic era dinosaurs dominated the Earth, but they all became extinct within a very short time. They may have been unable to cope with changes in vegetation brought about by severe effects on climate of a collision between the Earth and a giant meteorite.

Another example is the mammoth, which was abundant on the Earth until about 10 000 years ago. It is likely that the extinction of the mammoth coincided with the end of the last Ice Age – mammoths were well adapted to low temperatures but were at a disadvantage as the Earth warmed up.

Most extinctions have been the result of natural environmental change. Human activities may cause many more organisms to become extinct, as we shall see on page 268.

This exercise might test your skills as a palaeontologist! Look at the diagram above left.

1. How much taller is the modern horse than its earliest ancestor? Express your answer as a percentage.

2. Describe the major change to the feet of the horse during its evolution.

3. The teeth of the modern horse have very obvious hardened ridges. Compare this with the ancient horse. Which of the two would be better suited to chewing coarse vegetation such as grass?

4. Ancient horses lived in swampy areas, but modern horses live on open plains. How does the taller body and single toe of the modern horse suit it to its present-day habitat?

5. Assume that a horse can breed successfully at five years of age. How many generations could have passed between *Hyracotherium* and *Equus*?

6. Use the terms adaptation, variation, survival of the fittest and natural selection to describe how the modern form of the horse might have evolved from its ancestors.

Artificial selection

Making organisms useful to humans

Variation occurs naturally and randomly in all living organisms, but the natural environment is not the only agent of selection. Ever since early humans began to domesticate animals and plants, they have been trying to improve them. This improvement is brought about by selecting those individuals that have the most useful characteristics and allowing only these individuals to breed. This process is called **artificial selection**. Humans have replaced the environment as the agents of selection. There are many important examples of selective breeding:

▪ **Jersey cattle** have been bred to produce milk with a very high cream content.

▪ All domestic **dogs** are the same species, but some have been bred for appearance (e.g. Pekinese), some for hunting (springer spaniels) and some as aggressive guards (Rottweilers).

▪ **Wheat** has been bred so that all the stems are the same height (making harvesting easier) and the ears separate easily from the stalk (making collection of the grain easier).

Some examples of artificial selection are shown below and opposite. The same species can be bred in different ways for different purposes. Early horses have become specialised as carthorses or for racing, for example.

Maintaining variation

What appears to humans as a valuable characteristic might not always be valuable in a natural situation. For example, a Chihuahua dog would probably not survive in the wild because its hunting instincts have been bred out to make it more suitable as a pet. It is very important that humans preserve animal and plant genes for characteristics that do not offer any advantage to us at the moment. A cow with a limited milk yield may carry a gene that makes it resistant to a disease which is not yet a problem in domestic herds, for example. This resistance gene might be extremely valuable if ever such a disease did become established. For this reason many varieties of animals and plants are kept in small numbers in rare-breed centres up and down the country. Plant genes may be conserved as seeds, which are easy to store, and some animal genes may be kept as frozen eggs, sperm or embryos.

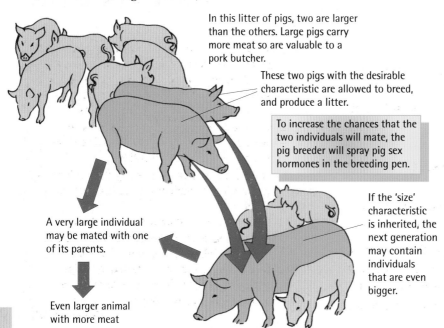

In this litter of pigs, two are larger than the others. Large pigs carry more meat so are valuable to a pork butcher.

These two pigs with the desirable characteristic are allowed to breed, and produce a litter.

To increase the chances that the two individuals will mate, the pig breeder will spray pig sex hormones in the breeding pen.

A very large individual may be mated with one of its parents.

Even larger animal with more meat

If the 'size' characteristic is inherited, the next generation may contain individuals that are even bigger.

Techniques of artificial selection

Artificial insemination

Male animals, no matter how many useful characteristics they have, **cannot give birth to young animals!** So:

▪ Most male offspring will be fattened up for selling as meat.

▪ 'Desirable' males may be electrically stimulated to ejaculate – the sperm is collected and frozen. One male can easily produce several hundred samples.

▪ The sperm can be taken to a pig breeding farm and used to inseminate many females.

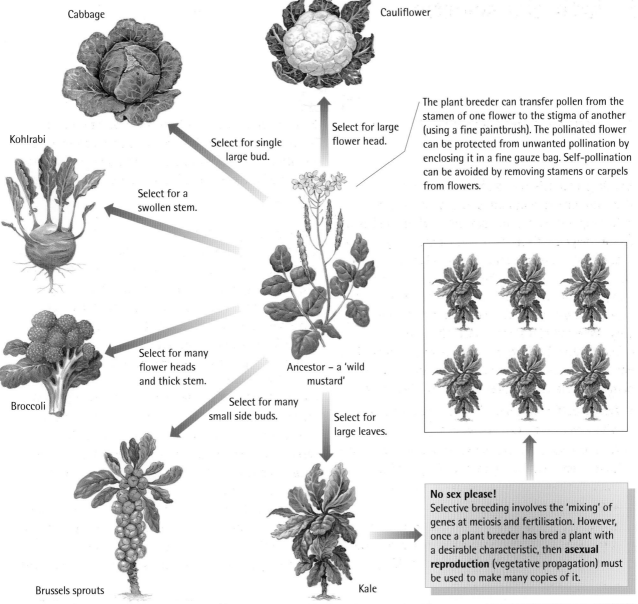

Cabbage

Cauliflower

Kohlrabi

Select for single large bud.

Select for large flower head.

The plant breeder can transfer pollen from the stamen of one flower to the stigma of another (using a fine paintbrush). The pollinated flower can be protected from unwanted pollination by enclosing it in a fine gauze bag. Self-pollination can be avoided by removing stamens or carpels from flowers.

Select for a swollen stem.

Select for many flower heads and thick stem.

Broccoli

Ancestor – a 'wild mustard'

Select for many small side buds.

Select for large leaves.

Brussels sprouts

Kale

No sex please!
Selective breeding involves the 'mixing' of genes at meiosis and fertilisation. However, once a plant breeder has bred a plant with a desirable characteristic, then **asexual reproduction** (vegetative propagation) must be used to make many copies of it.

Artificial selection has produced many vegetables from one ancestor species.

Three major differences between artificial and natural selection

- In artificial selection, humans are the agents of selection, while natural selection depends upon the natural environment.
- Artificial selection is much quicker than natural selection.
- Artificial selection offers no advantage to the animal or plant in its natural environment.

It is likely that selective breeding will be replaced by genetic engineering in the future. This technique, explained on page 218, is much more predictable than selective breeding and produces useful results more quickly.

1 A potato grower wanted to produce a new variety of potato which grows quickly and makes good chips. She has one variety which grows quickly but makes poor chips, and another which grows more slowly but makes good chips.

When plants of these two varieties produce flowers she crosses the two varieties. Later she collects the seeds and plants them.

a To cross the two varieties, the grower pollinates a flower of one variety with pollen from the other.
Describe how the grower should do this.

b From the seeds she collects, she finds that one of the new plants grows very quickly and produces potatoes which make good chips. How would she produce a crop of potatoes which are exactly the same?

(NEAB June 1992)

11·16 Genetic engineering

Objectives
- To understand the term genetic engineering
- To understand the value of enzymes in genetic engineering
- To be able to describe a technique in genetic engineering
- To list some products of genetic engineering that are of value to humans

What is genetic engineering?

The examples of selective breeding described on page 216 are a form of genetic engineering, since humans are interfering with the natural flow of genetic material from one generation to the next when they choose the animals or plants that will be allowed to reproduce (and pass on their genes). However, what we now call genetic engineering is a much more predictable and refined process than selective breeding. In this process:

- Genes that code for characteristics valuable to humans are identified.
- These genes are removed from the animal or plant that normally shows this characteristic.
- The genes are transferred to another organism, usually one that grows very quickly.
- This organism 'reads' the gene it has received, and shows the characteristic that is valuable to humans.

Recombinant DNA technology

In many cases the characteristic is the ability to manufacture a product that has some medical or industrial value. Because DNA (a gene) from one organism is being transferred to the DNA of another organism to make a new combination of DNA, this 'modern' genetic engineering is often referred to as **recombinant DNA technology**. The principle of this technique sounds very straightforward, but in practice it is extremely difficult.

- The genetic material is microscopic in size. A technician can't use a pair of scissors to cut out a gene!
- The **host** organism, that is, the one that will receive the valuable gene, would not normally take in DNA from another organism.

- The host organism might not show the valuable characteristic, for example it may not make a particular protein, even though it now has the DNA that codes for the protein.

Technological advances have overcome these potential problems. Key to success has been the discovery of:

- **enzymes** that can cut DNA from one chromosome and paste it into another, acting like scissors and glue
- **vectors** that can carry the gene from one organism to another
- **culture techniques** that allow large quantities of the valuable product to be produced and collected, even if the host organism would not normally produce it.

Many compounds can be manufactured by genetically engineered bacteria, including insulin and other products which are used directly by humans. These products are otherwise often taken from animals. For example insulin can be isolated from the pancreas of a pig.

Recombinant DNA technology has several advantages:

- The product is very pure, and can be the human version of a protein rather than a version produced by another animal. The human protein is likely to work more efficiently in a person, and is less likely to be rejected by the body's defences.
- The product can be made in large quantities, making it less expensive and more readily available. Insulin produced in this way costs about 1% as much as insulin produced from pig pancreas.
- The process can be switched on or off easily as the bacteria can be stored until needed again. The product can be made as required rather than just when animal carcasses are available.

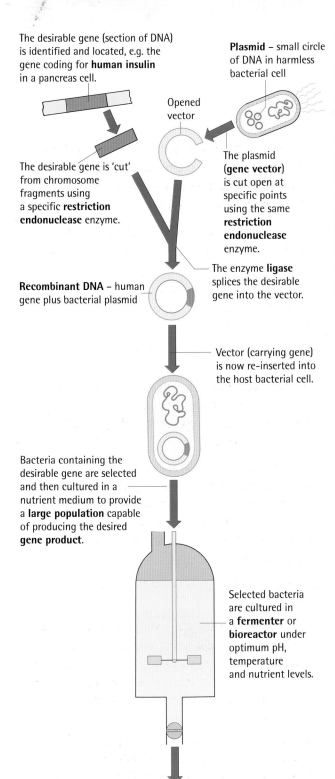

The desirable gene (section of DNA) is identified and located, e.g. the gene coding for **human insulin** in a pancreas cell.

Plasmid – small circle of DNA in harmless bacterial cell

Opened vector

The desirable gene is 'cut' from chromosome fragments using a specific **restriction endonuclease** enzyme.

The plasmid (**gene vector**) is cut open at specific points using the same **restriction endonuclease** enzyme.

The enzyme **ligase** splices the desirable gene into the vector.

Recombinant DNA – human gene plus bacterial plasmid

Vector (carrying gene) is now re-inserted into the host bacterial cell.

Bacteria containing the desirable gene are selected and then cultured in a nutrient medium to provide a **large population** capable of producing the desired **gene product**.

Selected bacteria are cultured in a **fermenter** or **bioreactor** under optimum pH, temperature and nutrient levels.

Product

After some processing, for example to remove the bacterial cells for recycling, the product is extremely pure and relatively inexpensive. Important examples of such gene products are:

■ **insulin** (required for the treatment of diabetes)
■ **human growth hormone**
■ **factor VIII** (blood clotting factor for haemophilia)
■ **BST** is an important animal hormone used to speed up the growth of beef cattle.

Genetic engineering (recombinant DNA technology) depends on enzymes and the culture of microorganisms.

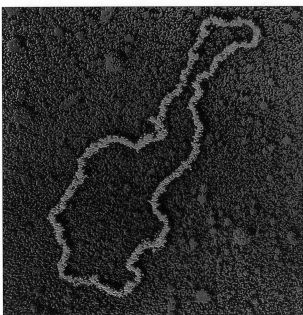

A plasmid of bacterial DNA

1. The following table lists events from the identification of a human gene coding for a hormone "X" to the commercial production of hormone "X".

   Genes can be transferred into plasmids, tiny circles of DNA which are found in bacteria.

   Show the correct sequence of events 1 to 8 by copying the table below and writing the appropriate number in each box provided. The first (number 1) and last (number 8) have been completed for you.

Event	Number
Cutting of a bacterial plasmid using restriction endonuclease	3
Cutting of human DNA with restriction endonuclease	2
Identification of the human DNA which codes for hormone "X"	1
Many identical plasmids, complete with human gene, are produced inside the bacterium	
Mixing together human gene and "cut" plasmids to splice the human gene into the plasmid	
Some of the cloned bacteria are put into an industrial fermenter where they breed and secrete the hormone.	8
The bacterium is cloned.	
Using the plasmid as a vector, inserting it, complete with human gene, into a bacterium	

(Edexcel Nov. 1994 [part])

Inheritance and evolution

11·17 Gene transfer in higher organisms

Objectives

- To describe how organisms other than bacteria may be altered by genetic engineering
- To appreciate that there are moral and environmental problems associated with the use of genetic engineering

Transgenic organisms

Bacteria are not the only organisms that can be modified by gene transfer. Genetic engineers have been able to transfer genes into flowering plants, fungi and mammals and thus alter the characteristics of these higher organisms. An organism that has received genes from a different species is called a **transgenic** organism. The major problem is finding a vector that can carry the gene into the new host. Different vectors have been used for different hosts, as described on the page opposite.

Genetic modification

The bacterium *Agrobacterium tumefaciens* has proved to be a very useful organism in gene transfer work, for two reasons:

- It carries plasmids, and using the techniques described on page 219 these plasmids can be recombined with a useful gene.
- The plasmid in this organism is called the **Ti plasmid**. It has has the ability to force cells infected with it to divide very rapidly to form a tumour (called a **crown gall** in plants).

Gene transfer in animals

Scientists can keep ova alive in a Petri dish. Transgenic animals are produced by introducing a desirable gene into the nucleus of a fertilised ovum using a fine pipette. When the fertilised ova containing the transferred gene have divided a few times, the ball of cells is implanted into a female animal and grows into a transgenic animal. This animal will be able to manufacture the protein coded for by the desirable gene.

Scientists arrange for the transferred gene to be 'read' in the cells of the mammary glands, so that the desirable product is released in the milk. The product, for example **factor VIII** which is used to treat haemophilia or **α-antitrypsin** which is used to treat inefficient immune systems, can then be purified from the milk.

Gene therapy

Gene therapy is the transfer of healthy human genes into a person's cells that contain mutant alleles which cause disease. The principle of gene therapy is outlined at the bottom of the page opposite.

Moral and environmental concerns about genetic modification

The benefits claimed for genetically modified products, and potential problems, are shown in the table below.

Benefits	Problems
Engineered organisms can offer higher yields from fewer resources. With plants, for example, this might reduce the need for pesticides and fertilisers.	Plants engineered for pesticide resistance could cross-pollinate with wild relatives, creating 'superweeds'
Crops engineered to cope with extreme environmental conditions will open up new areas for cultivation, and reduce the risk of famine	Engineered bacteria may escape from the laboratory or the factory, with unpredictable consequences
Genetic engineering gives much more predictable results than selective breeding	'New' organisms might be patented. A company that has spent a lot of money on developing such an organism might refuse to share its benefits with other consumers, making the company very powerful.
Foods can be engineered to be more convenient, such as potatoes which absorb less fat when crisps are made, or even to contain medicinal products such as vaccines	How far should we allow research into human gene transfer to go? Will we allow the production of 'perfect' children, with characteristics seen to be desirable by parents?

Inheritance and evolution

How plants may be genetically modified using *Agrobacterium tumefaciens* as a vector

Improved shelf life – a gene has been introduced into tomatoes which inhibits the enzymes causing deterioration. 'Flavr Savr' tomatoes keep for several weeks. Less wastage should mean lower prices.

Resistance to pests and herbicides
A gene is inserted into the crop plant which enables it to make **insecticidal crystal protein** (ICP) which affects the guts of caterpillars so that they cannot feed and eventually die.
A gene is inserted which makes the crop plant resistant to herbicides. The field of growing crop can then be sprayed with the herbicide, which will selectively kill the weeds.

Resistance to environmental conditions – gene transfer has produced:
drought resistance – plants with thicker, more waxy cuticles which can grow well in dry areas
uniform fruiting – plants produce flowers and fruits in response to daylight. Soya bean plants have been engineered to produce beans even in temperate regions of the world with a different light pattern to their normal habitat.
resistance to wind damage – soya plants have been engineered to have stronger stems of a more uniform height which makes them more resistant to wind damage and makes machine harvesting of the beans more efficient.

Transferring genes with *Agrobacterium tumefaciens*

Desirable gene introduced into Ti plasmid using **restriction endonuclease** and **ligase** enzymes.

Plasmid returned to bacterium.

Bacterium infects plant – plant produces a tumour (crown gall). Each cell contains the plasmid with the desired gene.

Fragments of gall grow into identical plants, each containing the desirable gene.

Nitrogen fixation – this is the conversion of nitrogen gas from the atmosphere into a form that plants can use (see page 256).

$$N_2 \text{ from atmosphere} \longrightarrow NH_4^+ \text{ ammonium ions} \longrightarrow \text{amino acids and other compounds}$$

This key step is controlled by enzymes coded for by 12 genes called the *Nif* genes

Most plants cannot fix nitrogen but gene transfer might either:
insert these *Nif* genes directly into a plant, or make a plant more likely to form root nodules with nitrogen-fixing bacteria.
This could:
■ produce cereal crops which also manufacture large amounts of protein
■ reduce the need for nitrogenous fertilisers.

Gene therapy may be able to repair diseased human cells.

Empty virus coat to act as gene vector

Virus takes up healthy gene.

Virus infects 'diseased' cell and releases healthy gene.

Healthy copy of gene

Cell can now make protein product, and no longer has disease.

Healthy gene 'repairs' diseased cell.

Cystic fibrosis is a good candidate for gene therapy because:
■ the healthy gene has been identified and is easily obtained
■ the diseased tissue in the lungs is easy to reach via trachea and bronchi
■ the coat of an influenza virus can be used as a gene vector.

1 Why is *Agrobacterium tumefaciens* a useful organism to genetic engineers?

2 What might be the benefits of transferring nitrogen-fixing genes from bacteria to other organisms?

3 Describe one example of gene therapy. Explain why this form of treatment is thought likely to be successful in the example which you describe.

Inheritance and evolution

1 Radiotherapy involves killing cancer cells by exposing them to ionising radiation. The radioactive isotope cobalt-60 is often used as a source of gamma rays. The gamma rays are directed at the tumour with great accuracy by the use of computer-controlled apparatus and highly trained staff.

Sometimes a radioactive isotope is used because the substance will be absorbed by the affected organ or tissue. For example, a radioactive isotope of iodine is used to treat cancer of the thyroid gland, because the thyroid gland manufactures the hormone thyroxine and thyroxine contains iodine.

a Explain the terms radioactive and isotope.

b Different types of radiation have differing degrees of penetration. This table lists the material and thickness necessary to stop three types of radiation.

Radiation type	Material and thickness necessary to stop radiation
Alpha	Paper 20 µm
Beta	Aluminium foil 2–3 mm
Gamma	Concrete 1–2 m

   i Which type of radiation has the greatest penetrating power?

   ii Which type of radiation would be used to treat lung cancer? Explain your answer.

   iii What precaution should a radiotherapist take when treating a patient with lung cancer?

c A person with cancer treated by radiotherapy may lose hair, have stomach upsets and possibly become anaemic. Explain the basis of each of these side-effects.

d A radioactive isotope of phosphorus is used to treat cancer of the bone. Explain why this is a suitable source of radiation for treating this form of cancer.

2 The diagram shows the nucleus of an animal cell.

nuclear 'membrane'

a When one nucleus divides, what is the normal number of nuclei formed from this nucleus as a result of division by

   i mitosis?   **ii** meiosis?

b **i** Name the structures seen inside the nucleus in the diagram.

   ii Draw the correct number and types of these structures as they would appear **1** after mitosis **2** after meiosis of the nucleus shown in the diagram.

(IGCSE Nov. 1997)

3 The diagram below shows a cell containing the diploid number of chromosomes. One pair of alleles on each pair of chromosomes has been shown.

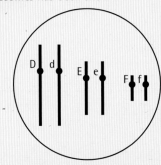

a How many genetically **different** types of gamete can be produced following meiosis of this cell? Choose from: 3, 4, 6 or 8.

b THREE of the following diagrams (A, B, C, D, E and F) show stages in meiosis in this cell.

A 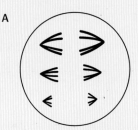   B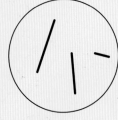

C 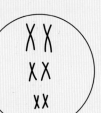   D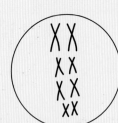

E 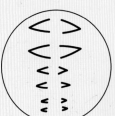   F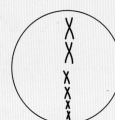

Write the letter of each diagram which shows a stage in meiosis in this cell.

(Edexcel June 1998)

4 In mice, a gene for body size has two alleles. There is a dominant allele, N, for normal body size and a recessive allele, n, for being fat.

a i Copy the table below and use this information to complete it.

ii The genetic diagram below shows a cross between a normal size heterozygous mouse and a fat homozygous mouse.

Copy the genetic diagram and complete it by writing correct letters in the circles.

(Edexcel June 1998)

Size of mouse	Genotype of mouse
Normal size (homozygous)	NN
Normal size (heterozygous)	Nn
Fat (homozygous)	nn

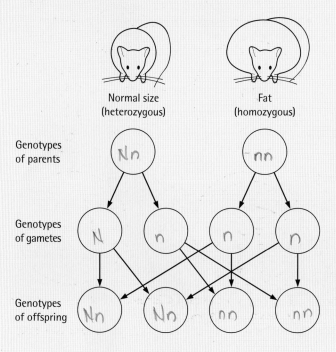

Normal size (heterozygous)   Fat (homozygous)

Genotypes of parents: Nn   nn

Genotypes of gametes: N n n n

Genotypes of offspring: Nn Nn nn nn

5 The diagram shows stages of an experiment in which a large number of genetically identical frogs were developed from unfertilised frog eggs.

The nucleus of each unfertilised egg was destroyed and replaced by a nucleus obtained from a body cell obtained from frog X.

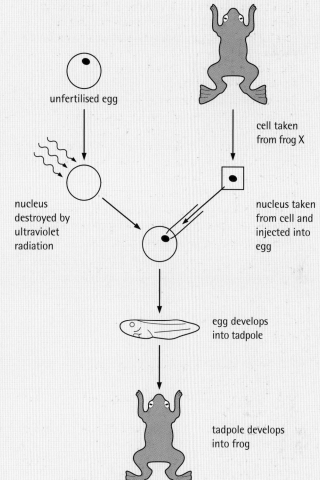

unfertilised egg

cell taken from frog X

nucleus destroyed by ultraviolet radiation

nucleus taken from cell and injected into egg

egg develops into tadpole

tadpole develops into frog

a i Explain why the eggs containing a nucleus from a body cell of a frog are able to develop into tadpoles whereas the unfertilised eggs are unable to do so.

ii Body cells of the frog contain 26 chromosomes. How many chromosomes would be likely to be present in each of the following?
- the unfertilised egg
- the eggs containing body cell nuclei

b i Explain fully why all the frogs produced from the treated eggs are genetically identical.

ii What is the name given to this method of producing genetically identical offspring?

iii Describe briefly the process of cell division which ensures that all the cells developing from an egg are identical.

c Some people object strongly to the sort of experiment shown in the diagram. Develop one argument for and one argument against this point of view.

(MEG June 1996)

Objectives

- To understand that evolution provides a basis for classification
- To appreciate why classification is necessary
- To understand the use of a key
- To be able to name the five kingdoms, and describe their distinguishing characteristics
- To understand the hierarchy of classification
- To know why a binomial system of nomenclature is valuable

The need to classify living things

Variation and natural selection lead to evolution. Evolution, and the isolation of populations, leads to the development of new species. Each species has different characteristics, and some of these characteristics can be inherited by successive generations of this species. Observing these inherited characteristics allows scientists to put all living organisms into categories. The science of placing organisms into categories on the basis of their observable characteristics is called **classification**. There are so many different types of living organism (an enormous variety of life) that the study of these organisms would be impossible without an ordered way of describing them.

Classification keys

Taxonomists (people who study classification) place organisms into groups by asking questions about their characteristics, such as 'Does the organism photosynthesise?' or 'Does the organism contain many cells?'. A series of questions like this is called a **classification key**. Examples of such keys are shown below.

Natural and artificial classification

The two types of classification key shown on this page are based on differences between organisms – at each step organisms with one particular feature are separated from all of the other organisms and placed in their own subgroup. This may group together organisms that are not very closely related – for example, if the branching point question was 'Does it have wings?' birds, bats and bees would end up in the same group! This type of classification is extremely useful for identification of organisms but it doesn't tell us much about their evolutionary relationships: it is known as an **artificial classification system**. If organisms are grouped according to their basic similarities they will have the same evolutionary origin. For example, the wing of a bird, the forelimb of a mole, the flipper of a dolphin and the hand of a human have all evolved from the same basic structure. A system based on similarities tells us a great deal about evolution, but may not be very helpful in identification. This is called a **natural classification system**.

This kind of key, with only two answers to each question (in this case, YES or NO), is called a dichotomous key ('dichotomous' means branching). It can be written as a branching or spider key, or as a list.

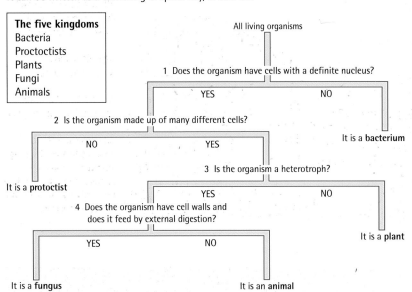

The five kingdoms
Bacteria
Proctoctists
Plants
Fungi
Animals

All living organisms

1 Does the organism have cells with a definite nucleus?
  YES   NO
2 Is the organism made up of many different cells?
  NO   YES   It is a **bacterium**
It is a **protoctist**
3 Is the organism a heterotroph?
  YES   NO
4 Does the organism have cell walls and does it feed by external digestion?
  YES   NO   It is a **plant**
It is a **fungus**   It is an **animal**

Banching keys are easy to use, but take up a lot of space when fully drawn out. For this reason this **listed form** of a dichotomous key is usually used for identification of organisms outside the laboratory.

1	Does the organism have cells with a definite nucleus?	YES	Go to question 2
		NO	It is a **bacterium**
2	Is the organism made up of many different cells?	YES	Go to question 3
		NO	It is a **protoctist**
3	Is the organism a heterotroph?	YES	Go to question 4
		NO	It is a **plant**
4	Does the organism have cell walls and does it feed by external digestion?	YES	It is a fungus
		NO	It is an **animal**

A key may be used to place an organism in one of the five kingdoms.

Five kingdoms

Using the key opposite, it is possible to place any living organism into one of five very large groups. These groups, distinguished from one another by major and obvious characteristics, are called the **five kingdoms**. Each of these kingdoms contains an enormous number of different species, and keys can be used within a kingdom to place any individual species into further groups. The diagram below shows the names of these groups, and how the lion is classified within the Animal Kingdom. The sequence of kingdom, **phylum, class, order, family, genus** and **species** is called a **hierarchy of classification**.

Notice that each classification group is given a name. Lions belong to the class Mammalia and the order Carnivora, for example. The final two group names are written in *italics* – this is a worldwide convention amongst scientists. The lion is called simba in Swahili, león in Spanish and leu in Romanian but is known as *Panthera leo* to scientists in each of these countries. This convention of giving organisms a two-part name made up of their genus and species was introduced by the Swedish biologist Carolus Linnaeus. In his book *Systemae naturae* he gave every organism known to science a two-part name based entirely on the body structure of the organism. This **binomial system of nomenclature** is still in use today. New species today may be named based on characteristics such as chromosome number or gene sequence, which Linnaeus knew nothing about.

The pages that follow describe the characteristics that distinguish living organisms in some of the most important phyla and classes.

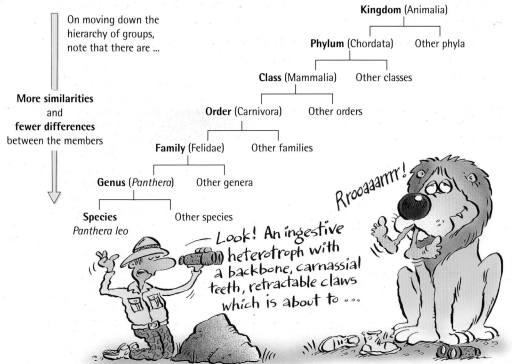

On moving down the hierarchy of groups, note that there are …

More similarities and **fewer differences** between the members

Kingdom (Animalia)

Phylum (Chordata) — Other phyla

Class (Mammalia) — Other classes

Order (Carnivora) — Other orders

Family (Felidae) — Other families

Genus (*Panthera*) — Other genera

Species *Panthera leo* — Other species

All animals are ingestive heterotrophs.

All chordates have a notochord (becomes the backbone).

All mammals have fur and mammary glands.

All carnivores have well developed carnassial (flesh-cutting) teeth.

All Felidae have retractable claws.

All *Panthera* (big cats) can roar but cannot purr.

All lions can mate and produce fertile offspring with other lions. The English scientist John Ray used this feature to define the term 'species'.

Look! An ingestive heterotroph with a backbone, carnassial teeth, retractable claws which is about to …

Rrooaaarrrr!

The hierarchical classification of the lion

---

1 The scientific names for the weasel and mink are *Mustela nivalis* and *Mustela vison*, respectively. Both of these animals belong to the order Carnivora, as do the fox (*Vulpes vulpes*) and otter (*Lutra lutra*). The otter, mink and weasel all belong to the family Mustelidae.

a Which feature must they have in common to belong to the order Carnivora?

b Which two animals are most closely related?

c Which animal is the most different from the other three?

d Suggest one feature that places all of these organisms in the Animal Kingdom.

2 The scientific name for the human is *Homo sapiens*. Try to find out the meaning of this name.

12·2 Bacteria and viruses

Objectives

■ To know the structure of a typical bacterial cell and a typical virus

■ To know the requirements for bacterial growth

■ To know how bacteria reproduce

■ To understand some of the ways in which bacteria and viruses affect human activities

■ To understand why viruses do not fit into the five kingdoms of living organisms

Bacterial structure

Bacteria (singular: bacterium) are single-celled organisms that **have no true nucleus**. Bacterial cells do not contain organelles like those found in typical animal and plant cells (see page 18), but are able to carry out all of their life processes without them. Bacteria are very small, usually about 1–2 μm in length, and so are only visible using a high-powered microscope. The structure of a typical bacterium is shown in the diagram below.

Bacteria exist in a number of different shapes, some of which are shown below right.

Requirements of bacteria

Bacteria have certain requirements that their environment must provide. An understanding of these requirements (see page 283) has been important in biotechnology and in the control of disease. If the environment supplies these needs, the

bacteria can multiply rapidly by **binary fission**. In this process each bacterium divides into two, then each of the two divides again and so on, until very large populations are built up. A bacterial colony can quickly dominate its environment, making great demands on food and oxygen and perhaps producing large quantities of waste materials. This process is summarised at the top of the next page.

The importance of bacteria

Bacteria are important to humans in many ways.

■ Some are **pathogenic** – they cause disease (see page 282). All pathogenic bacteria are parasites.

■ Some are involved in **nutrient cycles** (see pages 254–7).

■ Some are exploited by humans in **food production** and in **biotechnology** (see page 306).

Bacteria are probably the organisms that carry out the largest number of different activities, and are the most numerous organisms on Earth. There may be as many as 5000 undiscovered bacterial species in 1 m^3 of woodland soil!

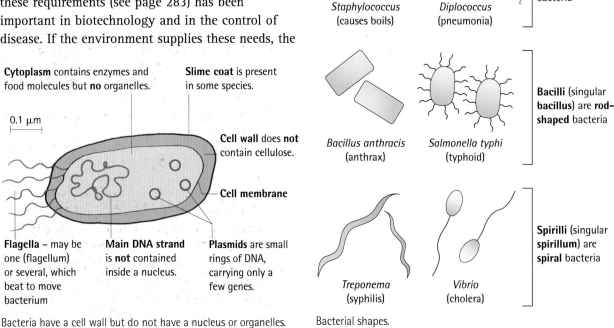

Cytoplasm contains enzymes and food molecules but **no** organelles.

Slime coat is present in some species.

0.1 μm

Cell wall does **not** contain cellulose.

Cell membrane

Flagella – may be one (flagellum) or several, which beat to move bacterium

Main DNA strand is **not** contained inside a nucleus.

Plasmids are small rings of DNA, carrying only a few genes.

Bacteria have a cell wall but do not have a nucleus or organelles.

Staphylococcus (causes boils)

Diplococcus (pneumonia)

Cocci (singular **coccus**) are spherical bacteria

Bacillus anthracis (anthrax)

Salmonella typhi (typhoid)

Bacilli (singular **bacillus**) are **rod-shaped** bacteria

Treponema (syphilis)

Vibrio (cholera)

Spirilli (singular **spirillum**) are **spiral** bacteria

Bacterial shapes.

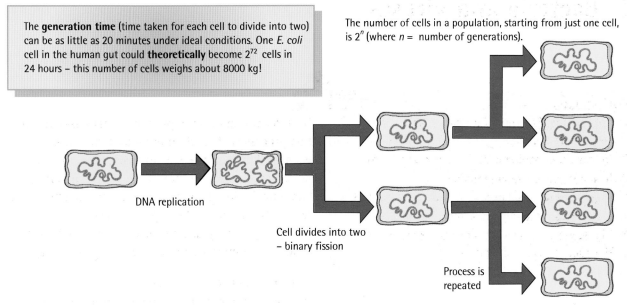

The **generation time** (time taken for each cell to divide into two) can be as little as 20 minutes under ideal conditions. One *E. coli* cell in the human gut could **theoretically** become 2^{72} cells in 24 hours – this number of cells weighs about 8000 kg!

The number of cells in a population, starting from just one cell, is 2^n (where $n =$ number of generations).

DNA replication

Cell divides into two – binary fission

Process is repeated

Binary fission in bacteria – a form of asexual reproduction

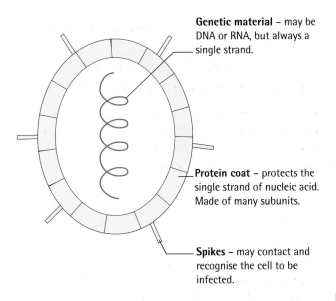

Genetic material – may be DNA or RNA, but always a single strand.

Protein coat – protects the single strand of nucleic acid. Made of many subunits.

Spikes – may contact and recognise the cell to be infected.

A typical virus has genetic material and a protein coat, but cannot carry out its life processes. It has no cytoplasm.

Viruses

When the five-kingdom system of classification was devised, no one was able to find a place for the group of organisms called the **viruses**. This is because viruses do not show the typical features of living things – respiration, nutrition and reproduction, for example – unless they are inside the cells of another living organism. In other words, all viruses are parasites and therefore cause harm to their host. Some taxonomists have suggested that viruses belong in a sixth kingdom. There is great variation in the structure of viruses, but they all have certain common features. The structure of a typical virus is shown on the left.

Most viruses cause disease – they may infect humans, domestic animals or plants (see page 280).

1. Look at the diagram of bacterial shapes. Make a dichotomous key that would enable a biologist to distinguish the different bacterial types on the basis of their structure.

2. Make a table to show which of the following structures are present in:
   a an animal cell **b** a plant cell **c** a bacterial cell.
   Write + if the structure is present and − if it is absent.
   Cell wall, slime capsule, cell membrane, nucleus, chloroplast, mitochondrion, DNA, cytoplasm

3. Why is it difficult to classify viruses into one of the five kingdoms of living organisms?

4. If ten bacteria landed on a bowl of soup, and reproduced every 30 minutes, how many would be present after 5 hours?

The variety of life

12·3 Fungi

Fungal cells have a common structure

The fungi are a very large group of organisms. They range in size from single-celled yeasts to enormous fungi whose underground parts may occupy an area greater than a football or hockey field.

Fungal cells have a cell wall made of a mixture of substances including **chitin**. The cytoplasm contains many organelles, since the fungus manufactures digestive enzymes. It feeds by **saprotrophic** ('dead-feeding') **nutrition**, as illustrated below.

Reproduction in fungi

Single-celled yeasts reproduce asexually by binary fission, but all other fungi reproduce by the production of **spores**, as shown above right and at the top of the opposite page.

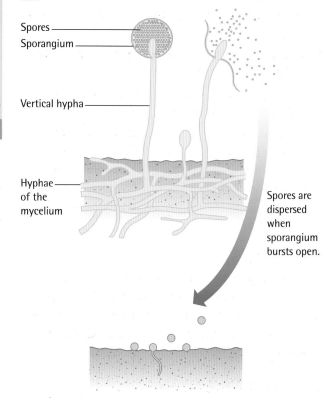

Spores are dispersed when sporangium bursts open.

Spore lands on food source – it can germinate and a new mycelium can develop.

Spore formation in a pin mould fungus

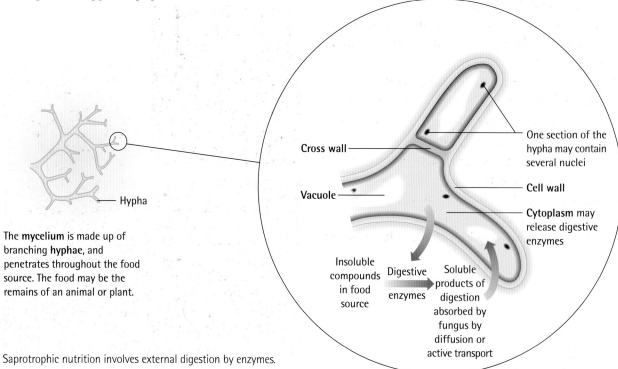

The **mycelium** is made up of branching **hyphae**, and penetrates throughout the food source. The food may be the remains of an animal or plant.

Saprotrophic nutrition involves external digestion by enzymes.

Requirements of fungi

Two examples of fungi, the pin mould and a toadstool, are described in the diagrams on the left and the right page. Fungi have very similar requirements to those of bacteria, that is:

- a moist environment, so that they can absorb the soluble products of digestion of their food source in solution
- a warm environment, so that enzymes can work at their optimum temperature
- a nutrient source to provide the raw materials and energy required for growth
- Fungi do not require light since they do not rely on photosynthesis for the production of food compounds. This means that fungi are rarely found in light environments, since such environments are usually too warm and dry for fungal growth.

Parasitic fungi

Fungi may also feed by parasitic methods. These fungi produce digestive enzymes, but only once they have killed the host and can no longer obtain soluble foods directly from its tissues. An example of a parasitic fungus is shown right.

The importance of fungi

Fungi have a number of effects on the lives of humans, for example:

- They are **decomposers**, and play a vital role in **nutrient cycles** (see page 256).
- Their decomposing action may destroy materials. Wooden buildings, in particular, are at risk from wet and dry rot.
- Mould fungi consume food which might otherwise be eaten by humans (see page 290).
- Fungi may be agents of disease, as in athlete's foot for example (see page 284).
- They may themselves be a source of food, for example mushrooms.
- Fungi are used in biotechnology – the brewing and baking industries (see page 302) are entirely dependent on the activities of yeast, for example.

Spore formation in a toadstool

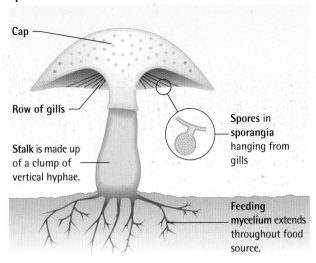

Cap

Row of gills

Stalk is made up of a clump of vertical hyphae.

Spores in sporangia hanging from gills

Feeding mycelium extends throughout food source.

Parasitic fungus

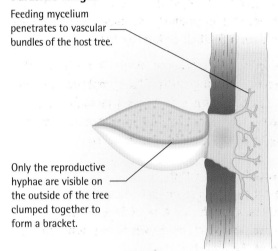

Feeding mycelium penetrates to vascular bundles of the host tree.

Only the reproductive hyphae are visible on the outside of the tree clumped together to form a bracket.

The best of both worlds! A bracket fungus eventually weakens and kills its host. It then feeds as a saprotroph on the **dead remains** of the tree.

1. Suggest why toadstools are likely to be found in dark areas of woodland where green plants are very limited.

2. Some fungi are saprotrophs, and secrete enzymes onto their food source. Suggest three such enzymes and name their substrates and products.

3. List, with examples, four ways in which fungi affect the lives of humans.

The variety of life

229

12·4 Plants

Plants are autotrophs

As **autotrophs**, plants manufacture food molecules from simple, inorganic sources by the process of photosynthesis using light as a source of energy. Plants all **contain the light-absorbing pigment chlorophyll** (or similar molecules which perform the same function) inside cells which **have a definite cellulose cell wall.**

Adaptations to life on land

The first plants lived in water, but as living organisms evolved, plant forms developed that could live on land. The classification of plants into groups follows this sequence of evolution, as described on these two pages.

The Plant Kingdom may be divided into four main groups (phyla): **algae, mosses, ferns** and **seed plants.**

Algae

These plants have no proper roots, stems, leaves or vascular tissue. They are therefore only found in water, in both freshwater and marine (saltwater) habitats. Two examples are shown below.

Mosses

Mosses have a stem and very simple leaves, but they do not have specialised vascular tissue (xylem or phloem). Instead of roots they have simple, unbranched structures called **rhizoids**. Mosses can live on land, although they cannot grow far from water. One adaptation to life on land is the production of dry, light spores for reproduction. The structure of a moss is outlined above right.

Ferns

Ferns are much better adapted to life on land than either mosses or algae. They have roots, stems, complex leaves and vascular tissues. They are able to produce spores for wide dispersal. However, they do not have very thick cuticles and can only survive in shady, humid areas. The gametes of ferns, like those of mosses, must swim through a film of moisture to reach the site of fertilisation. An example of a fern is described on the right.

Algae have no stem, root or leaves, and are confined to water.

Some algae are large, e.g. bladderwrack, a seaweed. Many seaweeds are brown algae – instead of chlorophyll they contain a brown pigment which is very efficient at absorbing light under water.

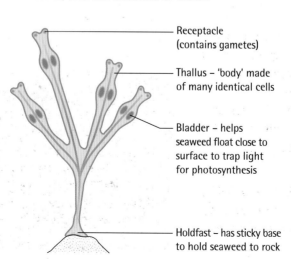

Receptacle (contains gametes)

Thallus – 'body' made of many identical cells

Bladder – helps seaweed float close to surface to trap light for photosynthesis

Holdfast – has sticky base to hold seaweed to rock

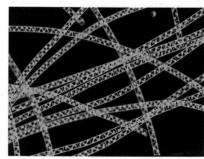

Some algae are long **filaments** made up of many cells, e.g. *Spirogyra*.

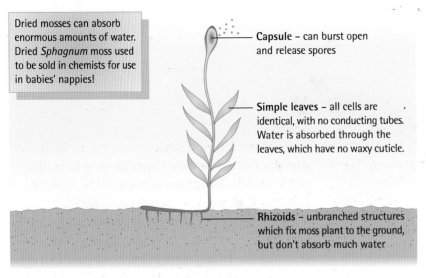

Dried mosses can absorb enormous amounts of water. Dried *Sphagnum* moss used to be sold in chemists for use in babies' nappies!

Capsule – can burst open and release spores

Simple leaves – all cells are identical, with no conducting tubes. Water is absorbed through the leaves, which have no waxy cuticle.

Rhizoids – unbranched structures which fix moss plant to the ground, but don't absorb much water

Moss plants can form a dense carpet in shaded, humid habitats.

Mosses have simple leaves but no vascular tissue or true roots. They reproduce by producing spores.

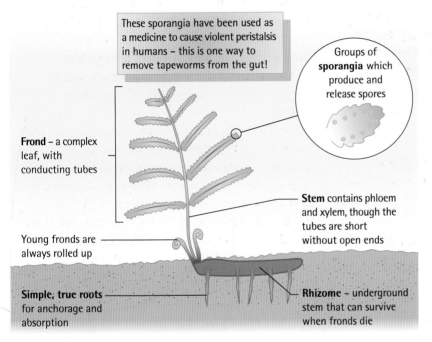

These sporangia have been used as a medicine to cause violent peristalsis in humans – this is one way to remove tapeworms from the gut!

Groups of **sporangia** which produce and release spores

Frond – a complex leaf, with conducting tubes

Stem contains phloem and xylem, though the tubes are short without open ends

Young fronds are always rolled up

Simple, true roots for anchorage and absorption

Rhizome – underground stem that can survive when fronds die

Each brown patch on the underside of the leaf is made up of many sporangia, which produce and release spores.

Ferns have complex leaves, vascular tissues and true roots. They reproduce by producing spores.

Seed plants

Algae, mosses and ferns all depend to some extent on a moist environment, especially for the transfer of gametes. The seed plants have proper roots, stems, leaves, vascular tissues and waterproof coverings, and **their gametes can be transferred without a film of moisture**. As a result the seed plants are able to live and reproduce in dry environments.

The two groups of plants that dominate our fields, woods and gardens are the **conifers** (cone bearers) and the **angiosperms** (flowering plants). We shall look at these in more detail on the next page.

1 Name the four different plant groups. Why are algae confined to water, whilst ferns are well adapted to life on land?

2 Seed plants are well adapted to live and to reproduce in dry environments. What major adaptation allows reproduction on dry land?

3 Why should humans be particularly concerned with the conservation of plants?

The variety of life

12·5 The seed plants

Objectives
- To be able to distinguish between conifers and flowering plants, and understand why flowering plants are so successful
- To recall the differences between monocotyledons and dicotyledons

Conifers

The **conifers** dominate the landscape in colder climates where flowering plants cannot compete. Conifers have needle-like leaves with a very thick cuticle which prevents water loss (it is very difficult to absorb water from cold soil). They do not rely on insects for pollination (flying insects are uncommon in cold areas) – conifers reproduce using structures called **cones**. The features of a conifer are described below.

Angiosperms

The angiosperms or flowering plants are the most successful of plants – they have evolved into many species and have colonised almost every available habitat. More than 80% of all plants are angiosperms (plants with enclosed seeds). Many features of the lives of flowering plants are covered elsewhere in this book (see Chapters 9 and 10, for example). The diagram at the top of the opposite page summarises these features, and emphasises the adaptations of flowering plants to a successful life on land, including warmer habitats.

Two groups of angiosperms

There are two major subgroups within the angiosperms. In one group there is a single cotyledon in the seed (see page 181) – these are the **monocotyledons**. In the other group there are two cotyledons – these are the **dicotyledons**. There are other differences between monocotyledons and dicotyledons, as shown in the diagram at the bottom of the opposite page.

Conifers have needle-like leaves and reproduce sexually using cones.

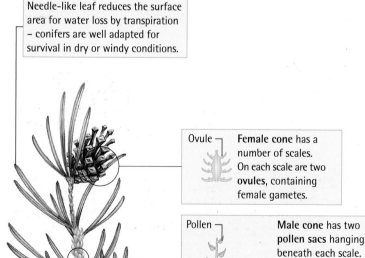

Needle-like leaf reduces the surface area for water loss by transpiration – conifers are well adapted for survival in dry or windy conditions.

Ovule — **Female cone** has a number of scales. On each scale are two **ovules**, containing female gametes.

Pollen — **Male cone** has two **pollen sacs** hanging beneath each scale. Pollen is very light, with air sacs, and is distributed by wind.

Seeds of the Scots pine are an important food source for red squirrels – see page 271.

Two 'naked' seeds on scale of mature cone

After pollination, each fertilised ovule develops into a seed but the seed is 'naked' (not inside a fruit as in the flowering plants).

Angiosperm adaptations

Growth, particularly of reproductive structures, can be very rapid. For example, pollination, pollen tube formation and fertilisation may take only one hour (compared with one year in some conifers), and some bamboos can grow 1m per day.

Flowers – the colour, pattern, shape, scent or nectar of the flower may attract insects, birds or mammals. These animals transfer pollen from male to female flower parts much more efficiently than wind or water.

Large **leaf surface** allows high rate of photosynthesis to supply energy for growth and fruit production. However, water losses by evaporation and diffusion through stomata are high.

Xylem vessels have no end walls and conduct water efficiently.

Roots form beneficial associations with other organisms. For example, legumes such as peas and beans form root nodules with nitrogen-fixing *Rhizobium* bacteria. Many angiosperms form ion-absorbing mycorrhizae with some fungi.

The **ovary** protects the ovules and developing embryo, particularly from drying out. ('Angiosperm' means 'enclosed seed').

Endosperm is a store of nutrients for the developing plant embryo. It does not develop until after fertilisation so that food stores are not wasted, as they might be in conifers.

Fruits are formed from ripened ovaries. Their specialised shapes, colours, smells and textures aid seed dispersal by wind, water and animals.

Stomata with guard cells regulate loss of water vapour and exchange of oxygen and carbon dioxide between plant and atmosphere

Waterproof **cuticle** reduces water loss to atmosphere

Vascular system transports water, ions and organic solutes

Specialised **supporting tissues** (air has a low density and does not offer support as water does)

Extensive root systems anchor the shoot systems and absorb water and ions

Monocotyledons and dicotyledons – two groups of angiosperms (flowering plants)

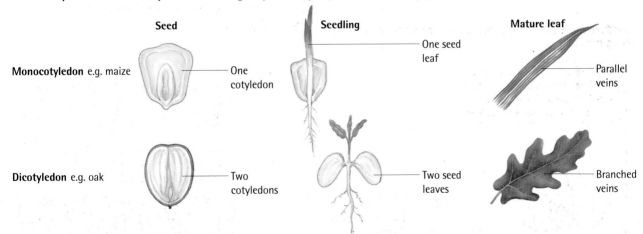

	Seed	Seedling	Mature leaf
Monocotyledon e.g. maize	One cotyledon	One seed leaf	Parallel veins
Dicotyledon e.g. oak	Two cotyledons	Two seed leaves	Branched veins

---

1. Copy and complete the table on the right, by writing 'yes' or 'no' in the spaces provided.

2. Use your table to produce a dichotomous key that would allow you to classify members of the Plant Kingdom. Add a question to distinguish between monocotyledons and dicotyledons.

	Type of plant				
Feature	Algae	Moss	Fern	Conifer	Angiosperm
True roots					
Complex leaves					
Xylem and phloem					
Produces spores					
Exposed seeds in cone					
Enclosed seeds in fruit					

12·6 Invertebrate animals

Objectives

- To know the difference between a vertebrate animal and an invertebrate animal
- To be able to describe the main characteristics of three invertebrate groups – annelids, molluscs, and and arthropods
- To be able to distinguish between insects and spiders
- To understand the importance of metamorphosis in insects

Vertebrates and invertebrates

All animals share one characteristic – **they feed on organic molecules** (see page 10). Members of the Animal Kingdom can be divided into two large groups based on whether they have a backbone as part of a bony skeleton. Animals with a backbone are called **vertebrates** and those without a backbone are called **invertebrates**. Three groups of invertebrates are described here:

- **annelids** have a body with obvious segments, and use chaetae (bristles) for movement
- **molluscs** have a soft body and a hard shell
- **arthropods** have a body with segments grouped into regions, a hard exoskeleton and a number of pairs of jointed limbs.

Annelids

Annelids such as the earthworm have a long segmented body and chaetae.

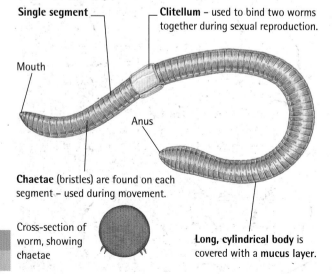

Single segment

Clitellum – used to bind two worms together during sexual reproduction.

Mouth

Anus

Chaetae (bristles) are found on each segment – used during movement.

Cross-section of worm, showing chaetae

Long, cylindrical body is covered with a **mucus layer**.

Molluscs

Molluscs have a hard shell protecting a soft body with no limbs.

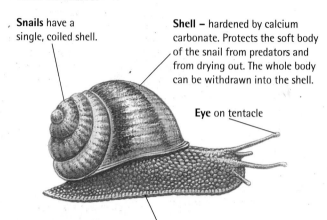

Snails have a single, coiled shell.

Shell – hardened by calcium carbonate. Protects the soft body of the snail from predators and from drying out. The whole body can be withdrawn into the shell.

Eye on tentacle

Foot – muscle with a slimy covering so that snail can move by creeping over the surface.

Arthropods

The arthropods are the most numerous of all animals, both in terms of the number of different species and the number of individuals in any one species. The insects are athropods that show an interesting adaptation in their life cycle called **metamorphosis** that allows them to use the resources of their habitat to the maximum.

Apart from insects, the arthropod phylum includes three other classes – **arachnids** (spiders, for example), **crustaceans** (crabs, for example) and **myriapods** (millipedes and centipedes). The diagrams opposite compare insects and spiders. Amongst the arthropods, insects and spiders are sometimes confused with one another. The table below highlights the difference.

	Insects	Spiders
Body sections	3	2
Legs	3 pairs	4 pairs
Wings	Usually 2 pairs	None
Eyes	Compound	Simple

Insects

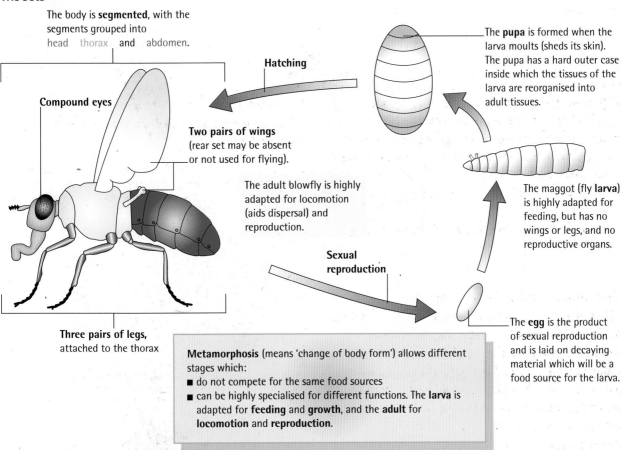

The body is **segmented**, with the segments grouped into head thorax and abdomen.

Compound eyes

Hatching

Two pairs of wings (rear set may be absent or not used for flying).

The adult blowfly is highly adapted for locomotion (aids dispersal) and reproduction.

Three pairs of legs, attached to the thorax

The **pupa** is formed when the larva moults (sheds its skin). The pupa has a hard outer case inside which the tissues of the larva are reorganised into adult tissues.

The maggot (fly **larva**) is highly adapted for feeding, but has no wings or legs, and no reproductive organs.

Sexual reproduction

The **egg** is the product of sexual reproduction and is laid on decaying material which will be a food source for the larva.

Metamorphosis (means 'change of body form') allows different stages which:
- do not compete for the same food sources
- can be highly specialised for different functions. The **larva** is adapted for **feeding** and **growth**, and the **adult** for **locomotion** and **reproduction**.

The blowfly is an insect that shows **complete metamorphosis** between larva and adult. Some insects, such as the locust, show **incomplete metamorphosis** in which the young stages look like smaller adults (although they have no wings or reproductive organs).

Arachnids

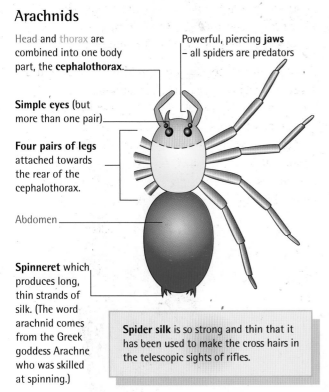

Head and thorax are combined into one body part, the **cephalothorax**.

Powerful, piercing **jaws** – all spiders are predators

Simple eyes (but more than one pair)

Four pairs of legs attached towards the rear of the cephalothorax.

Abdomen

Spinneret which produces long, thin strands of silk. (The word arachnid comes from the Greek goddess Arachne who was skilled at spinning.)

Spider silk is so strong and thin that it has been used to make the cross hairs in the telescopic sights of rifles.

Arachnids are arthropods with four pairs of legs and no wings.

1 Copy and complete the following paragraph. All animals have one common characteristic – _____. The invertebrates are animals that do not have _____. Examples of important invertebrate groups are _____, which are very clearly segmented with bristles called _____ to aid in movement; _____, which have a soft body inside one or two hard shells; and _____, which are the most numerous of all.

2 The arthropods include four classes – insects, arachnids, crustaceans and myriapods.
   a List three features that all of these classes possess.
   b List three features that only insects possess.
   c Compare insects and spiders under the headings 'Number of legs', 'Number of body sections', 'Number of wings' and 'Type of eyes'.

3 Insects are the most abundant of all animals on land. Many of them show an adaptation called complete metamorphosis. What does this term mean, and how does it help to explain why there are so many insect species?

12·7 Vertebrate animals: five classes

If asked to name an animal, most people would probably name a mammal because these are the most familiar animals to us. Mammals are just one class of the phylum **Chordata**. The chordates are often called the **vertebrates**, although strictly speaking there are a few chordates that aren't vertebrates. Vertebrates have a hard, usually bony, internal skeleton with a backbone. The backbone is made up of separate bones called **vertebrae** which allow these animals to move with great ease.

There are five classes of vertebrates, which, like the members of the Plant Kingdom, show gradual adaptations to life on land. The classes are **fish**, **amphibians**, **reptiles**, **birds** and **mammals**.

Fish
All fish are aquatic and are **ectothermic** which means that their body temperature changes with that of their surroundings. In sexual reproduction, they produce large numbers of eggs. The eggs and sperm are released into the water and so fertilisation happens outside the body (externally). Many eggs are not fertilised because sperm do not reach them.

Amphibians and reptiles
Amphibians and reptiles are all **ectothermic**. This restricts their range of habitats. Amphibians go through metamorphosis. The adults may spend much of their life on land, but must always return to water to breed. Sexual reproduction involves external fertilisation, but the adults hold on to one another so that the male and female gametes are released at the same time and place. This means that fewer gametes are lost than with fish. Reptiles are ectothermic but are well adapted to life on dry land. The characteristics of amphibians and reptiles are illustrated on the opposite page.

Birds and mammals
Birds and mammals are **endothermic**. They can use internal heat to maintain a constant body temperature (see page 112). This allows them to remain alert and active in a wide range of habitats. Birds and mammals have evolved rapidly and are to be found in every part of the Earth. Mammals are described on pages 238 and 239. Birds have many adaptations for flight (see page 126). They reproduce sexually using internal fertilisation, and lay a relatively small number of eggs protected by a hard shell. The young are cared for by the parents.

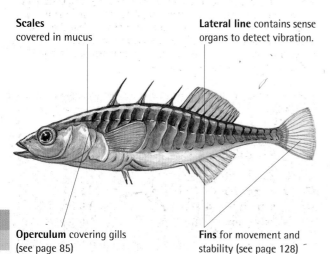

Scales covered in mucus

Lateral line contains sense organs to detect vibration.

Operculum covering gills (see page 85)

Fins for movement and stability (see page 128)

Forelimbs are modified as **wings**.

Nostril, leading to **lungs** which are the organs of gas exchange

Beak

Feathers, vital for flight and for endothermy

Scales on legs

The variety of life

Amphibians

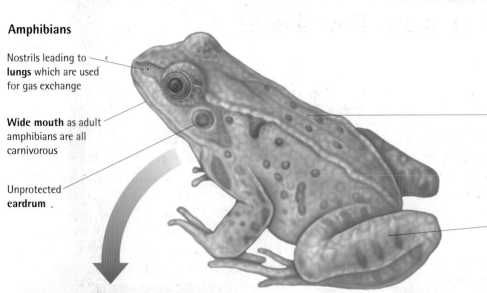

Nostrils leading to **lungs** which are used for gas exchange

Wide mouth as adult amphibians are all carnivorous

Unprotected **eardrum**

Moist skin (also used for gas exchange)

Four limbs, with hind limbs webbed

The male's thumbs have pads which help him grip the female during mating.

This **metamorphosis** means that:
- the two forms do not compete for food – the adult is carnivorous on land but the larva is herbivorous or carnivorous in water
- larvae can grow rapidly as they waste no energy in reproduction.

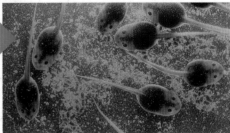

Tadpoles are aquatic larvae of amphibians.

Reptiles

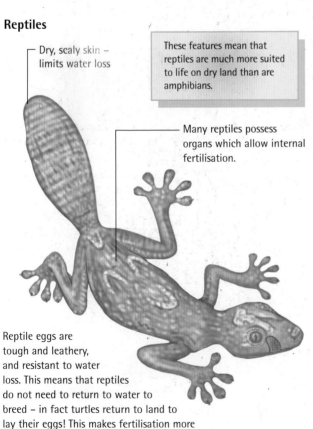

Dry, scaly skin – limits water loss

These features mean that reptiles are much more suited to life on dry land than are amphibians.

Many reptiles possess organs which allow internal fertilisation.

Reptile eggs are tough and leathery, and resistant to water loss. This means that reptiles do not need to return to water to breed – in fact turtles return to land to lay their eggs! This makes fertilisation more successful so that fewer gametes need be produced.

Although reptiles cannot maintain a constant body temperature by internal methods, they can partially regulate their temperature by behaviour. They can bask in the sun to gain heat, or 'gape' to lose heat by evaporation, for example. This regulation of body temperature enables them to be active for long periods, to hunt and to develop eggs very successfully.

1. Fish, amphibians, reptiles and birds are all vertebrate animals. Give two characteristics that they have in common, and two characteristics that would enable you to tell them apart.

2. In what ways is the reproductive method of a reptile more advanced than that of a fish or amphibian?

12·8 Vertebrate animals: mammals

Objectives
- To appreciate how mammals have exploited many environments, and how they have become well adapted to them
- To understand that humans are mammals, but have the unique ability to considerably modify their environment

Mammals are endothermic vertebrates that have the characteristics shown in the diagram below.

A wide range of adaptations has allowed mammals to colonise many habitats as diverse as the polar wastes and the Arabian desert, as shown opposite.

Humans are mammals
Humans show the typical mammalian characteristics of hair, mammary glands and a diaphragm, for example. Humans, though, are unique amongst all animals in that the adaptations they show allow them to modify their environment so that it is suitable for human occupation. As a result humans have been able to live and work in many habitats – no animal has a wider range. Human adaptation has allowed advanced development of the brain, and of all the complex activities that the brain can coordinate. The human brain is extremely sensitive to changes in temperature. Human adaptations include many that are concerned with the fine regulation of blood temperature (see page 112). Other features that make humans very special mammals include an upright posture, freeing the hands for complex movements including the use of tools.

Diaphragm – a sheet of muscle which separates the chest (with lungs) from abdomen (with many other organs). Only mammals have this structure, which makes breathing more efficient.

Pinna on ear – can be moved for maximum efficiency in sound detection.

Whiskers are sensitive to touch and vibration.

Fur – body covering which allows endothermy as a means of keeping a constant body temperature.

Penis – an organ of the male that enables efficient internal fertilisation.

Uterus – an organ of the female that allows internal development of the young, and connection to the mother at the **placenta**.

Mammals are endotherms with fur, whiskers and mammary glands.

Many young mammals are born blind, hairless and defenceless. **All** are fed on milk, produced in **mammary glands**, i.e. mammals **suckle their young.**

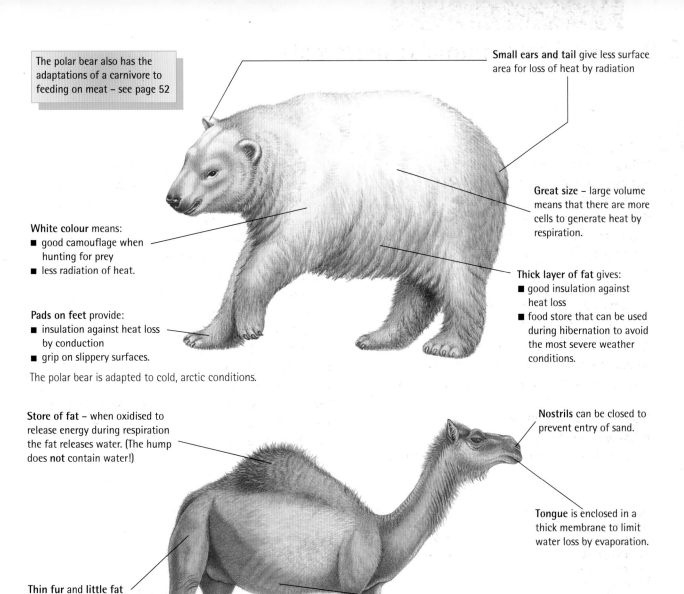

The polar bear also has the adaptations of a carnivore to feeding on meat – see page 52

Small ears and tail give less surface area for loss of heat by radiation

Great size – large volume means that there are more cells to generate heat by respiration.

White colour means:
■ good camouflage when hunting for prey
■ less radiation of heat.

Thick layer of fat gives:
■ good insulation against heat loss
■ food store that can be used during hibernation to avoid the most severe weather conditions.

Pads on feet provide:
■ insulation against heat loss by conduction
■ grip on slippery surfaces.

The polar bear is adapted to cold, arctic conditions.

Store of fat – when oxidised to release energy during respiration the fat releases water. (The hump does **not** contain water!)

Nostrils can be closed to prevent entry of sand.

Tongue is enclosed in a thick membrane to limit water loss by evaporation.

Thin fur and little fat beneath skin allow loss of heat since little insulation.

Large stomach – the camel can drink up to 100 litres of water in 10 minutes when water becomes available.

Large feet with membrane between toes – camel can walk on sandy surfaces without sinking.

The camel is adapted to dry, desert conditions.

1 Copy and complete this table.
   Use information from the table to explain why mammals, birds and reptiles are well adapted to life on land.

2 What is endothermy? How does endothermy make an animal more adapted for life on land?

Class of vertebrate	Eggs laid on land or in water?	Fertilisation internal or external?	Development of young internal or external?
Fish			
Amphibians			
Reptiles			
Birds			

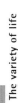

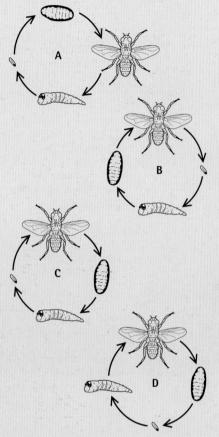

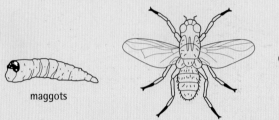

1 This question is about insect life cycles.
a Look at the four diagrams on the left.
 i Write the letter of the diagram which shows the correct life cycle of the blowfly.
 ii The diagrams below show stages in the life cycle of a blowfly. Write down the name of each stage. One has been done for you.

maggots

 iii The life cycle of the blowfly shows metamorphosis. Explain what **metamorphosis** means.
 iv Suggest **two** reasons why different stages eat different foods.
b Blowfly maggots feed on dead and decaying matter.
In 1500 it was found that placing live maggots of blowflies in infected wounds often helped the healing process.
In 1917, during the First World War, soldiers had wounds which were naturally infected with maggots. The maggots helped to heal their wounds more quickly.
In 1930 doctors used maggots to help heal the wounds of some children with bone disease.
Suggest why the wounds healed more quickly when infected with maggots.

(MEG June 1998)

2 Use the key to identify the five fish shown in the drawings. Write down the letter of each fish and its name.

(SEG June 1992)

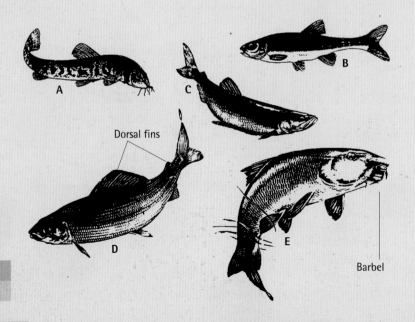

Dorsal fins

Barbel

Key		
1. One dorsal fin	2	
Two dorsal fins	4	
2. Barbels (fleshy extensions) at corners of mouth	3	
No barbels at corners of mouth	*Phoxinus phoxinus*	
3. Four barbels	*Barbus barbus*	
Six barbels	*Noemacheilus barbatulus*	
4. More than 10 bony rays in first dorsal fin	*Thymallus thymallus*	
10 or fewer bony rays in first dorsal fin	*Osmerus eperlanus*	

Keys and classification

3 **a** What are you? Follow the branch points at 1, 3, 4, 8, 9 and 11 to identify yourself as a mammal.

b Name **two** additional characteristics of mammals.

c In what way are humans **special** mammals?

A key enables identification of an organism by observation of its characteristics. Close observation allows a series of questions (the branch points in this key) to be answered, eventually leading to the organism being studied.

*the FIVE KINGDOMS

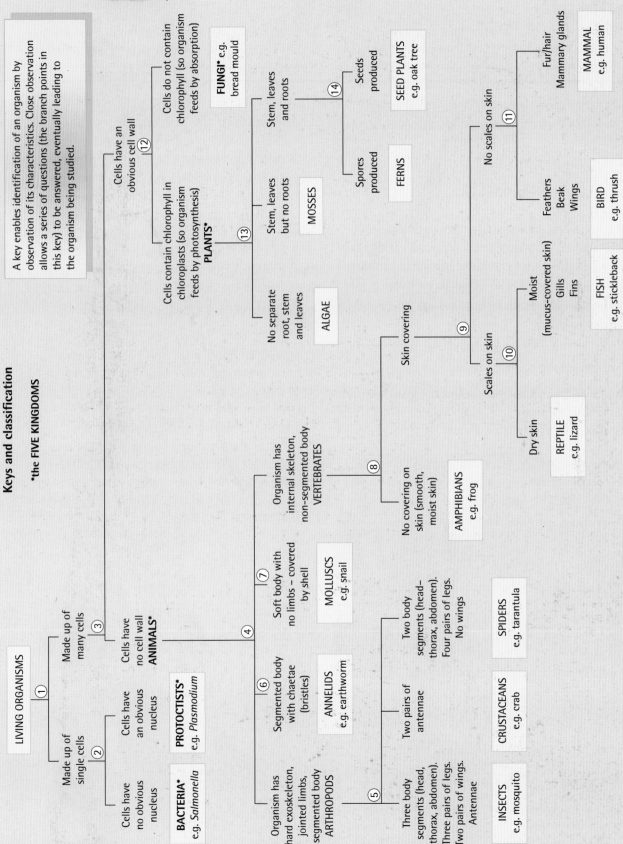

LIVING ORGANISMS

① Made up of single cells

② Cells have no obvious nucleus

BACTERIA* e.g. *Salmonella*

Cells have an obvious nucleus

PROTOCTISTS* e.g. *Plasmodium*

Made up of many cells

③ Cells have no cell wall

ANIMALS*

④ Soft body with no limbs – covered by shell

MOLLUSCS e.g. snail

⑥ Segmented body with chaetae (bristles)

ANNELIDS e.g. earthworm

Organism has hard exoskeleton, jointed limbs, segmented body

ARTHROPODS

⑤ Two pairs of antennae

CRUSTACEANS e.g. crab

Three body segments (head, thorax, abdomen). Three pairs of legs. Two pairs of wings. Antennae

INSECTS e.g. mosquito

Two body segments (head-thorax, abdomen). Four pairs of legs. No wings

SPIDERS e.g. tarantula

⑦ Organism has internal skeleton, non-segmented body

VERTEBRATES

⑧ No covering on skin (smooth, moist skin)

AMPHIBIANS e.g. frog

Skin covering

⑨ Scales on skin

⑩ Dry skin

REPTILE e.g. lizard

Moist (mucus-covered skin) Gills Fins

FISH e.g. stickleback

No scales on skin

⑪ Feathers Beak Wings

BIRD e.g. thrush

Fur/hair Mammary glands

MAMMAL e.g. human

Cells have an obvious cell wall

⑫ Cells do not contain chlorophyll (so organism feeds by absorption)

FUNGI* e.g. bread mould

Cells contain chlorophyll in chloroplasts (so organism feeds by photosynthesis)

PLANTS*

⑬ No separate root, stem and leaves

ALGAE

Stem, leaves but no roots

MOSSES

Stem, leaves and roots

⑭ Spores produced

FERNS

Seeds produced

SEED PLANTS e.g. oak tree

13·1 Ecology and ecosystems

Objectives

- To understand that living organisms require certain conditions for their survival
- To understand that living organisms interact with one another, and with their non-living environment
- To define population, community and ecosystem
- To realise that available resources change through the year

Environmental survival kit

All living organisms depend upon their environment for three 'survival essentials'. These are a **supply of food, shelter** from undesirable physical conditions and a **breeding site.** The living organism **interacts** with its environment – for example, a living plant:

- removes carbon dioxide, water and light energy from its habitat
- may be eaten by an animal or a parasite
- depends upon soil for support.

Factors in the environment affect the growth of the plant. Some of these factors are **biotic** – other living organisms – and some are **abiotic** – the non-living

components of the habitat. **Ecology** is the study of living organisms in relation to their environment. The interactions between the organism and its environment are summarised below.

Changing with the seasons

The ability of the habitat to supply living organisms with their requirements may vary at different times of year. The ecosystem in the photograph opposite will only exist for a certain period of time – as food or water becomes exhausted some animals may leave. These will then be followed by the predators which feed on them. The great animal migrations seen in East Africa result from the changing conditions in the animals' environment, for example:

- poor rain means little growth of grass
- herbivores leave for areas of fresh growth
- carnivores follow herbivores
- (then scavengers follow carnivores!).

Living together

Living organisms normally exist in groups. The names given to these groups, and the way they interact with the abiotic environment, are explained opposite.

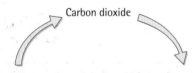

Carbon dioxide

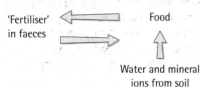

'Fertiliser' in faeces

Food

Water and mineral ions from soil

A giraffe feeds on a thorn tree. The tree requires water, mineral ions, carbon dioxide and light to grow. The giraffe may provide carbon dioxide from respiration, and ions from decomposition of its faeces.

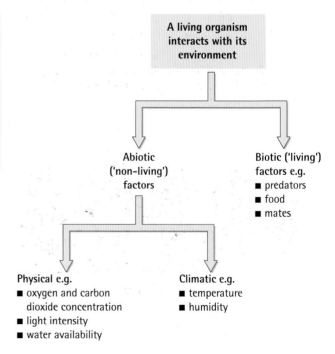

A living organism interacts with its environment

Abiotic ('non-living') factors

Biotic ('living') factors e.g.
- predators
- food
- mates

Physical e.g.
- oxygen and carbon dioxide concentration
- light intensity
- water availability

Climatic e.g.
- temperature
- humidity

Ecology

A **population** is all of the members of the same species (e.g. flamingoes) in a particular area.

A **community** is all of the populations of living organisms in one area (e.g. flamingoes, zebra, wildebeest and grass). The community is the **biotic environment**.

Air, water and soil make up the **abiotic environment**.

An **ecosystem** is all the living organisms and the non-living factors in a particular part of the environment.

A **habitat** is a part of the environment that can provide food, shelter and a breeding site for a living organism (e.g. a patch of grassland).

Organisms exist in groups within an ecosystem.

1 Define the terms population, community and ecosystem.

2 Name two abiotic factors that might determine whether or not a habitat is suitable for a living organism.

3 Suggest two ways in which a plant and an animal in the same habitat may interact.

4 What must a habitat provide?

5 How are the following observations related?
- Very few flying insects are found in Britain during the winter.
- Swallows migrate to Africa during the winter.
- Hobbies (small bird-eating falcons) leave Britain in late autumn.

6 What is meant by the term ecology?

7 **a** A group of pupils were studying a forest. They noticed that the plants grew in two main layers. They called these the tree layer and the ground layer.

tree layer

ground layer

The pupils measured the amount of sunlight reaching each layer at different times in the year. Their results are shown on the graph.

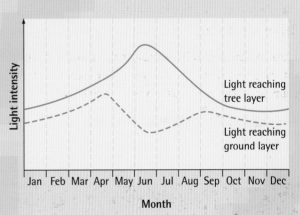

Light reaching tree layer

Light reaching ground layer

i During which month did most light reach the tree layer?

ii During which month did most light reach the ground layer?

iii Suggest why the amount of sunlight reaching the ground layer is lower in mid-summer than in the spring.

b The pupils found bluebells growing in the ground layer. Bluebells grow rapidly from bulbs. They flower in April and by June their leaves have died.

i Suggest why bluebells grow rapidly in April.

ii Suggest why the bluebell leaves have died by June.

(MEG June 1998 [part])

13·2 Feeding relationships: food chains and food webs

Objectives

- To know that the feeding relationships in an ecosystem can be expressed as food chains
- To understand why energy transfer through an ecosystem is inefficient
- To understand why complex food webs are the most stable

Food chains

The most obvious interaction between different organisms in an ecosystem is feeding. During feeding, one organism is obtaining food – energy and raw materials – from another one. Usually one organism eats another, but then may itself be food for a third species. The feeding relationships of the different organisms in the ecosystem can be shown in a **food chain**, as in the diagram below.

Energy transfer is inefficient

The amount of energy that is passed on in a food chain is reduced at every step. Since energy can be neither created nor destroyed, it is not lost but is converted into some other form. During respiration, some energy is transferred to the environment as heat. The flow of energy through a food chain, and the heat losses to the environment, are illustrated in the diagram opposite.

Food webs

Since so little energy is transferred from the base to the top of a food chain, a top carnivore must eat many herbivores. These herbivores are probably not all of the same species. In turn, each herbivore is likely to feed on many different plant species. All these different feeding relationships can be shown in a **food web.**

The more complicated a food web, the more stable the community is. For example, in the woodland food web shown opposite, if the number of squirrels fell, the owls could eat more worms, mice and rabbits. The mice and rabbits would have less competition for food from squirrels, and so might reproduce more successfully.

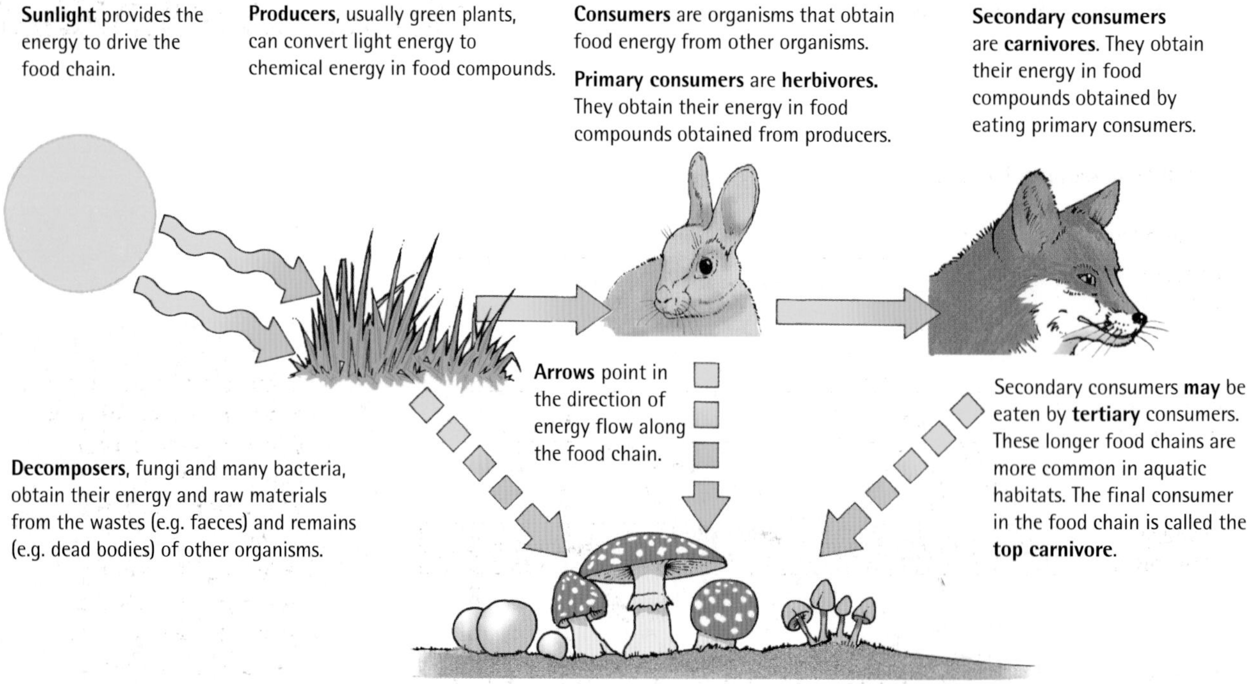

Sunlight provides the energy to drive the food chain.
Producers, usually green plants, can convert light energy to chemical energy in food compounds.
Consumers are organisms that obtain food energy from other organisms.
Primary consumers are **herbivores.** They obtain their energy in food compounds obtained from producers.
Secondary consumers are **carnivores.** They obtain their energy in food compounds obtained by eating primary consumers.
Arrows point in the direction of energy flow along the food chain.
Decomposers, fungi and many bacteria, obtain their energy and raw materials from the wastes (e.g. faeces) and remains (e.g. dead bodies) of other organisms.
Secondary consumers **may** be eaten by **tertiary** consumers. These longer food chains are more common in aquatic habitats. The final consumer in the food chain is called the **top carnivore**.

Food chains show energy flow through an ecosystem. Each organism in the food chain represents a different **trophic** (feeding) **level**.

Energy transfer

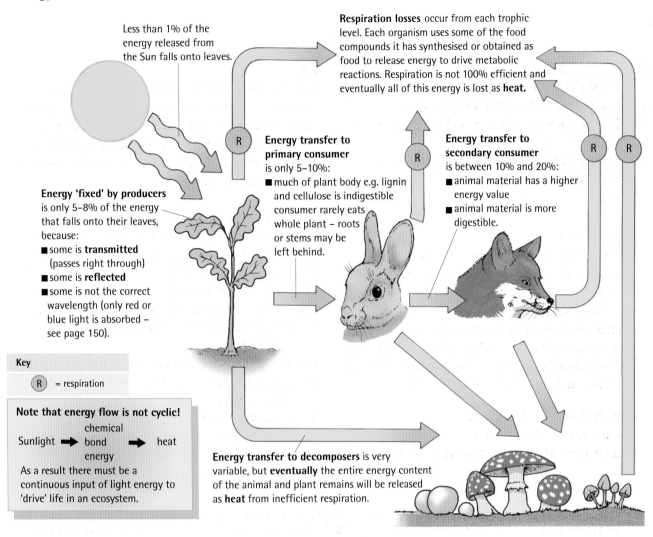

Less than 1% of the energy released from the Sun falls onto leaves.

Respiration losses occur from each trophic level. Each organism uses some of the food compounds it has synthesised or obtained as food to release energy to drive metabolic reactions. Respiration is not 100% efficient and eventually all of this energy is lost as **heat.**

Energy 'fixed' by producers is only 5–8% of the energy that falls onto their leaves, because:
■ some is **transmitted** (passes right through)
■ some is **reflected**
■ some is not the correct wavelength (only red or blue light is absorbed – see page 150).

Energy transfer to primary consumer is only 5–10%:
■ much of plant body e.g. lignin and cellulose is indigestible consumer rarely eats whole plant – roots or stems may be left behind.

Energy transfer to secondary consumer is between 10% and 20%:
■ animal material has a higher energy value
■ animal material is more digestible.

Key

(R) = respiration

Note that energy flow is not cyclic!

Sunlight ➡ chemical bond energy ➡ heat

As a result there must be a continuous input of light energy to 'drive' life in an ecosystem.

Energy transfer to decomposers is very variable, but **eventually** the entire energy content of the animal and plant remains will be released as **heat** from inefficient respiration.

A simple woodland food web

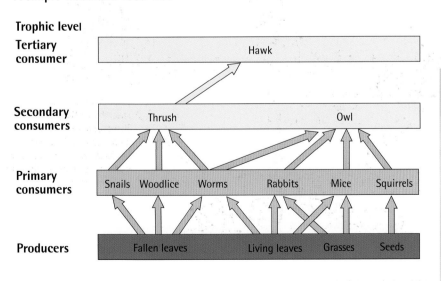

Trophic level

Tertiary consumer — Hawk

Secondary consumers — Thrush — Owl

Primary consumers — Snails Woodlice Worms Rabbits Mice Squirrels

Producers — Fallen leaves Living leaves Grasses Seeds

1 Define the terms producer, consumer and decomposer. Which of these could be omitted from an ecosystem? Explain your answer.
2 Write out a food chain from a named ecosystem which you have studied.
3 Why are food chains usually restricted to three or four trophic levels?

13·3 Feeding relationships: pyramids of numbers and of biomass

Objectives

▸ To be able to describe pyramids of numbers and of biomass

▸ To understand how data can be gathered to make ecological pyramids

Pyramids of numbers

Look at the food chain on page 244. Two things should be clear:

▸ The organisms tend to get bigger moving along the food chain. Predators, such as the fox, need to be large enough to overcome their prey, such as the rabbit.

▸ Energy is 'lost' as heat on moving from one trophic level to the next, so an animal to the right of a food chain needs to eat several organisms 'below' it in order to obtain enough energy. For example, a rabbit eats many blades of grass.

Food chains and food webs provide **qualitative** information about an ecosystem – they show which organism feeds on which other organism. How do we show **quantitative** information, for example how many predators can be supported by a certain number of plants at the start of the chain? We can use a **pyramid of numbers** or a **pyramid of biomass**, as shown in the diagram below.

Gathering data for ecological pyramids

To construct a pyramid of numbers or of biomass, organisms must be captured, counted and (perhaps) weighed. This is done on a **sample** (a small number) of the organisms in an ecosystem. Counting every individual organism in a habitat would be extremely time-consuming and could considerably damage the environment.

Pyramid of numbers – a diagrammatic representation of the number of different organisms at each trophic level in an ecosystem **at any one time**

Note

1 The number of organisms at any trophic level is represented by the length (or the area) of a rectangle.
2 Moving up the pyramid, the **number** of organisms generally **decreases**, but the **size** of each individual **increases**.

Problems

a The range of numbers may be enormous – 500 000 grass plants may only support a single top carnivore – so that drawing the pyramid to scale may be very difficult
b Pyramids may be **inverted**, particularly if the **producer is very large** (e.g. an oak tree) or **parasites feed on the consumers** (e.g. bird lice on an owl).

Pyramid of biomass–which represents the **biomass** (number of individuals × mass of each individual) at each trophic level **at any one time**. This should solve the scale and inversion problems of the pyramid of numbers.

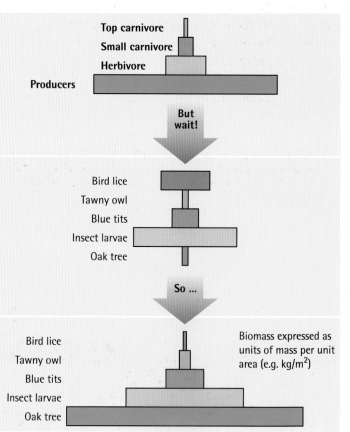

Ecological pyramids represent numerical relationships between successive trophic levels. The pyramid of biomass is useful because the biomass gives a good idea of how much energy is passed on to the next trophic level.

The sample should give an accurate estimate of the total population size. To do this:

- The sampling must be **random** to avoid any bias. For example, it is tempting to collect a large number of organisms, by looking for the areas where they are most common. To avoid this, the possible sampling sites can each be given a number and then chosen using random number generators on a computer.

- The sample must be the **right size** so that any 'rogue' results can be eliminated. For example, a single sample might be taken from a bare patch of earth, whereas all other sites are covered with vegetation. The single sample from the bare patch should not be ignored, but its effects on the results will be lessened if another nine samples are taken. A **mean value** can then be used.

Different techniques must be used for plants (which tend to stay where they are) and for animals (which usually do not). The diagrams on this page and overleaf describe some of these sampling methods.

Sampling plants and sessile animals

Once the organisms in a sample have been identified and counted, the population size can be estimated. For example, if 10 quadrats gave a mean of 8 plants per quadrat, and each quadrat is one-hundredth of the area of the total site, then the total plant population in that area is $8 \times 100 = 800$.

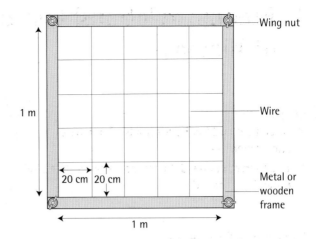

A quadrat is a square frame made of wood or metal. It is simply laid on the ground and the number of organisms inside it is counted.

A quadrat is used most commonly for estimating the size of plant populations, but may also be valuable for the study of populations of sessile or slow-moving animals (e.g. limpets).

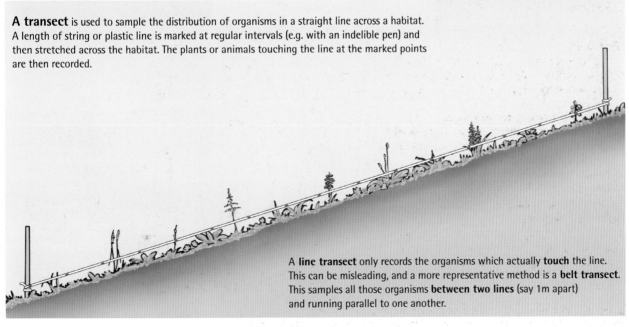

A transect is used to sample the distribution of organisms in a straight line across a habitat. A length of string or plastic line is marked at regular intervals (e.g. with an indelible pen) and then stretched across the habitat. The plants or animals touching the line at the marked points are then recorded.

A **line transect** only records the organisms which actually **touch** the line. This can be misleading, and a more representative method is a **belt transect**. This samples all those organisms **between two lines** (say 1m apart) and running parallel to one another.

Quadrats and transects sample populations of non-motile organisms.

Sampling motile animals

Tullgren funnel –
used to collect small organisms from the air spaces of the soil or from leaf litter. The lamp is a source of heat and dehydration – organisms move to escape from it and fall through the sieve. The mesh is fine enough to retain the soil or litter. The animals slip down the smooth-sided funnel and are immobilised in the alcohol. They may then be removed for identification.

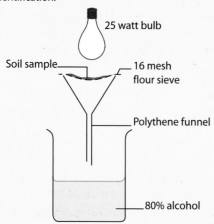

- 25 watt bulb
- Soil sample
- 16 mesh flour sieve
- Polythene funnel
- 80% alcohol

A group of Tullgren funnels in use

Pitfall traps –
used to sample arthropods moving over the soil surface. The roof prevents rain from flooding the trap, and also limits access to certain predators. Any trapped predators can be prevented from eating other trapped animals if a small quantity of methanol is added to the trap. Bait of meat or ripe fruit can be placed in the trap. Pitfall traps are often set up on a grid system to investigate the movements of ground animals more systematically.

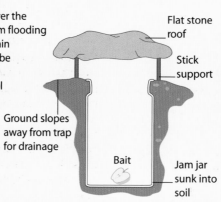

- Flat stone roof
- Stick support
- Ground slopes away from trap for drainage
- Bait
- Jam jar sunk into soil

Pooter –
used to collect specimens of insects and other arthropods. Trees or bushes are beaten and the animals fall on a sheet or tray underneath. They are then collected in the pooter. Sucking on the mouthpiece pulls the organism along the collecting tube and into the specimen tube. This does not harm the organism, and it can then be returned to its natural habitat.

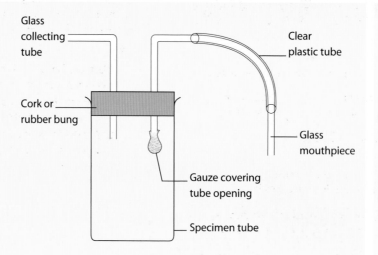

- Glass collecting tube
- Cork or rubber bung
- Clear plastic tube
- Glass mouthpiece
- Gauze covering tube opening
- Specimen tube

Other methods of collection are numerous. Many are based on some form of netting – for example, large mist nets may be used to collect migrating birds for identification and ringing, and sweep nets may be used to capture flying or aquatic arthropods.

Methods for the capture of motile organisms

The mark-recapture method

The diagram below shows one useful technique for estimating populations of motile animals.

1 Sample the population by capturing a number of organisms

2 Mark the sample in some way which:
- causes no harm
- does not make the organism conspicuous to predators
- does not affect the organism rejoining the population

e.g. mice can have a small mark clipped into their fur

3 Release the organism to rejoin its population

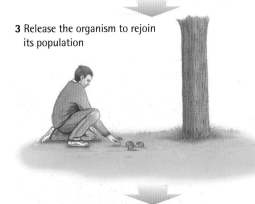

4 A second sample of the population is collected at a later date and counted. The number of previously marked organisms is noted.

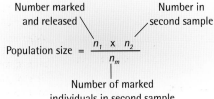

5 The population size is estimated using the **Lincoln index**:

Number marked and released   Number in second sample

$$\text{Population size} = \frac{n_1 \times n_2}{n_m}$$

Number of marked individuals in second sample

This method might be used, for example, when comparing populations **before** and **after** a conservation management plan (see page 270)

The mark-recapture method

(see page 270)

Recording and analysis

Two students wished to investigate the invertebrate populations present in an area of woodland. They set out pitfall traps in the evening, with rotting meat as a bait. They returned to count the collected animals next morning. The table shows their results.

Animal type	Number recorded by students	Total
Beetles	I/III \III I/I/II IIIII I/II III/II IIII I/I II III II	
Centipedes	II/II II IIII II	
Millipedes	II	
Spiders	II/II IIIII II	
Earthworms	/II	
Woodlice	II/II II/I	
Snails	I	

1 **a** Copy the table and complete it to show the total number of each animal collected.

    b Plot a bar chart of your results from part **a**.

    c Suggest a function of the trap lid, apart from preventing entry of rain.

    d The students used rotting meat in their traps. Suggest how the types and numbers of animals collected might be different if they had used rotting leaves.

The teacher suggested that a mark-recapture method might give a more accurate estimate of the beetle population. The students set up the pitfall traps with meat as bait and then marked the beetles they collected with a small spot of brown water-soluble paint. They released the beetles into the area they had been collected from, and that evening reset the traps. On the following day the numbers of marked and unmarked beetles in the traps were recorded, as shown below.

	Number of	
beetles in first sample – marked then released	marked beetles in second sample	unmarked beetles in second sample
30	12	40

    e Use the Lincoln index to calculate the total beetle population in the area.

    f Why did the students use brown paint, not yellow or red paint?

    g Why did the students use a water-soluble paint rather than an oil-based paint?

Factors affecting population size

Environmental resistance

By taking samples and counting the numbers of organisms in a particular habitat, an ecologist can study how any factor affects the size of a population. For example, a woodland manager might wish to know whether thinning the trees in the wood affects the population of low-growing plants, or a farmer might wish to know whether the time of grass-cutting affects the population of bank voles. These factors may be **living (biotic)** or **non-living (abiotic)**. Together they affect the rate at which a population grows, and also its final size. All the factors that affect population growth and size together make up the **environmental resistance**.

Some significant **biotic** factors that affect population growth include:

- **Food** – both the quantity and the quality of food are important. Snails, for example, cannot reproduce successfully in an environment low in calcium, no matter how much food there is, because they need this mineral for shell growth.

- **Predators** – as a prey population becomes larger, it becomes easier for predators to find the prey. If the number of predators suddenly falls, the prey species might increase in number extremely quickly. The relationship between predators and prey is described on page 272.

- **Competitors** – other organisms may require the same resources from the environment, and so reduce the growth of a population. For example, all plants compete for light. Competition for territory and for mates can drastically reduce the growth of individual organisms.

- **Parasites** – these may cause disease, and slow down the growth and reproductive rate of organisms within a population.

Important **abiotic** factors affecting population growth include:

- **Temperature** – higher temperatures speed up enzyme-catalysed reactions and increase growth.

- **Oxygen availability** – affects the rate of energy production by respiration.

- **Light availability** – for photosynthesis. Light may also control breeding cycles in animals and plants.

- **Toxins and pollutants** – tissue growth can be reduced by the presence of, for example, sulphur dioxide (see page 260), and reproductive success may be affected by pollutants such as oestrogen-like substances.

Growth curves and carrying capacity

When a small population begins to grow in a particular environment, the environmental resistance is almost non-existent – there may be plenty of food and no accumulation of poisonous wastes. The diagram opposite shows how environmental resistance eventually limits population growth, and the environment reaches its **carrying capacity**. Unless the environmental resistance is changed, perhaps by a new disease organism, the size of the population will only fluctuate slightly. Organisms that are able to maintain their population, or even increase it, must be well adapted to their particular environment.

Humans exploit environmental resistance

People use their understanding of environmental resistance to manage populations. For example:

- Preditors are eliminated from farm situations.

- More food is made available to domestic animals.

- Nitrogen fertilisers and artificial light are used to boost plant growth.

- Predators may be used to control pests.

- Anaerobic conditions or low temperatures are used to prevent populations of microbes from consuming our food.

- Competitors are eliminated from crops using pesticides.

Examples can be found on pages 272, 274 and 310.

Ecology

Factors affecting population growth

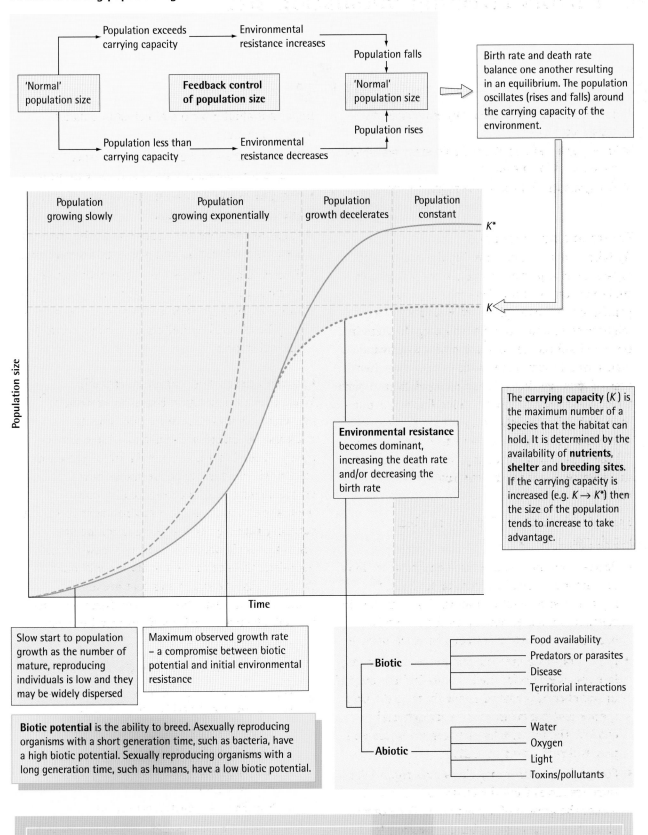

Feedback control of population size

'Normal' population size → Population exceeds carrying capacity → Environmental resistance increases → Population falls → 'Normal' population size

'Normal' population size → Population less than carrying capacity → Environmental resistance decreases → Population rises → 'Normal' population size

Birth rate and death rate balance one another resulting in an equilibrium. The population oscillates (rises and falls) around the carrying capacity of the environment.

Population size (y-axis) vs Time (x-axis)

- Population growing slowly
- Population growing exponentially
- Population growth decelerates
- Population constant

K^*

K

Environmental resistance becomes dominant, increasing the death rate and/or decreasing the birth rate

The **carrying capacity** (K) is the maximum number of a species that the habitat can hold. It is determined by the availability of **nutrients**, **shelter** and **breeding sites**. If the carrying capacity is increased (e.g. $K \rightarrow K^*$) then the size of the population tends to increase to take advantage.

Slow start to population growth as the number of mature, reproducing individuals is low and they may be widely dispersed

Maximum observed growth rate – a compromise between biotic potential and initial environmental resistance

Biotic potential is the ability to breed. Asexually reproducing organisms with a short generation time, such as bacteria, have a high biotic potential. Sexually reproducing organisms with a long generation time, such as humans, have a low biotic potential.

- Biotic
  - Food availability
  - Predators or parasites
  - Disease
  - Territorial interactions
- Abiotic
  - Water
  - Oxygen
  - Light
  - Toxins/pollutants

---

1 What is meant by the term environmental resistance? Give an example.

2 Define the terms biotic and abiotic factors, and give examples of each.

3 Give examples of the ways in which humans exploit their knowledge of the factors affecting population growth.

13·5 Decay is a natural process

Recycling nutrients

Humans have an unusual skill – they can modify their environment to suit themselves. For example, we cut down forests and plant crops, and we build houses. Many building materials are natural, such as wood and straw, and the environment treats these materials as the dead remains of once-living organisms – the environment reclaims the nutrients and returns them to the ecosystem.

Starting with scavengers

When an organism dies, the nutrients in its body are returned to the environment to be reused. The nutrients are recycled by a series of processes carried out by other living organisms. The first ones to appear are usually the **scavengers** which break up the dead bodies into more manageable pieces. Scavengers eat some of the dead body, but leave behind blood or small pieces of tissue.

Scavengers such as the vulture feed on dead bodies.

Decomposition by microorganisms

The remains that are left are **decomposed** by the feeding activities of microorganisms. These fungi and bacteria feed by secreting enzymes onto the remains and absorbing the digested products. This form of nutrition is called saprotrophic feeding (see page 228).

The diagram on the opposite page illustrates some of the features of the decomposition process. The decay process provides energy and raw materials for the decomposers. It also releases nutrients from the bodies of dead animals and plants, which can then be reused by other organisms, for example:

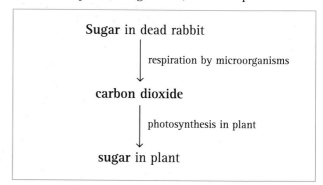

Sugar in dead rabbit

↓ respiration by microorganisms

carbon dioxide

↓ photosynthesis in plant

sugar in plant

In this way substances pass through **nutrient cycles** as microbes convert them from large, complex molecules in animal and plant remains to simpler compounds in the soil and the atmosphere. The next sections describe the recycling of the elements carbon and nitrogen.

Importance of decomposition processes to humans

- Organic waste in sewage is decomposed and made 'safe' in water treatment plants (see page 287).
- Organic pollutants such as spilled oil may be removed from the environment by decomposing bacteria (see page 266).
- Food is spoiled due to decomposition by fungi and bacteria. Many food treatments alter physical conditions to inhibit enzyme activity (see page 290).
- Wounds may become infected by saprotrophs, leading to tissue loss or even to death. Many medical treatments inhibit the multiplication or metabolism of saprotrophs.

Ecology

Saprotrophs cause decay.

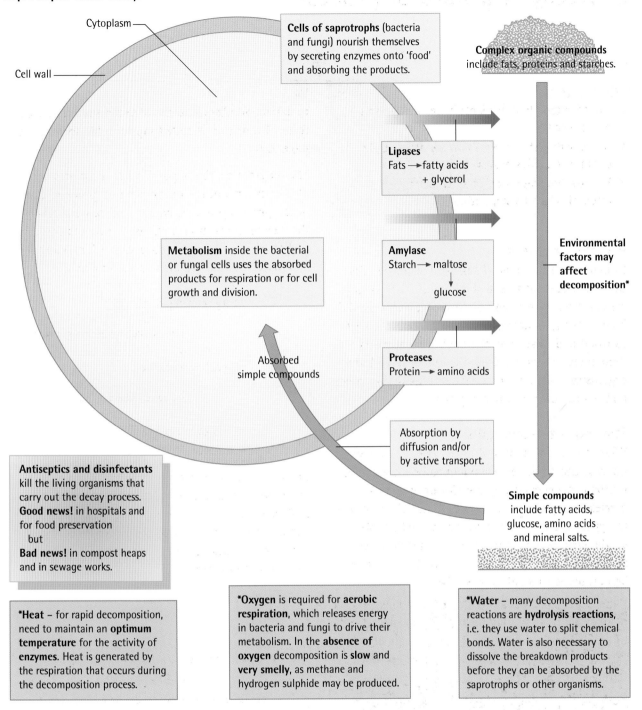

Cytoplasm

Cell wall

Cells of saprotrophs (bacteria and fungi) nourish themselves by secreting enzymes onto 'food' and absorbing the products.

Complex organic compounds include fats, proteins and starches.

Lipases
Fats → fatty acids + glycerol

Metabolism inside the bacterial or fungal cells uses the absorbed products for respiration or for cell growth and division.

Amylase
Starch → maltose
↓
glucose

Environmental factors may affect decomposition*

Proteases
Protein → amino acids

Absorbed simple compounds

Absorption by diffusion and/or by active transport.

Simple compounds include fatty acids, glucose, amino acids and mineral salts.

Antiseptics and disinfectants kill the living organisms that carry out the decay process.
Good news! in hospitals and for food preservation
   but
Bad news! in compost heaps and in sewage works.

*****Heat** – for rapid decomposition, need to maintain an **optimum temperature** for the activity of **enzymes**. Heat is generated by the respiration that occurs during the decomposition process.

*****Oxygen** is required for **aerobic respiration**, which releases energy in bacteria and fungi to drive their metabolism. In the **absence of oxygen** decomposition is **slow** and **very smelly**, as methane and hydrogen sulphide may be produced.

*****Water** – many decomposition reactions are **hydrolysis reactions**, i.e. they use water to split chemical bonds. Water is also necessary to dissolve the breakdown products before they can be absorbed by the saprotrophs or other organisms.

1 Copy and complete the following paragraph.
   During the process of decay, _____ and _____ convert complex chemicals into _____ ones. For example, proteins are converted to _____ , and _____ to fatty acids and glycerol. These decay processes involve the biological catalysts called _____ , and so the processes are affected by changes in _____ and _____ . Humans exploit decay, for example in the treatment of _____ to provide drinking water, and may deliberately limit decay, for example in the preservation of _____ .

2 Gardeners often place vegetable waste on a compost heap. Over the course of time the waste will be decomposed.
   a What do gardeners gain from the decomposed waste?
   b Why do gardeners sometimes spray water over the heap in warm summer weather?
   c Why do gardeners often build compost heaps on a pile of loose-fitting sticks or bricks?

Ecology

13·6 The carbon cycle

- To recall why living organisms need carbon-containing compounds
- To appreciate that carbon is cycled between complex and simple forms by the biochemical processes of photosynthesis and respiration
- To understand that formation and combustion of fossil fuels may distort the pattern of the carbon cycle

Carbon-containing nutrients – a reminder

The Sun keeps supplying *energy* to food chains. However, the supply of *chemical elements* to living organisms is limited, and these elements must be recycled. The nutrient elements are cycled between simple forms in the non-living (abiotic) environment and more complex forms in the bodies of living organisms (the biotic component of an ecosystem). Living organisms require carbon-containing compounds as:

- a source of **energy**, released when carbon-containing compounds are oxidised during respiration (particularly carbohydrates and fats)
- **raw materials** for the growth of cells (particularly fats and proteins).

Recycling carbon compounds

Plants, and some bacteria, manufacture these compounds from carbon dioxide during the process of photosynthesis (see page 148). Animals obtain them in a ready-made form by feeding on other living organisms (see page 38), and decomposers obtain them as they break down the dead bodies or wastes of other living organisms. These processes of feeding, respiration, photosynthesis and decomposition **recycle** the carbon over and over again. Theoretically, the amount of carbon dioxide fixed by photosynthesis should equal the amount released by respiration. As a result the most accessible form of carbon in the non-living environment, that is **carbon dioxide**, remains at about the same concentration year after year after year (about 0.03% of the atmosphere). Other processes may affect this regular cycling of carbon.

- Sometimes conditions are not suitable for respiration by decomposers, and carbon dioxide remains 'locked up' in complex carbon compounds in the bodies of organisms. For example, anaerobic, low pH or extreme temperature conditions will inhibit decomposition – this is how fossil fuels have been laid down in environments where decomposition is not favoured.

- Over millions of years the formation of fossil fuels has removed carbon dioxide from the environment. Humans have exploited fossil fuels as a source of energy over a relatively short time, and the **combustion** of oil, gas, coal and peat has returned enormous volumes of carbon dioxide to the atmosphere. As a result carbon dioxide concentrations are increasing (see page 260).

- The burning of biomass fuels such as wood and alcohol also returns carbon dioxide to the atmosphere, and can have a very severe local effect although worldwide it is less significant than the combustion of fossil fuels.

The way in which these different processes contribute to the cycling of carbon is illustrated opposite.

---

1 Refer to the carbon cycle opposite.
   a Name the simple carbon compound present in the abiotic part of the ecosystem.
   b Name two compounds present in the biotic part of the ecosystem.
   c Which processes raise the concentration of carbon dioxide in the atmosphere?
   d Which process reduces carbon dioxide concentration in the atmosphere?
   e Name the process that distributes carbon dioxide throughout the atmosphere from places where it is released.
   f Suggest a reason why some fossil fuels were formed as sediments at the bottom of ancient seas.

Ecology

The processes of photosynthesis, feeding, death, excretion and respiration lead to the cycling of carbon between living organisms and their environment. Fossil fuel formation and combustion affect the concentration of carbon dioxide in the atmosphere.

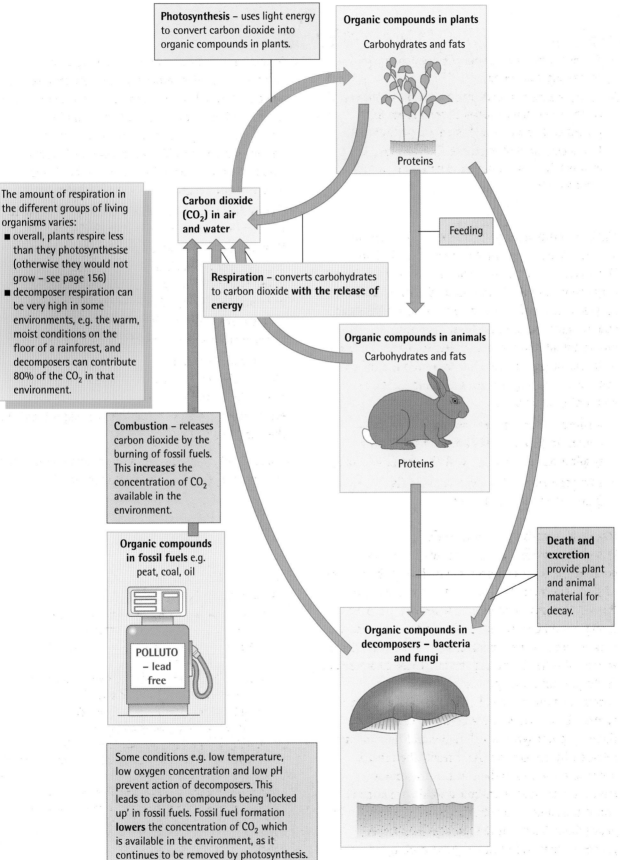

Photosynthesis – uses light energy to convert carbon dioxide into organic compounds in plants.

Organic compounds in plants

Carbohydrates and fats

Proteins

The amount of respiration in the different groups of living organisms varies:
■ overall, plants respire less than they photosynthesise (otherwise they would not grow – see page 156)
■ decomposer respiration can be very high in some environments, e.g. the warm, moist conditions on the floor of a rainforest, and decomposers can contribute 80% of the CO_2 in that environment.

Carbon dioxide (CO_2) in air and water

Feeding

Respiration – converts carbohydrates to carbon dioxide **with the release of energy**

Organic compounds in animals

Carbohydrates and fats

Proteins

Combustion – releases carbon dioxide by the burning of fossil fuels. This **increases** the concentration of CO_2 available in the environment.

Organic compounds in fossil fuels e.g. peat, coal, oil

POLLUTO – lead free

Death and excretion provide plant and animal material for decay.

Organic compounds in decomposers – bacteria and fungi

Some conditions e.g. low temperature, low oxygen concentration and low pH prevent action of decomposers. This leads to carbon compounds being 'locked up' in fossil fuels. Fossil fuel formation **lowers** the concentration of CO_2 which is available in the environment, as it continues to be removed by photosynthesis.

The carbon cycle

13·7 The nitrogen cycle

Objectives
- To recall why nitrate is an essential mineral for plant growth
- To know how nitrate is made available in the soil
- To understand that a series of biochemical processes results in the cycling of nitrogen between living organisms and the environment
- To appreciate the part played by microorganisms in the cycling of nitrogen

Plants need nitrate

Plants need nitrogen for the synthesis of proteins and other compounds, including DNA and vitamins. Nitrogen gas makes up about 80% of the Earth's atmosphere, but plants do not have the enzymes necessary to use the nitrogen directly – instead they must absorb it as **nitrate**. Nitrate is formed by two sets of processes carried out by microorganisms – **nitrogen fixation** and **nitrification**.

Nitrogen fixation

In **nitrogen fixation**, nitrogen and hydrogen are combined to form ammonium ions and then nitrate. The process depends upon enzymes that are only possessed by certain bacteria called **nitrogen-fixing**  **bacteria**. Some of these bacteria live free in the soil, but a very important species called *Rhizobium leguminosarum* lives in swellings called **nodules** on the roots of leguminous plants such as peas, beans and clover. Nitrogen fixation only happens if oxygen is present. It also occurs naturally in the atmosphere when the energy from lightning combines nitrogen directly with oxygen. Farmers can plant legumes in a crop rotation scheme to avoid having to use so much nitrogen-containing fertiliser. This saves money, and also limits pollution of water (see page 264).

Nitrification

In **nitrification**, ammonium ions produced by the decomposition of amino acids and proteins are oxidised, first to **nitrite** and then to nitrate. The process is carried out by **nitrifying bacteria** which live in the soil. Nitrification only happens if oxygen is present. In the absence of oxygen the process is reversed, and **denitrifying bacteria** obtain their energy by converting nitrate to nitrogen gas. This is why waterlogged soils, for example, tend to lose nitrate as nitrogen gas.

Recycling nitrogen

Once nitrate has been formed by either nitrogen fixation or nitrification, it can be absorbed by plants through their roots. Eventually the plant dies, and its body is added to the animal wastes and remains in the soil. Decomposers break down the nitrogen compounds in these wastes and remains and the formation of nitrate can begin again.

In a typical ecosystem the processes shown opposite recycle nitrogen between living organisms and the environment. However, some processes cause the loss of nitrate from the environment. This happens naturally as a result of **denitrification** (see above), and less naturally when crops are **harvested** and removed from the site where they have grown. These losses of nitrate can be made up either by nitrogen fixation or by adding nitrate in the form of fertilisers (see page 158).

---

1 Use your knowledge of the nitrogen cycle to explain how the following farming practices might improve soil fertility.
  a ploughing in stubble rather than burning it
  b draining waterlogged fields
  c planting peas or beans every third year
  d adding NPK fertiliser
  e adding well-rotted compost

2 Explain why farmers drain waterlogged fields.

The nitrogen cycle

The processes of nitrification, absorption, feeding, death, excretion and decay lead
to the cycling of nitrogen between living organisms and their environment. In a natural
ecosystem nitrogen fixation can 'top up' the cycle and make up for losses by denitrification.

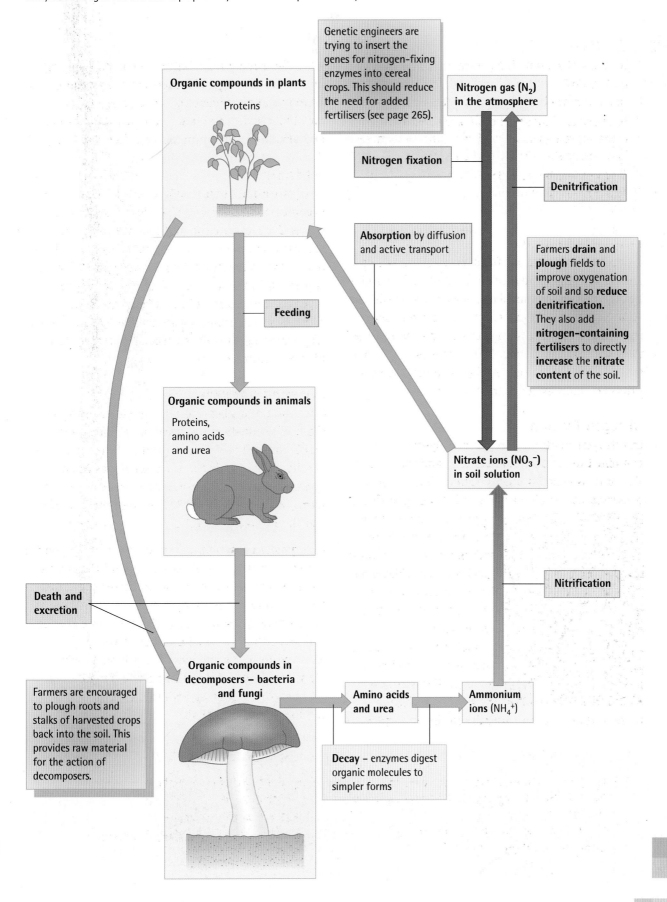

Organic compounds in plants

Proteins

Genetic engineers are
trying to insert the
genes for nitrogen-fixing
enzymes into cereal
crops. This should reduce
the need for added
fertilisers (see page 265).

**Nitrogen gas (N$_2$)
in the atmosphere**

Nitrogen fixation

Denitrification

Absorption by diffusion
and active transport

Farmers **drain** and
plough fields to
improve oxygenation
of soil and so **reduce
denitrification.**
They also add
**nitrogen-containing
fertilisers** to directly
**increase the nitrate
content** of the soil.

Feeding

Organic compounds in animals

Proteins,
amino acids
and urea

**Nitrate ions (NO$_3^-$)
in soil solution**

**Death and
excretion**

Nitrification

Farmers are encouraged
to plough roots and
stalks of harvested crops
back into the soil. This
provides raw material
for the action of
decomposers.

**Organic compounds in
decomposers – bacteria
and fungi**

**Amino acids
and urea**

**Ammonium
ions (NH$_4^+$)**

Decay – enzymes digest
organic molecules to
simpler forms

13.8 Human population growth

Objectives
- To know that the evolution of humans from hunter-gatherers to permanent settlers caused changes in the environment
- To understand the form of a human population growth curve

Humans, like other organisms, must find **food**, **shelter** and a **place to breed**. The first humans were hunter-gatherers who moved from place to place, taking what they needed to satisfy these requirements (but allowing the environment to recover once they moved on). After the most recent Ice Age this method of living became more difficult and humans began to settle in the most suitable areas. This meant that the environment did not have time to recover.

Growth of the human population

As with other organisms, the growth of the human population can be presented as a population growth curve (see page 251). The number of humans increases, by reproduction, until the carrying capacity of the environment has been reached. Humans have the ability to alter their environment to raise the carrying capacity. Three major changes in human activities led to significant surges in the world population, as shown below.

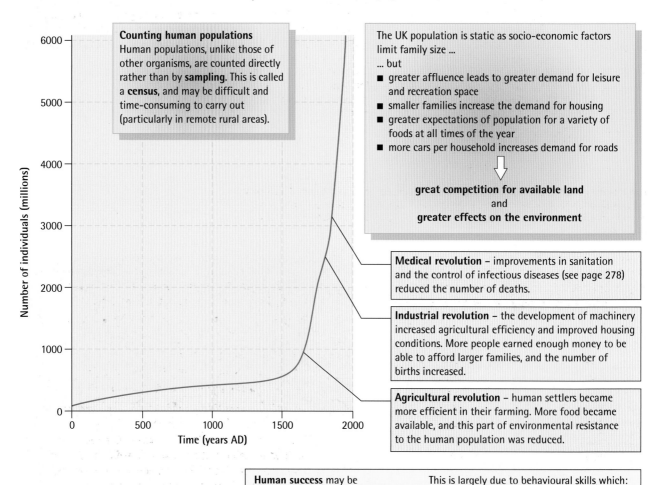

Counting human populations
Human populations, unlike those of other organisms, are counted directly rather than by **sampling**. This is called a **census**, and may be difficult and time-consuming to carry out (particularly in remote rural areas).

The UK population is static as socio-economic factors limit family size …
… but
- greater affluence leads to greater demand for leisure and recreation space
- smaller families increase the demand for housing
- greater expectations of population for a variety of foods at all times of the year
- more cars per household increases demand for roads

↓

great competition for available land
and
greater effects on the environment

Medical revolution – improvements in sanitation and the control of infectious diseases (see page 278) reduced the number of deaths.

Industrial revolution – the development of machinery increased agricultural efficiency and improved housing conditions. More people earned enough money to be able to afford larger families, and the number of births increased.

Agricultural revolution – human settlers became more efficient in their farming. More food became available, and this part of environmental resistance to the human population was reduced.

Human success may be measured as:
- worldwide distribution
- large number of individuals
- dominance over other species.

This is largely due to behavioural skills which:
- allow solution of complex problems
- allow control/modification of environment
leading to **changes in carrying capacity** of the environment.

Human population of the world

Population structure

Census figures show how many people of each age group are present in a population. These figures may be plotted to give a **population pyramid (age pyramid)**, as shown here.

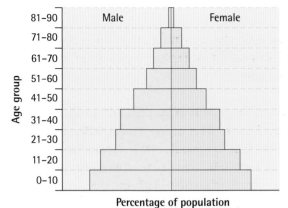

An increasing population
There are many individuals in the younger age groups. When these grow up and reproduce the population will increase in size. This pyramid might be seen in developing countries e.g. the Kenyan or Brazilian populations.

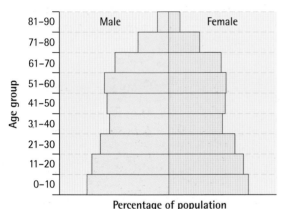

A stable population
Most of the age groups are of a similar size. When allowance is made for a few deaths in the younger age groups, there is little overall change in the population size. This pyramid would be typical of a western European population.

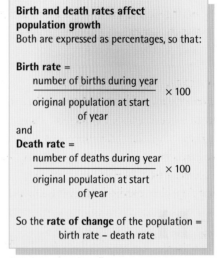

Birth and death rates affect population growth
Both are expressed as percentages, so that:

Birth rate =
$$\frac{\text{number of births during year}}{\substack{\text{original population at start} \\ \text{of year}}} \times 100$$

and

Death rate =
$$\frac{\text{number of deaths during year}}{\substack{\text{original population at start} \\ \text{of year}}} \times 100$$

So the **rate of change** of the population = birth rate – death rate

Population pyramids are important in planning use of resources. If scientists and politicians are making plans for the best use of a region's resources, they need to know whether the population is increasing or decreasing. A population pyramid gives this information from only one census.

---

1 The following table contains information on human population changes since the year 1700.

Year	Population (millions)
1700	700
1750	800
1800	900
1850	1200
1900	1600
1950	2500
1980	4450
1990	5300

a Plot these data in the form of a graph.

b Calculate the likely world population in the year 2050 if the growth rate shown between 1700 and 1800 had remained constant.

c Calculate the likely world population in the year 2050 if the trend in your graph continues.

d Explain the difference between your answers to b and c.

2 a What is an age pyramid?

b How could an age pyramid be constructed?

c How would an age pyramid for a country in western Europe differ from one for a developing country such as Brazil or Nigeria?

3 Describe how you could use a mark-recapture method to estimate the size of a crowd at a sporting fixture. Assume that the crowd could only enter and leave by a single route, but that they can move about freely inside the sportsground.

13·9 Humans and the environment: pollution of the atmosphere

Objectives

- To suggest why humans have such great effects on the environment
- To understand that human activities have affected water, land and the air
- To consider human effects in terms of cause, effect and possible remedies

Our demands on the environment

Human success, measured as an increase in population size, is largely due to our ability to solve complex problems and modify the environment for our benefit. This places great demands on the environment causing changes in **the atmosphere, the aquatic environment** and **the land.**

Humans have also, intentionally or otherwise, seriously upset the balance of populations of other living organisms.

Causes, effects and remedies for pollution

Pollution is any effect of human activities upon the environment, and a **pollutant** is any product of human activities that has a harmful effect on the environment. When looking at pollution, we shall consider three key points:

- What is the **cause?**
- What are the **effects?**
- What are the **solutions?**

Causes of the increased greenhouse effect

Greenhouse gases trap infrared radiation ('heat') close to the Earth's surface. Solar radiation is allowed to enter the lower atmosphere but is not allowed to escape. The greenhouse effect is increasing because of raised levels of these greenhouse gases:

- **carbon dioxide** released by combustion of fossil fuels in power stations and internal combustion engines (in cars and lorries, for example)
- **methane** produced in the guts of ruminants such as cows, and in the waterlogged conditions of swamps and rice fields
- **CFCs (chlorofluorocarbons)** from aerosol propellants and refrigerator coolants.

> More methane is produced by **termites** than by all the ruminant mammals on the Earth!

Effects

Good and bad results
Global warming (raised temperatures close to the Earth's surface) causes:

- greater climatic extremes – strong winds, heavier rainfall and unseasonal weather
- melting of polar ice and changes in density of sea water – rising sea levels and flooding
- evaporation of water from fertile areas – deserts form
- pests may spread to new areas

} all may cause loss of crops

But
- higher temperatures and more carbon dioxide mean **more photosynthesis** and **more food production.**

Solutions

To limit the effects of greenhouse gases, humans should:
- reduce burning of fossil fuels – explore alternative energy sources
- reduce cutting of forests for cattle ranching or rice growing
- replant forests.

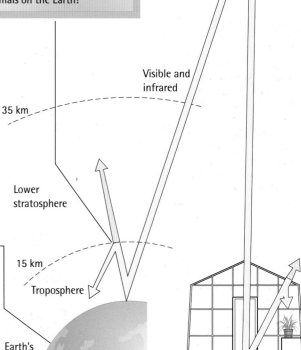

Solar radiation

Visible and infrared

35 km

Lower stratosphere

15 km

Troposphere

Earth's surface

Some gases added to the atmosphere act like the panes of glass in a greenhouse and raise the temperature close to the Earth's surface.

Ecology

Pollution of the atmosphere

There are three main problems with the Earth's atmosphere:

- the **greenhouse effect**
- changes to the **ozone layer**
- production of **acid rain**.

Burning of fossil fuels has a major effect on the atmosphere. The combustion process oxidises elements and compounds in the fuel, as shown in the equations on the right.

These oxides affect the atmosphere – carbon dioxide is a greenhouse gas, sulphur dioxide contributes to acid rain, and the oxides of nitrogen increase amounts of both low-level ozone and acid rain. The other major pollutants of the atmosphere are the chlorofluorocarbons (CFCs).

There are also localised problems with lead compounds, and with smoke. The causes and effects of, and possible solutions to, each of these problems are outlined in the diagrams here and on page 262.

Carbon oxygen	$+ \longrightarrow$	carbon monoxide (CO) and carbon dioxide (CO_2)
Sulphur oxygen	$+ \longrightarrow$	sulphur dioxide (SO_2)
Nitrogen oxygen	$+ \longrightarrow$	nitrogen monoxide (NO) and nitrogen dioxide (NO_2)

The ozone layer

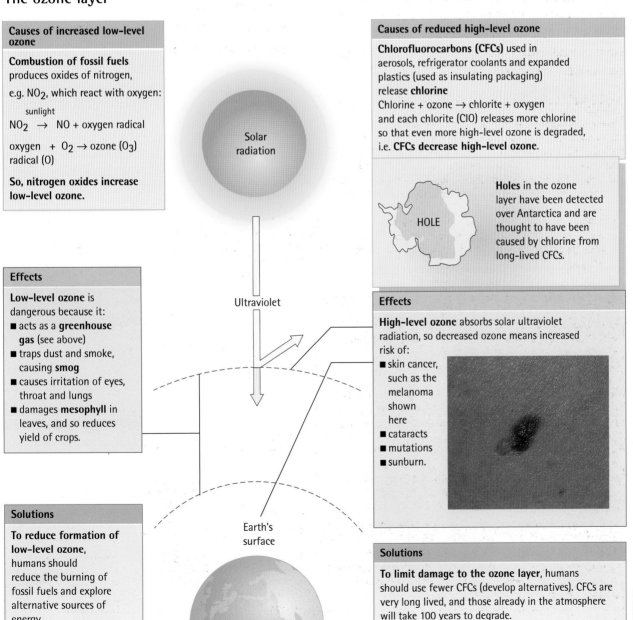

Causes of increased low-level ozone

Combustion of fossil fuels produces oxides of nitrogen, e.g. NO_2, which react with oxygen:

$$NO_2 \xrightarrow{\text{sunlight}} NO + \text{oxygen radical}$$

$$\text{oxygen radical (O)} + O_2 \rightarrow \text{ozone } (O_3)$$

So, nitrogen oxides increase low-level ozone.

Effects

Low-level ozone is dangerous because it:
- acts as a **greenhouse gas** (see above)
- traps dust and smoke, causing **smog**
- causes irritation of eyes, throat and lungs
- damages **mesophyll** in leaves, and so reduces yield of crops.

Solutions

To reduce formation of low-level ozone, humans should reduce the burning of fossil fuels and explore alternative sources of energy.

Solar radiation

Ultraviolet

Earth's surface

Causes of reduced high-level ozone

Chlorofluorocarbons (CFCs) used in aerosols, refrigerator coolants and expanded plastics (used as insulating packaging) release **chlorine**

Chlorine + ozone → chlorite + oxygen and each chlorite (ClO) releases more chlorine so that even more high-level ozone is degraded, i.e. **CFCs decrease high-level ozone**.

HOLE

Holes in the ozone layer have been detected over Antarctica and are thought to have been caused by chlorine from long-lived CFCs.

Effects

High-level ozone absorbs solar ultraviolet radiation, so decreased ozone means increased risk of:
- skin cancer, such as the melanoma shown here
- cataracts
- mutations
- sunburn.

Solutions

To limit damage to the ozone layer, humans should use fewer CFCs (develop alternatives). CFCs are very long lived, and those already in the atmosphere will take 100 years to degrade.

Acid rain

Causes

Human activities release acidic gases
- Sulphur and nitrogen in fossil fuels are converted to oxides during combustion.
- More oxidation occurs in the clouds. Oxidation is catalysed by ozone and by unburnt hydrocarbon fuels.
- The oxides dissolve in water, and fall as **acid rain**.

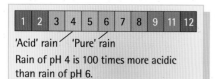

Sulphur dioxide and nitrogen oxides $\xrightarrow{H_2O}$ sulphuric and nitric acids

Effects

Acid rain causes problems
- **Soils** become very acidic. This causes **leaching of minerals** and **inhibition of decomposition**.
- **Water in lakes and rivers** collects excess minerals. This causes **death of fish and invertebrates** so that food chains are disrupted.
- **Forest trees** suffer **starvation** because of leaching of ions and destruction of photosynthetic tissue.

| 1 | 2 | 3 | 4 | 5 | 6 | 7 | 8 | 9 | 11 | 12 |

'Acid' rain   'Pure' rain

Rain of pH 4 is 100 times more acidic than rain of pH 6.

Solutions

Acid rain can be reduced
- Clean up emissions from power stations with **scrubbers**.
- Clean up emissions from car exhausts with **catalytic converters**.

Scrubber

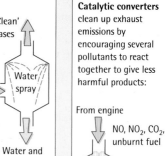

'Clean' gases

Polluted gases → Water spray

Water and dissolved pollutants

Catalytic converters clean up exhaust emissions by encouraging several pollutants to react together to give less harmful products:

From engine

NO, NO_2, CO_2, unburnt fuel

Metal catalysts

CO_2, H_2O, and N_2

To exhaust

'Acid' lakes and fields can be improved by the addition of crushed limestone ($CaCO_3$) – this is very expensive and time consuming.

Acid rain damages both living organisms and buildings made by humans.

Lead

Causes

Lead compounds are added to petrol to prevent 'knocking' (inefficient burning of the petrol–air mixture). They are released into the atmosphere from exhaust gases.

Effects

Lead compounds are absorbed into the body from inhaled air and may:
- slow down mental development
- damage the liver.

Solutions

Reduce the use of 'leaded' petrol. Most cars now run on unleaded petrol, and leaded petrol is becoming less readily available.

Poisonous lead compounds enter the atmosphere when fuels are burned.

Smoke

Causes

Inefficient and incomplete combustion of fossil fuels, e.g. bonfires or clearing stubble from fields. Severe 'smoke' pollution occurred following burning of oil wells during the Gulf War.

Effects

- Less light can penetrate atmosphere.
- Smoke deposits cover leaves.

Both these effects lead to reduced photosynthesis, and so to reduced crop yield.

- Particles in smoke also irritate eyes, nose and lungs. Some, e.g. from burning plastic, can be very poisonous.

Solutions

Smoke emissions are reduced by:
- more efficient burning, in well designed furnaces
- burning 'smokeless' fuels.

Toxic materials – some plastics and foams, for example – should never be burned in the open.

Smoke can affect both plants and animals.

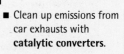

Analysis of data

Two students decided to investigate the effect of sulphur dioxide on the germination of oat seeds. They set up trays of germinating seeds under a clear plastic cover along with five different concentrations of sodium disulphate(IV) solution (sometimes called sodium metabisulphate). Sodium disulphate(IV) breaks down to release sulphur dioxide into the atmosphere. The table below contains the results after one week.

1 a Copy the table and complete it to show the percentage germination of the oat seeds at each sodium disulphate(IV) concentration.

Concentration of sodium disulphate(IV) (%)	Number of seeds germinated out of 20 (five experiments)					Percentage germination
0.00	19	19	17	20	18	
0.05	18	19	18	19	19	
0.10	12	13	14	11	12	
0.50	0	1	0	0	1	
2.50	0	0	0	0	0	

b Present the results in the form of a bar chart.

c Why was the experiment repeated five times at each concentration?

d Water (= 0% sodium disulphate(IV) solution) is a control. What is the purpose of this control?

e What is the lowest concentration of sodium disulphate(IV) that had a harmful effect on seed germination?

f How could the students modify the experiment to find a more accurate value for the concentration of sodium disulphate(IV) which had a harmful effect on seed germination?

g State the manipulated and responding variables in this experiment. Suggest two factors which might affect seed germination and are fixed variables in this experiment.

h The sodium disulphate(IV) in the experiment released sulphur dioxide into the apparatus.
  i What human activity releases large amounts of sulphur dioxide into the natural environment?
  ii Suggest two other effects, apart from reducing seed germination, of sulphur dioxide on living organisms.

2 The following table contains information about the sources and effects of greenhouse gases.

a Present this data in the form of a bar chart.

b The other greenhouse gas is water. Use the data in the table to calculate the greenhouse effect of water.

c Which of the gases shown in the table is produced by natural processes?

d What, exactly, is a greenhouse gas?

e Suggest three possibly harmful effects of greenhouse gases.

f Use the data in the table to suggest why the following are valuable conservation measures:
  i reducing forest clearances for cattle ranches
  ii improved insulation for houses
  iii the use of alternative energy sources such as windmills and wave machines.

g In 1900 the concentration of carbon dioxide in the atmosphere was 0.030%. In 1990 this had risen to 0.035%, and is expected to rise to 0.055% by 2030.
  i By how much did the carbon dioxide concentration increase between 1900 and 1990?
  ii What is the expected increase in carbon dioxide concentration between 1990 and 2030?
  iii Suggest why there is a difference between your answers to i and ii.

3 This photograph shows the ozone concentration over different parts of the Earth's surface.

a From the data in the diagram above, suggest the value for ozone concentration that counts as a 'hole' in the ozone layer above Antarctica.

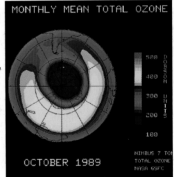

b Why must researchers in Antarctica wear skin-protecting creams when working outdoors?

c What are CFCs, and how do they affect the high-level ozone layer?

d How can humans limit future damage to the high-level ozone layer?

e In what ways is low-level ozone a risk to humans?

Gas	Sources	Overall contribution to greenhouse effect (% total)
Carbon dioxide	Burning forests, burning fossil fuels, production of cement	54
Chlorofluorocarbons (CFCs)	Aerosol propellants, refrigerants, coolants in air conditioners	21
Methane	Waste gases from domestic animals, rotting vegetation, rice growing	14
Nitrogen oxides	Exhaust gases from internal combustion engines, breakdown of fertilisers	7
Low level ozone	Combination of nitrogen oxides with oxygen	2

Ecology

13·10 Pollution of water

Objectives
- To recall why water is important to living organisms
- To understand that water supplies oxygen to living organisms
- To know how excess nutrients in water lead to depletion of oxygen levels
- To recall other aspects of water pollution

The causes of oxygen depletion

All living organisms depend on a supply of water, as we saw on page 8. Many organisms actually live in water. Most of these **aquatic** organisms respire aerobically and so require oxygen from their environment. Any change that alters the amount of oxygen in the water can seriously affect the suitability of the water as a habitat. The two pollutants that most often reduce oxygen in water are:

- **fertilisers** – nitrates and phosphates are added to soil by farmers (see page 158). Some of the fertiliser is washed from the soil by rain into the nearest pond, lake or river. This process is called **leaching**.
- **sewage** – this contains an excellent source of organic food for bacteria, and also contains phosphates from detergents.

Pollution reduces the dissolved oxygen in water as rooted plants are unable to photosynthesise because of the algal bloom.

How fertilisers and sewage affect the oxygen concentration

Water that contains few nutrients is rich in oxygen and supports a wide variety of living organisms. The oxygen enters the water from the atmosphere by diffusion and from photosynthesising aquatic plants. Simpler forms of life, such as algae and bacteria, are controlled because the low concentration of nutrients such as nitrate is a limiting factor for their growth. If more nutrients are made available, from fertiliser run off or from sewage, then:

- Algae and other surface plants grow very rapidly, and block out light to plants rooted on the bottom of the river or pond.
- The rooted plants die, and their bodies provide even more nutrients.
- The population of bacteria increases rapidly. As they multiply, the bacteria consume oxygen for aerobic respiration. There is now a biological oxygen demand (or BOD) in the water because of oxygen consumed by these microbes.
- Other living creatures cannot obtain enough oxygen. They must leave the area, if they can, or they will die. Their bodies provide even more food for bacteria, and the situation becomes even worse. This is an example of **positive feedback** – the change from ideal conditions causes an even greater change from ideal conditions.

The lower diagram opposite shows what happens if a pond or river receives too many nutrients. The process is called **eutrophication**. The pond or river soon becomes depleted of living organisms. Only a few animals, such as *Tubifex* (sewage worms), can respire at the very low oxygen concentrations that are available. The solution to this problem is straightforward – **do not allow excess nutrients into the water.**

A well balanced natural pond or river

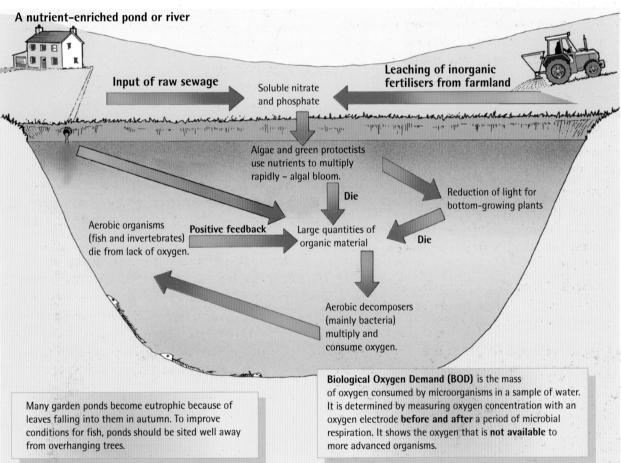

Populations of algae and bacteria are limited by low levels of nutrients.

Light penetrates to rooted plants which photosynthesise, producing oxygen.

Invertebrates and fish can obtain enough oxygen for aerobic respiration.

A nutrient-enriched pond or river

Input of raw sewage

Soluble nitrate and phosphate

Leaching of inorganic fertilisers from farmland

Algae and green protoctists use nutrients to multiply rapidly – algal bloom.

Die

Reduction of light for bottom-growing plants

Aerobic organisms (fish and invertebrates) die from lack of oxygen.

Positive feedback

Large quantities of organic material

Die

Aerobic decomposers (mainly bacteria) multiply and consume oxygen.

Many garden ponds become eutrophic because of leaves falling into them in autumn. To improve conditions for fish, ponds should be sited well away from overhanging trees.

Biological Oxygen Demand (BOD) is the mass of oxygen consumed by microorganisms in a sample of water. It is determined by measuring oxygen concentration with an oxygen electrode **before and after** a period of microbial respiration. It shows the oxygen that is **not available** to more advanced organisms.

Causes of eutrophication

Unnaturally high levels of nutrients:
- from leaching of fertilisers
- from input of raw sewage
- from liquid manure (slurry) washed out of farmyards.

Effects

Depleted oxygen levels in water cause death of fish and most invertebrates. High nitrate levels can be dangerous to human babies.

Solutions

- Treat sewage before it enters rivers (see page 286).
- Prevent farmyard drainage entering rivers and ponds.
- Control use of fertilisers:
  - apply only when crops are growing
  - never apply to bare fields
  - do not apply when rain is forecast
  - do not dispose of waste fertiliser into rivers and ponds.
- Bubble a stream of air through badly polluted ponds.

Water is affected in other ways by human activities

Industry, leisure and transport all produce more and more wastes which are often dumped in the most convenient body of water. Some other effects of humans on water are outlined below and opposite.

Oil pollution

Causes	Effects	Solutions
Oil tankers spill their contents, by accident or deliberately (during cleaning of their storage tanks), into the sea. Occasionally damage to pipelines at oil terminals causes enormous discharge of oil into the environment.	Most of the oil floats on the surface of the water, causing: ■ death of sea birds since feathers lose their ability to insulate when they are coated with oil ■ fish are directly poisoned ■ marine mammals are killed by eating poisoned food or by loss of fur's insulating capacity. Oil is also washed onto beaches, causing: ■ death of organisms such as limpets, periwinkles and seaweeds ■ loss of income from tourism.	■ Strict control of oil handling ■ Severe fines for breaking the rules concerning oil handling ■ **Bioremediation** – using living organisms to clear up pollution. For example, some bacteria can consume oil if fed with a source of sugar. ■ Volunteers may wash sea birds and mammals with detergents to remove oil.

Thermal pollution

Causes	Effects	Solutions
Water is used as a coolant: ■ in power stations ■ in industries, especially metal working and chemical production. The water cools the process but is itself warmed up. This hot water is then discharged into rivers or the sea.	Temperature of river is raised, which: ■ lowers the oxygen concentration of the water because the solubility of oxygen in water falls as temperature rises. ■ causes fish, invertebrates and bacteria to become more active, so they respire more and consume even more oxygen! ■ allows colonisation by 'foreign' species, which may affect food chains.	■ Control output of hot water so that it is rapidly cooled by river or sea. ■ Do not allow discharge of hot water into still or slow-moving rivers or canals.

There are now populations of terrapins and piranha fish in some British canals. These have been released by pet keepers, and do well in the warm waters near to outlets from power stations.

Metals

Causes	Effects	Solutions
Lead enters water because: ■ it dissolves from lead pipes which were traditionally used in plumbing ■ lead weights are discarded by anglers.	Lead compounds are toxic, and accumulate via aquatic food chains.	■ Replacement of lead pipes used in plumbing. ■ Strict control of angling – use of alternatives to lead weights. ■ Planting of reeds around ponds and lakes – these remove many toxic compounds from water without themselves being affected.

Mercury was discharged from a chemicals factory on Minimata Bay in Japan. Mercury passed through the food chain to fishermen. Many had severe damage to their nervous system, and more than 80 died of 'Minimata disease'.

Pesticides

Causes

Over-use of pesticides on agricultural land (e.g. to protect a crop from insects) or directly on water (e.g. to kill an aquatic stage of an insect) can raise pesticide levels in water. The pesticide levels are then **amplified** as they pass through food chains. For example, one stickleback may consume 500 *Daphnia*. The living matter in the *Daphnia* will be used for raw materials or lost as heat but the pesticide remains **concentrated in the tissues** of the stickleback.

DDT concentration in parts per million:

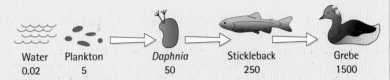

Water	Plankton	*Daphnia*	Stickleback	Grebe
0.02	5	50	250	1500

Effects

High concentrations of pesticides may accumulate in the tissues of top carnivores. The pesticide may be toxic (and kill the carnivore) or may affect its metabolism. DDT, used to control mosquitoes in malarial zones, severely reduced breeding success in birds of prey.

Solutions

- Use degradable pesticides – DDT, for example, lasts for a long time and so its use is banned in the UK.
- Explore alternative methods, such as biological pest control (see page 272).
- Crops that are **genetically modified** to resist attack by insects may reduce the need to use insecticides (see page 221).

Acid rain (see page 262) also causes significant pollution of water. Some lakes are almost empty of life as a result of pH levels as low as 4 or 5.

---

1 Sea otters eat fish, and fish eat small crustaceans such as shrimps. The shrimps feed by filtering algae from the water.

a Write out a food chain that links these organisms.

b Pesticides are washed from nearby farmland into rivers and then into the sea. Farmers say that the concentration of the pesticides is too low to directly affect the otters. Explain how the pesticides might still cause the death of the otters.

2 Untreated human sewage should not enter river water, but occasionally an overflow from a water treatment plant occurs. The tables below contain information on the changes that occurred in river water downstream from a sewage overflow.

a Plot these data in the form of a line graph. Choose axes to display the information in the way that best relates the abiotic factor to the biotic factors.

b Suggest why the number of bacteria was high at 0 m.

c Explain the shape of the curve for algae.

d How is it possible for fish numbers to fall to zero and then recover?

e Describe the changes in the concentration of oxygen dissolved in the water downstream from the point of sewage entry.

f Explain what might have caused these changes in oxygen concentration.

Distance downstream (m)	Concentration of dissolved oxygen (percentage of maximum)
0 (point of sewage entry)	95
100	30
200	20
300	28
400	42
500	58
600	70
700	80
800	89
900	95
1000	100

Table 1

Distance downstream (m)	Number (arbitrary units) of		
	bacteria	algae	fish
0 (point of sewage entry)	88	20	20
100	79	8	6
200	74	7	1
300	60	21	0
400	51	40	0
500	48	70	0
600	44	83	0
700	42	90	0
800	39	84	0
900	36	68	4
1000	35	55	20

Table 2

Ecology

Many of the pollutants already described have an effect on land, as well as on the air or water, for example:

▪ lead and mercury compounds may poison areas of land

▪ pesticides may enter land-based food chains

▪ acid rain can affect the availability of minerals in the soil.

Pollution also includes the loss of wildlife habitat that results from human competition for land.

Removal of hedges

Farmers remove hedges to increase the area where they can grow crops. The benefits of hedgerows as habitats, and the reasons why farmers feel justified in removing them, are outlined below.

Deforestation

The removal of woodland provides firewood, building materials, cleared land for crops or for grazing of cattle. For our first settler ancestors, it also removed the habitat of predators of domestic animals.

The technique used to clear forest today is often called **slash and burn**. The largest trees may be removed for sale as timber for furnishings but the less valuable woods are simply chopped down (slashed) and then burned. The humans using the land gain a short-term benefit, but the damage to

Advantages

Hedges act as **windbreaks** which provide shelter for domestic animals, protect fragile crops, limit soil erosion and reduce water losses by evaporation from soil. A hedge 1 m in height provides these benefits for approximately 2 m to its sheltered side.

Taller hedges offer secure nesting sites for up to 65 **bird species**. These species may be important predators on pest species on local crops.

Fallen leaves and fruits provide **nutrient enrichment** for soil.

Grassy strip provides **shelter** for game birds and overwintering insects, and **nesting sites** for small animals (e.g. voles).

Hedges and associated herbs provide **feeding and breeding** opportunities for **pollinating insects** (including 23 species of butterfly).

Roots improve **soil stability** and limit both wind and water erosion.

Disadvantages

A hedge takes up spaces that could be occupied by crops and reduces economic use of modern agricultural machinery.

Hedge may shade crop species (compete with them for light).

May be a source of insects, and viral and fungal pests (although such species are often specific and are therefore unlikely to be pests of local crop species).

May act as a reservoir of weed species which then invade and compete with crops.

Hedge banks offer burrowing opportunities to rabbits which may then consume crops, especially in the young stages.

Roots may consume water and nutrients which otherwise would be available to crop plants.

Maintenance of hedges is **labour intensive** compared with barbed-wire boundaries.

The removal of hedgerows in Britain has averaged 8000 km per year in the twentieth century. This represents a disaster for wildlife.

wildlife habitats is immediate and humans also suffer in the long term. Newspaper and television headlines emphasise the loss of forest in tropical areas of the world, but it should be remembered that most of the UK was once forested! Some of the penalties of large-scale deforestation are illustrated below.

Urbanisation

The concentration of humans and their machines into small areas creates disturbance so that animals may stop breeding. In addition, roads separate one area of suitable habitat from another, and wildlife areas become fragmented into pieces that are too small to support stable populations of animals and plants. In order to construct roads and buildings, materials must be extracted from the land. The effects of quarrying to extract building materials can be devastating to wildlife.

1 It has been estimated that 100 000 miles of hedgerow have been removed from around Britain's fields since the Second World War. Why has this been done? What are the possible effects on wildlife?

2 What is deforestation? Give reasons why humans should be anxious about this process.

3 Why has urbanisation occurred? List the ways in which urbanisation:
a benefits humans
b is harmful to wildlife.
Suggest one way in which the effects of urbanisation can be reduced.

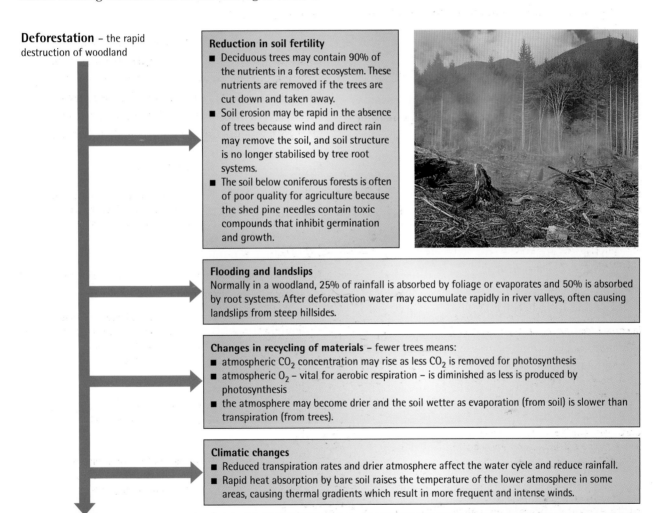

Deforestation – the rapid destruction of woodland

Reduction in soil fertility
- Deciduous trees may contain 90% of the nutrients in a forest ecosystem. These nutrients are removed if the trees are cut down and taken away.
- Soil erosion may be rapid in the absence of trees because wind and direct rain may remove the soil, and soil structure is no longer stabilised by tree root systems.
- The soil below coniferous forests is often of poor quality for agriculture because the shed pine needles contain toxic compounds that inhibit germination and growth.

Flooding and landslips
Normally in a woodland, 25% of rainfall is absorbed by foliage or evaporates and 50% is absorbed by root systems. After deforestation water may accumulate rapidly in river valleys, often causing landslips from steep hillsides.

Changes in recycling of materials – fewer trees means:
- atmospheric CO_2 concentration may rise as less CO_2 is removed for photosynthesis
- atmospheric O_2 – vital for aerobic respiration – is diminished as less is produced by photosynthesis
- the atmosphere may become drier and the soil wetter as evaporation (from soil) is slower than transpiration (from trees).

Climatic changes
- Reduced transpiration rates and drier atmosphere affect the water cycle and reduce rainfall.
- Rapid heat absorption by bare soil raises the temperature of the lower atmosphere in some areas, causing thermal gradients which result in more frequent and intense winds.

Species extinction Many species are dependent on forest conditions:
- mountain gorillas depend on cloud forest of central Africa
- golden lion tamarins depend on coastal rainforest of Brazil
- ospreys depend on mature pine forests in northern Europe.

It is estimated that one plant and one animal species become extinct every 30 minutes due to deforestation.

Many plant species may have medicinal properties, e.g. as tranquillisers, reproductive hormones, anticoagulants, pain-killers and antibiotics.
The Madagascan periwinkle, for example, yields a potent drug used to treat leukaemia.

Ecology

Humans may have a positive effect on the environment: conservation

Humans do not always damage the environment – growing numbers of **conservationists** try to balance the human demands on the environment with the need to maintain wildlife habitat. They will try to assess the likely effects of any human activity by producing an **Environmental Impact Statement**.

Forest management

Humans have been responsible for deforestation of much of the Earth's surface. Humans have also set up schemes for the large-scale planting of trees – in areas that have been cleared (**reforestation**) or in a new site (**afforestation**). There are a number of reasons for planting trees:

- as a cash crop, providing timber for building (coniferous plantations in the UK) or for fuel (quick-growing eucalyptus trees are widely planted in central Africa)
- to reverse soil erosion, particularly valuable in areas that have become deserts
- to provide valuable wildlife habitats – for example, Scots pine plantations are important habitats for red squirrels
- as recreational areas, providing leisure activities such as camping and mountain-biking.

A well managed forest can combine all of these functions. The Forestry Commission in the UK applies biological knowledge to the management of forests, as illustrated in the programme for conservation of red squirrels outlined opposite.

Endangered species

Competition between humans and other living organisms means that many species have disappeared or declined in number. The reasons for this are not always understood, but the following may be to blame:

- **Pest control** – the term pest includes any species that causes inconvenience to humans. Many species have been hunted ruthlessly, such as red deer (which damage trees), and also predators such as pine martens and red kites.
- **Commercial exploitation** – species of value to humans have been exploited, such as the beaver which was hunted and trapped to extinction for fur in the sixteenth century.
- **Loss of habitat** – more land is being used for agriculture, including previously unusable land that has been drained. This removes habitats for many species, such as cranes in East Anglia.

Conservationists work to slow down or stop the decline in **biodiversity** (the number of different species), and also to raise public awareness of the need to maintain species and their habitats. The number of different species in a community of living organisms can be described by a formula called the **Species Diversity Index**.

Conservation strategies

Conservation involves management of an area, and may include a number of strategies:

- **preservation** – keeping some part of the environment unchanged. This might be possible in Antarctica, but is less significant in a densely populated area like Britain than ...
- **reclamation** – the restoration of damaged habitats such as replacing hedgerows or recovering former industrial sites, and ...
- **creation** – producing new habitats, for example by digging a garden pond, or planting a forest.

A **conservation plan** involves several stages:

- **sampling** to assess the number of organisms
- **devising a management plan** – for example, trying to increase a species' population based on knowledge of its breeding requirements
- **carrying out the plan**
- **re-sampling** to assess the number of the 'conserved' species once more, and find out whether the conservation plan has worked.

The red squirrel in Britain

The red squirrel (*Sciurus vulgaris*) used to be widespread in Britain, but in most areas it has now been replaced by the larger grey squirrel (*Sciurus carolinensis*) which was introduced into Britain from North America. There are a number of possible reasons for the decline of the red squirrel:

- **Competition with the grey squirrel** – the red squirrel feeds mainly on seeds from pine cones. The grey squirrel eats a wider range of foods.

- **Disease** – the grey squirrel may carry a virus which harms red squirrels.

- **Habitat loss** – many recent forest plantings have been composed of trees all of the same age, and have often been of sitka spruce, which produces small seeds and sheds them early in the year, leaving little food for red squirrels in the winter.

Conservation plans to support red squirrel numbers are shown in the diagram below. Introducing a species from another country often causes problems for native wildlife. Wildlife is also affected by hunters and collectors. The organisation CITES (Convention on International Trade in Endangered Species of Wild Fauna and Flora) exists to try to prevent this trade.

1. Briefly describe why red squirrels are endangered in Britain. Outline a conservation strategy which might help to guarantee their survival.

2. What is meant by the term conservation? Why is conservation necessary?

3. It is sometimes stated that 'Conservation is a compromise'. Explain whether you think that this statement is a valid one. Use examples to illustrate your answer.

Tree species chosen to provide a food source that favours red squirrels, such as broad-leaved species that produce small seeds and are less attractive to the grey squirrels. Species favoured by the grey squirrels may be removed. Coniferous species might include Norway spruce and Scots pine, both of which shed their seeds late and thus provide a year-round supply of food for the red squirrels.

Competitor grey squirrels can be poisoned using warfarin-baited food in a 'grey-squirrel-selective' hopper. This strategy is restricted by legislation, but many landowners favour it because of damage to trees by grey squirrels.

Immunosterilisation – a vaccine could sterilise both male and female grey squirrels whilst leaving red squirrels unaffected. This could reduce the grey squirrel population in a humane way because it has little effect on the squirrels other than to make them sterile.

Supplementary feeding using hoppers that only allow access to red squirrels. These are placed in clusters of two or three about 20–30 m apart, and filled with a mixture of yellow maize, wheat, peanuts and sunflower seeds. They must be inspected and filled frequently.

Reintroduction of red squirrels – survival and behaviour of the introduced red squirrels must be carefully monitored by radio tracking and field observation.

Habitat management – red-squirrel reserves should be surrounded by at least 3 km of conifer forest or open land to act as a buffer against the entry of grey squirrels.

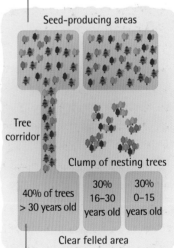

Forest management to provide both food and shelter. When clear felling, some single seed-producing trees should be left, and some small groups as nesting sites. Seed-producing areas should be connected by corridors of trees to prevent isolation and allow movement between one area and the next.

Conservation plans to support red squirrel populations involve habitat management for food provision.

Human management of ecosystems: biological pest control

Humans can control environmental resistance

The biotic component of an ecosystem interacts with the non-living or abiotic factors to eventually produce a stable and balanced ecosystem. Humans have the power to *un*balance an ecosystem – this might be seen as negative (for example, when pollutants affect animal populations) or as positive (for example, the management of a nature reserve to protect a particular population). Humans affect ecosystems by changing environmental resistance (see page 250).

Pest control

The control of **pests**, which compete for food or cause disease, is an important example of human management of ecosystems. Humans have a number of ways of controlling pests.

Cultural control involves removing pests physically, for example by weeding with a hoe, or preventing pests establishing themselves, for example by growing a plant species that deters pests amongst a crop.

Chemical control uses chemicals called **pesticides** to limit pest populations. Pesticides are not always **selective**, and sometimes kill harmless animals as well as the pest species. They may be **persistent** and remain in the environment for long periods. Some of them affect whole food chains (see page 267). Pests may develop **resistance**, and ever-increasing doses of pesticide will be required to have the same effect. Pesticides may be extremely expensive. Some crop species have been genetically modified to allow the crop to be protected with much less use of pesticide (see page 221).

In a **biological control** system, humans control the pest species using one of its natural predators. The principle of biological pest control is outlined below.

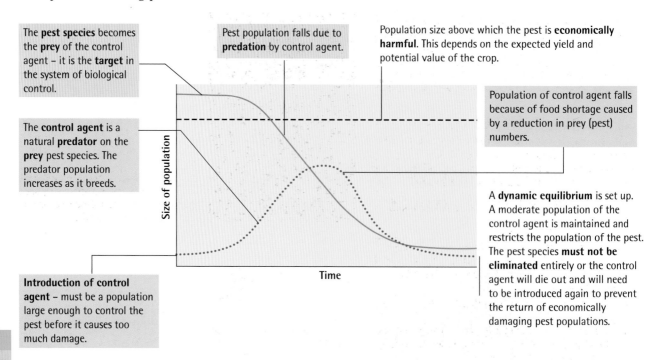

The **pest species** becomes the **prey** of the control agent – it is the **target** in the system of biological control.

The **control agent** is a natural **predator** on the **prey** pest species. The predator population increases as it breeds.

Introduction of control agent – must be a population large enough to control the pest before it causes too much damage.

Pest population falls due to **predation** by control agent.

Population size above which the pest is **economically harmful**. This depends on the expected yield and potential value of the crop.

Population of control agent falls because of food shortage caused by a reduction in prey (pest) numbers.

A **dynamic equilibrium** is set up. A moderate population of the control agent is maintained and restricts the population of the pest. The pest species **must not be eliminated** entirely or the control agent will die out and will need to be introduced again to prevent the return of economically damaging pest populations.

Size of population / *Time*

Biological control – the ideal relationship between a pest and its control agent

Cactoblastis cactorum

One of the earliest uses of biological control was the caterpillar *Cactoblastis cactorum* which was used to control the prickly pear cactus. The cactus was originally planted as cattle-proof hedges around farms in eastern Australia, but grew so quickly that it invaded the farmland itself. The biological control of the cactus was effective because the caterpillar fed only on the prickly pear. Remaining *Cactoblastis* moths could reproduce quickly and control any further outbreaks of cacti. The different techniques in biological control are outlined below.

Techniques in biological control

1 Use a **herbivore** to control a **weed** species e.g. *Cactoblastis* larvae to control prickly pear.

2 Use a **carnivore** to control a **herbivorous pest** e.g. hoverfly larvae to control aphids.

3 Use a **parasite** to control its **host** e.g. *Encarsia*, a parasitic wasp, to control the greenhouse whitefly *Trialeurodes vaporariorum*.

4 Disrupt the **breeding cycle** of a pest if it mates once only in its life e.g. release of irradiation-sterilised males of the screw worm fly, a flesh-eating parasite of cattle.

5 Control **pest behaviour** e.g. chemicals called pheromones are used to attract apple codling moths into lethal traps.

Failures with biological control

Any potential biological control agent must be tested thoroughly before its release. Sometimes scientists are so anxious to introduce a control that insufficient research is done, and problems arise.

If the link between the predator (the control agent) and the prey (the pest) is not close enough, the control agent may become a pest in its own right! Some examples of failed biological controls are illustrated at the bottom of the page.

Although setting up a successful biological control system is complicated, many conservationists prefer to use biological control systems rather than chemical control. Biological control is particularly useful in enclosed areas such as greenhouses (see page 274).

---

1 Make a table comparing biological and chemical pest control. Use the column headings:
specificity,
accumulation in ecosystems,
permanence of control,
development of resistance,
financial cost.

2 What are the features of an ideal biological pest control system? Explain, with examples, why some biological control systems have failed.

Failures in biological control

Cats and stoats were introduced to offshore islands of Britain and New Zealand to limit populations of rodents. The rodents were threatening rare ground-nesting birds. However, the cats and stoats ate the chicks of the rare birds!

House sparrows were introduced into California to control larvae on fruit trees. Sparrows are very successful at exploiting other food sources, and:
■ did not successfully control the insect larvae
■ reproduced very rapidly and now do enormous damage to crops.

Hawaiian cane toads were introduced into Queensland, Australia, to control the greyback beetle, a pest on sugar cane. The toads are now a serious threat to Australian wildlife. The toads:
■ eat many native insects and worms, and frogs (see right).
■ displace native frogs and toads from breeding pools
■ poison larger animals which try to eat them because their skin is extremely toxic.

Hawaiian cane toads pose a great threat to native Australian wildlife having been introduced into Queensland (see map) to control the greyback beetle.

13·14 Human management of ecosystems: fish farming and horticulture

Objectives

▪ To understand how humans can control environmental resistance

▪ To describe examples of maximising yields in the commercial management of ecosystems

Greenhouse management involves an understanding of the limiting factors that control photosynthesis (see page 155). Maximum photosynthesis means maximum plant growth.

Carbon dioxide concentration is a major limiting factor in photosynthesis. In a greenhouse plants may photosynthesise very quickly and CO_2 is rapidly used up. The CO_2 level is usually raised to about 0.1% of the atmosphere (about three times higher than in normal air). This gives an increase in yield of about 50%. The extra CO_2 can be provided by burning paraffin (which also raises the temperature) or by releasing it from a cylinder.

Computer control is widely used in large commercial greenhouses. Sensors provide information about air temperature, CO_2 concentration, water available to roots, humidity and mineral concentration, and the control centre ensures that any changes are corrected.

Temperature sensor → [computer] → Heater

High-yielding strains of crop are used. Selective breeding and/or genetic engineering can develop crop strains which:
▪ give a high yield
▪ produce fruit of a desirable colour/texture/size
▪ produce fruit at the same time
▪ may have genetic pest resistance.

Temperature affects plant growth because of its effect on the enzymes of photosynthesis. High temperatures may also speed up the life cycle of pests. Sunlight provides some heat (shading may be necessary in summer) but thermostatically regulated heaters provide greater control.

Humans exploit many other organisms, often as sources of food. Our understanding of population growth and the effect of environmental resistance allows us to maximise yields of 'food' populations by minimising environmental resistance. Two examples of the use of biological principles in the management of food-producing ecosystems are described here – greenhouse and fish farming.

Illumination – it is important to control:
▪ **intensity** – Higher light intensity → more photosynthesis until some other limiting factor intervenes.
▪ **quality** – photosynthesis is most efficient at red and blue wavelengths; white light contains some wavelengths (green) which are not useful.
▪ **duration** – if fruit is the desired product, the plant must flower. Flowering is controlled by day length (the duration of light in a 24-hour period).
Sunlight provides some illumination but artificial lighting systems are more controllable (though more expensive).

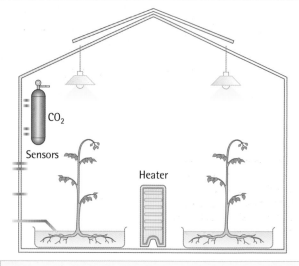

Pest control is particularly important – pest species can quickly spread through a greenhouse containing only a single crop.

---

1 Study the diagram on the opposite page and answer the following questions.

  a Suggest three biotic and two abiotic factors which might affect the productivity of the fish farm.

  b Why are salmon and trout the most widely farmed fish in the UK?

  c Suggest three ways in which biological knowledge is used to maximise the profits from the fish farm.

  d Some fish farmers put air bubblers in their enclosures. Why might this be necessary?

  e Why would doctors be anxious if growth hormones and antibiotics were added to the water in the enclosures?

  f Suggest one advantage and one disadvantage of feeding protein pellets instead of live food to the fish in the farm.

Ecology

Managing ecosystems

Fish farming maximises profit by minimising environmental resistance.

Suspended net keeps out aerial predators such as cormorant, heron and osprey.

Prepared food fed to the fish
- Pellets are easily transported and easily measured out.
- Usually made from fish caught in nets but not used for human consumption – **very high in protein** (gives rapid growth) but very expensive.
- May include **colouring agent** (turns fish pink – favoured by consumers) and **antibiotic** (disease control).

GRO-A-LOT PELLETS

Hanging net
- Keeps out **aquatic predators** such as otter and pike.
- Keeps out other fish and so **reduces competition** for the pelleted food.

Species – the 'farmed' species must:
- grow well under captive conditions
- accept prepared (non-living) food
- have a high **conversion ratio** i.e. convert food ⟶ flesh efficiently
- ideally be able to breed under captive conditions
- not be particularly susceptible to disease.

It is usually **expensive** to farm fish so the product should command a **high price**. For this reason the main farmed species in Britain are members of the salmon family.

Fry production
- Fish are often spawned in aquaria using added reproductive hormones.
- Temperature is controlled while fry are 'grown on' (higher temperature gives rapid growth). Oxygen levels are kept high with aerators. Growth hormones may be added to water.
- Fry of **uniform size** are released into the farming pens. This reduces the chance of the fish eating each other!

Disease control – close confinement makes diseases more likely to spread. Pesticides are added to water to control fish lice and fungal infections, and antibiotics are added to food.

Problems
- Very high food costs.
- Poor control of temperature and oxygen availability in large outdoor farming pens.
- Much more research necessary to obtain highest yields – **selective breeding** programmes to develop new fish varieties with improved growth rates and conversion ratios.

Environmental concerns
- Pollution by pesticides which may kill organisms that are foods for wild species.
- Excess food and fish faeces create nutrient-rich environment below netted area ⟶ growth of bacterial population ⟶ increased **biological oxygen demand**.

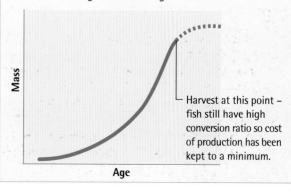

Age for harvesting

Harvest at this point – fish still have high conversion ratio so cost of production has been kept to a minimum.

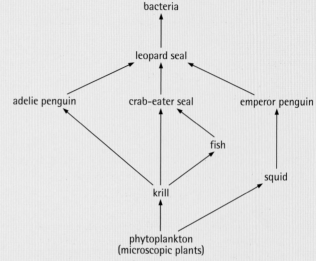

1 The diagram on the right represents a food web in the Southern Ocean.

 a i From the diagram, identify an example of each of the following

 a carnivore   a decomposer

 a herbivore   a producer

  ii Draw a food chain of **five** organisms selected from the food web.

 b In most food chains, the number of individuals decreases at each stage in the chain whilst the size of individuals increases. State the stage in the diagram at which this rule does **not** apply. Explain your answer.

 c Explain, with reference to the transfer of energy in food chains, why it might be more efficient for humans to eat herbivores rather than to eat carnivores.

(IGCSE June 1997)

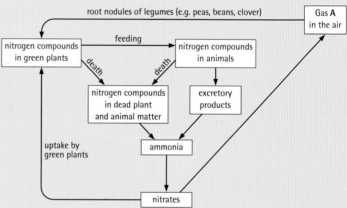

2 The diagram on the right shows part of the nitrogen cycle.

 a i Name the gas **A**.

  ii Copy the diagram and write the letter **B** next to **two** of the arrows in the cycle which represent stages involving bacteria.

  iii On your copy, label with an **X** the arrow which represents the process of denitrification.

 b i Name a chemical which is made by plants from the nitrates they absorb from the soil.

  ii Name an excretory product containing nitrogen, which is produced by animals.

(IGCSE Nov. 1997)

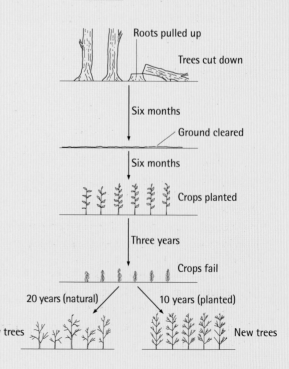

3 The drawings on the right show some of the changes which can take place in a tropical rain forest because of human activity.

 a Give TWO reasons why rain forests have been cut down.

 b The amount of rain falling on the forest area decreases after the trees have been cut down. Suggest the possible reason for this.

 c Describe the effects that removing the trees has on the animal life in the area.

 d Why do the crops fail after a few years?

 e Some of the world's mixed forests have been cut down and the area replanted with only one or two species of tree.

 Explain the disadvantage of this compared with allowing the forest to regrow naturally with many species of tree.

(Edexcel June 1997)

4 The red squirrel is a small rodent which feeds largely on pine cones. Two ecologists were interested in the conservation of the red squirrel, and particularly in the reasons for its decline in number. They studied the number of deaths of red squirrels in a large sampling area. The data in the table refer to the number of deaths in one year.

Month	Number of deaths
Jan	22
Feb	29
Mar	32
Apr	20
May	14
Jun	17
Jul	10
Aug	12
Sep	10
Oct	22
Nov	26
Dec	36

a Plot this data as a bar chart.

b Calculate the total number of deaths in this year.

c In which two months did most deaths occur? Suggest why.

d The scientists believed that the maximum population existed in August (the young are born in April–May). They sampled the population, using the mark–recapture method, and obtained the following data.

Number in first sample, marked and released	Number in second sample	Number of marked animals in second sample
100	80	25

Calculate the total population size at the time of the sample.

e The population of red squirrels in Britain has fallen rapidly during this century. They are protected under the Wildlife and Countryside Act, so cannot legally be killed by humans. Grey squirrels do not enjoy the same protection. Suggest two measures which could be taken to increase the number of red squirrels.

5 Red spider mites are common and troublesome pests in greenhouses where tomatoes are growing. The numbers of red spider mites may be controlled by a predator called Spidex™.

a What term is used to describe this way of controlling pests?

In an experiment tomato growers placed a Spidex™ on a piece of string.

They measured its speed of walking along the string.

They did more speed measurements using stems of different varieties of tomatoes instead of string.

b In this experiment there must be no red spider mites on the tomato stems. Suggest a reason for this.

Their results are shown in the bar chart.

c Use the information in the bar chart to help you to answer these questions.

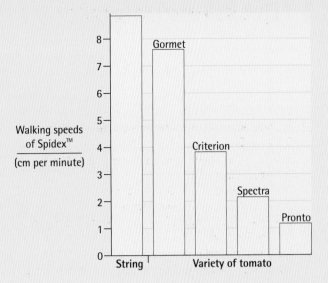

i Name the variety of tomato on which the predator moved at about 40% of its average speed on string.

ii From the results of the experiment suggest which variety of tomato has the hairiest stem. Give a reason for your choice.

d Suggest why tomato growers have been interested in measuring the speed that Spidex™ walks on tomato stems.

Red spider mites occur in patches in greenhouses. Tomato growers prefer to use another predator, Fightamites B™ to control red spider mites. Fightamites B™ are insects.

e Suggest why Fightamites B™ will find the red spider mites before Spidex™ finds them.

f Sometimes tomato growers use pesticides at the same time as they are using Spidex™ and Fightamites B™. Explain why growers may need to use pesticides as well as Spidex™ and Fightamites B™.

(MEG June 1998)

- To understand what is meant by disease
- To appreciate that disease may have a number of causes
- To understand that some microorganisms may cause disease

What is disease?

The process of homeostasis maintains optimum conditions for body function (see page 112). However, sometimes the mechanisms of homeostasis cannot cope with changes in the internal environment of the body. A person in this situation will show **signs** (such as a raised body temperature) and experience **symptoms** (such as feeling tired). The person is no longer 'at ease' but is 'dis-eased'. **Disease**, then, is the state of the body when it cannot cope with changes by the normal homeostatic methods.

Classification of diseases

There are two main classes of disease – **infectious** and **non-infectious. Infectious diseases** can be 'caught', or passed on from one individual to another. These diseases are caused by some other living organism, usually a microorganism. Infectious diseases can be classified according to how the disease-causing organism is passed from one individual to another, as illustrated below.

Non-infectious diseases are not 'caught' from another individual. These diseases may have a number of causes, illustrated opposite.

Patterns of disease vary in time and space

In the eighteenth century many British children died from bacterial infections. With the development of antibiotics, immunisation programmes and improved public hygiene, deaths from infectious

Infectious diseases

These are caused by organisms, which may spread in a number of ways:

In infected water e.g. *Cholera* bacteria
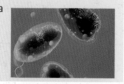

In droplets in the air e.g. influenza virus

By direct contact (contagious) e.g. athlete's foot fungus or head lice – insects

In contaminated food (causes food poisoning) e.g. *Salmonella* bacteria or pork tapeworm

By animal vectors e.g. *Plasmodium* protoctist (causes malaria) via *Anopheles* mosquito

Via body fluids e.g. hepatitis B virus or human immunodeficiency virus (HIV) (causes AIDS)
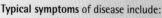

Typical symptoms of disease include:
- **sweating/fever** due to resetting of body's thermostat
- **vomiting/diarrhoea** due to body's attempts to clear gut of irritants
- **pain** due to release of toxins by pathogens.

A doctor might use a thermometer to recognise a sign such as raised body temperature.

Infectious diseases. Parasites such as tapeworms and head lice are not considered to cause 'diseases' by some people, but they do cause distress to the person affected by them and the body is less 'at ease' when it has been colonised by such a parasite. Parasites may be thought of as causing long-term disease.

Non-infectious diseases

Degenerative – organs and tissues work less well as they age. This is thought to be due to changes in body chemicals caused by **free radicals** such as the peroxide ion
e.g. heart attacks, cataracts, hardening of the arteries.

Deficiency – poor diet may deprive the body of some essential substance e.g. scurvy is caused by lack of vitamin C – see page 36.

Allergy – sensitivity to some antigen in the environment, e.g. hay fever (pollen is the antigen) – see page 299.

Environmental – some factor in the environment may trigger a dangerous or abnormal reaction e.g. overexposure to ultraviolet radiation may cause abnormal cell division leading to skin cancer – see page 196.

Inherited/metabolic – some failure in the body's normal set of chemical reactions, e.g.
- sickle cell anaemia (abnormal haemoglobin, page 206)
- cystic fibrosis (production of thick mucus, page 206)
- diabetes (failure to produce enough insulin, page 106).
These conditions are due to alterations in the genes.

Psychological/mental – changes in the working of the brain may lead to abnormal behaviour, e.g. schizophrenia, depression.

Self-induced – some abuse of the body may affect its function, e.g. lung cancer caused by cigarette smoking, cirrhosis of the liver caused by alcohol abuse, see page 98.

diseases in the UK are now much less common. Smallpox was a major killer worldwide until the 1960s, but effective vaccination has now eliminated this disease (see page 292).

In the Western world the major killers are now 'diseases of affluence', caused by our relatively wealthy lifestyle. Along with accidents, coronary heart disease and cancer cause most deaths in Britain, largely the result of smoking, eating too many sugary and fatty foods, and lack of exercise.

Infectious diseases that are spread by **vectors** (e.g. malaria spread by mosquitoes) are naturally confined to those parts of the world in which the vector can live and breed. In the same way, diseases spread by contact are limited by the number of people likely to meet an infected individual. In recent years there has been concern over the possible spread of infectious diseases because:

- Easier travel by air means that diseases can be carried from one country to another before the infected person develops any symptoms.
- Global warming has increased the range of some insect vectors.
- A greater dependence on communal eating and fast food has led to the easier transmission of organisms that cause food poisoning.

1. Suggest three ways in which microbes might be harmful to humans, and three ways in which they might be helpful. Give examples to support your suggestions.

2. Suggest three causes of non-infectious diseases, and give one example of each.

3. How can infectious diseases spread? Give examples to support your answer.

4. What is the difference between the signs and the symptoms of a disease? What are the causes of 'typical' disease symptoms?

5. Suggest why measles is very rarely fatal in Britain, yet still ranks among the top five killer diseases in the developing world.

6. How have changes in human lifestyle contributed to the spread of infectious diseases?

14·2 Pathogens are organisms that cause disease

Objectives
▪ To recall that a pathogen is an organism that causes disease
▪ To give examples of different types of pathogen and the diseases they cause
▪ To understand the virus life cycle, and how viruses can be controlled

Pathogens are parasites

Any organism that affects the body to cause disease is a **pathogen** (or **pathogenic organism**). Pathogens are **parasites**, that is, they live on the body of a host and cause it some harm:

▪ **by secreting poisons (toxins)** – this is especially common from bacteria. The toxins have different effects, for example the organism *Clostridium botulinum* produces a deadly nerve poison, whereas bacteria of the *Salmonella* group release a toxin which irritates the lining of the gut.

▪ **as a result of multiplication** – the organism may reproduce quickly and produce such a large colony that it damages cells directly, as in malaria, or it uses up compounds which should be used by the host cell, as in polio. Many viruses multiply and cause host cells to burst.

▪ **as a result of the immune response** – when the host detects pathogens it directs more blood to the site of infection. This can cause swelling and soreness, and usually causes a rise in body temperature.

There are many pathogens that are parasites on humans, causing diseases. The following table illustrates the range of pathogenic organisms.

Pathogen type	Size	Disease in humans
Virus	About 1 nm (1/1000 μm)	Influenza AIDS
Bacterium	About 1 μm	Cholera Food poisoning
Protoctist	Up to 1 mm	Dysentery Malaria
Fungus	May be extensive	Athlete's foot Ringworm
'Worms'	Up to several metres	Tapeworm *Toxocara*

Viruses

Viruses are responsible for many of the most serious human diseases. Viruses differ from the true living organisms in that they cannot survive and reproduce outside the cells of their host – every virus is a parasite. The structure of viruses was described on page 227. Remember that viruses are so small that they can pass through filters and screens which will trap any other organism. We use the electron microscope to study viruses. The life cycle of a virus is outlined in the diagram opposite.

Measles is an important viral disease

In the 1950s and 1960s measles was widespread in Britain. Cooperation between scientists, doctors and health authorities has reduced the number of cases of this disease, and also its severity. Measles is still an extremely important disease in developing countries, where the poor health and malnutrition of many of the children makes its effects far more serious. The most frequent viral infection in Britain is probably the common cold. The table opposite describes how measles and the common cold are controlled.

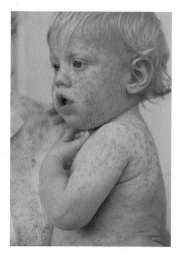

A child with measles

Viruses affect other organisms as well as humans

Viruses also cause diseases in domestic animals and in crops. The **tobacco mosaic virus**, as its name suggests, infects tobacco plants and can devastate tobacco crops.

Virus reproduction destroys host cells.

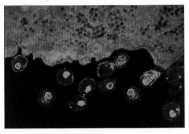

The electron micrograph was taken shortly after a cell had been invaded by a virus. The virus has reproduced, using the host cell's metabolic processes, and a large number of viruses are now about to be released as the host cell bursts.

1 Virus sticks to surface membrane of selected host cell.

The virus recognises the host cell by protein markers on the host cell surface membrane. Influenza viruses, for example, select the cells lining the human respiratory passages.

Some viruses have genes made of RNA, not DNA. Their RNA genes must be converted into DNA genes before they can be incorporated into host genetic material.

Nucleus

2 Virus genes enter host cell and become incorporated into host genetic material.

3 Virus uses host cell **transcription** to produce a 'virus' messenger RNA.

4 Host cell ribosomes read virus messenger RNA to produce many copies of viral protein coat.

6 Host cell assembles virus genes and protein coats into many new viruses.

5 Virus uses host cell **replication** to produce many copies of virus genes.

7 Host cell bursts to release many new viruses. Each new virus can then infect another host cell.

The fragments of the burst host cell irritate the lining of the nose and throat. This is what causes the sneezes associated with colds and flu.

Mutations (see page 200) occur at this stage, so new strains of virus arise. These can often evade the prepared defences of the immune system (see page 296).

Measles and the common cold are viral diseases.

Disease	Symptoms	Transmission	Control
Measles	Fever Red, blotchy skin rash Cough	Droplet, and sometimes by direct contact with soiled clothes	There is **no reservoir organism**, i.e. the virus lives only in humans. The simplest control is to limit contact between people with the disease and those without it. **Lifelong immunity** results from injection with a live vaccine (see page 296) or from accidental infection. ANTIBIOTICS HAVE NO EFFECT as they kill only **bacteria**
Common cold	Mild fever Fatigue Sore throat and runny nose Sneezing	Droplet and close personal contact	Transfer of infection is most likely from close personal contact (e.g. nasal mucus on hands) or from droplet infection. Control therefore involves good personal hygiene, e.g. sneezing into handkerchiefs or, preferably, disposable tissues. **Lifelong immunity** results from infection, but virus strains change and new strains cause further infection

1 Name three different types of pathogen. In each case state one example of a disease caused by this type of pathogen.

2 How do viruses cause disease?

3 Explain, giving an example, how knowledge of a virus life cycle can help to control the disease caused by the virus.

Humans and microorganisms

14·3 Bacteria have no distinct nucleus but carry out metabolic processes

Objectives

▶ To recall the structure of a typical bacterial cell
▶ To give examples of pathogenic bacteria and the diseases they cause in humans
▶ To understand the form of a bacterial growth curve
▶ To appreciate the need for safe techniques of culturing bacteria

Bacterial diseases

The structure of bacteria and their importance to humans are outlined on page 226. Some bacteria cause serious human diseases. The table below gives some examples.

Bacterial growth curves

Bacteria can reproduce extremely rapidly (see page 226). A **growth curve** for a bacterial population is plotted by counting the number of bacteria in a culture vessel at fixed time intervals; the results can be frightening (see opposite). Bacteria make huge demands on their environment during rapid reproduction under ideal conditions, which may cause problems for human hosts. To control bacterial disease, this rapid increase in population must be prevented.

The culture of microorganisms

Scientists often need to study the growth and characteristics of microorganisms such as bacteria. The growing (culture) of microbes must be carried out extremely carefully, since:

▶ The microbes under study might be dangerous.
▶ The food sources used by the cultured microbes could be colonised by other more dangerous species.
▶ The results obtained will only be useful if the experimental conditions are strictly controlled to prevent contamination by other organisms.

The techniques used to culture uncontaminated populations of bacteria in a safe and controlled way are called **aseptic techniques**, described on the opposite page.

Bacterial diseases

Disease	Symptoms	Transmission	Control
Cholera	Diarrhoea Thirst Severe gut pains	Contamination of food and water by the faeces of an infected person	Good sanitation Personal hygiene (washing hands after defaecation) Boiling drinking water Vaccine is available Sufferers **must** rehydrate or disease is fatal.
Whooping cough	Uncontrollable outbursts of coughing – 'whooping' sound as breaths are taken	Droplet	Isolation of infected individuals A vaccine is available, and natural immunity develops following an attack.
Tetanus	Severe muscle spasms (the common name for this disease is lockjaw)	Contact of deep wound with spores, usually from the soil	**Vaccination**, repeated every five years An **antitoxin** can be used for people who have contracted the disease. The disease can be fatal if untreated.
Tuberculosis (TB)	Can cause respiratory failure if breathing muscles are affected	Droplet in mucus Consumption of infected milk (cows can have bovine TB)	BCG vaccination (but only 70% effective) is now given to 6-week-old babies since TB is very severe in children. Overcrowding and 'spitting up' mucus make transmission more likely.

Any bacterial disease can be treated with **antibiotics**. Children exposed to whooping cough are given antibiotics as a **preventive** measure.

TB is now the infectious disease that causes most deaths worldwide, due to:
■ poor disease control programmes
■ resistance to antibiotics (see page 310)
■ co-infection with HIV (see page 292)
■ a rapid increase in the population of young adults, the age group most at risk from TB

Humans and microorganisms

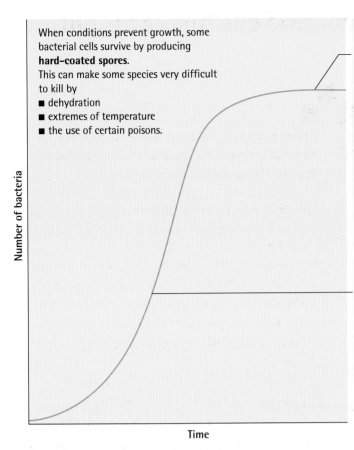

When conditions prevent growth, some bacterial cells survive by producing **hard-coated spores**.
This can make some species very difficult to kill by
- dehydration
- extremes of temperature
- the use of certain poisons.

Stationary phase – population remains constant as the number that die is balanced by the number produced by binary fission. The rate of binary fission is limited by:
- availability of nutrients
- availability of oxygen, in aerobic species
- temperature
- availability of water
- pH.

The number of deaths may be increased by:
- production of waste which increases in concentration as population becomes more dense.

Exponential phase – population grows rapidly, doubling perhaps as often as every 20 minutes.
The bacteria require:
- amino acids, for the synthesis of proteins
- carbohydrate, e.g. glucose, for the release of energy by respiration
- water, as a solvent and a reagent in biochemical reactions
- a suitable temperature, for optimum enzyme activity.

Understanding what bacteria need to reproduce can be useful in:
- preventing food spoilage
- controlling infections
- providing the best conditions for growth of useful bacteria.

Safe techniques in microbiology

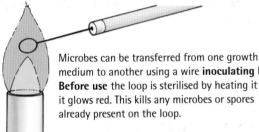

Microbes can be transferred from one growth medium to another using a wire **inoculating loop**. **Before use** the loop is sterilised by heating it until it glows red. This kills any microbes or spores already present on the loop.

The transferred microbes are 'streaked' onto the fresh agar plate. The lid is removed for as short a time as possible, to reduce the risk of contamination by microbes in the air.

The sterile loop is dipped into a source of microbes (e.g. from food, such as milk, water samples, skin, or pure cultures from suppliers) and touched onto a sterile agar plate.

Microbes such as bacteria can be grown in **Petri dishes** containing a layer of agar gel. This provides nutrients and water for the microbes to feed on.

Cultures growing on agar are observed from above.

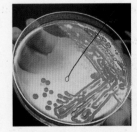

Labelling on bottom of plate, **in case** lids become mixed up!

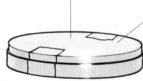

The dish is:
- sealed with tape
- placed upside down (to prevent any condensation falling back onto the agar)
- put in an incubating oven. 25°C allows growth of many microbes but **not** those that colonise the human body, which would be more dangerous.

---

1 Name two bacterial diseases in humans, and state their symptoms. What does the control of all bacterial diseases have in common?

2 Name one bacterial disease that affects domestic animals. How could this disease affect humans?

3 What are the requirements for the rapid growth of a bacterial population? State the function of each of these requirements.

4 Describe how you would safely collect any bacteria present in a sample of river water.

14·4 Fungi, worms and protoctists can also cause disease

Objectives
- To understand that some larger organisms may also cause disease
- To know examples of diseases caused by fungi, worms and protoctists
- To understand how study of an organism's life cycle can offer effective methods of disease control

Many important diseases are caused by microorganisms that are not viruses or bacteria, or larger organisms.

Fungi

Fungi colonise new habitats by producing huge numbers of spores (see page 228). Fungal infections are common in warm, moist conditions. Two important fungal diseases are outlined below.

Worms

Worms are not microorganisms, but they can cause disease. **Tapeworms** are parasites that live in the guts of other animals, including humans.

Another worm responsible for disease in humans is *Toxocara*. The adult worm lives in dogs and cats, and the larva, which causes the symptoms, can invade the liver, lungs and sometimes the eyes of humans. Without treatment this can cause serious, permanent damage.

Protoctists

Protoctists are single-celled organisms, sometimes large enough to be seen with the naked eye (see page 224). They cause some devastating diseases in humans. The diagram on the opposite page describes how the disease **malaria** (so called because it was once believed to be caused by 'bad air') is caused by infection with a protoctist called *Plasmodium*. Understanding the life cycle of *Plasmodium* offers methods of controlling the spread of malaria.

Malaria has killed more humans than any other disease. The mosquito carries the protoctist – it is the vector. The mosquito does not itself cause the disease.

Disease	Symptoms	Transmission	Control
Athlete's foot	Itching between toes Flaking of skin	Direct contact Contact with towels Via damp surfaces (e.g. at swimming pools or changing rooms)	Personal hygiene – not sharing towels, for example Thorough drying between toes Using fungicidal creams on the affected area

In the mid-1840s the Irish potato crop was ruined by a disease, potato blight, caused by the fungus *Phytophthora infestans*. The hyphae of the fungus penetrate the leaves of the potato plant and feed on the cells there.
The disease is now rare, because:
- resistant strains of potato have been developed
- potatoes are rarely grown in warm, humid conditions
- fungicide sprays kill the spores
- legislation prevents re-sowing in infected areas.

The life cycle of *Plasmodium*

The *Anopheles* mosquito is the **vector** for the pathogen *Plasmodium*. *Plasmodium* multiplies in the stomach wall of the mosquito, then migrates to the salivary glands.

Adult mosquitoes can be controlled by insecticides, such as DDT, sprayed onto their resting places.

Plasmodium is the protoctist that causes malaria.

It can reproduce sexually inside the mosquito, and the resulting variation (see page 200) makes the production of successful vaccines very difficult.

☐ = point of control

1
An infected mosquito passes on parasites to an uninfected human. *Plasmodium* passes down the piercing mouthparts (see page 55) from the mosquito's salivary glands.

Control methods include:
- sleeping under mosquito nets to prevent biting
- spraying of insect-repellent chemicals onto the skin
- wearing long sleeved clothes during the evening (time when most likely to be bitten).

4
An uninfected mosquito picks up parasites from the blood of an infected person.

Plasmodium

Liver

3
Parasites released from the liver invade red blood cells where they feed on haemoglobin and divide by **multiple fission**. The red blood cells filled with parasites burst and release the parasites into the blood.

Effects on the red blood cells cause many of the symptoms of malaria:
- tiredness, since fewer red blood cells means less oxygen is transported
- fever, as the red blood cells burst.

2
Parasites multiply rapidly in the human's liver, and are then released into the blood.

Drugs such as Paludrin and Larium control the disease by limiting entry of *Plasmodium* to the liver and reducing multiplication of the parasite.

Mosquitoes breed in bodies of still water, such as lakes and ponds. Rafts of eggs are laid which hatch into larvae, then pupae, which hang just below the water's surface to obtain oxygen through a short air tube.

This is a weak point in the vector's life cycle, and control methods include:
- spraying oil on the surface of the water, to block the breathing tubes
- draining marshes and swamps
- introducing small fish, called mosquito fish, which feed on larvae and pupae

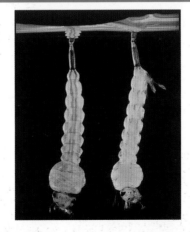

Tonic water contains **quinine**, an anti-malarial drug. Early colonists of malarial areas could justify drinking gin and tonic!

People with sickle cell anaemia are protected from malaria. The parasite cannot feed so well inside 'sickle' cells (see page 206).

1 Use the headings Disease, Causative agent, (Symptoms), Transmission and Control to describe the disease potato blight. Why does it make sense to replace the term symptoms with signs for this disease?

2 Two of the symptoms of malaria are fever and fatigue. What causes these symptoms?

3 Why are children more likely to become infected with *Toxocara* than adults?

Objectives
- To recall that pathogens cause disease only when they gain access to body tissues
- To recognise that food and water are possible means of entry to body tissues
- To understand the processes involved in the provision of a safe water supply

Limiting the spread of diseases

Pathogenic microbes can only cause disease if they are able to enter the body and invade the tissues. The body has defences against disease, but there are a number of weaknesses (see page 294). For example, food and water may contain pathogenic microbes. *Salmonella* and *Escherichia coli* (*E. coli*), which cause food poisoning, enter the body in this way, and so do *Cholera vibrio* and *Amoeba* which are waterborne organisms causing cholera and dysentery, respectively. We try to protect ourselves from these diseases by making sure our drinking water, milk and foods are pathogen free.

Safe water: sanitation and water treatment

Living organisms need water for a number of reasons (see page 8). Water can be lost very rapidly from the human body and we need access to a supply of drinking water. Water supplies are kept **potable** (pathogen-free and drinkable) by both **sanitation** and by **sewage treatment**.

Sanitation is the removal of faeces from waste water so that any pathogens they contain cannot infect drinking water. Where a good water supply is available, a flush WC is connected to the water carriage system and a flow of water carries the waste away. The waste is then treated at a **sewage treatment plant** so that the valuable water can be recycled. The page opposite shows one type of sewage treatment plant called the **activated sludge system**.

The treatment of the sewage has two functions:

- to destroy or eliminate potential pathogens – either by the high temperature in the anaerobic digestion tank, or by chlorination of the water before it is discharged

- to remove organic compounds (mainly in faeces and urine). These might otherwise contribute to the **biological oxygen demand** (BOD – see page 264) of the water into which the treated sewage is discharged. Organic compounds are digested by fungi and bacteria.

In the activated sludge chamber, powerful jets of air keep the sludge aerated so that the processes of decomposition and nitrification (see page 256) can be completed in 8–12 hours. This means that large quantities of sewage can be processed very quickly.

Storms and floods can be extremely dangerous! Main sewers can become overloaded and 'back up' so that faeces may be deposited onto land by the flood water. Many people may die of waterborne diseases following such natural disasters.

1. Why is a supply of water essential to humans? What dangers might be present in a water supply?

2. How does the treatment of sewage benefit both humans and the environment?

3. Name two waterborne diseases. Why are these diseases common in poor rural areas of developing countries, and in cities following very heavy rainfall?

4. a 'Sewage treatment involves both physical and biological processes'. Explain this statement.

   b The supply of safe water also involves some chemical treatment. Why would a Health Authority insist on the addition of:
   i chlorine and   ii fluoride to water supplies?

Humans and microorganisms

Sewage treatment provides clean water by a combination of physical and biological methods

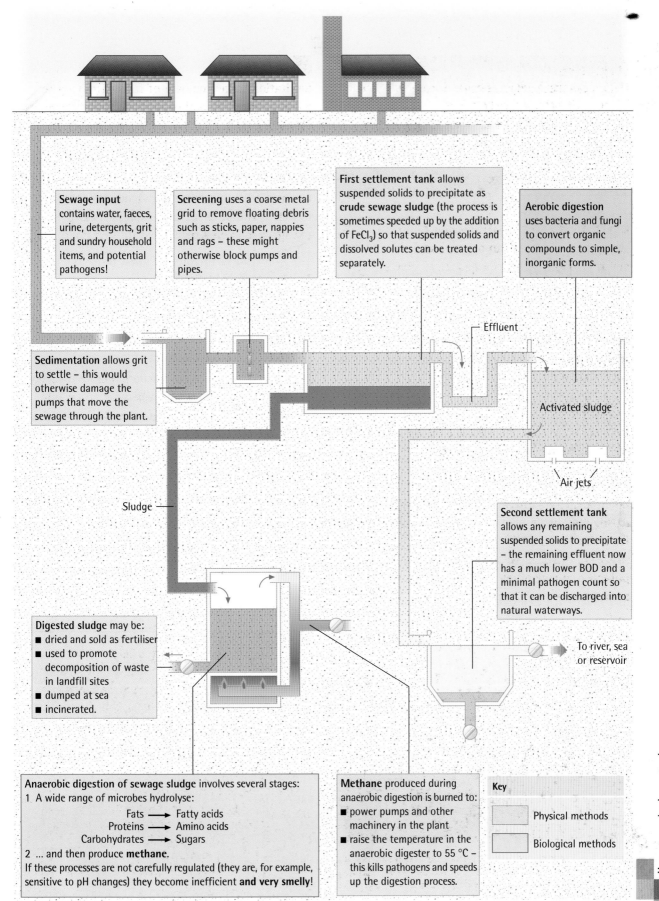

Sewage input contains water, faeces, urine, detergents, grit and sundry household items, and potential pathogens!

Screening uses a coarse metal grid to remove floating debris such as sticks, paper, nappies and rags – these might otherwise block pumps and pipes.

First settlement tank allows suspended solids to precipitate as **crude sewage sludge** (the process is sometimes speeded up by the addition of $FeCl_3$) so that suspended solids and dissolved solutes can be treated separately.

Aerobic digestion uses bacteria and fungi to convert organic compounds to simple, inorganic forms.

Effluent

Sedimentation allows grit to settle – this would otherwise damage the pumps that move the sewage through the plant.

Activated sludge

Air jets

Sludge

Second settlement tank allows any remaining suspended solids to precipitate – the remaining effluent now has a much lower BOD and a minimal pathogen count so that it can be discharged into natural waterways.

Digested sludge may be:
■ dried and sold as fertiliser
■ used to promote decomposition of waste in landfill sites
■ dumped at sea
■ incinerated.

To river, sea or reservoir

Anaerobic digestion of sewage sludge involves several stages:
1 A wide range of microbes hydrolyse:

Fats ⟶ Fatty acids
Proteins ⟶ Amino acids
Carbohydrates ⟶ Sugars

2 ... and then produce **methane**.
If these processes are not carefully regulated (they are, for example, sensitive to pH changes) they become inefficient **and very smelly!**

Methane produced during anaerobic digestion is burned to:
■ power pumps and other machinery in the plant
■ raise the temperature in the anaerobic digester to 55 °C – this kills pathogens and speeds up the digestion process.

Key

Physical methods

Biological methods

Humans and microorganisms

14·6 Preventing disease: safe food

Objectives
- To understand how microorganisms can affect human food supplies
- To know how safe supplies of milk are provided
- To understand the dangers of food poisoning
- To understand how the risks of food poisoning can be minimised

Human foods need to be protected from microorganisms for two reasons:

- the microorganisms might be decomposers and **spoil the food**
- the microorganisms might be pathogenic and **cause disease**.

Food poisoning

Food poisoning is caused by eating contaminated food which contains harmful numbers of food-poisoning microbes. The symptoms of food poisoning may be due to:

- the microorganism 'feeding' on the host tissues as it reproduces
- toxins released onto the food by the microorganism or released inside the host as the microbe reproduces.

A number of bacteria can cause food poisoning, including *Clostridium botulinum* (found in soil, fish and meat – it makes the most deadly nerve toxin produced by a living organism), *Listeria monocytogenes* (found in soft cheeses and pâtés, and becoming more common as we eat more 'convenience foods') and the *Salmonella* group. The diagram below shows some questions and answers about bacteria and food poisoning. Thorough cooking kills any bacteria in food, but food may become contaminated after being cooked, or may not be cooked well enough.

The following **principles of good food hygiene** help to prevent food poisoning:

- Avoid contamination of food by bacteria – wash hands, cooking utensils and surfaces carefully during food preparation, and package food carefully during transport and storage.
- Prevent any bacteria that do gain entry to food from multiplying – see page 290.
- Destroy any remaining bacteria – cook the food thoroughly.

Flash pasteurisation preserves milk

Milk is an excellent food, and it is readily available in large quantities. Bacteria may act on the milk sugar and milk protein to make it go sour and reduce its food value. The benefits of **sterilisation** and **flash pasteurisation** are outlined on the page opposite. The *controlled* spoilage of milk is important in cheese and yoghurt production – see page 307.

The causes and symptoms of food poisoning

How do the bacteria get into the food?	**Which are the high-risk foods?**	**What are the characteristic symptoms?**

Contaminated water used during preparation

Poor hygiene e.g. unwashed hands during preparation

- cooked meats and poultry
- cooked rice
- shellfish
- dishes made with raw eggs, e.g. custard, ice cream

- **abdominal pain**
- **diarrhoea**
- **vomiting**

Contamination during storage e.g. uncooked foods stored alongside cooked foods

Symptoms usually develop 8–36 hours after eating the food, and diarrhoea and vomiting may lead to **dehydration**.

Humans and microorganisms

Milk treatments

Fresh milk from cow contains very few bacteria

Some bacteria are picked up from:
■ surface of udder
■ milking machinery

Milk is refrigerated and transported to factory

At the factory the milk may contain 10 thousand million bacteria per litre

Milk is a valuable food
It contains:
■ protein, carbohydrate and fat
■ vitamins A and D
■ calcium
but has no dietary fibre or iron.
These nutrients also make milk an excellent food for the growth of microorganisms!

Infection of milk with pathogens e.g. *E. coli* 0154 is most likely when the preservation unit is on the farm itself, rather than in a highly controlled factory environment

Without any preservation

Fats and some **proteins**

Other bacteria

Alcohol, hydrogen sulphide, amine

Unpleasant smell and taste

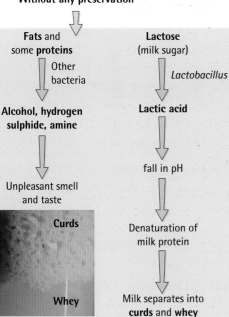

Curds

Whey

Lactose (milk sugar)

Lactobacillus

Lactic acid

fall in pH

Denaturation of milk protein

Milk separates into **curds** and **whey**

Preservation

Ultra-heat treatment (sterilisation) 130 °C for 2 seconds

Milk with:
■ no bacteria
■ 6-month storage life
but
■ altered taste

Flash pasteurisation 72 °C for 15 seconds

Milk with:
■ no pathogens (but some *Lactobacillus* remain)
■ storage time of 6–10 days if refrigerated
■ no alteration to taste

Milk can be processed further!
■ **Skimmed milk** has the fat removed
■ **Fortified milk** has added calcium and vitamins
■ **Evaporated milk** is sterilised and has its water content reduced by 30%
■ **Condensed milk** has added sugar and its water content reduced by 65%

---

1 a Before being sold to the public milk is usually treated in one of several ways. The table below shows three different methods of treating milk and the effects of these treatments.

  i During which treatment is the milk heated to the highest temperature?

  ii Which treatment requires the longest time to complete?

  iii Why do sterilised and UHT milk not go sour in the unopened containers?

  iv Why might the milk distributors find the sterilisation process a disadvantage?

b Staff working at the cooked meat counter of a large store are instructed to place a new piece of plastic film on the scales before weighing each portion of meat. Tongs must be used when meat is moved from the display area to the scales. Explain clearly why these instructions are given to the staff.

(CCEA June 1988 [part])

Method	Temperature of treatment/°C	Time of treatment/s	Effect of treatment on bacteria in milk	Effect of treatment on taste
Pasteurisation	71.6	15	Kills some bacteria	No effect
Sterilisation	104.5	15	Kills all bacteria	Changed
UHT	132.0	2	Kills all bacteria	Slight change

14·7 Food preservation techniques

Objectives

▪ To understand how the risks of food poisoning can be minimised

▪ To recognise that food preservation techniques depend on a knowledge of the growth requirements of microorganisms

Microbes, like any other living organism, demand certain factors from their environment – they require food, water, the correct atmosphere, a suitable temperature for enzyme action and reproduction, and conditions of pH and solute

Dehydration – one of the most efficient methods involves **freeze–drying.** Food is frozen rapidly then rewarmed under reduced pressure, giving an open granular structure (e.g. in coffee or dried milk).
Benefits: freeze-dried foods rehydrate well when carried out in a nitrogen-containing atmosphere, offers 2–3 years' storage
Drawback: any fats present are easily oxidised (rancidity) because of open structure.

Canning – heat sterilisation kills microorganisms and their spores. If the sterilised food is to be stored for long periods, it must be sterilised in a sealed container which will prevent recolonisation by new microbes.

High osmolarity – salt or sugar can be added to create high solute concentrations in foods. Microorganisms lose water by osmosis and do not grow.

Coffee noir

JAMINSON

VIT C DRINK

BEANZ 57

Heat – steam drives out air

Can closed – falling volume should suck ends inwards

'Bulge' – evidence of a 'blown' can due to gas released by respiring microbes

Cans of food are cooled in water after closing – any gap in the sealing might allow entry of microbes as water would be drawn inwards. Cooling waters are chlorinated to prevent accidental reintroduction of microbes.

Freezing – most fresh foods contain over 60% water. If water is frozen it cannot be used by microorganisms.

Control of pH – microbes may grow more slowly under acidic conditions.
Yoghurt: lactic acid is produced by lactose fermentation.
Pickles: preserved by adding vinegar (aqueous solution of ethanoic acid).

Irradiation – sterilisation by radiation is permitted for medical supplies and drugs, but not for food preservation in the UK (although currently it is the only effective method for reducing *Salmonella* in frozen meat). This process is expensive.

cobalt-60 ⎤
⎥ **gamma-radiation** – dose required to kill microbes is usually greater than dose permitted for humans, but radiation does not stay in
caesium-137 ⎦ the food.

Chemical preservatives –
■ typically act as **antioxidants**
■ removal of O_2 gas and lower pH both limit growth of microbes
■ sulphur dioxide/sulphites: used in soft drinks but may cause **asthma** attacks in sensitive individuals
■ nitrates: meats such as ham and bacon are **cured** using nitrate but there is some danger that nitrates react with amino acids in foods to produce **cancer-causing chemicals.**

Food preservation techniques may kill microbes or prevent their reproduction. Different preservation techniques are suitable for different food types.

concentration which do not damage them. Any technique for the preservation of food must remove one or more of these factors from the microbes' environment. At the same time, the technique must not:

- affect the nutritional value or taste of the food
- cause any harm to the potential consumer
- be so costly that profits are lost.

Some techniques

In a **refrigerator** the food is kept between 0 °C and 4 °C. This slows down the reproduction of microorganisms. A variety of other food preservation techniques is outlined on the page opposite.

Preventing *Salmonella* food poisoning

The *Salmonella* group of bacteria is widespread in eggs and poultry. Salmonella is responsible for many cases of food poisoning, but the dangers can be minimised. Controlling the *Salmonella* group of food-poisoning bacteria depends on using correct techniques of hygiene, storage and preservation, as shown below.

Salmonella **control**

Correct cooking – cooking at 68 °C kills *Salmonella* in meat. The cooking time must be long enough for the centre of the chicken to reach this temperature.

Intensive rearing of chickens makes it easy for *Salmonella* bacteria to spread. Infected chickens pass the bacterium from their gut to their faeces, which drop to the floor of the rearing shed. Poor hygiene may then allow these bacteria to pass via hands and working surfaces to the chicken carcasses.

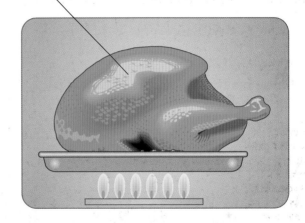

The *Salmonella* bacteria are not very active – an intake of 10 000 000 is needed to start an infection. The multiplying bacteria release a toxin, and this causes a severe inflammation of the gut. The inflammation causes diarrhoea, vomiting, fever and pain, leading to dehydration and even death.

Treatment – antibiotics are not very effective because they do not reach the gut lining. The sufferer must rest and replace lost body fluids with a mixture of water, glucose and salts.

Irradiation may control *Salmonella*
- this kills the bacteria
- there may be some danger to consumers from induced radiation
- it is very expensive, and there is some loss of vitamin content
- this treatment may leave the toxin produced by the bacteria behind.

---

1 a List the requirements that microorganisms have for growth and multiplication.
  b Explain how three named methods of food preservation deny these requirements to microorganisms.

  c Mountaineers and hillwalkers often carry dehydrated foods, because they are very light. What other benefits does food dehydration offer?

14.8 Individuals and the community can fight disease together

Objectives
- To understand that the fight against disease involves several levels of responsibility
- To provide examples of individual, community and worldwide responsibilities

The fight against disease has three levels:

- **personal** – for example, each individual can take responsibility for his or her own social habits
- **community** – for example, local health services must be correctly managed and financed
- **worldwide** – for example, many nations carry out vaccination programmes (see page 297).

Personal responsibility

The **individual** can reduce his or her chances of contracting some diseases by:

- **personal hygiene**
- **balanced diet**
- **regular exercise**
- **not smoking**
- **controlling alcohol intake**

Community responsibility

Living close together in towns and cities means we share many facilities which affect our health. **Community health responsibilities** include:

- Providing safe drinking water and treating sewage (see page 286)
- removing refuse (see diagrams below and right)
- providing medical care for the unwell
- monitoring standards of health and hygiene.

Worldwide responsibility

The **World Health Organisation** (WHO) aims to raise the level of health of all the citizens of the world so that they can lead socially productive lives. They have had some successes:

- reduced infant mortality, by providing a better diet for mothers and their infants
- elimination of smallpox, by a well coordinated vaccination programme
- reduction in malaria, by a variety of control measures (see page 285)
- improved provision of safe water, by the construction of water-treatment plants.

Refuse disposal in land-fill sites

Advantages
- Can help **land reclamation** e.g. in filling old quarry workings.
- Can be made economical in terms of space:
  - lorries use rams to compress rubbish
  - very deep pits can be used.
- Can be situated well away from residential areas, reducing impact of smells and unsightly rubbish.

Disadvantages
- Sites can attract **pests**, such as flies, rats and gulls. These might spread disease (e.g. flies contaminate food) or leave a mess (e.g. gulls leave droppings).
- Ecologically important areas such as marshes and heathland may be used as dumps.

Refuse may be buried under 0.5m of soil. This
- reduces access to pests
- allows bacteria and fungi to decompose organic compounds
- generates **biogas** which can be used to fuel machinery.

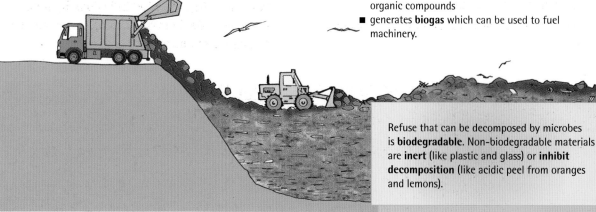

Refuse that can be decomposed by microbes is **biodegradable**. Non-biodegradable materials are **inert** (like plastic and glass) or **inhibit decomposition** (like acidic peel from oranges and lemons).

Humans and microorganisms

Refuse disposal by incineration

Advantages
- Incineration plant is quite small, so valuable land not used.
- No attraction to pests, so less risk of disease.
- Heat generated can be used – incinerators built as part of housing projects can save energy.

Disadvantages
- May generate toxic fumes (especially from burning plastics).
- Can be very expensive to build.
- Seepage of wastes may pollute groundwater.
- Fuel is consumed to begin the combustion process.

Sexually transmitted diseases (STDs)

The control of **sexually transmitted diseases** requires the interaction of individuals and communities. These diseases, some of which are listed on the right, are most likely to be contracted by sexual contact (the responsibility of the individual) but can only be controlled by a concerted effort both locally and worldwide.

Individuals must take care with sexual habits. A STD can be transmitted quickly through a population, so individuals should:

- know the sexual history of their partners
- use a condom for barrier protection
- have a medical check if any symptoms occur.

Communities must offer testing and treatment, e.g. by family doctors.

- Individuals at greatest risk, (e.g. drug users), can be offered testing for HIV.
- Sexual contacts can be traced to identify sources of infection.

Worldwide involvement can include, for example,

- education programmes to prevent infection
- provision of antibiotics
- development of vaccines and antiviral drugs.

Here are some examples of bacterial STD:

- Chlamydia is the most common STD worldwide.
- Gonorrhoea is the second most common, but is declining in developing countries.

Both of these have symptoms of a runny discharge from the urethra, and pain on urination.

- Syphilis is now rare in developed countries. It may have severe long-term symptoms, including damage to the central nervous system.

Bacterial STDs are treated with antibiotics (e.g penicillin, see page 310) but resistant strains are developing.

Viral STDs are increasing in frequency. These include.

- genital warts
- herpes
  Both become more severe with repeated infection.
- AIDS (acquired immune deficiency syndrome):
- is caused by human immunodeficiency virus (HIV)
- is transmitted sexually, or from mother to child, in contaminated blood or organ transplants, or by sharing of needles by intravenous drug users
- causes severe depression of the immune system (see page 296), allowing infections by other pathogens. Death may result from pneumonia, fungal infections or cancer.

---

1 Suggest two steps an individual can take to reduce the risk of named diseases.

2 What are the responsibilities of a community health service?

3 Name one viral and one bacterial sexually transmitted disease (STD).

4 For any one named STD suggest how individuals, local communities and scientists worldwide might be involved in its control.

14·9 Combating infection

Objectives
- To recall what is meant by disease
- To recall that disease can be caused by pathogens, which must first invade the body
- To understand that the body may be able to defend itself against pathogens

Disease (see page 278) is often caused by the invasion of the body by another organism. Organisms that cause disease in this way are called **pathogens** and their attacks on the body result in **infections**.

The skin and defence against disease

The outer layer of the skin, the epidermis, is waxy and impermeable to water and to pathogens (although microorganisms can live on its surface). Natural 'gaps' in the skin may be protected by **chemical** secretions, for example:

- the mouth leads to the gut which is protected by hydrochloric acid in the stomach

- the eyes are protected by lysozyme, an enzyme that destroys bacterial cell walls, in the tears

- the ears are protected by bactericidal ('bacteria-killing') wax.

Physical defences against the entry of microorganisms include the cilia and mucus-secreting cells of the respiratory pathways (see page 76). If the potential pathogens do penetrate these first lines of defence, they might reproduce quickly in the warm, moist, nutrient-filled tissues. Further defence depends upon the **blood**.

Bleeding and clot formation

Blood clotting seals wounds. The blood clot limits the loss of blood and also prevents entry of any pathogens. Clotting depends on **platelets** and **blood proteins**, as outlined in the diagram below.

White blood cells and defence

Organisms that gain entry to the tissues are removed or destroyed by **white blood cells**. These white blood cells must attack only invading organisms and not the body's own cells (although this does happen sometimes, see page 299). The white blood cells recognise foreign particles such as bacteria, or perhaps large molecules such as snake venom, and react against them. These foreign particles are called **antigens**. Potential pathogens have antigens on their surface, and they are

Blood clotting reduces loss of blood and seals the wound against pathogens.

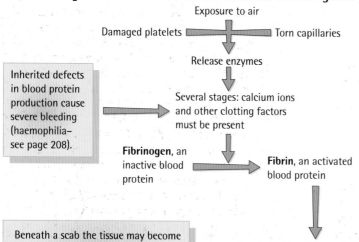

Exposure to air

Damaged platelets ——————— Torn capillaries

Release enzymes

Inherited defects in blood protein production cause severe bleeding (haemophilia– see page 208).

Several stages: calcium ions and other clotting factors must be present

Fibrinogen, an inactive blood protein

Fibrin, an activated blood protein

Beneath a scab the tissue may become red and inflamed. Certain white blood cells release **histamine**, a chemical messenger which allows plasma to leak out of the capillaries. The extra plasma dilutes any toxins which may have entered the wound.

Forms a mesh of fibres which traps red blood cells. These dry out to form a **scab** which closes the wound and prevents the entry of pathogens.

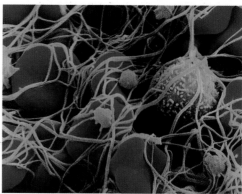

Fibrin fibres trap blood cells to form a scab.

Phagocyte action

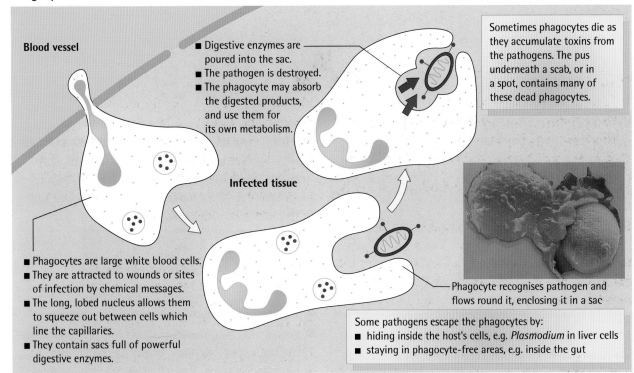

Blood vessel

- Digestive enzymes are poured into the sac.
- The pathogen is destroyed.
- The phagocyte may absorb the digested products, and use them for its own metabolism.

Sometimes phagocytes die as they accumulate toxins from the pathogens. The pus underneath a scab, or in a spot, contains many of these dead phagocytes.

Infected tissue

- Phagocytes are large white blood cells.
- They are attracted to wounds or sites of infection by chemical messages.
- The long, lobed nucleus allows them to squeeze out between cells which line the capillaries.
- They contain sacs full of powerful digestive enzymes.

Phagocyte recognises pathogen and flows round it, enclosing it in a sac

Some pathogens escape the phagocytes by:
- hiding inside the host's cells, e.g. *Plasmodium* in liver cells
- staying in phagocyte-free areas, e.g. inside the gut

recognised and destroyed by **phagocytes** and by **antibodies**. Phagocytes engulf and then destroy the pathogens with digestive enzymes, as outlined above. Antibodies are described on page 296.

There are many phagocytes present in areas of the body likely to suffer infection. The exposed surfaces of the lungs, for example, are patrolled by phagocytes. If the lungs are regularly attacked by the free radicals in tobacco smoke, large numbers of phagocytes collect and may become disorganised.

They can destroy lung tissue rather than foreign particles, leading to the disease **emphysema** (see page 80).

First aid can save lives

Severe blood loss, or haemorrhage, can cause a number of problems. Following an accident there may be so much blood loss that the blood pressure falls to dangerously low levels. This may affect the function of vital organs such as the heart, brain and kidney.

If the victim has no pulse or is not breathing, steps are taken to restart these essential functions.

If there is considerable bleeding, the first-aider applies firm pressure to the site of the injury. The victim should not be moved unless he or she is in danger. No attempt should be made to clean wounds – this may force a foreign body such as a glass fragment deeper into the wound.

Organisations such as the St John's Ambulance Brigade provide training in first aid.

1. Suggest how the skin may limit the entry of pathogens to the body. Why is it necessary to prevent the entry of pathogens?

2. This question concerns the process of blood clotting.
   a Why might blood clotting be necessary?
   b When could blood clotting be a disadvantage?
   c Blood clotting occurs in a number of stages. This is quite common in biological processes, since it allows **amplification**. Each step produces a product which can trigger many repeats of the next step – for example, each enzyme molecule released from a platelet can catalyse the conversion of 100 inactive protein molecules to their active form.
      i Suggest how this amplification might be an advantage in a rapid response to wounding.
      ii If there were five steps, each allowing an amplification of 100, how many 'product' molecules would be present at the end of the complete process for each 'signal' molecule released at the start of the process?

3. Describe the process of phagocytosis. Suggest two ways in which the structure of a phagocyte is related to its function. Suggest two ways in which a pathogen might avoid phagocytosis.

14·10 Antibodies and the immune response

Objectives
- To know what an antibody is
- To understand how antibodies are involved in defence against disease
- To understand how memory cells protect against infections
- To know how the immune response can be enhanced

An antibody is a protein

An **antibody** is a protein produced by the body in response to an antigen. Each different antigen stimulates the production of the particular type of antibody that will destroy that antigen. Antibodies are made by white blood cells called **lymphocytes**. They defend the body as shown below.

Once the lymphocytes have learnt to make a particular type of antibody in response to the antigens on an infective organism, the body begins to recover as the organisms are destroyed. It takes a few days to produce antibodies, so the infected individual will show some symptoms of the disease.

Immunity

After an infection, some lymphocytes are kept as a 'memory', which helps the body to defend itself against further attacks by the same antigen. This 'memory' may last for years, and the body is said to be **immune** to the disease. There are different types of immunity, as shown opposite.

Vaccines

Vaccines are produced in several ways:
- dead pathogens, e.g. whooping cough vaccine
- weakened pathogens, e.g. oral polio vaccine
- genetically engineered fragments – proteins from the pathogen's surface which are recognised by lymphocytes, e.g. hepatitis B viral coat protein.

Some vaccines are given two or three times at intervals, to build up more antibodies on each occasion. A booster dose may be needed after a time to ensure that there are enough memory cells to maintain the immunity. The antibody count following vaccination or infection is described opposite.

Lymphocyte action

There are several types of lymphocyte:
- only **B-lymphocytes** produce antibodies
- **T-lymphocytes** either attack pathogens directly, or produce chemicals which coordinate the activity of all cells in the immune system
- one kind of T-lymphocyte, T-helper cells, are invaded by HIV to cause AIDS (see page 293).

Scientists estimate that humans can make up to 1 000 000 different antibodies – enough to account for every pathogen or 'foreign' substance we might ever meet

This end of the antibody acts as a signal to phagocytes, or to T-lymphocytes, to destroy the pathogen.

The forked end of the antibody recognises and binds to the surface antigen on the pathogen to 'label' it.

Lymphocytes are a type of white blood cell:
- found in circulating blood and in the lymph nodes (see page 67)
- have a large nucleus and no granules in the cytoplasm
- stimulated by contact with pathogens to produce **antibodies**.

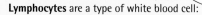

Antibodies are:
- proteins produced by lymphocytes
- able to recognise, bind to and help to destroy pathogens
- always Y-shaped.

'Labelled' pathogens may be destroyed by:
- sticking together in clumps so they can be **ingested by phagocytes**
- T-lymphocytes, which **burst membranes around the pathogen**
- antibodies directly – a few antibodies may actually destroy the pathogen's cell walls or membranes.

An **antigen** is:
- a protein or carbohydrate on the surface of the pathogen
- able to provoke the immune system of the host.

Pathogens may evade the immune system by mutation – they change and produce different antigens which the host has not learned to recognise and has no antibodies for.

Immunity may be

Active: individual makes his or her own antibodies

Passive: individual is given ready-made antibodies

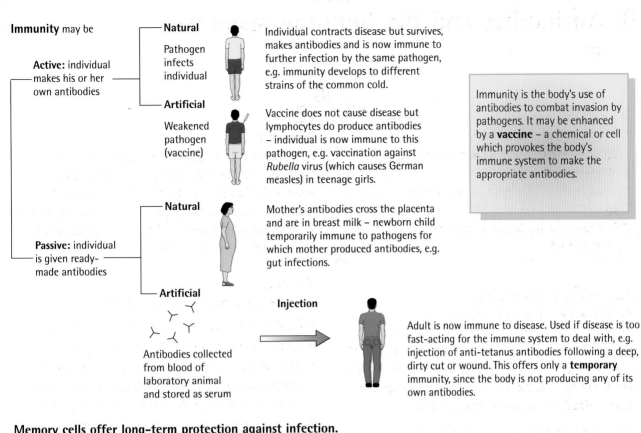

- **Natural**

  Pathogen infects individual

  Individual contracts disease but survives, makes antibodies and is now immune to further infection by the same pathogen, e.g. immunity develops to different strains of the common cold.

- **Artificial**

  Weakened pathogen (vaccine)

  Vaccine does not cause disease but lymphocytes do produce antibodies – individual is now immune to this pathogen, e.g. vaccination against *Rubella* virus (which causes German measles) in teenage girls.

- **Natural**

  Mother's antibodies cross the placenta and are in breast milk – newborn child temporarily immune to pathogens for which mother produced antibodies, e.g. gut infections.

- **Artificial**

  Antibodies collected from blood of laboratory animal and stored as serum

  Injection

  Adult is now immune to disease. Used if disease is too fast-acting for the immune system to deal with, e.g. injection of anti-tetanus antibodies following a deep, dirty cut or wound. This offers only a **temporary** immunity, since the body is not producing any of its own antibodies.

Immunity is the body's use of antibodies to combat invasion by pathogens. It may be enhanced by a **vaccine** – a chemical or cell which provokes the body's immune system to make the appropriate antibodies.

Memory cells offer long-term protection against infection.

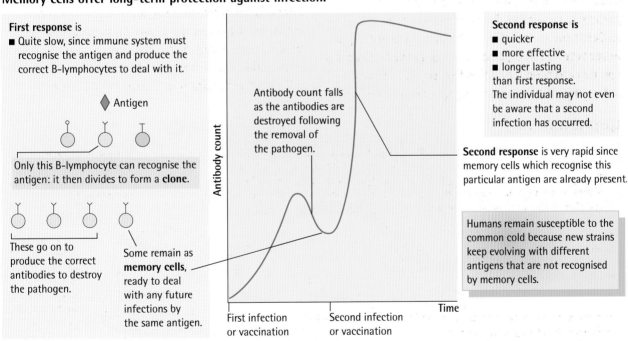

First response is
- Quite slow, since immune system must recognise the antigen and produce the correct B-lymphocytes to deal with it.

◆ Antigen

Only this B-lymphocyte can recognise the antigen: it then divides to form a **clone**.

These go on to produce the correct antibodies to destroy the pathogen.

Some remain as **memory cells**, ready to deal with any future infections by the same antigen.

Antibody count falls as the antibodies are destroyed following the removal of the pathogen.

Antibody count

First infection or vaccination

Second infection or vaccination

Time

Second response is
- quicker
- more effective
- longer lasting
than first response. The individual may not even be aware that a second infection has occurred.

Second response is very rapid since memory cells which recognise this particular antigen are already present.

Humans remain susceptible to the common cold because new strains keep evolving with different antigens that are not recognised by memory cells.

1. How do antibodies recognise pathogens?
2. State one difference in structure between a lymphocyte and a phagocyte, and one difference in function between a B-lymphocyte and a T-lymphocyte.
3. Explain how a single infection by a pathogen can provide lifelong protection against a disease.

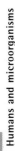

Humans and microorganisms

14·11 Applications of immunology

Objectives
- To understand how genetic engineering can produce safe vaccines
- To understand the production and use of monoclonal antibodies
- To appreciate that the immune response may cause problems
- To understand how problems with the immune response may be overcome

Genetic engineering is used to produce vaccines

The vaccine used to give people artificial immunity must be:

- effective – it must protect against the disease
- safe – it should not cause health problems.

Hepatitis B is a serious disease of the liver, caused by a virus. The production of the hepatitis B vaccine is described below.

Monoclonal antibodies are produced by fused tumour–lymphocyte cells

Scientists need a good supply of 'pure' antibodies to work with. They produce these by combining the properties of two types of cell:

- **lymphocytes** are very efficient at producing antibodies but cannot be grown in large numbers outside the human body
- **tumour cells** cannot produce antibodies but divide very well in artificial cultures.

Cells formed by joining together lymphocytes and tumour cells – called **hybridomas** – can produce enormous quantities of one desirable kind of antibody *and* survive for long periods in artificial culture. The antibodies produced in this way are called **monoclonal antibodies** ('mono' means one type and 'clonal' means a group of identical dividing cells). They have many uses in medicine, industry and research, as outlined opposite.

Hepatitis B
Worldwide over 2000 million people are infected by this virus. The virus spreads through body fluids and causes acute infection of the liver.

Antigen on surface of hepatitis B virus

Gene which codes for surface antigen in genetic material of virus.

Antigen gene is isolated from hepatitis B virus – other virus molecules are discarded.

Antigen gene from virus is incorporated into the DNA of a yeast cell.

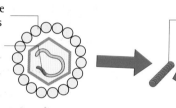

Yeast cells are removed from the medium. They can be recycled for further antigen production.

Anti-Hepatitis B vaccine

Purified vaccine contains only surface antigen, and:
- provokes immune system to make anti-hepatitis B antibodies
- cannot itself cause disease since no whole virus is present
- is usually given in two doses – first gives 1 year's protection, second (one year later) boosts this to 10 years' protection.

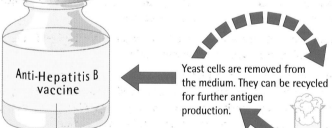

Yeast cells grow and multiply in culture medium containing all nutrients at correct pH and temperature.

Yeast cells manufacture virus antigen. They do not need it so they secrete it into their growth medium.

Genetic engineering provides a safe vaccine against hepatitis B, given to people likely to be exposed to this virus (such as a surgeon who might come into contact with patients' blood).

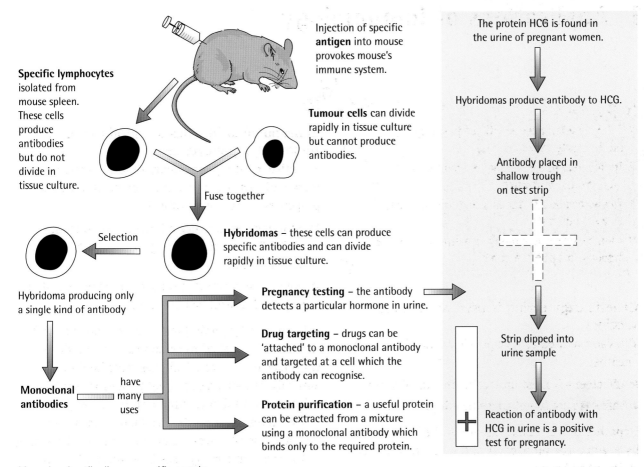

Specific lymphocytes isolated from mouse spleen. These cells produce antibodies but do not divide in tissue culture.

Injection of specific **antigen** into mouse provokes mouse's immune system.

Tumour cells can divide rapidly in tissue culture but cannot produce antibodies.

Fuse together

Selection

Hybridomas – these cells can produce specific antibodies and can divide rapidly in tissue culture.

Hybridoma producing only a single kind of antibody

Monoclonal antibodies have many uses

Pregnancy testing – the antibody detects a particular hormone in urine.

Drug targeting – drugs can be 'attached' to a monoclonal antibody and targeted at a cell which the antibody can recognise.

Protein purification – a useful protein can be extracted from a mixture using a monoclonal antibody which binds only to the required protein.

The protein HCG is found in the urine of pregnant women.

Hybridomas produce antibody to HCG.

Antibody placed in shallow trough on test strip

Strip dipped into urine sample

Reaction of antibody with HCG in urine is a positive test for pregnancy.

Monoclonal antibodies are specific protein molecules with important medical and industrial uses.

Some problems with the immune response

The activity of the immune system saves all our lives, many times over. There are occasions, however, when it may actually reduce the likelihood of survival. These are described below.

Autoimmune diseases are caused by the body producing antibodies which destroy its own cells. Why this should happen is not known. Examples include:

- diabetes – underactive pancreatic gland – the body destroys its own insulin-producing cells by an immune reaction
- rheumatoid arthritis – white blood cells destroy connective tissues in joints and make movement extremely painful.

Allergies are conditions in which the body becomes sensitive to a substance and over-reacts to it. This may cause swelling and tissue damage. Examples include hay fever and sensitivity to bee and wasp stings. Allergies are treated with drugs such as antihistamines to reduce the immune response.

Transplant rejection – the most common organ transplant in Britain is the kidney transplant (see page 117), but heart, intestine, lung, liver and pancreas transplants are becoming more common. The recipient's lymphocytes may recognise antigens on the surface of the donor organ as foreign and slowly destroy it. This problem of rejection is being overcome by:

- drugs that suppress the immune system of the recipient long enough to allow the transplanted organ to become established.
- matching tissues wherever possible, for example by seeking out relatives of people needing bone marrow transplants, since relatives are more likely to have similar antigens to the recipient.

Blood transfusions

The transfusion of blood from one person (the **donor**) to another (the **recipient**) is the most common 'tissue transplant'. It has to be carried out carefully because red blood cells carry **antigens** on their surface membrane, and blood plasma carries **antibodies** to these antigens. The blood types of the donor and recipient must be carefully matched. This matching can ignore the antibodies from the donor, but must consider the antibodies of the recipient and the antigens of the donor.

There are two sets of antigen–antibody interactions to consider. One concerns the **ABO groups** (see page 207 for a description of the inheritance of the genes controlling this characteristic); the other concerns the **rhesus factor**. These interactions, and the effects they have on blood transfusion, are outlined opposite.

---

1 A vaccine against hepatitis B can be made by genetic engineering. In this process:

a **i** What part of the virus is put into a yeast cell?

    ii What part of the virus is produced by the yeast cell?

b Before genetic engineering was developed, vaccines contained viruses that had been heated or treated chemically to stop them reproducing. Whole virus particles were present in the vaccine.
Explain why a genetically engineered vaccine is safer than a vaccine made directly from the hepatitis B virus.

2 The graph shows information about kidney transplants.

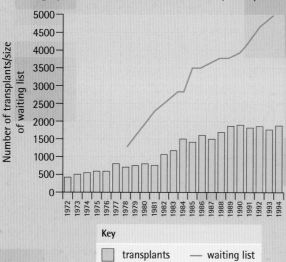

Key
  ☐ transplants   — waiting list

Use this information to answer the following questions.

a Calculate the percentage increase in the number of people on the waiting list in 1994 compared to 1978.
Show how you work out your answer.

b What problem does the graph show?

A big problem with all organ transplants is that the person receiving the organ may reject it.

c What type of cell is involved in rejecting the organ which has been transplanted?

d How do these cells lead to the transplanted organ being rejected?

(MEG June 1998)

3 **a** When giving blood transfusions, doctors must cross match the donor blood to make sure it is compatible with the recipient blood.

Use the information in the table and your knowledge to answer the following questions.

  i Which group is known as the Universal recipient and which is known as the Universal donor? Give reasons for your answers.

  ii Explain why it is important to screen all donated blood.

	Blood group			
	Recipient		Donor	
	O	A	B	AB
O	✓	✗	✗	✗
A	✓	✓	✗	✗
B	✓	✗	✓	✗
AB	✓	✓	✓	✓

Key
✓ compatible with recipient
✗ incompatible with recipient

b Human blood carries a rhesus factor. People with rhesus negative (Rh−) blood do not have antibodies to the rhesus factor but would produce antibodies if they were in contact with rhesus positive (Rh+) blood.
Explain why this can be dangerous for a rhesus positive baby (Rh+) carried by a rhesus negative mother (Rh−).

(NICCEA June 1995 [part])

Blood groups and blood transfusions

ABO blood groups

The **ABO blood grouping** is based on:

- two **antigens** called **agglutinogens**, symbolised as **A** and **B**, which are genetically determined carbohydrate molecules carried on the surface membrane of the **red blood cells**
- two **antibodies** called **agglutinins**, anti-A and **anti-B**, carried in the blood plasma.

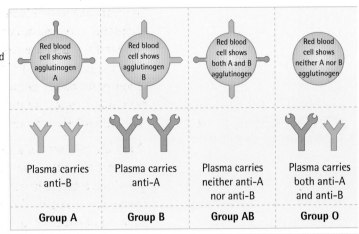

Red blood cell shows agglutinogen A	Red blood cell shows agglutinogen B	Red blood cell shows both A and B agglutinogen	Red blood cell shows neither A nor B agglutinogen
Plasma carries anti-B	Plasma carries anti-A	Plasma carries neither anti-A nor anti-B	Plasma carries both anti-A and anti-B
Group A	**Group B**	**Group AB**	**Group O**

A **blood transfusion** may be necessary to make up blood volume following haemorrhage or during surgery.
Only **compatible** blood should be transfused, or **agglutination** and **haemolysis** may occur. Agglutinated (clumped) cells may block capillaries and cause kidney or brain damage, or even death. Haemolysed cells 'leak' haemoglobin so oxygen transport is affected.

An **incompatible transfusion**: blood group B red blood cells are **clumped** by anti-B agglutinins in plasma of blood group A.

The agglutinins in the donor blood are ignored – they are in too low a concentration to cause major damage.

About 80% 0f the population – called **secretors** – release ABO type antigens in saliva and semen. This has been useful in some criminal investigations.

Recipient	Donor			
	A	B	AB	O
A (anti-B)				
B (anti-A)				
AB (neither)				
O (both)				

AB is the **universal recipient** since its plasma contains no agglutinins to clump donor red blood cells.

An enzyme, α-galactosidase, isolated from green coffee beans, can be used to convert type B blood to type O, the most useful for transfusions.

O is the **universal donor** since its red blood cells carry no agglutinogens to be clumped by recipient antibodies.

The rhesus factor

The **rhesus (Rh) system** of **blood grouping** is so named because it was first worked out in the blood of the rhesus monkey.
Some people's red blood cells have the **rhesus factor** on their membranes. They are **rhesus positive** (Rh⁺) and make up about 85% of the population. A **rhesus negative** individual does not normally have anti-Rh antibody in the plasma, but can make it quickly once exposed to Rh⁺ cells.

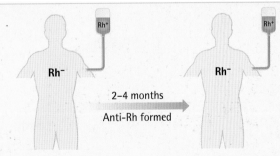

2–4 months
Anti-Rh formed

First transfusion: no anti-Rh present – **no problem**

Second transfusion: anti-Rh in plasma – **severe reaction**

The most severe cases concern the fetus and the newborn child.

Leakage of blood from an Rh⁺ baby may cause an Rh⁻ mother to make anti-Rh antibodies. These cross the placenta into the blood of the fetus of a second or subsequent pregnancy: this fetus suffers from burst red blood cells (haemolytic disease of the newborn).

Humans and microorganisms

14·12 The economic importance of microorganisms: baking and brewing

Objectives
- To appreciate that some microorganisms are useful to humans
- To recall an equation for anaerobic respiration
- To understand the industrial production of alcohol and bread

Bread production

Flour, sugar, water and salt are mixed with **yeast**. This process is called **kneading** and produces **dough**.

If a loaf is not left to rise, it will be small and dense.

The dough is rolled into shape, then kept in a warm (about 28 °C), moist environment. The yeast ferments the sugar, and the bubbles of carbon dioxide are trapped by the sticky proteins of the dough. The dough expands or **rises**.

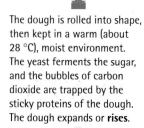

If a loaf is left to rise for too long too much carbon dioxide is produced and there are too many large holes.

Cooking at 180 °C – **baking**:
- kills the yeast and stops fermentation
- causes alcohol to evaporate
- hardens the outer surface to form a crust.

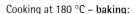

The product is **bread**, which should be:
- spongy in texture, because of trapped carbon dioxide
- fresh smelling (partly alcohol vapour!).

The perfect loaf.

'Wholemeal' bread is made with flour which has **not** had the husk removed from the wheat – hence 'whole' meal. It is rich in B vitamins and dietary fibre.

Bread may be fortified – in Britain, bread often has added protein, calcium and vitamins A and D – not to mention preservatives and whitening agents.

Yeast performs alcoholic fermentation

Much of the commercial use of microorganisms is based on the process of **fermentation**. This term covers *any* metabolic process carried out by microorganisms using carbohydrate as a starting material. The best known fermentation reaction is the anaerobic respiration of glucose by the single-celled fungus **yeast**:

$$\text{Glucose} \longrightarrow \text{carbon dioxide} + \text{ethanol} + \text{energy}$$

Since one of the products is ethanol (ethyl alcohol), this process is often known as **alcoholic fermentation**. As well as making alcohol, the carbon dioxide produced is valuable commercially. For the yeast, the useful product is energy – the alcohol and carbon dioxide are by-products.

Alcohol has a high energy content and is toxic

Alcohol contains a great deal of energy, a fact that is exploited when alcohol is used as a fuel source (see page 309). Alcohol is also toxic (poisonous) and the yeast excretes it into the surrounding liquid medium. If the alcohol concentration in the medium gets higher than 8–9%, the yeast is killed and fermentation stops.

Baking and brewing use fermentation

The processes of **baking** and **brewing** have both been around for thousands of years. These processes are outlined on the left and opposite.

Fine tuning the fermentation process

Because of the enormous commercial significance of these processes, much research has gone into making them as efficient as possible. For example:

- strains of yeast that are tolerant to higher concentrations of alcohol have been developed
- high-yielding strains of barley have been selectively bred
- genetic engineers have developed yeasts which can convert starch to maltose, and thus remove the need for the 'malting' stages.

Humans and microorganisms

Brewing

Barley is the source of **sugar**.

Barley is **ground** to separate husks from starchy interior.

Husks are collected, dried and sold to make cattle food

Enzymes in the barley convert

Starch → **maltose** (sugar)

Roasted hops and **colourings** (e.g. caramel)

Hops provide the **flavouring** and **bitterness**.

Hops are **roasted** – time depends on type of beer

Yeast and **extra sugar** – different yeast strains for different beers, e.g. *Saccharomyces carlsbergensis* for lager

WINE MAKING uses similar processes. Grapes provide the sugar, and are 'pressed' to allow enzymes to begin the fermentation. Only 'sparkling' wines such as Champagne have a second 'in the bottle' fermentation.

Fermentation vat
- copper for beer (wood for wine)
- yeast + hops + sugar = **wort**
- here sugar is fermented to alcohol. The carbon dioxide escapes to form a froth which keeps the mixture anaerobic.

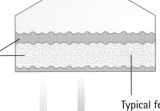

Typical fermentation temperature: 28–30 °C

'Live' beers – some yeast remains so that a second fermentation occurs in the barrel or bottle. CO_2 cannot escape and gives 'fizz' to beer.

As the alcohol rises to 9 or 10% the beer yeast are killed. Much higher alcohol concentrations are achieved by:
- **distillation** – to remove water, as in the production of spirits such as whisky and gin
- **fortification** – addition of alcohol, as in production of port and sherry (fortified wines).

'Container' beers – fermented wort is sterilised to kill yeast. CO_2 is added from gas cylinders.

---

1 Yeast ferments glucose ($C_6H_{12}O_6$) to ethanol (C_2H_5OH) and carbon dioxide. Write out a balanced chemical equation for this process.

2 Bread may be fortified with vitamins A and D, and the mineral calcium. What benefit would these give to the consumer? Suggest why bakers often add: **a** preservative and **b** whitener to their product.

3 Brewing is a very competitive business. Name two possible by-products of the process which might generate some income for the brewer.

14·13 Food from microorganisms: mycoprotein

Objectives

▪ To understand that microorganisms may be cultivated in large numbers as a source of foodstuffs

▪ To outline the conditions needed for the successful cultivation of microorganisms

▪ To describe an important industrial application of the cultivation of microorganisms

Microorganisms other than brewer's yeast can also carry out fermentation reactions, to produce food. The advantages of this compared to other production methods are:

▪ the reactions can be carried out at the relatively low temperatures found in living organisms, usually about 30 °C, offering great savings in fuel costs

▪ the processes are carried out more efficiently by the living organism (natural selection would eliminate the inefficient organisms!) meaning less waste and less need for purification of products

▪ the organisms can be genetically engineered so that they manufacture products useful to humans which they would not naturally produce.

Some of these processes are carried out on an enormous scale in special factories. The microbes (most commonly bacteria or fungi) are usually cultured separately and then added to their food source in a very large sterilised container. These containers are called **fermenters** or **bioreactors**, and the principles involved in their efficient use are described on the page opposite.

Fermentation may be used to produce food

Excess yeast produced during alcoholic fermentation is sometimes used as cattle food – the cattle are actually eating the bodies of the fungus. Fungi may also be grown in a bioreactor to produce food for humans. The product is called **mycoprotein**, and is made from the compacted hyphae (see page 228) of the fungus *Fusarium graminearum*. This fungus offers a number of advantages as a food source:

▪ it can be produced very quickly – the fungus doubles its mass within hours

▪ it can be produced cheaply – the fungus can grow on waste materials from other processes, such as the waste carbohydrate from flour production or cheaply available 'foods' such as sugar beet

▪ fermenters take up very little land area, so valuable agricultural land is not used

▪ fermenters offer a controlled environment, independent of the local weather conditions

▪ the product is always of the same quality

▪ it has a high protein content (40%), at least as high as beef steak

▪ it has a much lower fat content (only 13%) but much higher fibre content than meat, offering numerous health advantages to humans

▪ the mycelium of hyphae can easily be shaped and flavoured.

Fusarium is grown in continuous culture, with a 'harvest' being collected every two or three weeks. The collected fungus is separated from the culture medium, washed in steam and then frozen or dried before processing into other food products. Mycoprotein is marketed as a product called **Quorn**®, and is used widely in soups and biscuits, and as a substitute for chicken and ham.

1. Why must the nutrient input to a bioreactor contain a source of nitrogen?

2. Why is it important that the temperature of the fermentation is closely controlled?

3. The fermentation process is less efficient if the mixture is not well stirred. Why is this?

4. The computer could be described as the 'brain' of the bioreactor. Is this description justified?

5. If you were the manager of an industrial fermentation plant, what factors would you have to take into account if you wished to set up a new bioreactor?

6. Suggest three advantages of using microorganisms in food production.

A bioreactor

Paddle stirrers continuously mix the contents of the bioreactor:
- ensures microorganisms are always in contact with nutrients
- ensures an even temperature throughout the fermentation mixture
- for aerobic (oxygen-requiring) fermentations the mixing may be carried out by an **airstream**.

Microbe input – the organisms that will carry out the fermentation process are cultured separately until they are growing well.

Nutrient input –
the microorganisms require:
- an energy source – usually carbohydrate
- growth materials – amino acids (or ammonium salts which can be converted to amino acids) for protein synthesis.

Heating/cooling water out

Sterile conditions are essential.
The culture must be pure and all nutrients/equipment sterile to:
- avoid competition for expensive nutrients
- limit the danger of disease-causing organisms contaminating the product.

Gas outlet – gas may be evolved during fermentation. This must be released to avoid pressure build-up, and may be a valuable by-product, e.g. carbon dioxide is collected and sold for use in fizzy drinks.

Constant temperature water jacket – the temperature is controlled so that it is high enough to promote enzyme activity but not so high that enzymes and other proteins in the microbes are denatured.

Probes monitor condition such as pH, temperature and oxygen concentration. Information is sent to computer control systems which correct any changes to maintain the optimum conditions for fermentation.

Heating/cooling water in

In **batch culture** there is a fixed input of nutrients and the products are collected by emptying the bioreactor. The process is then repeated. This method is **expensive**, since the culture must be replaced and the reactor must be sterilised between batches, but has the **advantages** that:
- the vessels can be switched to other uses
- any contamination results in the loss of only a single batch.

In **continuous culture** fresh nutrients are added as soon as they are consumed, and the reactor may run for long periods. Products are run off at intervals while the process continues. This is **more economical** but has the **disadvantages** that:
- contamination causes greater losses
- the culture may block inlet or outlet pipes.

Further processing of product
may be necessary:
- to separate the microorganism from the desired product. In some fermentation systems these microorganisms may then be returned to the vessel to continue the process.
- to prepare the product for sale or distribution – this often involves **drying** or **crystallisation**.

Bacteria carry out useful metabolic processes

Most bacteria are **heterotrophic** – they take in ready-made food molecules from their environment. Like fungi such as yeast and *Fusarium*, some bacteria secrete enzymes onto their food source, absorb the digested products and then use these products in their metabolism – they are **saprotrophic**. The enzymes they secrete, and any toxic or excess products which they excrete, may be of use to humans. This makes some bacteria useful in food production, for example:

- *Acetobacter* in vinegar manufacture
- *Lactobacillus* in yoghurt and cheese production
- 'Ripening' bacteria in cheese production
- *Lactobacillus* (and the fungus *Aspergillus*) in soy sauce.

The role of these bacteria in food production is outlined on the opposite page.

Commercial food production

The fermentation processes used to grow the bacteria must be economical and efficient, and methods are always being improved.

Bacterial **single cell protein** is used as cattle food. It is produced using a cheap and readily available food source – methanol, which is fermented by the bacterium *Methylophilus methylotrophus* (meaning methane lover, methane feeder).

Cheese production is a traditional process that has been updated by the use of modern scientific techniques. The curds are formed more quickly if the coagulation of the milk protein casein is catalysed by an enzyme. Traditionally **rennin** was used, extracted from the stomach contents of calves slaughtered for meat. Genetic engineers have now produced a strain of the bacterium *E. coli* which contains the gene for the enzyme **chymosin**. This enzyme can be used instead of rennin to produce a cheese that is acceptable to vegetarians.

The second phase of cheese production also involves the action of bacteria or fungi – hard cheeses such as Stilton are formed by bacterial action from the *inside*, whereas soft cheeses are usually the result of fungal action from the *outside*. The characteristic smells of strong cheeses are usually due to metabolism of fatty acids, sometimes the same as those found on human skin. The warm, moist conditions on the feet produce an odour which the producers of Camembert cheese call 'les pieds de dieu' (God's feet).

A wide range of fermentations is used in food production, but they all share common features:

- The organisms require a source of food, including carbohydrate for energy and amino acids for protein synthesis.
- The organisms require optimum conditions of temperature, pH, oxygen concentration and water availability for most efficient activity.

1. What is meant by the term fermentation?
2. Several bacterial processes use milk as a starting point. Why is it important to pasteurise this milk?
3. Make a table to summarise the processes described on the opposite page. Use these headings: Product, Starting material, Bacteria involved, Special conditions.
4. Give one example of the importance of:
   a genetic engineering
   b technology
   in the commercial production of foods.
5. Both cheese and soy sauce are available in many flavours. How do you think these different flavours might be obtained?

Bacteria are involved in the production of food. **Vinegar** is produced by **aerobic fermentation of alcohol** in a suitable bioreactor (see page 305).

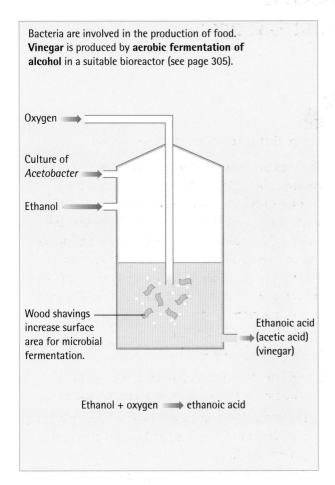

Oxygen

Culture of *Acetobacter*

Ethanol

Wood shavings increase surface area for microbial fermentation.

Ethanoic acid (acetic acid) (vinegar)

Ethanol + oxygen ⟹ ethanoic acid

Cheese production involves several stages to provide both texture and flavour.

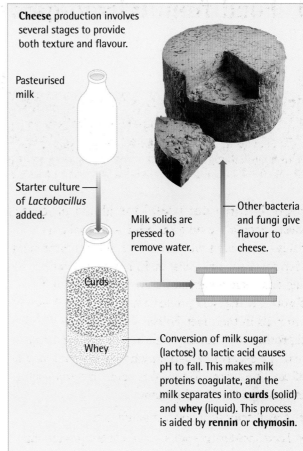

Pasteurised milk

Starter culture of *Lactobacillus* added.

Milk solids are pressed to remove water.

Other bacteria and fungi give flavour to cheese.

Curds

Whey

Conversion of milk sugar (lactose) to lactic acid causes pH to fall. This makes milk proteins coagulate, and the milk separates into **curds** (solid) and **whey** (liquid). This process is aided by **rennin** or **chymosin**.

Yoghurt is milk that has been soured by **fermentation of lactose** and thickened by **denaturation of protein**.

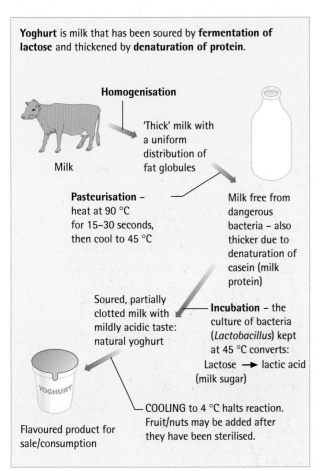

Homogenisation

Milk

'Thick' milk with a uniform distribution of fat globules

Pasteurisation – heat at 90 °C for 15–30 seconds, then cool to 45 °C

Milk free from dangerous bacteria – also thicker due to denaturation of casein (milk protein)

Soured, partially clotted milk with mildly acidic taste: natural yoghurt

Incubation – the culture of bacteria (*Lactobacillus*) kept at 45 °C converts:
Lactose ⟶ lactic acid (milk sugar)

COOLING to 4 °C halts reaction. Fruit/nuts may be added after they have been sterilised.

Flavoured product for sale/consumption

Production of **soy sauce** involves both aerobic and anaerobic fermentation:

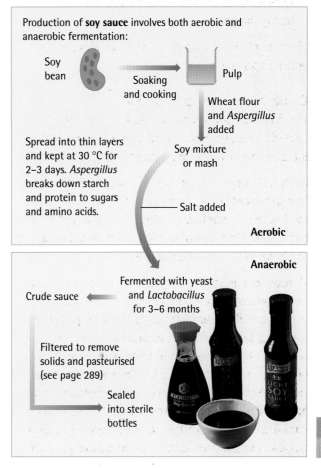

Soy bean

Soaking and cooking

Pulp

Wheat flour and *Aspergillus* added

Spread into thin layers and kept at 30 °C for 2–3 days. *Aspergillus* breaks down starch and protein to sugars and amino acids.

Soy mixture or mash

Salt added

Aerobic

Anaerobic

Fermented with yeast and *Lactobacillus* for 3–6 months

Crude sauce

Filtered to remove solids and pasteurised (see page 289)

Sealed into sterile bottles

14·15 Fuel from fermentation

Fermentations make products which can be used as **fuel**. **Biomass fuels** use raw materials produced by photosynthesis. These materials are from plants and can therefore be regenerated. Biomass fuels include:

▪ **solid fuels** – wood, charcoal and vegetable waste

▪ **liquid fuels** – alcohol and vegetable oil

▪ **gaseous fuel** – biogas (a methane/carbon dioxide mixture).

The production of these biomass fuels is described in the following diagrams.

1 What is a biomass fuel? What advantages might the use of biomass fuels offer?

2 What are the environmental benefits of quick-growing species of tree?

3 Look at the diagram opposite.

 a Suggest three products which could be sold, apart from the alcohol produced.

 b Both amylase and cellulase are involved in the preparation of the glucose feedstock for a gasohol generator. Suggest the exact function of these enzymes.

 c How has genetic engineering helped the gasohol industry?

 d A typical American car travels 10 000 miles a year at 15 m.p.g. This consumes the alcohol generated by the fermentation of 5000 kg of grain. A human on a subsistence diet consumes about 200 kg of grain per year. Comment on these figures.

4 Give two benefits that biogas generators offer to rural communities in poor countries.

5 Why are biogas generators built underground?

6 Why would it be inefficient to add disinfected household waste to the biogas generator?

Solid fuel using natural woodland causes environmental problems but there are alternatives.

Natural woodland – live cutting: see **deforestation** (page 268)

Fallen, dead wood: lesser environmental problem, but still loss of habitat and nutrients

Cut wood: may have to be carried long distances. Heavy because of water content – much time/energy spent in wood-gathering.

Heating wood without air present produces almost pure carbon, called **charcoal**.
This fuel:
■ burns slowly, releasing much heat
■ causes very little pollution.

Producing charcoal

Wood slowly burning

Turf covering wood to keep out air

Quick-growing tree species may provide renewable fuel
e.g. eucalyptus in Zaire ...

Erect, regular growth habit means easy cutting and storing.
Rapid growth – 8 m in 3 years.
High resin/oil content means it is clean burning, giving out much heat.

... and **sweet chestnut** from coppices in Kent may fuel local power stations.

Liquid fuel – ethanol

Liquid fuel – ethanol
The raw material is called feedstock

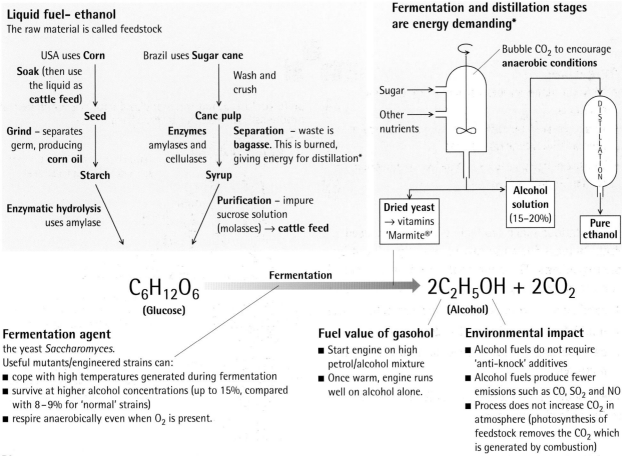

USA uses **Corn**

Soak (then use
the liquid as
cattle feed)
↓
Seed
↓
Grind – separates
germ, producing
corn oil
↓
Starch
↓
Enzymatic hydrolysis
uses amylase

Brazil uses **Sugar cane**
↓
Wash and
crush
↓
Cane pulp

Enzymes
amylases and
cellulases
↓
Syrup

Separation – waste is
bagasse. This is burned,
giving energy for distillation*

Purification – impure
sucrose solution
(molasses) → **cattle feed**

Fermentation and distillation stages are energy demanding*

Bubble CO_2 to encourage **anaerobic conditions**

Sugar →
Other → nutrients

Dried yeast
→ vitamins
'Marmite®'

**Alcohol
solution**
(15–20%)

DISTILLATION

**Pure
ethanol**

$$C_6H_{12}O_6 \xrightarrow{\text{Fermentation}} 2C_2H_5OH + 2CO_2$$
(Glucose)   (Alcohol)

Fermentation agent
the yeast *Saccharomyces*.
Useful mutants/engineered strains can:
- cope with high temperatures generated during fermentation
- survive at higher alcohol concentrations (up to 15%, compared with 8–9% for 'normal' strains)
- respire anaerobically even when O_2 is present.

Fuel value of gasohol
- Start engine on high petrol/alcohol mixture
- Once warm, engine runs well on alcohol alone.

Environmental impact
- Alcohol fuels do not require 'anti-knock' additives
- Alcohol fuels produce fewer emissions such as CO, SO_2 and NO
- Process does not increase CO_2 in atmosphere (photosynthesis of feedstock removes the CO_2 which is generated by combustion)

Biogas

Benefits of biogas
- **Cheap** – using surplus materials
- **Disposes** of human waste
- **Reduces** landfill problems
- **Reduces** use of other sources of power.

What are ideal conditions?
- Temperature of 20–30 °C: fermentation rate doubles per 10 °C rise
- Anaerobic conditions: oxygen is toxic to methanogenic bacteria
- Underground position → low O_2/stable temperature

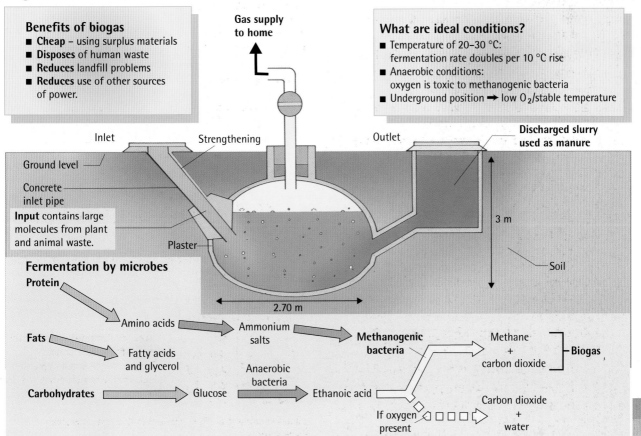

Gas supply to home

Inlet

Strengthening

Outlet

Discharged slurry used as manure

Ground level

Concrete
inlet pipe

Input contains large
molecules from plant
and animal waste.

Plaster

3 m

Soil

2.70 m

Fermentation by microbes

Protein → Amino acids → Ammonium salts → **Methanogenic bacteria** → Methane + carbon dioxide ⎤ Biogas

Fats → Fatty acids and glycerol

Carbohydrates → Glucose → Anaerobic bacteria → Ethanoic acid

If oxygen present → Carbon dioxide + water

14·16 Fungi can be used to produce antibiotics

Objectives

- To recall the mode of nutrition of fungi
- To understand that fungi may produce antibiotics as part of their normal metabolic processes
- To define the term antibiotic
- To understand how penicillin works as an antibiotic
- To describe the large-scale production of antibiotics
- To understand the problems of antibiotic resistance

Natural antibiotics: penicillin

A fungus such as *Penicillium* absorbs food molecules from its environment, and then uses these molecules for its own metabolism. Sometimes a *Penicillium* mould will make substances that it secretes into its environment to kill off any disease-causing or competitive microorganisms. A product made by one microorganism to kill off another microorganism is called an **antibiotic**.

The first antibiotic to be discovered was called **penicillin** after the organism *Penicillium* that produced it (see page 315). Antibiotics used in medicine work in various ways to inhibit the development of bacterial infections, without harming human cells. Penicillin prevents the bacterial cell walls forming (human cells do not have cell walls). Antibiotics only affect bacterial cells – there is no benefit in taking antibiotics to treat viral or fungal diseases.

Production of penicillin

The large-scale production of penicillin takes place in industrial fermenters. Penicillin is a **secondary metabolic product** – it is made when growth of the producer organism is slowing down rather than when it is at its maximum, as shown in the diagram below.

Antibiotics do not always kill bacteria

Bactericidal antibiotics kill the pathogen directly, whereas **bacteriostatic** ones prevent it reproducing, leaving the host's defences to kill the existing pathogens. The diagram opposite illustrates the different effects of a bactericidal agent and a bacteriostatic agent.

Antibiotic resistance

As the use of antibiotics increases, strains of bacteria that are **resistant** to the antibodies are developing, as shown opposite.

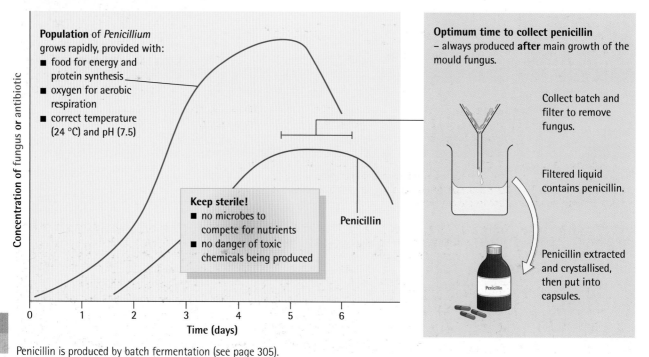

Penicillin is produced by batch fermentation (see page 305).

Antiseptics are not the same as antibiotics

An **antibiotic** is used to **treat** a bacterial infection. An **antiseptic** can be used to **prevent** infection ('anti' = prevent, 'sepsis' = infection). Antiseptics are chemicals applied to the outside of the body, such as the skin, to kill microbes. The development of antiseptic surgery is outlined on page 315.

Disinfectants are also chemicals that kill microbes, but they are more powerful and are generally used on worksurfaces or lavatory bowls, where potentially harmful bacteria may be growing.

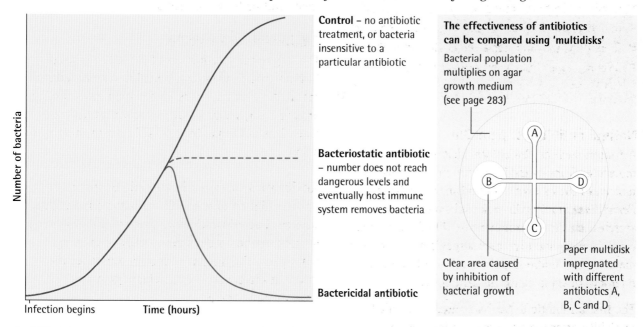

Control – no antibiotic treatment, or bacteria insensitive to a particular antibiotic

Bacteriostatic antibiotic – number does not reach dangerous levels and eventually host immune system removes bacteria

Bactericidal antibiotic

Number of bacteria

Infection begins   Time (hours)

The effectiveness of antibiotics can be compared using 'multidisks'

Bacterial population multiplies on agar growth medium (see page 283)

Clear area caused by inhibition of bacterial growth

Paper multidisk impregnated with different antibiotics A, B, C and D

Penicillin is bactericidal at high concentrations, but these may have some side-effects in humans (and may lead to **resistance** – see below) so penicillin is usually given at bacteriostatic doses.

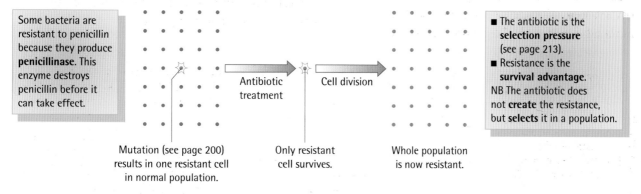

Some bacteria are resistant to penicillin because they produce **penicillinase**. This enzyme destroys penicillin before it can take effect.

Antibiotic treatment

Cell division

Mutation (see page 200) results in one resistant cell in normal population.

Only resistant cell survives.

Whole population is now resistant.

■ The antibiotic is the **selection pressure** (see page 213).
■ Resistance is the **survival advantage**. NB The antibiotic does not **create** the resistance, but **selects** it in a population.

Antibiotic-resistant strains of bacteria are formed by artificial selection. This is more likely to happen if antibiotics are used unnecessarily, or if people do not finish a course of prescribed antibiotics. This allows some of the bacterial population to recover, and possibly develop strains that are resistant to the antibiotic.

---

1 Distinguish clearly between the following pairs of terms:
   a antiseptic and antibiotic
   b antibiotic and antibody
   c resistance and immunity.

2 Purified penicillin is normally taken orally (by mouth). The crystals of the drug are enclosed in a capsule for distribution. Suggest three important properties of the material used to make the capsules.

14·17 Microorganisms are a source of enzymes

Objectives
- To understand that enzymes have many roles which benefit humans
- To know examples of a range of uses of enzymes
- To understand the benefits of enzyme immobilisation

Enzymes in industry

Enzymes are biological catalysts that operate at the temperatures, pressures and moderate pH values found in living organisms (see page 14). Using enzymes for industrial processes therefore does not require extreme (and expensive) conditions. For example, the Haber process for producing ammonia requires a temperature of 750 °C and a pressure of 30 times atmospheric pressure whereas nitrogen-fixing bacteria can perform this process at 25 °C and at atmospheric pressure.

In industry, the enzymes are often extracted from the living organisms before they are used. This has several advantages:

- There is no loss of raw materials for growth of the organism
- Optimum conditions for a particular enzyme can be used, which may not be the same as optimum conditions for the whole organism

- Wasteful side-reactions within the organism are eliminated
- Purification of the product is easier – the remains of the whole cells need not be removed.

The majority of enzymes used commercially are obtained from microbial sources, usually fungi or bacteria. Sometimes the organism naturally secretes the enzymes onto its substrate; sometimes the microbial cells must be broken open to release the enzymes. Using genetic engineering (see page 218), genes for desirable enzymes such as chymosin (see page 308) can be inserted into organisms that do not use this enzyme, and so they secrete it into their environment.

Immobilised enzymes

Enzymes are unstable – they can break down very quickly when used to catalyse industrial processes. Enzymes can now be protected and stabilised by **immobilisation**, a technique which fixes the enzyme to a non-reactive support material, as shown below. When using immobilised enzymes, the product of the reaction does not contain enzyme molecules, so purification is simple and inexpensive. Immobilised enzymes also allow continuous production rather than batch production, again reducing costs.

Enzyme molecules E may be fixed onto beads made of **resin**...

or onto **fibres**.

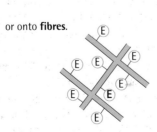

The carrier substance must be **inert**, i.e. it must not react with the enzyme or with the raw materials.

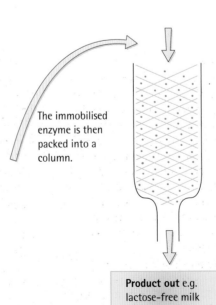

The immobilised enzyme is then packed into a column.

Raw materials in e.g. milk containing lactose

Immobilised lactase (breaks down lactose)

Some people become ill if they consume lactose – they are **lactose intolerant**.

Product out e.g. lactose-free milk

Humans and microorganisms

Commercial applications of enzymes

Pharmaceuticals

The enzyme **catalase** is used in wound dressings. Catalase converts hydrogen peroxide in the dressing to oxygen and water. Oxygen speeds up healing and inhibits dangerous, anaerobic bacteria such as the species which causes gas gangrene.

Analysis

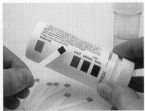

Dip-sticks such as Clinistix® and Albustix® use enzymes to detect biological compounds in mixtures. The biological compound is oxidised to a product which causes a colour change in a dye.

Pad at the end of stick contains enzyme + dye

Glucose + dye → (Glucose oxidase) → Changed dye

This is used by people with diabetes to test blood or urine for the presence of glucose.

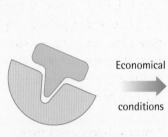

Enzyme + substrate → Economical conditions → Enzyme + products

Biological washing powders can operate at lower temperatures:
- less costly water heating
- less risk of clothes shrinking

Food production

- A **protease** from bacteria softens gluten, making the rolling of biscuits easier.
- **Isomerase** converts glucose to fructose – this is sweeter so less needs to be used in slimmers' biscuits.
- A **lipase** from fungi helps chocolate coverings to flow.

Textiles

Leather for clothing is softened using a **protease** from bacteria.

Stains are removed using **lipase, amylase** and **protease**.

---

1 Read the following passage.

An enzyme implant has successfully reduced the level of particles of the fatty substance, cholesterol, in the blood of rabbits by 40% within 70 minutes. Scientists have developed a way of implanting the enzyme PLA2 into the body without affecting the cholesterol needed in cell membranes. The enzyme is immobilised inside thin hollow fibres. Pores in the walls of the fibre are large enough for cholesterol particles to diffuse through, but too small for blood cells to enter. The enzyme breaks down the cholesterol, and the products are rapidly taken up by liver cells and removed from the bloodstream.

The scientists are cautious about using enzyme therapy in humans. 'We need to know exactly what happens to the products from the cholesterol in the body', says the head of the laboratory that developed the technique. 'Several drugs already on the market can safely be used to lower cholesterol levels. However an implant of the immobilised enzyme PLA2 could be easily inserted and could last for years.'

a Explain the advantage of lowering the level of the fatty substance, cholesterol, in the blood.

b Suggest how the enzyme might be immobilised inside the fibres.

c Suggest why it is an advantage to immobilise the enzyme inside hollow fibres.

d The enzyme PLA2 occurs naturally in humans. Explain why the enzyme could not be used as an implant if it did not occur naturally in the human body.

(NEAB June 1996 [part])

14·18 Pioneers of medicine

Objectives

▪ To understand that developments in medicine often involve the cooperation of many scientists

▪ To be able to describe the contribution to medicine of Lister, Jenner, Pasteur, Fleming, and Harvey

The war between humans and disease-causing organisms has had many battles. None of these battles has been won by an individual – scientists usually work as members of a team – but the following names will always be associated with advances in medicine that have made significant differences to the quality of life for all of us.

Jenner: vaccination against smallpox

Edward Jenner was the son of a country parson who went to London to study medicine. During his studies he received the valuable advice: 'Why think or speculate – why not try the experiment?' He followed this valuable scientific guideline throughout his life.

The disease **smallpox** was widespread in the eighteenth century, and some outbreaks resulted in very high death rates. Those who survived were often horribly disfigured. The only means of combating the disease was to inject material from a person with a mild attack of the disease into another person without the disease. Unfortunately there were two problems:

▪ The transmitted disease did not always remain mild, and many deaths occurred.

▪ The inoculated person could pass on the disease to others, causing further infection.

It was well known that people who had had **cowpox** – a relatively harmless disease contracted from cattle – could not catch smallpox. In 1796 Jenner found a young milkmaid with fresh cowpox sores on her hands. He took matter from these sores and inoculated an eight-year-old boy by scratching the matter into his arm. The boy developed a slight fever and a few mild sores. Six weeks later he injected the boy again, but this time with smallpox matter! No disease developed – he had been protected. Jenner later demonstrated his faith in the procedure by repeating the experiment on his own son.

Despite many initial setbacks – largely due to a shortage of fresh cowpox matter, and an inability to preserve it successfully – this technique became widespread. It was named **vaccination** because the cowpox ('vaccus' means cow in Latin) matter offered protection. At one time the Spanish colonists of South America used boy orphans as reservoirs of cowpox to provide them with enough vaccine to protect their armies! At one time the Spanish colonists of South America used boy orphans as reservoirs of cowpox to provide them with enough vaccine to protect their armies! The

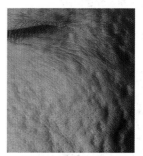

relatively wealthy countries achieved good control over smallpox, but it was not until the development of techniques to preserve the vaccine, such as freeze-drying, that people in poorer countries could be protected. Smallpox was finally eliminated from the human population in 1977.

Smallpox was a killer disease, and it scarred people who survived.

Pasteur: vaccination against rabies

In the 1860s Louis Pasteur proved, using the 'swan-necked flask experiment', that food only decomposes if it is exposed to microbes from the air. Pasteur went on to demonstrate that it was possible to prevent decomposition if food was treated to kill the microbes. His **pasteurisation** process probably saved the wine and vinegar industries in France, and also made it possible to transport British-brewed beer as far as India without it deteriorating! Pasteur also demonstrated that disease in silkworms was always accompanied by infection by microbes, and he devised a way of preventing the spread of these microbes.

In 1882 Pasteur began his most spectacular research – the prevention of **rabies**.

▪ He noted that the rabies virus was present in the brains of infected animals, and that injection of brain tissue into uninfected animals gave them the disease.

▪ He dried tissues of infected animals, and after experiments on the effect of temperature on these tissues, was able to develop a weakened form of the virus which he could use for inoculation.

▪ In 1885 he inoculated a nine-year-old boy, Joseph Meister, who had been bitten by a rabid dog and would certainly have died in agony. The boy recovered almost immediately.

The Pasteur Institute was set up in Paris in 1888 to carry on research into the prevention and treatment of rabies. It is well known nowadays for its work on AIDS, and is a fitting memorial to a man who revolutionised scientific method and its application to the problem of disease.

Lister: surgery and antiseptics

In the mid-nineteenth century the American dentist Thomas Morton and the Scottish physician James Simpson developed the use of ether as an anaesthetic. This allowed pain-free surgery for patients, and allowed surgeons to perform longer and more complex operations. Unfortunately many patients survived operations only to die of wound infections.

In 1865 **Joseph Lister**, an Edinburgh doctor, heard of Pasteur's observations that meat broth was turned 'bad' only after infection by airborne microbes. Lister believed that airborne microbes might also be responsible for **sepsis** – wounds turning 'bad' following surgery. **Carbolic acid** was used to treat foul-smelling drains and so he tried this compound as a means of killing microbes. He sprayed it onto the area of the body where the surgeon was operating. It was a spectacular success and marked the beginning of **antiseptic surgery**.

Modern surgery is no longer antiseptic – it does not aim to kill microbes – but instead it is **aseptic** and aims to prevent the entry of microbes to wounds. Aseptic surgery involves:

- ■ filtration of air entering the operating theatre to prevent entry of microbes
- ■ use of disinfectants to clean all surfaces in the operating theatre
- ■ use of sterilised clothing by surgeons and their assistants
- ■ use of sterilised equipment for all surgical procedures.

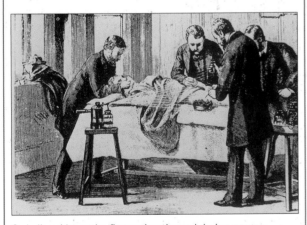

Carbolic acid was the first antiseptic used during surgery.

---

1. Make a table to describe the medical work of Lister, Jenner, Pasteur and Fleming. Use the following headings: Date, Name, Discovery, Significance of discovery.

2. Which of these pioneers do you think made the greatest contribution to medicine? Explain your choice.

Fleming, Florey and Chain: penicillin was the first available antibiotic

The British bacteriologist **Alexander Fleming** was working on cultures of bacteria grown on agar plates. In 1928 he noticed that some of his plates were contaminated with mould – this was a common occurrence – but, more importantly, he noticed that the bacteria could not grow close to the mould. Fleming identified the mould as *Penicillium notatum* and suggested that it produced a substance which killed the bacteria. He isolated a small quantity of the substance, and called it **penicillin**. Fleming believed that penicillin might be useful in fighting bacterial infections, but was not able to overcome the difficulties of isolating it in large enough quantities for use in medicine.

In 1938 two chemists, **Howard Florey** and **Ernst Chain**, started to work on techniques for growing large quantities of the mould and for isolating penicillin from it. The Second World War made it difficult to obtain laboratory equipment, so they carried out many of their experiments in milk bottles, jam jars and even bedpans borrowed from the nearby hospital! They found that *Penicillium chrysogenum* was a better strain than *P. notatum* for producing penicillin, and manufactured enough of the drug to carry out the first clinical trials. The first person to be successfully treated with penicillin, in 1940, was a policeman who had a bad wound infection and was close to death. Penicillin cleared the infection, but unfortunately there wasn't enough available for continued treatment and many of the early patients died after showing signs of recovery.

The urgent need to treat wounded soldiers stepped up the production of penicillin. The work moved to the USA – it is said that strains of *Penicillium* were soaked into clothing in case the couriers were intercepted by foreign agents!

By 1944, doctors had enough penicillin to treat all the British and American casualties of the Normandy landings. The knowledge of this 'wonder drug' was a great morale-booster for the Allied troops.

By the 1950s penicillin was available for widespread use throughout the general population. The large-scale production techniques described on page 305, and the continued development of high-yielding strains of *Penicillium*, have made penicillin the most widely available antibiotic.

Although Alexander Fleming was awarded the Nobel prize for his work on penicillin, he always acknowledged that the greater credit should have gone to Florey and Chain for their persistence in isolating the antibiotic and producing large enough quantities for clinical trials.

William Harvey grew up in Kent and worked as a physician to King James I. He made several contributions to medicine – the most important of these concerned the mechanism for the movement of blood through the body.

At the time Harvey began his studies most people believed that blood 'ebbed and flowed' through the body, passing through the arteries and veins and in and out of the heart rather like the tide coming in and out. Harvey, however, believed that blood flowed in a circulation – through veins, the heart, arteries and then round again. Other people had similar ideas, but Harvey differed from his contemporaries because he decided to seek experimental evidence to support his ideas. The following pieces of evidence supported Harvey's ideas:

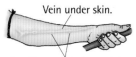

1 Swellings mark the positions of the veins.

Vein under skin.

2 Block vein with fingers as shown.

3 Keep right finger where it is, then push blood to the next swelling with left finger.

4 Take left finger away. Note that blood does not flow back . . .

5 . . . even if you try pushing it with your finger.

Harvey's famous experiment showing that blood in the veins flows in one direction – towards the heart.

◗ There are valves in the veins (see page 70) and between the atria and ventricles of the heart (see page 68). Harvey argued that these valves would make certain that blood could only flow in one direction through the heart and vessels – in other words, the blood could not 'ebb and flow'. Harvey suggested that the blood flowed towards the heart in the veins and away from the heart in the arteries, and he demonstrated this flow in many animals, including humans. One of Harvey's famous experiments is outlined in the diagram (below left).

◗ There are no channels in the septum (the wall between the left and right side of the heart) – blood can't flow directly between the two sides. Harvey pointed out that the blood would have to flow from the right side of the heart to the lungs and then return to the left side of the heart. He called this the 'lesser' circulation, and called the blood flow from the heart to the other tissues the 'greater' circulation. We now use the terms **pulmonary** and **systemic** circulation for these two circuits. Harvey didn't know as much about oxygen and carbon dioxide as we do today, and made the quite reasonable suggestion that the blood went to the lungs to be cooled.

◗ Harvey measured the maximum volume that can be pumped from the heart with each beat – in humans that is about 70 cm³ with each heartbeat. He then estimated that if there were 60 beats per minute the heart would pump $70 \times 60 \times 60$ cm³ in an hour, or about 6000 dm³ per day. Harvey deduced that such an amount of blood could not be produced or consumed in a day; therefore it must circulate out in the arteries and back in the veins, over and over again, as long as the human is alive.

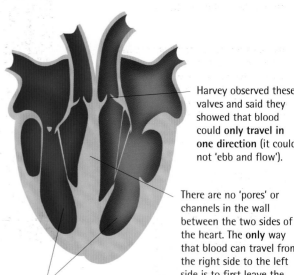

Harvey observed these valves and said they showed that blood could **only travel in one direction** (it could not 'ebb and flow').

There are no 'pores' or channels in the wall between the two sides of the heart. The **only** way that blood can travel from the right side to the left side is to first leave the heart and travel to the lungs before returning.

Harvey noted that the two ventricles always contracted **at the same time**. This would not be possible if blood 'ebbed and flowed' between the two sides of the heart.

Harvey dissected the heart and showed that blood circulates around the body.

Harvey concluded that there must be tiny connections to link the ends of the arteries with the beginnings of the veins to form a true circulatory system – we now call these 'connections' the capillaries. Harvey, then, was the first true experimental scientist. He was prepared to back up his theories with observations and measurements. He published his findings in 1628 in a short book *On the workings of the heart and blood* – this was the first book on the science of physiology.

Christiaan Barnard and heart transplants

Christiaan Barnard (1922–2001) was born in South Africa, studied heart surgery in the USA, and returned to South Africa to set up a cardiac unit in Cape Town. In 1967 he transplanted the heart of a road accident victim into a 59-year-old man, Louis Washkansky. Washkansky died after just 14 days – the drugs used to reduce the risk of rejection of his new heart unfortunately lowered his resistance to infection. Christiaan Barnard continued his work, and in 1974 research workers in Norway discovered a drug, cyclosporin, which prevented rejection of transplanted organs without lowering the patients' resistance to infection. Christiaan Barnard had taken the first steps into a form of surgery – organ transplantation – which is now routine in medical practice.

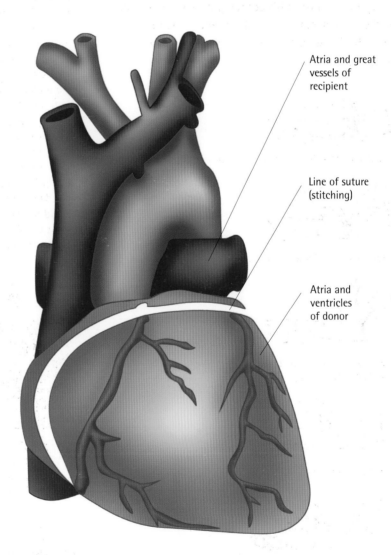

The **surgery** is relatively simple, with much of the recipient's atria and great vessels left intact.

Donors are accident victims who are 'brain dead' but with functioning hearts – they are size-matched with the recipients (to ensure compatible heart size), must have no heart disease, and must be matched for ABO blood type and one particular HLA (human leucocyte antigen) characteristic.

The **donor heart** is stopped by an injection of K^+ ions, cooled and usually transplanted within 3–5 hours.

Immunosuppressive drugs are necessary to prevent host rejection of the transplanted tissue. These may have side-effects – a higher incidence of cancer, especially of the lymphatic system, a high risk of infection and an accelerated rate of atherosclerosis.

Clinical trials are currently underway with artificial hearts which may be used to support a diseased natural heart.

Atria and great vessels of recipient

Line of suture (stitching)

Atria and ventricles of donor

Heart transplants first took place in the late 1960s and there is now an 80% chance of survival for one year in patients under 40.

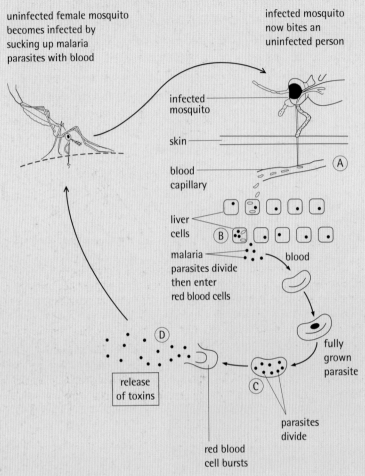

uninfected female mosquito becomes infected by sucking up malaria parasites with blood

infected mosquito now bites an uninfected person

infected mosquito

skin

blood capillary

(A)

liver cells

(B)

malaria parasites divide then enter red blood cells

blood

fully grown parasite

(C)

(D)

release of toxins

parasites divide

red blood cell bursts

1 Malaria is a tropical disease spread by mosquitoes.

a Here are five sentences describing the spread of malaria. They are in the wrong order.

  A The mosquito sucks up the blood of the infected person. The blood carries the malaria parasite (*Plasmodium*).

  B Eggs hatch into tiny larvae which live just below the water surface. Later young mosquitoes hatch out.

  C Female mosquitoes lay eggs on the surface of ponds.

  D The mosquito transmits the disease to any healthy person it bites.

  E The female mosquito bites a person infected with malaria.

  i Write the letters in order to describe the spread of malaria. The first one is C.

  ii The mosquito is a **vector**. What does this mean?

b The diagram shows the life cycle of the malaria parasite (*Plasmodium*).

  i In which human body cells of man does the parasite reproduce?

  ii At which stage **A**, **B**, **C** or **D** would you expect the patient to start suffering with a fever?

c Describe two methods of controlling the spread of malaria and explain how each method works.

(MEG June 1998)

2 a Some bacteria are pathogenic and parasitic. Explain the terms "pathogenic" and "parasitic".

b 1 cm³ of a bacterial culture was placed in a sterile petri dish containing sterile nutrient agar. Three wells of equal size were cut with a sterile cork borer and were then filled with equal volumes of different hand cleansers. The petri dish was incubated at 20 °C for 72 hours and the results are shown in the diagram.

  i Describe and explain the results shown in the diagram.

  ii Why was sterile nutrient agar used?

  iii How is sterilisation achieved in the laboratory?

  iv Explain why the petri dish was not incubated at 37 °C.

  v The hand cleansers had antiseptic properties. What does the term "antiseptic" mean?

(CCEA June 1994 [part])

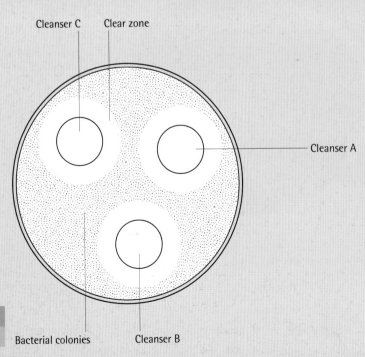

Cleanser C

Clear zone

Cleanser A

Bacterial colonies

Cleanser B

3 a Give THREE natural ways in which the body can prevent the entry of pathogens.

b How can a baby acquire immunity from its mother after birth?

c The diagram below shows how the human body can respond to the entry of a pathogen by producing B and T lymphocytes.

   i Explain how the B lymphocytes protect the body from pathogens.

   ii Describe ONE way in which the T lymphocytes protect the body after a second infection by the same pathogen.

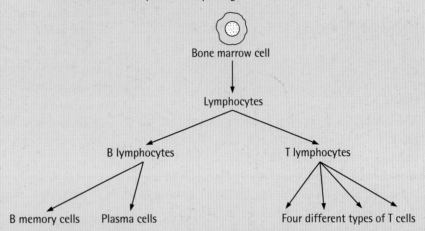

Bone marrow cell

Lymphocytes

B lymphocytes   T lymphocytes

B memory cells   Plasma cells   Four different types of T cells

d Mr Jones landed at the airport after a holiday abroad. He read in a newspaper that typhoid had broken out in the town where he spent the last three days of his holiday. Typhoid is a dangerous disease which usually causes illness between 7 and 14 days after infection.

The graphs below show two ways in which a person can acquire artificial immunity. Method A involves the injection of an antigen, method B an injection of antibody.

Which of the methods shown in the graphs would provide the best protection, from typhoid, for Mr Jones? Give a reason for your answer.

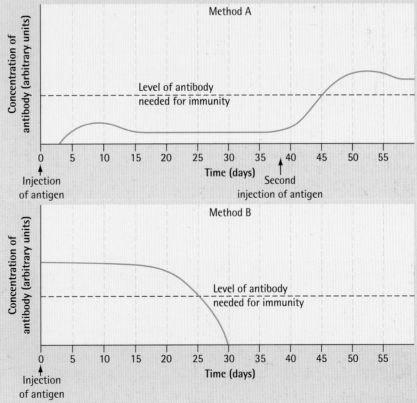

(Edexcel June 1996)

15·1 Understanding soil

Objectives

- To understand what soil is made of
- To appreciate the importance of soil in agriculture
- To understand how humans can alter the composition and properties of soil

What is soil?

The **biosphere** is the thin layer on the surface of the Earth that can support life. Life on Earth requires, amongst other things, water, minerals, carbon dioxide and a source of energy (usually sunlight). The **soil** is the thin layer of the biosphere that covers the land, and can often supply a suitable combination of these requirements. Living organisms are not distributed uniformly over the Earth's surface, and the varying composition of the soil in different areas goes a long way towards explaining this uneven distribution. The soil provides nutrients, water and support for an enormous number of plants, which in turn are the base of food chains. The soil also provides a habitat for many microorganisms, including those responsible for maintaining the carbon and nitrogen cycles (see pages 255 and 257).

A complete soil is a mixture of many things, as illustrated below.

Manipulation of the soil composition

The components of a particular soil will greatly affect which organisms can flourish within it. The activities of humans can influence the nature of a soil, and so can affect its fertility (ability to support plant growth). Soil scientists are able to analyse the composition of soil, and can advise farmers on the need to adjust the soil for maximum fertility. Important adjustments to soil properties include:

- alteration of soil pH
- alteration of air content
- addition of fertilisers.

These techniques are outlined in the table opposite.

Agriculture – matching crops and soils

Farmers try to adjust the fertility of soil so that it can support **crops** – plants that can be used by humans (most importantly as food), or by their domestic animals. Agricultural scientists have been able to match particular crops to certain soil types to make sure that the crop yield is at a maximum. Crops have been developed by **selective breeding** (page 217) so that they can grow well in particular types of soil. It is likely that genetic engineering (page 221) will become increasingly important in developing new strains of crops.

Decaying organic material – decomposition releases sticky organic compounds which help to bind particles together to form crumbs. The decaying matter is also called **humus**.

Hypha of fungus – one of many living organisms feeding on organic remains in the soil. There are also many microbes involved in the cycling of nutrients, earthworms which drag leaves into the soil and maintain aeration and plant roots which help to prevent soil becoming compacted.

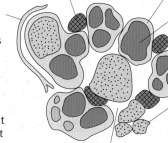

Film of water – coats surface of soil crumbs. Provides the habitat for most of the soil microbes, and also dissolves mineral ions so that they are available for uptake by roots.

Soil crumbs – small mineral particles bound together by sticky organic compounds from humus. A good crumb structure means that soil is well aerated, has good drainage and is easily penetrated by small animals, plant roots and hyphae of fungi.

Clay particles – individual particles are extremely small and tightly bound to one another. As a result, air spaces are few in number and very limited in volume.

Soil air – provides oxygen (and nitrogen if required) for soil organisms. Badly aerated soils favour the action of denitrifying bacteria (nitrates → nitrogen and oxygen), and also inhibit decomposition. Acidic soils often have relatively few air pockets.

Soil structure

Soil component	How it is analysed	Why it is adjusted	How it is adjusted
Air content	By measurement of the volume of air displaced from a soil sample when mixed with water. Agricultural engineers can use electronic probes to measure the amount of **oxygen** in the soil.	Anaerobic conditions favour the action of denitrifying bacteria (page 257) and inhibit decomposition (page 255). Soils with a low air content often have a high water content, and so are heavy and difficult to work.	By **drainage** (the Government gives farmers grants to do this) and by **ploughing**. The drainage of soils is very controversial, since it destroys wetland habitats and the specialised animals and plants which live there.
Mineral ions	A sample is collected and analysed in a machine called a flame photometer. This machine can be adjusted to give a direct reading of the content of any important mineral in the soil sample.	To supply essential minerals, such as nitrate, phosphate, potassium and magnesium (see page 159).	By the addition of **fertilisers** (see page 158). N.B. these inorganic fertilisers can cause environmental damage (see page 264) and can alter the soil structure (the soil crumbs are destroyed), increasing the risk of soil erosion.
pH (acidity and alkalinity)	By using an **indicator solution**: orange colour indicates acidic soil; blue-green colour indicates alkaline soil. Special pH probes can also be used (see photo below).	pH affects the ability of the plant roots to take up minerals from the soil (see page 262) and low pH (acidic conditions) also reduces the effect of decomposers (see page 255).	Lime (calcium carbonate) is added to acidic soils to raise the pH (make soil more alkaline). Lime also makes small particles of soil combine to produce ideal-sized crumbs (flocculation) and, of course, provides the mineral calcium. Liming is an important treatment for soils damaged by acid rain (page 262). Peat is added to alkaline soils to lower the pH (make soil more acidic). The addition of peat also improves the crumb structure of the soil.

A pH meter testing the acidity or alkalinity of soil. The meter displays a pH of 4, meaning that this is an acid soil.

To summarise:

Agricultural scientists can analyse the composition of soil, and can advise on the adjustment of composition to provide maximum fertility. Plant breeders and genetic engineers can develop new strains of plant to maximise yields of crop.

1. Give three reasons why a gardener would add lime to the soil. Explain your answers carefully.
2. The effect of pH on the uptake of ions was measured in a carefully controlled experiment.
   a Plot the results opposite as a set of line graphs.
   b Which mineral ion is least affected by pH?
   c What is the best pH for the maximum uptake of all four mineral ions?
   d A gardener tested a sample of soil with indicator solution. The soil gave a blue-green colour. Explain how the gardener could adjust the soil pH so that it would be at the value identified in part (c).

pH	Ion uptake in arbitrary units			
	Potassium	Phosphate	Calcium	Magnesium
4	1	6	2	5
5	4	15	3	7
6	9	19	5	8
7	15	11	8	7
8	17	7	19	7
9	12	1	17	6

3. a Explain how the technique of selective breeding would be used to produce a valuable cereal crop from a simple grass.
   b Name another crop that has been produced by selective breeding.
   c Give two examples of characteristics that have been introduced into crops by the use of genetic engineering techniques.

Biology in action

321

15.2 DNA provides an unique profile

Objectives

- To appreciate that the DNA profile is unique to each individual
- To understand how a DNA profile or fingerprint is produced
- To know some of the applications of DNA profiling
- To understand the use of gene probes and the polymerase chain reaction

DNA is the genetic information

DNA provides the information which allows cells to produce proteins. These proteins, in turn, are responsible for the development of the characteristics of the cell and the organism of which the cell is a part (see page 190). It should be clear that, because each organism has different inherited characteristics from each other organism (except for an identical twin), the DNA content of each individual organism is unique.

This 'uniqueness' means that, in theory, an individual organism can be identified by the DNA it contains in its cell nuclei. In the past twenty years an enormous amount of research has gone on into how humans can identify the unique DNA in each organism. The results of this research mean that we can now produce a **DNA profile** or **genetic fingerprint** for any individual organism. This ability has many important applications – in medicine, forensic science, agriculture and conservation, for example.

Producing a genetic fingerprint

This is a quite complex and expensive process, but it does follow a clear sequence which means that special laboratories can be set up to carry it out in the most efficient and economical way. The basic procedure involves the following steps:

- **Extraction of DNA:** this involves collection of a sample of, for example, blood, hair or semen. In blood, white cells are required since the red cells have no nucleus.
- **DNA digestion:** restriction enzymes (see page 219) are used to cut the DNA into fragments.

- **Electrophoresis:** separates the DNA fragments according to their size.
- **Blotting:** the DNA fragments are transferred from the electrophoresis gel to a nylon membrane.
- **Probing:** DNA probes are used to identify genes within the DNA fragments.
- **Printing:** the DNA probes bound to the DNA fragments are 'shown up' on X-ray film or under ultraviolet light.

These steps are outlined below.

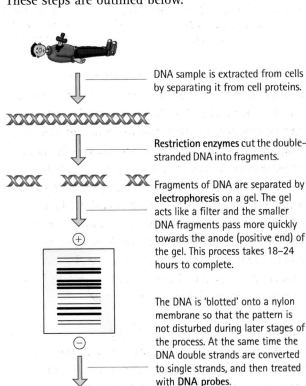

DNA sample is extracted from cells by separating it from cell proteins.

Restriction enzymes cut the double-stranded DNA into fragments.

Fragments of DNA are separated by **electrophoresis** on a gel. The gel acts like a filter and the smaller DNA fragments pass more quickly towards the anode (positive end) of the gel. This process takes 18–24 hours to complete.

The DNA is 'blotted' onto a nylon membrane so that the pattern is not disturbed during later stages of the process. At the same time the DNA double strands are converted to single strands, and then treated with **DNA probes**.

An X-ray film is held against the nylon membrane. Any radioactive probes bound to the DNA cause the X-ray film to 'fog'. Safer 'chemical probes' can be used – these show up under ultraviolet light.

Only DNA fragments that are bound to the radioactive DNA probe show up on the X-ray film. The pattern which results is a **DNA profile (genetic fingerprint).**

Steps in DNA profiling

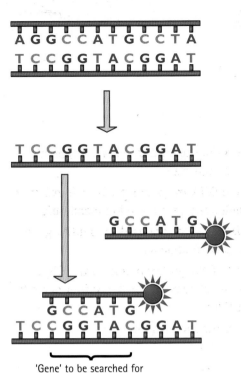

A short section of DNA. The DNA is double stranded – each strand is a sequence of bases, shown by their initial letters A, G, C and T. The two strands are linked by bonds beteen **complementary** bases: A–T and G–C.

The strands are separated to give single-stranded DNA with the bases 'exposed' (ready to form bonds with their complementary bases).

A **DNA probe** is introduced. This has a short sequence of bases which is complementary to a base sequence in the gene being searched for. The probe also has a label ( ), which might be a radioactive isotope or a chemical which shows up under ultraviolet light.

The DNA probe will bind to the single-stranded DNA **if the complementary sequence is present** (i.e. if the 'gene' is present). The DNA is now labelled, and can be detected. Only DNA strands which contain the complementary sequence will be detected.

'Gene' to be searched for

N.B. Genes are actually much bigger than this – from 200 to 20 000 bases long! Gene probes may be quite short, and only bind to a small section of the gene.

How a DNA probe labels a gene

Once a DNA profile has been made it can be compared with another one. For example, a profile obtained from the blood of a suspected murderer can be compared with a sample from beneath the fingernails of the victim. Depending on the number of gene probes used (see diagram above), it is possible to narrow down the DNA profile to one in a million people. Once an identification like this has been made, the scientists can conduct even more detailed analysis of the DNA (a technique which involves working out the actual base sequence in a piece of DNA!) until a unique DNA fingerprint is available for comparison.

Applications of DNA profiling

Despite the expense of the process, and the fact that it takes several days to obtain results, there are many important uses of DNA profiling. These include

- **Resolution of paternity disputes:** DNA profiling is much more accurate than blood-grouping in identifying the father of a particular child. This process is relatively easy, since large amounts of sample DNA are available.

- **Apprehension of criminals:** suspected rapists, murderers, burglars and arsonists have all been identified using this technique. One problem is that the criminal does not deliberately leave behind large quantities of DNA for profiling!

This means that the profiling is not very accurate, unless more DNA can be obtained. Fortunately, there is a technique – the **polymerase chain reaction** – which can produce large quantities of DNA from a tiny sample. The polymerase chain reaction is outlined in the diagram overleaf.

- **Diagnosis of disease:** the Human Genome Project has identified the positions of all human genes, and it has been possible to locate genes that can be linked to particular inherited disease. Gene probes can be used to search for the presence of a 'disease-gene' in a sample of DNA from any individual. This may make it possible to give treatment to such a person before the disease actually develops to a dangerous stage. One disease which can be identified by this method is **cystic fibrosis** (see page 206) – the faulty gene may be identified and may, one day, be replaced by **gene therapy** (see page 221).

- **Identification of wild animal family trees:** this may be significant in devising breeding programmes between zoo animals which reduce the risk of inbreeding. DNA profiles have also been useful in the conviction of people who have taken endangered species from the wild – for example, samples from the feathers of peregrine falcons have shown whether the birds have been bred in captivity or have been taken from the wild population.

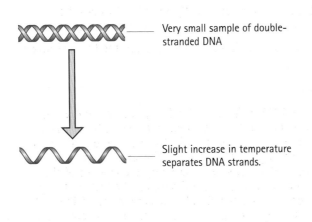

Very small sample of double-stranded DNA

Slight increase in temperature separates DNA strands.

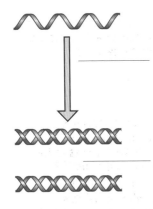

Mixture of bases is added, and allowed to bind to DNA single strands. The reaction is catalysed by **DNA polymerase** enzyme.

The mixture is cooled, and double-stranded DNA reforms.
There is now twice as much DNA. The cycle can be repeated many times to give large quantities of DNA for profiling.

The polymerase chain reaction can provide large DNA samples for genetic fingerprinting.

Building a DNA library

Scientists are interested in building a 'library' of DNA. For example, it could be very important in disease treatment to have a copy of the altered gene in a 'library' for comparison with a sample from the affected person. Police scientists would also like to keep a record of DNA profiles from convicted criminals so that future crimes might be solved more easily. Many people would accept this, but are not willing to accept the building up of a DNA library or databank of people who have not been convicted of a crime. For example, police investigating a rape might interview several hundred young men and take DNA samples from all of them. Many people feel that profiles made from these samples should not be kept by the police, as this is an infringement of the freedom of an individual.

Another application of DNA profiling which causes moral concerns is the use of genetic information by the insurance industry. It is already possible to identify certain lethal inherited conditions (Huntington's disease, for example – see page 206) using gene probes, and many people are worried

that insurance companies will refuse insurance cover to individuals carrying these lethal genes. Employers might also be unwilling to offer jobs to people with a DNA profile that indicates that they might become ill in the future.

Finally, scientists urge caution since the DNA profiling process is not yet foolproof!

Problems with contamination

One reason given for caution in interpretation of DNA profiles is that the samples may be contaminated. Forensic samples are rarely pure because:

- They may contain DNA from the vagina of rape victims.
- DNA from fungi and bacteria is often present in samples collected from crime sites.
- Dyes from clothes may affect the specificity of the restriction enzymes.
- Environmental contaminants from the crime site may bind to fragments of DNA and affect their rate of movement under electrophoresis.

Despite these problems it is likely that DNA profiling will provide an increasingly sophisticated amount of forensic evidence for police scientists.

The Human Genome Project

The human genome – the total length of DNA in a diploid human cell nucleus – is about 3×10^9 base pairs. This corresponds to about 2 metres of DNA per nucleus. In general, the more complex the organism the longer the DNA, although this is not a fixed rule – some amphibians and some plants have even longer genomes.

The genome of the bacterium *Haemophilus influenzae* was sequenced in July 1995. The bacterium can cause ear infections and meningitis. The DNA sequence is 1.8×10^6 base pairs long, comprising 1743 genes, and the experimental approach used was rather revolutionary, involving complex computer programming which made the whole process much quicker.

Wednesday 24 April 1996 marked the end of a huge project involving scientists in 37 laboratories to sequence the entire genome of a eukaryotic organism, baker's yeast. The sequence contains about 14 000 000 bases arranged in about 6000 genes.

Sequencing the 3×10^9 base pairs of the human genome represented a problem of a completely different order. To put this into perspective, a typical A4 page of print could represent the sequence of bases on the DNA of a small bacteriophage virus (ϕX174) that attacks the *E. coli* bacterium – about 5000 base pairs. On the same scale as this, the genome of *E. coli* would occupy 500 pages and the human genome about 250 000 times this!

What about mice?

Scientists have recently announced the completion of the map of the mouse genome. It is thought that scientists will be able to use this knowledge to transfer genes for human diseases into mice, and then to test possible treatments on the mice. This will:

- allow scientists to gain a great deal of useful information much more quickly than if they had to use human data
- be much safer for humans!

Improvements in automation and computing made it possible to complete the sequencing of the human genome early in 2000. More than 100 genes leading to specific diseases have been identified, and it is hoped that knowing the DNA sequence and location of all the human genes will allow a whole new range of therapeutic drugs to be developed. It may be possible to produce transgenic cells which will secrete virtually any human protein, and new molecules may be designed specifically to block metabolic pathways that lead to disease.

A DNA profile allows forensic scientists to determine which suspect, if any, is responsible for the crime.

It has proved technically possible to map the human genome, but this possibility raises a number of important issues. These are outlined in the boxes below.

The cost

The 1996 estimate of the likely cost of completing the Human Genome Project was about $1 per base for chemicals and technical assistance, plus the cost of sorting the short DNA chains and writing the computer software to speed up the analysis of the data. A conservative estimate for the total cost was about £6 000 000 000 ($6 billion), much of the cost resulting from the enormous demand on computer time and hardware.

A similar project, in terms of finance, was putting the first human on the moon, and comparable sums are spent on the NASA programme for landing exploratory vehicles on Mars.

Ethical issues

Now that the complete human DNA sequence is available, questions can be posed about who 'owns' the information. Who will be allowed access to the information, and who will be allowed to use it?

- Much of the information was gathered by privately funded research. Who 'owns' this information – the private company or humankind in general?
- How should the information be used? Should we limit further research into areas with direct medical benefit?
- Once DNA sequences are known, gene probes can be developed. Who will decide who should be 'screened' for the presence of potentially harmful genes?
- Should we limit prenatal screening? Should we allow parents to select zygotes carrying 'good' combinations of genes, and reject those carrying 'less good' combinations? In 2000, scientists announced that intelligence has a largely genetic basis – should parents be allowed to screen zygotes for 'intelligence' genes?
- Who should be employed? Should we discriminate against those more likely to be ill and to place demands on employment benefit schemes?
- Who should be insured? Will insurance companies have the right to demand genetic screening before issuing life cover? Will doctors be required to maintain confidentiality about results of genetic screening?

Such issues need to be widely discussed. Interested parties include parents of children with genetic diseases, science educators, religious groups, people from ethnic minorities, doctors, lawyers and insurance underwriters.

Science and the fishing industry

- To understand the value of fish as a food source
- To know how fishing methods increase yield
- To understand how overfishing has reduced fish stocks
- To appreciate that the mangement of fish stocks depends on scientific research

Fish as a source of food

Fish has been a valuable food source for humans for thousands of years. Fish is an excellent source of protein and, depending on species, of oils. Scientists are becoming more aware of the value of fish oils in preventing some of the 'diseases of affluence', such as coronary heart disease (see page 72). It is very important that humans include certain oily compounds (especially unsaturated fatty acids) in their diet, and these oily compounds are extremely abundant in some fish species.

Science and fishing

Scientists make many contributions to our understanding of the value of fishing. These include

- **Identification of valuable species:** the 'oily' fish are typically those which swim actively near the surface of the sea (pelagic species). These species have a high lipid content in their bodies because they need to use these stores of energy in their lengthy periods of rapid swimming. Of these species, the herring has been a particularly significant source of food to those nations bordering the North Atlantic Ocean.

- **Study of fish populations:** scientists are able to show how the population of any species changes over the course of time (see page 251). They are able to predict how many fish can be removed from a population without reducing the overall numbers, and they can estimate how long a population will take to recover from overfishing.

- **Knowledge of the growth pattern of individual fish:** it is possible to study small groups of fish to work out how long they take to reach breeding age, what their maximum size will be and which diseases they might be susceptible to. This allows

scientists to advise on net mesh sizes which should be used to catch adult fish, and to suggest fishing methods which will limit the catch of 'trash' fish (fish which are not used for human food). Fishing methods and mesh sizes used in herring fishing are shown below.

Seine ('purse-seine') netting – the net is towed to the school of herring by two boats. The fish are surrounded by the net and the bottom of the 'purse' is sealed by pulling on the rope. The net is slowly tightened so that the fish are concentrated in a small volume of water - the immature fish have time to escape. The captured fish are lifted from the water using hand nets - this limits the damage to the fish and so reduces wastage.

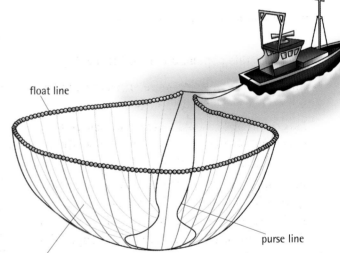

float line

purse line

Mesh – square mesh does not close up to trap small fish whereas older diamond mesh did.

120mm mesh size catches mature herring but allows small cod and haddock to escape.

Mesh and methods used in herring fishing.

- **Understanding of fish migratory patterns:** ecologists have been able to 'tag' fish and release them. These fish are sometimes recaptured at a later date, and the ecologists are able to work out the patterns of migration of the fish. They can then advise the fishing fleet about where and when they are likely to obtain the best catches of mature fish.

Biology in action

Overfishing and the herring population

Herring fishing became extremely efficient in the mid- to late-1960s. As a result the North Atlantic herring population fell dramatically, as shown in the graph below.

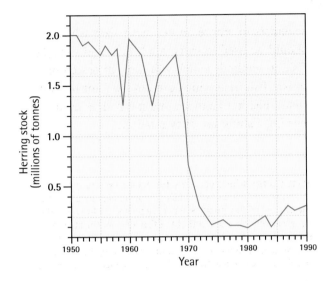

Herring population changes in the North Atlantic

Reasons for this population crash included:

- Shoal location became more efficient as radar systems became freely available.
- Larger and safer boats meant that fisheries extended as boats could remain further from port even in bad weather.
- Fishing was often 'mixed' i.e. fishing for one species would often catch other species of similar size. These other species might not be at the same growth stage, and so their population could not be maintained.

The situation became so severe that herring fishing is now very tightly controlled by the European Union. Some of the measures designed to limit overfishing are listed below.

- **Control of mesh:** both the **size** and the **shape** of the mesh are designed to allow immature fish to escape.
- **Setting of quotas:** the EU set up a Common Fisheries Policy in 1983 in an attempt to limit the size of catches. Unfortunately scientists now believe that initial quotas were too high, and even the reduced quotas now in force have not allowed herring populations to recover. The fishermen were tempted to catch more than their quota but to throw back the smaller, less marketable fish. Unfortunately these fish were often damaged by capture and did not survive to reproduce.
- **Protection of fisheries:** the EU set a limit of 320 km around their waters in an attempt to control fishing by non-EU countries. These limits have been very difficult to enforce, and have often led to confrontation between fishermen and governments from different countries.
- **Reduction of fishing fleets:** Governments are encouraged to provide subsidies to fishermen whose livelihood has been threatened (or even destroyed) by the measures listed above. The British Government has been reluctant to support these schemes, and many fishing communities have been devastated by the strict control of herring fishing.

As with many situations, there are no clear-cut answers. Fishermen understand that herring stocks must be allowed to recover but are naturally anxious about making a living. The scientists can only advise, the governments must act on this advice!

1 The table shows the chemical composition of some common fish species.

Species	Protein (%)	Lipid (%)
Cod	17	0.7
Herring	17	19
Mackerel	18	11
Salmon	22	9

a Plot this information in the form of a bar chart.
b Which compound will make up the bulk of the rest of the fish?
c Why are oily fish beneficial to health?
d Fish are also rich in minerals such as iron. How does this help in a healthy diet?

2 a Studies of individual fish species such as herring indicate the age and size at which they reach maturity. Why is it better to catch herring after they reach maturity rather than before?
b What is the advantage in fish conservation of using purse-seine netting?
c Describe how ecologists can provide information that might lead to conservation of fish stocks.
d Suggest three ways in which the British Government can help stocks of herring in the North Atlantic to recover.

15·4 Biology and behaviour

- To understand what is meant by 'behaviour'
- To know that some behaviour is inherited and some is learned
- To understand how some examples of behaviour can be studied
- To appreciate the contribution made by biologists to our understanding of behaviour

What is behaviour?

Many of us use the term 'behaviour' without ever thinking what the term really means! A biologist could define behaviour as:

'the course of action produced by an organism in response to a stimulus'.

All living organisms show a variety of behavioural activity – the extent of their behaviour depends on how much they are able to respond to stimuli. A biological scientist would be interested in the sense organs and their links to the central nervous system – he or she might try to explain behaviour on the basis of biochemical or physiological changes (see page 91). A behavioural scientist would probably be more interested in the stimuli themselves, and the way in which the organism's response to the stimuli allows it to do well in its environment. Both of these groups have a contribution to make to our understanding of how and why we respond to our environment.

Behavioural scientists sometimes distinguish two types of behaviour. **Innate behaviour** is inherited, is not changed by the environment and is inflexible (always the same response to a given stimulus). **Learned behaviour**, on the other hand, is not inherited, is changed by the environment and may be quickly adapted to new circumstances.

A choice chamber can be used to investigate orientation behaviour in woodlice.

N.B. Ensure that only one choice is offered. A dark cover on one chamber might make it darker and cooler.

Surface view

Two Petri dishes glued or welded together

Hole for introducing animals to chamber: can be closed with rubber bung

Sheet of fine mesh gauze: animals can't fall through but air can pass freely between upper and lower chamber

Simple organisms such as woodlice or blowfly larvae

Side view

Granules of anhydrous calcium chloride: create dry environment

Moist cotton wool: creates dry environment

Woodlice and choice chambers – orientation movements are an example of innate behaviour.

Investigating hydrotaxis

1. Introduce 10 woodlice into the centre of the choice chamber.
2. Count the number of animals in each half of the chamber, every minute for 10 minutes.
3. Record results in a table.

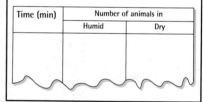

| Time (min) | Number of animals in | |
	Humid	Dry

A **taxis** is a movement of the whole organism in response to the **direction** of an external stimulus.

A movement **towards** the stimulus is a **positive** taxis e.g. **positive hydrotaxis** – towards a damp stimulus.

A **kinesis** is a **non-directional** movement – the **rate** of movement depends on the strength of the stimulus.

e.g. Woodlice move more rapidly and frequently in a dry environment – this may be part of searching for a more suitable damp environment.

Innate behaviour

Innate behaviour depends on 'built-in' nerve pathways – as a result of these 'built-in' pathways a given stimulus will always produce the same response. Innate behaviour includes simple reflexes, orientation movements and instincts. It is possible to design equipment which will allow study of some innate behaviour in the laboratory. The biologist Niko Tinbergen observed the instinctive courtship behaviour of the three-spined stickleback. The use of choice chambers in the study of orientation behaviour is outlined on the opposite page, and a well known study of instinctive courtship behaviour is described below.

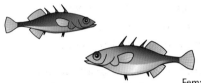

Female fish with belly swollen with eggs enters territory occupied by male.

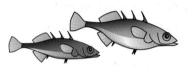

Male responds to the stimulus of the female's swollen belly with a zig-zag dance towards the nest.

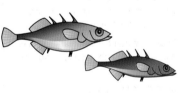

The stimulus of the nest and pointing by the male attracts the female so that she enters the nest.

When the female is in the nest the male becomes excited. He makes a trembling motion against the side of the female – this movement induces the female to spawn (lay eggs).

The sight of the eggs induces the male to enter the nest and fertilise them. The female swims away.

Tinbergen's sticklebacks – instinctive innate behaviour.

Learning

Learning can be defined as a change in behaviour caused by experience. There are increasing levels of complexity of learned behaviour. Simple examples include **habituation** (birds 'learning' to ignore a scarecrow, for example) and **imprinting** (ducklings following the first animal they see after they hatch from an egg, for example). Slightly more complex is the example studied by Pavlov (see page 93) in which the 'normal' stimulus which sets off a piece of behaviour is replaced by another stimulus – the organism shows **conditioning** to the second stimulus. The animal must be regularly exposed to the second stimulus or it 'forgets' what it has learned. The most complex forms of learned behaviour involve the organism 'storing away' experiences and then calling upon them later. For example, a mouse will learn where its burrow is and then use this stored information at a later date when trying to escape from a predator. Complex behaviour of this type depends on the presence of **association centres** in the brain (see pages 94–5) and the development of memory.

Human behaviour

The study of human behaviour is extremely widespread, involving psychologists, criminologists and advertising executives – not forgetting parents! Psychologists may use **conditioning** in **behaviour therapy** to help people with phobias. For example, in the technique known as systematic desensitisation a person is first taught a relaxation technique so that they can relax whenever they choose. They are then exposed to a mild form of whatever phobia they experience, and helped to relax. The severity of the phobic stimulus is increased until they are able to relax through the entire experience.

Behaviour therapy may help sufferers of arachnophobia

Parents often use presents to reward children for good behaviour or punishments to show their disapproval of inappropriate behaviour. This is a form of conditioning, but is less successful than the 'training' of Pavlov's dogs since humans can often see the motives behind other people's behaviour and may resist the attempt at conditioning!

Using sex to sell a product – two products, same advertising agency.

Advertising agencies employ behavioural scientists to help them sell their products. Potential customers will be taught to associate new stimuli with particular responses. These responses often involve social acceptance or sexual activity – a young man may associate buying a particular product with an image of a beautiful girl, for example.

Sociologists study the behaviour of whole populations of humans. They might be interested, for example, in why one leader can convince a group of people to behave in a way that none of them would accept as an individual. The biologist Desmond Morris has made extensive studies of groups of football supporters and has shown that the group behaviour is quite predictable.

Biologists of all types will have an increasing part to play in our understanding of what makes us humans.

Training a dog – becoming a pack leader

Understanding the behaviour patterns of dogs is important in their domestication. Without humans being able to manage the behaviour of dogs, it would not be possible to keep these animals as pets. All dogs still display the same patterns of behaviour as their distant ancestors – if we realised that our pet has all the instincts of a wolf we might not be so willing to accept it into our family!

Dogs are pack animals – for the social structure of the pack to hold together, every pack needs an **alpha** (leader) **figure**. In a wolf pack, understanding the rules is easy because every member of the pack has an established position in the pecking order. If a lower-ranking individual tries to take a privilege reserved for the alpha figure, order is quickly maintained with little more than a withering look from the alpha. For domestic dogs, understanding the rules becomes confusing because it is living in a mixed-species 'pack'. Humans behave towards each other in a way that is different from the way they behave towards the dog, but the dog doesn't easily understand this! The dog can only reason in a canine way, yet people often expect it to appreciate human values. Consider some of the mistakes people make:

- letting the dog jump up alongside them as they watch television
- varying their mealtimes, but tending to feed the dog at a fixed time
- playing tug-of-war with the dog, either in a game or at the end of his lead, and usually giving up before he does
- letting the dog run upstairs ahead, and then look back down at them
- letting the dog push past through a doorway, or lie in the middle of the floor.

Without thinking about this people give their pet the 'rights' of the alpha figure. The dog doesn't ask for these rights – the owners inadvertently promote him to this rank and so he takes on the responsibilities of the job.

Understanding this behaviour allows people to reverse the role and to 'train' the dog.

Group behaviour is quite predictable.

A dog should be made to earn any privileges from the alpha figure. Any demands should be met by a simple instruction such as to 'Sit' or 'Stay' – this ensures that if the dog wants something, he has to earn it first. Simple procedures establish people as 'leaders' and dogs as 'followers' – if a dog has bad habits and the pecking order needs to be rearranged, the human should deny the dog any privileges reserved for the alpha figure.

How the dog interprets human mistakes

Alpha behaviour

Denying the dog the privileges of the alpha figure

Modifying dog behaviour!
The sexual behaviour of dogs is controlled by hormones. Removing young male dogs' testes prevents production of testosterone and makes them less likely to roam in search of a sexually receptive female. OUCH!

- Don't let the dog sleep on your chair or bed, but sometimes sit in his basket!
- Prepare the dog's food, but then eat something before you allow the dog to have its meal.
- Control all games e.g. throwing a ball but **never** enter into trials of strength.
- Always climb the stairs, or go through a door, before you allow your dog to do so.
- Make the dog move out of the way as you move around the house.

1 What is the difference between **learned** and **innate** behaviour? Give one example of each type of behaviour in a human.

2 Some scientists believe that blowfly larvae (maggots) burrow into rotting meat in an attempt to escape from the light.
   a What is the name given to these orientation movements?
   b Describe an experiment you could perform to find out whether blowfly larvae naturally move away from the light. Include a diagram of the apparatus you would use, and draw out a table for presenting the results.
   c An alternative hypothesis suggests that the larvae are moving towards a damp environment. How would you find out whether 'dampness' or 'darkness' is the stronger stimulus for the larvae?
   d What name would be given to behaviour in which a woodlouse moves away from light?

3 Select one advertisement currently showing on television. State what the product is, and explain how the advertiser is using conditioning to sell this product.

4 Use a series of annotated diagrams (diagrams with brief notes) to describe the experiments carried out by Ivan Pavlov. What conclusions did Pavlov draw from his results?

1 a The graph shows the mass of herring caught in the North Sea between 1935 and 1975.

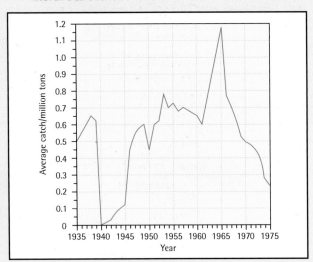

i Which year had the largest catch?

ii What was the herring catch in 1950?

iii Describe the trend in the herring catch from 1945 to 1975.

iv Suggest and explain **two** ways governments have attempted to reduce overfishing of herring.

(CCEA June 1996)

2 a The diagram shows the nitrogen cycle.

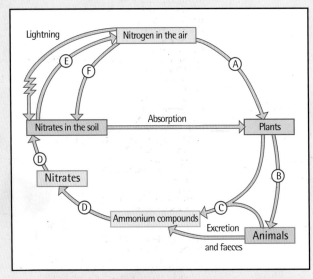

Use the diagram and your knowledge to answer the following questions.

i Name the processes B and E.

ii Some of the processes in the nitrogen cycle involve bacteria. Which process represents:
bacteria producing nitrates in the root nodules?
bacteria increasing the nitrates available for plants?

iii Name the process and the organisms involved in C.

b Farmers use fertilisers to supplement the nitrogen content of their land. The table shows some information about fertilisers.

	Natural fertiliser	Artificial fertiliser
Cost	Low	High
Speed of action	Slow	Fast
Availability	Limited availability	Always available

i Give an example of a natural fertiliser.

ii Using your own knowledge and the information in the table, suggest why the majority of farmers do not use natural fertilisers despite their advantages.

(CCEA June 1995)

3 Samples of soil, **A**, **B** and **C**, were collected from different places. The soil samples were each of equal mass. The samples were shaken with the same amount of water and allowed to settle for 12 hours.

The figure below shows the results of the investigation.

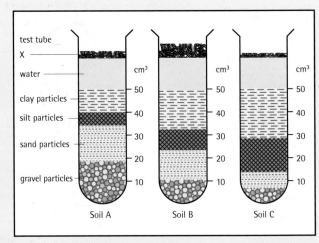

a i Which one of the soils **A**, **B** or **C** would **NOT** be likely to contain a large earthworm population? Explain your answer giving **THREE** reasons for your choice.

ii State **TWO** other ways in which the sample of soil chosen in (a)(i) would not be as fertile as the other two soil samples.

b Using graph paper, construct a bar graph to show the relative proportions of mineral particles in **Soil A**.

c i Name the material labelled **X**.

ii State **TWO** functions of this material in improving the fertility of a soil.

d If re-cycling of nutrients did not occur, a soil would be almost completely emptied of mineral salts after millions of years.

i Describe **TWO** main ways in which mineral salts are removed from the soil.

ii Describe in detail **ONE** re-cycling process which restores mineral salts to the soil.

(MEG November 1992)

Index